CASE.

D1567600

Handbook
of Institutional
Advancement

THIRD EDITION

Peter McE. Buchanan, Editor

The Council for Advancement and Support of Education is the largest
international association of educational institutions, with more than 2,900
colleges, universities, independent elementary and secondary schools in
the United States, Canada, Mexico, the United Kingdom, and 29 other
countries as members. Since 1974, CASE has helped its members build
relationships with their communities, raise funds, market their institutions
to prospective students, diversify the profession, and foster public support
of education. CASE also offers various advancement resources, provides
standards and an ethical framework for the profession, and works with
other organizations to respond to public issues, while promoting education
worldwide.

To find out more information, or to receive our catalog, call (202) 328-2273.
Visit CASE Books online at www.case.org/books.

CASE Books

Book designer: Fletcher Design
Senior Editor: Bridget Booher
Editors: Nancy Raley, Shannon Joyce, and Karla Taylor
Researcher: Laurie Calhoun
Indexer: Deborah Patton

Appreciation

It is a high privilege to extend to more than one hundred current and former advancement professionals, the volunteer leaders of the Council for Advancement and Support of Education (CASE), a handful of CASE's current staff and consultants, and several special colleagues, heartfelt appreciation for their efforts in making this edition possible.

This third edition of the *Handbook of Institutional Advancement* is a gift to the profession from a wide cross section of advancement professionals speaking in their own voices. Without recompense, they have devoted countless hours to share their experience, expertise, and wisdom about the past, present, and future practice of educational advancement worldwide with their colleagues and students of our profession. Their names and current professional positions appear in the "Contributors" section; I salute them.

Special thanks are owed to the 1997 and 1998 members of the CASE District Chairs Council, the CASE Commissions on Alumni Relations, Communications, and Fund Raising, and of the CASE Board of Trustees. They reviewed early drafts of the structure and content of the *Handbook,* and contributed many helpful suggestions to its development.

Led by the indefatigable Nancy Raley, director of CASE Books, the CASE staff has done an extraordinary job organizing the authors' material, helping with the editing, and proofing a large volume within a very difficult timetable. I want to thank Shannon Joyce, Laurie Calhoun, and consultants Bridget Booher and Karla Taylor who supported Nancy's diplomatic and editorial leadership.

I will always be especially indebted to the eight section editors who carried the major burden of this endeavor. They recruited their chapter authors and oversaw the composition of each section. Warmest thanks to Rick Nahm, who insisted only my name should be on the first section of the *Handbook* when I combined two sections into one, even though he edited nearly half the material appearing in that section; special appreciation to Eric Johnson who never missed a beat about leadership and management while moving from Pittsburgh to Houston; gratitude to Steve Grafton for heading up alumni relations in the midst of a most demanding schedule of club events; appreciation to Roger Williams for a communications section of superb substance and writing and for his advice on what the overall *Handbook* should encompass; my most sincere thanks to Mike Worth

Appreciation

for, in effect, writing nearly a second book about fund raising in less than three years; special thanks to Larry Lauer for pioneering marketing in our profession with insight and sensitive determination; gratitude to John Taylor for spearheading the writing about a new advancement discipline he did much to create; my great appreciation to Pat Jackson for her insight into how advancement is altered by the widely differing institutional settings in which it is practiced; and, deepest appreciation to Linda Weimer for editing the section on the roles of key institutional leaders in advancement while relocating to Wisconsin.

I also want to acknowledge the contributions that Susan Washburn and Bill McGoldrick unmistakably made to this book by sharing with me their insights and knowledge of our field. There are no better professional colleagues. My heartfelt thanks go also to Ed Crawford for his foreword and other assistance; no one has served the best interests of our field so well. I want also to thank and acknowledge A. Westley Rowland for whom I have great admiration. He edited the previous editions of this handbook.

Finally, the first chapter of the first section of this edition was written by Michael Hooker, then chancellor of the University of North Carolina at Chapel Hill. He was one of the first educational leaders to speak and write about technology's impact on society, and especially its impact on higher education. He never lived to see his chapter in print, lost to cancer in the prime of his life. We remember him and his eloquent expression of concern and hope for the academy with profound gratitude.

Peter McE. Buchanan
June 2000

Contents

SECTION I

The Environment and the Changing Face of Advancement

Peter McE. Buchanan, Editor

SECTION II

Leadership and Management

Eric C. Johnson, Editor

Foreword

My interest in CASE began in the late 1950s while I was with the Southern Regional Education Board in Atlanta. In 1959, Howard Curtis from Brown University, chair of the American College Public Relations Association, invited American Alumni Council Chair Brad Ansley from Emory University and I to dinner at a district ACPRA meeting.

At dinner, the chairs talked at length about the fact that both organizations often duplicated services. They conducted meetings that covered similar issues and sometimes even booked the same speakers, and their magazines often published comparable and duplicative articles. Everyone at dinner agreed that merger could produce greater efficiencies and more and better services for the membership of both organizations. But the time was not quite right.

The courtship continued for 15 years with steps forward and backward before both parties got really serious. A joint–study committee in 1972 did the heavy-lifting that finally led to merger in 1974. This committee and the organizing board (of which I was a member) representing both organizations focused on the reasons for and advantages of merger. Herman B. Wells, the late president and chancellor of Indiana University, was asked to serve as the facilitator for the committee's work. He was a great diplomat who kept the committee on course and persuaded us to sell the values of merger before we settled the more sensitive questions like selecting a name, appointing the first president, or establishing dues. This was a brilliant stroke on his part because at the end of two years of self-study and reasoned debate, about 95 percent of each organization's members supported the merger.

By September 23, 1974, the search committee and new board of trustees unanimously selected Alice Beeman as the first president. She was well-known for her public relations work at Vanderbilt University and the universities of Michigan and Texas. Her six-year presidency of the American Association of University Women gave her extra credibility. She became the first female president at One Dupont Circle (site of so many education associations) and instituted a number of sound programs for the new Council for Advancement and Support of Education.

Among her first creations was the *Handbook of Institutional Advancement* in 1977. She persuaded A. Westley Rowland, vice president of university relations at the State University of New York at Buffalo, to serve as editor with 30 contributing members. As Rowland noted, it was the hope of the authors that the first *Handbook* would be another element in the maturing of the institutional advancement function as CASE sought to interpret, support, and develop understanding of higher education.

Rowland also served as editor of the second edition of the *Handbook,* published in 1986, with a new group of section editors and chapter authors. In addition, he commissioned chapters on important and timely topics not covered in the earlier work. As President James L. Fisher, CASE's second president, noted in his foreword to the second edition, "The resulting volume is truly a new book, not a revision. Reading this volume and comparing it with the first edition gives an interesting perspective on how advancement has matured in the past decades." Ginny Carter Smith, whom I am pleased to say I suggested Alice Beeman hire as a CASE vice president, helped to edit both early editions of the *Handbook.*

I am honored to be asked to prepare the foreword for this third edition of the *Handbook of Institutional Advancement,* which has been orchestrated under the skilled direction of CASE President Emeritus Peter McE. Buchanan. In this

edition, he presents the many diverse voices of advancement in 2000 in order to provide a snapshot of the CASE constituency in its richness and complexity. The new edition, with 96 contributors, offers views of the important support that advancement provides for educational institutions, especially for its CEOs.

Early in my career, I was honored to have had a part in shaping the organization that would become CASE. Serving as founding chair of the board, as an advancement professional at several distinguished institutions, and as a CASE volunteer, and late in my career, as a staff member at the invitation of Peter Buchanan, I have a unique perspective on CASE. While the organization has developed and grown into a complex entity, its basic philosophy remains the same. Alice Beeman noted that the unified organization of advancement must begin on the campus. Offices and personnel responsible for the diverse functions of fund raising, alumni administration, institutional relations, and government relations must work as a team to be successful. And as we near CASE's third decade, this philosophy remains as valid and visionary as it was in 1974.

Edwin M. Crawford
June 2000

Contributors

GENERAL EDITOR

Peter McEachin Buchanan, President Emeritus of the Council for Advancement and Support of Education and Associate, Washburn & McGoldrick, Inc.

A veteran academic administrator, Buchanan served as president of CASE (1991-97), an international association of over 2,900 educational institutions that provides training for some 20,000 campus professionals in alumni relations, communications, and fund raising. He also served as vice president at Columbia University (1969-77, 1982-90) and Wellesley College (1977-82). Buchanan has led three comprehensive fund-raising campaigns ranging from $70 million to $1.15 billion. As a trustee, he has served on the boards of CASE, Independent Sector, The Wellesley College Center for Research on Women, the Dana Hall School, and the Episcopal Divinity School.

Buchanan is a chapter author in Michael Worth's book, *Educational Fund Raising: Principles and Practice,* and Sondra Gray's *Vision of Evaluation.* He has written several articles about campaign fund raising and philanthropy published in CURRENTS and *Planning* magazines and wrote an unpublished history of the origins and early years of CASE for its 25th anniversary celebration in 1999.

In addition to his consulting work, Buchanan currently serves one overseas and four U.S. institutional clients. These include three research universities, one comprehensive university, and a specialized two-year college. He is a trained facilitator in fund raising for the Association of Governing Boards of Colleges and Universities (AGB) and continues to participate in CASE programs as a volunteer.

A graduate of Deerfield Academy, he received his B.A. from Cornell University, his M.B.A. degree from Columbia University, and his Ed.D. from Teachers College, Columbia University.

EDITORS

Steve Grafton, Executive Director, Alumni Association, University of Michigan

Since taking his current position at the University of Michigan in 1994, the alumni association of 100,000 members has undergone radical structural changes, resulting in innovative online and print communications, ground-breaking alumni lifestage research, alumni Web communities, broader regional programming, a diversification of the travel program, new alumni career services, and dynamic partnerships with senior university leadership. Before coming to UM, Grafton headed the alumni association at Mississippi State University and prior to that, worked for U.S. Senator John Stennis, D-MS. He has served CASE in many capacities, including trustee, district director, conference faculty member, and chair of the Commission on Alumni Relations. He is also a charter member and current member of the board for the Council of Alumni Association Executives. Grafton received bachelor's and master's degrees from Mississippi State University.

Patricia King Jackson, Assistant Head of School for Development and Alumni Relations, Sidwell Friends School

Pat King Jackson started in advancement in 1971 at Bryn Mawr College, where she created the institution's first foundation and corporation relations program. In subsequent chief development officer roles, at Dartmouth Medical School, Fox Chase Cancer Center, and Sidwell Friends School, Jackson has successfully used campaigns as strategies for greatly increasing the institutions' fund-raising plateaus. From 1983 to 1992, she served as vice president of Grenzebach/Glier & Associates, Inc. There she worked with a variety of college and university clients on campaign fund raising and other advancement issues.

Eric C. Johnson, Vice President for Resource Development, Rice University

Before coming to Rice in 1999, Johnson was the vice president for development at Carnegie Mellon University for seven years. There he planned and implemented a successful, comprehensive $350 million campaign. He worked 20 years at the Massachusetts Institute of Technology (M.I.T.), including four years as director of corporate relations where he had responsibility for the Industrial Liaison Program and all corporate gifts. He has extensive experience in university-industry relations in the United States, Europe, and Asia. He earned his bachelor's degree in metallurgy at M.I.T. and his master's degree in

operations research at Case Western Reserve University.

Larry D. Lauer, Vice Chancellor for Marketing and Communication and Assistant Professor of Corporate and Marketing Communications, Texas Christian University

A member of the chancellor's cabinet, Lauer also heads TCU's marketing advisory board, and is director of The Commission on the Future of TCU, the university's strategic planning initiative. Lauer was founding chair of CASE's advanced Seminar on Integrated Marketing and is chair of the 2000 CASE Summer Institute on Communications and Marketing at Duke University. He has worked with more than 20 campuses on integrated marketing initiatives in the USA, Canada, South America, and the United Kingdom and has been a presenter at numerous regional, national, and international conferences. He is the author of *Communication Power* (Aspen Publishers, 1997) and more than 25 journal articles and book chapters on institutional marketing and communications.

John H. Taylor, Director, Alumni and Development Records, Duke University

Taylor holds a B.A. degree in mass communications and socio-political change from Vanderbilt University, and has completed his work for a master of arts degree in liberal studies at Duke. Before coming to Duke, Taylor was an officer at First Wachovia in Atlanta. In 1987, he joined Duke as the manager of university payrolls and assumed his current position in 1988. During his tenure as gifts director, Taylor has guided Duke's gifting process to an industry benchmark of efficiency and accuracy. He is the author of articles in *Cash Management Forum, The Chronicle of Philanthropy*, and CURRENTS, and is consulted frequently by authors regarding charitable gifts and gift tax-related issues. He has spoken at numerous CASE conferences across the country and has been the chair for the CASE Summer Institute in Advancement Services. Taylor frequently consults for educational institutions, foundations, and other nonprofit organizations focusing on the areas of systems, policies and procedures, IRS and accounting regulations, and general gift processing issues.

Linda Weimer, Vice President for University Relations, University of Wisconsin System

Weimer has spent 25 years in the field of university advancement. She previously was assistant vice chancellor for public affairs at University of California-Berkeley and, before that, was director of university relations at the University of Wisconsin-Madison. Former chair of CASE's national Commission on Communications, Weimer is the author of *Reaching Out: How Academic Leaders Can Communicate More Effectively with their Constituencies.*

Roger L. Williams, Associate Vice Chancellor of University Relations, University of Arkansas

In addition to his position at the University of Arkansas, Williams also is counsel with Dick Jones Communications and serves as adjunct assistant professor of higher education at Pennsylvania State University. With more than 22 years of experience in higher education communications, Williams previously served as associate vice president for communications at Georgetown University and as assistant vice president for university relations at Penn State. He holds a doctorate in higher education from Penn State and is author of *The Origins of Federal Support for Higher Education: George W. Atherton and the Land-Grant College Movement.* He serves on the editorial board of *The History of Higher Education Annual.*

Michael J. Worth, Vice President for Development and Alumni Affairs, The George Washington University

Worth has more than 25 years of experience in institutional advancement. He served as director of development at the University of Maryland College Park before accepting his current position in 1983. At GW, he has planned and directed two major campaigns. In addition to serving as vice president, Worth holds an appointment as professor of education and has taught graduate courses on higher education and institutional advancement. He has written or edited numerous articles and three books, including *Educational Fund Raising: Principles and Practice.* He received CASE's Alice L. Beeman Award for Advancement Writing in 1995 and has served as a member of CASE's Commission on Philanthropy. A graduate of Wilkes College, he holds a Ph.D. from the University of Maryland.

AUTHORS

Thomas W. Anderson
Fellow, The Center for Professional Ethics, Case Western Reserve University

Lynne D. Becker
Assistant Vice President for Development, Development Services, University of Washington

Diane Benninghoff
Director, Alumni and Parent Programs, Colorado College

Richard B. Boardman
Executive Director of the Harvard College Fund, Harvard University

Colin Boswell
Senior Consultant, Brakeley Europe and Former Executive Director, CASE Europe

Sue Boswell
Head of Alumni Relations, Queen Mary & Westfield College, University of London

Keith E. Brant
Executive Director, UCLA Alumni Association, University of California, Los Angeles

Jeffrey Brenzel
Executive Director, Association of Yale Alumni, Yale University

Contributors

Midge Wood Brittingham
Executive Director, Oberlin College Alumni
Association

Peter McE. Buchanan
Associate, Washburn & McGoldrick, Inc and
President Emeritus, CASE and
Former Vice President of Columbia University
and Wellesley College

Steven L. Calvert
Executive Director of Alumni Relations,
Northeastern University

Margaret Sughrue Carlson
Executive Director, University of Minnesota
Alumni Association and Associate Vice President,
University of Minnesota

John B. Carter, Jr.
President and CEO, Georgia Tech Foundation
and Former Vice President and Executive
Director, Georgia Tech Alumni Association

Tom Chaves
General Manager, SCT Global Education
Solutions

Paul B. Chewning
Vice President, Professional Development, CASE

Virginia B. Clark
Vice President, Development and Alumni
Relations, University of Pennsylvania

J. Todd Coleman
Executive Director, University of Missouri
Alumni Association and Assistant Vice Chancellor,
University of Missouri

Edward G. Coll, Jr.
President, Alfred University

Helen A. Colson
President, Helen Colson Development Associates

Sandra Conn
Director of Communications and Marketing,
Indiana University

Bruce Darling
Vice President, University and External Relations,
University of California

Kenneth N. Dayton
President, Oak Leaf Foundation (Minneapolis,
MN)

Terry Denbow
Vice President for University Relations, Michigan
State University

Douglas S. Dibbert
President, General Alumni Association, The
University of North Carolina

Susan Clouse Dolbert
President and Executive Director, Arizona State
University Alumni Association

David R. Dunlop
Former Senior Development Officer, Cornell
University

Jan Pruitt Duvall
Associate Director of University Relations and
Director of Marketing Communications, The
University of Alabama

Gary A. Evans
Vice President, Development and College
Relations, Lafayette College

Albert C. Friedman
Director, University Publications, University of
Wisconsin-Madison

Laney Funderburk
Associate Vice President, Alumni Affairs and
Director, Alumni Affairs, Duke University

Kathleen Casey Gigl
Vice President for Institutional Advancement,
Texas Woman's University

Steve Grafton
Executive Director, Alumni Association of the
University of Michigan

Linda Gray
Assistant Vice President and Director of News &
Public Affairs, University of Florida

Patricia Gregory
Senior Director of Corporate and Foundation
Relations, Washington University School of
Medicine in St. Louis

William R. Haden
President, West Virginia Wesleyan College

Don Hale
Vice President for University Relations, Carnegie
Mellon University

Margarete (Peg) Rooney Hall
Associate Professor of Public Relations, College of
Journalism and Communications, University of
Florida and former Vice President of
Advancement, Gallaudet University

Karen K. Hansen
Executive Director of the Center for Lifelong
Learning and Former Director of Alumni/ae and
Parent Relations, St. Olaf College

April L. Harris
Director of Alumni Relations, University of
Alabama in Huntsville

Dan L. Heinlen,
President/CEO, The Ohio State University
Alumni Association, Inc.

Jonathan R. Heintzelman
Assistant Vice President for University
Development and Director of Planned and Major
Gifts, Northwestern University

Jeffrey T. Hermann
University Editor and Director of Publications,
The Pennsylvania State University

Lynn K. Hogan
Executive Director, Medical Affairs Development,
University of Washington

Terry M. Holcombe
Former Vice President for Development, Yale
University

Michael Hooker
Chancellor (Deceased), University of North
Carolina at Chapel Hill

Patricia King Jackson
Assistant Head of School for Development and
Alumni Relations, Sidwell Friends School

Harvey K. Jacobson
Professor Emeritus of Journalism, University of
Wisconsin-Oshkosh and Former Institutional
Advancement Officer, University of Michigan

Eric C. Johnson
Vice President for Resource Development, Rice
University

Robert E. Johnson
Vice President for Enrollment, Albion College

Dick Jones
Principal, Dick Jones Communications

Robert E. Kelley
Adjunct Professor, Graduate School of Industrial
Administration, Carnegie Mellon University

Thomas F. Kelly
Vice President for External Affairs and Professor
of Management, Binghamton University, State
University of New York

Sharon Kha
Associate Vice President for Communications,
University of Arizona

Roland King
Vice President for Public Affairs, National
Association of Independent Colleges and
Universities

Patricia Ann LaSalle
Associate Vice President and Executive Director
of Public Affairs and Editor, *SMU Magazine*,
Southern Methodist University

Larry D. Lauer
Vice Chancellor, Marketing and
Communication, Texas Christian University

Annette Hannon Lee
Director of Public Information, Georgia
Southwestern State University

Judith Jasper Leicht
Associate Vice Chancellor and Executive Director
of University Communications, Washington
University in St. Louis

Charles F. Lennon, Jr.
Executive Director, Alumni Association, Associate
Vice President for University Relations, University
of Notre Dame

Walter K. Lindenmann
Specialist in Public Relations Research and
Management and Former Senior Vice President
and Director of Research, Ketchum

Jonathan A. Lindsey
Director, Donor Information Services, University
Development, Baylor University

Deirdre A. Ling
Head, Middlesex School

Karen M. MacArthur
Executive Director of Institutional Advancement,
Delta College Foundation

Charles S. Madden
Vice President for University Relations and Ben
H. Williams Professor of Marketing, Baylor
University

Bruce R. McClintock
Chairman, Marts & Lundy, Inc.

James H. Melton
President, Florida State University Alumni
Association

Susan G. Montague
Director of Development and Public Relations,
University of New Brunswick

David Morse
Director of Public Affairs, The Pew Charitable
Trusts

Mary Kay Murphy
Vice President for Institutional Advancement,
Morris Brown College

Frederick C. Nahm
Acting President, Colonial Williamsburg
Foundation

Jerry Nunnally
Vice President for Institute Relations, California
Institute of Technology

Alison L. Paul
Attorney, Montana Legal Services Association

Harry L. Peterson
President, Western State College of Colorado

Judith Turner Phair
Vice President for Institutional Advancement,
University of Maryland Biotechnology Institute

Gary R. Ratcliff
Director, University Center and Adjunct Assistant
Professor of Educational Leadership and
Counseling, University of Montana

Amy Button Renz
President, Kansas State University Alumni
Association

John A. Roush
President, Centre College

Janet Sailian
Director of International Programs, CASE

Carolyn S. Sanzone
Assistant Vice Chancellor, Science & Technology
Advancement, Corporate & Foundation
Relations, University of Massachusetts Amherst

Tracy Savage
Assistant Head of School for Development and
Public Relations, National Cathedral School

Fritz W. Schroeder
Executive Director of Annual Programs and
Alumni Relations, The Johns Hopkins University

Robert A. Sevier
Vice President for Research and Marketing,
Stamats Communications, Inc.

Terry Shepard
Vice President for Public Affairs, Rice University

Reggie Simpson
Head of Alumni Relations, London School of
Economics

Kathy Stanford
Director, Gift Policy and Administration,
University of California, Irvine

Michael Stoner
Vice President for New Media, Lipman Hearne
Inc.

John Taylor
Director, Alumni and Development Records,
Duke University

Debra J. Thomas
Director of Public Relations, Jesse H. Jones
Graduate School of Management, Rice University

Jeffrey S. Todd
Director of Alumni Relations and The Wooster
Fund, The College of Wooster

Stephen Joel Trachtenberg
President, The George Washington University

Donna A. Van De Water
Vice President for Research, Lipman Hearne, Inc.

M. Fredric Volkmann
Vice Chancellor for Public Affairs, Washington
University in St. Louis

Linda Weimer
Vice President for University Relations, University
of Wisconsin System

Robert L. Weiner
Director of Product Strategies, MyPersonal.com,
Inc.

Eric B. Wentworth
Former Director of the National Center for
Institutionally Related Foundations, CASE

Roger L. Williams
Associate Vice Chancellor for University
Relations, University of Arkansas

Michael J. Worth
Vice President for Development and Alumni
Affairs, The George Washington University

The advancement leader of tomorrow will have to be a creative thinker, a person who understands the difference between flexibility and capitulation in a rapidly changing environment, an individual who exemplifies collaboration in approach without compromising principle, and a professional who is devoted first and foremost to the cause of education.

—*Peter McE. Buchanan*

The Environment and the Changing Face of Advancement

Edited by Peter McE. Buchanan

Introduction

Peter McE. Buchanan
President Emeritus
CASE and

Associate
Washburn & McGoldrick, Inc.

American higher education stands at the dawn of a new millennium as one of the nation's most remarkable achievements. Widely considered the finest tertiary system of education in the world, it educates more of its citizens than any other nation, welcomes more students from other nations than any other, and produces an extraordinary and continuing array of world class research in virtually every field of intellectual inquiry. Uniquely created by private initiative and public support, it provides the widest spectrum of educational offerings in the world.

The character of the American free enterprise system in which the individual is free to pursue any future course with few restrictions, other than those to protect the general welfare, is strongly evident in higher education. Its institutions, whether privately or publicly chartered, compete in local, regional, national, and international markets for resources, human and monetary, and reputation just as individuals do…with only two notable exceptions. They are generally exempted from paying taxes, and private gifts to them are tax deductible. These are privileges of serving the public interest.

While higher education was largely a creature of private initiative in the first century of the Republic—it is important to remember that government had no responsibility for education in the Constitution of the United States—it is today a complex system of publicly supported, state not federal, institutions educating more than 85 percent of entering undergraduates and 60 percent of graduate students, with a somewhat smaller number of privately supported institutions educating the remainder.

As the perceived value of higher education has shifted from one that primarily benefits society to one that primarily benefits the individual—as was the case in the nation's first century—the relative importance of private and public financial support has shifted as well. For example, in the early 1990's, state support for many publicly chartered universities actually declined as public tuitions rose and federal financial aid shifted more and more from outright scholarships to loans. Public concerns about welfare, crime prevention, and facilities for criminal incarceration also contributed to that shift. As the demand and outcome expectations of students, parents, employers, legislators, and governors for higher education have increased, college and university leaders are competing for private and public monetary support and visibility as never before.

If that competition alone was not sufficiently challenging for educational leaders, they also are in the midst of, or more likely at the very beginning of, an information revolution, the parameters of which few can barely see nor understand. It is certainly a communications revolution at its very least. It is doubtless a scientific revolution, the dimensions of which we cannot perceive because of the capacity of the technology to change the very essence of what we know and do, and, therefore, what we teach and learn. It is a human revolution with no clear outcome. If the whole of humanity is not its beneficiary, then it could be catastrophic. Its potential for both good and evil is unbounded. Because it is also a learning revolution, it is up to the academy and the generations it educates to prepare students to make certain the coming changes benefit the public as a whole.

Never has education loomed more important for the welfare of the individual, for the welfare of each nation, and for the welfare of the global community. Only an educated world citizenry will be able to confront successfully the problems of poverty, disease, injustice, ethnic and racial conflict, and degradation of the environment. Given this unprecedented responsibility in a competition for resources and reputation within a revolution of unknown power and complexity, it is little wonder that the field of institutional advancement has become increasingly important to the academy. It is a field of endeavor now considered one of the three or four most important administrative portfolios in American higher edu-

cation. How education, and especially higher education, fares will likely determine our global destiny.

Michael Hooker, the late chancellor of the University of North Carolina at Chapel Hill and Stephen Joel Trachtenberg, president of George Washington University speak eloquently about the educational environment of the future. Together, their writings in Chapters 1 and 2 outline the likely environment in which advancement will function in the United States.

Increasingly important to educational institutions in the United States, advancement also has gained a foothold internationally. More and more leaders of other nations concluded that the predominant world model in which federal government provided a free higher education to a small elite was inadequate to compete successfully in the world market. As a result, these leaders have begun to adapt the American model of higher education, including the institutional advancement model, albeit somewhat haltingly. Colin and Sue Boswell have been participants in the global privatization of higher education and speak to that subject from their professional experience in the United Kingdom in Chapter 3.

The signal event in the advancement profession in the post World War II period was the Greenbrier Conference of 1958. The report of that conference recommended that the various functions and activities performed in the academy to develop understanding and support from all constituencies should be directed and coordinated by a senior administrative officer reporting to the campus chief executive. In most institutions, those functions, henceforth to be called "advancement," were distributed at that time in many different organizational structures.

The organizational and functional diversities of professional staff inevitably created competition, confusion, and often confrontation. It took nearly 16 years after the Greenbrier conference for the two largest professional organizations in the field of advancement to merge their resources and energies. In 1974, the American Alumni Council (AAC) and the American College Public Relations Association (ACPRA) joined together to form the Council for Advancement and Support of Education (CASE). It took that organization nearly 22 years before it defined its functional territory as alumni relations, communications, and fund raising, and produced a curriculum to reflect those choices. Even so, enrollment management, except for admissions communications, was not included. A.Westley Rowland's definition in the second edition of the *Handbook*, namely "it is all activities and programs undertaken by an institution to develop understanding and support from all its constituencies in order to achieve its goals in securing such resources as students, faculty, and dollars" is far more encompassing than any present reality. Advancement has often been described as an evolving profession. It is still evolving.

With over a century of combined professional experience, Rick Nahm of the Colonial Williamsburg Foundation; Fred Volkmann, vice chancellor of public affairs at Washington University in St. Louis; Steve Calvert, executive director of alumni relations at Northeastern University; and David Morse of the Pew Charitable Trusts trace respectively the changing nature of fund raising, communications, alumni relations, and government relations in Chapters 4, 5, 6 and 7. They provide a perceptive analysis of how advancement's most important components have evolved since the publication of the *Handbook's* second edition in 1986.

Because many thoughtful observers agree that the most dramatic change in advancement in the next decade will result from employing the Web to build relationships between and among institutional constituents, Robert Johnson, vice

president for enrollment at Albion College, provides in Chapter 8 an interim status report of the Web's employment and early impact upon the field.

The century-old debate about the proper place for intercollegiate athletics in the academy in the United States has never been more hotly contested than in the recent past. Advancement professionals have become more and more involved, as institutional leaders have tried, with very mixed results, to exert their authority over the direction of the debate. John Roush, president of Centre College, writes in Chapter 9 a particularly balanced perspective on intercollegiate athletics that provides insight into what promises to be one of the most time consuming and increasingly complex issues on campus in the future.

From the very outset, advancement has been viewed as a delegation of presidential duty and responsibility. The president, vice chancellor, or head of an institution is still the "chief advancement officer" of that institution. How he or she chooses to delegate that responsibility—in what organizational framework and to which individual(s)—determines how advancement will develop within that institution. In the future, it appears that campus leaders will choose to adopt a broader, more encompassing role than ever before. CASE recently conducted a study of the public relations function of institutions. The information contained in the final analysis will be available in a CASE book in Winter 2000. It suggests that the field will require professionals with broad rather than narrow experience, with hands-on leadership of several advancement functions rather than just one, and with a broad rather than narrow perspective of their proper role in the academy. I conclude Section I in Chapter 10 with one view of what the future may portend for the field and those who will lead it in a new century.

America's colleges and universities must be prepared to embrace and meet the resulting challenges of living in a new world with new rules. Trying to live by the old rules in a changed context will not work.

Higher Education in the New Millennium

Michael Hooker
Chancellor (Deceased)
University of North Carolina at Chapel Hill

Editor's Note: Michael Hooker died in 1999, a few months after he contributed this chapter. A special tribute to him appears in the Editor's Appreciation.

An undergraduate sits in her dorm room at a computer, deftly strokes keys for a few hours and, if she is clever and lucky, creates a new piece of software, ready to spring to life from a tiny disk. She used little energy and no raw material: just the electricity to power the computer and whatever she ate for breakfast to fuel her brain cells.

This simple scenario—reminiscent of how Mitchell Kapor, founder of the Lotus Development Corporation, became one of America's most famous high-technology entrepreneurs—illustrates the change facing our nation's economy and our universities in the 21st century. The world is undergoing a transformation as profound as anything since the harnessing of fire. For the first time, the driving force of economic activity is shifting from energy to knowledge. Brain power, not muscle power, is becoming the genesis of economic value, and knowledge is assuming the role of value creation that energy once held.

America's colleges and universities must be prepared to embrace and meet the resulting challenges of living in a new world with new rules. Trying to live by the old rules in a changed context will not work. Technology is dramatically altering the economic, social, and political environment in which we provide higher education.

Consider the differences between the energy-based, manufacturing economy of the 20th century and the knowledge-based economy of the future, and you begin to see what awaits higher education. The manufacture of nearly every product consumers demanded during the past century required an energy-intensive process: energy was needed to collect the raw material, transport it, transform it into the finished product, market it, and sell the product.

Steel production offers an excellent example. Energy is required to mine the ore, deliver it to a plant, and fuel the blast furnace, all of which boost at each stage of the process the economic value of the finished steel beam sold in the marketplace. Compare that process to the brainpower required when a student writes software—software that can hold even more potential economic value than the steel beam. In the new, high-tech society, we can create enormous economic value with little or no raw material and minimal energy.

In the 21st century, the only thing that will confer competitive advantage on the economy of a nation or state will be the cultivation of intellectual capital. That job falls squarely on the shoulders of higher education. University leaders have a moral obligation to support and nurture the knowledge-based economy and to ready our students to be productive citizens who can live meaningful lives in the new economy.

Convincing critical campus decision makers—trustees, presidents, administrators, faculty, staff, and students—of the necessity of responding to this new economic environment will not be easy. Community college systems increasingly are being recognized as important players in the economic development equation. Even K-12 education is beginning to respond. But we in the ivory tower are known for being slow to accept change, particularly if it threatens the status quo. "Why fix something that's not broken?" many argue. Higher education has served our nation exceptionally well over the years. It has helped build a strong economy and arguably is the United States' best export product. But assuming that the future will be like the past is exceedingly risky.

This new era arrives as a silent revolution. There are no bloody battlefields, no clashes of artillery or rumbles of heavy armament to mark its advance. The opening volleys have been fired, however. Colleges and universities that fail to respond will be left in the revolution's wake.

Management guru and philosopher Peter Drucker forecast in a June 1997 *Forbes* article written by Gubernick and Ebeling, "Universities won't survive. The future is outside the traditional campus, outside the traditional classroom. Distance learning is coming on fast." While some institutions will undoubtedly fall and others will founder, I am not as pessimistic—if universities respond quickly. I am convinced that only those institutions that embrace change will prosper, and probably only they will survive. Universities must get in front of the curve, adapt to the changes, and put them to work for their students. In addition, campuses must be ready to supply the fuel rods—the new knowledge for product development and process innova-

● ● ●

I am convinced that only those institutions that embrace change will prosper, and probably only they will survive.

tion—that will drive economic change. Students must be properly equipped to live and work in this new economic environment. We must rethink how we teach, whom we teach, what we teach, and how we perform our other roles in society.

HOW WE TEACH

In the emerging knowledge economy, digital technology permeates every aspect of society, including online courses, stock trading, retail sales, entertainment, and how we receive our news. Professors are referring students to Web sites that enrich and enhance the classroom experience. E-mail is supplanting face-to-face faculty office hours. Students are participating in asynchronous, electronically mediated discussions about course material through online discussion forums. A tiny CD can replace a four-pound textbook and offer the interactive bells and whistles that make learning not only easier, but also more interesting.

According to one national survey, the cost of integrating those activities into the curriculum and related administrative and support services totaled $2.8 billion for hardware and software alone in 1998—an average of $176 per student (American Association of State Colleges and Universities, 1998). Such spending is sure to grow rapidly given the importance of delivering education more efficiently and with greater quality.

Digital technology also has given birth to the virtual university—individual schools or consortia of schools that are harnessing technology to deliver education to students studying on campus or half a world away. For-profit institutions, such as the University of Phoenix, a pioneer of traditional distance education, have taken up the challenge of sustaining quality while delivering lower-cost, consumer-convenient education. New York University has created a for-profit spin-off company to sell online continuing education courses. Other entrepreneurs and businesses are marketing ways to help schools place and sell their academic courses and other services online. All told, 75 percent of campuses planned to offer some courses through digital distance education in the near future, according to a 1997 report by the National Center for Education

Statistics and reported on in a 1998 *Association of Governing Boards Priorities* article by James Mingle. The die is cast, and there is no turning back. Digital pedagogy must be reckoned with by all of us, and it will change us at the most basic level.

The Internet, already pervasive in society, soon will be a fundamental in our new educational toolbox. A U.S. Department of Commerce report, "The Emerging Digital Economy," noted that in 1994, three million people, primarily in the United States, used the Internet. Just four years later, some 100 million people worldwide had tapped into the technology. Colleges and universities increasingly are using Internet technology both as an educational delivery system and as a resource that puts a world of knowledge at students' fingertips. In a very few years, almost all of our distance education will be delivered via the Internet, primarily because of its "anytime and anywhere" availability.

A host of other universities and consortia are creating cyberspace classrooms, accessible wherever students boot up their computers and log onto a World Wide Web site. For example, Western Governors University (WGU) is a partnership of 17 states and Guam, and the Southern Regional Electronic Campus (SREC) has more than 175 participating colleges in 16 states; these two entities are among a rapidly growing new breed of virtual universities that expect to attract hundreds of thousands of students each year to their electronic catalogs of courses. WGU *(www.wgu.edu)* aims to be competency-based, degree-granting and offer access to campuses as well as corporate training programs. SREC *(www.srec.sreb.org)* functions as an electronic marketplace where students first find basic information about courses and then move by "hot link" from a central electronic campus to the individual institution that best meets their need.

California Virtual University connects students to hundreds of online courses, as well as certificate and degree programs, offered through the state's colleges and universities. Some virtual universities operate under the auspices of existing university systems, while in other cases entrepreneurs have contracted with campuses to place courses and student services online. Nearly all highlight the educational availability, flexibility, and relatively low cost that virtual universities offer.

Universities must look beyond hardware and software when they determine how to deliver courses in the future. They must bring faculty firmly on board, both philosophically and technologically. They must prepare to use the new tools as they teach freshmen from the MTV generation who were weaned on a PC. Likewise, continuing education students are bringing computer literacy gleaned on the job that may far surpass what professors are accustomed to encountering in the traditional classroom. Each group will demand professors who are as comfortable with the computer as they are.

As one of my own faculty members aptly put it, we may have digital students on our doorstep, but we're not yet digital faculty members. I place myself in that category, too. Nightly e-mail homework sessions with my high school-age daughter who lives 200 miles away have driven that point home. She thinks and communicates in ways that I do not, ways that have been strongly influenced by computers and television. Training our faculty to use these new tools and, just as importantly, to feel confident teaching with them, must be a priority that includes finding the proper funding, time, and other support to make teachers comfortable. This "ramping up" process won't come easily to professors who are convinced that face-to-face pedagogy is a sacred trust and essential to the learning process.

Faculty must be convinced that online classes can be an engaging, interactive form of high-quality education that have the potential to be as rigorous as traditional forms. In almost every case, faculty can enhance or improve the traditional lecture or seminar format with the use of digital technology.

Professors must realize that students who choose this form of education can no longer rely on the often passive learning experience of simply showing up in a classroom. Online learning makes all students active participants—they must write and think constructively in all that they do online, whether working on a paper or exam or participating in a chat room discussion, according to a 1998 *Real Education Chronicles* article by Bell and Helmick. Such online interaction can bring out the best in those shy students who normally would not participate in a traditional classroom discussion.

WHO WE TEACH

The top-caliber undergraduate and graduate students who come to our campuses to learn in a residential setting will remain the bread and butter of many institutions. This traditional market will continue to swell as we feel the reverberations of the Baby Boom echo. The U.S. Department of Education has predicted a 17 percent increase in the number of public high school graduates by 2008. Some states will see even more astonishing leaps: 78 percent in Nevada, 39 percent in Hawaii, and 38 percent in Florida (Riley, 1998). On average, full-time college enrollment is expected to rise by 15 percent during this decade, a trend that poses particularly difficult issues for public universities that exist first and foremost to serve the qualified students from their home state.

Computer-mediated distance learning has the potential to help universities cope with burgeoning enrollments that campuses cannot physically accommodate. Online courses do not require the classroom space, the beds, or many of the student services associated with more traditional campus learning. While online distance learning cannot replace the residential experience—where students learn as much outside the classroom as in—it can help ease the burden of the rising enrollment tide.

At the same time, the demands of the high-tech workplace, coupled with the convenience of the virtual university, will entice new groups of students to seek college degrees. Older students who hold associate degrees from community or junior colleges, and even those who have never pursued higher education, will see a degree or certificate from a four-year institution as not only necessary or highly desirable, but within their grasp.

The New York Times, in a 1998 article by Karen Arenson, cited the case of a single mother in California who worked nights and weekends while pursuing her bachelor's degree online from the University of Phoenix. "I do a lot at night when my children are in bed," she told the reporter. "That's the beauty of this stuff—you can do it at 3 a.m." That access and flexibility is what many non-traditional students seek from online courses and degree programs. In many cases, these men and women are productive members of the workforce. They have families to support and mortgages to pay. As

tomorrow's job market changes, they need to retool their skills and update their knowledge base. These workers often cannot afford to pull up stakes and move to a college town to pursue the degree or the advanced training they need to move ahead. Distance learning offers them a chance to be life-long learners and the vehicle for advancement without leaving their home, their family, their job, or their community. Even the alumni of our four-year colleges and universities, faced with a rapidly evolving workplace and shifting professional knowledge, will return to the classroom online to update their skills. They will expect our institutions to teach them while they continue to work.

Statistics from *Peterson's: Distance Learning* (1998) show that most distance learning students are over age 25, employed, and have some previous post-secondary learning. This trend will only increase as our population ages and we move into a more technologically infused society. For older students, turning to distance learning to keep abreast of the skills necessary for job success, the Internet will provide a vehicle to extend their education in untold ways. These students no longer will have to leave the comfort of their home or office to receive a top-quality education.

New distance learning technologies and virtual universities will open even broader markets for universities, markets that know no state or national boundaries. Today, the United States makes up only about 4.5 percent of the world's population. Residents of many foreign countries are clamoring for an education from an American university. While few of these potential students can travel to the United States, the Internet, videoconferencing, and related technologies offer outstanding alternatives for taking our classes to them quickly, efficiently, and affordably. Registering one million students for a single class is not as far-fetched an idea as it might once have sounded.

Moreover, the marginal increase in cost to actually deliver an Internet course to one million students rather than 100 is zero. That fact will change the economics of higher education. To provide a quality educational experience for a million students, of course, will be daunting, since it will require personnel to answer questions, grade exams, and attend to other needs, but the economies of scale clearly are operative.

Why dive into foreign markets when U.S. universities face an enrollment crunch and resource shortfalls? One answer in large part derives from the dollars at stake in this new market and universities' increasing need for alternative revenues. Higher education purse strings—especially at the federal and state levels—likely will draw only tighter in the future. Few new sources of revenue will be available beyond private donations and revenue associated with tuition increases. Entrepreneurial activities such as distance learning will become increasingly critical sources of funding. The global market is ripe for harvest.

Universities stand to gain tremendous revenue by providing distance education to the global population, particularly compared to the relatively low cost of delivering online courses—many of them the same courses already developed for our own students. Universities can reinvest profits from such programs to better compete with their peers in traditional arenas. Such ventures can bring in money to help institutions attract top faculty by bolstering salaries, recruit the best students by supplementing scholarship or financial aid coffers, and provide premier facilities by strengthening building funds. In addition, the more involvement we have with foreign students, the better we ultimately prepare our residential students for life in the global village and for competing in the global economy.

Success in international markets will change the political landscape, at least for public universities. When state legislatures realize that universities have access to these new sources of revenue, they will ask, "Why don't you become more entrepreneurial like your neighbor and fund more of your own activities?" Many policymakers—like some of those behind Western Governor's University—will see online courses as an alternative to funding their traditional state universities. Initially, these politicians and legislators will not understand that distance education is not really an acceptable alternative for traditional students. We must be able to explain why the traditional residential, liberal arts education remains vitally important for 18- to 22-year-olds.

> ● ● ●
> **Success in international markets will change the political landscape, at least for public universities.**

WHAT WE TEACH

For most of its history in the United States, the primary purpose of higher education has been to enrich permanently a student's life and to give him or her the wherewithal to live life more fully and more meaningfully. In the Jeffersonian ideal, a democracy is only as strong as the education of its citizens. Lately, we have moved toward seeing the purpose of education as enabling students to live productive lives in a highly competitive economy. In my judgment, the best way to educate students to live productive lives in a technology-infused economy is to provide them a classical liberal arts education. The liberal arts teach students to think reflectively, analytically, critically, and creatively—the very skills that will help them keep abreast of changing technology and function in a complex, rapidly changing environment.

Consider a new graduate, well versed in molecular biology and knowledgeable in the latest laboratory skills. When she is hired by a major pharmaceutical company fresh out of college, she is more than equipped to do the job and is maximally valuable to her employer. But skills and knowledge have an increasingly short half-life in a technological society. Even the most technically sophisticated knowledge base will be obsolete in a few short years.

Ultimately, it is far more valuable for universities to give students the know-how to continue to upgrade their workplace skills and revise their knowledge to meet the demands of a continually evolving world. The classical liberal arts curriculum provides students a strong foundation, and it cultivates desirable and useful habits of the intellect. At the same time, they become prepared to serve as the next generation of the brightest managers and leaders in society and the high-tech economy.

As universities increasingly come to rely on online education, we must be ever mindful of controlling the quality of courses and programs or risk irreparable damage to the hard-earned reputations of our institutions. Students need to feel secure in the value of the courses they take and the degrees they pursue. We also have an obligation to employers to ensure that our graduates can serve them well in the workplace. We must consider new methods of granting accreditation or certifying skill-based programs to assure quality in a world where students and teachers meet only in cyberspace.

Donald Langenberg, chancellor of the university system of Maryland, envisions the day when computers will help us customize the educational experience to meet the needs of individuals, break down artificial barriers that exist between learners at all levels, and create "a seamless, cradle-to-grave educational system." He's right. We will drift away from the baccalaureate degree as the gold standard of education and move toward certificates or other measures that will tell the external world what a person knows and what he or she can do.

Above all, quality must remain a cornerstone of all of our educational efforts—whether it's teaching a student sitting in front of us in the lecture hall or one who relies on technology to become part of our university. Members of my own faculty have questioned how we can maintain the rigor that is a hallmark of our on-campus education as we move the classroom into cyberspace. They want to know how we can verify who is sitting at a keyboard thousands of miles away submitting a paper or answering exam questions, as well as the authenticity of the work. And they have asked how we can steer the virtual university away from the role of the old matchbook-cover diploma mills, some of which have continued to flourish in the age of the Internet, where a Web address and post office box are all unscrupulous entrepreneurs need to set up money-making schemes. These are very valid questions and concerns, and we will provide the answers, in large part, as we explore the frontiers of what technology makes possible.

IMPLICATIONS FOR UNIVERSITY ADVANCEMENT

In the world of university advancement, these technological trends already are dramatically changing the way in which professionals—including chancellors or presidents—work to compete effectively for philanthropic dollars and position their campuses with key audiences. Rethinking how colleges and universities communicate, especially with alumni who are arguably our most receptive "public," is fundamental.

The promise of distance learning will bring

with it radical shifts in our alumni bases. What happens when new graduates no longer have that all-important sentimental connection to the physical campus, especially for institutions that are known and respected for the quality of their residential experiences? Does that mean alumni of the strictly digital age will be less inclined to think or act favorably toward their university, either in terms of attitude or in their willingness to give? The strategic challenge is to find new ways to engender and sustain the loyalty of distance learning alumni. The very technology that enabled us to educate them will enable us to stay in touch with them. So it is obvious that variations in the alumni base also have implications for campaign planning and media relations strategy for many schools.

Despite these vexing challenges, technology can make it easier for us to communicate with alumni, prospective students, key volunteers or legislators, as well as internal audiences, through e-mail, electronic newsletters, listservs, Web pages, and the like. Those channels of communication have the potential to make advancement professionals even more cost-effective and efficient in reaching out to their constituencies. Technology can also enable us to prospect for new development constituencies beyond our traditional supporters. Once we find them, it can help us cultivate them. We also must continue to remain "high touch"—rather than simply high-tech—when communicating with our publics. The best technology applications can make that easier to ensure.

Technology will not replace the value of face-to-face interaction, but it can help fill in significant gaps when that preferred form of communication is not practical. To remain successful in fund raising, alumni relations, and public relations activities, campuses should recruit advancement professionals who can identify audience needs and be flexible in delivering information. And those successes will play a major role in determining which colleges and universities flourish or fail in the 21st century.

EMBRACING HIGH-TECH CHANGE

Consider the birth of health-maintenance organizations (HMOs) as a parallel to these new forces now shaping higher education. Spiraling costs in a fee-for-service environment quickly exceed the corresponding increases in the overall cost of living. That also has been the case in higher education. Third parties—employers or the federal government—paid for on-demand health care, eventually driving up prices. Federal financial aid programs, state appropriations, and even corporations footing tuition bills for employees enrolling in pricey MBA programs have had much the same effect in higher education. Those trends and the popularity of college loan programs helped defer the real impact of college costs.

HMOs sprang up to contain costs at a time when the public was increasingly reluctant to pay more without receiving higher-quality care. HMOs increased competition and reduced costs. The University of Phoenix, the for-profit "virtual university," competes with traditional campuses by delivering its product efficiently and holding down costs. Phoenix relies on part-time faculty and others who are more interested in teaching than in producing original scholarship. Its administrators are thinking creatively and coming up with new ways to deliver education, ways that are foreign to old-school campus officials who don't think of a college or university as a business, with customers and products. We have much to learn from the business model. Those who dismiss it do so at their own peril and risk the survival of their institutions.

Distance learning represents an opportunity for those of us who run America's higher education system to lead—not by resisting change but by welcoming it in order to command our own futures. Over time, we must learn how to balance the mutual goals of guaranteeing a high-quality product with offering access to the largest number of students at the smallest possible cost.

The Spirit of St. Louis didn't carry 300 passengers across the Atlantic in five hours, but it was a first step. That's where the virtual university and online learning are now—the rudimentary stages

of a revolution. One prominent administrator has compared it to the wildest of roller coaster rides, and I think that description is quite apt. To make sure diplomas, certificates, and the other results of lifelong learning in this new age of technology are truly worthy of bearing the names of our campuses, we must take part in the experiment.

REFERENCES

American Association of State Colleges and Universities. "Campus Technology: Colleges Scramble and Stumble to Keep Pace With Demand," *Memo to the President* 38, no. 11 (Nov. 1998): 1, 3.

Arenson, Karen W. "N.Y.U. Sees Profits in Virtual Classes," *New York Times* (Oct. 7, 1998): A20.

Arenson, Karen W. "More Colleges Plunging Into Unchartered Waters of On-Line Courses," *New York Times* (Nov. 2, 1998): A14.

Bell, Daniel M. and Robert Helmick. "Online Instruction: An Evaluative Report of What Works," *Real Education Chronicles*. http://rs.realeducation.com (Oct. 12, 1998).

Gubernick, Lisa and Ashlea Ebeling. "I Got My Degree Through E-mail," *Forbes* (June 16, 1997): 84.

Hooker, Michael. "Don't Ignore The On-Line University," *Trusteeship, Association of Governing Boards of Universities and Colleges* 5, no. 23 (May/June 1997): 4.

Hooker, Michael. "The Transformation of Higher Education," In *The Learning Revolution: The Challenge of Information Technology in the Academy*. Bolton, MA: Anker Publishing, Inc., 1997. 20-34.

Langenberg, Donald N. "Diplomas and Degrees are Obsolescent," *The Chronicle of Higher Education* 44, no. 3 (Sept. 12, 1997): A64.

Mingle, James R. "Responding to the New Market for Higher Education," *Association of Governing Boards Priorities*, no. 11 (Summer 1998): 1-15.

Riley, Richard. *A Back to School Special Report on the Baby Boom Echo: America's Schools Are Overcrowded and Wearing Out*. Washington, DC: U.S. Department of Education (Sept. 8, 1998).

"Who is Learning at a Distance?" In *Guide to Distance Learning Programs 1999*. Princeton, NJ: Peterson's, 1998. (*www.petersons.com*)

● ● ●

If the older ideal consisted of faithful alumni who could always be counted on for generous contributions, the newer and more effective ideal may be a university audience of individuals who welcome the university as an "ongoing argument," where debate is ceaseless.

Institutional Advancement and Higher Education in the Future

Stephen Joel Trachtenberg
President
The George Washington University

The ground rules for institutional advancement are in serious flux. "Rules of the game" that once seemed immutable are melting away before our eyes. And the paradoxical cause of the stresses now falling upon individual advancement is successful institutional advancement. The fact that so many Americans have either graduated from or feel connected with our colleges and universities means that we are now dealing with a very highly informed audience that needs to be addressed in terms for which we have no real precedent.

A college-educated America! What a triumph! Only don't expect your graduates and those they influence to leave their skepticism and their knowledge at the door on Graduation Day. And depend upon it: In today's business-savvy American environment, alumni and friends of your school are going to know a great deal about its actual and possible policies.

One challenge facing colleges and universities today is having to adapt to information transfer modes like the Internet, a challenge we have begun to successfully face. The bigger challenge is the pace, rather than the content, of the electronic media. The notion of being online, and, therefore,

having your "facts" changed several times each day, runs in a direction almost diametrically contrary to the ethos of most colleges and universities. The historical drama of the university library, after all, has often been thought of as the centuries-long quest for an entirely accurate text. Today, scarcely a discursive sentence can be spoken or written that is not accompanied with an understood parenthesis: "for the time being."

Our institutions of higher education must somehow adapt to a world of frantic and ceaseless revisionism. Book reviewers sniff without pause after the most earthshaking literary and cultural events. Frontline researchers in the natural sciences often communicate via e-mail rather than print. Courses at my own university and other schools encourage their students to immerse themselves, via the Internet, in the global hurly-burly that has replaced more traditional visions of scholarship.

Is it any wonder, therefore, that colleges and universities are apt to project—via institutional advancement or some other office—a blurred and shaky image? On the one hand, they continue to be haunted by the sense of timeless solidity that was once regarded as "the academic tone" but is most likely to be cited today as a sign of nearly colonial obsolescence. On the other hand, our colleges and universities are often portrayed as places that have gone gaga with the drugs known as "student preferences." The fact that the kids "like it," anguished scholars keep insisting, is not automatically synonymous with its being true.

This may not be the first time in history that colleges and universities have been perceived as places employing a standard all their own. But it definitely is the first time in history that "intramural" has meant the opposite, almost, of "invisible." When a majority of the American population has experienced higher education to some extent, often in the quest for a two-year degree, issues involving tenure or curriculum inevitably find their way onto the front pages of our newspapers or into prime-time TV.

Publications that once focused on political and crime news are finding their readers and listeners to be avid consumers of news from our colleges and universities. It's hard to read or listen to or watch the media these days without a sense of academic Sturm und Drang—and of the embarrassment felt for institutions suddenly splurged with media attention. The relationship between this nation and its schools of higher education seems to be in a state of terrifying openness. It's not uncommon to hear that campus-based universities are an anachronism in our electronic age. Nor is it rare to be told that our universities have lost the precious integrity they laid claim to in the distant past, and have turned into schools of fashion, guided by a sense of panic, rather than places devoted to the "eternal verities."

A NEW STRATEGY IN ADVANCEMENT

Appealing to such a world for contributions and kindly opinion can sometimes feel like a labor out of Dante's *Inferno*. Alumni who must be solicited for kindness are themselves likely to be highly skilled professionals. They need to be talked to in a tone of such radiant intelligence that it cannot be disputed by hostile faculty members or distrustful graduates. This makes the job of a modern institutional advancement professional difficult. On the one hand, the fact that so many Americans care about our higher education system implies a colossal social triumph for our universities: They have convinced most Americans that they seriously mat-

ter. On the other hand, their acknowledged importance inevitably carries with it the seeds for outside criticism. College-educated Americans in particular are not shy about expressing doubt and disagreement with regard to our higher education system.

So different is today's academic scene from that of half a century ago that we must ask ourselves whether our ways of structuring institutional advancement still make sense or are due for dramatic revision. For example, it has long been an axiom of this field that the confusion and "ragged edges" of the academic reality need to be cautiously shaped and pruned before our alumni and other supporters can feel inspired by them. Meanwhile, those same supporters are deluged with news stories about academic life that are considerably less flattering—including the suggestion that the Internet has rendered university campuses and perhaps university curricula obsolete.

What this implies for institutional advancement strategy is a new tone altogether, one whose rhetorical norms are far more open and unrelenting. Is the university engaged in a passionate debate over its core curriculum for undergraduates? In that case, perhaps the faculty advocates for diametrically different proposals should be offered "raw" to the school's alumni and outside supporters. To argue in public is, of course, to risk embarrassment. Those willing to run that risk are also testifying to their courage—and to the seriousness of the discussion. If the results don't "read smoothly," that's all the better in an age that above all distrusts slick and seamless surfaces.

But doesn't a strategy of that kind call into question the very metaphor implied by "advancement"? Theoretically, institutional advancement is the art of moving the institution forward, to the point at which it has to worry far less about receiving financial and ideological support from those who know it best.

But "forward" is, of course, a slippery concept. If the older ideal consisted of faithful alumni who could always be counted on for generous contributions, the newer and more effective ideal may be a university audience of individuals who welcome the university as an "ongoing argument," where debate is ceaseless. Inelegant as the image may be, the school is a bubbling pot.

Such a state of affairs is inevitable if we contemplate our planet as an orb devoted to, among other things, ceaseless scholarship in every field of knowledge, much of it coming from places once regarded as "remote." This implies a new stage in the psychological evolution of our species: a stage in which all judgments are widely accepted as merely temporary, and in which "truth" is ceaselessly in motion.

One temptation posed by such a new intellectual order is a flight into religious or political absolutism. Flights of this kind remain rare. Another temptation is for citizens to reject the news as mere acts of manipulation, severed from truth. This extreme attitude is also rare in today's America.

One eroding axiom is that a college or university is necessarily engaged in a quest for public attention. A contrary axiom has partly replaced this old one: that a school can all too readily count on the kind of public attention that ceaselessly quests after failure and scandal—and that particularly rejoices when people with lots of higher degrees can be convicted of primal stupidity or ignorance. In this marketplace, does a university that makes mistakes—of all things!—really deserve to survive?

As I have already implied, the pacing and ubiquity of the electronic media increasingly determines the effectiveness of our institutional advancement efforts. In the newly developing relationships between universities and their supporters, there is no significant hiatus between what goes on at the school and what gets thought about it. This new state of affairs allows less and less time in which policies can be debated and meticulously developed. Let the school commit an error of sufficient magnitude, and suddenly the school is in a grueling "uphill race" in quest of a less negative image.

Academic Communications

Among other things, this implies a reversal in the relationship between academic media and outside media. For many decades, the assumption tended to be that academic media specialists were shadows of their profit-making counterparts in the "outside world." The latter were forever racing to meet tight

● ● ●

Is the university engaged in a passionate debate over its core curriculum for undergraduates? In that case, perhaps the faculty advocates for diametrically different proposals should be offered "raw" to the school's alumni and outside supporters.

deadlines and nearly impossible demands. Their academic equivalents could console themselves for their relatively modest salaries by reflecting on their comfortable surroundings and good vacations. But in a world increasingly dominated by the pace of electronic communication, college and university publications are now expected to manifest a competitively high level of productivity and speed.

Campuses will also increasingly be hiring in a marketplace that includes communication specialists from radio, television, the newspapers, and major corporations, as rapid marketplace consolidations make unemployment increasingly likely even for the most qualified journalists. Communications specialists will routinely move back and forth between the profit-making sector and the non-profit sector, including the world of higher education.

The new world of institutional advancement will pose special challenges for university presidents and chancellors. Where creative cooperation with institutional advancement professionals is concerned, presidents and chancellors have a very uneven track record. Often they have been more concerned not to give away information confined to the school's senior managers than to work hand in glove with those who are communicating the school's activities to the world outside.

This is not a challenge that can be met by mere mechanical adjustments. What is needed is steady, ongoing contact, at least some of which may not have a localized and direct purpose. Good ideas are often hatched in the space created by an open conversation. To further that process, the relationship of trust between president and the public affairs staff needs to preclude the possibility of someone "blabbing." If the president says that the time is not ripe for revealing some point to the media, then the president should not be second-guessed. Conversely, the "go" button, once pushed, should be treated as something close to the opening of the stall doors at a horse race. It means that hard running and the well-directed enthusiasm, is now appropriate.

The day is quickly passing when academic

public affairs departments could be forgiven a certain lack of sophistication. The American public—through the syndication of stories and columns by newspapers of record, among other phenomena—has come to expect instant analysis of a highly revealing and accurate kind.

Has an Islamic nation announced that it will be pursuing a particular line of national policy? Then right next to the major story on that subject, today's readers expect articles by specialists in the Koran, in the history of the Middle East, and in the records of 19th- and 20th-century Muslim statespersons. Instantaneous sophistication of this sort can no longer be regarded as beyond academic media capacities. It has become a minimum for attracting public attention.

Campuses that continue to limit their capacities—to argue that "that's beyond our means"—may soon be embarrassed by the capacities of their wealthier or braver rivals. Indeed, consortia of academic institutions may be devoted, within a few years, to building the kind of information technology base that can be shared by all of the participants.

Fund Raising

A similar revolution is in the works for academic fund raising. Universities' internal finances are not a mystery to college-educated Americans, whose personal finances are no longer in a different sphere from those of large organizations. The functioning of an endowment and the significance of campus maintenance and renovation—subjects once regarded as beyond the public's perceptions or interests—are now familiar to Americans, whose investment portfolios have taken on a global look, and whose ability to detect underlying weaknesses is honed daily by news from the world of finance.

This, in turn, calls attention to a force that cannot be minimized when thinking about the academic future: competition. Once considered not quite right for a respectable college or university, competition is today a recognized and growing power as campuses struggle to gain various edges on each other. The design of catalogs, brochures, applications, and other printed and electronic materials is just one competitive area.

● ● ●
Campuses that continue to limit their capacities—to argue that "that's beyond our means"—may soon be embarrassed by the capacities of their wealthier or braver rivals.

Rising competitiveness reflects a development in the national spirit that will leave few academic activities untouched: the legitimization of what was once known as "selfishness." Colleges and universities feel this, most obviously, where corporate donors are concerned. Profit-making organizations have long gotten used to making their generosity dependent on some arguable connection between what they give and why they are giving it. If the training in question is likely to produce more applicants for the jobs the company is most concerned about staffing, well and good. The proposal for an Institute of Sanskrit Philology, meanwhile, is likely to be greeted with the suggestion that another donor may be more appropriate (assuming that the company does not earn its profits by exporting audiocassettes to the universities of India!).

Historically, the only other kind of selfishness permitted to colleges and universities was that involved in team sports. More recently, the struggle for position in lists of various kinds— notably those compiled by *U.S. News & World Report*—has made Americans realize that no aspect of university life is free from outside observers.

Higher education must deal with selfishness, both enlightened and unenlightened. This is particularly obvious to colleges and universities located in major cities, where even the smallest addition to a campus—a Center for Electronic Communication, say—is likely to stir up opposition in the surrounding neighborhood. The occasionally predatory atmosphere of the business world can also find its way into the academic context. Where institutional advancement is concerned, this mandates a "new realism" in discussions with alumni and other supporters, many of whom have never heard their campus describe itself in terms other than those that can be traced back to religious parables.

THE CAMPUS AS A "BUBBLING POT"

The legitimization of "selfishness," as a broad cultural tendency is closely related to the new positive known as "entrepreneurship." Notably, our model for the optimal undergraduate has changed from "the student who gets good grades" to "the student who makes good use of school resources." Imagine the reaction, as recently as the 1950s, to the news that Student X is using something called the Internet to build a global electronic magazine devoted to forms of activism, some of whose readers may be potential felons. Shock, incredulity, and dismay would have resulted back then—and a summons to Student X from the dean of students!

Today, tactful suggestions to the effect that Student X scrutinize his or her readership more closely, combined with admiration for his or her "initiative," are considerably more likely. Student X is demonstrating, after all, that the students of "our school" learn how to be competitive entrepreneurs—and that will hardly come as bad news to their parents and families. The recent article about Student X in *The Los Angeles Times* is already being photocopied for general circulation by the admissions department, potential contributors will be told. And the student will be featured in the remarks that the campus president will deliver today to the parents and families of applicants for next year's freshman class.

Institutional advancement personnel must get used to the notion of the college or university as a seething, bubbling collection of possibilities. The traditional image of the campus as a place for undergraduates to "develop" is having to adapt to a world that increasingly thinks of development as a lifelong process, in the course of which an individual may glide through three or four careers, a sequence of foreign languages, and all kinds of higher education (including that represented by distance learning).

In today's society, success is less often seen as the product of five or six decades of employment by a major organization. Institutional advancement specialists must recognize that the "entrepreneurial undergraduate" is the key not only to donations but also to academic news. They will have to become adept at dealing with an internal "scene" in which traditional academic departments feel threatened by the initiatives of their own students. The professor as an authority will have to cope with a steady leakage of authority—an interesting story in its own right, if it can be presented in ways that do not instigate heart failure in senior administra-

tors or encourage alumni wallets and purses to snap impenetrably shut.

In short, our definition of a "campus" is steadily disintegrating. In part, this has resulted from the rise of distance learning. Theoretically, a student sitting in his or her bedroom thousands of miles away—in a totally different country, perhaps—can earn the same diploma or certificate as a student living in one of the campus residences.

But the total picture goes much further than that. With e-mail, an undergraduate or graduate student doing research from the banks of the Amazon or the Ganges can get in touch with his professor with just a few keyboard button-pushes. (Is the student therefore on-campus or off-campus?) A college or university president traveling in Europe or East Asia may find a faxed communication waiting at her hotel to update her on the internal squabbles she had allegedly escaped. Alumni living in South America or South Africa may find themselves playing a role in the next admissions drive, which seeks to increase applications from their land. Potential undergraduates in Finland or Brazil may receive specialized e-mail written in their own languages, providing them with details on how the central campus offers them opportunities attuned to their cultural backgrounds.

Such tendencies, by traditional standards, represent fragmentation. They seem coincidental, also, with expansion—especially the expansion to a global perspective. Students from outside the United States represent a substantial and highly valued set of financial gains for our colleges and universities. In turn, they create foreign alumni who are often eager to keep in touch. Some of these alumni will also become serious development opportunities whose contributions may someday mean the creation of new facilities and programs.

INTEGRATING INTERNAL PROCESSES

It is tempting to think of these developments as adding up to a "genial chaos" in which a college or university can become all kinds of things if it is only willing to surrender such previous ideals as coherence and good sense. Such an assumption is inaccurate because it ignores what will prove to be, in the years ahead, a countervailing institutional force: the struggle to integrate more successfully our institutions' internal processes, often through the use of information technology. Many academic operations, after all, mainly see themselves as reporting upward to the campus president and the campus's board of trustees. Too few are able to keep lateral contact going with those whom they may well regard as their institutional rivals for funding and other forms of patronage.

But all one has to do is to name such departments as admissions, alumni affairs, public affairs, development, and campus maintenance, and the instinctive response will be: "Those departments are all involved in doing the same thing: making this school a viable and competitive entity!" Some of the most aggravating situations in academic life occur through failures of lateral communication. E-mail and the Intranet may make more rare such gross failures of information-sharing. But even in our electronic age, there is no substitute for departmental chiefs who stay in sympathetic touch with each other's needs because they refuse to see each other as rivals.

Thus, those responsible for campus maintenance are obviously serving the needs of those responsible for fund raising. A foundation officer who unexpectedly arrives for a campus visit is unlikely to become more enthusiastic when she notices campus trees that are dying because they haven't been pruned since Dwight Eisenhower was president of Columbia. Those who work to keep students happy with their lives on campus are working with future alumni. Those engaged in laying fiber-optic cable are appealing as strongly to involved parents as to their children (also known as students). And if a school's public affairs specialists are alert, they can bring the institution to the attention of potential students and faculty members—as well as potential donors—by promoting in media outlets the work of faculty members doing the most advanced kinds of medical research.

Once we focus on internal integration as an ideal, the roles of those at both the bottom and the top of the organizational table take on more advanced status. Those who happen to answer the telephone can shape a caller's attitude toward the school. A wrong number, if handled with sufficient

● ● ●
A foundation officer who unexpectedly arrives for a campus visit is unlikely to become more enthusiastic when she notices campus trees that are dying because they haven't been pruned since Dwight Eisenhower was president of Columbia.

tact and finesse, might turn into a grateful payer of tuition. Meanwhile, the president of the school can become a public affairs specialist with whom the school's reporters and writers can barely keep up. That implies a workaholic president who regards each piece of mail in the in-box, and each phone call, as an opportunity for advancing the institution.

In other words, the efforts of those formally identified as working for institutional advancement can be seconded and strengthened by countless others on the school payroll, all of whom understand how essential it is to make a good impression on the general public. Less and less often does one encounter academicians who feel that "selling" the campus is someone else's job.

STRATEGIES TO AVOID, STRATEGIES TO PURSUE, IN OUR COLLEGE-EDUCATED AMERICA

As those who lead armies or build empires have long known, success seldom comes without a price of some kind. The spectacular success of our colleges and universities, which are now attended by a majority of our citizens, and which influence even those who do not attend, is a case in point.

Our campuses have produced a country that often looks like an expanded university. They issue "credentials" for every serious profession. They train and employ authorities on every serious subject. Each new step they take with regard to curriculum or admission is immediate big news, which often leads to extensive editorial comment.

The population of the United States, in short, consists of people who already know a great deal about how colleges and universities function. Colleges and universities are no longer distant "halls of ivy," populated by Anglophiles with mellow voices, pipes, and tweed jackets. The close connection between higher education and paid employment is obvious to every American, including those still attending grade school. The issue is whether the campuses themselves are living up to so awesome a responsibility.

A highly knowledgeable public can easily be perceived as a cause of discomfort. A campus president, for example, must deal with reporters who have multiple degrees. They are all too capable of asking the president embarrassing questions. Even the humblest employee of a large foundation may be a Ph.D. who failed to gain (or decided not to pursue) an academic position. He or she does not need an extensive review of the basics of postgraduate research. Meanwhile, personal protests elicited by some line of academic activity appear, not uncommonly, on stationery garlanded with credentials, and will often be signed by former students or faculty members of the very institution they are protesting against.

This is quite a contrast to the institutional advancement universe of only two or three decades ago. I can recall hearing, in that earlier world, an expression of anguish on the part of a public affairs employee who kept hearing from development personnel that they had completed such-and-such an application and now had to "put in the boilerplate" about the history of the school and its local, regional, and national position. Back then, boilerplate was a bad habit that a foundation or government executive could easily spot. The struggle was to give an application, from beginning to end, a custom-tailored look reflecting the willingness to work hard and think at a pervasively high level. (This, in turn, made the potential donor more likely to think the requested grant would be put to good use.)

Today, any American whose academic training has proceeded beyond high school can probably spot a boilerplate. In a college-educated America, institutional advancement personnel, as well as all other parts of a college or university, must communicate respect for one's audience and avoid condescension. There is no way of successfully talking down to people who regard themselves as your intellectual equals.

The challenge this represents for institutional advancement will be felt with particular sensitivity among those who edit academic newspapers, magazines, press releases, and Web pages. On the one hand, they must write clearly, but not condescendingly. If it is abstruse research they are describing, their role is to communicate it in such a way that even the researcher is impressed with the resulting clarity. (A common literary strategy is to create a "persona"

within the story who at one time could barely grasp the complexity of the work being performed, but finally understood it when it was presented in terms that are then inserted into the story.)

But, of course, the consequences of a college-educated America extend throughout the academic structure. For example, most of us hear all too much about the extent to which faculty distrust administrators. What we do not hear enough about are the talents and credentials taken for granted among faculty members, which are increasingly those also considered normative for members of the administration.

Administrators responsible for marketing a campus are increasingly aware of their intended audience's sophistication. Families considering a college or university for their high school senior are no longer incapable of judging its relative standing in an academic hierarchy based on research skills (or teaching skills that are compatible with research skills). Perhaps Dad received his doctorate in physics from M.I.T., while Mom got her M.A. in counseling from The George Washington University. Folks with credentials like that can dig up on the Internet all kinds of details about a campus, its faculty, and its finances. They must be talked to in ways that assume they already know most of what a college or university likes to boast about, as well as everything it prefers to conceal.

One theme becoming central to those who work in institutional advancement is the role that a college or university now plays with regard to our national economy. This will be an obvious theme when a campus is applying for a grant from a corporate foundation or the "corporate responsibility" department of a nearby manufacturer. But it should find its way even into applications aimed at bigger (i.e. national) fish. Potential donors need to be reminded of their gift's potentially global impact. Genetic technology is one example of an innovative field that joins the higher education sector with the corporate sector.

We are living at a moment in history when those who work in institutional advancement must set ever-higher standards for themselves. They should see major newspaper reporters as rivals rather than superiors. They should not be too surprised if some of their colleagues have entered academic employment from the "major leagues." And when seeking contributions from their institution's alumni, they should be able to draw a swift but careful connection between what the campus will do with that money and the needs of the alumnus's own children.

The words "criticism" and "self-criticism" have been a leitmotif throughout my text. Self-critical institutional advancement departments, dealing with an increasingly and effectively critical public, can all too easily turn into nasty workplaces that flicker with barely controlled resentment. Special efforts should be made to prevent this from happening. Collegiality and civility are qualities that help to keep even the most talented personnel on campus. They also lower stress in ways that serve creative and original writing in the academic media as well as on applications for funding. A spirit of pleasure—of fun—should never be driven from the academic environment, especially the portion of it devoted to institutional advancement.

Such a spirit may be easier to sustain if we keep in mind the fact that institutional advancement, by its very nature, ranks with the elite American and international professions. As many of us know, the salaries paid in professions like publishing, public relations, and customer relations are often relatively modest—because these professions are considered intrinsically desirable. To sit comfortably behind a desk while seeking the creative touch looks remarkably like paradise to those who must drive for thousands of miles in order to sell stainless steel widgets, or deliver newspapers at 6 a.m. on a winter day, or have every bin loaded with bagels before the breakfast crowd arrives.

But let there be no mistake about it: Those fortunate enough to be doing interesting work under comfortable conditions are at great risk when an error is committed. An American public concerned with personal advancement, or the advancement of children and grandchildren, can be mercilessly unforgiving when those who enjoy good working conditions can somehow be convicted of failure.

The only way to avoid such unhappiness is to be more critical of one's own efforts than any outside monitor. In a college-educated America, institutional advancement personnel need to empathize

with skeptics who are all too ready to "flare up"—not a maneuver routinely taught to those who earn their livings by convincing a broad public of their employer's virtues!

ELECTRONIC RESOURCES MUST BE RESISTED AS WELL AS WELCOMED.

I choose this as my closing note because it is forcing itself into our consciousness on such a broad scale. Institutional advancement personnel can joyfully welcome the revolution represented by computerization and the Internet. It enables them to contact more people, with more relevant data, than was conceivable only a few decades ago. But it carries some risks as well.

Desktop publishing, like e-mail communication, so often looks wonderful. When the typewriter reigned supreme, only printed books could boast carefully chosen typefaces and justified margins. The distance separating a typewritten page from its eventual printed incarnation was huge, and required a whole stratum of carefully trained professionals who called themselves printers. Today, on the other hand, even an institutional advancement "freshman" can unfold his or her thoughts in an early typeface once employed for the works of Descartes or Alexander Pope.

And therein lies a risk. How often, these days, do we receive splendid-looking documents that close inspection reveals to be tepid and uninspired? Writers must learn to resist the appearance—as opposed to the substance—of their own prose. Meanwhile, a gorgeous illustration, precisely because it rivals the most recent ad for an automobile or a dishwasher, may even today strike many viewers as insufficiently academic.

Though the gap has greatly narrowed between the academic and the corporate sectors of our national economy, colleges and universities continue to be regarded by most Americans as places whose functioning is pervaded with idealism. Even those who spend much of their time attacking our colleges and universities begin their diatribes with an overture devoted to disappointment: The virtues of yesteryear are gone, they lament. A debased generation of professors and administrators has utterly reversed the splendid accomplishments of [fill in date].

To work in institutional advancement is to be hardheaded without forgetting that there are contexts in which hardheadedness is not enough. Because they train our young, and retrain our not-so-young, colleges and universities seem to be in the process of regaining their connections with the European Middle Ages. At that time, university students were clergy in "minor orders," were crucial in keeping their societies functional, and would often quote an old Latin saying: "Laborare est orare" ("to work is to pray").

For colleges and universities, such connections mean that giving a bit extra ought to be a reflex rather than a remote option. Tempting as it is to argue that higher education helps to keep the United States competitive with its industrial rivals, we must be sure to add that it does so in a spirit of often-unrewarded benevolence. Our joy is to watch our world becoming a better place, in part because of the work being done by our colleges and universities. Relevance combined with creative pleasure: Has there ever been a better field in which to work than institutional advancement?

FURTHER READINGS

Daniel, John S. "Why Universities Need Technology Strategies," *Change: The Magazine of Higher Learning* 29, no. 4 (July/August 1997): 11-17.

Finn, Chester E. Jr. "The Conflicting Values of Consumers and Producers," *Educational Record* 78, no. 1 (Winter 1997): 10-16.

Footlick, Jerrold K. "The Holy Cow! Story: How the News Media Cover College Costs," *The Presidency* 1, no. 1 (Spring 1998): 29-33.

Jackson, Patrick. "The Unforgiving Era: Why Higher Education Will Be the Next Target in an Age of Increasing Public Outrage—and What PR Pros Can Do About It," CURRENTS 24, no. 9 (October 1998): 12-15.

Norris, Donald M. and James L. Morrison, eds. *Mobilizing for Transformation: How Campuses are Preparing for the Knowledge Age: New Directions for Institutional Research*, no. 94. San Francisco, CA: Jossey-Bass Publishers, 1997.

The changes in the UK since 1986 have stimulated a growing interest in institutional advancement as schools, colleges, and universities realize that they exist in an increasingly competitive world and must seek enhanced public understanding and support from all their constituencies.

Global Privatization of Education: The UK Model

Colin Boswell
Senior Consultant, *Brakeley Europe* and
Former Executive Director, *CASE Europe*

Sue Boswell
Head of Alumni Relations
Queen Mary & Westfield College, University of London

"Institutional advancement is a uniquely American component of higher education," wrote Steven Muller in 1986 in the second edition of the *Handbook of Institutional Advancement.* He went on to say, "These activities (external and internal communications, government and public relations, fund raising, and alumni relations), regarded as necessary on every American campus, are not generally found in colleges and universities of other countries."

Yet by April 1999, nearly 150 European institutions were members of the Council for Advancement and Support of Education (CASE), accounting for a quarter of the organization's newest members worldwide. Clearly, institutional advancement has spread well beyond the United States.

The trend toward global privatization of higher education is widely recognized. The United Kingdom is an interesting and early example of that new direction for what once was a universally government-provided service.

Muller's thesis was that most universities outside the United States were agencies of central government and that higher education in those countries was a benefit conferred upon the individual by the state. He argued that American state universities were more like American private universities than like state universities in other nations. Muller identified five key factors that distinguished American higher education and created a unique climate for institutional advancement:

1. The role of the church in founding colleges and universities and the separation of church and state.

2. The commercial character of American society in which higher education was a commodity to be purchased (through tuition fees) rather than a benefit to be conferred by society.

3. The general acceptance of the need for private contributions to sustain public causes.

4. The American emphasis on individual initiative and enterprise that has limited government to being a regulator, rather than principal executor, of the public interest.

5. The competition between American colleges and universities, not only for resources but also for students and, to some degree, for faculty members.

Applied to the UK, Muller's analysis was broadly correct a decade ago. At the time he published his analysis, taxpayers had assumed a major responsibility for higher education, paying the tuition fees of the majority of the 6 percent of 18-year-olds who went to university as well as providing generous, income-dependent maintenance grants for room and board and other living expenses.

However, some advancement functions did exist in the UK and elsewhere in the world. For example, many UK universities and polytechnics have had information officers and professional networks since the 1960s. Many universities, particularly those in Scotland, communicated regularly with their alumni and a number of Scottish universities had also created development offices. International student recruitment has been an important function for several decades.

There was also the important private sector in school-level education in the UK. In 1986, about 7 percent of the 11-18-year-old population was educated in fee-paying schools, and pupils from these schools accounted for more than 50 percent of entrants to the Universities of Oxford and Cambridge, according to the Universities and Colleges Admissions Service. Independent schools communicated regularly with their alumni and were adept at fund raising, particularly from the parents of current students. In addition, a significant number of the maintained state schools were "voluntary-aided." A voluntary body (usually the church) had founded these schools. Their governors hired the teachers, made their own admission arrangements, and maintained the buildings. They had a degree of independence not conceded in Muller's analysis.

Influenced by the economic theories of Professor Milton Friedmann and the apparent political success of Reaganomics in California, Margaret Thatcher's Conservative government in the 1980s introduced wholesale privatization of public utilities (telecommunications, electricity, gas) and other major companies, such as British Airways and British Petroleum. The government also led the introduction of market mechanisms into state-funded health and education services.

● ● ●
By the mid-1990s, British universities were casting envious eyes at Australia, where tuition fees were introduced, and a general consensus was growing that the UK should follow suit.

PRIVATIZATION IN THE UK

In British higher education, outright privatization, the complete independence from state funding, remains a limited phenomenon. The University College at Buckingham, founded in 1976, educates fee-paying undergraduates to first degree level in two intensive years. In 1983, it was granted its Royal Charter and became the University of Buckingham. This is not a trend. Buckingham still remains the only private British university and, although it has carved out a niche market, it does not feature prominently in the rankings that regularly appear in the press. Other private universities in the UK are American-style international universities, a good example of which is Richmond, the American International University in London, founded in 1972. With only 6 percent of its undergraduates from the UK, Richmond is clearly not seen as a major player by British students.

While there is little likelihood more private universities will be newly established in the UK, there may be a case when a state-funded university will opt for independence. And mainland Europe already has one. In 1999, the second independent university in Germany was created, the private English-language International University Bremen, a collaboration between the state-funded German University of Bremen and the city-state of Bremen, encouraged and advised by the private Rice University in the United States.

Fees

If the UK has so far not been a testbed for outright privatization of higher education, it is a country where there has been much partial privatization, principally in the area of university tuition fees. Fees had existed previously, but from the post-war period until 1979, local education authorities had paid the nominal tuition fees of full-time undergraduate students. The first serious change was in 1979, when the first Thatcher Conservative government introduced full-cost tuition fees for students from outside the European Union (EU). Overseas student fees have now become a major source of income for many universities.

Although all postgraduate students and part-time undergraduate students paid tuition fees, most full-time EU undergraduates did not. By the mid-1990s, UK universities were experiencing severe financial difficulties. The government had encouraged a massive increase in the proportion of 18-year-olds entering higher education but since the early 1980s had constantly driven down the per capita grant from the state to an institution. At the same time, the value of the student maintenance grant had eroded and student loans were introduced. British universities were casting envious eyes at Australia, where tuition fees were introduced. There was a growing consensus that the UK should follow suit.

One of the first acts of the new Labour government that came to power in May 1997 was to introduce tuition fees, subject to income-level eligibility of $1,600 per year for undergraduates, and to abolish what remained of the maintenance grant, replacing it entirely by a student loan. This fee is uniform across all universities and all courses, and was increased with inflation for 1999-2000.

The current debate centers on whether to maintain this fee or whether a free market will emerge, with prestigious universities and/or prestigious courses charging premium fees. The general feeling is that the present system is not sustainable. The dean of the Said Business School at the University of Oxford, for example, is proposing an undergraduate course in business studies with tuition fees of $22,500 per year.

Other Examples of Privatization

Other aspects of partial privatization include increased commercial activity of all kinds—contract research and consultancy, technology transfer, university companies, and conference business, among others. Some universities have funded major building schemes through the Private Finance Initiative (PFI) in which the university pays a private provider a regular service charge, covering capital and facilities management costs, for the use of a fully operating facility with specified service standards.

Fund raising is also becoming increasingly important. Most British universities now have a professionally-staffed development office, and many are launching capital campaigns to finance a portion of their research and facility needs.

There has also been much change in the way public funding has been administered in British higher education. Successive governments have changed funding mechanisms from formulaic block grants to competitive systems where the more successful (in research, teaching, and recruitment) are rewarded. As a result, British universities are now fiercely competitive. On March 12, 1999, *The Chronicle of Higher Education* reported that the University of Cambridge would significantly increase faculty salaries to make the salaries more competitive. The concepts of accountability and customer service have become almost commonplace, and the reintroduction of undergraduate tuition fees will accelerate this process.

In 1986, the UK already had a flourishing independent sector at primary and secondary school level. The sector had been strengthened in the late 1970s when the Labour government abolished the state-supported, direct-grant grammar schools and many of them opted for total independence. The Thatcher years did not see a huge expansion of independent schools and the proportion of the school-age population attending them remained fairly constant at 7 percent. In some inner cities, however, where middle-class parents viewed the state-funded non-selective comprehensive schools as unsuitable for their offspring, the percentage was higher.

The Assisted Places Scheme, introduced by the first Thatcher government, was the major aspect of partial privatization. This allowed independent schools to designate a proportion of their places for able children whose parents could not afford the fees. These were paid, in whole or in part, by the state. The scheme gave a significant financial boost to independent schools and helped them to maintain high academic standards. It was abolished in 1997 as one of the first acts of the new Labour government, in order to fulfill a major election pledge to reduce class sizes in maintained schools. As a result, independent schools have increased fund raising to create their own scholarships to replace the lost assisted places.

The creation of City Technology Colleges (CTCs) in the 1980s and 1990s, is another example of partial privatization. These are paid for jointly by central government and private sector sponsors, with no involvement of the local authority. They teach the national curriculum but with emphasis on mathematics, technology, and science.

A good example of public funding change was the creation, from 1990 on, of grant-maintained (GM) schools, state schools that receive their income directly from the government rather than their local education authority. They have considerably more independence than other maintained schools. The new Labour government will keep them, but under the new name of "foundation" schools.

CTCs and GM schools were used by the Conservative governments to weaken the influence of local education authorities, a process that was extended by shifting many powers from the authorities to school heads and governors through the Local Management of Schools (LMS) initiatives. So far, the new Labour government has not sought to reverse this trend. In fact, private companies will now contract to take over the running of failing schools and failing local authorities in education "action zones."

THE FUTURE OF INSTITUTIONAL ADVANCEMENT IN THE UK AND ELSEWHERE

The changes in the UK since 1986 have stimulated a growing interest in institutional advancement as schools, colleges, and universities realize that they exist in an increasingly competitive world and must seek enhanced public understanding and support from all their constituencies. In 1995, CASE opened an office in London to serve its European membership, which has increased by 232 percent in six years. The term "advancement" is still seen as a neologism and is less widely used than, for example, the term "external relations." But even this may be changing: the London Business School already has an associate dean for institutional advancement and, early in 1999, the University of Central Lancashire advertised for a director of university advancement.

The global trend toward privatization of edu-

cation is likely to increase as governments realize that they cannot afford the educated citizenry their nations need to compete successfully in world markets. The UK's experience is indicative of the changes that may be expected elsewhere in the new century.

FURTHER READINGS

Ainley, Patrick. *Degrees of Difference: Higher Education in the 1990s*. London: Lawrence and Wishart, 1998.

Beney, Adrian. "Awakening the Philanthropic Spirit," CURRENTS 25, No. 9 (October 1999): 68.

Beresford-Hill, Paul. *Education and Privatisation in Eastern Europe and the Baltic Republics, Oxford Studies in Comparative Education*. London: Symposium Books, 1998.

Bollag, Burton. "Higher Education in Europe Moves Away From State Control: As Share of Operating Funds From Governments Falls, Institutions Become Entrepreneurial," *Chronicle of Higher Education* 44, no. 11 (November 7, 1997): A47-A48.

Bollag, Burton. "Looking for New Money: As Government Support Lags, Europe's Universities Cultivate Other Sources," *Chronicle of Higher Education* 41, no. 41 (June 23, 1995): A33, A35.

Chitty, C. "Education Action Zones: test-beds for Privatisation," *Forum* 40, no 3 (1998): 79 – 81.

Darvas, Peter. *Higher Education in Europe*. New York, NY: Garland Publishing Inc., 1997.

Finegold, David, Laurel McFarland and William Richardson. *Something Borrowed, Something Blue? A Study of the Thatcher Government's Appropriation of American Education and Training Policy, Oxford Series in Comparative Education*. London: Symposium Books, 1993.

Gearhart, G. David and Roger L. Williams. "The British are Coming: Fund Raising in the United Kingdom is Catching Up Fast—And That Means Competition," CURRENTS 16, no. 9 (October 1990): 72.

Muller, Steven. "The Definition and Philosophy of Institutional Advancement," in *Handbook of Institutional Advancement*. 2nd ed. Edited by A. Westley Rowland. San Francisco, CA: Jossey-Bass Publishers, 1986.

Nichols, Judith. *Lessons From Abroad: Fresh Ideas From Fund-Raising Experts in the United Kingdom*. Chicago, IL: Bonus Books, June 1997.

Pollack, Rachel H. "A View From Across the Pond," CURRENTS 25, no. 5 (May 1999): 32-35.

It is our responsibility to guarantee that all volunteers who work with us feel valued and their efforts recognized. The same recognition should be given to colleagues in other areas of advancement with whom we work.

Educational Fund Raising

Frederick C. Nahm

Acting President
Colonial Williamsburg Foundation and

Former President
Knox College

Over the past two decades, all elements of institutional advancement have become increasingly professionalized. CASE's commissions on alumni relations, fund raising, and communications continue to update a core set of competencies for the field. We can now take university courses and earn degrees in fund raising and advancement. Those of us working in the field have developed increasingly specialized skills; our colleagues are more often women and minorities; and public relations is considered an adjunct to advancement, not a separate function. Technological tools allow us to access and manipulate far more data about our constituents and potential donors than ever before.

No longer is fund raising primarily the purview of academia; nonprofits, large and small, community agencies and foundations, even public institutions such as town libraries, have moved aggressively into fund raising to supplement their public funding dollars and to better fulfill their missions. The increasing numbers of institutions engaging in fund raising should not concern us. Increased competition has not diminished the generosity of Americans one iota. It has only meant that we must

be more effective, more accountable, and more conscientious in gaining public understanding and support for the institutions we represent.

Central to all of our efforts, especially during a comprehensive or capital campaign, is the annual fund. The importance of enlarging that base, without which the institution cannot move forward, should not be underestimated. Student bodies are increasingly diverse and international. Alumni relations programs (also more diverse) have expanded their focus to also include programs for undergraduates and young alumni who need to be taught about philanthropy—including what the annual fund is—and their future role as alumni. In addition, in order to "grow" your annual fund base, they require increasingly sophisticated and targeted-by-segment direct mail.

Volunteers need to know that our expectations of them include their time, their talents, and their leadership participation in the annual fund. While we depend more on volunteers today than ever, they are more difficult to recruit because of demands upon their time. We need to ask volunteers to perform discrete tasks that offer them satisfaction. An early investment in time spent training volunteers will pay big dividends down the line.

It is our responsibility to guarantee that all

volunteers who work with us feel valued and their efforts recognized. The same recognition should be given to colleagues in other areas of advancement with whom we work.

CASE reminds us that the "three-legged stool" metaphor has re-emerged; alumni relations, communications, and fund raising working together comprise the institutional advancement team. Together, we work more professionally, we build on our strengths, and we share information. Today, some of the most powerful partnerships are between alumni, communications, and development offices. Each must be clear about its goals and focused on achieving its long-term objectives.

While our lives have all been changed—and will continue to change— by rapid developments in technology, I am confident that fund raising over the next decade will, at heart, remain a "people profession." Craig Sweetan, one of my predecessors as vice president for development at the University of Pennsylvania, said it best: "Nothing will come along to replace the three-by-five cards in your pocket."

Just as it's been said that all politics is local, all good institutional advancement is, in the end, personal. Despite our embrace of PCs, the Internet, online searches, and e-commerce, we are also more intent than ever on keeping in touch with one another using cell phones, pagers, e-mail, alumni magazines, special donor newsletters—and fountain pens. When it's time for a development officer on the advancement team to make that big ask, there is no more effective way to do that than meeting face-to-face with a prospect. A great deal of groundwork by staff members, often requiring the effective use of technology, is necessary to reach that critical point when you know someone is ready to be asked. But, after that, it is person-to-person. Only then can we know whether the time is right to ask for a large gift, to issue an invitation to join the board, or to present our case for more government support.

Once a donor has made a gift or a constituent a commitment to our institution, our task is to convince her or him that it was the right decision. Keeping donors, alumni, board members, and volunteers informed at regular intervals is essential. All of us involved in institutional advancement—fund raisers, alumni, government, and public relations officers—owe our constituents careful, attentive stewardship. We have learned that the greatest gift we can give our strong supporters is personal access. They usually do not want us to spend a lot of money on them, but recognition of their contributions and publicity about their gifts are important. A handwritten note from the president, invitations to special events that offer inside glimpses of our institutions, access to our institution's leaders, and prominently placed donor plaques and contributors' lists in alumni magazines are all powerful and effective means of conveying gratitude for their support. Tomorrow, stewardship must receive the same attention and priority as solicitation does today.

● ● ●

Once a donor has made a gift or a constituent a commitment to our institution, our task is to convince her or him that it was the right decision.

Student bodies on college campuses are becoming more multi-ethnic and international. More women are controlling assets and making philanthropic decisions. We must be equipped to embrace and encourage that diversity.

A hallmark of the new millennium is that more people have more disposable income at a younger age. We are also witnessing the most significant transfer of wealth in history from aging Baby Boomers to their heirs. Our role is to help them learn how to be philanthropic and to demonstrate how rewarding that can be. I know I'll continue to use my three-by-five cards along with the new technological tools in development's arsenal for prospecting, tracking, and communicating. And I know that I can succeed only by working in close collaboration with the communications and alumni/constituent relations staff as part of the advancement team.

FURTHER READINGS

Brehmer, Dianne A., ed. *Communicating Effectively with Major Donors: New Directions for Philanthropic Fundraising,* no. 10. San Francisco, CA: Jossey-Bass Publishers, 1995.

Carter, Lindy Keane and Stewart Saltonstall. "Group Dynamics—Despite Their Differences, Your Development Committee Volunteers Can Work as a Team for Solid Fund-Raising Results," CURRENTS 24, no. 1 (January 1998): 34-39.

Heuermann, Robert. "A Higher Calling: Your Fund-Raising Efforts Are Crucial to the Future.Here's Why," CURRENTS 23, no. 4 (April 1997): 16-18.

Holton, Carlotta. "Major Gifts Are Philanthropy's Future: Nonprofits Seek Checks With Big Zeros," *Nonprofit Times* 10, no. 10 (October 1996): 1, 12, 14.

House, Michael L. "Structured Stewardship: How One Campus Plugged In a System to Thank, Inform, and Remember Its Top Donors—All Year, Every Year," CURRENTS 22, no. 4 (April 1996): 40-42, 44.

King, David H. "What Development Professionals Can Learn From Tyrannosaurus Rex," *Fund Raising Management* 28, no. 1 (March 1997): 28-30.

Toward, Christopher. "The Young and the Restless—Alumni in Their 20s, 30s, and 40s Can Be an Untapped Source of Major Gifts for Your Campus, But They May Not Sit Still for the Usual Appeals," CURRENTS 25, no. 2 (February 1999): 26-31.

Educational
Fund Raising

Our goal as advancement communicators should be to help the offices we serve generate effective strategies for accomplishing a one-to-one relationship with a carefully targeted audience—whether it be a donor, a prospective student, an editor, a reporter, a graduate, an employee, or the general public.

Effective Communication in the Information Age: High-Touch or High-Tech?

M. Fredric Volkmann
Vice Chancellor for Public Relations
Washington University in St. Louis

"The more things change, the more they remain the same."

Alphonse Karr, Les Guêpes, 1849

A medical scientist reported in late 1998 that he had achieved the first successful direct link between a human brain and a computer—something that was the stuff of science fiction only a decade ago. Has technology induced a massive change in how we think and make decisions in the Information Age? Perhaps history can teach us what the future will bring.

HOW WE COMMUNICATED BEFORE THE INFORMATION AGE

Let's journey back in time to the 1450s when Gütenberg perfected movable type and forever changed our access to information by making it easier and cheaper to print. Then, as now, knowledge was power—an avenue to information that previously had been limited to the privileged few who could read and afford to own hand-lettered books. The ensuing revolution in printing and writing helped create a society where written language and ideas were now available to almost anyone. Yet these new tools of communication did little to alter how important personal or business decisions were made.

By the 1800s, the invention of the telegraph and then the telephone changed message transmission times from days and weeks to seconds and minutes. Fast forward to the early 1940s when the first attempts at computing resulted in a giant, noisy agglomeration of telephone relay switches and vacuum tubes. By this time, the cost of reproducing and sending printed information had dropped dramatically as linotype and then electronic typesetting technology streamlined much of the preparatory process. After World War II, the cost of producing newspapers was driven down even further because advertisers began to see them as a good place to send their messages to an educated, reading public. Just a few years earlier, in the 1920s and 1930s, the world saw the advent of commercial radio, followed by the emergence of television. While these communications tools were revolutionary, they did not profoundly change the actual personal messages we communicated and the important business decisions we made.

In the 1980s, we saw another major technological revolution in the methods of communication. The fax machine, the personal computer, and the Internet struck a chord with a world eager for vastly cheaper, faster ways of processing and transferring data. The results have been exponential annual improvements in speed and quality of data transmission. In seconds, entire books and newspapers can be sent anywhere on earth, complete with illustrations, photographs, Web site links, video segments, and audio embellishments. Access to personal computers and Internet connections are necessary for communication and for any sort of business operation today.

VALUE OF PERSONAL COMMUNICATION

Given these technological breakthroughs, it's not surprising that we are able now to link a computer with a human brain. The tools of communication—the methods of conveying and storing information—have changed dramatically. Yet, have these technological breakthroughs truly changed the value of a personal message? I would argue that the value of human contact has risen faster than we can say "World Wide Web." As technology pervades our culture, people crave personal contact as an antidote to the deluge of messages that rain down on all of us every day—by early 1999, it was estimated that one could access more than 800 million Web pages. Predictions say that this number will exceed 3 billion by 2002. Education has embraced this revolution as a tool to speed up learning and research, but not as a replacement for face-to-face communication.

Here are a few examples of how personal communication still holds its own in the Information Age:

- Sales of writing papers and greeting cards have skyrocketed in the last two decades as people seek truly personal messages from others.
- Fountain pens and other writing instruments are now more highly prized than ever.
- Personal cell phones and beepers are ubiquitous, demonstrating peoples' need to have contact with others at all times.
- E-mail users demand individualized answers from other users and protection from electronic junk mail because they don't want unsolicited impersonal messages interfering with their personal and professional e-mail.
- Computer software that imitates an individual's

handwriting is now available so that the laser printer output looks as if it were produced by a person putting pen to paper.

Indeed, for educational institutions, mass-produced words in either electronic or printed form may be one of the worst ways to communicate effectively with internal and external audiences. Development, public relations, admissions, government relations, and alumni relations programs still depend too heavily on alumni magazines, newsletters, tabloid newspapers, news releases, press conferences, announcements, viewbooks, catalogs, brochures, pamphlets, Web sites, and mass-produced letters. Most of us know from experience that such techniques are not always the best ways of solving a communications, marketing, or fundraising problem, but we often ignore more effective strategies when a specific result or outcome is needed.

People talking to people is how important decisions are accomplished—not by deluging one another with more paper or electronic messages. The battle is high-tech versus high-touch. Most major donors being cultivated for a large gift prefer being approached face-to-face. If a new university initiative deserves wide attention, the president will brief the local newspaper editor in person, rather than sending a news release or making a telephone call. Should important legislation be needed to solve a resource or funding problem, the government relations office will go personally to Congressional leaders to argue the institution's case. When the alumni magazine plans a feature about a famous graduate, the writer (and the subject) invariably prefers a personal interview. Admissions professionals and athletics coaches know that a personalized campus visit is invaluable in recruiting a prospect.

We want to occupy the same space as another human being because we are driven by our need to use all of our senses when dealing with consequential matters. We see in three dimensions; we hear in two-eared stereo; we talk and listen not just with our voices but with our facial expressions and body gestures; we often converse while sharing the act of eating; we use our sense of touch when we shake hands; we even process information about each other based on the scent of one's cologne or perfume. No computers can replicate and communicate these uniquely human sensations that build trust and respect, or repulsion.

Face-to-face experiences help us gather information we cannot acquire through technology and allow us to use our human instincts. Did she manage good eye contact? Is that a firm handshake? Did his posture coincide with his tone of voice and the level of interest he expressed? Did I believe what was said, based on the presenter's deportment?

Perhaps the best evidence of the value of personal contact is right on our campuses where millions of students still attend classes every day to hear live human beings give lectures or conduct tutorials; they could opt to view these sessions by videotape or read about them on a Web site. This is why distance learning is never likely to totally replace in-class experiences, at least for traditional-age students.

USING HIGH-TOUCH COMMUNICATION IN ADVANCEMENT

In this age of high-tech, high-touch remains extraordinarily powerful and effective. Obviously, communicators in institutional advancement cannot possibly afford to use face-to-face communications all the time.

Compare communications to a ladder with the top rung representing the most effective and the most costly way to send or receive messages; this top rung would indeed be one-on-one, face-to-face communications. For example, if a major crisis were to occur on our campus and we wanted to do the best job possible in explaining some difficult and sensitive aspect of the problem, we would start by personally informing those who are most affected by the event. Another example of the importance of face-to-face communication is with prospective students. Most decide on which college to attend only after visiting the schools and meeting faculty and students; it's not the viewbook, the flashy video, or the catalog that makes their choice—it's the people.

The second rung from the top would be the small groups or meetings in which two-way com-

● ● ●

We want to occupy the same space as another human being because we are driven by our need to use all of our senses when dealing with consequential matters.

munication is encouraged. Human beings require one another's presence to make decisions effectively and to deal with issues promptly and efficiently. Think about why so many advancement professionals travel to attend seminars, institutes, and workshops—when the information shared is available via manuscript, video, or Web formats.

The third rung is a person speaking before a large group such as in a lecture hall, or at a religious service, or political rally. Even though two-way communication is difficult in this setting, something about the "chemistry" of being in the same place with hundreds or thousands of others can have a catalyzing effect on communications. An example in educational advancement is a fundraising campaign kickoff.

Sharing fourth rung on the ladder are the telephone and e-mail; they allow the continuation of two-way discussion, but with no ability to look into one another's eyes to determine the level or credibility of each message. As more and more people install answering machines and other ways of blunting invasive behavior, the phone is less useful. E-mail is enjoying a heyday, but the sheer volume of messages is already causing people to review e-mail marketing with skepticism.

The personal letter is the fifth rung down the ladder. The best way to send a personal message in this high-tech world is to handwrite it. Testing has shown time and again that the recipients of handwritten notes and letters give them much higher credibility and value than any other form of mailed communication. Make sure that all the computer-generated letters you send are personalized and individually tailored so that the recipient doesn't feel as though he or she is hearing from a machine. Laser output and ink-jet technology test less favorably with letter readers than the good old typewriter or the outdated computer wheel printer.

The next rung down this ladder of communication would be a mass-produced, non-personal letter, fax, or e-mail sent out with a salutation like, "Dear Employee, Dear Colleague, Dear Student, Dear Graduate, or Dear Occupant."

Of even lower value is a brochure or pamphlet sent out as a direct-mail piece without a cover letter, and ranking below it are articles in your institutional newsletter, magazine, tabloid, or on junk electronic mail.

News carried in the media can rank lower yet, including printed and electronic newspapers, radio, television, magazines, and Web sites.

The very bottom rung of this communications ladder is paid advertising in virtually any media, followed in turn by billboards, skywriting, bulletin boards, graffiti, window decals, posters, and the like.

Some readers may be skeptical of this ladder of communications, because in our everyday life, we are inundated with thousands of messages from many sources, and it may seem like there is no order to this message madness.

Alumni expect to be treated personally by their institutions, simply because they experienced personalized and inspiring service as students. We indeed have to practice the same sort of attentiveness in our advancement communications that students have come to expect from their educational experience.

Some leading US organizations provide examples of successfully using personal communications. The Republican and Democratic parties and the National Organization for Women appeal to a wide range of citizens for gift support, yet they don't generally use brochures or newsletters as their initial contacts with potential members. Instead, they send personalized letters, carefully stating the reasons why one should support their efforts and become an active member.

At Washington University in St. Louis, we have seen a dramatic increase in responses to initial mailings to prospective high school students when only a "personal" letter is sent. If we add a brochure, the response rate drops. Why is this? Because people respond positively to being given personal and sincere attention.

Then why do so many educational communication and promotion projects concentrate the greatest part of their efforts on some of the least productive forms of mass communication—especially mass mail and lots of printed literature? The answer is lack of strategy.

Our goal as advancement communicators should be to help the offices we serve generate effective strategies for accomplishing a one-to-one relationship with a carefully targeted audience—whether it be a donor, a prospective student, an editor, a reporter, a graduate, an employee, or the general public.

When your chief executive suggests that we should "get out a publication, an e-mail, or a news release" to solve a problem or blunt a crisis, think twice about the desired result. A meeting might be more successful. A client comes into your office seeking to enroll 10 students for a specialized program; these students can be chosen only from a group of 200 students. Is it really necessary to do a publication, a news release, or a Web page when a simple, personalized letter will do the trick? If you are going to announce a new personnel policy that affects 50 people in your institution, should you send out an e-mailed generic memorandum, rather than sending a personalized letter or holding a series of meetings?

For important issues or needs, invest time and money in making telephone calls, writing letters, sending personalized e-mail, making one-to-one contacts, or holding group meetings. An effective communications plan will narrow the audience to a manageable size so that you can deliver the message, wherever possible, using a one-to-one method.

For the old hands among us in media relations, we know sending a news release is often a huge waste of time and money—not to mention adding to the endless mail and e-mail that inundate reporters. Making a telephone call to a reporter or editor, or hand-delivering a message is often vastly more effective in getting attention for a worthwhile effort or newsworthy program. What works in development, works in human resources, works in news, works in everyday life. So next time, stop and ask yourself three questions:

1. What is the desired result?
2. If it requires a personal touch, is there a more results-oriented but cost-effective way of communicating than a brochure, a news release, a Web site, or a memorandum?
3. Will investment in one-to-one, high-touch communications solve the problem, sell the product, communicate the message, or fill the need best?

By answering these questions, I contend that our efforts will be more productive in support of admissions, development, government relations, human resources, and the other vital public affairs areas we serve. It is important to look beyond conventional, inadequate solutions to better communicate in the complex world surrounding our colleges, universities, and schools.

Gutenberg's printing press did not replace our need for face-to-face communication any more than the computer will. Let's not confuse tools like printing presses, PC's, or the Internet with the core content of messages and the strategies that make them effective. In the world of educational communication and advancement, we must put the message before the medium—especially when we know that personalized messages are the most powerful tools. And where we can use technologies like the cell phone and e-mail to improve interpersonal communication, by all means do so. Make technology your servant, without becoming its slave.

FURTHER READINGS

Gilbert, Laura-Jean. "Gains and Losses: A Publications Director Explores the Pluses and Minuses of Communicating Via E-Mail," CURRENTS 21, no. 5 (May 1995): 16.

Langley, James M. "Voices That Ring Loud & Clear—With Proper Cultivation, Opinion Leaders Will Carry Your Campus Message Far and Wide," CURRENTS 25, no. 8 (September 1999): 21-25.

Netherton, Robin. "Face to Face: An Expert Argues That One-on-One Communication is the Single Defining Factor in Public Relations Success," CURRENTS 21, no. 5 (May 1995): 8-11.

Netherton, Robin. "Get Real: Five Practical Steps for Putting Personal Contact into Your PR Program," CURRENTS 21, no. 5 (May 1995): 12-14.

"Relationship Marketing: A New Marketing Concept for Higher Education," *Marketing Higher Education* 10, no. 4 (April 1996): 1-5.

"The Right Tools for the Right Jobs: A Chart Showing the Best Uses for 17 Different Communication Strategies," CURRENTS 21, no. 5 (May 1995): 25.

In many attractive, nerve-wracking, important ways,
our campuses are becoming the experimental theaters
where we begin to act out the drama of "one world."

The Changing Face of Alumni Relations: Future Trends in the Profession, 1984–2010

Steven L. Calvert
Executive Director of Alumni Relations
Northeastern University

George Orwell's attempt in his book *1984* to predict the future ought to instruct us in two ways. First, writing in 1948, his dyslexic trick gave him a date 36 years into a future he could not accurately forecast. We should keep in mind that in looking just 10 years ahead in alumni relations, we, too, will miss a lot. Second, Orwell feared humans would abuse one another through technology. We also need to deal with technology; like Orwell, we can affect our future by being conscious about how we use technology in our high-touch alumni relations profession.

The date 2010 may look intimidating; but we are preparing for it. In response to the loud voices claiming the Internet will change alumni relations and higher education, some of us are admitting that change might be appropriate. Our traditional face-to-face programs may always have a place in alumni relations; but we should also take advantage of technology's ability to connect alumni to our campuses.

You don't have to be a Luddite (those 19th-century English who destroyed early manufacturing machinery as the Industrial Age supplanted agriculture) to see the advantage of stability and very slow change in alumni relations, while fund raising, communications, and government relations weather sea-change.

Our brand of stability differs from thoughtless adherence to the past. While we trade on tradition and nostalgia, we are listening to our customers. The change we experience comes methodically. This century, we, in the field of alumni relations, have added one new program type every 20 years in our efforts to connect alumni to alma mater. We created alumni magazines and alumni councils right around World War I, established annual funds around World War II, developed alumni continuing education just before and during Vietnam, and began alumni community service programs in the 1980s. So, before we explore trends in alumni relations, let us recognize—celebrate, even—that our profession's strength lies partly in its stability. Prove this to yourself by watching alumni at reunions. These programs have changed little since Yale's first one in 1792.

STRONGEST TRENDS, BIGGEST HEADACHES, GREATEST JOYS

Here are four factors I predict will have the greatest effect on alumni relations in the future:

The Changing
Face of Alumni
Relations:
Future Trends in
the Profession,
1984-2010

■ *Diversity:* An emphasis on diversity will change everything, from programs to the way we communicate with one another. Universities can be the laboratories where diversity will be tested for the outside world.

■ *Technology and electronic communications:* The challenge will lie not in keeping up with advancing technologies (although that will be hard enough), but in knowing when to use technology and when to use more traditional means of connecting alumni to one another and to their institutions.

■ *Professionalism:* This focuses on knowing our business, and competing for and making best uses of our volunteers' time.

■ *Leadership:* We may face a crisis in alumni relations leadership, in building powerfully diverse staffs, in balancing alumni and nonalumni on staff, and in keeping our visionary managers.

Diversity

It's a megatrend. Since 1984, our alumni groups have rapidly become diverse and international. After a decade of trying, most institutions finally reached numeric male-female equality in student enrollment in the late 1980s. Women now outnumber men in the population and in higher education. They control an increasing share of the wealth, wealth that could be directed towards our institutions. As a result, we may expect to see fewer alumni programs that center around alcohol, social club events, and spectator sports, and more programs that add value to alumni lives—career services, educational programming, and community service.

Achieving gender equity placed even greater emphasis on the unresolved issues of race and ethnicity, disabilities, sexual preference, and more. In many attractive, nerve-wracking, important ways, our campuses are becoming the experimental theaters where we begin to act out the drama of "one world."

We are doing substantially better serving the diversity in our student and alumni bodies than we are with serving our international alumni. We still have work to do in figuring out how to connect international alumni and how to make them regular donors.

Just as all young people take computers for granted, many seem to take difference for granted. And, as with computers, our students are the ones who will teach us acceptance of differences. An increasing diversity in our student populations will force program trends for students and young alumni.

Young people arrive on campus already knowing more about diversity than we will ever understand—but they also know less about philanthropy, how higher education is funded, or their future roles as alumni. We can't assume they already understand the concept of annual funds, for example. Students from other countries, for instance, do not understand the U.S. brand of philanthropy. We have to teach them, because without an ongoing commitment to annual funds, the base of the alumni constituency will inevitably deteriorate to the detriment of the future quality of education itself.

We can support our students and emulate our younger alumni by applying "diversity impact assessments" to all alumni programs and communications, thus testing and adapting everything for appropriateness with a diverse audience. By 2010, we will be led by a younger generation, for whom diversity, we hope, will begin to be a way of life.

● ● ●

In response to the loud voices claiming the Internet will change alumni relations and higher education, some of us are admitting that change might be appropriate.

Technology and Electronic Communications

Technology always costs (never saves) time and money. One faculty expert in the history of technology pointed out that the last humans with real disposable time were hunter-gatherers. The wheel, the mill, the vacuum cleaner, and the computer, he reminds us, complicate our lives, and steal our disposable time.

Technology has serious implications for alumni relations. It helps to explain why our volunteers are so much busier and less likely to take on a club or class presidency than they were in 1984. Our cell phones, the Internet, the World Wide Web, and e-mail offer very mixed blessings. Yes, we can benchmark a dozen institutions in a day. But one recent study showed that in some industries, a

1000 percent increase in personal computers increased individual productivity zero percent. Never mind the human cost of hours at a keypad.

With the advent of e-mail (in about 1984), some of us realized that this new form of communication could keep us from doing each day the one thing we came to work to do. In desperation, a few of us hired students just to triage our e-mail. We had long conversations by e-mail with colleagues sitting in the next office, when a real visit would have been quicker, more effective, and a lot more fun. Cell phones are not just dangerous on the highway. Like e-mail, they tempt us to do what seems "urgent," instead of what is "important." They interrupt our face-to-face conversations with our favorite alumni, and they interrupt reading to our children.

In the broad area of electronic communications and services, the Web lets us offer "lifetime" vanity e-mail addresses, social and professional networking, and educational programs to our alumni. The concept of "lifetime" vanity e-mail addresses is noted in double quotation marks because nothing is for life in the fast-changing world of electronic communications. Some colleagues predict that the U.S. Postal Service will give us long-term e-mail addresses, and that new Internet rules will forbid e-mail forwarding to curtail "spamming." One way or another, we will get used to electronic communications, and so will our alumni. The result will be ever-changing uses, standards, benefits, and risks.

It is too soon to predict when (after 2010, probably) technology might change higher education so much that alumni relations might also be forever changed. Two things might happen simultaneously, along futurist John Naisbitt's line of high-tech, high-touch thinking. First, technology will allow the delivery of higher education without campuses, athletic facilities, dormitories, student centers, or tenure. Business does not need philanthropy. In this scenario, alumni are reduced to repeat customers. Second, and quite the opposite, "activity-oriented" and "learning-oriented" (Cyril Houle, *The Inquiring Mind*, 1961) students of all ages will demand a campus, first-rate classrooms, real books, and mentor-teachers. In these higher education settings, alumni relations can still play a powerful role.

Professionalism

CASE's Commission on Alumni Relations voted in 1993 that alumni relations professionals should decide for themselves how to measure alumni relations, instead of being subject to external judgment. This reflected a desire to bring an increased level of professionalism to alumni relations work.

As a result, the Commission created the "Alumni Support Index," a database of comprehensive and comparative information on alumni programs that strengthens the way in which we measure the institutional effects of our programs. The ASI collects measurements outside alumni relations that should improve if the alumni office does its job well. It counts not only the percentage giving to the annual fund, but other development measures; and it adds reputational (public relations) measures, and key data from alumni programs. The ASI helps us manage alumni relations in three ways:

- We will measure our own campus's current effectiveness, and our progress over time.
- We will measure ourselves against peer institutions.
- And (with several years' data in the ASI) we will measure our strength compared with other institutions when they were at our current stage of growth—more helpful for short-term planning than taking aim at institutions more advanced than we.

We know that our mission is to connect alumni to one another and to their alma mater for life, and that this can only be done through a variety of communications and programs. We are learning the difference between efficiency and effectiveness, and how to focus on what's important while pushing aside the merely urgent. We adopt "total quality management," "meeting skills," and "continuous improvement." We now see that even smart people cannot just "make it up" anymore. We increasingly agree that the retired coach does not necessarily make a good alumni director (we can't rule it out, either; coaches are better managers and marketers these days, too). We address the problem that alumni may know their institution without understanding alumni relations. More directors these days are not alumni where they work. They

The Changing
Face of Alumni
Relations:
Future Trends in
the Profession,
1984-2010

hold more Ph.D.s and Ed.D.s. They bring stronger business skills and track IRS and USPS regulations. They manage programs barely known in 1984: career services, community service, and electronic communications.

All alumni officers today experience management challenges that directors of independent, separately-operated alumni associations have faced all along: raising their own revenues, paying their staff, and funding alumni programs and communications. All directors now deal with legal, postal, tax, and business issues. Even at our wealthiest institutions, alumni relations funding has been tight. We must prove that budgets are effectively spent to connect alumni with alma mater.

Alumni relations is no longer just about programs, and we organize our offices to prove it. In some alumni offices, in fact, "alumni programs" is just one of several alumni-related offices. Other staff members work with alumni services (from travel programs to Web networking). We now staff "operations" (human resources, the budget, order and program fulfillment); communications (no longer just magazines, communications now includes newsletters, Web sites, and listservs); and research and new product development. The research department is where we benchmark one another, and look outside advancement for ideas to help us manage (like TQM or outsourcing to vendors). New product development means starting new programs, or improving old ones—for example, adding seminars to reunions, or career panels for alumni clubs. At some point, our vendors may provide financial services to alumni.

All of these new functions and new skills contribute to greater professionalism, and we can continue to do better. Here is one example. We often still fail to start new programs correctly, that is, with business plans and heavy front-end investment in staff, volunteers, and operating capital. We often don't invest enough in recruiting and training volunteers to get to that magical state where volunteers do their jobs with little staff support. In any program that fails to reach volunteer critical mass, the staff gets trapped in start-up mode, runs out of time, and the overall alumni relations effort stagnates. If, in the next 10 years, the only lesson we learn from our past is how much investment in vol-

unteers will produce "ultra-volunteerism," then we will have made significant progress.

Leadership

Like the business world, alumni relations is getting harder and busier than it was 10 years ago, with no relief in sight. We travel and work long hours and weekends. Personnel and budget decisions get harder with more government regulation and public pressure to cut higher education costs. Stretching valuable staff time, we depend more on volunteers, but their lives offer less disposable time, making them harder to recruit, especially for long-term jobs.

We still pay junior officers less than they can make in the business world. At senior levels, our trend is toward nonalumni in the corner staff office. Alumni find this hard to understand. Fund raising was becoming a "hired-gun" profession in 1984; alumni relations is heading in the same direction. Will any alumni directors be graduates of their own institutions in 2010? We may be facing an alumni relations leadership crisis in these next 10 years.

We should imagine using our past to build a desired state of alumni relations for the future. In this ideal scenario, alumni and nonalumni professionals in our alumni offices, diverse in every way, will more effectively manage programs and communications for our heterogeneous alumni populations. Alumni activities will continue to expand in type and scope. The alumni profession will itself stabilize. Staff members will be paid well enough to raise families and send their own children to college on the campuses where they work. Our volunteers will be much better managed—recruited for very specific purposes, supported, rewarded, and reassigned as they pass through stages of their volunteer life. And in this ideal alumni world, we will educate incoming students to be supportive lifelong alumni who know how higher education works, how it is funded, and their lifelong role in it. Technology will benefit our institutions, our alumni, and our staffs because we will control it, not the other way around. And for each one of us alumni professionals, our work will be valued, and our own volunteer roles will be as rewarding as our work.

On the occasion of his retirement, Bob Forman, who served the University of Michigan's alumni association for 30 years, noted a lesson he learned through his work. This lesson reminds us of the importance of our work in alumni relations, and of the stability we should cherish and preserve in our profession:

"Alumni volunteers are not a means to an end, but friends for life."

FURTHER READINGS

Benninghoff, Diane, Dan Heinlen, and Keith H. Brant. "How Critical Are Family Ties?" CURRENTS 26, no. 3 (March 2000): 32-36.

Bickel, Kathy. "Proceed With Caution: Societal Trends Like Cocooning and Clanning May Hinder Your Ability to Reach Alumni. Use These Four Maneuvers to Steer Clear of Trouble," CURRENTS 24, no. 8 (September 1998): 9-13.

Cleary, Sean. "A New Order of Things—The University of Michigan Alumni Association Reinvents Itself as a Market-focused Organization," CURRENTS 25, no. 6 (June 1999): 38-43.

Jackson, Laura Christion. "Setting Your Sights: Looking to Make It Big in Alumni Relations? Start with These Three Strategies from the Big 12's First Female Alumni President," CURRENTS 23, no. 2 (February 1997): 12-16.

Jackson, Laura Christion. "What's That Up Ahead? Alumni Directors Predict Trends and Challenges That Will Affect the Alumni Profession," CURRENTS 24, no. 8 (September 1998): 14-18.

Stoner, Michael. "Coming Up Next: If You Manage Your Alumni Office Web Site, Watch for These Trends: More Valuable Features, More Outside Expertise, and More Evaluation," CURRENTS 24, no. 3 (March 1998): 10-15.

Williams, Roger L. "CASE's Special Cases: A Close-Up Look at Four Groups' Progress and Pay," CURRENTS 22, no. 2 (February 1996): 20-22.

Colleges' increasing attention and commitment to campus-based government relations is a favorable and necessary trend that comports with a local focus on politics and policy.

SECTION I

The Environment and the Changing Face of Advancement

Best Practices and Trends in Government Relations

David Morse
Director of Public Affairs
The Pew Charitable Trusts and

Former Associate Vice President for Policy Planning
University of Pennsylvania

In government relations and in other professional venues, we tend to be "presentists," that is, we think of our times or the challenges we currently face as far more complex and turbulent than those our predecessors experienced. And indeed, it certainly appears that the environment for campus government relations is, if not more complicated, at least very different from that of 15 years ago, when the last *Handbook of Institutional Advancement* was published.

Still, at least one condition that overlays the world of higher education government relations seems to be immutable. As Tip O'Neill, the late speaker of the House of Representatives, was fond of noting, "all politics is local." Although the locus of campaign fund raising that serves as the "mother's milk" of the new politics usually goes far beyond the boundaries of the precinct, local issues and concerns still drive both elective and legislative politics in all policy domains, including those of higher education.

Dick Kennedy, in his chapter in the second edition of the *Handbook,* made a compelling case for a clearly delineated campus or system-based government relations function. He wanted to convince colleges and universities to establish and sus-

tain an identifiable, institution-based approach that would reflect policymakers' needs to support and promote their local interests. Whether or not it is due to Kennedy's convincing argument, what has developed since then is a clear trend toward the proliferation and professionalization of institution-based government relations personnel and activities.

Colleges' increasing attention and commitment to campus-based government relations is a favorable and necessary trend that comports with a local focus on politics and policy. As the campus, and its associated students, faculty, and staff, is the elected representative's constituent, that institution, more than the larger and more amorphous higher education association, is best able to evaluate a particular policy initiative's impact at the micro, "real world" level.

As I will suggest later, however, this trend may further fractionalize a collective or community-wide approach to advocacy for higher education. As Constance Cook indicates in *Lobbying for Higher Education: How Colleges and Universities Influence Federal Policy* (1998), the higher education associations' role in setting and advancing the collective interests of a diverse set of more than 3,000 institutions and an even greater number of sub-units is a necessary but far from sufficient condition for effective advocacy.

Each of the "imperatives for effective government relations" that Kennedy described in 1986 still applies today. But both the external political dynamics and internal dynamics of campuses that are conducive to an effective government relations approach have changed somewhat in the intervening years.

KEY OPERATING PRINCIPLES

In this chapter, I will highlight several key operating principles or rules of the road; suggest some new rules and observations based on my own and my colleagues' experiences at the federal, state, and local levels of campus government relations; and describe some of the changes in the political and higher education landscape and their implications.

Understand the Role of Communication

Today it seems obvious, but both Dick Kennedy and Ed Crawford, who wrote the chapter on government relations in the first edition of the *Handbook,* emphasized the singular importance of being an effective communicator with policymakers, both as presenter of information and as listener. It's not simply a matter of the institutional official who is principally responsible for government relations developing that relationship; bringing your president, faculty, or students to city hall, the state house, or Washington to meet with key policymakers is also essential, as is creating opportunities for policymakers to visit the campus to meet with those whom their policies are affecting.

Changing Faces

Knowing who on your campus are the most effective policy messengers is critically important.

To demonstrate the pitfalls of inadequate pre-screening of potential messengers, I recall my third day as the University of Pennsylvania's newly minted director of federal relations. I had received an irate call from a director of a National Institutes of Health-funded center at Penn who had been informed by NIH that it was phasing out his cen-

ter's support in the third year of a five-year commitment in order to fund more investigator-initiated projects. I was young and eager-to-please, and quickly arranged for the center director to meet with NIH's deputy director for extramural research. I hoped to have the NIH see the error of its ways and change the decision. We had a legitimate and cogent case to make and I was confident that reason (and we) would easily prevail.

At the meeting, our center director screamed at the top of his lungs, calling for the immediate firing, drawing, and quartering of the Institute director who had proposed the new policy. Needless to say, we didn't get what we wanted through constructive jawboning. Washington and Bethesda quickly became off-limits for my center director. Later, we took another, less direct route and the existing grant agreements were "grandfathered" by Congress.

● ● ●

What has developed is a clear trend toward the proliferation and professionalization of institution-based government relations personnel and activities.

Building effective personal communications with policymakers takes a considerable investment of resources, the most important of which may be time. Increasing rates of turnover among legislators and legislative staff in Washington in recent years have made the forging of strong, stable connections difficult. With each new election may come not only a shift in who represents a particular district in which a college or university is a constituent, but a reverberating change in key staff and committee assignments. In particular, the change in congressional leadership, especially in the House of Representatives in 1994, meant that an entire cadre of legislators, largely unknown to the higher education associations and to the colleges in their districts, would be taking on the responsibility of making policy affecting higher education. The effect of such turnover is a considerable loss of institutional memory about the purposes of higher education policy. Optimists may say this leads to a healthy rethinking of those purposes.

This increasing rate of turnover among policymakers at the congressional level is compounded by a recent phenomenon in many states—term limits for legislators, both statutory and self-imposed. Higher education issues—student aid, institutional allocations, assessment and accountability, research policy, tax policy—like most public policy issues, are complex and take time and effort to master, time that a six- or eight-year term may not afford even the most astute legislators. Even though many term-limited legislators may attain a new office and still be involved in higher education policymaking, there is still a net loss in institutional memory and a change in perspective. It would be prudent, therefore, whenever there is a change in a legislative seat, that the chief campus government relations officer visit new legislators as soon as possible after the election and before they officially take office. This would offer an opportunity to introduce the institution and to help legislators understand its importance to their districts.

This external phenomenon of policymaker turnover is even further exacerbated by a growing loss of institutional memory and personal relationships at the campus level, particularly as the average tenure of college and university and system presidents and chancellors declines. To policymakers, presidents usually personify their institutions (although faculty and students might quibble with that observation). And while presidents should typically serve as their institutions' principal spokespersons with policymakers on policy matters, it is also wise to identify respected surrogates who can step in when the president can't be, or should not be, the main spokesperson. The instances in which the president is not the principal representative for government or public affairs purposes may be rare, but it is important to conserve the use of the chief executive as a resource, lest he or she become the point person or lightning rod for all issues.

Changing Methods
Individual institutions and groups of colleges are increasingly turning to sophisticated and entrepreneurial communications techniques to mobilize public and policymaker opinion to affect public policy. Institutions and their associations now often use focus groups and polling to develop effective messages, and use advertising (although still an uncommon method) to build public and policymaker support, particularly in creating *ad hoc* campaigns to oppose or promote specific budget actions or state referenda.

Similarly, higher education institutions are increasingly using sophisticated economic impact data—economic multipliers, including numbers of jobs or businesses created; taxes paid by employees; results and applications from scientific research; numbers of visitors to local communities—to build support for public investments. Among the best and most effective of these economic impact studies are ones done for the University of Illinois and the Massachusetts Institute of Technology. (These studies supplement data that indicate a growing individual economic premium to a college degree.)

Know the Institution
Twenty-five or even 15 years ago, campus government relations officers most commonly came from the ranks of faculty or administrators who took on a new or additional role of representing their college or university. They knew their institutions and their institution's priorities well, if not the arcane process for achieving policy objectives.

Today, government relations officers typically come to higher education with experience in the policymaking world, and are often more familiar with the political process than with the institutions they represent. Government relations work on behalf of colleges has become a profession in which practitioners have gained their credentials in the political trenches in Austin or Washington rather than in Old Main or College Hall. That valuable experience is nonetheless fairly alien to the campus, which makes it all the more important that these highly-skilled policy professionals learn and know the priorities, inner workings, people, and institutional politics of their colleges and understand almost intuitively the impact of a proposed policy initiative or at least know where to go to find out. Simply put, they need to be able to interpret for the campus the blips on the political radar screen and craft their strategy accordingly.

I do not mean to suggest that the new college government relations officers are simply political strategists or lobbyists who would be just as content representing Union Carbide as Union College. They clearly have an affinity for the special mission and character of higher education and of their institutions, and typically think of their representation of their campuses as an extension of their earlier public service.

Campus government relations officers who come from the world of politics must also quickly learn to appreciate the ambiguity that derives from a shared governance approach to decision making. Few, if any, colleges or universities are clear hierarchies in which there is only one position publicly expressed on a policy issue. The president may speak *ex cathedra* on the college's behalf, but so may faculty and students (and often staff) publicly and passionately express, without fear of reprisal, contrary opinions that may receive equal or greater attention from policymakers. When Harvard's Neil Rudenstine talks on affirmative action, people may listen, but they may also listen to Harvey Mansfield, a Harvard professor of government with very different views on that subject.

Tolerance on the part of government relations officers for such ambiguity is essential. During Congress' debate over the landmark Tax Reform Act of 1986, Penn's position on one important aspect of that debate—the issue of tax treatment of gifts of appreciated property to 501(c)(3) organizations—was in direct conflict with the views of two faculty members, one the chairman of the Wharton School's Finance department and the other a highly-regarded junior member of the economics department. Each testified before the House Ways and Means Committee that prudent tax policy dictated that the appreciated portion of a taxpayer's gift to a college or other charitable organization be taxed as any other capital gain. The university's position was that the existing law, which provided that donors could take a full deduction for the fair market value of such gifts, was an appropriate incentive to encourage the transfer of private wealth for a public good.

While Penn's "official" communications never got to the Oz-like point of telling them to "pay no attention to that man behind the curtain," they consistently made it clear that the university's position to sustain the current law reflected efficient tax policy and good social policy, and presented case studies of gifts that would not have been made if appreciation were subject to taxation. (The faculty members' position prevailed, although fair market deductibility of such gifts was fully restored in 1993.)

● ● ●
Knowing who on your campus are the most effective policy messengers is critically important.

Issue Explosion

If there is one phenomenon that complicates effective advocacy by government relations officers, it is the exponential growth in the volume of issues that may affect a campus or system. The sheer number of policy concerns that touch campuses has made strategic focus and prioritization in government relations both more difficult and more essential than ever. The core funding issues of student aid, institutional support, charitable giving, and, for the larger institutions, research, are still prevalent; however, other permutations of these core issues are increasingly matters that institutions need to address.

Here are several examples of newly prominent policy concerns that affect many institutions: accreditation; campus security; hazardous waste disposal; health care reimbursement; immigration policy; local tax-exempt status; lobbying registration and disclosure; "right-to-know" legislation; antitrust policy; nondiscrimination and affirmative action policies; employment status of graduate students; faculty retirement; taxation of endowment income; local zoning procedures; intellectual property rights; and telecommunications legislation and regulation.

Knowing, and building alliances with, the appropriate actors, including faculty and students, at the campus level is as important as knowing the burgeoning set of current and potential issues. It may be difficult, particularly at a large private or state university or state system, to be omniscient about both the issues and the policy actors at the campus level.

Another way to describe the operating principle of knowing and being able to work with campus constituencies, may be to "first do no harm." Early in my tenure at Penn, a newly appointed professor invited a senior and influential member of Pennsylvania's congressional delegation to participate in an all-day symposium on adult literacy, one of that member's major concerns. As was occasionally the case on a campus of more than 20,000 students and 15,000 employees, I knew vaguely of the symposium but not of the congressman's participation. Late in the afternoon of the symposium, I got a call from the congressman's chief of staff telling me his boss was "furious" at having awakened before 5 a.m., driven over two hours to Philadelphia to participate, only to be given five minutes to make a statement and to be peremptorily whisked off the podium without so much as a "thank you." I spent a good part of the next year trying: (a) to convince the important representative that Penn was not an institution of ill-mannered boors and that we were worthy of his interest and attention, and (b) to convince the faculty member that if he wanted to regain the congressman's confidence and sustain his interest in Penn's adult literacy program, he'd best not act like an ill-mannered boor.

The lesson learned here is that making frequent calls or visits to faculty, students, and administrators who may occasionally be called on to testify before or advise policymakers helps the government relations officer keep track of key campus constituencies and their interests; assess and place those interests among institutional priorities; and offer guidance in helping them achieve their objectives.

Know the Process

Most government relations officers are knowledgeable about the process of government and governing. Understanding the political process and having a strategy for achieving institutional policy objectives are only preconditions for effective advocacy; they must also be adept at implementing that strategy. In implementing a strategic approach, government relations officers must know the interests and disposition of policy players, like-minded colleagues, and potential adversaries; they must also know whether, when, and what to compromise. The most effective government relations officers are those who are capable of serving as shapers and simultaneous translators of their campus' priorities in the realm of policymaking and politics (and vice-versa).

THE CHANGING RELATIONSHIP BETWEEN CAMPUS AND ASSOCIATION: MONITORING, STRATEGY, AND TACTICS

Knowledge about pending legislation or regulation and their potential opportunities or threats for higher education is essential. The policy landscape in higher education is replete with examples of critical amendments added by crafty legislators to obscure bills in the wee hours before dawn.

The proliferation of campus-based government relations officers, coupled with the advent of free or inexpensive information on policy developments available via the Internet, has changed the way campus officials get information. While higher education associations remain critical in building consensus within the higher education community and in supporting and carrying out direct advocacy, for many government relations officers, they are becoming less essential as a source of early warnings and as a synthesizer of policy developments. Increasingly, questions of whether, when, and how to act are being made on the basis of data gathered directly at the campus or system level rather than as a result of information presented or prompted by the myriad higher education associations. This phenomenon is leading to the formation of *ad hoc* or permanent sub-associational groupings of institutions with similar interests in a particular policy outcome, described below.

Cooperative Advocacy and Strategic Alliances

Organizations like the large state independent college associations and Washington's "Big Six" (American Council on Education, American Association of Community Colleges, American Association of State Colleges and Universities, Association of American Universities, National Association of State Universities and Land-Grant Colleges, and National Association of Independent Colleges and Universities) represent large numbers of very different types of institutions. Smaller institutions will often rely on their membership associations to alert them to policy developments and to help organize and execute their advocacy activities. As Constance Cook indicates in her book, *Lobbying for Higher Education*, since the operating principle of these associations (and of the presidents of their member institutions) is to achieve consensus before taking a position on a policy development, these presidential associations are commonly slow to act and their positions, particularly on contentious issues, *de facto*, often represent a common denominator that may not reflect the particular position of any one of their members.

In the past, there have been quasi-permanent sub-groupings of institutions organized to bring about policy outcomes, like the Ad Hoc Tax Group established in 1969 to promote incentives for charitable giving to colleges and universities. Still, the confluence of three factors—the growing professionalism of campus-based government relations operations, the advent of stricter federal budget rules, and the 1994 change in party control of Congress—has led many institutions to launch sophisticated *ad hoc* advocacy coalitions to supplement or circumvent association advocacy efforts in Washington. These new groups, which include the association-led Alliance to Save Student Aid and the institution-led Science Coalition (to support federal investment in basic science research), are narrowly focused on specific policy outcomes, and can thus act more quickly than the large associations.

At the state level, institutions have banded together to form temporary coalitions to advance or thwart ballot initiatives. They have successfully used communications techniques new to higher education—polling and focus groups, advertising and earned media, strategic alliances with third-party endorsers, and grass-roots advocacy. As institutions perceive major threats from proposed funding reductions, changes in tax-exempt status, and rollbacks in affirmative action, for example, such *ad hoc* arrangements are likely to become increasingly common.

Institutions and their *ad hoc* coalitions are beginning to effectively use grassroots or indirect advocacy techniques, including the building of strategic alliances with influential individuals and groups both in and outside of higher education. Such alliances can provide important third-party verification of institutional or collective advocacy efforts. For example, members of the Science Coalition, facing in 1995 a perceived threat to federal investments in basic research, allied with leaders of major corporations that benefited from publicly-supported research and successfully encouraged them to contact key policymakers and influential media on behalf of sustained science funding. Similarly, the Science Coalition arranged for several recent Nobel Laureates to meet with influential members of the House Science Committee and to

describe the effect of federal funding on their award-winning research as legislators considered budget recommendations for 1997.

Much as colleges and universities have turned to alumni and trustees for assistance with development efforts, so have they increasingly begun to use them for government relations purposes. The University of California system and the University of Michigan have established advocacy networks of alumni for both state and federal relations efforts, and the California system has, since the 1980's, invested major staff resources to build alumni advocacy. Creating such networks requires establishing ties and greater information-sharing between government and alumni relations staff and those responsible for trustee relations.

Express Appreciation to Those Who Help

As Dick Kennedy noted, what once seems to be common courtesy is often overlooked. A simple "thank you" goes a long way to convince policymakers that they've done, or are trying to do, the right thing.

Most colleges and universities are proscribed, by law or policy, from engaging in direct fund raising for officeholders or candidates, and most policymakers understand such restrictions. There are, however, many other things an institution can do to promote relationships with policymakers. Tom Wolanin, a veteran Capitol Hill education committee staff member and federal official who now teaches at The George Washington University, commented on alternatives to higher education political action committees (PACs):

> Higher education has the ability to shower…positive name recognition on members of Congress. Congressman Jones cuts ribbon at the new physics lab, throws out the first pitch in spring baseball, crowns the homecoming queen, chairs the mock convention or moot court, delivers a lecture, visits the financial aid office, receives an honorary degree, and so on. All of these events will be covered by the campus and public media. This coverage in the "free media" has greater credibility and penetration across the constituency, and therefore has much more value to the member of Congress than all the advertising that he or she might otherwise

purchase with campaign contributions from a higher education PAC. Did you ever wonder why presidents and cabinet members frequently choose campuses for their debates and major speeches? In short, colleges and universities have a potential political gold mine with which to participate in electoral politics: they can direct the resource at their command—positive name recognition—to the aid of their friends. They need to develop that resource and use it more consciously and systematically.

PACs remain rare in the higher education realm, except for those organized by proprietary schools and by for-profit firms, like financial institutions, that have interests in specific aspects of the enterprise (such as student loans and bond issues). As the cost of political campaigns and the proportion of legislators' time taken up by fund raising escalates, so too has the number of requests for political contributions from institutions or their representatives. Individuals who are associated with or employed by colleges may and do make contributions to candidates, but it is unclear to what extent the institution benefits from such political donations.

One government relations colleague who works with a small, institutionally-related PAC at the state level has suggested that higher education is at a distinct disadvantage in terms of access to and influence with policymakers:

> The volume and dollar requests have easily tripled in the last 10 years. Those of us with little or no access to funds in this area are becoming more and more at a disadvantage to the corporate and association lobbyists who have substantial resources. Unfortunately, for this reason, higher ed is not seen as a major player by many of our public officials. This trend has resulted in many colleges or universities hiring contract lobbyists to advocate their cause. It is interesting to note the proliferation of contract lobbying firms in the state capitol in the last 10 to 15 years, many of them being retained by nonprofit organizations.

The jury is still out on the issue of political contributions. In my opinion, individual contributions by government relations officers can be a useful means of thanking those who have helped your institution, but they are tricky and must be handled deftly. And, once started, making such contributions takes you down a slippery slope. Perhaps a better way to leverage contributions of others is, as described earlier, to build the kind of strategic alliances with those who can and do contribute regularly and to make sure that those allies associate their interests with your institution. Campaign finance reform may be the most effective antidote to the money chase/access problem.

EXTERNAL TRENDS

Funding Policies

At the federal level, the share of higher education funding as a proportion of the budget has remained relatively stable over the past two decades, and support for student financial aid and university-based research has fared fairly well in comparison to other parts of the federal budget. In the past 15 years, however, budget ceilings or "caps" for the domestic discretionary programs on which colleges and universities typically rely have become more prominent, and the competition for funding among programs subject to these caps, including student aid and research, has seemed to grow more fierce each year. The advent of a balanced federal budget has, in fact, exacerbated this competition. In order to maintain spending discipline, the 1997 federal budget agreement established extremely strict spending caps for the subsequent decade. Without considerable compromise on the part of congressional and executive branch leaders, substantial cuts in important federal higher education programs could ensue. While few expect that to be the result, the outlines of a compromise are not yet clear.

At the state level, higher education has been generally accorded a steadily declining share of appropriations, largely as the result of state attention and fiscal effort for medical and public assistance for indigent populations and for corrections. Funding in individual states has experienced considerable fluctuations, with substantial retrenchment in the early 1990s and restoration of support in the latter half of that decade. Generally, however, at the institutional level, state funding as a proportion of revenue has dropped; tuition and fees from services have increased; and institutions have become more reliant on non-governmental sources of revenue.

Thus, on the one hand, colleges and universities have become more market-driven and independent from their ties to state government; on the other, they have come under increasing pressure from state policymakers to demonstrate their accountability and "performance" as a precondition for receiving state funding.

At both the federal and state level, tax policy is fast becoming a co-equal and an often uncomfortable partner to student aid and institutional support policies. Federal tax credits to help middle-income families pay for college were not among the principal policy planks of the Washington higher education establishment, but in 1997, once the "Hope scholarship" (patterned on a Georgia program) appeared to have political momentum (and need-based student aid funding was sustained), the Washington-based associations and most institutions joined the bandwagon. Indeed, according to Cook (1998), many of higher education's representatives, from institutions and associations, indicated that it would be foolhardy not to support $40 billion in tax incentives that defrayed tuition costs.

Many states have established tuition prepayment plans to lock in or guarantee future tuition. Several states, most notably New York and New Hampshire, have created plans to promote individual tax-deferred investments to help cover the cost of future tuition. For New York residents, its plan also includes a considerable income tax deduction. Most of these efforts are quite new, and the long-term effects of federal and state tax initiatives on direct funding of student aid or of institutions are not yet clear.

Lobbying Registration

Prior to 1996, it was rare for campus or association government relations officers to register as lobbyists in Washington, although lobby registration was perhaps more common among representatives of institutions or higher education groups at the state level. The Lobbying Disclosure Act now requires institutions (and their lobbying staff) to register if they have staff that devote more than 20 percent of their time to lobbying and if they spend more than $20,000 on lobbying activities in a six-month period. A substantial proportion of the growing number of government relations staff of colleges and universities and of associations, who used to scrupulously avoid using the term "lobbyist" to describe themselves, are now registered as lobbyists.

Earmarking

Kennedy's 1986 *Handbook* chapter was critical of the legislative practice of "earmarking," the legislative designation by a member of Congress of funding for a particular campus program or initiative that bypasses the traditional process of peer or federal agency review. He put hope in "a major joint effort, working largely through the educational associations, …attempting to eliminate this 'end-run' approach, lest it split the higher education community and touch off a flurry of such activity that will surely work to everyone's disadvantage." Despite Kennedy's hopes, earmarking is not likely to go away soon.

Fourteen years later, the practice of earmarking still thrives, fueled by campus officials and hired consultants, as well as by elected officials' desire to demonstrate their ability to bring federal resources to their districts. One former university official who served in a high-level federal position told me that he had once vehemently opposed the practice of "earmarking," but that he eventually saw that, for a limited amount of funds, earmarking leveraged support among policymakers for the entire panoply of federal aid to higher education.

THE STRUCTURE OF INSTITUTIONAL GOVERNMENT RELATIONS

The structural arrangements of government relations programs at education institutions, as Kennedy noted, vary largely by size, type, and breadth of programmatic and governmental relationships. It remains crucial that the government relations function be: (a) clearly assigned, with a specific "point person" readily identifiable to facul-

> Regardless of the structure, I would strongly counsel a close functional relationship between the public affairs and government affairs units.

ty, staff, students, and policymakers; and (b) at the highest level of institutional governance and decision making.

Even in larger institutions, organizational arrangements differ considerably. There may be a vice president or vice chancellor for government relations, or the principal advocacy function might be vested in a senior officer whose duties incorporate other campus issues, like public relations, legal counsel, or development. Regardless of the administrative housing of government relations, the function should be closely linked with the institution's chief executive and it should be perceived that way on campus. It has been my experience that the institutions that are the most accomplished at government relations are those in which the president or chancellor takes an active advocacy role, rather than simply letting the professionals do it. Larger institutions may also have standing government relations committees involving senior faculty and administrative officers who meet regularly and can quickly assess the impact of a particular proposal to determine the institution's advocacy priorities.

Princeton University's Governmental Affairs Committee, chaired by its vice president for public affairs, is a good example of such a coordinating and monitoring body. According to Nan Wells and Nan Nixon, writing in a 1986 article in the *Journal for Higher Education Management*, in this committee "the regular involvement of members in reviewing the issues tends to discourage individual members from pursuing legislative initiatives independent of the offices primarily responsible for these activities and helps prevent conflicting and competing presentations" to policymakers. The risk of such "conflicting and competing presentations" is compounded when a university's academic health or medical center has a government relations structure that is separate from that of its core university.

The convergence of communications skills and advocacy techniques used in campus government relations and in public affairs suggests that an effective structure might join the government and public affairs functions. Indeed, among the larger universities, those whose government relations and public affairs staff members report through the same office seem to be unusually effective and accomplished in both the public relations and policy realms. Among the large private universities, I would place Cornell, Duke, Harvard, and Princeton in this category. Among the most successful publics are the University of Michigan and the University of California system and several of its campuses. Regardless of the structure, I would strongly counsel a close functional relationship between the public affairs and government affairs units.

FINAL CONSIDERATIONS

Several of the trends I have noted—namely the registration of college and university advocates as "lobbyists;" the professionalization of the government relations field; the increased pressure to provide campaign contributions; and earmarking—all combine to make higher education advocacy less distinguishable from that of other so-called "special interests."

This theory of the convergence of higher education with other "special" interests is supported by public survey results that show declining public confidence in most types of institutions, including higher education. The good news in these Gallup surveys is that higher education is still among the most "respected" institutions or professions, ranking close to the U.S. military and the clergy; these results suggest a relatively high value placed on higher education by the public. The bad news is that only the military and the clergy were deemed "respected" by more than 50 percent of survey respondents.

These recent phenomena, when viewed in light of an increasing tendency on the part of policymakers to consider higher education as much a private as a public good, suggest an uphill battle in developing favorable public policy. The trends toward student aid subsidies being devoted more to loans than to need-based grant aid, toward tax policy as an instrument of supporting students, toward the reduction of state government support relative to other sources, toward the rhetoric of "markets" and "customers," all suggest a new dynamic at play. The objective of college and university government relations officials, seeking to promote the public good through public policy, will continue to be ever more complicated and challenging in this new environment.

The views expressed in this chapter represent the author's opinions and not necessarily those of The Pew Charitable Trusts.

REFERENCES

Cook, Constance Ewing. *Lobbying for Higher Education: How Colleges and Universities Influence Federal Policy.* Nashville, TN: Vanderbilt University Press, 1998.

Council for Advancement and Support of Education. *Creating Effective Legislative Issue Papers: A CASE Issues Paper for Advancement Professionals,* No. 22. Washington, DC: Council for Advancement and Support of Education, 1995.

National Council of State Legislatures. *Inside the Legislative Process.* Denver, CO: National Council of State Legislatures, 1991.

Rowland, A. Westley, ed. *Handbook of Institutional Advancement.* 2nd ed. San Francisco: Jossey-Bass Publishers, 1986.

Wells, Nan and Nan Nixon. "Working with Washington," *Journal for Higher Education Management* (Summer/Fall 1986).

Wolanin, Thomas R., "Lobbying for Higher Education in Washington," *Change* 30, no. 5 (September/October 1998), pp. 58-62.

If our institutions skillfully use the Web and the "right stuff," we have an opportunity to build stronger institutional relationships with all your publics than ever before and reap the likely positive results.

Advancement and the Web: Thriving in a New World

Robert E. Johnson
Vice President for Enrollment
Albion College

The Web is home to millions of impatient people of all ages looking for information and interactive communication with people who share their interests. The best Web sites weave copy with animation, use limited visuals without long download times, and provide access to chat rooms where like-minded people can gather and exchange information and opinions.

No longer the domain of young white males, the Web is increasingly attracting young women and people over the age of 50. Users are still more affluent than the general population but even that is changing as access gradually expands to people at most income levels.

The Web is introducing the greatest change in the way people communicate since the telephone. In fact, today's youngest teenagers with Web access would rather talk to friends via e-mail than via a telephone. And that introduces an important message: As fascinated as we can all become with a "full featured" Web site, we should never forget that it is still the simplicity of e-mail communications that is the most attractive feature of the Internet. Web sites must be designed to take advantage of that attractiveness and not act as a barrier to it.

WHO'S USING THE WEB?

The annual survey of Web use conducted by the Graphic, Visualization, & Usability Center at Georgia Tech University is one of the easiest and most authoritative ways to keep up with Web usage. Results of the ninth and 10th surveys (1998) are available at *www.cc.gatech.edu/gvu/user_surveys/*. Although the survey is biased in favor of frequent Web users, this is a useful bias if you plan to increase the number of frequent users of your site. (The bias occurs because survey respondents are solicited with banner ads placed on Web sites. The more you use the Web, the more likely you are to be solicited and to respond.)

Note these significant findings from the ninth survey:

■ Web users are becoming more typical of the population as a whole. Female users continue to increase (now 38.7 percent) but at a much slower rate than between the seventh and eighth surveys. Average annual income continues to drop (now $52,000). Note especially that 43.8 percent of Web users between 11-20 years of age are female. New Web users (active for less than a year) are slightly more likely to be women than men (51.7 percent) and more likely to be under age 20 and over age 50 than in

Advancement
and the Web:
Thriving in a
New World

the years in between. Growth, therefore, is ideal for those contemplating communicating with prospective high school students and for deferred gifts from alumni.

■ E-mail is the most indispensable technology, according to survey respondents for the time since the surveys began. Usage rose 9 percentage points from the previous year.

■ Slow Web speed (measured by the time required to download a Web page) continues to frustrate 64.8 percent of respondents and this response level has been consistent over the previous two surveys. Note especially that 53 percent of respondents reported leaving a commercial Web site rather than waiting for a page to download. The dissatisfaction continues despite relatively constant upgrading of the modem in use. Web pages contain more images, animations, scripts, and programs, which decreases the impact of faster modems.

WHAT THE WEB MEANS FOR INSTITUTIONAL ADVANCEMENT

These findings obviously impact Web communications in institutional advancement. Consider, for example, the following lessons we could learn:

■ Your future annual fund contributors will communicate far differently than even your recent graduates. Teens' communications habits change constantly. Colleges with a primary dependency on traditional-age students need to pay close attention to the changing communication habits not only of teenagers but also preteens. By the time pre-teens are ready for college, Web use will most likely reflect the general population of college-bound students. That's less than 10 years from now.

■ People over the age of 50 are becoming more involved with the Web each year. This is a tremendous opportunity for college and university alumni relations offices.

■ Be cautious of the creative impulse to do everything that is technologically possible on your Web site. Technology is advancing far faster than access speed. Web designers should test the results of their creativity on a home PC connected to a medium-speed modem and a

phone line. If your Web site is slow to download, most people will leave it. Period.

■ Pay special attention to the power and speed of e-mail. People of every age love e-mail and the trend appears to be growing. Include it as a distinct part of your Web marketing plans.

■ Adopt the innovations possible with Java script. Visit the University of Dayton site to see what this can do for your Web site (*www.udayton.edu*).

New alumni will expect to keep in touch with friends and to donate to the annual fund using Web services provided by their alma mater. Maintain their connection with you by offering them:

■ personal Web sites that continue after graduation;

■ online employment searches;

■ athletic updates.

For alumni and other donors, the Web can be an ideal vehicle to cultivate long-term relationships that bring mutual benefits to both parties. And that, after all, is the essence of successful marketing communications.

In the areas of marketing and communications, there are endless possibilities for the Web. In just a few years, it will dramatically change the way you do your business. The problem is, we do not know exactly how. And that is both the challenge and the caveat of this essay. New advances in technology may soon overtake whatever is included now as we begin the new century. There is no way to make this chapter completely up-to-date when you read it. So why write it? Two reasons:

1. Internet communications, particularly the use of e-mail in conjunction with Web sites, is here, and increasing numbers of people are using it effectively.

2. To alert you to the awesome change that is about to happen.

Don Schultz of Northwestern University's McGill School of Journalism said it best in a January 15, 1997 column in *DM News*, "Integration and the Internet": "It is clear that the Internet is going to be a major factor in the communications system of

Advancement
and the Web:
Thriving in a
New World

the future. When that future will occur is anybody's guess. Best estimates put it at least 10 to 15 years from now."

Note that this Shultz column appeared in *DM* (for Direct Marketing) *News*. Direct marketers have been leading the exploration of the Internet's potential to enhance marketing communications. Most important principles of direct marketing have an application on Web sites and in e-mail. Both the "integrated marketing" and "one-to-one marketing" concepts have strong roots in direct marketing. The emphasis is on direct communication and interaction with potential customers on an individual basis. And the long-term goal is creating an ongoing relationship between the individual and a group or community of like-minded people. This concept of community is an excellent fit for what colleges and universities attempt to do when they enroll students and cultivate relationships with them from the time they graduate until they die. From initial annual giving to final estate planning, the Web offers excellent opportunities for alumni to remain involved with their alma mater.

SPEED AND ACCESS

Two technology-related developments in particular will influence the pace of the change in the way we use the Web to communicate in advancement.

First, and most important, is the speed with which people in their homes can access information on Web sites, especially videos. At present, this is annoyingly slow over any telephone modem and this lack of speed severely restricts what we can effectively do on Web sites. Web users of any age are very impatient; effective communication activities today must heed this impatience and be limited in scope.

This *is* changing. As I write, my cable TV company has already sent the first notice of the tremendous increase in download speed that is coming soon to my neighborhood. At a probable cost of twice what I am now paying for my monthly Internet connection (not counting the extra phone line charge), my Web access speed will increase more than 50 times over its present rate.

● ● ●

By the time pre-teens are ready for college, Web use will most likely reflect the general population of college-bound students.

Despite this coming improvement, don't expect speedy access to happen overnight. A November 1998 edition of the *Nua Internet Survey* reported this research by the Gartner Group: In 2003, 63 percent of 46 million Internet access lines in the United States will still be using analog modems or telephones. Of the remainder, it was estimated that only 14 percent will use a cable modem and 3 percent will use a satellite connection. The message is clear: In planning Web and Internet communications, don't overlook the great variation in access speed that will continue for some time.

Second is access to computers. Computers capable of effectively accessing the Web must cost no more than $500. Two years ago—even one year ago—this would have seemed a silly statement. Powerful computers (by yesterday's standard) with 200MH + operating speeds, 32MB of RAM, and large hard drives are available now for less than $1,000. As prices continue to fall, penetration in the marketplace will spread rapidly. I predict that, within 10 years, nearly every home in the United States will have Web access as a basic utility. The change will take place even sooner among middle to upper income families. In other words, successful college graduates will expect to communicate on a regular basis using the Web.

A CLEAR MESSAGE TO ADVANCEMENT PROFESSIONALS

The message at this point should be clear: If our institutions do not provide enough of the "right stuff" on our Web sites, alumni giving rates are likely to fall, general fund raising may drop off, and our connections with our publics will suffer. However, if our institutions skillfully use the Web and the "right stuff," we have an opportunity to build stronger institutional relationships with all our publics and reap the likely positive results.

FURTHER READINGS

Bates, Don and Paul Warren. *Using the Internet for Public Relations Purposes.* New York, NY: Public Relations Society of America, 1998.

Cornforth, Suzanne R. and William Koty. "Untangling the Web: It Takes More Than Counting Hits to Evaluate Your

Web Site's Successes—Or Troubles. Here's How to Find Out Who Your Visitors Are, What They Want, and How They Want It," CURRENTS 23, no. 7 (July/August 1997): 10-16.

Matros, Michael. "Getting Coverage That Counts: Reaching Your Audience in This Electronic Age Requires a Plan—and the Willingness to Experiment," CURRENTS 23, no. 3 (March 1997): 8-12.

Schultz, Don. "Integration and the Internet," *DM News* (Jan. 15, 1997).

Stoner, Michael. "Coming Up Next: If You Manage Your Alumni Office Web Site, Watch for These Trends: More Valuable Features, More Outside Expertise, and More Evaluation," CURRENTS 24, no. 3 (March 1998): 10-15.

Stoner, Michael and Phillip Cartwright. "Alumni, Public Relations, Admissions—And Technology," *Change: The Magazine of Higher Learning* 29, no. 3 (May/June 1997): 50-52.

●   ●   ●

In view of the place college sports occupy in American culture," reform that seems to limit any aspect of competition will be widely viewed as negative. That notwithstanding, we should do it because it's the right thing to do.

Intercollegiate Sports: Putting First Things Second

John A. Roush
President
Centre College

There is hardly a senior advancement officer in education, whether in alumni relations, communications, or fund raising, who has not had to deal with significant issues about intercollegiate athletics. Whether related to admissions policies, booster clubs, financial aid, athletic facilities, gender participation, and the most fundamental questions about educational values, the advancement professional inevitably will be called upon to address issues of this kind to members of the immediate academic community and its external publics. The following chapter is presented here as a balanced perspective about the state of intercollegiate athletics today, together with a rich source of references for further inquiry.

—PMB

I'm finishing this essay as I sit watching college bowl games on the first day of the new century. The afternoon's contests have been particularly good, and there have been many outstanding plays and extraordinary efforts by the young men competing. Some would argue that this is college football at its best. If you didn't know better, you could conclude that all's well with intercollegiate sport. Sadly, most of us closely associated with the pursuit know this isn't the case.

It's been seven years since the Knight Foundation released the last of its three seminal reports on the state of intercollegiate athletics. While the Knight report focused much of its attention on "about 100 schools in football and about 200 in basketball," most college presidents and others involved in the enterprise, knew then and know now there's much to be done at all levels of competition if we're to make intercollegiate athletics a more constructive component of America's colleges and universities.

It's clear even to the casual observer that many of the problems detailed in the Foundation's report—most of which boil down to putting the athlete first and the student second—persist and may have worsened. Bailey and Littleton (*Athletics and Academe*) go all the way back to the 1929 study of the Carnegie Foundation, which specified many of the same issues as the Knight report, in their assessment of the current situation: "Sixty years later the same problems, greatly magnified, persist and are exerting more deleterious effects on higher education than ever before." Given the long-term persistence of these conflicts, those among us who wish the nation's preoccupation with sport, or at least big-time college athletics, would somehow spontaneously recede to more reasonable levels need to get past this false hope.

A GROWTH INDUSTRY

A quick look at the data shows that intercollegiate competition has grown dramatically both in participation and revenues over the past few years. For example, NCAA records indicate that from 1983 to 1998, total participation increased by over 30 percent. Andrew Zimbalist, in *Unpaid Professionals*, points out that NCAA "corporate sponsorships have increased roughly sevenfold in the nineties..." and that "the NCAA's total budget, which surpassed $270 million in 1997-98, has grown at an annual rate of 15 percent since 1982."

The implementation of Title IX has generated a significant portion of the participation increase, but the simple truth, reflected by the upward-trending NCAA numbers, is that the nation's colleges and universities are increasing their commitment to intercollegiate sport. Today's young athletes want to compete at their colleges, and America's institutions of higher education have elected to accommodate this desire. And while some will argue that the current intense emphasis on competitive athletics for women and men is an anomaly of sorts in higher education, it's obvious that the decades-long growth in participation, expenditures, and revenues is not the exception but the rule.

A LIFETIME OF ATHLETICS

That said, I should say this: I'm an unabashed supporter of intercollegiate athletics. I believe involvement in competitive sport can provide an invaluable addition to a young person's educational experience. Competitive sport can be an exciting, community-building, educational element in the college environment.

I grew up caring deeply (probably too deeply for a time) about athletics of all types. And while academics, music, and theater also shaped me, it was through sport that I learned many of life's most important lessons. It was my good fortune to play and then coach football at the Division I level. I've had the chance to be involved administratively at two places—the University of Richmond (Division I) and now Centre College (Division

III)—that, quite simply, "do it right" by putting academics first. My wife and I have watched our two sons be influenced positively by sport, and as a family we've had the privilege of seeing our sons be recruited and signed to grants-in-aid at two of the country's outstanding institutions—Duke and Northwestern. So I'll be among the last to make a blanket indictment of intercollegiate athletics. Rather, I'll attempt to offer a balanced, challenging commentary about several issues that are timely and, in my opinion, are crucial to the future of collegiate sports at all levels.

BACK TO ORIGINAL REASONS

We need to recommit ourselves to the purposes for which intercollegiate athletics were established. The NCAA, the governing body affecting the great majority of colleges and universities, stated in its original constitution in 1906 that its purpose was to regulate and supervise U.S. college athletics "...in order that the athletic activities in the colleges and universities may be maintained on an ethical plane in keeping with the dignity and high moral purpose of education." (Goff, Tollison, and Fleisher: *The National Collegiate Athletic Association*) Today's NCAA Web site and literature include in the organization's first purpose, "to promote and develop educational leadership." While I'm confident intercollegiate sport is about education and leadership for the vast majority of men and women, some contemporary suggestions for "reform" would move the association even further away from its original and currently stated purpose.

THE FALSE PROMISE OF PROFESSIONALISM

I continue to marvel at those—smart, knowledgeable folks who should know better—who believe that college athletics, Division I programs in particular, need to become "more professional" in their operation. These men and women, who sincerely believe that athletes should share in the economic success of the higher-profile programs across the country, are seriously misguided, in my opinion.

Their contention is that student-athletes (young men who play college football and basketball in particular) should be paid to play, and be provided other amenities, even beyond the pampering many receive at America's colleges.

(Notwithstanding some attempts at reform, privileges include "special living conditions, meals, and curricula [that] reinforce a class system within the student body" (Zimbalist), not to mention what Paul Lawrence (*Unsportsmanlike Conduct*) calls the "educational shortcuts" of personal tutors, lax class attendance requirements, and even pressure on faculty to give unearned passing grades.) With direct pay, the reasoning goes, student-athletes will be encouraged to stay in college and complete their degrees. These ideas should be respectfully refuted.

Colleges and universities that offer grants-in-aid (Division I and II) should continue to do so—no more, no less. Affording a young person the chance to earn his or her education by participating on a collegiate team is enough. The notion that student-athletes deserve to be paid, deserve to be singled out for special treatment even more, and deserve to profit from whatever financial success their institution may experience is clearly outside the education-enhancing purpose of college athletics.

Historian Christopher Lasch put it well in a *New York Times* article: There's no need to be "...the least bit apologetic to the young warrior who goes out there and fights for alma mater..., and it doesn't bother me if the university is bringing in a fair amount of money and he isn't getting a big salary, provided he's getting something else of tremendous value and that something else is a good education." (as quoted in Bailey and Littleton) This—delivering a quality education—is where we should direct our reform efforts instead of promoting play for pay.

Some reformers also worry that too many of our athletes leave early for the pros. I don't. Based on NCAA statistics, less than one percent of college athletes move on—before or after graduation—to professional careers in men's basketball or football. Professional opportunities aren't the enemy. In the final analysis, colleges and universities can never compete with a professional pay structure that sometimes includes eight-figure packages. More importantly, as institutions dedicated first and foremost to education, we shouldn't try.

● ● ●

Under the guise of giving customers what they want (in this case the student-athletes and their families), we've allowed our institutions to chase after physical plant additions and renovations that have little to do with the academic mission.

In another instance of being lured to emulate professional athletics, we need to stop some of the competitive madness in the area of facilities (Zimbalist calls this a "sports facility construction boom...") Programs in all the NCAA divisions have launched a keeping-up-the-Joneses approach that's created expectations for customized locker rooms, lavish state-of-the-art weight-training areas with cable TV, and palatial playing facilities—gymnasiums, football stadiums, track and field and tennis complexes, baseball and softball diamonds, and swimming pavilions—most, extraordinarily expensive and beautiful beyond description.

Let me be clear: I'm in favor of safe and good equipment for athletes. I'm in favor of providing our student-athletes with well-designed, high-quality practice and game facilities. I'm absolutely in favor of first-rate training and medical services for these young men and women. But we've allowed our interest in "being competitive" to take us beyond reason, and we need to challenge each other to put an end to this nonsense. Under the guise of giving customers what they want (in this case the student-athletes and their families), we've allowed our institutions to chase after physical plant additions and renovations that have little to do with the academic mission.

YOUNG LIVES OUT OF BALANCE

America's preoccupation with determining who or what is No.1 in almost everything has had a negative effect on intercollegiate athletics, especially as it pertains to the overall experience of student-athletes. The result of this preoccupation in collegiate sports at all levels has been to make postseason play the measure by which one claims success. This development has diminished the importance of winning one's conference or league championship. It's also been a factor in allowing the competitive seasons of athletic teams to lengthen at a troubling rate. Zimbalist notes this season creep in "the number of football and basketball games per year that has found a way to keep growing," as well as common methods for circumventing the 20-hour-per-week practice limit that allow athletes to "spend 50 or 60 hours a week on their sport in season." (As this limit is by wide agreement ineffective, the rule should be rewritten to close all the loopholes and backed up by sanctions stringent enough to persuade coaches to comply.)

How has this affected the lives of our students? I would argue that it's narrowed their experience at all levels. And while the Division I and II programs might contend they have "the right" to demand this level of commitment given the investment they're making in these student-athletes (an arguable contention), this is clearly not true for Division III programs.

Here, too, we see a never-ending interest in extending the regular competitive seasons and expanding the non-traditional seasons. Because of the overlap of schedules in different forms of competition, the two- or three-sport athlete is a thing of the past. Worse yet, students choosing to compete in athletics are less and less able to engage in other aspects of the college that are of intellectual and social value. Their chances to do service-learning, study and travel abroad, participate in meaningful internships, compete for summer fellowships and work experiences, or just hang out in the residence hall are compromised by what's become an year-round commitment to athletic competition. This commitment is either "encouraged" by their coaches or by pressure from their teammates.

The argument that this is what the students want, and I believe they do in most cases, should be respectfully set aside. In this instance, more isn't better, and those who are in a position to keep some measure of moderation in the time student-athletes are allowed to compete and practice need to step forward and give back these young people a sense of balance in their lives. We must temper a system that, in the words of an anonymous college president quoted by Bailey and Littleton, "send[s] youngsters out who can no longer do the only thing that's been important in their life since middle school and they have no skill to do anything else."

● ● ●
While college presidents and others in responsible positions may not have caused this obsessive focus on sports and the men and women who coach, they've done little to exercise control over the situation.

STEPS TOWARD REFORM

Two, albeit simple, ways to bring some reason back into the athletic experience are to:

1) re-emphasize the importance of conference play in order to counterbalance the view that post-season play is the only thing that counts, and

2) begin to limit, not expand, the number of teams that qualify for post-season play.

The ideas are not new, but we need to return to them. Campus presidents and the NCAA should go after these reforms with determination, and they should expect little encouragement or cooperation from coaches, student-athletes, parents, or fans. As Bailey and Littleton point out: "In view of the place college sports occupy in American culture" [if not between motherhood and apple pie, certainly in the vicinity] reform that seems to limit any aspect of competition will be widely viewed as negative. That notwithstanding, we should do it because it's the right thing to do.

THE SUCCESS OF HIGHER EXPECTATIONS

There's already evidence that movement away from the athletics-before-everything approach can produce positive results. The increase of success by student athletes in the college classroom is due in large part to the standards imposed by Proposition 48 (which for freshman eligibility requires a 2.0 high school GPA in 11 core courses and a combined math/English SAT score of at least 700 or an ACT score of at least 15) beginning in 1986. This should be a point of pride for all who care about intercollegiate athletics.

The record of Prop 48 is, of course, far from perfect. As Murray Sperber points out in *College Sports, Inc.,* a number of institutions have cheated outright and found other ways to qualify academically weak athletes. Still, Prop 48 has been useful. Since 1986, NCAA records show that graduation rates of intercollegiate have trended upward.

Some contend that with this positive movement, we should claim victory and mute our emphasis on educational achievement. I think this is just a modest beginning and we need to look for other ways to emphasize academic preparation. Colleges and universities need to re-double their efforts to be sure the student-athletes they admit are, in fact, ready to achieve in the classroom as well as in the athletic arena. The importance of academic rigor across the American academy, which I view as the bedrock strength of our system, needs to be affirmed; all campuses should be focused on raising the academic standards of the student-athletes it chooses to admit and, even more importantly, be prepared to help these men and women be successful as college learners.

THE ACADEMY'S NEW ICONS

As focal figures of the ever-growing appetite in America for sports, Division I-A football coaches and Division I basketball coaches for men, and, in a few cases, women, are the academy's new superstars. The compensation these individuals command is extraordinary. The attention they garner for their institutions—both positive and negative—is enormous. The old example of the public knowing the name and a lot more about an institution's head coach than its president or the quality of its academic program is truer now than ever before. And while I'm not saying this is calamitous in and of itself, we should at least recognize the situation and ask whether it's ideal and if we're doing what we should to be sure these men and women understand and are committed to the academic mission of their institutions.

I should be clear that the media (combined with the willingness of most of these coaches to take advantage of media attention and its resultant rewards) has played a significant role in creating this situation. When it comes to intercollegiate sports, the media often reports out of both sides of its mouth. As Bailey and Littleton comment:

> There is perhaps no more conspicuous example of the conflict between serving as the conscience of intercollegiate athletics and using the publicity about sports to promote its own vested interest than in the [media's] voluminous reporting about recruiting of football and basketball players. It is the responsibility of the media to inform the public about the excesses of college sports. However, to do so while at the same time contributing to that excess is to be guilty of the same hypocrisy for which higher education is…[often] criticized.

While college presidents and others in responsible positions may not have caused this obsessive focus on sports and the men and women who coach, they've done little to exercise control over the situation. In truth, the coach-as-star train left the station a long time ago, and I'm not suggesting we can or should try to alter this part of the situation in a fundamental way. I do, however, believe presidents and others who care about the core purpose of educational institutions should redouble their efforts to be certain the coaches they hire understand and are committed to the academic purposes of the institution they serve. This isn't too much to ask. The men and women who coach our teams shouldn't be permitted to stand apart from the institutions they represent. Those who care most about college sport—administrators and faculty alike—need to look for substantive, creative ways to welcome coaches back into the life of the academy.

TIME TO TILT

Halting and reversing movement toward the athlete-student will be difficult and often unpopular. Big-time sports provides a kind of gratification-on-demand that's seductive to fans as well as the players who strive for the spotlight. Some argue convincingly that any effort at change is tilting at windmills. But this is a windmill at which we should tilt.

If we drift away from the ideal of the student-athlete and slouch toward the reality of the athlete-student, educational institutions run the risk of parodying rather than exemplifying their most deeply held values. Our actions will echo the plea attributed to a university president when he asked the state legislature for a substantial budget increase "to build a university of which our football team will be proud." (Zimbalist)

This short piece only begins the conversation, a small but essential step in putting first things first. If enough of us tell our truth with regularity, conviction, and respect, perhaps we can inspire further movement toward an intercollegiate athletic enterprise that's worthy of the young people it attempts to serve. College sport as a means of enriching the experience of students is an educational opportunity that shouldn't be missed. Today's and certainly tomorrow's student-athlete deserves our clearest thinking and our most courageous effort to do the right thing.

REFERENCES AND ADDITIONAL RESOURCES

Bailey, Wilford and Taylor D. Littleton. *Athletics and Academe: An Anatomy of Abuses and a Prescription for Reform.* New York: Macmillan Publishing Co., 1991.

Goof, Brian A., Arthur A. Fleisher, and Robert D. Tollison. *The National Collegiate Athletic Association: A Study in Cartel Behavior.* Chicago and London: The University of Chicago Press, 1992.

Lawrence, Paul R. *Unsportsmanlike Conduct: The National Collegiate Athletic Association and the Business of College Football.* New York: Praeger Publishers, 1987.

Sack, Allen L. and Ellen J. Staurowsky. *College Athletes For Hire: The Evolution and Legacy of the NCAA's Amateur Myth.* Westport, CT: Praeger Publishers, 1998.

Sperber, Murray. *College Sports Inc.: The Athletic Department vs The University.* New York: Henry Holt and Company, Inc., 1990.

Zimbalist, Andrew. *Unpaid Professionals: Commercialism and Conflict in Big-Time College Sports.* Princeton, NJ: Princeton University Press, 1994.

Thinking, what we call strategic planning, will become a very high art form, and prompt, pro active as well as responsive, action will be more important than ever before, if higher and independent school education are to flourish.

SECTION I
The Environment
and the Changing Face
of Advancement

The Evolution of Advancement in the 21st Century

Peter McE. Buchanan
President Emeritus,
CASE and

Associate
Washburn & McGoldrick, Inc.

I n the second edition of the *Handbook of Institutional Advancement*, A. Westley Rowland described advancement as, "all activities and programs undertaken by an institution to develop understanding and support from all its constituencies in order to achieve its goals in securing such resources as students, faculty, and dollars."

In this edition, Larry Lauer describes another field of endeavor, integrated marketing, as,

> "coordinating the planning and implementation of initiatives with the participation of all the areas of the institution that have a stake in its success. Its aim is to mobilize the total institution. It is a total organizational approach that stresses everyone's responsibility to help advance the institution's goals and objectives."

Ironically, these definitions of different fields, developed more than a decade apart, sound similar. This leads me to believe that our field of advancement is evolving into what we call today integrated marketing.

As currently structured by CASE, the field of advancement includes a vast amount of the territory that Lauer describes as integrated marketing, but not all of it. Yet, is it not reasonable to posit that the evolutionary direction of advancement is towards integrated marketing, rather than in any other direction? Here are some reasons why that is likely to be true in the 21st century.

Executive Decision

Because the field is composed of administrative functions, often highly personal in nature, delegated by the campus chief executive to advancement professionals, those functions are determined directly by the chief campus executive. They can be expanded by executive decision. There is no bureaucratic process involved, multiple permissions to be secured, or board approval required. It is up to each campus executive whether or not functions and activities should be added to or deleted from today's advancement portfolio.

A recent CASE Survey among presidents and public relations executives shows some evidence of the establishment of a senior officer for integrated institutional marketing. However, the sample size was too small to show more than a hint that such positions are emerging.

Competition

As technological competition is added to the competition for fiscal and human resources, and as

SECTION I: THE ENVIRONMENT AND THE CHANGING FACE OF ADVANCEMENT   **67** international competition arises in all three areas, the need for well-coordinated initiatives will become more acute than ever before. If the educational environment is competitive today, it is certain to be more so tomorrow. The competition for philanthropic dollars will not be so much among educational institutions as it will be among other worthy nonprofit organizations. That competition may be less acute than in other areas because of the staggering increase in the nation's wealth, but it still will be substantial. There also will be continuing competition for "the best" faculty and students among the great majority of institutions. Competition for public financial support, not so much among educational institutions but between education and other state funded priorities, is likely to be the most acute of all. Competition for technological superiority represents an unmeasured but formidable new source of competitive exposure for institutions, as does competition from for-profit educational institutions. These pressures will force institutions to be intentional in developing strategies and demand that all the institution's talent and energies be employed to implement those strategies successfully. This will require using integrated marketing principles.

Accountability

The increasing demand for public accountability will require institutions to make a much more powerful case for the support that they receive from private individual and institutional donors and legislatures alike. Educational leaders will have to spell out the deliverables of student outcomes, research monies, economic development, business employment, and public service to the community. The public demand for accountability will lead chief campus executives to ask for higher standards of accountability for, and integration of, each major administrative function in the academy.

Range of Responsibility

Chief advancement officers have an extraordinary range of responsibility for the relationships between and among the members of the immediate academic community and the members of all its external constituencies. Virtually no one else in the academy has that same breadth and depth of responsibility

for a whole host of relationships that together form much of the fabric, if you will, much of the very foundation of the institution's support. They are, therefore, better positioned to assume the added responsibility that an integrated marketing model requires.

Finally and perhaps more persuasive than any other reason, is the fact that institutions both in the United States and elsewhere are beginning to adopt integrated marketing at their institutions. As Lauer writes, marketing is more than a field of endeavor; it is a "way of thinking."

IMPLICATIONS FOR ADVANCEMENT PROFESSIONALS

The implications for individual professionals of advancement's evolution toward integrated marketing are especially important. The types of personality traits necessary to build institutional relationships are no different than those required to build personal ones—integrity, intelligence, competence, fidelity, commitment, sensitivity, and unselfishness, among others. If every advancement professional would approach people capable and interested in furthering the institution as if they were their most important major gift prospects, the field of advancement would be a good deal closer to achieving its full potential than it is today. Yet, as important as those qualities and approach are, they alone will hardly be sufficient to meet the challenges of an evolving field.

The future will require that each educational institution define in the most distinctive and powerful way its unique educational mission and the means by which it intends to pursue it. Thinking, what we call strategic planning, will become a very high art form, and prompt, pro active as well as responsive, action will be more important than ever before if higher and independent school education are to flourish.

Strategic thinking must also be accompanied by an institutional flexibility and responsiveness that few academic institutions appear to have in abundance. Colleges and universities are far better known for maintaining the status quo, for properly resisting fads, and being the repositories of the past and preservers of the culture. Nimble, prompt, and responsive are not adjectives linked to the academy in general, though there are certainly exceptions. The need for institutional flexibility in strategic thinking is nearly as important as the thinking itself. Without flexibility, strategic thinking will not be strategic for very long.

Such thinking will take place in an environment characterized by more rapid change than ever before. We know absolutely that what is known today, for example scientifically, will surely be amended, if not proved entirely obsolete, tomorrow. If today's knowledge will be substantially altered tomorrow, the academy per force will have to live in a constant state of change. Tomorrow's professionals must meet the increasing speed of change with increasing competencies and a far greater assurance that they "know what they're doing." Performance measures for every function, whether currently included or excluded from advancement, will be sought where they do not now exist. Benchmarking against one's own performance will have to be conducted against peer institutions' performance, and soon against standards of organizational or functional performance in fields other than education. They will be required, not only in fund raising, but in alumni relations, and communications.

Professionals will have to become expert in the field of evaluation. Continual evaluation of major institutional initiatives will be essential in a fast moving environment to be certain that those activities are truly effective. It is the only way professionals will know how well their institutions are performing. (See Independent Sector's *Evaluation with Power* by Sandra Trice Gray and Associates.)

Those who wish to be leaders in the field of advancement must see their primary roles as flexible strategists for the campus chief executive, capable of conceptualizing how to powerfully position their institutions to achieve their unique educational purposes. They must be sufficiently skillful to effectively lead the advancement functions for which they are directly responsible and successfully collaborate with others in charge of "other marketing functions" they do not lead. Tomorrow's successful advancement professional will understand that the ideal integrated marketing model for

● ● ●
Performance measures for every function whether currently included or excluded from advancement will be sought where they do not now exist.

advancement will never materialize in the academy until egos are discarded and credit is readily shared with others.

In the past few years, many senior advancement professionals have acknowledged that, given good professional competence, the integration of all the various disciplines of advancement is the single most important factor in the success of an advancement program. That does not imply, in theory or in fact, that those successful advancement programs are directed by one individual. In many cases, there are two or three individuals sharing the leadership of the advancement program as, for example, at Harvard, Duke University, the University of Michigan, the University of North Carolina at Chapel Hill, and Stanford, not to speak of literally hundreds of other institutions. It is the spirit of that collaboration that enables the kind of integration the marketing approach demands of different administrative units, no matter how large or small. That collaboration will suffice when old organizational structures cannot be changed, but integration of programs and activities is essential.

The advancement leader of tomorrow will have to be a creative thinker, a person who understands the difference between flexibility and capitulation in a rapidly changing environment, an individual who exemplifies collaboration in approach without compromising principle, and a professional who is devoted first and foremost to the cause of education. With those kinds of leaders, there is every possibility that the field of advancement will evolve into the field of strategic integrated marketing, if not by name or in organizational form, in the way the institution thinks and the spirit with which it acts.

REFERENCES

Lauer, Larry D. "Need Visibility? Get Integrated: Campus Communicators are Natural Leaders for Integrated Marketing Programs. Here's Why—And How to Pull It Off," CURRENTS 24, no. 1 (January 1998): 12-19.

Sandra Trice Gray and Associates (Independent Sector). *Evaluation with Power*. San Francisco: Jossey-Bass Publishers, 1998.

Sevier, Robert A. *Integrated Marketing for Colleges, Universities, and Schools: A Step-by-Step Planning Guide.*

Washington, DC: Council for Advancement and Support of Education, 1998.

Sevier, Robert A. *Integrated Marketing Communication: A Practical Guide to Developing Comprehensive Communication Strategies.* Washington, DC: Council for Advancement and Support of Education, 1999.

Rowland, Westley A., ed. *Handbook of Institutional Advancement.* 2nd ed. San Francisco: Jossey-Bass Publishers, 1986.

Ross, John and Carol Halstead (College Connections). *Preliminary Analysis: CASE Presidents and Chief PR Officers' Surveys.* CASE Books, 2000. [The information contained in this analysis will be available, in final form, in a CASE Book in Spring, 2001.]

Virginia Wesleyan College, Norfolk, Virginia

SECTION II
Leadership and Management

Edited by Eric C. Johnson

Introduction

Eric C. Johnson
Vice President for Resource Development
Rice University

Advancement is changing, and the rate of change is accelerating. Whether there are different demographics of our constituents, competition for qualified staff, technological innovations that were unimaginable just five years ago, or simply the increasingly complex environment in which we operate, change is placing new demands upon chief advancement officers. To be successful, they must have everstronger leadership and management skills.

It is appropriate that this section begins with a discussion of leadership because the most successful advancement officers are playing increasingly important leadership roles in their institutions.

Robert Kelley, author of the best-selling book, *How to be a Star at Work*, first gives a primer on leadership from extensive research he has conducted in the business community in Chapter 1. He says the old style command-and-control type of leadership, which he calls "big-L," is ineffective. He describes "small-l" leadership

as that depending heavily on teamwork, where effective leaders have strong knowledge and people skills and an ability to keep a project moving toward a goal.

In the second chapter, William Haden, president of West Virginia Wesleyan, explores the boundaries of leadership for a chief advancement officer, underscoring the importance of strong peer relationships with senior academic and administrative colleagues. He speaks eloquently also to the importance of an appropriately senior role for a chief advancement officer so that institutional policies are shaped to strengthen, least of all not damage, important relationships between the academic community and its surrounding publics.

Kathleen Casey Gigl, vice president for institutional advancement at Texas Woman's University, writes in Chapter 3 about the opportunity chief advancement officers have to lead in the strategic planning of the institution's future. She argues persuasively that no other senior officer understands important external constituencies and how they can best support the priority choices of the institution as well as the chief advancement officer.

In Chapter 4, Harvey Jacobson gives his unique perspective as professor and former development and alumni officer. Making full use of the breadth of books and articles written on management, Jacobson describes the qualities and skills necessary for successful transformational leadership.

In Chapter 5, the Vice President for Institute Relations at the California Institute of Technology, Jerry Nunnally, briefly, but forcefully, speaks to the absolute necessity of understanding organizational culture in great depth, the need to take risks, to try new things, to accept ambiguity in surroundings that are inherently ambiguous, and to communicate tirelessly and frequently with colleagues and stakeholders alike.

Michael Stoner, vice president for new media at Lipman Hearne, walks us through some valuable suggestions on how to adapt to the rapidly changing technological landscape in Chapter 6. His suggestions range from forming an internal technology group to implementing effective training and staff development so that technology can be truly harnessed to serve the advancement team.

The Vice President for Development of the University of Pennsylvania, Virginia Clark, addresses in Chapter 7 the most critical management issue in advancement today—the recruitment and development of staff. She begins with advice on how to recruit effectively, including tips on the interview process. Outlining key questions supervisors must answer about the professional development of staff, Clark concludes the chapter with advice about managing and measuring staff performance.

Thomas Anderson, former vice president at the California Institute of Technology and Case Western Reserve University and a fellow at the Center for Professional Ethics at Case Western, concludes the section with a chapter on creating an ethical environment. He notes that nonprofit leadership requires a well-grounded sense of morality, a finely tuned sense of ethical behavior, and a commitment to create an ethical environment.

Throughout these chapters, we learn that current trends in higher education offer leaders and managers in advancement an opportunity to redefine the field. We not only are poised to embrace the breathtaking changes that await our profession, but also to shape definitively the ways these changes will affect us all.

The small-l leader usually has no direct supervisory authority; no staff depends on his or her good graces in order to get a paycheck. Colleagues voluntarily cooperate with small-l leaders, because they trust that if they work together, important things will get done.

Leadership: With a Big-L or a little-l?

Robert E. Kelley
Adjunct Professor, Graduate School of Industrial Administration
Carnegie Mellon University

American organizations have an obsessive love affair with the notion of leadership. The signs are everywhere—front-page feature stories and TV talk-show gabfests with celebrity CEOs; $1,000-a-day cult seminars; best-selling autobiographies that highlight swagger over substance. We are drawn to these leader paradigms because they are packaged as larger than life. If we could learn their secrets, be more like them, then we, too, could advance to chair of the board or CEO, get our picture on the cover of *Fortune* magazine, or collect on stock options worth more than the government budgets of some foreign countries. Sure, we wouldn't be able to end world hunger, but at the very least, we could assign ourselves a coveted space in the parking lot.

LEADERSHIP WITH A BIG-L

We adore what I call leadership with a capital L—even though that big-L leadership style has the same relationship to organizational success

Adapted by permission of the publisher from How to Be a Star at Work *by Robert E. Kelley. Published by Times Books, a division of Random House, Inc. in 1998.*

as, to paraphrase the science fiction writer Robert Heinlein, "history has to truth, i.e. none to speak of." Certainly much of what has been written and taught on leadership over the past decade feeds the popular culture myth of the hard-driving, high-living CEO. In reality, much of the material is filtered through a sophisticated public relations strategy that seeks to market CEOs as much as the products their companies make.

Many training seminars and "self-help" books also embrace this cult-hero worship as the best way to teach organizational leadership. But consumers who hope to take on the traits of these titans end up with a mythological, rock-video version of leadership that can't possibly succeed in the workaday world. Charles de Gaulle must have been thinking about big-L leadership when he quipped, "The Great Leaders always stage-manage their effects… while the real leaders are down in the ranks, quietly changing the world."

Big-L leadership traits may make for an impressive show at times, but they're of little productive use to the 99 percent of brain-powered workers who have to deal with vexing problems in the trenches. Brain-powered workers know that they need no-nonsense leadership skills to be more productive, but they also know the big-L stuff being offered isn't going to help them much.

The star performers in the organizations we have studied were able to see big-L traits as unproductive posturing. [Editor's note: Mr. Kelley refers to a study of Bell Lab's knowledge workers and a later study of 3M workers.] The stars concentrated instead on a set of skills I have identified and labeled as small-l leadership behaviors.

Where big-L leaders noisily preside with an ego-centered, management-by-me leadership style, small-l leaders work quietly and unceremoniously side by side with their co-workers inside the system. The small-l leader may have no direct supervisory authority; no staff depends on his or her good graces in order to get a paycheck. Colleagues voluntarily cooperate with small-l leaders, because they trust that if they work together, important things will get done.

SMALL-L LEADERSHIP

Knowledge-intensive activities require a whole new form of leadership. Complex, specialized, and long-term projects performed by teams of brain-powered workers, often in different offices and diverse parts of the organization, define the environment in which small-l leaders operate. In addition, the heightened powers that brain-powered workers have been given in the workplace require a broader range of leadership skills.

Small-l leadership is practiced among peers, most often in teams. The degree of success has less to do with the power of a job title than the power of expertise, a credible reputation, influence, and persuasion. The small-l leader may run the entire effort or a portion of it in a roomful of co-leaders and co-followers. She may be a leader for a one-hour meeting or a six-month project, but it is clear to her and those who follow that this is a role she is filling temporarily. The small-l leader is a role, not a person, and the workers who assume that role know they don't own or define the job, as some big-L leaders pretend to do.

To be an effective small-l leader, a team member must secure the respect of co-workers in at least

● ● ●

Charles de Gaulle must have been thinking about big-L leadership when he quipped, "The Great Leaders always stage-manage their effects… while the real leaders are down in the ranks, quietly changing the world."

one of three areas covered by this critical skill:

1. Knowledge Quotient—respected expertise and proven judgment in areas relevant to the group's goals.
2. People-Skills Quotient—the leader cares about colleagues and values their goals as much as his or her own; as a result, co-workers are moved to work voluntarily to accomplish the goal.
3. Momentum Quotient—the leader will do whatever it takes to help the group actually achieve the goal.

These small-l leadership quotients—knowledge, people, momentum—were not simply pulled out of a hat or identified because they fit some theory of what leaders should do. These are the leadership activities that our star performers used on the job day in and day out to gain their productivity edge. Sometimes one star would engage in all three; other times, these activities would rotate from team member to team member. The bottom line, though, is that the stars made sure that all three activities were in play when needed, by the person most appropriate for the role.

In a brain-powered environment where the workers often have more specialized knowledge than the big-L leader, big-L leadership may be anachronistic. Instead, small-l leadership, with its grounding in the day-to-day realities of information intensive activities, responds better to the demands of this fast-changing world.

In the end, it all comes down to which type will both attract the right kind of followership and succeed. As a brain-powered worker, ask yourself: Whom would you rather follow? Do you want a big-L leader who thinks he or she has all the answers? Or do you prefer someone who has no formal power over you but who has won your support with a track record in getting things done in a way that includes you? Which group of employees will come out ahead on the productivity scale? The small-l star performers or the big-L wannabes?

The stars we studied found that an easy choice and were rewarded with striking increases in productivity and effectiveness.

The research information presented is based on an extensive study of Bell Labs' knowledge workers and supported by later research on 3M workers.

REFERENCES AND FURTHER READING

Crawford, Megan, Lesley Kydd, and Colin Riches, eds. *Leadership and Teams in Educational Management*. Bristol, PA: Open University Press, 1997.

Green, Madeleine F. and Sharon A. McDade. *Investing in Higher Education: A Handbook of Leadership Development*. Phoenix, AZ: ACE/Oryx Press, 1994.

Hesselbein, Frances, Marshall Goldsmith, and Richard Beckhard, eds. *The Leader of the Future: New Visions, Strategies, and Practices for the New Era*. San Francisco, CA: Jossey-Bass Publishers, 1996.

Kelley, Robert E. *The Power of Followership: How to Create Leaders People Want to Follow, and Followers Who Lead Themselves*. New York: Doubleday, 1992.

Kelley, Robert E. *How to Be a Star at Work*. New York: Time Books, 1998.

Wilson, Jeanne M. et al. *Leadership Trapeze: Strategies for Leadership in Team-Based Organizations*. San Francisco, CA: Jossey-Bass Publishers, 1995.

Leadership:
With a Big-L
or a little-l?

The chief advancement officer must be willing to participate actively and effectively in campus planning initiatives, in lectures and seminars, and in other similar activities. In sum, he or she must be engaged in the intellectual life of the institution.

Boundaries of Leadership: The President and the Chief Advancement Officer

William R. Haden
President
West Virginia Wesleyan College

A successful partnership between a nonprofit institution's president and chief advancement officer (CAO) can result in a dynamic relationship that serves both the institution and these two individuals well. Too restrictive or narrow a view of the chief advancement officer's role and the partnership will fail to serve effectively the institution's needs and aspirations.

The chief advancement officer should be a key spokesperson for the institution, and more specifically, a trusted representative of the president. In order for this role to work well, the chief advancement officer must be intimately aware of the inner workings, thinking, and deliberations of the institution's senior leadership. As a key spokesperson, the chief advancement officer does more than speak for the president. In many vital settings, his or her voice is understood to be the same as the president's. In my own current institution, the CAO does, in fact, speak for me in many community contexts.

Beyond this important relationship, though, the chief advancement officer also must have a clear and well-defined peer relationship with senior faculty and academic administrators. He or she is a

colleague, not just an expert assistant assigned to help achieve their goals. This is particularly true in research universities, but it applies to all types of institutions. Given the central role of private support in achieving academic and research objectives, the chief advancement officer must be knowledgeable, experienced, and have a deep and appreciative understanding of the intellectual enterprise.

SELECTING A CAO

In considering the matter of boundaries and relationships, the president should select a broadly prepared chief advancement officer, someone with whom he or she can develop a close and trusting partnership. This preparation should consist of a progressively enlarged portfolio of career responsibilities together with appropriate formal education. For example, the CAO should have experience in finance and general administration, and either a MBA or MPA degree can offer the appropriate formal educational background. Put simply, the president should select a chief development officer whose experience and education can make him or her a peer among the senior leaders of the institution.

Establishing appropriate credentials for the position also must include the chief advancement

Boundaries of
Leadership:
The President and
the Chief
Advancement
Officer

officer's commitment to know and understand the academic and, where relevant, the research character of the institution. How to do this? The chief advancement officer must be willing to participate actively and effectively in campus planning initiatives, in lectures and seminars, and in other similar activities. In sum, he or she must be engaged in the intellectual life of the institution. At one institution I know well, the CAO attends at least a half-dozen campus events weekly and always makes a point of showing up at concerts, plays, and lectures. The partnering required among the senior officers of the institution requires nothing less than a full measure of collegial confidence and trust, and this can only be established on the basis of complete engagement on the part of the chief advancement officer in the life of the institution.

The most effective presidents and chief advancement officers work in tandem, as partners. For this relationship to succeed, and for the institution to take full advantage of the chief advancement officer's skill and experience, engagement in general decision making and leadership must transcend the role of advancement. The chief advancement officer must be more than simply a "rainmaker" or "hired gun." At my institution, for instance, the CAO and I regularly take turns playing devil's advocate when we're trying to brainstorm challenging situations. She knows that I expect no less than her honest opinion and she gets honesty from me in return.

Of course, your CAO must be an accomplished, professional fund raiser. Beyond this, however, the president and the institution will benefit most when the chief advancement officer is also clearly perceived as an involved senior colleague whose views and knowledge of issues can significantly help in making decisions and addressing broader issues.

In choosing a chief advancement officer, the president faces two challenges: first, to identify and select someone whose skills and experience offer the broad preparation necessary to play this role; and, second, to give the chief advancement officer

● ● ●

In choosing a chief advancement officer, the president faces two challenges: first, to identify and select someone whose skills and experience offer the broad preparation necessary to play this role; and, second, to give the chief advancement officer the appropriate role in senior deliberations.

the appropriate role in senior deliberations. The president must have sufficient confidence in the judgment of the CAO to allow for a full consultative role in all aspects of institutional life.

ROLE OF A CAO

Assuming that the president and the chief advancement officer have come together in a close collegial partnership, the essential requirement becomes effectively engaging the chief advancement officer in substantive consultation and decision making. What does he or she bring to the table? First and foremost, you would hope for a detailed knowledge of major institutional constituencies that can help understand the likely consequences of specific decisions and outcomes.

Alumni, parents, corporate leaders, and other friends are more than just supporters or would-be supporters; they are also barometers of opinion and concern that are best taken into account in decision making. This does not mean that such opinions or views ought to be determinative; rather, they should be factors in assessing outcomes. The chief advancement officer is the one institutional officer most likely to have a feel for the pulse of external groups. This important fact is often overlooked or underestimated, particularly as the role of institutional funding and public relations grows more complex. For the president, this colleague is, or certainly ought to be, a "window onto the world" so vital to effective decision making and interpretation.

If the chief advancement officer truly knows these constituencies well, he or she can also be an intermediary in discussions with them. There are many occasions in the life of colleges, universities, and other nonprofit organizations when dealing effectively with external constituencies will be essential to successful outcomes. I observed closely one CAO's leadership in intense negotiations between a college and a community arts organization regarding the development of a performance space. Throughout these deliberations, the CAO was clearly speaking for the institution, and he brought the discussions to a highly satisfactory outcome.

The truly experienced and skilled chief advancement officer will often bring other talents to the table. If the chief advancement officer has had an increasingly responsible series of assignments, then it is likely that she will have developed managerial, financial, and leadership skills that can be beneficially engaged for larger responsibilities. Budgets and personnel requirements for advancement programs are routinely among the largest and most complex units within administrative structures. Senior development personnel can and will, when afforded the opportunity, transfer this experience to broader institutional contexts, and it is the wise chief executive who takes full advantage of their experience.

For example, a well prepared chief advancement officer who has developed a good understanding of institutional issues and achieved effective relationships with both the academic and administrative leaders, is in an exceptionally good position to lead strategic planning efforts. Other than the president, few of the senior officers of a complex nonprofit organization will have the opportunity or requirement to develop a comprehensive understanding of both internal issues and external constituencies.

In sum, the successful team of president and chief advancement officer is an amalgam of trust, experience, and mutual confidence that draws fully on the expertise and judgment of both parties. Given the array and extent of work that must be accomplished in this vital arena, the team approach is both useful and necessary. It is the wise president who can see the value of this colleagueship.

FURTHER READINGS

Bensimon, Estela Mara. *Redesigning Collegiate Leadership: Teams and Teamwork in Higher Education.* Baltimore, MD: Johns Hopkins University Press, 1993.

Davenport, David. "Teamwork at the Top: The President's View: When the President and the Chief Fund Raiser Share Ideas and Ideals, Money is Just One Result," CURRENTS 15, no. 7 (July/August 1989): 12-14.

Moore, H. Martin. "A Model of Cooperation: A Survey of Presidents and Chief Advancement Officers Shows Four Types of Relationships," CURRENTS 13, no. 7 (July/August 1987): 40-44.

Rhodes, Frank H. T., ed. *Successful Fund Raising for Higher Education: The Advancement of Learning.* Phoenix, AZ: ACE/Oryx Press, October 1997.

Smith, G. T. " The Chief Executive and Advancement." In *Handbook of Institutional Advancement.* 2nd ed. Edited by A. Westley Rowland. San Francisco, CA: Jossey-Bass Publishers, 1986.

Advancement professionals can help refine the planning process, advocate the positions and involvement of external stakeholders, maximize the public relations value of the process, and develop strategies for sharing the plan with internal and external audiences.

Strategic Planning and Institutional Advancement: Partners for Success

Kathleen Casey Gigl
Vice President for Institutional Advancement
Texas Woman's University

The information and technology age has opened the gates of academia to scrutiny by our stakeholders, as well as by any person or organization demanding accountability from our institutions. An institution that operates in this environment without a strategic plan will find itself ill-prepared for the future without clear goals and direction.

A strategic plan provides the context for defining the institution's goals and objectives. It provides the basis for defining the institution's own future through strategies that ensure the continuous quality and relevance of its teaching, research and service programs, and initiatives.

Advancement officers can contribute not only substantively but also uniquely to the strategic planning process of their educational institution. Advancement professionals are comfortable with, and knowledgeable about, planning. Their experience in assessing opportunities, developing strategies, implementing activities, and evaluating outcomes in the internal or external environment are valuable assets for strategic planning. They can help refine the planning process, advocate the positions and involvement of external stakeholders, maxi-

mize the public relations value of the process, and develop strategies for sharing the plan with internal and external audiences.

Refining the Planning Process

The process of creating or updating a strategic plan is fairly straightforward. It typically begins with an analysis of external factors—the economy, political agendas, demographics, marketplace characteristics, etc.—that affect your institution, along with an internal assessment, often described as a SWOT—strengths, weaknesses, opportunities, and threats. The proactive stages are: (1) developing a vision statement, which describes the institution's future directions; (2) affirming or redirecting the institution's mission; and (3) selecting the strategic directions and developing an action plan with a timeline and assignment of responsibilities, plus a methodology for evaluation and feedback.

Refine and enhance your institution's strategic planning process by involving representatives from all the traditional advancement areas—alumni relations, fund raising, communications, and perhaps other areas as defined by your institution, such as government relations and enrollment management. Advancement professionals are accustomed to viewing the realities of their institutions—academic programs, student and faculty achievements, research initiatives and partnerships, the physical environment—through the eyes of external constituencies. By the very nature of their jobs, advancement professionals keep one eye focused outside the institution and the other within the school, college, or university. Their involvement in the planning process brings a perspective that is not only introspective, but also balances the "view from the inside" with the expectations and perceptions of those external constituencies.

Advocates for External Stakeholders

Advancement professionals interact continuously with external constituencies—alumni, prospective and current donors, opinion leaders and community leaders, reporters, and elected and appointed officials. Whether discussing a proposal for funding with a foundation grants administrator, convincing a reporter of the merits of a news story, or engaging volunteers, the advancement staff is well aware that the "public" expects an honest accounting about your institution, including its blemishes.

The advancement representatives should advocate inviting these external stakeholders to participate in the strategic planning process. Developing an effective strategic plan requires an honest appraisal of your institution. Without the input of external constituents and, perhaps, their presence at the planning table, the analysis of external factors and the institutional assessment may result in inappropriate objectives and ineffective strategies. By involving external stakeholders, the end product will be supported by a wider variety of constituents in a position to help the institution achieve its goals and realize its objectives. Prospective donors and key volunteers are more likely to commit time, talent, and dollars when they believe their perspective and involvement will make a difference by moving the institution to a stronger position among its peers.

Maximizing the Public Relations Value of Strategic Planning

The strategic planning process, which can take anywhere from six to 12 months, is an opportunity for

● ● ●
By the very nature of their jobs, advancement professionals keep one eye focused outside the institution and the other within the school, college, or university.

an institution to strengthen its reputation and enhance its image. The advancement team should launch a carefully crafted communications plan to inform the public about the process. Prospective students and donors, friends, and even critics will welcome news of the institution's planning for the future.

The communications plan should keep all the stakeholders of the institution, internal and external, informed about the stages of the planning process and the role they can play in its formulation. It should provide regular updates about progress and relevant news of interest. In addition to special communications, the plan should place updates in publications distributed to students, faculty, and staff, as well as those sent to alumni and other external audiences. Awareness that your institution is evaluating the quality, relevance, and future prospects for all its programs and services should strengthen alumni affiliation, renew the confidence of donors, and encourage the support of opinion leaders and elected officials.

Announcing the Strategic Plan

With all functions of advancement involved in the planning process, the communication strategy and strategic plan should evolve simultaneously. There is no excuse for waiting until the final draft is crafted to plan its dissemination. Whether the president, executive cabinet, or the provost crafts the planning document, the advancement staff should recommend the most effective ways to communicate it to the diverse audiences who should receive it.

The communications strategy should include variations of the strategic plan for internal and external audiences. Usually, the plan is first disseminated internally, then externally. You might use existing publications or a new family of publications designed exclusively for the plan for both internal and external audiences. Special publications may be particularly effective when the plan calls for a comprehensive fund-raising campaign. This may also be the ideal time to produce a new video, Web site design, or other multi-media production to share the institution's vision and goals. Certainly, it provides a rationale for inviting a wide range of audiences to campus to learn personally about your institution's plans.

Disseminating the plan requires either a real-location or additional allocation of operating funds. It also places an increased demand upon the time of the president, and perhaps board members, who can most effectively share the institution's goals and objectives. Budget and schedule for these resources during the planning process. There is nothing less exciting than a plan that has been on the shelf for a year or more.

In today's competitive environment, educational institutions rely on advancement professionals to develop clearly delineated action plans that will achieve institutional objectives. Consequently, advancement professionals are comfortable with and knowledgeable about planning. Involve these professionals in the planning process at your school, college, or university, and you'll get both a superior end product and the enhanced commitment and support of your institution's alumni, donors, and friends.

FURTHER READINGS

Hunt, Carle M. et al. *Strategic Planning for Private Higher Education*. Binghamton, NY: Haworth Press, Inc., 1997.

Levenson-Wahl, Carrie, Lenora Brennan, and Kelly Williams. "Berkeley Carroll School Triumphs in 10-Year Strategic Plan," *Fund Raising Management* 28, no. 1 (March 1997): 18-26.

Maxwell, Kimera. "Foundation Takes Lead in Planning," *Foundation Focus* 1, no. 5 (Spring 1996): 8.

Ray, Douglas E. "Strategic Planning for Non-Profit Organizations: What is Strategic Planning? It is a Controlled Process in Which We Call to Mind Why the Organization Exists; We Determine Where We Want to Go; We Define the Strategies/Policies Necessary to Get There; and We Make the Specific Plans to Implement Those Policies," *Fund Raising Management* 28, no. 6 (August 1997): 22-23.

Welton, John and Bruce Cook. "Institutional Vision: A Prerequisite for Fund Raising Success: This Article Explains Why a Clear Institutional Vision is Often a Self-Fulfilling Prophecy for Successful Fund Raising," *Fund Raising Management* 28, no. 9 (November 1997): 28-30.

●　●　●

*Transformational management helps organizations
"recognize and apply newer managerial styles,
approaches and methods" to meet the challenges
they face.*

4

The Transformational Leader

Harvey K. Jacobson
Professor Emeritus of Journalism
University of Wisconsin-Oshkosh and

Former Institutional Advancement Officer
University of Michigan

Peter Drucker, in *Management Challenges for the 21st Century,* encourages us to think of management as the organizational function that aims "to make institutions capable of producing results." Planning, organizing, and other factors are important. But the key word is *results.*

This emphasis on results comes from the dominant concept in management today—transformational management and leadership. Transformational management helps organizations "recognize and apply newer managerial styles, approaches and methods" to meet the challenges they face, writes George Kozmetsky.

Concurrently, institutional advancement managers find themselves in a prime spot in this new order. They serve in significant "boundary spanner" roles between their organizations and their environments, observes Kathleen Kelly in *Effective Fund-Raising Management.* Indeed, advancement personnel occupy "the most synergistic seats in education," according to an article by Donna Shoemaker. Why so? Because these personnel are positioned strategically to "do the translating between the community at large and the academic community—to the mutual advantage of

both the institution and society."

Transformational management incorporates new terms and new emphases, which translate into a different organizational texture, according to Jerry Wind and Jeremy Main. It is vision-directed more than goal-directed; flat/empowered rather than hierarchical; customer-driven rather than program-driven; stakeholder-focused rather than shareholder-focused; speed-oriented rather than finance-oriented; entrepreneurial rather than stable; cross-functional rather than functional; networked/interdependent rather than vertically integrated; and global rather than local, regional, and national.

A MOVER AND SHAPER

In this world of transformational management, the advancement professional should strive to be a transformational leader. As Peter Drucker puts it, "One cannot manage change. One can only be ahead of it. . . . (U)nless it is seen as the task of the organization to lead change, the organization. . . will not survive." What is needed is people who know how to navigate unknown waters, "pilot test" new initiatives and services, and address change to meet systems goals.

The transformational leader is a mover and

shaper. The mover respects the short term, meets deadlines, and recognizes resource constraints. The shaper examines the long term; monitors social, economic, and other trends; and takes pride in being an analyst who is objective, curious, and relativistic. The mover is pragmatic with an ability to reject perfectionism. This person has "a bias for action: an insistence that more be done than talk," note Iain Somerville and Quinn Mills. The payoffs are results and resolution of the problem. The shaper has a sense of proportion and profession that acknowledges a need to learn and to modify the knowledge of others. The shaper uses the modification model, which blends empirical evidence with experience and common sense. "The manager is not forced to have his head in the clouds or his hands in the grease," writes Joseph Massie. The manager needs to achieve a proper balance between reason, orderly thinking that is rational, and "intuition—critical thinking at warp speed," suggest Spitzer and Evans.

THE SKILLS FOR TRANSFORMATIONAL LEADERSHIP

What skills are most important for transformational leadership? David Whetton and Kim Cameron studied 60 characteristics of effective managers in the public and private sectors. They concluded, "Whereas people with different styles and personalities may apply the skills differently, there are, nevertheless, a core set of observable attributes of effective skill performance that are common across a range of individual differences." They identify three major management skill areas as the most important:

1. *Personal Skills*, including increasing self-awareness, managing stress, and solving problems creatively;
2. *Interpersonal Skills*, including communicating supportively, gaining power and influence, motivating others, and managing conflict; and
3. *Applied Communication Skills*, including conducting meetings, making oral presentations, and interviewing.

Effective managers are "both participative and hard-driving, both nurturing and competitive.

They are able to be flexible and creative while also being controlled, stable, and rational." Research reviewed by Whetton and Cameron indicates that competence in personal and interpersonal skills contributes more to the long-term success of managers than does their proficiency in analytic and quantitative skills.

THE QUALITIES OF TRANSFORMATIONAL LEADERSHIP

These qualities characterize transformational leadership:

- *Mindset of mutual benefit.* Stephen Covey uses this phrase to capsulize the approach a successful leader needs to direct disparate persons or groups toward a common goal. The manager must create synergy. "Focus on *we* instead of *me*."
- *Flair for cutting through the fog.* In an era that is data rich and information poor, decision makers who excel will quickly reduce complex situations to their essentials, make their way through dense detail and obfuscation, and go straight to what seems the obvious course of action. More people will see the big picture if you speak in plain talk.
- *Ability to think globally.* International initiatives of individual institutions as well as national organizations such as CASE, PRSA, and the National Society of Fund Raising Executives remind us of the growing movement to globalize. Managers need to reassess how they network, how they learn, how they respond to societal demands, and how they redesign their infrastructure, advise Wind and Main.

One way to move from generalities toward specifics for action is to consider the lessons learned by international marketers. In making recommendations about multinational marketing, Masaaki Kotabe and Kristiaan Helsen discuss how to adapt to other languages and cultures, communicate with the world consumer, and deal with constraints on global media programming. You'll find insights on international public relations by Hugh Culbertson and Ni Chen in a book that

Effective managers are "both participative and hard-driving, both nurturing and competitive. They are able to be flexible and creative while also being controlled, stable, and rational."

concentrates on comparisons of public relations practices in various countries and also touches on the practice of public relations in a cross-cultural context. Lilya Wagner and Patrick Ryan offer a glimpse of globalization's impact on the priorities and practices of American fund raisers and donors.

■ *Dedication to diversity.* Institutional efforts to achieve diversity raise ethical concerns and social responsibility issues. Institutional advancement managers should lead by example as well as design communication programs that help internal and external publics understand why diversity deserves to be celebrated rather than ignored. Managers should select personnel with an ability to interact effectively with men and women who are physically challenged, or differ in race, gender, sexual orientation, or other factors. Managers can take steps to provide accurate information, overturn inaccurate stereotypes, arrange ongoing diversity training and education, and help develop an atmosphere in which people feel free to share differing perspectives.

■ *Receptivity to technological change.* As educational institutions become increasingly computer literate, they need to clarify what they want technology to accomplish. How do managers enhance the integration of technology into the life of their operations? They need not win blue ribbons in "geekspeak" or enroll for advanced degrees in computer science. Rather, suggests Stephen Covey, they should: (1) Understand how the intelligent use of new technology best contributes to institutional goals, (2) Recruit, develop, and maintain teams of technically competent people, (3) Learn how to make and manage investments in new technology, and (4) Serve as positive role models in leading the use of new technology.

■ *Anticipatory outlook.* Effective managers take steps to avoid crisis management and internal/external shock. They are proactive rather than reactive. Peter Drucker reminds us in his 1999 book that the discovery of trouble spots in their early stages helps managers "starve problems and feed innovations." In helping the organization adjust to change, managers need

to be askers, not pontificators. "Leaders do not need to know all the answers. They do need to ask the right questions," advise Ronald Heifetz and Donald Laurie.

■ *Temperament for transformation.* The successful manager must be able to "create a developmental climate," assert Cynthia McCauley and Martha Hughes. This approach helps members of the organization innovate, learn, and grow.

■ *Proficiency in leading co-workers.* Transformation management puts a premium on teamwork and collaboration. The successful manager has an ability to provide perspective, lead subordinates, motivate fellow workers, delegate unambiguously, and set clear performance expectations. He or she should have the ability to work well one-on-one and in groups, to listen, to give counsel, and to discover commonalities. The person should be understanding and compassionate and should help others reach their potential.

These characteristics are of signal importance to tomorrow's advancement leaders. Good judgment; compatibility with the chief executive officer; a true affection and respect for the academy's values; and the highest standards of institutional integrity, professional performance, and personal conduct will provide for all who incorporate them an unprecedented level of leadership in advancement.

REFERENCES

Covey, Stephen R. "The Mind-Set and Skill-Set of a Leader." In *Leading Beyond the Walls.* Edited by Frances Hesselbein, Marshall Goldsmith, and Iain Somerville. San Francisco, CA: Jossey-Bass Publishers, 1999.

Culbertson, Hugh M. and Ni Chen. *International Public Relations: A Comparative Analysis.* Mahwah, NJ: Lawrence Erlbaum Associates, 1996.

Drucker, Peter F. *Management Challenges for the 21st Century.* 1st ed. New York, NY: HarperCollins Publishers, 1999.

Heifetz, Ronald and Donald L. Laurie. "The Work of Leadership," *Harvard Business Review* 75, no.1 (January-February 1997): 124-134.

Kelly, Kathleen S. *Effective Fund-Raising Management.* Mahwah, NJ: Lawrence Erlbaum Associates, 1998.

Kotabe, Masaaki and Kristiaan Helsen. *Global Marketing Management*. New York, NY: John Wiley and Sons, 1998.

Kozmetsky, George. *Transformational Management*. Cambridge, MA: Ballinger, 1985.

Massie, Joseph L. *Essentials of Management*. 2nd ed. Englewood Cliffs, NJ: Prentice-Hall, 1971.

Shoemaker, Donna. "A Doer's Profile," CURRENTS 33, no. 9 (October 1997): 11-13.

Somerville, Iain and D. Quinn Mills. "Leading in a Leaderless World." In *Leading Beyond the Walls*. 1st ed. Edited by Frances Hesselbein, Marshall Goldsmith, and Iain Somerville. San Francisco, CA: Jossey-Bass, 1999. 227-241.

Spitzer, Quinn and Ron Evans. "The New Business Leader: Socrates with a Baton," *Strategy and Leadership* 25, no. 5 (September-October 1997): 32-41.

Wagner, Lilya and J. Patrick Ryan. "The Global Community," *Advancing Philanthropy* 7, no. 1 (Spring 1999): 36-39.

Whetten, David A. and Kim S. Cameron. *Developing Management Skills*. 2nd ed. New York, NY: HarperCollins Publishers, 1991.

Wind, Jerry Yoram and Jeremy Main. *Driving Change: How the Best Companies Are Preparing for the 21st Century*. New York, NY: Free Press, 1998.

FURTHER READINGS

Barrett, Katherine and Richard Greene. "No One Runs the Place: The Sorry Mismanagement of America's Colleges and Universities," *Financial World* 163, no. 6 (March 15, 1994).

Barton, David W., Jr. "Events by Objectives," CURRENTS 6, no. 6 (June 1980).

Bryson, John M. *Strategic Planning for Public and Nonprofit Organizations*. San Francisco, CA: Jossey-Bass Publishers, 1995.

Carbone, Robert F. *An Agenda for Research on Fund-raising*. College Park, MD: Clearinghouse for Research on Fund-raising, University of Maryland—College Park, 1986.

Crowder, Nancy L. *Academic Centers and Research Programs Focusing on the Study of Philanthropy, Voluntarism and Not-for-Profit Activity: A Progress Report, 1990-1991*. 2nd ed. Washington, DC: Independent Sector, 1991.

Cutlip, Scott M. *Fund Raising in the United States: Its Role in America's Philanthropy*. New Brunswick, NJ: Transaction Publishers, 1990. (Original work published in 1965.)

Cutlip, Scott M. *Public Relations History: From the 17th to the 20th Century. The Antecedents*. Hillsdale, NJ: Lawrence Erlbaum Associates, 1995.

Cutlip, Scott M. *The Unseen Power: Public Relations. A History*. Hillsdale, NJ: Lawrence Erlbaum Associates, 1994.

Cutlip, Scott M., Allen H. Center, and Glen M. Broom.

Effective Public Relations. 6th ed. Englewood Cliffs, NJ: Prentice-Hall, 1985.

David, Fred R. *Strategic Management: Concepts and Cases*. 7th ed. Upper Saddle River, NJ: Prentice-Hall, 1999.

Drucker, Peter F. *Managing the Non-Profit Organization: Practices and Principles*. 1st ed. New York, NY: HarperCollins Publishers, 1990.

Dunlop, David R. "Special Concerns of Major Gift Fund-Raising." In *Handbook of Institutional Advancement*. 2nd ed. Edited by A. Westley Rowland. San Francisco, CA: Jossey-Bass Publishers, 1986.

Ehling, William P. "PR Administration, Management Science, and Purposive Systems," *Public Relations Review* 1, no. 2 (Fall 1975).

Grunig, James E. and Todd Hunt. *Managing Public Relations*. New York, NY: Holt, Rinehart and Winston, 1984.

Herman, Robert D., ed. *The Jossey-Bass Handbook of Nonprofit Leadership and Management*. San Francisco: Jossey-Bass Publishers, 1994.

Hock, D. "The Birth of the Chaotic Century: Out of Control and Into Order." Presented at the Extension National Leadership Conference, Washington, DC (March 11, 1996).

Jacobson, Harvey K., ed. "The Economy of Information: Priority of Communication in the Allocation of Scarce Resources." Presented at the annual assembly of the Council for Advancement and Support of Education, Chicago, IL (July 10, 1975).

Jacobson, Harvey K. (ed.) *Evaluating Advancement Programs*. New Directions for Institutional Advancement, no. 1. San Francisco, CA: Jossey-Bass Publishers, 1978.

Jacobson, Harvey K. *The Evolution of Institutional Advancement on American Campuses, 1636-1989*. Oshkosh, WI: Journalism Research Bureau, University of Wisconsin-Oshkosh, 1990a).

Jacobson, Harvey K. "Research on Institutional Advancement: A Review of Progress and a Guide to the Literature," *The Review of Higher Education* 13, no. 4 (Summer 1990b).

Jacobson, Harvey K. "Toward an Economy of Information for Organizations in a Limited-Growth Environment." Presented at the annual conference of the International Communication Association, Portland, OR (April 17, 1976).

Jones, Gareth R., Jennifer M. George, and Charles W. L. Hill. *Contemporary Management*. 2nd ed. Boston, MA: Irwin McGraw-Hill, 2000.

Keller, George. *Academic Strategy: The Management Revolution in American Higher Education*. Baltimore, MD: Johns Hopkins University Press, 1983.

Kelly, Kathleen S. *Fund Raising and Public Relations: A Critical Analysis*. Hillsdale, NJ: Lawrence Erlbaum Associates, 1991.

Kennedy, Larry W. *Quality Management in the Nonprofit World: Combining Compassion and Performance to Meet Client Needs and Improve Finances.* San Francisco, CA: Jossey-Bass Publishers, 1991.

Kotler, Philip. *Strategic Marketing for Educational Institutions.* Englewood Cliffs, NJ: Prentice-Hall, 1985.

Kotler, Philip and Alan R. Andreasen. *Strategic Marketing for Nonprofit Organizations.* 5th ed. Upper Saddle River, NJ: Prentice-Hall, 1996.

Mali, Paul, ed. *Management Handbook: Operating Guidelines, Techniques and Practices.* New York, NY: John Wiley and Sons, 1981.

Malone, Thomas W. "Is Empowerment Just a Fad? Control and Decision Making, and IT," *Sloan Management Review* 38, no. 2 (Winter 1997).

Mixer, Joseph R. *Principles of Professional Fundraising: Useful Foundations for Successful Practice.* San Francisco, CA: Jossey-Bass Publishers, 1993.

Nanus, Burt and Stephen M. Dobbs. *Leaders Who Make a Difference.* San Francisco, CA: Jossey-Bass Publishers, 1999.

Nutt, Paul C. and Robert W. Backoff. *Strategic Management of Public and Third Sector Organizations.* San Francisco, CA: Jossey-Bass Publishers, 1992.

Oblinger, Diana G. and Sean C. Rush, eds. *The Learning Revolution: The Challenge of Information Technology in the Academy.* Bolton, MA: Anker Publishing Company, 1997.

Pappas, Alceste T. *Reengineering Your Nonprofit Organization: A Guide to Strategic Transformation.* New York, NY: John Wiley and Sons, 1996.

Richards, M. D. and G. R. Sherratt, *Institutional Advancement Strategies in Hard Times.* American Association for Higher Education/Educational Resources Information Center Higher Education Research Report No. 2. Washington, D.C.: American Association for Higher Education, 1981.

Ryan, Joseph E. "Profitability in the Nonprofit Environment," *Journal of Systems Management* 30, no. 8 (August 1980).

Taylor, Barbara E., Richard P. Chait and Thomas P. Holland. "The New Work of the Nonprofit Board," *Harvard Business Review* 74, no. 5 (September-October 1996).

Taylor, Karla. "Sudden Impact: CASE's New President Promises to Concentrate on More and Better Services—And Be Quick About It," CURRENTS 23, no. 10 (November-December 1997).

Young, Denis R., Robert M. Hollister, and Virginia A. Hodgkinson and Associates, eds. *Governing, Leading, and Managing Nonprofit Organizations: New Insights from Research and Practice.* San Francisco, CA: Jossey-Bass Publishers, 1993.

● ● ●

Opening one's own ideas to a sort of peer review takes a secure mind. It is what is done in the academic process. Institutional advancement professionals should do nothing less when managing their staffs.

Managing in a Complex Environment: Swimming with the Dolphins

Jerry Nunnally
Vice President for Institute Relations
California Institute of Technology

"No successful businessman has ever made his fortune without the dedicated help of his employees. The realization of almost every idea requires the intelligent work and cooperation of all involved. An ambitious executive must know how to summon the best from those around him, regardless of the pressure or lack of it. This is the essential skill that comes naturally to some, but can also be learned."

J. Paul Getty
(*How To Be Rich*, 1965)

How many times in our careers have we heard that higher education and business techniques are two divergent paradigms? That the policies, practices, and procedures of one are not compatible with the other? While the cultures are different, I do not believe that successful management is a different process for the academy from that for business. Early in my career, I had a brief stint in banking. Though just an interlude, some 23 years later, much of what I know about managing an advancement office draws heavily from my management experience in banking

Of the 10 critical ingredients for successful management in any organization, in this chapter I will address individually:
■ Environment,
■ Taking risks,
■ Learning new things,
■ Ability to navigate through ambiguity, and
■ Communication.

(The others are leadership, vision, colleagues who share and are inspired by the vision, eagerness to give recognition to those who contribute to success, and capable staff.)

THE ENVIRONMENT

All organizations have cultures. They view themselves through a particular cultural prism. Understanding the work environment in the prism is as essential as understanding the organization's mission. A manager helps staff members interpret that environment in order to help them become successful in it. In academia, the mission may be the same or similar to that of another university, college, or independent school, but the culture invariably will differ. Failure to understand that unique culture will adversely affect your management. Taking the time to appreciate that cultures

Managing in a
Complex
Environment:
Swimming
with the
Dolphins

differ from campus to campus may determine whether you succeed or fail. Advancement professionals cannot work in isolation; they must be able to navigate through their environment with the precision of a dolphin swimming in the ocean.

When I worked in the private sector, one of my greatest challenges was to understand what my boss and the bank expected of me. This meant asking questions and lots of them. It meant not being afraid to ask the simplest question without feeling stupid. What I have learned over the years is that many times the simplest question is often the most pertinent one. With the encouragement of a mentor, Don Campbell, and my boss in banking, I sought out people who were considered the best managers in the bank. As long as they were willing conversants, I asked questions. This proved to be a good device for understanding the bank as well as my role in it. Each person I spoke with had a slightly different twist on his (they were all men then) description of the bank, but all had a common message: "To be successful here, you need to know the place and how it works." You can only learn about the environment if you are persistently inquisitive about how your institution works.

TAKING RISKS

Once you understand your environment, how do you manage in it? In order to manage successfully in the academic culture, a manager must have a clear sense of priority coupled with an excitement for the task to be accomplished. And you must effectively communicate both messages to the staff. Managing is not always cheerleading. It must provide the reality check for the organization in the face of grandiose ideas. In other words, being a good manager does not mean always saying yes. Nor does it mean saying no to unconventional ideas. What it means to me is balance. It means making decisions in a way that encourages creative initiative while minimizing the chance of failure. Don Campbell once told me that everyone deserves an opportunity to fail. How many times have we been told in our lives not to be afraid of failure? I believe a good manager is neither afraid of failure nor does he or she penalize staff members for taking risks.

If advancement professionals are to be seen as

players in the larger institutional environment, they must be willing to take risks. Once, during my days in banking, my division manager raised this question in a staff meeting: "Does being successful at your job mean never having egg on your face in front of your boss?" My initial reaction to the question was yes (I was 24 then). However, as I examined the question more closely through the years, the answer has to be no. I have come to believe that one of the greatest inhibitors to personal growth in academia, at least administratively, is the mindset "we don't do it that way here." When I hear this, it signifies that the person is opposed to taking risks or change. Earlier, I wrote about the need to understand your environment. Understanding your environment and taking risks are not incompatible ideas. One helps you with the other.

LEARNING NEW THINGS

A manager should learn from the staff and enable the staff to learn from her or him. A good manager should encourage the exchange of new ideas, which are devices for motivating staff. The old General Motors maxim that if it were not invented here it is not worthy of consideration is a dinosaur. Some of the best ideas that I have heard over the years have come from discussions with staff members inspired by an open dialogue. Opening your own ideas to a sort of peer review takes a secure mind. It is what is done in the academic process. Institutional advancement professionals should do nothing less.

Learning is a life-long process, which does not stop when you receive your diploma. While this is not news, it is worth reminding yourself that there are always new and better ways to do things. Who would have thought a few years ago that the World Wide Web would play as important a role as it does now in academia? There are many ways advancement managers can hone their skills. Professional conferences such as those offered by CASE and other groups, executive programs, or additional formal study are all conventional ways of learning. However, when managing in the complex environment, the informal process is a particularly effective but often overlooked tool. Talking regularly with faculty, deans, other administrators, and colleagues from other institutions may well be

Managing in a
Complex
Environment:
Swimming
with the
Dolphins

the easiest route to professional growth. Several years ago, while working at Dartmouth College, a dean asked whether I thought I was in fund raising or education. We engaged in a spirited discussion about the difference between the two. My conclusion was that institutional advancement officers are educators who work in development, public relations, alumni relations, or government and community relations. That recognition will help guide us through the interstices of our institutions. Seeing ourselves any other way disserves the institutions we represent and ourselves. Do not reject the new because it is different; do not retain the old because it is comfortable.

NAVIGATING THROUGH AND MANAGING AMBIGUITY

Academia is known for being unwilling to make decisions about priorities. This can frustrate the orderly managerial mind. Once I asked a dean at one of the universities where I have worked, "How do I get my hands around this place?" He responded, "To know this place is to know that it is complex and that no one can completely understand it in its entirety." He went on to suggest that I become expert at my piece of the organization and that that would help me understand the whole. In their book, *In Search of Excellence,* Thomas J. Peters and Robert H. Waterman, Jr. write about the changing face of management models in successful companies. They conclude that managers who do not take into account the complexities of corporate cultures, and who do not understand the cultures' evolution, are at risk of not succeeding in the future. This assertion seems to fit the academic world as well. In research universities where I have spent most of my advancement career, things tend not to be clear-cut. They are filled with an array of decision-making processes that are at best vague. By its nature, the academy is in a constant state of discovery, seeking answers, knowing that what will be discovered tomorrow will forever change what we believe is true today. Understanding that there are many competing interests with potential positive outcomes has helped me to understand why universities have both clarity and confusion. Trying to fit

● ● ●
Being a good manager does not mean always saying yes. Nor does it mean saying no to unconventional ideas. What it means to me is balance.

them into a box can only lead to frustration.

Colleges and universities are complex and perplexing entities. Research universities, in particular, can be a labyrinth of decision making, even to an experienced manager. Just getting your arms around the vision and priorities can be difficult. How many times have you or your colleagues complained about not having an institutional vision? If only the president or school head would just define it, your job could be much easier. As an advancement manager, your input into the process is more important now than it was for those who preceded you. In any organization, you need to know where you are going so that you will know when you have arrived. This means advancement professionals as well as presidents and school heads need to be a part of the process of determining that vision.

How do you participate in the process? Most institutions have administrative councils on which the chief advancement officer usually sits. However, the beginning point is with your boss and the informal connections you have with the rest of the leadership in your institution. A key is to bring to the table the right issues, and to bring them along with proposed solutions. To busy academic executives, there is nothing more deafening than the words "We have a problem" without any recommendation of how to solve it. Here are some pointers: Don't manage up! Don't be unnecessarily negative. Be balanced in your views. Make your recommendations in terms of what is best for your institution, not what is best for you. Stay focused on institutional outcomes, not yours.

A few years ago, Henry Rosovsky, a popular and internationally renowned former dean of the Faculty of Arts and Sciences at Harvard, wrote a book titled *The University, An Owner's Manual.* In the chapter on governance, Rosovsky lists seven principles of how a university is governed. Principles four and seven offer some sanguine guidance for anyone in university, college, or school administration. They are, respectively: "In a university, those with knowledge are entitled to a greater say." and "To function well, a hierarchical system of governance requires explicit mechanisms of consultation

Managing in a
Complex
Environment:
Swimming
with the
Dolphins

and accountability." Institutional advancement managers have the obligation and responsibility to their employers to acquire as much knowledge as they possibly can about their universities. They must act on that knowledge for the good of the whole while involving the proper persons in the process. Understanding the innate complexities of your institution, participating in defining the vision, and staying knowledgeable about your field will help you navigate the ambiguities that inevitably exist in an academic environment.

COMMUNICATION

This is probably the most difficult aspect of academia, no matter how large or small the institution. The rise of e-mail has helped communications, but, in some cases, it has exacerbated the problem of effective communication. Some of my colleagues have complained over the years that e-mail interferes with face-to-face dialogue. They also worry that e-mail volume continues to proliferate. While I can appreciate these concerns, e-mail does offer fast and broad coverage when time is critical. At Caltech, we operate on a principle of "no surprises." What this means is that each staff member and manager endeavors to keep informed the appropriate parties in the decision tree. While it is impossible for a manager on a daily basis to keep the masses apprised of all they would like to know,

it is critically important to develop a mechanism for disseminating timely information that articulates the institution's position. Remember Rosovsky's fourth principle. It can make all the difference in how well you navigate and manage.

In each of the foregoing areas, I believe a willingness to communicate constantly the goals and objectives throughout the advancement unit and the organization is the first prerequisite to successful management. If it is true that in the high-powered business world, the successful manager swims with the sharks, then the analogue in academia must be that the successful administrator swims with the dolphins in sometimes shark-infested waters. Having or developing good sonar is the key to a fruitful career in the academy.

FURTHER READINGS

Getty, J. Paul. *How To Be Rich*. New York, NY: Jove Books, 1965.

Peters, Thomas J. and Waterman, Robert H., Jr.. *In Search of Excellence*. New York, NY: Warner Books, 1982.

Labovitz, George, Yu Sang Change, and Victor Rosansky. *Making Quality Work*. New York, NY: HarperCollins, 1993.

Rosovsky, Henry. *The University: An Owner's Manual*. New York, NY: Norton and Company, Inc., 1991.

Smigel, Lloyd. *Management Plus: Leadership, Motivation, and Power in the Changing Marketplace*. New York, NY: Lowell House, 1994.

Rather than resisting or fearing change, embracing it—or at least acknowledging its inevitability—is the first step toward managing change constructively.

Managing Technological Change

Michael Stoner
Vice President for New Media
Lipman Hearne, Inc.

For most of the history of the human race, people struggled to adapt to changing climate. Now human-kind struggles to adapt to changes in technology. Accelerated development of new products, services, and processes affects every part of our lives. It makes managing staff and projecting expenses a major issue for every manager. New technologies, such as Web-based interfaces to information systems, can make managing people and processes easier and more efficient. In other cases, though, technology makes managing more complicated by offering an array of competing options that make choices difficult and expensive.

MANAGING TECHNOLOGY IN ADVANCEMENT

There are several reasons why this is particularly an issue in advancement. First, higher education institutions are slow to respond to change. Budget constraints force managers to be conservative and creative in responding to any changes in the internal or external environment. Second, staff may be suspicious of change or reluctant to change—while the constituencies that advancement serves may be clamoring for change. Finally, it is difficult to keep up with the rapid pace of

change and to know which innovations to adopt and which to shun.

Here are two ideas to help managers manage better:

■ **Accept change as a constant.** Change is a constant—and it will continue to be part of our lives. In fact, the pace of change will probably accelerate. So, rather than resist or fear change, embrace it—or at least acknowledge its inevitability. This is the first step toward managing change constructively.

While some staff in the advancement office may welcome change openly, others may not be so accommodating. Humans, after all, need time to adjust to new ways of doing things, not to mention new ways of thinking about how to do them. Managers must lead by demonstrating an interest in technology and encouraging staff members to explore applications and new developments that can improve how things are done.

In the Information Age, good leaders also must recognize that no one can keep up with the pace of technological change. Helping to allay staff anxieties about keeping up means recognizing that everyone is behind and that as long as reasonable steps are being taken to keep up, you can safely ignore headlines that encourage this anxiety. It's also important for managers to recognize that cutting-edge technology takes some time to trickle down and become a mass utility. Today, institutions must have good, well-organized Web pages. In 1995, however, this was not the case.

■ **Develop a "technology advisory group."** To help you manage changing technology effectively, identify staff members who are particularly interested in technology and appoint them as your in-house technology advisory group. Part of their jobs will be to monitor new advancements in technology and track these developments to see how they might have an impact on the way you do business. Ideally, this group should consist of both staff members with responsibilities for managing information technology and those who don't. Technology should always serve the needs of the office and, to do that, those responsible for managing technology need to have input from people who use it.

● ● ●
Since not every person on your staff needs the hottest machine on the market, develop a plan that allows you to replace machines on everyone's desk over a two-to-three-year period.

Buy the technology group subscriptions to magazines (I particularly recommend *Wired, Fast Company,* and *Technology Review*) and circulate these magazines among other staff members. Encourage your technology advisory group to subscribe to e-mail periodicals that report on technology developments. Send them to talk to faculty and alumni who are active in the information industries. Finally, have them report to you and their colleagues about what they learn. This creates buy-in among the staff, raises the overall level of awareness in the office, helps to develop in-house expertise, and encourages teamwork and self-development.

If you have a group of alumni or close friends of your institution who are active in the information industries, you might want to bring them together as an informal outside technology advisory group. Encourage them to meet with your staff during reunions or at other convenient times to help you and your staff recognize and harness the power of technology more effectively.

BUDGETING

Success in managing technology requires a plan for replacing computers and other hardware. Offices that are successful at using technology develop plans for replacing their computers periodically (every two to three years is normal in many industries). Since not every person on your staff needs the hottest machine on the market, develop a plan that allows you to replace machines on everyone's desk over a two-to-three-year period.

Typically, you'll want to replace the computers of "power" users (for example, your database manager or Web-based researchers) more frequently, giving them a next-generation machine, and shifting these users' older high-end computers to staff members who use their computers less intensively. Unfortunately, replacement is a recurring expense, so you must plan your budgets accordingly. Your budget must also include a line item for training and staff development.

TRAINING AND STAFF DEVELOPMENT

Perceptive managers must provide a climate in which staff are encouraged to learn about new developments, new technology, and the effects of these advancements on society and on how they do their job. Time and budget for training and staff development are necessities in an organization that wants to understand technology and manage it effectively. This is not a one-time expense, but an ongoing need. As the pace of change accelerates, your staff will need help in enhancing its skill sets and learning new approaches to its work. This mindset will be crucial to success in the future.

One of the main characteristics of the information age is that the model of top-down management is breaking down. Instead, people are working in cross-functional teams where information and responsibility are shared. This is a new way of working and staff members need help to understand it and develop the skills necessary for being effective team members and influencing their teammates.

There are plenty of opportunities on most campuses for training and staff development, often at relatively low expense. For example, on many campuses, the computing and information technology department provides training. In many cases, faculty members offer classes or do research at the cutting edge of technology. (This is true even at liberal arts colleges with few pretensions to being MIT, Carnegie Mellon, or Cal Tech.) There are also opportunities to learn about using new technologies from outside vendors, who can provide training to some staff members, who can then train their colleagues. Finally, alumni and friends can often offer their expertise and share their knowledge and experience with staff.

No matter where the training comes from, staff must be encouraged to share what they've learned in informal sessions such as brown-bag lunches or in more structured sessions. But staff members need encouragement from management—and release time—to take classes and to keep up on new developments that affect their fields.

There is a Chinese curse that says, "May you live in interesting times." The times we live in are interesting indeed. Embracing change, or even welcoming it, can provide us with an opportunity to learn, develop a culture of teamwork and support, and improve our institutions.

FURTHER READINGS

Additional resources to supplement the text of this chapter can be found on the Web at *www.lipmanhearne.com*.

Forbush, Dan and John Toon. "PR in the 21st Century: An Informal Survey Predicts How New Technology Will Affect the Field—And How Campus Communicators Can Prepare for Change," CURRENTS 20, no. 3 (March 1994): 44-48.

Miller, James D. and Deborah Strauss, eds. *Improving Fundraising with Technology: New Directions for Philanthropic Fundraising*, no. 11. San Francisco, CA: Jossey-Bass Publishers, 1996.

"Technology vs. Reality: The Real Deal on Eight Common Misconceptions About Hardware and Software," CURRENTS 24, no. 2 (February 1998): 9.

Warwick, Mal. "Technology and the Future of Fund Raising: The Business of Direct-Response Fund Raising is Changing in Genuinely Fundamental Ways Under the Onslaught of Emerging New Technologies," *Fund Raising Management* 25, no. 2 (April 1994): 38.

Staff, like potential donors, are most productive when their skills and interests align with the needs of the organization.

Staff Management: Strategies for Success

Virginia B. Clark
Vice President, Development and Alumni Relations
University of Pennsylvania

Every organization needs people with a wide variety of skills and competencies to succeed. Particularly adept organizations recognize they also need a rich diversity of personalities, people with varied work habits, temperaments, and personal goals. A great organization is likely to include entrepreneurs, methodical analysts, cage rattlers, consensus builders, bright stars, big-picture thinkers, and young drivers. It is important for leaders to be intentional about hiring staff to create such diverse talents and characteristics.

For the mature program, it may be time to bring in a cage rattler or someone who may not have direct experience but who can ask tough questions and adopt good new ideas taken from unexpected places. Or, the program may have just gone through a tremendous growth spurt, and it is now time to strengthen the infrastructure with people who are by temperament and attitude likely to give their best to the long term stability of the office.

TIPS ON RECRUITMENT

The type of employee you are looking for must inform the recruiting and interviewing process. It should not be the "kitchen-sink" approach to interviewing, where practically every staff member who has an interest in the candidates has a chance to meet them. Dispense with asking staff members to participate for reasons that have little to do with assuring the right candidate is chosen and more to do with assuring no one's feelings are hurt.

Match the interview team and process to the type of individual needed. A short, intense search can appeal to candidates who themselves make decisions quickly, have high energy, and like change. If the position requires a consensus builder or someone who needs to integrate various office functions, the process should be more involved. The interview team should meet frequently as candidates are interviewed. During these meetings, chaired by the hiring officer, impressions can be shared, differences aired, and issues identified that need further exploration. If a candidate seems overly aggressive, for example, the next interview should include some "what if" scenarios to test how aggressive the candidate would behave in two or three hypothetical situations that actually occurred or could occur in the future.

A final note on recruitment. I am convinced that checking references thoroughly is a dying art—if it ever lived. If your view of the world was based solely on references, the world would be filled exclusively with high-energy, smart, thoughtful people with excellent communications skills. With almost every call I get asking for references, it is clear that the caller has already made up his or her mind. The questions are perfunctory. Never does the caller probe or revisit a question to get clarity. Equally, I have found that when I am reference-checking, people are never very honest about an individual's weaknesses. It is important to do informal checking as soon as the candidate is likely to be a finalist for the position. That means checking in the middle of the process and calling upon colleagues' networks to get this information. The network usually gets it right when assessing people.

ORIENTATION AND PROFESSIONAL DEVELOPMENT

It is generally true, and should always be so, that when a person is hired and enters the organization from the outside, he or she receives a good orientation, including training on data systems, counseling on benefits, and a thorough introduction to, or review of, institutional goals and procedures. Ironic as it seems, this opportunity is not always provided to the employee selected from within the organization. Good training and development should be equally available to everyone in the organization, and every promoted person, whether appointed from outside or within the organization, should have an orientation opportunity.

What are the critical skills, competencies, management traits, or thinking processes that are key to this position? How and by whom is that knowledge imparted? How does the individual grow stronger in those areas? The more senior the staff member, the less likely orientation will be done through seminars, lectures, or training sessions. Instead, each senior staff member should have his or her own training program developed and modified annually, which articulates the skills to be further refined or developed.

For senior team members, a seminar on major gifts solicitation has little value to develop leadership skills. Yet, to develop leadership skills, a

⬤ ⬤ ⬤

Checking references thoroughly is a dying art—if it ever lived. With almost every call I get asking for references, it is clear that the caller has already made up his or her mind.

director could be asked to lead a task force on a department-wide issue that is not necessarily in her or his area of expertise. Representation on institution-wide committees or speaking engagements are other well-used methods of strengthening a senior staff member's leadership potential. A less public approach to leadership training is to give the staff member a chance to be "Boss for the Day." This doesn't mean the staff member takes over your office. Instead, bring the person into your confidence on a particularly challenging issue. Give her the opportunity to role-play the issue with you. Let him think through the problem, discuss the issues, and plot a course of action. Because all is done within the confines and confidences of your office, the staff member can safely practice asking questions—and making mistakes.

TURNOVER

Of course, no team remains the same forever. Some key staff members are recruited by other organizations or seek opportunities simply because no appropriate career path exists for them in your organization. While recruiting for entry-level or relatively junior-level positions will often be difficult, it can be even more trying to find good middle to upper-level staff members. Some positions, especially senior ones requiring a strong "institutional memory," will be best filled from within the organization—for example, the director of major gifts or the head of planned giving. Assuring continued strong leadership in these areas requires some planning both in the hiring for lower level vacancies, as well as in the career development of people already in place. Always have a strategy for filling these key positions should someone leave unexpectedly.

PERFORMANCE MANAGEMENT

Advancement organizations are coming under increasing pressure to do more with less—or at least to do more with what they have. While this may occasionally appear to be the equivalent of "squeezing blood out of stone," few organizations are so well tuned that they cannot benefit from closer attention to performance. Managing the performance of the advancement team or an individual member of the team requires a clear understanding of the overall goals and objectives of the organization. These goals and objectives should link performance exactly with expectations for the organization as a whole, the team unit, and the individual. Within these areas, long-term and short-term objectives should be outlined. Campaigns are often used to focus an institution on specific goals, but even in the absence of a campaign, clear goals and objectives are crucial.

The departments and individuals within the organization also need clarity about what their priorities should be to achieve the goals and objectives. Being clear on goals, objectives, and priorities is essential to managing performance. For example, if adding new, endowed professorships is a top priority of your institution, then major gift officers may need to focus more attention on the biggest prospects—perhaps at the expense of broadening the major donor base. If the top priority for alumni affairs is to increase alumni participation at reunions, other worthwhile initiatives may have to take a back seat while the reunion effort is improved. The director of alumni affairs needs to be clear about these trade-offs so that staff members know how to allocate their time and resources.

Finally, identify role models who embody the values and culture of the organization, and who have demonstrated consistent job accomplishment. Keep this directory of talents on hand when thinking about the organization's objectives and how to motivate high performance from others in the organization. Then, think about the various approaches to be taken to keep them all engaged. Just as there are multiple ways of bringing a potential donor to make a gift, you must have equally diverse approaches to assure staff members remain productive over the long term.

STRATEGY FOR SUCCESS

You might think of leading and managing a staff as something like managing a prospect pool. Staff, like potential donors, are most productive when their skills and interests align with the needs of the organization. You strive to both upgrade (maintain) your current donors and attract new ones. Likewise, the strongest program both promotes from within and brings in exciting new talent. Finally, good stewardship is vital for both donors and staff: express appreciation, provide opportunities for involvement, and communicate the impact of their good work.

FURTHER READINGS

Carter, Lindy Keane. "Basic Training: Point New Employees in the Right Direction With a Thorough Orientation," CURRENTS 15, no. 7 (July/August 1989): 26-29.

Ciervo, Arthur. "What to Look for in a PR Professional," CURRENTS 18, no. 8 (September 1992): 52-53.

Cook, Diana L., John B. Shorrock, and Isadore Newman. "Strike the Right Match: A New Test Can Help Spark Better Decisions in Hiring Development Staff," CURRENTS 16, no. 4 (April 1990): 44-46.

"On the Hiring Line," (Manager's Portfolio) CURRENTS 25, no. 3 (March 1999): 13-14.

Simpson, Kristen. "Please Don't Go," (Manager's Portfolio) CURRENTS 25, no. 2 (February 1999): 13-14.

Struck, Darla and Jeff Stratton, eds. *Build a Better Staff, Volume 1: Hiring, Evaluating and Firing Staff Members.* Frederick, MD: Aspen Publishers, 1992.

Sweeney, Robert D. and William E. Pearson. "The Orient Express: Strong Orientation and Training Help Get New Fund Raisers Up to Speed Fast," CURRENTS 18, no. 8 (September 1992): 58-61.

Leadership is a moral activity. Ethics cannot be separated from the day-to-day activities of any person who makes any claim to leadership responsibilities in the nonprofit community.

Creating an Ethical Environment

Thomas W. Anderson
Fellow, The Center for Professional Ethics
Case Western Reserve University

How often do we hear or use the canard, "Setting the ethical issues aside, we should do . . . ." That statement is usually followed by a series of ethical pronouncements be-cause, of course, the ethical issues can never be set aside. Ethics is that accumulation of religious and secular principles that guide and govern right conduct. Ethics not only helps us to know what we can do but, just as importantly, it instructs us on what we *should* do. It is the serious consideration of right and wrong, good and evil, rights and responsibilities, and virtue and vice. The scholarly study of ethics can be highly theoretical, but ethics can also be applied so that it is useful in the day-to-day lives of individuals and organizations. Nonprofit leadership requires a well-grounded sense of morality, a finely tuned sense of ethical behavior, and a willingness to create an ethical environment.

In *Nichomacean Ethics*, Aristotle helped us to know that ethics was and is as much about who we are—*being*—as it is about what actions we take or ends we serve—*doing*. If we seek virtue (justice, beneficence, courage, etc.) and pursue lives as virtuous persons, our actions will take care of themselves. The task of every human being is to achieve moral excellence through a life of conscious choices about what to do or not to do—what sort of person should I become? The objective for every human being should be to become an excellent person. And the reward for living an excellent and virtuous life will be happiness.

Perhaps Aristotle's most important contribution to applied ethics was his admonition to find virtue through "nothing in excess." Virtue is then found between the extremes of "too much" and "too little." The perfect moral choice lies in the Golden Mean between excess and deficiency. Thus, as noted in Albert Anderson's *Ethics for Fundraisers*, the virtue of beneficence can be found by a philanthropist who wishes to improve society through gift-giving that avoids both self-aggrandizement (excess) and penury (deficiency).

In *Nichomacean Ethics*, Aristotle told us that morality cannot be learned by reading a book on virtue. It is acquired by training, practice, and through the witness and conduct of a moral person. Today, we would call the "witness of another" something like "mentoring" or "role modeling." These terms have a familiar ring to them and represent experiences, both positive and negative, that we have all had in our work environment.

THEORIES OF LEADERSHIP

In creating an ethical environment, the lessons of Aristotle need to be applied to 21st century understandings of leadership. Leadership is not just about leaders. Rather, it is about a relationship between leaders and followers. Leadership is a process of influencing an organized group toward accomplishing the mutual goals of both leaders and followers. Leadership is a shared communal activity among all members of the group. Leadership is not a position, a title, or a status. What distinguishes followers from leaders is not intelligence, character, ethical behavior, or judgment. What distinguishes followers from leaders is the *role* they are playing at a particular point in time. We are all leaders and followers at different times and in different situations.

These understandings of contemporary leadership have a moral dimension that is perhaps best represented in historian James MacGregor Burns's theory of transformational leadership. In *Leadership*, Burns argues that "such leadership occurs when one or more persons engage with others in such a way that leaders and followers raise one another to higher levels of motivation and morality . . . ." For Burns, transformational leadership is a moral enterprise that "raises the level of human conduct and ethical aspirations of both leader and led, and thus it has a transforming effect on both." Another normative theory of leadership—Robert Greenleaf's "servant leadership"—represents a move from followers who serve leaders to leaders who are trusted as leaders because they serve their followers. According to *Servant Leadership: A Journey Into the Nature of Legitimate Power and Greatness*, servant leaders are moral agents whose concern is for their followers' highest priority needs. Servant leaders must pass the following test: Do those served grow as people? Do they, while being served, become healthier, wiser, freer, more autonomous, more likely themselves to become servants? And, what is the effect on the least privileged in society; will they benefit, or at least, not be further deprived? This is not a standard for the faint of heart or the self-interested or the autocrat. This is leadership as a moral journey.

ETHICS AND LEADERSHIP

Ethics is at the core of nonprofit leadership and all other kinds of leadership as well. Leadership is a moral activity. Ethics cannot be separated from the day-to-day activities of any person who makes any claim to leadership responsibilities in the nonprofit community.

Ethicist Joanne B. Ciulla in her book, *Ethics: The Heart of Leadership*, reminds us that the critical question is "What is good leadership?" Good is the operative word and, in the leadership context, it means "both morally good and technically good or effective." Put another way, a technically incompetent or ineffective leader who is moral is still incompetent. An immoral leader who is technically competent or effective is still immoral. And neither is a good leader.

If we accept the assertions that ethics is fundamental to leadership and that we are all leaders at one time or another in our organizations, then each of us has a responsibility to contribute to the ethical environment of the workplace. Each of us must live the Aristotelian principle of the "witness of another." Ethical behavior is a lifelong process of making decisions about virtue found between the excesses of "too much" and "too little." And, it is the process of both having a role model and being a role model.

So, how do we create an ethical environment? It is created one day at a time. While those having the role of leader at a particular point in time have a special responsibility both to model virtuous behavior and to institutionalize ethical practices, it is not their sole responsibility. Each person in the workplace has a duty to contribute to creating an ethical environment by asking not just "What should I do?" but asking the more profound question "What kind of person should I be?"

If ethics in its simplest form is "What ought to be?" and leadership in its simplest form is "leaders and followers moving an organization toward shared goals," then *good* leadership must be as much about virtue as it is about acts and consequences. It is as much about people of character as it is about duties and responsibilities. And it is as

> **If we accept the assertions that ethics is fundamental to leadership and that we are all leaders at one time or another in our organizations, then each of us has a responsibility to contribute to the ethical environment of the workplace.**

much about the daily struggle to be a good person as it is about the daily struggle to do the right thing. None of these are mutually exclusive and all contribute to creating and sustaining ethical leaders, ethical followers, and ethical organizations. Good leaders, good followers, and good nonprofit organizations can and must be defined as both ethically and technically good.

If we are going to be successful in creating ethical environments, every person in every nonprofit organization needs to spend time wrestling with the question "What kind of person should I be?" even while dealing on a daily basis with the question "What should I do?" As ethical and technical competence is modeled in our organizations and lives, it will not only be the practice of ethical nonprofit leadership, but it will also be—as Aristotle told us almost 2,400 years ago—the "witness of another" to the moral life. And, it will create the ethical environment that contributes to happiness and fulfillment in professional and personal lives.

REFERENCES

Anderson, Albert. *Ethics for Fundraisers*. Bloomington, IN: Indiana University Press, 1996.

Burns, James MacGregor. *Leadership*. New York, NY: HarperCollins Publishers, 1978.

Ciulla, Joanne B., ed. *Ethics: The Heart of Leadership*. Westport, CT: Quorum, 1998.

Gardner, John W. *On Leadership*. New York: Free Press, 1990.

Gini, Al. "Moral Leadership and Business Ethics." In *Ethics: The Heart of Leadership*. Westport, CT: Preager, 1998.

Greenleaf, Robert K. *Servant Leadership: A Journey Into the Nature of Legitimate Power and Greatness*. New York: Paulist Press, 1977.

Herman, Robert D., ed. *The Jossey-Bass Handbook of Nonprofit Leadership and Management*. San Francisco, CA: Jossey-Bass Publishers, 1994.

Ostwald, Martin (trans). *Aristotle: Nichomachean Ethics*. Englewood, NJ: Prentice Hall, 1962.

Pojman, Louis, ed. *Moral Philosophy: A Reader*. Indianapolis, IN: Hackett Publishing, 1993.

Smith, David H. *Entrusted: The Moral Responsibilities of Trusteeship*. Bloomington, IN: Indiana University Press, 1995.

Wren, J. Thomas, ed. *The Leader's Companion: Insights on Leadership Through the Ages*. New York, NY: Free Press, 1995.

Introduction

Roger L. Williams
Associate Vice Chancellor for University Relations
University of Arkansas

The astronomical theory of the ever-expanding universe might be just as aptly applied to the higher education communications profession. Since the last edition of the *Handbook* was published in 1986, expansion and increased complexity have underscored the changes in the communications field. Those megatrends will continue apace, as the next edition of the *Handbook* will surely demonstrate.

This section presents a host of new disciplines, skills, and areas of professional activity that were either unborn or fledgling in the mid-1980s: strategic communications, benchmarking, issues management, crisis management, the Internet and the World Wide Web, institutional identity, and development communications, to name just a few.

All of these new areas plus the foundational disciplines of communications—publications, periodicals, media relations, special events, and more—are addressed in the 15 chapters that follow.

As the authors point out, technological change—providing a host of exciting new tools—has revolutionized the communications disciplines. But there is much more that has expanded the portfolio and changed the nature of what communications professionals do. The roles, expectations, tasks, and skills are greater in number, wider in scope, and ever more complex.

The most basic shift in the profession, however, has been the rapid change from a mainly tactical to an increasingly strategic orientation. A 1991 CASE random-sample survey of 300 college and university presidents in the United States and Canada sought to gain a sense of what they thought about the role and effectiveness of public relations at their institutions. The presidents agreed that public relations was a major part of their responsibilities and an institutional priority. But they gave their communications staffs higher marks for tactical work such as media relations, special events, and publications than for the more strategic work related to interpreting the institution, enhancing community relations, marketing the institution and sharpening its image, and providing counsel and advice.

Beginning in the late 1980s, changes in the external environment—particularly in the way opinion leaders came to view higher education more critically—prompted communications professionals to think more strategically. Issues such as South African divestiture, rising tuition, teaching versus research, campus crime, indirect cost recovery, campus deficits and budget crises, ethnicity and multiculturalism, political correctness and, as the 20th century turned, concern about Third World sweatshops that manufacture items bearing campus logos necessitated a broader, strategic approach to the communications disciplines.

Add to that the rapid advent of the marketing imperative in higher education—with targeted communications initiatives now segmenting themselves down to the level of the individual. Mix in a healthy increase of communications research across all facets of our work, and the communications field looks far different in 2000 than in 1986. The Age of Innocence, if ever there were one in higher education communications, is gone forever. But the new age is more exciting, more challenging, more filled with possibilities and opportunities for communications professionals to serve their institutions at the strategic level.

In the opening chapter on strategic communications, Judith Jasper Leicht illustrates the rapid changes that occurred in the communications field in just six years—much of it fueled by developments in information technology and especially the proliferation of e-mail. She outlines 12 tips for practitioners who want to succeed at strategic communications, and poses key questions for the future—including how the communications media will find new ways to use the Internet.

In Chapter 2, "Organizing the Communications Operations," Roland King observes that the basic problem with higher education communications structures is that they traditionally have been organized along "skills" and "tools" lines rather than "task lines." This makes it hard for the communications operation to function strategically because the existing tools define the task, rather than the task (or strategic imperative) defining the tools.

The foundation of strategic communications is, of course, research. In Chapter 3, Walter K. Lindenmann provides a *tour de force* of communications research for planning and effectiveness. Lindenmann writes a legible prescription for what kinds of research projects work best for particular contexts or communications problems, and explains new research formats that have been opened up by technological advances.

A particular brand of communications research—benchmarking—came into vogue in the 1990s. In Chapter 4, Gary R. Ratcliff details how benchmarking can be especially useful to communications practitioners in comparing an organization's structure, functions, resources, and capabilities to a set of peer or higher-performing organizations.

In Chapter 5, Don Hale takes on the unenviable task of making sense of a world that will likely re-invent itself many times over in the early 21st century—communications technology. He outlines the changes e-mail, the Internet, and the World Wide Web have wrought, and provides practical tips for their use. Finally, he offers useful advice for public relations professionals who want to provide effective leadership for the sprawling electronic worlds-within-worlds that their campuses have become.

In Chapter 6, Terry Denbow provides a glimpse into his philosophy of how issues management is best approached. It is not so much a "skill" as a "philosophy and practice of professional life" for communications managers. To be most effective, issues management first requires a seat at the table with the institution's top decision makers, and assertion of our expertise as public relations professionals. It also requires the daily conduct of our work in a way that builds credibility among internal and external constituencies.

Linda Gray, as assistant vice president and director of news and public affairs for the University of Florida, managed communications during the nationally visible crisis created by the off-campus serial murders in Gainesville in 1991. In Chapter 7, "Crisis Communications: Planning, Executing, Surviving," Gray offers a series of recommendations for effective communications management before, during, and after a crisis.

In Chapter 8, Judith Turner Phair underscores the importance of communicating with what is arguably our most important constituency—our internal campus communities. Without their understanding, buy-in, and support, external communications initiatives can be severely undermined; with their understanding and support, all things are possible. Phair advises that internal communications be built into the institution's overall communications plan, and she offers many new high-tech methods as well as some tried-and-true low-tech approaches for doing so.

Institutional graphic identity is one of the newer additions to the higher education communications repertoire. In Chapter 9, Jan Pruitt Duvall and Jeffrey T. Hermann provide a comprehensive guide to putting such a program in place. Their approach is rooted in research, directed at reinforcing overarching institutional goals, sensitive to internal and external politics, and intended to serve for the long haul.

The real "driver" of the institutional identity program is, of course, the institution's department of publications. Yet identity is only one of

the major changes with which publications offices are dealing, as Al Friedman says in Chapter 10. Friedman discusses the new roles, mission, and the increased expectations for publications professionals today. He foresees a greater role for publications in the context of integrated marketing and the growing influence of the Web as the primary source of information for both external and internal audiences.

In Chapter 11, "Periodicals: Sources of Information and Inspiration," Patricia Ann LaSalle stresses the fundamental role of these communications vehicles as that of interpreting the institution in a compelling way to audiences with varying degrees of interest in those stories. Quality and integrity must remain the hallmarks of periodicals, whether they be printed or online newsletters, magazines, or tabloids. Periodicals, she adds, can add a strong measure of credibility to an institution's communications programs, whether telling the "bad news" about a campus controversy or the "good news" of a capital campaign.

In his chapter (12) on media relations, Dick Jones reminds us why media visibility remains so important to our institutions. He outlines the fundamentals of a successful media relations program, emphasizing how to find the stories on campus, how to market them to media through a variety of high-tech and low-tech approaches, and how to use the results (print and video clips) to an institution's best advantage.

In Chapter 13, "Broadcast Communications: Getting the Word Out," Annette Hannon Lee provides a comprehensive overview of television today and recommends ways of getting the institution's stories pitched and told. She provides extensive examples of how public universities create high visibility through programs tailored to broadcast media. Finally, she discusses how broadcast media are changing dramatically with their distribution and delivery capabilities, courtesy of new laws and advanced technology.

In Chapter 14, I discuss a new specialization that has come into being in recent years: development communications, which provides total public relations, communications, and marketing support to the educational fund-raising operation. Questions, imperatives, and activities are discussed for the three levels of development communications: contextual, which creates visibility and builds reputation for the institution so that fund raising can succeed; strategic, which resolves the fundamental "what are we going to do?" and "why are we going to do it" questions of fund-raising communications; and tactical, which determines how to flesh out the strategy with specific communications programs, initiatives, and events.

The communications section ends with Chapter 15 on special events. Here April Harris defines special events as strategic communications initiatives. She observes that guests at special events can usually infer more about an institution in one evening than they can through a year's worth of news articles, magazines, and brochures. She advocates doing special events in a goals-and-objectives framework, consistent with the institution's mission. Harris offers advice for specific events planning in the context of a larger master plan, while adhering to timeless planning principles.

Even the richest and most elite higher education institutions no longer operate under the illusion that they can excel at all things. A clear understanding of where your institution is today, and the directions it is taking in the future, is essential to strategic communications planning.

Strategic Communications: Working with Technology to Communicate a Single Message

Judith Jasper Leicht
Associate Vice Chancellor and Executive Director of University Communications
Washington University in St. Louis

When Washington University in St. Louis managed the 1992 Presidential Debate, we had only nine days to prepare. That was seven years ago. But it was light years ago in communication time.

When we managed both of Steve Fossett's Solo Spirit 1998 round-the-world balloon attempts, the world of communications was a very different place. The debate and the balloon flights generated enormous worldwide interest, but there the similarity ends. The variety and number of communications tools available to us—and the length, breadth, and speed of our communications—had moved from night to day.

In 1992, staff and volunteers stood at fax machines 18 hours a day—even meal breaks were covered by replacements—to get the press information out and the media credentialed. In 1998, we posted our information and photographs on *www.solospirit.wustl.edu,* our specially designed Web page that was updated every hour. It received 12 million hits from 126 countries and more than 200,000 different hosts in nine days. In 1992, we contacted the media on the telephone. In 1998, we

contacted them via e-mail.

The good news is that communications today are easier, faster, and less expensive. The bad news is that the number of e-mail messages received each day is growing exponentially. Pitney Bowes estimates that in 1998 at least four trillion e-mail messages were sent in the United States, and that seven trillion will be sent in the U.S. during the year 2000. While there is no accurate way to determine precisely how many users are on the Internet, estimates indicate that the Web has grown even faster as measured by the number of hosts. At the time of the 1992 Presidential Debate, the number of Web sites was estimated to be a little more than one million. By August 1998, that number approached 37 million, and by January 1999 it had grown to more than 43 million. According to *Web Content Report,* citing International Data Corporation as the source, more than 53 million people were using the Internet as of September 1999, and 44 million were using the Web; the difference is largely the result of those who use Internet e-mail but do not have access to the Web.

Media Dynamics of New York City estimates that the average city dweller encounters 1,500 commercial messages in various forms per day. Think about it—that's 1,500 commercial messages

Strategic
Communications:
Working with
Technology to
Communicate a
Single Message

to say nothing of personal contacts. The result is that we become selective and very good at filtering out unwanted messages. It's impossible to process all the data that hits every day. Instead, we select what's important to us and internalize it. It's a process of survival.

Herein lies the challenge for strategic communications in a rapidly changing environment. How can we harness technology and understand its impact to better plan, focus, and tailor messages, so that they make it across the information filters of our target audiences—potential and current students, alumni, donors, media, government and civic leaders, faculty and staff, or the general public? While medical researchers are working on finding chemical means to cross the physical brain barrier in order to develop cures for strokes and other brain impairments, communicators need to conduct ongoing research to determine current awareness and perceptions of our institutions and use the information to develop strategies that work.

Bob Brock, formerly assistant vice president of college relations at Metropolitan State College, says, "People take what they know about you—good, bad, or indifferent—and give you a place in their minds accordingly. That's your market position, whether you like it or not, and you need to understand it before you change it."

Brock, now president of Educational Marketing Group, Inc. incorporated the principles of integrated marketing into his strategic communications plan and swiftly moved Metropolitan State from last to first in Colorado in the number of first-time, full-time freshmen. He developed a simple message, based on research and designed to differentiate Metropolitan State from the competition. Here's the positioning statement: "We provide real-world education, so graduates get great careers." That was the internal statement, which was refined for positioning with other audiences. For students, it was, "We provide the skills and experiences you need to get a great job." For business and government leaders, the message was, "We provide the region with a well-trained work-

force to ensure economic health." For donors, the message was, "We improve our society by giving individuals new opportunities." The same strategic message—a clear signal, free of background noise with an enlightened self-interest component—made it across the information filters of Metropolitan State's target audiences and resulted in a significant behavior change.

Rapid change is the hallmark of the worldwide climate we operate in today. How do we manage to stay ahead? Here are 12 tips to consider when managing communications strategies in our complex and competitive higher education environment.

• • •
As the Web becomes a window to the world, partnerships between communications and technology staff are crucial. Ask yourself: Who controls the Web? What images, messages, and information are projected?

1. *Position yourself at the decision-making table.* Help your president understand the importance of strategic communications and advise him or her on how to make the right moves.

2. *Understand your institution's vision, mission, and future strategic directions.* Even the richest and most elite higher education institutions no longer operate under the illusion that they can excel at all things. A clear understanding of where your institution is today, and the directions it is taking in the future, is essential to strategic communications planning.

3. *Appreciate the power and importance of communications.* Of all the processes that drive our institutions, communication is the most important. Help others to overcome the fear of communicating. Repeat the same messages over and over again. You know where the institution is headed, but don't assume everyone else knows.

4. *Advocate for your program.* Know what threatens the communications program, such as budget and personnel cuts. Clarify expectations and educate others to the downside implications.

5. *Keep your eye on the future like never before.* Keeping up with changing technologies is not an easy task, even for large communications offices. When I was planning the CASE Annual Assembly several years ago, I asked a leading electrical engineering researcher and technology entrepreneur to speak on the future of communications 10 years out. He laughed heartily at my naive

request! When I limited the horizon to five years, he responded that even the cutting-edge experts would take only an educated guess! Overwhelming as that might be, it does not diminish the need for communicators to marshal all the resources at hand and stay abreast as much as possible, making the right long-term investments for our programs.

6. *Scan your environment frequently.* This will enable you to understand better the current landscape of perceptions and opinions about higher education. Understand the broader issues that affect our abilities to communicate and incorporate them into your strategic communications process. National surveys and issue-tracking reports by educational organizations, including CASE Flash Files, can provide valuable assistance. This CASE member service can be received electronically or through the mail, and is on the home page at *www.case.org*.

7. *Make informed decisions.* Research resulting in action plans with predictable outcomes is possible. Predicting the impact of change on customer satisfaction can help eliminate "best guess" management and inform management decisions. More sophisticated research techniques are moving from the corporate sector into higher education. For example, overnight package delivery giant United Parcel Service has long conducted business-to-business customer satisfaction surveys. Working with CFI Group of Ann Arbor, Michigan, UPS identified and assessed customer satisfaction scores for service categories and determined the importance of each category to overall customer satisfaction ratings. Areas with low customer scores but high impact on overall satisfaction were identified, and UPS concentrated its action plans on their improvement. This process enabled UPS to know with certainty the impact of improvements in each service category and meant that finite resources are not wasted on problem areas that had little effect on overall satisfaction.

Taking their lead from the for-profit world, Steve Grafton, executive director of the University of Michigan Alumni Association, and Clayton Wilhite, managing partner of CFI Group, currently are collaborating on a comprehensive association membership research project for UMAA. It will result in an action plan that leads to significant and predictable improvements in overall members' satisfaction levels.

8. *Develop new partnerships, internal and external.* In the past, communicators dealt with printers and mailing houses. Now we must develop and use new strategic communications technologies to our best advantage. As the Web becomes a window to the world, partnerships between communications and technology staff are crucial. Ask yourself: Who controls the Web? What images, messages, and information are projected? Five years ago, not even the most sophisticated institutions devoted significant resources to their Web sites. Yet, such resources will be among the most important priorities for communications programs in the next decade.

9. *Remember that internal audiences are essential players.* It's counterproductive to spend all your efforts conveying positive messages to external audiences if faculty, staff, and students are uninformed or, worse yet, negative. Remember that strategic communications begin in-house and good internal communications are vital.

10. *Follow multimedia technologies that influence communications practitioners.* Consider what these changes mean for office structures and staffing: What kinds of positions will be needed in the future? What kinds of employees with what skills will fill these positions? How will you recruit, reward, and motivate them?

11. *Look for weak places and unnecessary projects.* Eliminate or reduce them in order to focus resources of money, people, and time on the most important priorities. To do this, marry all the functions of the communications arena across the entire institution. Integrate all aspects of internal and external communications by coordinating publications, media relations, community relations, and alumni and parent communications, so they speak with one voice. Messages clearly, consistently, and uniformly delivered can bring significant results.

12. *Make attitudinal and satisfaction testing an ongoing process.* Readership studies and content analysis are important benchmarks. But the rubber hits the road when we measure behavioral change. Strategic communications are working if, for example, student applications are up, alumni participation is growing, and annual giving is increasing.

Strategic
Communications:
Working with
Technology to
Communicate a
Single Message

While our eye is on the future in strategic communications planning, the ground is shifting beneath us. Moving from tips to topics, here are a few "big picture" questions to ponder:

■ *Distance learning:* Will distance learning break the familiar mold for universities? More than 100,000 college courses already are available online, and by 2001 that number is projected to be more than three million. According to an article in the February 1999 issue of *Fortune*, there are 750,000 students taking online classes worldwide. Experts predict this figure will double by 2004. Many education leaders believe that virtual universities will enlarge the pool of potential students, fundamentally alter the classroom setting, and change the products schools offer. What are the implications for strategic communications?

■ *Libraries and dorms:* Will technology level the playing field, rendering the great research libraries of our most prestigious institutions obsolete? Will students at all colleges and universities have equal access to information? Colleges and universities are building dorms. Will we need them? And, if so, for how long? What technological changes will make them obsolete and how quickly? What are the implications for strategic communications?

■ *News media:* Newsroom and new media operations are now shared in more than half the nation's newsrooms. The 1999 Middleberg/Ross (*www.middleberg.com*) *Media in Cyberspace Study* indicates that Internet access by journalists now approaches universality. Middleberg says, "The exploding use of the Internet by journalists has forever transformed the practice of public relations. Public relations practitioners not truly incorporating Internet communications initiatives into their public relations strategies are doing a disservice to their clients and the media. To dismiss the new generation of media in cyberspace and the online communications they prefer is incompetent and borders on negligence." What are the implications for strategic communications?

Tracking results frequently and using the information to constantly alter our view, our thinking, and our plans is more important as we manage communications with the ground shifting beneath us.

Existing technologies improve and expand every hour. Virgil Renzulli, associate vice president for public affairs at Columbia University, reports that its New Media Technology Center is working on projects that, a few short years ago, only Mr. Wizard would have envisioned. To name a few:

■ computer languages to improve the quality of Internet multimedia information, allowing users to view an enormous variety of high-quality video and voice;

■ new visual Web search tools where users can enter words to describe an image they need or they can sketch the image and ask the software to match it;

■ new object-based editing software that will move a talking figure from one video sequence and paste it into another—much the way computer graphics software allows graphic designers to paste objects into photographs.

These are just a few technologies coming our way from Columbia. Other similar centers are developing a wide range of communication technologies coming soon to your institution and mine.

The process of strategic communications is more powerful, yet more complex than ever before. This unparalleled opportunity allows us to move from planning to communicate with our audiences by target group to communicating one-on-one with individuals. Not only can we target individuals, but we can do it globally, and do it in many languages.

For Steve Fossett's Solo Spirit balloon flights, Washington University in St. Louis posted all information in English and Spanish. We relied upon "human" translators, but effective language translation software will be available in the near future.

Tracking results frequently and using the information to constantly alter our view, our thinking, and our plans is more important as we manage communications with the ground shifting beneath us. But it can and must be done well and done effectively.

When I was director of public relations at the St. Louis Science Center, we made the strategic decision that all publications should support marketing. The Science Center is an educational institution. But the theory was that education took place in the center and, therefore, publications should focus on increasing attendance. Once that strategic decision was made, it was easy to eliminate the research journal and other educational publications and reallocate the previous resources to marketing. This, among other strategic communications initiatives, increased attendance from 780,000 to more than 1.1 million in 18 months, once again demonstrating the power of strategic communications planning when it follows and supports strategic initiatives.

Reputations are built over time. Educational institutions might appear to resemble a large ship at sea—even with a full rudder change and all engines at full speed, the turning radius is wide, and direction can be changed only over the course of many miles. It might well take considerable time to change the course of our institutions as a whole. But the rate of change for communications has accelerated dramatically in the past decade and will continue to do so, making strategic communications imperative as our institutions navigate the 21st century.

When I think about the new challenges and opportunities before us, I envision the communications office of 2050. I see in my crystal ball a vice president of university relations at a retirement dinner reflecting on a career that began with mass mailings of the printed word and ended in a place we cannot yet imagine, much less define.

Then, I remember my grandfather, who was born in 1890 and, near the end of his life, liked to reflect on the enormous changes that took place in his lifetime, from the horse-and-buggy era to a man walking on the moon. If the rate of change in communications between the 1992 Presidential Debate and the 1998 Fossett flights is any indication of things to come, the speed and scope of the changes my grandfather saw in his lifetime pale in comparison to the unknowns that lie ahead for us. The body of knowledge is expanding rapidly, and the speed of communications is equal to the speed of light. We have an awesome responsibility and an unparalleled opportunity ahead.

FURTHER READINGS

Botan, Carl. "Ethics in Strategic Communications Campaigns: The Case for a New Approach to Public Relations [Special Issue: Ethics in Business Communication]," *Journal of Business Communication* 34, no. 2 (April 1997): 188.

Kerkman, Larry and Karen Menicelli. *Strategic Communications for Nonprofits Series*. New York, NY: Benton Foundation and Center for Strategic Communications, 1992.

Lauer, Larry. "Eight Steps to a PR Plan: Follow These Directions to Develop a Strategic Communications Plan That Works," CURRENTS 12, no. 1 (January 1986): 28-31.

Mahoney, Jim. "The Accountability Game, " CURRENTS 26, no. 2 (February 2000): 30-35.

Radtke, Janel M. *Strategic Communications for Nonprofit Organizations: Seven Steps to Creating a Successful Plan*. New York, NY: John Wiley and Sons Inc., April 1998.

Schreiber, William. "The Proof is in the PR: Five Case Studies Offer Conclusive Evidence of the Value of Strategic Communications," CURRENTS 19, no. 9 (October 1993): 31-34.

Interpreting a college or university to its various constituents and the public is difficult when, from the inside, the view is often one of loosely organized chaos, warring factions, and institutional schizophrenia.

Organizing the Communications Operation

Roland King
Vice President for Public Affairs
National Association of Independent Colleges and Universities

The first edition of this handbook, published in 1977, included a chapter on organization and structure of the overall advancement function written by James M. Shea, then vice president for university relations at Temple University. In making the distinction between higher education and commercial enterprises, Shea quotes former Ohio State President Harold Enarson on the thesis that a university is not "just another organization. It is a very special kind of place. It is more like the Metropolitan Opera than the Metropolitan Life Insurance Company. It is more like a church than a factory, more like a research lab than the highway department. The university is an intensely human enterprise. And it is not so much managed as led."

Today, at least as much as in the 1970s, it is this very special nature of higher education that challenges professionals in public relations/communications (we will use the two terms interchangeably). Interpreting a college or university to its various constituents and the public is difficult when, from the inside, the view is often one of loosely organized chaos, warring factions, and institutional schizophrenia. The structure for this daunting communications task also must be

approached with an eye toward building a communications organization that reflects and responds to the special nature of the particular institution. This means there is no "one size fits all" answer for organizing communications activities; there are, however, some broad patterns and general guidelines that may be helpful in evaluating whether an appropriate structure is in place or might be modified for greater effectiveness.

From a 1999 e-mail survey that I conducted of 33 top public relations/communications officers from a wide range of institutions, there emerged a handful of forces affecting the shape of communications. In identifying the biggest structural changes they have noted in recent years, the public relations officers' responses neatly grouped into four major observations:

1. *A growing stature for the communications function.* One respondent noted, "I've seen [public relations] offices go from being seen as super-secretarial support to being included in the president's cabinet of senior officers." Another observed that "Today, compared to 10 years ago, I'll bet it's much more the rule than the exception that PR has a seat at the table."

2. *The increasing use of a strategic approach to communications.* Said one public relations officer,

"We now focus pretty heavily on strategy, proactive communications, internal communications, and speech writing in addition to the more established roles of working with reporters and publishing a magazine and [an internal] newspaper."

3. *The presence and potential of new technology* or, as one person put it, "The increasing ability to take your message directly to your audience through the Web, [electronic discussion groups], etc., rather than through intermediaries."

4. *The relatively new and not fully defined role of marketing.* "The lines between [marketing and communications] seem more blurred," said one respondent. "What it means for higher education in the long term, I'm not sure. I think, though, that the impact of marketing on our field is permanent."

These forces are not only redefining the role and the reach of the communications office, but are even influencing what we consider college and university communications to be.

The communications function is, at most colleges and universities, awash in parentheses. Certainly, relations with the news media is a part (and often the most visible part) of the communications operation, as is some (but not all) internal communications. The communications office also gets involved (at some institutions more, at other institutions less) in communications with key external constituents such as alumni, donors, prospective students, legislators, and business leaders. And there are a number of communications-laden functions (with current students, visitors to campus, or suppliers, for example) that could benefit from the insights of communications professionals but are handled unilaterally by other offices.

The parameters of the office are defined by each institution to encompass those communications functions deemed (1) most essential or (2) not easily or logically assigned to another administrative office. This is what media relations consul-

● ● ●
Electronic discussion groups, intranets, and electronic bulletin boards may be controlled by people with no knowledge of or responsibility for institutional communications. And e-mail is essentially "electronic word of mouth," but with far more reach than the old water-cooler version.

tant Dick Jones once described as the "toxic waste dump" aspect of the communications office.

Virtually all traditional college and university communications offices have three common functions.

■ media relations, which may be identified as public information or the news bureau;

■ publications, divided into editing and design with, in some larger offices, a periodicals sub-unit as well;

■ at least a limited form of internal communications, which may encompass only the internal newsletter or magazine.

Somewhat less common units of the communications office are marketing, advertising, special events, community relations, sports information, photography, and electronic media production (radio and television). Still less common are units or individuals dedicated to government relations, conference and visitors services, and in-house printing and mailing services.

This list of functions reveals a basic problem with the typical campus communications structure: It has been organized, primarily along skills or tools lines rather than task lines, as a series of self-contained "silos." This strongly vertical structure makes it difficult for communications offices to operate strategically, bringing all resources, talents, and tools to bear on a communications problem.

For years, the inefficiency of this approach was hidden by the limited number of channels used to communicate. As just one example, internal communications is a relatively simple task if defined only as producing and distributing the "official" newsletter or newspaper. An effective internal communications program, though, must use a multitude of channels and devices—from special events and videos, to articles in the local newspaper reaching faculty, staff, and non-residential students at home. The internal communications office also must monitor and counter the flood of information—or misinformation—from "unofficial" sources. Electronic discussion groups, intranets, and electronic bulletin boards may be controlled by people with no knowledge of or responsibility for institutional communications. And e-mail is essentially "electronic word of mouth," but with far more reach than the old water-cooler version. The world of communications certainly has, in the last years of the 20th century, become exponentially more complex.

Figure 2-1 lists the most common communications assignments ("Tasks") in a comprehensive communications office, then on the right, the communications functions ("Tools") that might be used in performing these tasks. At a smaller institution, many of these tools would be combined under one or two staff members and some are not likely to be available through the communications office at all.

It should be apparent that to accomplish the tasks listed, the communications office will likely need to use a selection of the listed tools. Yet because of the structure of most communications offices, tools take precedence over tasks. For exam-

---

TASKS

Leadership Counseling and Support
Environmental scanning and issues anticipation
Issues management and crisis prevention
Crisis communications

Institutional Image and Identity
Graphic identity development and standards
Institutional image definition and maintenance
Reputation assessment and promotion
Definition of institutional position

**Constituent Communications, Feedback,
 and Marketing**
Prospective students
Current students
Alumni
Development constituencies
Business and corporate leaders
Community leaders, residents, and
 campus neighbors
On-campus constituencies (faculty, staff, students)
Promotion of specialized services (continuing
 education, health programs, arts programs, etc.)
Assessment of constituent attitudes, concerns,
 misperceptions

Athletics Communication
Sports information
Fan/booster communication

TOOLS

Media Relations
Responding to media queries
Providing information actively to the media
 (publicity)
Media tours
Editorial board visits

Publications
Brochures
Periodicals
Posters

Writing Services
News releases
Speeches
Scripts
Position papers, issues papers, fact sheets, letters
General copy writing

Small Group and One-to-One Communications
Speeches
Letters
Meetings and visits

Special Events
Events planning and management

Electronic Communications
Broadcast (radio and TV) production
World Wide Web site design, content development,
 and maintenance
Multimedia production

Photography

Advertising

Research
Gathering of existing research
Conducting of qualitative and quantitative research

Figure 2-1. Communications Tasks and Tools

ple, communications support of undergraduate student recruitment is often thought of as a publications function, rather than as a broad-based marketing communications task that might require not just a new viewbook, but services such as speech writing, special events planning, and news media visibility.

In their classic public relations textbook, *Effective Public Relations*, authors Cutlip, Center, and Broom lay out a four-step problem-solving process for communications: (1) defining the problem (or opportunity), (2) planning and programming, (3) taking action and communicating, and (4) evaluating the program. The "silo" structure of a tool-oriented communications office can lead to an overemphasis of the third step, to the exclusion of the other three. It also can lead to a minimalist view by top administration of the communication staff's role as messengers instead of strategists and problem-solvers.

At least partially in response to the communications office's emphasis on tools, a number of colleges and universities have begun searching for a means to unify and focus the institution's outreach efforts. Much of the interest in marketing in the late 1990s has not been directed at improving the transactional relationships that define the marketing function. Rather, these efforts have sought to foster an integration of relationship-building efforts, and to build a thematic consistency across the institution's relationships through "integrated marketing communications" or similar terminology. While admirable goals, these efforts are no more or less than what an enlightened communications office should be doing day in and day out.

How does an established communications office reorient itself to operate strategically? Most often, the path has been through modification of the existing structure rather than a total dismantling and reinvention of the office. At the University of Maryland, College Park, a traditional public information office was reoriented by organizing the media relations specialists into "strategic initiative" teams dealing with broader issues. The teams researched assigned emerging issues, produced Q&A and fact sheets on the subjects, then developed action plans to deal with the most pressing issues.

In Maryland's case, members of the communications team included professionals from other offices, not just those narrowly defined as communications office staff. More than any other office on campus—with the possible exception of the president's office—the communications office depends on "dotted line" relationships to accomplish its work. In order to influence and improve communications in areas it does not organizationally "own," the office must add its expertise and insights to that of others with different skills, perspectives, and priorities. Political savvy, the ability to build informal partnerships, and professional respect are intangible but essential ingredients of an effective communications office.

Three communications developments have conspired to turn institutional communications on its head in recent years:

1. *Today, everyone has the potential to be a "great communicator."* Formerly, to reach a large number of people, a person had to have access to a printing press, a radio station, or some other form of complicated, expensive "machinery." Now, that machinery is as simple and inexpensive as a computer and an Internet connection. The multiplicity of channels available for individuals to use in reaching large numbers of people has made the traditional communications office role of "gatekeeper" no longer valid.

2. *Just as "all politics is local," increasingly, all communications is becoming individual.* The new channels such as Web sites, fax on demand, and electronic discussion groups have put the power of communications in the hands of the receiver and not the sender. Mass communication principles are being challenged by those in an institution's target audiences (and there are more of them every day) who decide what information they want, then how and when they want it.

3. *Growing public skepticism of all institutions has made it tougher to convince and motivate constituencies.* Citing the public's critical stance in an article on "The Unforgiving Era," public relations counselor Patrick Jackson sees a pressing need for college communications professionals to become more effective, and proposes that, if they don't, "...higher education will join

public schools, government, and health care as an object of public anger, with predictable outcomes: unfavorable legislation, decreased funding, alumni revolt, donor irritation, student riots, and more." (CURRENTS, October 1998)

In light of these long-term trends, a well-organized and appropriately-structured communications office should move well beyond the "get the word out" mantra of the past, devoting equal attention to what the institution wants to say and what the constituent wants to know. In its relationship to the rest of the organization, the office should operate at the strategic level within the institution, with the various skills of its staff being applied in a concerted and logical way to implement those strategies. It also should serve as the linchpin of an institution's contacts with its constituencies—coordinating communications across organizational lines and advising other offices of the messages and priorities that form the institution's communications foundation.

The university relations division at Carnegie Mellon University builds the strategic concept into its mission, which reads in part,

> We monitor and address the interests, perceptions and concerns of key constituencies, including alumni, media, prospective/current students and employees. We bring public relations perspectives and strategies into decision-making and planning, and we provide expertise and services that improve the quality and effectiveness of the university's communications efforts. We contribute to the achievement of the university's goals through programs and communications strategically planned to influence key customers and provoke desired behaviors.

A more recent convert to the strategic communications model, the University of Miami in the late 1990s revamped its office of media and external relations away from the old "news bureau" model and toward a broad-based strategic approach that focuses on communicating the university's core messages to key audiences. The transition meant that staff members would no longer just write press releases and pitch story ideas to reporters, but would actively form partnerships with administrators and faculty in developing comprehensive public relations strategies. This holistic approach includes combining media relations with publications, advertising, internal communications, community relations, special events, and Web marketing, with the staff member serving as consultant and facilitator on all pieces of the project.

North Carolina State University's news services office also actively works cooperatively with administrators and faculty members to determine the most important projects of the year. To introduce the new chancellor, for example, the office teamed up with donor relations, alumni relations, and student recruitment staff members to execute eight two-day visits by the chancellor and 21 N.C. State students to 17 communities across the state. The visits resulted in over 5,000 face-to-face interactions, extensive media coverage, and a byproduct of more than $750,000 in donor pledges.

A strategic and team-oriented approach is especially crucial in creating and maintaining World Wide Web sites. A leader in addressing this medium is the University at Buffalo, which, in 1997, created the UB Web Team. The team is comprised of three professional staff members with editing, design, and technical responsibilities, and is supported by undergraduate and graduate assistants. Team members are responsible for a whole range of tasks from implementing standards to providing expert assistance in developing an electronic communications strategy. They collaborate with the university's publications office, information technology office, and the various university units to develop Web site solutions. This cooperative approach offers a responsiveness and pervasiveness that would be impossible if the function were viewed as solely the purview of any one office. See their Web site at *www.buffalo.edu/webteam*.

Even under this emerging model, there is—and will continue to be—a need for specialists in the various tools used to communicate. The graphic designer will most likely work in tandem with an accomplished writer; the media relations person will probably draw upon a broadcast producer's skills in creating a video news release. Still, the contemporary college or university communications office functions less as a hierarchical unit than as a network of communications professionals who create *ad hoc* groups with the necessary expertise to address the particular communications challenge. This new structure may not be as neat as the old, but should prove to be infinitely more effective and rewarding.

REFERENCES AND FURTHER READINGS

Cornforth, Suzanne R. "Battle Cry of the Web Managers: So Much Work, So Few Resources, You and Staffing Your Online Efforts," CURRENTS 24, no. 8 (September 1998): 38-43.

Cutlip, Scott M., Allen H. Center, and Glen M. Broom. *Effective Public Relations.* 7th ed. Englewood Cliffs, N.J.: Prentice Hall, 1994.

Dilenschneider, Robert L., ed. *Dartnell's Public Relations Handbook.* 4th ed. Chicago, IL: Dartnell Corporation, 1996.

Hincker, Larry. "Finding the Perfect Fit—Five Ways to Structure the Communications Office," CURRENTS 25, no. 7 (July/August 1999): 46-52.

Jackson, Patrick. "The Unforgiving Era: Why Higher Education Will Be the Next Target in an Age of Increasing Public Outrage—and What PR Pros Can Do About It," CURRENTS 24, no. 9 (October 1998): 12-15.

Landsberg, Marc. "Smart Staffing: A Management Expert Tells How to Organize Employees in the PR Office for the Best Results," CURRENTS 21, no. 6 (June 1995): 40-43.

Shaffer, Jim. "Reinventing Communication," *Communication World* 14, no. 3 (February 1997): 20-23.

Simpson, Christopher. "The Day We Closed the News Bureau: How Indiana University Survived the Switch From Promotions-Oriented PR to Integrated Marketing," CURRENTS 24, no. 1 (January 1998): 26-32.

As part of the communications research effort, most institutional advancement officers are interested in measuring the believability of the information sources, including the relevance and overall importance of the messages being disseminated.

Communications Research For Planning and Evaluation

Walter K. Lindenmann

Specialist in Public Relations Research and Management and
Former Senior Vice President and Director of Research
Ketchum

Research is the key to any successful institutional advancement, communications, and/or marketing efforts. Without research, those who administer public relations, public affairs, fund raising, development initiatives, and related communications programs and activities for their organizations would be operating in the dark, without any guidance or clear sense of direction.

Communications research, as the name implies, focuses on the entire communications process and examines how individuals and institutions communicate with each other. For the institutional advancement officer, communications research is an essential tool for fact and opinion gathering—a systematic effort aimed at discovering, confirming, and understanding through objective appraisal the facts or opinions pertaining to a specified problem, situation, or opportunity.

Most institutional advancement officers have come to recognize the following as real "needs" for conducting communications research:

■ to collect information that communications professionals need to do their jobs more effectively;

■ to obtain benchmark data regarding the views of key target audience groups;

■ to plan, develop, or refine an institutional advancement program or activity;

■ to track or monitor programs, activities, or events that are important to the institution;

■ to evaluate the overall effectiveness of the institutional advancement program or activity by measuring outputs and outcomes against a predetermined set of objectives;

■ when facing a sudden and unexpected crisis, to put the issues involved into proper perspective through emergency monitoring or polling;

■ when circumstances allow, to provide appropriate support in publicizing or promoting a specific program, activity, or event.

For truly effective communications research, advance planning is necessary. Before you begin, clearly define your goals and objectives. Ask yourself what you want and need the research to do for you. Remember, finding out "why" things are the way they are, or the reasons individuals feel and act the way they do, is often much more important for communications planning and evaluation than simply finding out "what" the facts are or "how" people feel. When considering communications research, remember the classic one-sentence definition of the communications process first described by political scientist Harold D. Lasswell more than 50 years ago. He said if you can figure out *who says what, to whom, how, with what effect,* you will have come a long way in understanding how communications work.

The *who* refers to the sources, or disseminators, of information; the *what* to the messages that are being disseminated; the *to whom* to the targeted audiences or intended recipients of your messages; the *how* to the channels of communications; and the *with what effect* to the eventual outputs and outcomes of the communications or advancement effort.

As part of the communications research effort, most institutional advancement officers are interested in measuring the believability of the information sources, including the relevance and overall importance of the messages being disseminated. They should also find out as much as they possibly can about the opinions, attitudes, and behavior patterns of those in the target audience groups, as they respond—or do not respond—to the various messages being disseminated. Finally, they should pinpoint the best and most effective communications channels to use when disseminating messages.

PRIMARY AND SECONDARY RESEARCH

There are really only two types of communications research—*primary,* which involves doing an original study, and *secondary,* which involves examining data already available.

Secondary research ought always to come first. Don't reinvent the wheel. Any time you are considering a possible communications research assignment, do not automatically assume that you need a completely new study. There's a good chance that someone else has already done a similar study or gathered similar data.

Secondary Research

Start out with a review of what's already been done by doing a literature search and secondary analysis. With the growing wealth of data on the Internet and in printed source books and periodicals, there are hundreds of places to obtain background information. A logical starting point is academic, trade, and professional journals. Here are a few Web sites to start with.

- Census Bureau: *www.census.gov*
- Department of Education: *www.ed.gov*
- *American Demographics:* *www.marketingtools.com*
- Association for Education in Journalism and Mass Communication: *www.aejmc.sc.org*
- Pew Research Center for the People & The Press: *www.people-press.org*
- Roper Center for Public Opinion Research: *www.ropercenter.uconn.edu*
- Survey Research Laboratory at the University of Illinois: *www.srl.uic.edu*
- Survey Sampling, Inc.: *www.worldopinion.com*

The Commerce Department's 1,000-page reference book, *Statistical Abstract of the United States,* is a must for obtaining secondary data. Other invaluable periodicals include:

- *Research Alert,* a biweekly newsletter that summarizes recent public opinion polls, available from E.P.M. Communications in New York City;
- *The Public Perspective,* a bimonthly magazine that summarizes recent public opinion polls, available from the Roper Center for Public Opinion Research at the University of Connecticut;
- *The Polling Report,* a semi-monthly newsletter that summarizes recent public opinion polls, available from the Polling Report, Inc. in Washington, D.C.;
- *Survey Research,* a quarterly newsletter that summarizes public opinion studies carried out by academicians and those in the nonprofit sector, available from the Survey Research Laboratory at the University of Illinois.

For institutional advancement officers, the annual *The American Freshman* norm studies that have been designed and carried out since 1966 by the Higher Education Research Institute at UCLA, in cooperation with the American Council on Education, are a crucial source of information on the changing views of students entering college for the first time. For details, contact the Higher Education Research Institute at UCLA in Los Angeles.

Primary Research

Primary research is usually either *qualitative* or *quantitative* in form. Qualitative research usually refers to studies that are somewhat subjective, but nevertheless in-depth, using a probing, open-ended, free response format. Quantitative research usually refers to studies that are highly objective and projectable to the total population under study, using closed-end, forced-choice questionnaires. These studies tend to rely heavily on statistics and numerical measures.

Qualitative Research

When communications researchers consider doing qualitative studies, the data collection methodologies that come quickly to mind are *focus groups* and *depth interview studies*.

Focus groups are an exploratory technique in which a group of somewhere between eight and 12 individuals—under the guidance of a trained moderator—are encouraged, as a group, to discuss freely any and all of their feelings, concerns, problems, and frustrations relating to specific topics under discussion. Focus groups are ideal for brainstorming, idea gathering, and concept testing.

Depth interview studies rely on a probing, open-ended, largely unstructured interviewing format, and usually are carried out in person or by telephone. As part of the interview, respondents are encouraged to talk freely and in great detail about given subjects.

Other useful forms of qualitative research include *convenience polling, ethnographic research,* and *inquiry studies.*

As the name implies, a *convenience poll* is a type of non-probability study in which whoever happens to be available at a given point in time is included in the sample. It sometimes also is referred to as a "haphazard," "informal," or "quick-and-dirty" poll.

As you might expect, most researchers view *convenience polls* as highly unscientific, unreliable, and invalid, and the findings are certainly not projectable to the total population under study. However, they could be of some value to the institutional advancement officer—and, thus, are worth

● ● ●
Any time you are considering a possible communications research assignment, do not automatically assume that you need a completely new study.

considering—if all you need at a given point in time is a "quick read" of people's views, feelings, or sentiments regarding a particular issue. Recognize, too, that the data you collect in this manner is little more than a rough, informal "sounding board" pertaining to a handful of people's opinions.

Ethnographic research relies on the tools and techniques of cultural anthropologists and sociologists to better understand how individuals and groups function in their natural settings. Usually, this type of research is carried out by a team of impartial, trained researchers who "immerse" themselves into the daily routine of a campus setting, a neighborhood, or a community. Using a mix of observation, participation, and role-playing techniques, they try to assess what is really happening from a "cultural" perspective.

At one academic institution that was having major student recruitment problems, a researcher relied on *ethnographic* "role-playing" techniques to gain a better understanding of why prospective students were applying to other colleges and universities. The researcher had his daughter, a junior in high school, write a letter asking for enrollment information and background materials. She mailed the exact same letter on the same day to the institution that was having problems and 10 of its principal competitors. The 11 institutions' responses were then carefully monitored and analyzed, to come up with a portrait of how different colleges and universities respond to the unsolicited inquiries they receive from prospective students.

An *inquiry study* is a systematic review and analysis, using content analysis or sometimes telephone and mail interviewing, to study the range and types of unsolicited inquiries that an organization may receive from key audience groups with which it frequently communicates.

For educational institutions, for example, it could be of great benefit to conduct informal interviews with prospective students or even alumni who contact campus officials for information or guidance. Although those who contact the institution on their own would constitute an unscientific, self-selected sample, the mere fact that they are calling could provide the advancement office with a useful source of qualitative information about important target groups.

Quantitative Research

Quantitative studies can be carried out using a broad array of data collection techniques, including e-mail, fax, face-to-face interviewing, mail, mall intercepts, omnibus polling, panels, telephone, and Web sites. Most of these techniques are self-explanatory, but a few—conducting surveys via e-mail and Web sites, through omnibus polling, and using panels—are growing in popularity and warrant further comment.

E-mail surveys are exactly what the name implies: They are self-administered questionnaires that are sent directly to potential respondents electronically. Their major advantage: speed. Since e-mail questionnaires are sent to potential respondents' electronic mailboxes, they get immediate attention. Their major shortcomings: an inability to appropriately format the questionnaires, problems regarding "skip" questions, and the fact that the questionnaires are often sent back with incomplete or missing data.

Web-based surveys differ in that a specialized software program or system is needed to construct a questionnaire and to collect and eventually process the results. The benefit is that survey instruments can be attractively designed (with audio, video, and graphic concepts added, if desired) and can contain complex, built-in skip patterns. Survey responses are collected in databases, which eliminates the need for manual data entry. However, unlike e-mail surveys, Web-based surveys are more passive, relying on respondents to seek out the online questionnaire. This can have a major effect on respondent eligibility and on overall representation.

The major advantages of e-mail and Web-based surveys are that large samples are possible in a short amount of time; usually studies can be carried out much more quickly and far more cheaply than using other methods; and data can be analyzed continuously; that is, one can "port" directly into statistical tools and databases as the completed questionnaires are returned. The major disadvantages of e-mail and Web-based surveys are that respondents

usually are self-selected, so there is limited or often no control over sample design and selection; probability sampling is not yet (and may never be) achievable; and identity validation can be a problem.

An *omnibus survey* is an "all-purpose," general-public consumer poll, usually conducted nationally on a regular schedule—once a week or every other week—by major market research firms. These firms charge clients (institutions) to "buy" one or several proprietary questions to add to the basic questionnaire.

There are also many organizations that conduct omnibus polls in individual states, usually among a representative sample of adults in that state. State omnibus polls are usually conducted far less frequently than are national omnibus polls, with some organizations going "into the field" once a month or a few times a year.

For an academic institution, the major advantage of using an omnibus poll service is that answers to a small number of short, closed-end questions can be directed at the general public at a reasonable cost. This service usually costs the institution from $500 to $800 per question for a survey of a sample of up to 1,000 adults. The data can be gathered in a week or two without going through the hassle of worrying about sample design specifications, interview quality and control, and data processing and tabulation issues.

Panels are a type of research study in which a group of individuals, because of their special demographic characteristics, are deliberately recruited by a research firm to be periodically interviewed on a broad array of topics.

Consider fielding a panel study if you are trying to survey a hard-to-reach or hard-to-find audience segment. For example, assume you wanted to survey a sample of adult African-Americans. In 1999, African-Americans made up 13 percent of the U.S. population; that means to poll a representative sample of adult black Americans, you would need to place 100 phone calls for every 13 blacks you wanted to contact.

That can be very expensive. An alternative approach is to rely on a market research supplier that maintains a "panel" of known potential respondents, broken down by their demographic characteristics. Not only are there cost savings, but also savings in time, since the audience segment you are targeting can quickly be identified and found. There are "panels" available for practically every different type of potential respondent, from membership in certain organizations to various age categories, broken down by various education, income, household size, and product use variables.

Of the various quantitative data collection techniques listed above, the best methodologies to keep costs down are e-mail polls, fax polls, mail surveys, omnibus polls, panels, and simple telephone polls.

If your primary consideration is quick-turnaround of the study from start to finish, the best methodologies are e-mail polls, omnibus polling, telephone polls, and Web-site surveys.

If your study is involved and complex and involves showing potential respondents a set of promotional materials or other items, consider face-to-face interviewing and mall intercept studies.

RESEARCH FOR STRATEGIC PLANNING AND PROGRAM DEVELOPMENT

All of the data collection tools and techniques that we have described are appropriate to use when designing and carrying out communications research, both for strategic planning and program development purposes. They also are appropriate for measuring and evaluating the effectiveness of your marketing and communications activities.

For communications research to provide support and assistance to the strategic planning and program development process, a mix of both qualitative and quantitative research is preferable. Qualitative research (e.g. focus groups, depth interviews, etc.) is usually carried out first, to obtain "exploratory" information, followed by quantitative research (e.g. a telephone, mail, or Internet survey, with representatives of key constituent groups.) Using this approach, you will obtain information that is both "descriptive" and "explanatory" in nature.

The two together—qualitative research followed by quantitative research—will give you a good mix of in-depth information that will tell you not only "how" and "what" people think, but "why" they hold the views they do. You can use this in-depth information for strategic planning and program development.

RESEARCH FOR MEASUREMENT AND EVALUATION

For research to provide assistance in measuring and evaluating the effectiveness of communications and marketing efforts, it is far better to emphasize quantitative data collection (although qualitative research can provide some useful information). The quantitative approach allows you to obtain statistically valid numbers to pinpoint clearly any changes that have taken place as a result of the communications effort.

In recent years, there's been a growing interest in measuring and evaluating an organization's communications effectiveness. In the business sector, CEOs now demand that their communications officers document—through research—that the communications programs they have designed and implemented really work; that the "needle has moved" in a positive direction.

Campus advancement officers are now confronting the same pressures.

For any communications measurement and evaluation research to be credible, four major components of the process need to be taken into consideration. They are:

1. **Setting specific measurable communications goals and objectives.** Practitioners cannot really measure the effectiveness of anything unless they first figure out exactly what it is they are measuring that something against.

The institutional advancement officer should begin by asking: What are or were the goals or objectives of their communications, marketing, and development activities? What exactly did their program hope to accomplish through its communications component?

2. **Measuring communications outputs.** *Outputs* are usually the short-term or immediate results of a particular communications program or activity; often outputs are what are readily apparent to the eye. They measure how well an organization presents itself to others, and the amount of attention or exposure that the organization receives.

In media relations efforts, outputs can be the total number of stories, articles, or "placements" that appear in the media; the total number of those who might have been exposed to the story; and an assessment of the overall content that has appeared. Media content analysis is one of the principal methodologies used to measure media outputs.

For other facets of communications, outputs can be white papers, speaking engagements, the number of times a spokesperson is quoted, specific messages communicated, specific positioning on an important issue, or any number of quantifiable items that are generated as a result of the effort.

Outputs also might include an assessment of a specific event, a direct mail campaign, the number of people who participated in a given activity, how an institutional administrator or faculty member handles himself or herself at a press conference, or the appearance and contents of a brochure or booklet.

You can measure and evaluate both the quantity and quality of all outputs. Media can be evaluated for content; an event for whether the right people were there; a brochure for its visual appeal and substance.

3. Measuring communications outcomes. As important as it might be to measure communications outputs, it is far more important to measure communications *outcomes*.

These measure whether target audience groups actually received the messages directed at them, paid attention to them, understood them, and retained them. Outcomes also measure whether the messages have resulted in any opinion, attitude, or behavior changes on the part of those targeted audiences.

It is usually much more difficult and generally more expensive to measure communications outcomes than it is to measure communications outputs. This is because more sophisticated data-gathering research tools and techniques are required.

Research techniques used to measure communications outcomes include quantitative surveys (face-to-face, by telephone, by mail, by fax, via e-mail, via the Internet, in malls, etc.); qualitative depth attitude surveys of elite audience groups; pre-test/post-test studies (e.g. before-and-after polls); experimental and quasi-experimental research projects; and multi-variate studies that rely on advanced statistical applications such as correla-

tion and regression analyses, Q-sorts, and factor and cluster analysis studies.

4. Measuring institutional outcomes. Advancement officers must measure the effectiveness of what they, themselves, do in connection with their communications and/or marketing programs and activities. At the same time, it is imperative that they also take steps to link their public relations accomplishments to the ultimate goals, objectives, and accomplishments of the institution as a whole.

In other words, you must relate communications outcomes to such desired institutional outcomes as increased market penetration, improved market share, enrollment increases, and a successfully completed fund-raising campaign.

This is not easy to do. It requires a careful delineation of what the communications program seeks to accomplish in concert with what the institution as a whole seeks to accomplish. It also requires a good understanding of how and why the two processes are supposed to work together.

Once you understand the desired impact and how the process is supposed to work, many of the research tools and techniques reviewed in this chapter can be relied on to measure the desired outcomes.

CAN RESEARCH BE DONE IN-HOUSE, OR SHOULD OUTSIDE SPECIALISTS BE HIRED?

A good deal of the communications research we have discussed in this chapter can be done efficiently and effectively in-house, with a modest amount of internal training.

By relying on the services of marketing professors and statisticians who work in your institution's academic departments, as well on your own internal computer center, your students, and members of your support staff, it is possible to set up and conduct studies that involve such methodologies as depth interviewing; convenience polling; ethnographic research; inquiry studies; and quantitative surveys via e-mail, fax, and regular mail.

An obvious problem in conducting in-house communications research is that internal studies sometimes lack credibility. People tend to be skeptical about the objectivity of a research project created and analyzed by staff members who may have a vested interest in the outcome. If you choose to design and carry out communications research in-house, there are a number of excellent books to use as resources:

■ *Using Research in Public Relations: Applications to Program Management*, by Glen M. Broom and David M. Dozier;

■ *The Practice of Social Research*, by Earl P. Babbie;

■ *Mail and Telephone Surveys: The Total Design Method*, by Don A. Dillman;

■ *Asking Questions: A Practical Guide to Questionnaire Design*, by Seymour Sudman and Norman Bradburn; and

■ *The Advertising Research Foundation's Compendium of Guidelines to Good Advertising, Marketing and Media Research Practices*, by the ARF in New York.

You should rely on the services of an outside research supplier whenever you need to do sophisticated research involving specialized data analysis procedures (e.g. factor and cluster analysis); when you do communications measurement and evaluation research projects; and whenever you consider doing studies involving the following methodologies: focus groups; mall intercepts (or shopping center studies); omnibus polling; panel studies; telephone surveys; Web site surveys; pre-test/post-test studies (e.g. before-and-after polls); experimental and quasi-experimental research projects; and multi-variate studies that rely on advanced statistical applications such as correlation and regression analyses.

Two reference sources you way wish to turn to when "shopping" for a research supplier are:

■ *The Green Book (The International Directory of Marketing Research Companies and Services*, published annually by the New York Chapter of the American Marketing Association, 60 East 42nd Street, Suite 1765, New York, NY 10165).

■ *The Blue Book* (A listing of more than 200 research agencies and organizations published by the American Association for Public Opinion Research, P.O. Box 1248, Ann Arbor, Michigan 48106-1248).

For more detailed information on the growing and somewhat complicated area of communications measurement and evaluation, read *Guidelines and Standards For Measuring and Evaluating PR Effectiveness*, published in 1997 by the Institute for Public Relations. A copy can be obtained online from the Institute's Web site: www.instituteforpr. com.

REFERENCES AND FURTHER READINGS

Advertising Research Foundation. *ARF Guidelines Handbook: The Advertising Research Foundation Compendium of Guidelines to Good Advertising, Marketing and Media Research Practice.* New York, NY: Advertising Research Foundation, 1990.

Babbie, Earl P. *The Practice of Social Research.* 8th edition. Belmont, CA: Wadsworth, 1997

Broom, Glen M. and David M. Dozier. *Using Research In Public Relations: Applications to Program Management.* Englewood Cliffs, NJ: Prentice-Hall, 1990

Dillman, Don A. *Mail and Telephone Surveys: The Total Design Method,* New York, NY: Wiley, 1978.

Hiebert, Ray E., ed. *Precision Public Relations,* New York, NY: Longman, 1988.

Hon, Linda Childers. "Demonstrating Effectiveness in Public Relations:Goals, Objectives and Evaluation," *Journal of Public Relations Research* 10, no. 2 (Spring 1998): 103-135.

Institute for Public Relations. *Guidelines and Standards For Measuring And Evaluating PR Effectiveness.* Gainesville, FL: The Institute for Public Relations, University of Florida, 1997.

Lasswell, Harold D. "The Structure and Function of Communication Society." In *The Communication of Ideas.* Edited by Lyman Bryson. New York, NY: Harper, 1948.

Lindenmann, Walter K. *A Guide to Public Relations Research.* New York, NY: Ketchum, 1999.

Miller, Delbert C. *Handbook of Research Design and Social Measurement.* 5th Edition. Newbury Park, CA: Sage Publications, 1991.

Rayburn, J.D. II and Thomas L. Preston. "The Science Behind Public Relations: We Need Rigorous Research, Not More News Release, to Get the Results We Want," CURRENTS 16, no. 2 (February 1990): 26-29.

Schreiber, William. "All Roads Lead to Research: Systematic Evaluation Will Point Your PR Program in the Right Direction," CURRENTS 19, no. 9 (October 1993): 24-28.

Sudman, Seymour and Norman M. Bradburn. *Asking Questions: A Practical Guide to Questionnaire Design.* San Francisco: Jossey-Bass Publishers, 1982.

Yancey, Bernard D. *Applying Statistics in Institutional Research: New Directions for Institutional Research, no. 58.* Edited by Bernard D. Yancey. San Francisco, CA: Jossey-Bass Publishers, 1988.

Benchmarking is an ongoing systematic approach by which communications departments measure and compare themselves with higher-performing departments to generate knowledge about communications practices, products, services, or strategies that will lead to improvement.

Communications Benchmarking

Gary R. Ratcliff
Director, University Center and Adjunct Assistant Professor of
Educational Leadership and Counseling
University of Montana

In an era of constrained resources, public relations professionals have come under mounting pressure to demonstrate their worth to upper management. This is especially true for communications professionals reporting to senior managers who embrace the principles of Total Quality Management and its use of empirical data for performance measurement. In today's business climate, it takes concrete evidence of effectiveness to convince senior managers of the need to support PR activities.

MOVEMENT TO MEASURE EFFECTIVENESS AND IMPROVE QUALITY IN PUBLIC RELATIONS

To its credit, the communications profession has become more sophisticated in measuring its effectiveness. In 1996, the Institute for Public Relations Research and Education gathered two dozen leading practitioners and academics to produce the publication, *Guidelines and Standards for Measuring and Evaluating PR Effectiveness*. The authors make a critical distinction between public relations outputs, which pertain to immediate results such as amount of press coverage and public relations outcomes, which refer to lasting results such as changes in opinion or behavior. Outputs are relatively easy to measure; outcomes, however, which are far more important than outputs, are more difficult and expensive to measure. To measure outcomes, research such as before-and-after opinion surveys is required. Senior managers who are communications-savvy expect information on both public relations outputs and outcomes, but realize that unless research to measure outcomes is funded, the information provided will most likely be anecdotal or inferred from events.

Senior managers also look for assurance that their public relations departments are innovative, productive, and efficient. In recent years, these departments have provided this assurance by using benchmarking as a tool to measure their performance and identify best practices.

Benchmarking is an ongoing systematic approach by which communications departments measure and compare themselves with higher-performing departments to generate knowledge about communications practices, products, services, or strategies that will lead to improvement. It is a fact-finding activity that identifies gaps in performance and sometimes triggers innovations that leapfrog communications departments ahead of their peers.

EVOLUTION OF BENCHMARKING

Benchmarking first emerged in the 1980s as a survival tool for Xerox in response to increased competition in the industry. By looking outside its industry for best practice leaders, Xerox substantially improved its operations.

Within higher education, benchmarking is gaining currency. The first major benchmarking study in higher education was sponsored by CASE in 1990 and involved examining the fund-raising expenses of 51 universities. In 1992, the National Association of College and University Business Officers (NACUBO) recruited 120 institutions to participate in a national benchmarking project on administrative services. Now, more than 300 institutions have participated in the NACUBO program and benchmarks have been developed for services ranging from admissions to purchasing. The program not only measures productivity and efficiency but also measures quality through the use of customer satisfaction surveys.

Benchmarking has been widely adopted in communications. In 1996, the Foundation for Public Affairs surveyed 264 public affairs departments and found that nearly half had undertaken benchmarking within the past year. In 1994-95, the university relations office of Penn State University conducted a series of benchmark studies on the public information, issues management, marketing, and publication development processes of 15 universities. A review of these studies found that most of these processes were driven by the desire to pursue strategic or operational changes, perceptions of gaps in performances compared to other organizations, and senior managers' interest in performance measures.

STEPS TO BENCHMARKING

The steps to conducting a benchmark study are described in a number of books, several of which are referenced at the end of this chapter. Most identify the following five steps to benchmarking:

1. **Planning:** Deciding what topics to benchmark.
2. **Identifying target organizations:** Deciding what organizations to recruit to participate in the study.
3. **Data collection:** Deciding what methods to use.
4. **Analysis:** Determining strengths and gaps in performance and what factors contribute to them.
5. **Implementation:** Using what has been learned.

Each of these steps is summarized below.

Step 1. Planning

When planning a benchmark study, limit the study to those practices, products, services, or issues that are crucial to the performance of the communications department. Rely on input from staff members and clients to identify those crucial success factors. Functions viewed as strategically significant but that do not meet expectations are excellent candidates for benchmarking. Do not rule out functions that are already distinctive competencies. Through benchmarking, you can bolster the strategic advantage of these functions.

Within public relations, a broad range of functions can benefit from benchmarking. A department can benchmark how public relations departments generate a specific type of the news coverage, such as science coverage. It can examine how public relations departments generate coverage in a particular medium, such as network news. It can research what reporters regard as the most useful Web sites and benchmark how campuses develop and maintain them. Examples of topics that are ripe for benchmarking include:

- types of news coverage (e.g., state, sports, op-ed),
- production of media guides and other campus news bureau products,
- practices related to managing issues and crisis management,
- practices related to employee relations such as the production of faculty/staff newspaper,
- academic and career background of staff and job training and professional development experiences,
- relations between PR departments and senior administrators, and
- quality control of campus publications.

When determining the scope of a project, think small—benchmarking projects often expand as they go on, but they seldom contract. It takes time to review the operations of benchmark partners in depth. A topic such as public relations is too broad and complex to explore. Even the topic of how campuses maintain good relations with employees may be too unwieldy. In contrast, what faculty and staff regard as important and useful in a faculty/staff newspaper and how top-performers produce it is a manageable topic.

Successful planning also requires support from upper management and putting relevant staff members on the benchmark team. Inattention to these concerns may sink a study. When pulling together the benchmark team, include staff members who are most familiar with the organizational processes under study and who would be responsible for implementing any changes in response to the findings.

Step 2. Identifying target organizations
Approaches to benchmarking vary depending on the type of benchmark partners targeted. The three most common approaches to benchmarking are internal, industry, and generic benchmarking. Internal benchmarking looks at departments within an organization. This approach suits large organizations with departments that perform related similar functions. Industry benchmarking compares a department's practices and performance with peer organizations. Generic benchmarking examines the best practices of organizations regardless of the industry. This approach promotes out-of-the-box thinking but requires an understanding of how functions can translate across industries.

When identifying prospective benchmark partners, consider several factors. First and foremost, select only recognized leaders in the area chosen for benchmarking. Resources for identifying top performers include CASE awards, survey results, publications, and colleagues.

Because factors beyond internal processes mitigate the performance of public relations departments, consider recruiting campuses in similar circumstances. For example, national press coverage is influenced not only by media relations practices but also by proximity to major news bureaus. Hence, universities in rural locations

⬤ ⬤ ⬤
When planning a benchmark study, limit the study to those practices, products, services, or issues that are crucial to the performance of the public relations department. Rely on input from staff members and clients to identify those crucial success factors.

should recruit high-performing universities in comparable settings rather than in urban news centers.

To ease the recruiting process, consider institutions that affiliate with one another in some manner. Institutions with a history of sharing information make good benchmark partners. Recruit communications departments from campuses that are in the same athletic conference, CASE district, or institutional association.

Once you have identified the benchmark partners, secure their cooperation by ensuring confidentiality, minimizing the investment of time in the study, and promising to share the results. To ensure confidentiality in the Penn State study, numbers were assigned to the 15 universities in the study. The results were presented using the numeric designations.

Step 3. Data collection
The objective of data collection in benchmarking is to examine processes and measure performance. Examining processes entails using research methods, such as interviews and site visits, to identify how benchmark partners perform their work. Measuring performance involves developing metrics, such as satisfaction surveys, to compare performance. Both pieces of information are critical. To institute improvements, information is needed on what processes are linked to superior performance and how those processes are performed.

Performance measures used internally by communications departments can be refined and used in benchmarking studies. For example, Penn State's benchmark study of publications departments found that nearly every department used a client satisfaction survey to measure performance. Penn State recommended that a common survey be developed for benchmarking.

When developing metrics of performance, ask the following questions about organizational processes:
■ What is the measure of quality for this process?
■ What are the criteria used to define excellence in performing this process?

■ How do you measure the quality of the output of this process?

Several research methods can be used to study the processes of communications departments; each possesses strengths and weaknesses. Surveys are easy to administer and are relatively inexpensive but are limited in their ability to measure how communications departments conduct their work. Telephone interviews are more time- consuming to conduct but allow for processes to be discussed in greater detail. Meetings at conferences are another useful means of gathering data but are difficult to coordinate. Finally, site visits yield the richest data but require the greatest investment of time.

Step 4. Analysis

In the analysis phase, the communications department identifies its strengths and weaknesses relative to its benchmark partners. Depending on the focus of the study, the department may analyze differences in satisfaction levels, levels of service, or service quality. It also may analyze the quality of its communications product line and its breadth and depth.

The analysis may compare efficiency levels by examining communications outputs relative to budget and staffing levels. However, be cautious when combining cost and performance data. Communications departments often use different methods of allocating costs and it is important to account for these differences in your comparisons.

The analysis should reveal the factors that contribute to the differences between the communications department and its benchmark partners. These factors may be internal and relate directly to organizational roles, strategies, and processes or they may be external and pertain to the environment of the organization. In-depth data collection through such means as site visits may be required to fully identify these factors.

Step 5. Implementation

The analysis phase generally culminates in a documented action plan. The plan should identify the strengths and weaknesses of the communications department relative to its benchmark partners and contain recommendations to improve its performance. These recommendations should target products, practices, or roles that can be refined or added. They should be short-term and long-term in nature, with short-term recommendations including initiatives that can be undertaken with minimum disruption or expense.

Because benchmarking focuses on quality improvement, higher education leaders contend that it is here to stay. A review of organizations that have conducted benchmark studies testifies to the benefits of the process. While benchmarking does not promise "magic bullet" answers, it can help communications professionals improve the operations of their departments.

BENCHMARKING RESOURCES

A number of books have been published on how to conduct benchmark studies. Several are particularly relevant to higher education, public agencies, and public relations. They include:

Alsete, J. *Benchmarking in Higher Education*. ASHE-ERIC Higher Education Report No. 5. Washington, DC: The George Washington University Graduate School of Education and Human Development, 1995.

Fleisher, C. S. *Public Affairs Benchmarking: A Comprehensive Guide*. Washington, DC: Public Affairs Council, 1995.

Keechly, P., Medlin, S., and Longmire, L. *Benchmarking for Best Practices in the Public Sector: Achieving Performance Breakthroughs in Federal, State, and Local Agencies*. San Francisco: Jossey-Bass, 1997.

For information about the evaluation of public relations effectiveness, read *Guidelines and Standards for Measuring and Evaluating PR Effectiveness*, published by the Institute for Public Relations Research and Education, University of Florida, P.O. Box 118400, Gainesville, FL, 32611-8400.

Several firms, associations, and higher education consultants specialize in benchmarking and evaluation. Here is a partial list of names to start with.

Delahaye Group is a leading firm in the measurement and evaluation of public relations. In addition to consulting, the firm sponsors conferences and sells publications on public relations evaluation. For information, visit their Web site at: *www.delahaye.com*.

Educational Benchmarking Inc. (EBI) is a private higher education consulting firm that has conducted national benchmark studies for business schools, residence halls, student unions, and other administrative services. For information, visit EBI's Web site at: *www.webebi.com*.

International Benchmarking Clearinghouse (IBC) is a division of of the American Productivity and Quality Center

(APQC). For information, visit APQC's Web site at: *www.apqc.org*.

The National Association of College and University Business Officers (NACUBO) coordinates a national benchmarking program. For information, visit NACUBO's Web site at: *www.nacubo.org*.

OTHER REFERENCES

Blumenstyck, G. "Measuring Productivity and Efficiency." *The Chronicle of Higher Education*. (September 1, 1993): A41.

Camp, R. C. *Benchmarking: The Search for Industry Best Practices that Lead to Superior Performance*. Milwaukee, WI: ASQC Quality Press, 1989.

Douglas, B., P.G. Shaw, and R. Shepko. "Seventh Inning Stretch: A Retrospective on the NACUBO Benchmark Program." *NACUBO Business Officer* (December 1997).

Fleisher, C.S. and D. Mahaffy. "A Balanced Scorecard Approach to Public Relations Management Assessment." *Public Relations Review* 23, no. 2(1997):117-143.

Fleisher, C.S. and S. Burton. "Taking Stock of Corporate Benchmarking Practices: Panacea or Pandora's Box?" *Public Relations Review* 21, no. 1 (1995): 1-20.

Halloway, J., G. Francis, M. Hinton, and D. Mayle. "Best Practice Benchmarking: Delivering the Goods?" *Total Quality Management* 9, nos. 4-5 (July 1998): 121-126.

Lindenmann, W.K. "Setting Minimum Standards for Measuring Public Relations Effectiveness." *Public Relations Review* 27, no.1 (1997): 391-410.

Ratcliff, G.R. and R. L. Williams. (1997). "Are You Worth It?" CURRENTS. 23, no. 9 (October 1997): 20-26.

Ryan, E. (1990). "The Costs of Raising a Dollar." CURRENTS 16, no.8 (September 1987): 58-62.

Watson, G.H. *Benchmarking Workbook: Adapting Best Practices for Performance Improvement*. Portland, OR: Productivity Press, 1992.

Weisendanger, B. Benchmarking Intelligence Fuels Management Moves. *Public Relations Journal* 49, no. 11 (1993): 20-23.

Is this the last printed edition of the Handbook of Institutional Advancement? *Probably not, but its days are surely numbered. It's only a matter of time before you'll be pulling this chapter up on your computer or television screen just as you do today's newspaper.*

5

Using Communications Technology and New Media

Don Hale
Vice President for University Relations
Carnegie Mellon University

My first introduction to technology in communications came when I went to work for a wire service immediately after college. With a telephone headset clamped to my head, I sat among clacking teletype machines, my fingers racing across my typewriter keyboard.

Those fingers were racing because standing over my shoulder was the bureau manager, who ripped the paper from the typewriter carriage each time I hacked out a paragraph of a breaking story on the hospitalization of a major political figure. He'd tear out a page, I'd put another in, and he'd hand the page to the teletype operator, who would type it again in teletype "code" for shipment to the main editorial office in New York and transmission to waiting wire service clients around the nation.

Even at a wire service, where the adage was that you had a deadline a minute, that was about as fast as we could deliver.

Today it's hard to even find a manual typewriter, and if you want to see a teletype machine, you'll need to visit a museum. Teletype operators are using their fast hands as court reporters or casino card dealers.

Meanwhile, as the 21st century begins, the world of communication is changing more rapidly than at any time in history. Modern technology has transformed forever the way public relations professionals and journalists share information with their audiences. The change has been so fast, in fact, that we're still trying to figure out what happened. But one thing is certain. Even as we struggle to adapt, we must be sure to integrate two of the newest communications tools into our daily work: e-mail (especially for media relations) and the World Wide Web (for external relations of every sort).

PUTTING E-MAIL'S EFFICIENCY TO WORK

Several years back, I participated in a study to determine how people communicate during a typical workday. Participants had to record each communication transaction in a log provided by the researchers. I went into this study knowing that, like many PR folks, I spent an inordinate amount of my day on the telephone.

To my surprise, my log revealed that the vast majority of my communications took place on e-mail. The telephone was a distant second.

Because of e-mail's tremendous advantages, its popularity will only increase for us in public relations. For one thing, it's among the most efficient two-way communication tools ever developed. You can receive messages and respond to them when you want. You don't have to engage in the small talk that accompanies a telephone conversation. You need not worry about catching your subject at "a bad time." There's no telephone tag.

For another thing, e-mail has emerged as an essential tool for communicating with members of the news media, who especially like it for all the reasons noted above.

"Ninety-nine percent of the reporters I work with like and use e-mail," George Simpson, president of George Simpson Public Relations in New York, told *Editor & Publisher* magazine. "There are a few who still want faxes or pitch letters, but they are a dying breed. After all, who these days has the luxury of waiting a week for a letter?"

E-mail lists are as crucial in today's communications office as the traditional media mailing list. E-mail communication enables us to move information more quickly and at lower cost than "snail" mail. And in the not-too-distant future, you will be able to ship electronically everything you now include in that slick printed press kit.

E-mail shares one big characteristic with snail mail: It can be useful or useless, depending on how wisely you put it to work. The February 13, 1999, edition of *Editor & Publisher* magazine provided this list of three tips for today's "cyber publicists":

- Don't send attachments. Not only can they transmit viruses to computers, but your recipients may not be able to open them.
- Don't overcommunicate. Even e-mail press releases should be pithy. And use good judgment about whether to follow up with a call; often journalists don't have time for phone pitches.
- Keep your e-mail lists up to date, just as you should with fax, phone, and mail lists. Many journalists still get press releases from beats they covered years ago.

Here's a more skeptical list of press relations tips

from the March 29, 1999, edition of *pr reporter.*

- Realize that e-mail is not the magic ticket; it's a delete key closer to not being read at all. So keep the phone calls and faxes coming as needed.
- Don't overlook how crucial the subject line is to making sure an e-mail gets opened.
- Always include your phone numbers when you send e-mail to avoid "e-mail tag."
- When a journalist asks to be removed from a distribution list, do it.

THE INTERNET'S PROMISE—AND PITFALLS

In addition to including a strategy aimed at increasing personal contact via e-mail, every public relations toolkit needs a wider Internet component. One important part should be maintaining a section of your Web site to provide information exclusively for reporters and editors, especially since many journalists will turn to your site when they can't reach a live source by phone. Another vital strategy is to take advantage of sites and services, including ProfNet, Newswise, PR Newswire, and the American Association for the Advancement of Science's EurekAlert, as well as others more targeted to specific fields. Also take advantage of LEXIS-NEXIS, a useful research tool for media relations professionals and journalists alike.

> ● ● ●
> **Generally, the annual maintenance budget (including staff) for a Web site should be about the same as the initial cost of building the site, with 50 percent of that total the absolute minimum you should budget.**

While new technology has certainly had an immense impact on the publicity field, its greatest impact—and greatest promise—lies in the opportunities it offers us in reaching and influencing our organizations' key audiences directly.

At the Public Relations Society of America's Technology Conference in 1998, counselor Don Middleberg said flatly, "If you want to influence anyone born after 1980, the Internet is the only method."

That statement should speak volumes to us in education. Above all other tools of modern technology, the Internet holds the keys to the kingdom for public relations, not just because of the opportunities it offers today but because of its vast potential. In the not-too-distant future, it's quite possible that all prospective students, alumni, and journalists will want to transact business through the Internet.

We will no longer publish paper versions of routine documents, from course catalogs to alumni magazines to news releases. Our audiences' primary window to our institutions will be their computer screens.

Is this the last printed edition of the *Handbook of Institutional Advancement*? Probably not, but its days are surely numbered. It's only a matter of time before you'll be pulling this chapter up on your computer or television screen just as you do today's newspaper.

Unfortunately, the great benefits of technology come at a cost. Along with lightning-fast tools comes the expectation that your office will move information more rapidly and update more frequently. And with the ability to target your audiences more effectively comes the challenge of dealing with an ever-widening universe of media outlets—not just newspapers, magazines, radio, and network TV but also cable TV and Web sites. This fragmentation will only get worse, warns Michael Stoner, vice president for new media at Lipman Hearne Inc. "In some ways it's just a big mess. Public relations people have to pay more attention to what they're doing and how they're doing it."

Beyond the Web's external challenges come the problems of managing internally. The Internet today is the Wild West of communications, a sprawling frontier of unbridled opinion, innuendo, and misinformation. It's a wilderness of Web sites inhabited by a disparate army of pioneers all seeking to get their messages out there. Given the Internet's rapidly growing importance in communication, you might think the typical public relations department would play the role of "new sheriff in town," bringing order to this "shoot-'em-up."

But you'd be wrong. In many cases, the public relations office has the sheriff title but no bullets in its guns. It lacks the financial resources and the institutional clout to bring coherence to the way a campus is represented on the Web. And it must take on a wild bunch that shoots down any attempt at unity of message or purpose. Among them: the technical staff, who control computer networking at many institutions; deans and department heads, who want the independence of their own sites; and student designers, who offer to produce a boffo Web site more cheaply than any professional de-

signer on your staff.

It's apparent, unfortunately, that high school students who visit campus Web sites are most likely to visit student and faculty home pages, which are the parts of the institutional site that PR people manage the least. This makes for the most confusion at one of your campus's most popular entry points—and makes it clear that it's time to take a firm hand.

TAMING THE NEW TECHNOLOGICAL FRONTIER

How to bring control to this lawless landscape? Here are some of the most common problems in Web design and management, followed by solutions you can use to enhance this exceedingly valuable communications tool.

■ **Problem: Many institutions mount a Web site without considering what their objectives are.**

Solution: Overseeing the strategy and development of the site should be a principal role for public relations. Putting the communications staff in charge is the best way to make sure the Web ties in with your campus's public relations and marketing plans.

Before designing (or redesigning) your Web site, consider the impressions you are trying to create among different segments of your viewers. More important, think about how your Web site might both serve those visitors and convince them to act on behalf of your institution, whether by applying for admission or featuring campus research in news reports.

In addition, as Stoner says, "no matter what size of institution we're talking about, you must focus on developing an effective navigation route and feature set for your site. The material has to have integrity, it must be accurate and, above all, it must reflect the institutional message and mission."

■ **Problem: Too many sites are organized around the interests and needs of the senders of information rather than the receivers.**

Solution: Plan every part of your site around this guiding principle: What does our visitor want, and how can we best deliver it?

The Web provides ample opportunity to track visitors' use patterns. Put that research to work in developing navigation routes that get your visitors where they want to go in the most direct way. Because the Web has given people the power to explore an institution in new ways, it has put a lot more power in the hands of these consumers. Make sure they use that power in ways that serve both themselves and your institution.

■ **Related problem: Some sites are simply Web-based organizational charts.** Even though most folks visiting your site don't care which department provides what service, often their route through the site is determined by an institution's departmental structure.

Solution: Revise that structure according to the tasks Web users want to perform, even if it means grouping disparate departments together.

■ **Problem: Multiple designers create multiple impressions.**

Solution: The answer sounds simple, though it's often politically challenging: Have one office responsible for the design of the entire site. Constantly remind your colleagues that users get annoyed when they move through pages on a site and find drastically varying designs and navigational patterns. As in all communications, consistency is crucial to successful Web management.

■ **Problem: Web sites get old real fast.** This problem is aggravated because even though institutions are willing to put resources into constructing a Web site, they're often reluctant to invest in an equally important second step—Web maintenance.

Solution: Someone needs to be assigned to frequently update Web content. Ideally, this would be an additional staff position in the PR office. Where can you find the money to pay for this staffer? Perhaps you can redirect money that you're currently spending on campus publications no one wants or reads. The design of

the site probably needs to be evaluated at least once a year. A rule of thumb: Generally, the annual maintenance budget (including staff) for a Web site should be about the same as the initial cost of building the site, with 50 percent of that total the absolute minimum you should budget.

■ **Problem: Web sites fail to motivate visitors to come back again,** despite the fact that your Web site—like commercial sites—gains in value when visitors frequently come back to take a look.

Solution: Get "sticky." As explained in the February 11, 1999, issue of the *Wall Street Journal,* "A shrinking list of rivals are scrambling to create what is almost impossible in cyberspace: Web properties so enticing and all-encompassing that users wouldn't dream of going anywhere else. The ultimate goal is to create sites worthy of the hot buzzword 'sticky,' commanding Web surfers' attention for minutes, even hours, in a medium where people jump from site to site in seconds."

Educational institutions can't offer the entertainment value of *gamesville.com* or the thrill of the online auctions at *ebay.com.* But they can offer visitors entertaining and perhaps thrilling ways to interact with their sites. Can your visitors easily find information on your site about the latest developments at your institution? Or are you cranking out that same old litany of visions and missions and commitment to students? Does your site engage your visitors? Is it interactive? Consider adding some games, trivia, tests, virtual tours, or promotional gimmicks.

■ **Problem: The Web continues to be viewed as a secondary medium.**

Solution: Dumping your alumni magazine, your campus newspaper, or other printed materials on the Web is not the answer. Instead, Web designers and content experts have to create new ways to convey information appropriate for the interactive, non-linear nature of the Web.

■ **Problem: Those aforementioned student**

and faculty home pages, which are both popular and hard to rein in.

Solution: You've got no chance of controlling the individual pages created by your students and faculty. But a reasonable goal is to unify these sites by requiring faculty departments to use common identifiers and useful pathways to and from your institutional front door.

THE NEW MEDIA FORECAST: GREATER DISCIPLINE AND DIRECTION

Despite campus disputes over control of the Web, public relations professionals are likely to prevail eventually. As the Web's value as a communications and business tool becomes increasingly evident, institutional leaders will be forced to pursue greater discipline and direction in the way their institutions are portrayed on the Web.

At the same time, we as public relations professionals will have to bring a new set of skills to the task, even beyond strategy and management. Mounting text on the Web will come to seem relatively simple as everyone, at home or at the office, gains the capability of viewing video or hearing audio on a Web site. Teleconferencing will be commonplace. And we public relations pros will need audio and video production skills. The good news is that we will be able to apply them in editing suites that will be as easy to use as the word processor of today.

In the future, all our publics will use the Internet. They'll be able to filter out messages they don't want. They'll create their own Web pages to provide them with feeds of information related to their interests. They'll watch TV programs whenever they wish, not at a predetermined time. They'll share fewer common experiences, such as reading the town newspaper. And their new habits will make breaking through in this consumer-driven medium even more of a challenge.

To succeed, we public relations professionals must call on a time-honored skill that has nothing to do with technology—a skill we've demonstrated time and again on paper and in the airwaves. The Internet, with its mix of text, video, and audio, will give us a new creative freedom to display our craft. We will be storytellers for a new age, unfolding like never before the ideas, images, and impressions that touch hearts and minds.

REFERENCES

Editor & Publisher. New York, NY: ASM Communications, (February 13, 1999): 20.

Anders, George. "The Race for 'Sticky' Web Sites," *Wall Street Journal* (11 February 1999): B1.

Bates, Don and Paul Warren. *Using the Internet for Public Relations Purposes.* New York, NY: Public Relations Society of America, June 1998.

Cartwright, G. Phillip. "Creating a Web Policy: What You Need to Know," *Change: The Magazine of Higher Learning* 28, no. 5 (September/October 1996): 53-55.

Cornforth, Suzanne R. and William Koty. "Untangling the Web: It Takes More Than Counting Hits to Evaluate Your Web Site's Successes—Or Troubles. Here's How to Find Out Who Your Visitors Are, What They Want, and How They Want It," CURRENTS 23, no. 7 (July/August 1997): 10-16.

Klassen, Frank W. and Wendy S. Bresler. "What's So Hard About the World-Wide Web? Two Media Experts Offer Advice on Making Your Jump Onto the World-Wide Web Faster and More Effective," *Designer* (Winter 1996): 18-20.

Stubbee, Melinda. "The FAQs on Intranets: You've Heard of These Hot New Tools. Now Consider Whether Building One Can Make Internal Communication on Your Campus Easier, Faster, and Cheaper," CURRENTS 23, no. 7 (July/August 1997): 18-20, 22.

"Technology: Heavy On Media, Lacks Organizational Integration," *pr reporter.* (March 29, 1999). (*www.prpublishing.com*)

Issues management requires the public relations officer to be an expert and a risk taker, to be efficient and effective, to be pragmatic and visionary, and, most crucially, to be there.

Issues Management:
Balancing on a High Wire

Terry Denbow
Vice President for University Relations
Michigan State University

First and foremost, there is no formula, equation, or set of dogmas that assure the successful management of issues on campus in the 21st century. This chapter focuses on what issues management is and isn't, a view of the role the public affairs office must play, and some pragmatic advice about issues and managing them. This subject requires an appreciation for ambiguity, periodic failure, uncertainty, and tolerance for unrealistic expectations by one's self and others.

If you want to be an issues manager in education today, and you surely must if you are to fulfill your professional obligations, you should realize that the responsibility requires you to be second-guessed on a regular basis. You should also realize that, if you are not subject to unrealistic expectations, blame, and second-guessing, you probably are not doing your job. Make no mistake, issues management often puts the public relations officer in a precarious position, on the floor of the arena (or on a high-wire above it), in the spotlight, in front of the cameras, across the desk from the president, or all of the above.

Issues management requires the public relations officer to be an expert and a risk taker, to be efficient and effective, to be pragmatic and visionary, and, most crucially, to be *there*. Just like Teddy Roosevelt's "Man in the Arena": ". . .who at best knows achievement and who at the worst if he fails at least fails while daring greatly so that his place shall never be with those cold and timid souls who know neither victory nor defeat."

DEFINING THE TERMS

Not everyone agrees upon what the component terms "issues management" represent, disagreeing on what an "issue" is or what "management" is.

To some, an issue is anything—from a campus event to an educational philosophy—that challenges the status quo, that defies conventional wisdom. To others, it is anyone or anything that causes a problem. Any kind of problem. To them, "negative issue" is redundant, "positive issue" is an oxymoron. To yet others, an issue is any concept or idea that has sharply defined intra-campus conflict; if there are not clearly understood enemy camps, it's not really an issue. In our jobs, of course, we are asked to deal with situations that meet all these criteria; they defy conventional wisdom while causing problems that result in open campus conflict! But they may or may not be issues. Ally yourself with those who consider an issue a trend, cycle, or environmental challenge (problem and/or opportunity) that you can help to predict, frame, shape, influence, and evaluate.

Management, to some, means taking central control of an issue, quickly winnowing options, proclaiming a decision, and declaring the issue over. To these people, an issue is something to be "solved." To others, management means minimizing risk at all cost, with decision deferral and even denial as options, especially when "this isn't an issue we chose." These are the ones who tell the public relations office, "It's not an issue unless we make it an issue," which usually can be translated as "Why are you PR people always inventing trouble?" Be prepared, then, to have your advance counsel blamed for "creating" the alleged issue at hand. To yet others, management means risk-taking leadership no matter what the cost or how long it takes to address. These leaders know that deferred gratification might be the best outcome, and they are willing to risk rejecting placebo-like responses to ease the pain of the moment. Ally with them.

A PLACE AT THE TABLE

Key to the role of the public relations professional in issues management is the requirement that public relations expertise be represented everywhere strategic discussions take place. Surely, there is risk in entering that arena. But there is greater risk in remaining outside looking in. The security of observation and silence is not an acceptable component of the public relations role in effective issues management. Ideally, those in our profession are at the very core of our administration's issues management team. They want to be members of the cabinet. In fact, they wouldn't have accepted the job if they weren't. They sit at the table where existing and anticipated issues are identified, analyzed, debated, and prioritized. They listen at that table; and they are heard at that table. They help to plan, strategize, and make decisions. They help to determine audiences and markets affected. Their "with-the-bark-off" counsel on issues is heard at the top, not relayed to the top. The ideal? At the tables where these folks reside, there is a universal understanding that effective public relations counsel and issues management are inseparable.

Regretfully, too many of our public relations professionals are not yet perceived as rightful members of the issues management starting lineup. In baseball terms, they are either designated hitters or relief pitchers, summoned off the bench for a big hit or called in from the bullpen with orders to stem the tide. On their campuses, they are perceived as agenda specialists, not visionary generalists. They are told to know their place!

■ They were never part of the enrollment strategy meetings, but they are called in to "get us 200 more freshmen by August."

■ They are seen as aliens by the medical dean, but he summons them when a malpractice suit, inevitable for months, hits the morning paper.

■ They were never involved in capital campaign planning, but are ordered to put out a brochure to increase deferred giving.

■ The liberal arts dean considers them issues managers for the president only, but needs immediate help in getting her op-ed piece in tomorrow's *Washington Post*, preferably above the fold.

■ The vice president for research hasn't met "a flak I like," but wonders if maybe the reason federal grants are down is because of bad PR.

The Perils of Opting Out

It is even more regretful that too many public relations administrators have not sought a starting-lineup role as members of the cabinet or have opted out of that crucial role in frustration or, perhaps, exhaustion. Some of these folks simply do not believe that policy shaping is part of their mandate, choosing to believe—often based on experience—that the expectation of the administration is for them merely to reflect what others decide. They naturally see issues management, at least for the public relations office, as inherently a *post-facto* activity, something akin to after-battle triage. Just stop the bleeding.

There is another problem. It is the ironic, false, and dangerous supposition that an effective communicator of campus issues must be perceived as above-the-fray-neutral, both on and off campus. I've heard it. "If the media/faculty knew I was sitting at the right hand of the president or provost, I'd lose my credibility with those media and faculty." Such a stance denies an issues management verity for public relations professionals: it is our proximity to others at that table—not our distance from them—that gives us our credibility, our clout, and our effectiveness, on or off the campus. Father Ted Hesburgh, the legendary former president of Notre Dame, used to say that any president who isn't regularly heard off the campus isn't worth being heard on it. In the same vein, the public relations administrator who isn't heard at the table isn't worth being heard away from it.

One cannot be a credible advocate—or an effective issues manager—unless one is known to be a willing and active "player" at the center of the action.

It is more than helpful, then, that the chief public relations officer be at the table as a person who reports directly to the president or chancellor.

It is true that access is based on an attitude, not an organizational chart. Thus it's possible that a direct report can have little access and a middle manager can be granted regular access. But all in all, the impact of the public relations officer in issues management is significantly enhanced when communication with the CEO, the chief academic officer, and others is direct and solid, organizationally or otherwise. If an administrator who is not the chief public relations administrator has to convey to that officer a translation of what happened at the cabinet meeting, too much is lost along the way. And, similarly, if the chief executive regularly hears filtered or superficial summary representations of what the chief public relations officer thinks, much is lost as well. The result can be what Walter Cronkite called information "distortion by compression." Beware of those who seek to be communication buffers between the CEO and the public affairs office. Yes, their intentions often are salutary, but their contributions to the issues management process are just as frequently counterproductive.

More than Media Relations

To be fair, some of our best-intentioned peers have just quit asking to be seated or heard at the table.

● ● ●

To some, an issue is anything—from a campus event to an educational philosophy—that challenges the status quo, that defies conventional wisdom. To others, it is anyone or anything that causes a problem.

They recall those occasions when their voice didn't count when policy issues were debated at the top, hearing one too many times, "We set the policy in motion; you PR folks merely add the spin." Behind such a misguided order is the outmoded belief that media relations is the *raison d'etre* for a public relations office. To be sure, media are crucial audiences for our messages and our advocacy. But if media are viewed as the sole targets of our public relations planning, our roles are diluted. Effective public relations requires that we be involved in issues management that takes into consideration numerous constituencies, including faculty, students, donors and potential donors, taxpayers, alumni, legislators, other colleges and universities, ranking agencies, accrediting boards, special interest groups, political parties, and many others.

If we are called upon to consider only media that filter our messages, we are not valid issues managers, no matter what the issue. In such an environment, we are thereby limited to being the public information office without the clout or directive to be involved as counselors with constituent service, marketing, research and analysis, student recruitment, fund raising, legislative relations, and other considerations for which others should look to us.

Confusion over Issues Management

Let's get back to definition of terms. Too frequently and always lamentably, "issues management" is misconstrued as a term synonymous with "crisis communication" or "emergency preparedness." Indeed, when panel discussions on issues management are held, they inevitably focus on public relations strategies to be employed in times of imminent, ongoing, or recent peril.

This widely accepted myth is based in part upon the false notion that public relations exists to follow rather than to lead, to react rather than to anticipate, and to clean up rather than to build up. This view of our role leads to negative stereotyping: We're the bad news folks. The myth is also supported by a widely held notion that an issue is something that lives only in the "now." Arthur Miller once wrote that the now is a time bomb tossed through an open window. And it's ticking. Many consider an issue as a ticking time bomb thrown through the window of the public affairs office.

Therefore, the issues management panel discussions at CASE conferences or in less formal dialogues tend to end up analyzing:

■ How last spring's drunken riot ruined our image.

■ What to do when a young female faculty member is charged by her male mentor with research misconduct.

■ Why are all those editorial writers blasting us over tuition?

■ How could we have better handled the takeover of the administration building by the Hispanic students?

■ Why such fallout from the health center boycott?

■ How could we have responded better to the NCAA investigation?

■ Where did we go wrong in our media relations after the law dean unexpectedly resigned?

Inevitably, after panel discussion by experts on how such things have been or might be handled, someone asks, apologetically but eagerly, "Can I get a copy of your plan?" as if a magical, guaranteed blueprint exists in the files at Penn State or Washington University or UCLA to avert or assuage the pain of alumni, avoid bad press, and calm down the faculty and students. To be sure, most have plans in the form of press policies (for example, MAP, the Media Assistance Plan at MSU) and crisis and emergency plans (what happens when a meningitis case is reported or when the Cyclotron has a radiation leak?). But issues management goes far beyond crisis communication. Consider this: what if the issue is not an event or an episode or anything temporally defined? Or consider this radical thought: What if the issue could provide a positive result for you? As the ancient proverb goes, "Even the other side has an other side."

The Analytical Depth to Issues Management

Is last May's riot the issue, or is it alcohol abuse? Or

long-term town/gown mistrust? What are we going to do about it? Is the young assistant professor's data manipulation the issue, or is it inordinate pressure on non-tenured faculty to produce journal articles? Or gender bias in the life sciences? What are we going to do about it? Is next fall's big tuition hike the issue, or is it lack of private support? Or over-dependence on student fees? What are we going to do about it?

So, the "issue" the PR office must be concerned with isn't so much the Hispanic students' takeover of the administration building; it's the issue of diversity and pluralism, of demographics, of institutional commitment to access. Yes, the protest is today's perceived "issue." And maybe you are doing a lousy job retaining Hispanic students after the freshman year. Maybe your Hispanic population doesn't mirror the state's. If so, talk about it. A lot. And do something about it. But maybe the rest of the story is how well you're doing in improving overall minority enrollment, diversifying curricula, and increasing scholarships. Maybe years of issues management brought more solutions than problems.

Finding the True Issue

The "issue" the PR office should be concerned with is student medical care delivery, not just the health center boycott.

Yes, the boycott is in the headlines. And, yes, you recognize that students are justifiably upset over insufficient emergency care services. Their parents are e-mailing you in volume. Admit it. Do something about it. But maybe the rest of the story includes the satisfaction survey conducted by an external firm that shows over the past five years students have come to know and love the health center, that they're using it more, and that health problems have decreased among both women and men.

The "issue" isn't the current NCAA investigation, it's the growing presence of unscrupulous agents.

Yes, the athletic boosters are complaining about the investigation. And, yes, its regrettable your blue-chip recruit might well have a relationship with an agent. You'll probably lose him and still badly need a power forward. But maybe your athletic department's compliance staff is having investigative success in identifying problems earlier and bringing to light more solutions than problems. And that's a more substantive tale.

The "issue" isn't the long-serving law dean's surprise resignation, it's the issue of the law school's time-honored mission to serve practicing attorneys in the region.

Yes, the dean's quitting in a huff has legislators—many of them her former students—calling the provost. And, yes, you are losing a brilliant, nationally renowned anti-trust expert who's regularly quoted in the *New York Times*. Don't downplay the loss. But maybe she quit because she didn't think the law school should reach out to attorneys with continuing legal education programs, and the resignation is great news to the law alumni, state bar, and potential donors to the law school.

ADVICE FOR ISSUES MANAGEMENT SUCCESS

In summary, here are some guides to the role of the public relations officer in issues management:

- Be in the arena…in the starting lineup.
- Identify issues on the horizon, on the back burner, or on the desk of the president.
- Understand there is risk in your candid advice.
- Bring solutions as well as problems.

- Realize that an issue might still be there long after you aren't.
- Know that a crisis is not necessarily an issue, and vice versa.
- Resist those who limit your role to media adviser.
- Evaluate your counsel.
- If not you, who?

FURTHER READINGS

Bray, Sarah Hardesty. *Issues Papers Digests,* I, II, III, IV, V. Washington, DC: Council for Advancement and Support of Education, 1995.

Bryan, Jerry L. "The Coming Revolution in Issues Management: Elevate and Simplify," *Communication World* 14, no. 7 (July 1997): 12-14.

Hirsch, Peter. "Mapping Out Issues Management: When an Organization Has Abundant and High-Quality Information, the Ability to Identify Future Issues and to Design Appropriate Responses is Correspondingly Good," *Communication World* 14, no. 7 (July 1997): 15-18.

Kanzler, Ford. "The Positioning Statement: Have One Before You Start Communicating," *Public Relations Quarterly* 42, no. 4 (Winter 1997-1998): 18-22.

Public Relations Society of America. *Professional Practice Center Profolio: Crisis Planning and Management.* New York, NY: Public Relations Society of America, 1998.

Shea, Susan C. "Take It From the Top—Campus CEOs Tell PR Officers What It Takes to Get a Seat at the Executive Table," CURRENTS 25, no. 4 (April 1999): 30-35

An unknown institution, or one with unsatisfactory media relationships, will have a much more difficult time handling a crisis than an institution that has dealt honestly and regularly with the media.

Crisis Communications: Planning, Executing, Surviving

Linda Gray
Assistant Vice President and Director of News & Public Affairs
University of Florida

When it comes to dealing with crises at educational institutions, there is bad news and there is good news. The bad news is that every institution will, at some time in its existence, have crises. The nature of the crises may vary in intensity but because of human nature and our complex society, trouble is inevitable.

The good news is that thinking in advance about how to cope with crisis will inevitably ameliorate the negative results. Whether an institution has a detailed plan, loosely based guidelines, or has only discussed the possibility of crisis minimally, that anticipation will have a positive influence on the result. The nature of all crises, both small and large, requires that some decisions be made immediately and that a plan be formulated quickly to deal with a specific crisis at hand. However, thinking in advance about the "what if's" inevitably will allow those coping with the crisis to make decisions more quickly and more effectively.

Crisis can be defined as any situation, event, or activity affecting individuals closely associated with the institution that will reflect negatively on that institution and that could produce unfavorable media and public attention. Crises can become more severe, or can be minimized, by the way in which they are approached, the speed of response, and the judgment used in their resolution. Crises are fluid, and plans to deal with them must be fluid as well.

While crises such as the off-campus serial killings of students experienced by the University of Florida, the on-campus shootings of more than a dozen women at Ecole Polytechnique de Montreal, and the earthquake that demolished the University of California at Northridge are rare, the more likely ones are the misappropriation of school funds, student protests, alcohol abuse-related incidents, or sexual harassment cases.

Regardless of the severity of these crises, institutions that deal well with them usually have credibility with the media and the public in advance of the event. An unknown institution, or one with unsatisfactory media relationships, will have a much more difficult time handling a crisis than an institution that has dealt honestly and regularly with the media, and has a reputation for fairness and openness in its dealings.

In building relationships, it takes time for individuals to get to know and trust one another. The relationships between media representatives and communications personnel and administrators are no different. The middle of a crisis is not the time to try to establish credibility or convince the media and the public that institutional representatives are truthful and believable.

THE BASICS

The best preparation for a crisis is to conduct everyday business with the media and the public in a professional and credible manner.

The basic tenets for working with the media are simple, common-sense rules. Failure to adhere to them will inevitably bring disastrous results at some point and will affect how an institution is treated by media thereafter.

These cardinal rules are:

1. *Never lie* to the media. You will almost surely be found out and your credibility will be forever lost.

2. *Respond and respond quickly* to the media when you are contacted. Not responding almost always prevents you from telling your side of the story; in many cases, journalists will think you are hiding something or will portray you as evasive. You may need to consult with others before contacting media. Also, you can prepare in advance what you will say to media (though you should never read to them). But you should respond, even if it is only to say, "I'm sorry, the matter is in litigation, and university attorneys indicated there's nothing further we can say at this time."

3. *Don't pretend to know* something you don't or talk before you find out what a media representative is seeking. It is not only acceptable, but preferable, to say, "I don't know." But follow quickly with " . . . but I can find out for you, and I'll get back to you as soon as possible." Talking to media before you know the information they really seek can result in your saying things you shouldn't or causing a reporter to inquire about information that wasn't pertinent to the issue at hand.

4. *Cultivate media contacts.* Get to know the members of the media who regularly cover your institution, and develop new contacts on a continuing basis. Be friendly and cooperative. Develop amiable relations where possible. People who like one another are more apt to work well together. When a crisis occurs, reporters who have good relationships with an institution will be much more understanding and cooperative.

5. *Never say "no comment."* Reporters (and those who see or hear these words in the media) will think you are hiding something. This is a contrived phrase used in fictional drama; it does not work in practice.

6. *Think ahead,* discuss contingencies, and prepare for how your institution would handle a media frenzy in a crisis situation.

Before the Crisis

In preparing for a crisis, having something written down can reassure many people at your institution. Additionally, it serves as a reminder that members of the institution need to be aware of and think about what they would do in a crisis situation. Advance work should involve the following:

■ *A written plan* that can include: teams that can be called together, depending upon the nature of the crisis; information on who speaks for the institution, who releases material and who decides what information is released; and what role the institution's media relations/communications staff will have in the process. A plan can be simple or complex but should reflect the nature and character of the individual institution.

■ *Up-to-date computer lists (preferably with office, home, and beeper numbers) of media (state, national, and local)*; and contacts during a crisis, including crisis team members, administrators, media relations staff, local people, related government or agency personnel, boards related to the institution, close friends of the institution, key alumni, donors, politicians, etc.

■ *Specification of as many logistical details as possible.* While it's impossible to plan in advance for every detail, there are a number of things you can do to prepare for any crisis. Identify locations where press conferences/media availabilities can be held (how many a room can hold, whom to call to reserve rooms). Take an inventory of equipment and space available (What phones do you have and would they be enough for your use, for media use? Where could you get more? Where could media plug laptops into phones? Where could TV media plug in their cameras?). Draw up diagrams and parking plans (if you had a major media onslaught, where would media, visitors, others park?) Advance work with campus police, security, or local officials can help. (Administrators at the University of Florida never thought they would need to worry where 21 satellite uplink trucks could park, but when five students were murdered off campus by a serial killer, the resulting media convergence on campus called for a plan.) Make a list of available staff support (Whom would you call on to help type information, make copies, fax materials, help make calls?) Advance planning can be invaluable. Make lists of area hotels/motels to which you could refer members of the media covering a long-term story at your institution.

■ *Consideration of worst-case scenarios.* What would your institution do if it were without electricity, water, or supplies? When Hurricane Andrew struck south Florida, Florida International University, the University of Miami, and others in the area found themselves in just that situation as their institutions were forced to close temporarily. Consider in advance where an emergency command center could be established, and where auxiliary power sources are on campus.

In the Midst of Crisis

The cardinal rules listed on page 156 hold even more importance when an institution is in crisis mode: Never lie. Be proactive and friendly. Respond to calls quickly and stick to what you know when talking with reporters.

■ *Monitor what is happening and tell the media.* In most cases, the more that is known and the quicker it is explained, the less intense and serious a crisis will seem.

■ *Listen to the media as well as talk to them.* You may glean helpful information or learn how your story is being covered and perhaps positively influence that coverage. And while it is sometimes difficult to maintain composure in a crisis, it is important not to be irritable or antagonistic.

■ *Be flexible during crisis situations.* Try to have a heightened awareness of what is happening

around you. What are the needs of your institution; what are the needs of the media? How can you make things better? For example, if hundreds of calls are coming in, can you devise a system to handle them? Would a dedicated call-in line that offers information be helpful? Would a rumor-control hotline help? Should additional staff be hired or called in to deal with a problem? Think on your feet.

■ *Consider how information released to the media may affect others.* If you release information containing the names of individuals, call them and let them know. If information released will result in media calling other agencies or individuals, warn them of impending calls.

■ *Be sure to give credit to other agencies, groups, or individuals working on the crisis.* For example, credit the firemen who put out the fire, the police who uncovered the crime, the doctors who saved the victim, the bystander who reported the theft, or other institutions or entities that assisted you. Don't forget to mention your own staff and others at your institution who were helpful. This is simply the right thing to do and will reflect well on your institution, but it can also enhance your relationships with others.

Press Conference Details

If a crisis demands a news conference or press availability, here are some useful guidelines.

■ *Define the nature of the event.* If you announce a news conference, media will expect you to provide them with new information. A press availability simply means you are making an individual available to the media to answer whatever questions they may have.

■ *Do not set up false expectations.* If media believe their time is being wasted or you are trying to use them inappropriately to diminish the crisis, you may put your institution in hot water.

■ *Decide in advance what format and agenda the press conference will have.* Provide handouts when possible and as much advance information as you can. Try to present the newest or latest information first, especially in ongoing events. Decide who will introduce speakers; who will decide when the question/answer period ends; and who will decide where cameras are set up, whether lights can be used, and who will stand where.

■ *Remember media deadlines* when determining the time of a press conference; know when newspapers are "put to bed" and when TV must have footage for the evening news. Check to see that nothing else is scheduled in your community that would interfere. Consider whether you need to notify any other agencies or organizations of the event (you may wish to invite individuals from outside your institution to participate). Try to notify media 24 hours in advance, though breaking events usually don't allow for that luxury. If there are to be any restrictions on the event, communicate them in writing prior to the press conference.

■ *Preplan still-photo opportunities.* Know that media photographers will be looking for photo opportunities, so think in advance what image of your institution (people, places, etc.) you would like to see on the front page of tomorrow's paper.

■ *Maintain a sense of humor and professional dignity.* Institutional representatives who talk with the media, particularly in front of television cameras, should dress professionally and convey a dignified, helpful attitude. Mussed clothing, frantic speech—anything that says you or your institution are not in control—will have negative results.

Those handling details of the crisis may want to keep notes of day-to-day activities, jotting down vital information. These notes may be useful after the crisis, in recalling the events and in planning how to deal with any future problems.

After the Crisis

After the crisis, it is important to have a debriefing. Gather together those people involved in handling the crisis. Discuss mistakes and how to correct them in the future, and review those things that worked well. Consider writing an article, a paper, or some other record of the crisis to benefit others who will face similar circumstances in the future.

● ● ●
In most cases, the more that is known and the quicker it is explained, the less intense and serious a crisis will seem.

An institution also may want to edit, revise, or change in some way its plans for handling crises. The lessons learned during a specific crisis can give members of an educational community a new perspective on what their needs and concerns may be in certain pressured situations.

When the worst of a crisis is over, media relations personnel should send notes of appreciation to those who were of service during the crisis, both outside and inside the institution. Notes of thanks to your own staff are also important. People who perform well in crises deserve to be recognized.

Additionally, you may wish to send a note to a reporter or two whose coverage of the crisis was exceptional. Reporters do not need to be thanked for doing their job. But media representatives who were fair and unbiased, and who went out of their way to tell the story of the crisis appropriately, might well appreciate a note sent directly to them, specifically delineating what you believe to be a mark of professionalism in their work.

Unfortunately, a crisis situation may mean that those handling it have to abandon other work temporarily to focus on its resolution. So you may need to apologize to individuals whose correspondence, projects, or other work you had to temporarily lay aside.

Crisis situations have a way of bringing personnel together and back to reality. Crises remind us that most of the time we exist in fortunate circumstances, that we are privileged to do the work we do, and that sometimes things are not as bad in our day-to-day work as we may have thought.

It is a rare institution that has gone through a crisis and is not better for the experience. Campuses that have experienced violence usually are safer places afterward and personnel are more vigilant. Institutions that have suffered financial loss usually put in place methods to prevent future loss. Schools that have had personnel who conduct themselves improperly usually remove those people and are more careful about whom they hire or appoint in the future. Staff at institutions experiencing crises resulting from acts of nature—hurricane, tornado, earthquake—certainly can do nothing to prevent recurrence. But they do have the knowledge that the institution is more important than the crisis and that it continues and survives, even if wounded. In every crisis, the institution must be proactive and responsive, never passive or in paralysis. Institutions are stronger than events that plague them. They need to act accordingly.

Given the choice, none of us would choose to endure another crisis, no matter how much we learn. Those who have endured intense crises believe the word should probably be spelled more accurately as "cry-sis" but feeling the institution's pain means those who endured the crisis truly care and have done their best. Ultimately, that is all that any professional can do.

FURTHER READINGS

Ahles, Catherine B. "Handle With Care—Student Affairs Crises Require Extra-Gentle Management Strategies," CURRENTS 25, no. 6 (June 1999): 32-37.

"Campuses Under Siege: The Author of a New Book on Campus Crises Talks About the Stories Behind the Scandals—and Offers Advice on How to Head Off the Same Mistakes," CURRENTS 23, no. 5 (May 1997): 28-30.

Footlick, Jerrold K. "Doing the Right Things: In Times of Crisis, Campuses Should Be as Open With the Media as Possible—and That Requires Skillful Public Relations," CURRENTS 23, no. 5 (May 1997): 31-34.

Footlick, Jerrold K. *Truth and Consequences: How American Colleges and Universities Respond Publicly to Crises*. Phoenix, AZ: ACE/Oryx Press, 1997.

Larson, Wendy Ann. *When Crisis Strikes on Campus*. Washington, DC: Council for Advancement and Support of Education and the University of Florida, 1994.

Lukaszewski, James E. "Establishing Individual and Corporate Crisis Communication Standards: The Principles and Protocols," *Public Relations Quarterly* 42, no. 3 (Fall 1997): 7-14.

Internal communications matters. In fact, it is one of the most powerful means a university has to create a genuine community from internal constituencies that may differ considerably in gender, ethnicity, educational background, responsibilities, aspirations, and expectations.

Internal Communications: Creating a Community

Judith Turner Phair
Vice President for Institutional Advancement
University of Maryland Biotechnology Institute

The day was sunny and mild—perfect for a campus open house welcoming prospective students and their parents. Some had undoubtedly been lured by admissions materials sporting a catchy new slogan linking this prestigious—but not household-word—university to the nation's elite. What campus administrators didn't expect was a demonstration outside the admissions office by a group of students protesting the new slogan. More than 2,000 brightly-colored posters, appearing across campus overnight, declared similar sentiments.

The marketing message—penned with the help of an outside firm—had effectively reached external audiences, but an important internal constituency had been left in the cold. They hadn't participated in the process, didn't buy into it, and were not about to keep their displeasure under wraps. Poor internal communications were torpedoing an expensive new recruitment campaign.

Meanwhile, in another part of the country, a state university system had just finished negotiations with the top candidate for the presidency of one of its member campuses. The bargaining was tough, and the final salary was considerably higher than the new recruit's predecessor—and higher than that of any other president in the system. A press conference announced the new president, but not his salary. A local paper, however, found the magic number, and included the information in its story. The other presidents and the key members of the state legislature who were currently considering the system's budget were surprised and angry to get the news first from the media. A chance to celebrate the successful recruitment of a truly top-notch candidate had turned into an embarrassing occasion that could increase divisions between member campuses and presidents and imperil the higher education state budget—all because internal constituencies had been forgotten in the communications process.

Internal communications matters. In fact, it is one of the most powerful means a university has to create a genuine community from internal constituencies that may differ considerably in gender, ethnicity, educational background, responsibilities, aspirations, and expectations. When that sense of community exists, it can be the key to effectively communicating essential messages to the world outside. Internal audiences are our best ambassadors—and our loudest critics.

Forging an effective program of internal communications requires a clear understanding of why—as well as when and how. It calls for a structure that is interactive, personal, organized, and flexible, with full commitment coming from the top down. Like all good public relations programs, it is rooted in research and nurtured by constant monitoring and evaluation. It utilizes the latest technology—and some of the oldest means of communication as well. Most importantly, an effective internal communications program must be an integral and equal part of an overall institutional communications plan.

INTERNAL COMMUNICATIONS BEGINS WITH RESEARCH

Research consistently shows the value of internal communications. A 1999 study by The Hay Group, a multinational management consulting firm, examined more than 75 key components of employee satisfaction and discovered a clear link between employee satisfaction and the communication skills of an organization's top leadership. Bruce Pfau, Hay's research practice leader and managing director, says, "Our findings confirm what many leadership experts have been saying for years. Leaders must create a clear, compelling business vision and provide the work force with consistent feedback on where the organization stands relative to that vision." Peter Fleischer, director of Ketchum's Global Workplace Communication Practice, hailed the findings as "a powerful new tool" for showing that effective communications win employee support. "More companies are beginning to understand the connection between culture and business performance... Communication ... is the responsibility of top leadership," he adds.

Similarly, *PR Tactics* reported in its May 1998 issue that, among critical areas outlined in a survey of 259 major U.S. corporations on best practices in internal communication, were communication of leadership with all levels, involvement of internal audiences in the communications process, and recognition and celebration of internal audiences.

These studies confirm the results of countless other research studies over the years. Internal communications makes a difference. It must come from the top. It must be an integral part of a com-

munications program. And it must be grounded in an atmosphere of trust.

How can an institution build a new model of internal communications or make an existing program better? Again, research must set the agenda. Colleges and universities have a more complicated internal communications task than most corporations, because the internal audiences are so widespread and complex and the channels for delivering messages, and receiving messages, so varied.

DEFINING COMPLEX AUDIENCES IS CRITICAL

The internal audiences of a typical educational institution are complex combinations of widely disparate socioeconomic groups of varying educational achievement," points out M. Fredric Volkmann in *Excellence in Advancement* (Aspen Publishers, Inc., 1988). Indeed they are. Administrators, students, faculty, staff, alumni, donors, and boards of regents or trustees are key groups. Others may include prospective students and their families, members of the local community, and state legislators. As Volkmann also notes, these groups may vary greatly in terms of needs, expectations, and biases. Territoriality can play a role, too. The University of Maryland, in its 1997 study, *Promoting Open Communication: Improving Internal Communication at the University of Maryland*, chronicled some significant challenges to internal communication, including variations in literacy levels (some staff members could not read English; some had no reading skills in any language); diverse locations of campus units; and territoriality. As the report explained, "Our large university of loosely coupled, semi-autonomous colleges, schools, and departments naturally promotes an identification with unit or discipline, at the expense of university-level identification."

TIMING, METHOD ARE KEYS TO EFFECTIVE DELIVERY

Clearly, to reach such disparate audiences, an internal communications program must be multi-faceted, based on the needs and wants of various constituencies. An examination of when internal communications does, and should, occur, can provide important guidelines for tailoring messages and choosing the right vehicles for the process.

Internal communications occurs most commonly in these situations:

■ Daily information—a parking lot is closed because of construction, open enrollment begins for health benefits, a major speaker is visiting the campus, an open house will take place for prospective students;

■ Crisis—there has been a crime on campus, the president is resigning, the director of the foundation is under investigation, students are occupying the president's office, a case of racial/gender/sexual orientation discrimination has occurred;

■ Big news—a new president has been selected, a national news magazine has given top ranking to a department or school, a faculty member has won the Nobel Prize, an alumnus has given a sizable gift to the university;

■ Critical issues—the administration needs to correct misperceptions, counter rumors, or present a point of view.

The most effective mode of communication may differ according to the situation and the audience. Indeed, the ways to communicate in each of these situations with internal audiences are greater than ever before—but so are the expectations and sophistication of these audiences. One-way communication may be sufficient in some instances, but contemporary audiences want to be more than passive receptacles of information from above. They want timely information from credible sources, and they want to be heard from as well as to hear. As reported in the May 1998 issue of *PR Tactics*, "face to face must be the backbone of a communications program...communicators need to harness and feed the 'grapevine.'"

A look at the rapidly-growing options for internal communications, from e-mail, electronic discussion groups, and Intranet to the more traditional modes, offers expanded opportunities to match audiences, situations, and messages to greatest advantage. Increasingly, the faculty/staff newsletter has been labeled "outmoded" by some critics. *The Wall Street Journal*, in a March 1997 article headlined "Employee Newsletters Are Rapidly Becoming Obsolete," cited the increased use of other communications tools, such as internal

TV, e-mail, and faxes, to inform employees. But most public relations professionals are not ready to consign the newsletter to obsolescence. Instead, many institutions are adapting this "workhorse" to supplement and complement other communications vehicles.

E-mail and Intranet newsletters are one adaptation especially suited to breaking news. Still, these cannot completely replace a publication that can be carried from place to place, brought home to family members, and read by employees who do not have ready access to computers. The format of the traditional newsletter also lends itself to the more detailed story and to human-interest material. It is sent to the consumer—it doesn't require action on the consumer's part to access it, as do Intranet newsletters. In its study, the University of Maryland found its printed weekly newsletter, *Outlook*, particularly effective for routine communications and for spotlighting important university messages on critical issues. In fact, a separate research survey on the newsletter indicated that 83 percent of the faculty and staff surveyed had seen the publication in the past three months, and 71 percent had read at least some of it. The university survey disclosed that, while the newsletter was not always considered the most credible source of information, it was the most widely read source.

MEDIA MIX REACHES MAXIMUM AUDIENCES

Ellen Kindle, vice president of internal communication, BancOne Corporation, makes another compelling argument for a mix of media in an internal communications program. As she notes, "As far as replacing print communication...our experience has shown us that you can never drive your employee communication down a single channel. Some people are paper learners and some learn from video."(*PR Tactics*, May 1997).

Student-run media, including the student newspaper, radio, and television stations, are also important vehicles for communicating with internal audiences in all situations. Experienced campus communicators know the value of treating student media as professionals, according them the same respect and responsiveness as that given to the daily press.

For routine communications, other appropriate media may include campus bulletin boards, inserts in pay envelopes, and posters, along with e-mail and Web-based communications. In a crisis, immediacy is of utmost importance. It has been well documented that people remember best the first version they hear of a story. Thus, unless you want your students, faculty, staff, alumni, and others to have their initial impressions formed by the report on the 6 p.m. news, it is imperative that you get the word to them first. In this instance, advancements in technology have left little excuse for slipping up with inside audiences. A crisis is the time to bring numerous vehicles into play to reach large numbers concurrently, to ensure message consistency, and to counter rumor, misperception, and misinformation. E-mail, fax, bulletins on internal radio and TV stations, "push technology" (messages that appear without prompting on the computer screen), telephone "hot lines," and broadcast voice may all be brought into play. Many of these same vehicles are equally adaptable to "big news" stories (although one large university experienced some faculty backlash for "invasion of privacy" when it used broadcast voice—technology that sends the same message to the voice mail of every telephone on campus—to promote a symposium).

● ● ●

In a crisis, immediacy is of utmost importance. . . . Unless you want your students, faculty, staff, alumni, and others to have their initial impressions formed by the report on the 6 p.m. news, it is imperative that you get the word to them first.

KEEPING THE PERSONAL TOUCH IN AN ERA OF TECHNOLOGICAL DOMINANCE

While these new ways to communicate with internal audiences should make this function easier and more effective than ever, there are a few drawbacks that have, indeed, been exacerbated in our era of instant information. First, although the modes of communication have proliferated, most are still passive. They require the receiver to seek out information, and they offer no means of response. In an increasingly impersonal age, when e-mail communication has, for many, replaced the telephone call or the personal visit, internal audiences may feel more alienated than ever from university leadership. More than ever, two-way, personal contact must be a key component of a successful college or university internal communications effort.

Fortunately, many campuses are recognizing the need for their important internal audiences to feel connected and they are responding in a variety of ways. Several hold periodic "town meetings" to discuss key issues. Parents' associations and alumni groups have open meetings with university leadership on "hot topics." Savvy presidents meet weekly or semi-weekly with student media representatives. The University of Maryland study urged the adoption of a series of "Celebrate Maryland" events with required participation by campus leadership. Many campuses have also implemented special events and programs that thank and recognize internal audiences for their efforts. Some presidents schedule "open house" hours for all comers each week, or set up interactive e-mail dialogues at pre-announced times.

Effective internal communications is, finally, active as well as reactive. Many institutional advancement leaders credit old-fashioned "walking around" and paying attention to signs in halls; conversations among students, faculty, and staff; and the reading and viewing habits of their colleagues with providing the best cues to current and emerging concerns and the best modes of communication. Observation, responsiveness, and the commitment of key leadership are all critical elements in crafting an effective internal communications program that will thrive in an environment of trust and confidence.

REFERENCES

Anderson, C. "Crisis Communication on the Intranet," *PR Tactics* (May 1997): 15.

"Are Employee Newsletters Rapidly Becoming Obsolete?" *PR Tactics* (May 1997): 30.

"Best Practices in Internal Communication," *PR Tactics* (May 1998): 10.

Boyle, M. "Internal PR Vital to Staff Retention," *PR Week* (March 8, 1999): 1.

Council for Advancement and Support of Education. *Creating Campus Community: A CASE Issues Paper for Advancement Professionals,* No. 10. Washington, DC: Council for Advancement and Support of Education, 1992.

Davidson, M., Chair, University of Maryland Continuous Improvement Team. *Promoting Open Communication:*

Improving Internal Communication at the University of Maryland (study). December 15, 1997.

Denbow, Terry. "Breaking Out of the Box: How to Stop Closing Yourself Off from Reality," CURRENTS 17, no. 2 (February 1991): 6-10.

"Employee Newsletters Are Rapidly Becoming Obsolete," *Wall Street Journal* (March 24, 1997): 1.

Hale, Don. "High-Tech PR: Five Case Studies in Computerized Communications: A Campuswide Network Helps Carnegie Mellon Shop Around for Better Internal Communications," CURRENTS 19, no. 4 (April 1993): 18-19.

Hollander, Cohen & McBride. *University of Maryland Outlook Study,* February 1997.

Shoemaker, Donna. "They Pledge Allegiance: PR People and Their Presidents Tell How They Forge a Bond Through Open, Honest Communication," CURRENTS 19, no. 9 (October 1993): 20-23.

Stubbee, Melinda. "The FAQs on Intranets: You've Heard of These Hot New Tools. Now Consider Whether Building One Can Make Internal Communication on Your Campus Easier, Faster, and Cheaper," CURRENTS 23, no. 7 (July/August 1997): 18-20, 22.

Volkmann, M. Fredric. "Public Relations Begin at Home: Why Good Internal Communications are Vital." In *Excellence in Advancement.* Edited by W.W. Tromble. Gaithersburg, MD: Aspen Publishers, Inc., 1998.

Your job in creating an identity system is to provide consistent visual and verbal stimuli to help your constituents form an image in line with the image that your institution wishes to have.

Image and Institutional Identity

Jan Pruitt Duvall
Associate Director of University Relations and
Director of Marketing Communications
The University of Alabama

Jeffrey T. Hermann
University Editor and Director of Publications
The Pennsylvania State University

Ever since Transylvanian potters began inscribing their pots with their personal marks 7,000 years ago, humans have been using "logos" to mark their products. The practice continued in one form or another through history into the 15th and 16th centuries, when craftsmen guilds began to use symbols to represent the professional qualifications needed to perform a particular skill. Identifying products with visual marks continued into the Industrial Revolution when corporations began to use symbols to represent an entire business.

Today, logos are one part of overall identity systems that are intended to convey at a glance the individuality, traditions, and mission of a corporation or institution. Visually, the logo must be easy to reproduce in a variety of media, from business cards to the Internet, and it must balance modern design trends with the timelessness necessary to gain recognition with the intended customers or audience. In addition to the logo, graphic identity systems include consistent editorial style guides, color palates, and other common elements. These and many other factors of identity work together to form an image of the institution.

What is image? In *Institutional Image: How to Define, Improve, Market It*, Bob Topor says that an institution's image "consists of many individual sets of perceptions in the minds of its constituents. Your constituents, of course, are many—the alumni, faculty, students, donors, legislators, staff members and the general public, etc. Each of these constituents—past, present, and future—has formed, or will form, an image based on many stimuli." Your job in creating an identity system is to provide consistent visual and verbal stimuli to help your constituents form an image in line with the image that your institution wishes to have.

Not every institution has a formal graphic identity system. Some are reaching the students they want, receiving the donations they want, and generally happy with what the public says about them—and all of this without an institutional logo. However, those institutions are few. Most institutions want more, or better, students, to increase their endowment or state appropriation, and to improve the image of their worth among the public. These institutions need to coordinate their planning into one overarching mission for the future, and to coordinate their visual and editorial messages into one that reflects the institutional mission and traditions. Most institutions need a graphic identity.

HOW TO ESTABLISH AN INSTITUTIONAL GRAPHIC IDENTITY: FINDING THE FIT

Within the halls of academe, there exists a deep-seated but crumbling resistance to applying the language of commerce to the operations of educational institutions. Referring to students as "customers" deserving of "first-class service" is certain to draw ridicule from at least some members of the faculty and staff. However, they likely would endorse the idea that every student should be treated with courtesy and equity by an efficient staff and a challenging, expert faculty. Similarly, upon surveying the competition faced by your campus for students, funding, and donors, they might have no hesitation in declaring, "We need to do a better job of marketing our institution! We need to be telling our story!"

And therein lie the good news and the bad news. Our institutions increasingly recognize the need for marketing. But they are inclined to think of it as merely promotion or advertising, rather than "the analysis, planning, implementation, and control of carefully formulated programs designed to bring about voluntary exchanges of values with target markets for the purpose of achieving organizational objectives," as marketing expert Robert A. Sevier puts it.

Still, the good news outweighs the bad. Recognizing the necessity of marketing can provide a starting point from which to introduce the full spectrum of integrated marketing to our campuses. The call for your institution's story to be told can be answered with the practice of integrated marketing communication, founded on a strong institutional image made cohesive and memorable through unifying graphic standards.

Setting the Agenda

As your campus's marketing communications officer (by whatever title), you have the responsibility to ensure that your institution's written and online communications present a cohesive, positive, and accurate image. In almost all institutions, that responsibility must be fulfilled through a process of collaboration and negotiation with colleagues in all divisions across the campus, starting at the top.

If your CEO and his or her executive council do not realize the importance to your campus of a cohesive visual identity, make it your mission to bring institutional image to their agenda and recommend the process by which it can be improved. Will your administrators be inclined to invest in the beginning step of that process, which is the assessment of your current graphic image? In their foundational 1979 work on communication auditing, *Auditing Organizational Communication Systems: The ICA Communication Audit.* (Kendall/Hunt Publishing Company, 1979), Gerald Goldhaber and Donald Rogers caution:

> The results and recommendations of a communication audit will be useful to an administrator if (and only if) at least two of these three conditions are met: (1) the college must be under pressure to improve its performance (2) the college must be faced with the problem of coordinating (and controlling) complex operations, and (3) the college must have the slack resources (time, money, and people) to support an intensive diagnosis of its condition.

Any attempt to develop and implement a visual identity program across an institution must have the support of the highest levels of administration if it is to succeed. The reality of turn-of-the-millennium educational life is that Goldhaber and Rogers's first two motivational conditions are compelling givens for most institutions. Competition for students, funding, and gifts, coupled with ever-mounting public and donor demands for accountability, require continually improved performance. As technological options multiply the ways in which courses are offered and internal procedures conducted, the operations that institutions must coordinate and control are increasingly complex.

"Slack resources" is today an alien concept to most campus communications professionals, so perhaps the third condition should be updated to " recognizing the necessity of the most effective use of all resources," a need universally clear to competent executives. By presenting pertinent case studies, you can help your leaders understand that marketing is an essential

As your campus's marketing communications officer (by whatever title), you have the responsibility to ensure that your institution's written and online communications present a cohesive, positive, and accurate image.

way to, in institutional advancement professional Larry Lauer's apt phrase, "mobilize, not commercialize" your institution, and that an appropriate and memorable graphic identity is one key to such mobilization. Good sources of such studies are CURRENTS and the proceedings of the American Marketing Association's annual symposia on higher education marketing.

Develop a graphic identity only if your administration is willing to invest personnel hours, money, or at least its blessing. A variety of institutions have used the following steps to develop successful and compelling visual identities.

Discovering Together Where We Are

While executive support of the graphic identity program is a prerequisite for success, it is by no means a guarantee. For a graphic identity program to be appropriate and long-lasting, people at every level in the institution must have a part in its creation and understand the reasons for, if not embracing, at least complying with the standards. As Carole A. Custer summarized to the 1996 American Marketing Association symposium on marketing higher education, the graphic identity program must be research-based and represent the integral university rather than the current administration or a single department.

This does not mean that an identity system should be created through a design contest or ratified by campus referendum. (Under no circumstances should either be done! If suggested, follow marketing consultant Patti Crane's advice to a client at the University of Alabama in August 1998, and make the point that your visual identity is as real an asset as your financial base. Then ask whether your institution would hold a contest to decide how to invest your endowment.) Instead, the process should begin with a commission from your president to assemble a representative group to assess your campus's marketing communications position and practices, and to make recommendations regarding its improvement, including a particular focus on visual identity.

This group's composition will vary from institution to institution. In a recent effort at The University of Alabama, the "marketing council" included all vice-presidents, the athletic director,

the university registrar and head of admissions, the director of university relations, the director of publications, the director of media relations, the head of licensing, the dean of the college of continuing studies, a professor of marketing from the business school, a representative of the faculty senate, the director of university relations for the University of Alabama system, the secretary to the board of trustees, the university lobbyist, and the director of the alumni association.

The assessment group must carry out or direct three kinds of research to assess and enhance the institution's graphic identity and overall marketing communications program. These include: 1) a publications inventory (a version of a communications audit); 2) quantitative research dealing with targeted market segments; and 3) qualitative research with internal and external constituencies.

Conducting the publications inventory will be the major hands-on task of the assessment group. The process is simple but time-consuming for everyone involved, and because of its magnitude is best carried out over a period of months. Gather and review an example of, and information about, publications produced by every division of your college or university. For this inventory, "publication" is defined as print, online, video, broadcast, and specialty items such as T-shirts, pencils, and mugs.

Steps for carrying out the inventory and review are as follows, according to the *1989 Report of the Publications Review Board* by Penn State's Department of University Publications:

1. Send to all department heads a memorandum from the president asking for a copy of every publication, including stationery and business cards, to be sent to the chair of the assessment group by a given date at least eight weeks in the future. Include a reproducible information sheet for the purpose of gathering information about the purpose, frequency, audience, and cost of each piece.

2. As the pieces come in, key-number the sheets and attachments and enter the information into a database.

3. Once the material is catalogued, with database summary sheets in hand, begin a series of three to five monthly, day-long meetings of your

group to review the submissions for content and quality, noting any duplications or gaps in information across the institution.

4. Once your review is complete, send data print-outs to your senior administrators to review for accuracy and completeness in their reporting channels. Allow them at least a month to review the information and return their amendments to you.

5. When amended information is received, convene the group in a series of meetings to discuss it in light of the results of the qualitative and quantitative research. Within three months, issue recommendations for revising institutional image by implementing cohesive institutional messages and graphic standards in publications.

The publications inventory will help you assess the messages your institution is sending out through its various paid materials. The inventory should be done by a balanced group of volunteer personnel to avoid any appearance of bias by one area of the institution. However, other research initiatives should be commissioned by the group but carried out by professional research teams because of time, resources, and techniques that must be employed to achieve optimal results.

Such professional teams may be found easily on your campus, whether it's faculty members working through on-campus institutes or pertinent classes looking for projects to carry out. This research may be costly, but it is essential if you want to develop a graphic identity that is truly reflective of the institution's values, and is truly responsive to its communication needs. Quantitative and qualitative research should be carried out with the first half of the publications review timeline so that all results will be available for synthesis simultaneously.

Quantitative research into the targeted audience's attitudes toward, and impressions of, your institution will outline the messages your various publics are receiving. Cover as broad a spectrum as possible within your budget, but concentrate on the constituencies most important to you: prospective students, current students, prospective donors, alumni, and so on. Work with your researchers to create a survey instrument to assess the perception

of your institution's quality and value.

Qualitative research will help clearly define your institution's strengths and values that can most effectively differentiate your campus from its competitors. Be sure that every type and level of institutional personnel are included in the focus groups. In addition to setting up groups that are representative of your personnel in race, gender, and length of time with the institution, issue an open invitation for anyone who would like to participate. These groups are the avenue through which employees will have input into the new graphic identity. It is important that all employees are represented, and that they know they are. Throughout the research phase, communicate across campus through every available medium to let everyone know where the process stands. Remind them they can contribute through focus group participation or messages to you by note, telephone, or e-mail.

Creating the System

Once the program intelligence is gathered, you are ready to begin design of the new system.

Inside or Out?

Should you use in-house designers or hire an outside agency for this crucial task? Either method can yield successful results, and agency work on identity programs can seem prohibitively expensive. However, there are several advantages to choosing an experienced outside agency.

■ The agency's staff members come to the work with fresh eyes and the ability to assimilate the research results without preconceived notions of how your institution should be represented.

■ They are able to concentrate their time on your project without the ongoing responsibilities and distractions your in-house staff members face.

■ They are experienced in the creation of stationery systems and can apply that prior knowledge to the construction of your system, avoiding pitfalls that might not be obvious to less specifically experienced designers.

On the down side, while the actual costs will be roughly the same once personnel time and opportunity costs are factored in, a payment to an outside agency is a possible target for media scrutiny, particularly for public institutions. Consider which of these factors have the greatest import for your situation and decide accordingly. Choose whether you will stay with inside talent or call on external expertise before commissioning your research, since some agencies offer research capabilities and would want to participate in gathering the qualitative data that informs their work.

Who Can Say No?

Design by committee is not design at all—it is mutation. While some genetic mutations have happy results, that fortunate circumstance seldom extends to designs subjected to tinkering. For this reason, it is important to pare down the number of people on campus whose "no" can stop the adoption of a design on the basis of personal preference rather than concern that the design does not meet the agreed-upon, research-distilled objectives. .

Your assessment group, in concert with the president, should have the initial approval of the design to be presented to the campus community. While you and other members of the group might react to sketches during the design process, do not ask to be shown two or three designs among which to choose, and do not offer that option to the rest of the community. Your designers should use their professional expertise to create the elements that best meet the objectives for your graphic design program. Therefore, the key question to ask when assessing a proposed design is not, "Do I like it?" but "Does it work to represent my institution as having the values we defined?" It is perfectly all right to send your designers back to the drawing board, but only after articulating to them how the impact of their design falls short of your stated objectives.

Once you agree on the design, show it to campus opinion leaders, including your deans and those who participated in the focus groups. Outline the principles and show how the design meets the objectives. Attend to their comments and enlist their aid in testing the letterhead design. Particularly if you are changing stationery formats, enlist the help of those opinion leaders and their staff assistants in testing the new one. Going from a centered design to an off-center one, or changing to one whose first and second sheets use different margins, can be very difficult for many individuals. Provide test users with 50 sheets of generic stationery in the new design and ask them to give you their comments after three days of working with it. This can go a long way toward defusing the anxiety of change, as well as discovering if there are flaws in the system that should be addressed before it is released campus wide.

INTRODUCING THE NEW LOOK TO CAMPUS

While this true story is more instructive to public than private institutions, it bears repeating:

In the mid-1980s, a public university in the West paid an agency $29,000 to create a new graphic identity. The resulting work was unveiled to great fanfare while the state legislature was in session just down the street. The legislators got wind of the payment, became incensed at the perceived waste of the taxpayers' money, and cut the university's appropriation by—can you guess?—$29,000.

Think of your institution's new graphic identity as the equivalent of an individual sporting a perfect haircut while wearing his or her sharpest suit. The desired effect is not that he or she will be stopped on the street and asked where the cut or the clothes were acquired and how much they cost, but that people will look at that individual and think, "Wow! What a great-looking person! I'll bet he/she is not only well-dressed, but also intelligent, compassionate, principled, and fun."

The same is true of the "new clothes" of an identity program. Its creation is not news, just a normal part of carrying on the institution's operations. Don't throw a party for it. Introduce it as a working tool by putting it in the hands of every departmental secretary and department head, accompanied by a manual and letter from the president stating the expectations for its use. Disseminate it widely on campus and off, and through the Web. While you may encounter some resistance to the new standards, keep everyone informed of the process to ease assimilation.

HOW TO KEEP IT GOING

You have put countless hours and dollars into conceiving and launching your institutional identity system. But how do you keep it going? A host of factors may make consistent implementation of your identity system difficult. Maybe some staff or faculty members don't agree with the need for the system. Maybe a department head wants to maintain her own departmental identity. And maybe others, for whatever reasons, just don't like the logo. What can you do?

Stay Focused

Make sure the administration stays focused on the identity. Your president and top administration have been paying a lot of attention during the development and launching of your identity and now that it has been announced, they assume they can get back to the business at hand. Well, they can't. Now more than ever, effort from the top is needed during the period when the identity takes root. The identity program will either become an intrinsic part of the institution or sputter and die. When an identity system dies, it is usually because it is not properly managed or supported, not because there are those who don't like the logo.

To properly manage the identity, you need to put someone in charge of it. Many times this is the vice president for university relations because that is where most communications and graphic departments report. The administrator responsible for the identity system should assign a staff member to implement the graphic identity. This person will take care of myriad tasks that deal with stationery and signage. However, the vice president should concentrate on the larger issues of identity and should be the voice within the president's cabinet reminding everyone what the goals are, and how to stay focused.

Create a Manual

To successfully launch and maintain an identity system, you must create a graphic standards manual. This manual should include all of the rules for logo usage, as well as examples of stationery, signage,

publications, advertisements, vehicle identification, and so on. While the manual should be printed with enough inks to accurately show the color(s) needed to reproduce the logo, it should not be so expensive that wide distribution is prohibitive. Often, identity manuals wind up on administrator's shelves and not in the hands of printers, sign makers, and others who need the guidelines to make the system work.

Put the manual on your Web site for use by the majority of people, and then print enough copies to distribute to suppliers and others outside of the institution who may not have access to the Web. The Web, of course, affords an easy distribution for camera-ready copies of the logo.

Be Flexible

The graphic system itself should be flexible. For example, while the institution should have specific official colors, do not mandate that the logo always appear in these colors. This will limit the designers who create the communications, and will incur added expense. Imagine if your school colors were gold and green and every brochure had to either be printed in gold and green, or you had to bear the added cost of those two colors in every brochure.

A common misperception about identity systems is that all brochures must be designed to look exactly the same. Systems that demand this type of conformity risk boring the designers and not reaching their target audiences.

A brochure that would appeal to a prospective engineering student is not likely to appeal to one who is interested in the art department.

Any identity manager should understand that the various departments and units have individual needs. Even with thorough planning and research, not everything will have been thought of when your system is introduced. There will be a federally-funded center that must use the logo of the Department of the Interior on all of its communications. Rather than telling this center, "Sorry, all individual departments must use the standard institutional stationery," you should listen

> **Your president and top administration have been paying a lot of attention during the development and launching of your identity and now that it has been announced, they assume they can get back to the business at hand. Well, they can't.**

to why they need to have some visual connection with the Washington funding agency. If the need is real, first determine which should be the dominant symbol and then work out a special design that uses both logos. However, you must be consistent. If one person or department gets an exception or special design, have a rationale you can apply to a similar situation that arises later. More to the point, be able to explain why one department was special and another one was not.

Remember that every institution evolves over time and the graphic identity system should, too. Colors, graphic elements, and signage all need to be changeable with styles and fashion of the times. In some cases, the business cards and stationery may also need to be redesigned to fit organizational changes.

REFRESHING AN INSTITUTIONAL IDENTITY

Developing and implementing a graphic identity program takes many months, even years, depending on the size and complexity of your institution. Given the investment in time and resources necessary to create a system and put it in place, why would you choose to change a thoughtfully established graphic identity? Why risk losing brand equity by changing recognized symbols?

Robert Sevier identifies two, and only two, reasons for taking this drastic step. First, if the look you have isn't working to communicate the finest values and aspirations of your campus, either because your institution has undergone a major realignment of mission or because the marketplace has changed, then it is time for your graphics to change as well. Second, if a particular opportunity such as a signal anniversary, a name change, or a special event provides an opportunity to energize your campus and share that energy with your constituents, then it may be time to freshen a dated look.

However, some of the most frequently encountered reasons for change (three cited by Carole Custer: "the new president just doesn't like the logo/wants her own stationery design/says his wife doesn't like the color") are not valid and should be resisted at all cost. When confronted with such reasons, take a deep breath. Then share with the person making the request or issuing the order the thorough process by which your institution's graphic standards were set and how your current program expresses your institutional values. Mention that a strong brand identity is the first step in keeping a favorable position in the market.

And hang in there!

REFERENCES

Custer, Carole A. "So, Someone Thinks You Need a New Logo for Your University?: A Research-Based Approach Used at a Public University." Proceedings of the 1996 Symposium for the Marketing of Higher Education. Chicago, IL: American Marketing Association, 1996.

Goldhaber, Gerald M. and Donald P. Rogers. *Auditing Organizational Communication Systems: The ICA Communication Audit*. Dubuque, IA: Kendall/Hunt Publishing Company, 1979.

Hermann, Jeffrey. "Report of the Publications Review Board" (May 26, 1989) The Pennsylvania State University Department of Publications. (Handout)

Lauer, Larry D. Presentation to CASE Leadership Summit. Toronto, Canada. (March 13, 1999.)

Sevier, Robert A. and Robert E. Johnson, eds. *Integrated Marketing Communication—A Practical Guide to Developing Comprehensive Communication Strategies*. Washington, DC: Council for Advancement and Support of Education, 1999.

Sevier, Robert A. *Integrated Marketing for Colleges, Universities, and Schools: A Step-by-Step Planning Guide*. Washington, DC: Council for Advancement and Support of Education, 1998.

Topor, Robert. *Institutional Image: How to Define, Improve, Market It*. Washington, DC: Council for Advancement and Support of Education, 1986.

The advent of desktop editorial and design tools, digital printing techniques, and Internet publishing completely changed the publications office in a single decade.

Publications: A New Chapter

Albert C. Friedman
Director, University Publications
University of Wisconsin-Madison

The traditional campus publications office would be enjoying a slow and natural evolution, satisfying to both the studious editor and the contemplative designer, if not for simultaneous and major changes in the publishing industry. The advent of desktop editorial and design tools, digital printing techniques, and Internet publishing completely changed the publications office in a single decade.

While all of these technological shifts were occurring in the 1990s, the environment in which campus publications are created was undergoing dramatic change as well. Today, institutions are approaching planning, funding, and student and faculty recruitment with increasingly sophisticated strategies. Many campuses now realize the need to employ strategic planning, which in turn results in integrated marketing and communication plans that greatly affect publications.

Outside our institutions, a number of other trends have had an impact on both campuses and our publications offices. One is the Total Quality Management movement, parts of which have become embedded in the way we work. Through quality management and process improvement,

many publications offices now participate in planning, perhaps at higher levels than before. As an outgrowth of TQM's focus on satisfying customers, it is almost impossible to convene a committee today without some discussion of surveys, focus groups, and the need for more data. Publications offices have always needed this kind of information but seldom received it in the past. We are now less isolated and have more information about core institutional projects.

A second influential trend is the networked office (and campus). Writing, editing, and design still take human time—but the networked office has greatly enhanced production output steps.

A third trend is the speed that society now demands. People expect to receive information when they want it, and quickly. Even though desktop publishing and the early "publishing-on-demand" efforts never exactly delivered on this front, the Internet has. Internet publishing, in whatever primordial form it is in today, positions the communications office to meet people's need for information when and where they want it.

New management and analytical techniques, as well as supporting technologies, have been put in place to do the job. Given all these changes, what is the job of the publications office, and the publications professional, today?

To a certain extent, the job is unchanged. The traditional work of writing, editing, designing, and printing is still at the core of publications' mission and role. Even so, the sphere in which the publications office operates has, to a great and happy degree, broadened. While the changes mentioned above might make things confusing at times, the times are filled with opportunity. To take advantage of those opportunities, we in publications must be sure we're doing the right things. Asking yourself the questions that follow is vital to making sure your office functions wisely and well, both in the way you structure your mission and role, and in how you handle basic publications practices.

STRUCTURAL QUESTIONS

1. What is the mission of your publications office? This question is crucial. Obviously, at the core is responsibility for traditional projects related to student recruitment, alumni affairs, development, the president's office, and, on larger campuses, freestanding divisions ranging from libraries to the arts.

But much has changed, fortunately, since the days when publication offices were merely brochure publishers. In settings where campuses have implemented strategic planning and integrated marketing approaches, publications offices' missions must expand to include involvement in these new areas as well as Web publishing.

To check your mission, ask a simple question: If you were going to establish, or even fund, a publication office on your campus, what would you have it do? Answer the question as if you were your boss; as if you were the college president or school head. If you are not sure how he or she would answer, your mission is not clear. If this is the case, you must clarify your mission. The mission might be so narrow as to include only traditional publications work. Ideally, the accepted mission for a publications office is to participate in communications at many levels. Where a publications office was once pigeonholed as the purveyor of a finite set of materials, opportunities now exist to do much more.

2. What is the role of your publications office? If your mission is understood, you and your campus must understand your role in implementation. The role of the office relates to exactly how and what is done by the publications staff. Think about questions like these to explore the roles for your office:

- *To what extent should your publications office be involved in market research?* Is there a market research group available on campus? If so, you need not fill that role. Can you lead an effort to get students in a marketing class to conduct research for you? Perhaps you can be on a team designing the research project. If others are conducting the research, it is important to receive the results in a timely manner, establishing your office as a customer of the research team. The publications office should always be aware of student and alumni surveys and focus groups. Making your data needs known will put you at the table when the decisions are being made.

- *To what extent should your publications staff be involved in campus marketing overall?* Knowing what activities are being launched on behalf of the alumni should dovetail with messages aimed at prospective students. Without being directly involved in every program, a publications office still needs to know what populations are being targeted, by whom, and what vehicles are being used. This not only helps refine the messages, but also can reduce duplication and prevent over-solicitation. Most publications offices have a breadth of campus knowledge and experience and have much to offer the overall marketing effort.

- *What is the publications office's role with the Web?* Who takes responsibility for the institution's World Wide Web presence can be a source of conflict. Though many principles of design, production, and publishing are transferable to the Web, some campuses do not involve publications offices in Web planning at all. At the other end of the spectrum, some publications offices have primary oversight of Web content. Though struggles may ensue over who is involved in certain decisions and activities, ultimately it is as important to know the division of labor among offices as it is to know the division of labor within an office. Ideally, the publications office will be responsible for, and funded for, maintaining core institutional publications on the Web. Other roles may include developing Web templates, style guides, and helpful links.

3. What should your publications office do when the workload grows? If institutional expectations of your office do not match your mission, and particularly your roles, this confusion can create conflict. For example, if you're in a small office where responsibility is limited to a finite set of materials, what happens when additional offices expect service? Feeling obligated to serve each and every campus customer (which is common) generally creates over-commitment problems. Then everything suffers. Though the solution is complicated, you can resolve these situations only through clarification and good internal communication.

A major cause of over-commitment is the institutional desire to keep control of all publications. However, outsourcing is perfectly acceptable as long as your publications office does the main work the institution expects. Rather than committing to any and every project, it is best to know what is within your mission and excel at those projects. Skillful, carefully chosen freelance writers, editors, designers, and production people can do the rest.

An alternative to outsourcing is to set up a charge-back operation and ask various campus offices to pay fees for service. Though it is complicated to operate a business within an office (and not something that every editor and designer can or should be able to do), establishing a charge-back operation allows the publications office to guarantee institutional standards in a setting where responsibility and demand are growing. In the interest of adding value (and not cost), institutional or administrative publications may be done best internally. The purpose of the charge-back is only to gain the staff and equipment necessary to meet the campus needs—not to make money.

Charge-back systems can work well as long as

> ● ● ●
>
> **In settings where campuses have implemented strategic planning and integrated marketing approaches, publications offices' missions must expand to include involvement in these new areas as well as Web publishing.**

campus clients don't view them as a deterrent to publishing. By charging fees, an institution tacitly discourages the production of lesser or frivolous materials. Yet getting information published or disseminated is of utmost importance to campus departments large and small. It is always best for the publications professional to be a facilitator of communication, not a prohibitor. If the project cannot run through the publications office, offer suggestions for how and where else it might be done.

4. Should your publications office be centralized or decentralized? Each way has its advantages and disadvantages.

The main advantage of centralization is control. From an institutional perspective, it is important to have an identifiable office responsible for "official" publications and Web pages. While everything an institution publishes may be considered official, unquestionably, there are core institutional materials that must be managed most responsibly to meet the campus's highest standards of quality.

In addition to being an identifiable place where faculty, staff, and sometimes students can come for help, a central publications operation provides many value-added services. Foremost is the publication professional's role as a consultant, particularly in an integrated marketing environment. Having early involvement of a central publications staff can increase quality and effectiveness and reduce time, work, and cost.

In addition, centralized publications professionals will be aware of other departments involved in or producing similar materials, edit and design materials according to applicable standards, and attend to legal details (such as copyright, affirmative action statements and the Americans with Disabilities Act.) They will also manage the production schedule, text development, photo selection, final editing, and in some cases, printing. Finally, they will make sure appropriate materials are archived in hard copy and digital format. Access to digital versions of materials is important for historical and practical reasons, particularly since so many materials are updated on an annual or ongoing basis.

The advantages of a decentralized office mirror the disadvantages of the centralized one. The centralized staff will, by necessity, place lower priority on non-institutional projects. Especially on large campuses, lesser units may grow impatient with their rank. They see publications assistance as something they can easily buy from the private sector. What's more, they may be happier with timetables they can control and products they can target to the audiences they feel they know best.

Even on decentralized campuses, a central publications office must concern itself with ensuring that everything that goes out over the campus's name adheres to institutional identity and quality standards. In larger settings, a main publications office can co-exist with other decentralized offices. Coordination among unrelated offices can have good results with good internal communication. At its worst, it can be an acrimonious effort with minimal results.

So, centralized or decentralized? Your institution's highest-level executives must decide the kinds of publication services to provide, the extent of centralization, and the authority of the publications office. Access to and dissemination of information are at the core of any corporate entity. Underestimating the importance of this activity inevitably leads to reduced effectiveness in the communications arena.

GOOD-PRACTICE QUESTIONS

Here are six good questions to ask about any publication project.

1. Who is your audience?

Unfortunately, too often the answer to this question is, "Everyone." This is usually the first indication that no one has thought about this question. The text and design depend on an audience. Without an audience, text and design are weakened.

In addition to knowing the target audience, you must also answer such questions as: what do readers need to know now? What should they do as a result? How can they get more information? Is this a stand-alone booklet or part of a family of publications that readers will see? If it's part of a family, how important is institutional identity? Is there a Web equivalent of this information that needs to be coordinated to serve readers better?

2. What's the best way to fit content to the audience?

When developing content, first find out as much as possible about the reader's need for information. Staff can often develop responses based on the most common requests they receive. At other times, audience expectations are not as well known. In either case, the design and substance of the response have great importance. Always make sure your communication is appropriate and consistent with your image.

For example, a prospect who expresses interest in making a major gift will be disappointed with an impersonal postcard thanking him for his interest. A student wanting basic information about a particular major might be overwhelmed if she receives an entire course catalog. To the greatest extent possible, you must tailor publications, including Web pages, to the audience.

Some budgets do not permit multiple, stratified publications. Such programs are forced by budget and staff realities to have a single, general brochure. This solution is common enough, and fairly effective—provided that you give the reader an address or phone number for more information. In smaller programs where this is the case, personal attention tends to be in greater supply and most effective in closing the communications loop.

If you have the budget, segmenting your target populations is ideal for matching audience to content. True, segmenting audiences and creating specific messages requires more resources, more research, and thorough evaluation—but the results justify all three. Recent graduates may have different feelings about their alma mater than the class of 1950. Finding out what those differences are and speaking meaningfully to each audience is well worth the effort when you get a bigger response.

Alumni, as a finite and known population, are generally easier to segment and categorize than prospective students. Assuming that the best admissions prospects have much in common with already-enrolled students, many campuses create general recruitment publications to reflect their current-student profile. If your campus decides instead to segment your recruitment publications for a diverse prospective population, you'll have to do more strategic planning. This goes well beyond the realm of traditional publications planning. If you approach business and community leaders, high school personnel, and parents in a concerted effort to interest new students, each group (leaders, counselors, parents, and students) may well require separate communications and publications. In an integrated marketing environment, your campus may employ special community-development activities supported by news, publications, and Web pages.

● ● ●

Delivering a well-planned orientation program booklet to a vice president for human resources can give the publications office the most important kind of internal visibility.

3. What's the best way to handle design?

A strong institutional look maximizes your institution's visual identity. This doesn't mean that the entire family of publications must all look the same. If they do, the materials (printed or electronic) become indistinguishable from one another and confuse the institution as well as the audiences. To combine unity and diversity, vary your publications' size, format, color, and medium, but standardize other visual cues, such as paper, typefaces, and recognizable graphic identity standards.

4. What's the best format for any given information—and what's the role of the Web?

As already mentioned, some campuses may not have the luxury of creating as many materials as they would like. In this case, a general brochure is the answer. But beware of the omnibus publication—the giant catalog of everything there is to know (regardless of whether it was requested or not). Not only are these kinds of publications expensive to produce and distribute, but they are also difficult to keep up-to-date. Publications planners should remember to consider the hidden costs of staff time elsewhere on campus when such a compendium is proposed. Every time departments are asked to submit or approve text, it consumes staff time in each office.

Web usage has already changed the ways many campuses manage institutional documents. The initial rush to put information on the Web caused many publications offices to post electronically the same materials they produced in printed form. In many cases, these long text documents contained few useful links and failed to fit the needs of the new medium and new users. But as Web use increases and matures, institutions are now creating texts specifically for Web sites.

To strengthen the relationship between printed and Web publications, many publications professionals are developing posters and shorter brochures to promote Web sites where readers can gain access to specific information on demand.

While printed materials will always have their place, the growing sophistication of Web development and improved content will make the Web the primary source of information in many instances. The publications professional, in collaboration with information technology professionals, has much to offer in the design and organization of Web products. Just as with conventional materials, the publications staff should weigh in on everything from creating reader-friendly design to maintaining good production values, always asking, "Is this the best way to convey this information?"

5. Are you paying enough attention to internal communications?

Never forget the importance of internal communications, which too often is relegated to the second tier. The complete publications professional, as a communications specialist, will always advocate internal communication and coordination first and not let external needs detract from quality internal materials. After all, good internal communications sets the stage for good external communications. A better informed and enfranchised faculty and staff will help spread positive messages. Without their help, the burden falls on too few shoulders.

The Web has had a tremendously positive impact on what you can provide to internal audiences and the speed with which messages can be disseminated. Much internal information, such as directories, employment rules, benefits books, and orientation information, is suited perfectly for Web publishing. This is one area where electronic publishing has shown definite early benefits in terms of service to a specific audience as well as significant savings in document management and printing.

Of course, you'll also want to promote campus initiatives and events on both the campus Web site and in the campus newspaper. While the Web may someday eclipse the student and campus tabloids, newsprint is still a primary source for many readers. Over time, internal communications may favor electronic media, but this needs to be phased in carefully.

There is yet another advantage in making internal communications a high priority. Participating in and adding value to internal programs put your publications office in closer contact with appreciative campus executives. Delivering a well-planned orientation program booklet to a vice president for human resources can give the publications office the most important kind of internal visibility. That vice president's positive, firsthand experience with your staff will help determine your reputation and credibility level—supporting or negating impressions elsewhere on campus.

FINAL THOUGHTS ON POSITIONING YOUR OFFICE

Building a sound internal reputation is the only reliable means of making sure that your publications office enjoys the support it needs. Regardless of whether campus units use your office, the goal is to be so good that they want to use your office—not just for production but for other marketing services and advice as well.

The emergence of the new technologies puts your publications office in an odd position. You must use the most advanced techniques to write, design, and print your campus's materials. Your staff will feel justifiably proud of being on top of the latest technologies. But few outside the publications office will care which layout program you use, if you take a file to the printer via cab or send it electronically, or whether you print the job offset or on a plateless digital press. In fact, the more opaque these methods are to the client, the better. Discussing technology and technique only tends to pigeonhole

your publications office as a conduit to printing.

Answering the questions raised in this chapter should help you accomplish a major goal: to break away from traditional perceptions, and position your publications office as an indispensable part of internal and external communications. Every time your institution develops a communication project and assembles the team, your publications staff should be there at the beginning—not just at the end when the brochure is needed. The sooner your campus executives recognize your broad expertise, the sooner your publications office will be part of the integrated marketing team that is, and will be, so necessary to campuses.

FURTHER READINGS

Arden, Kelvin J. and William J. Whalen. *Your Guide to Effective Publications: A Handbook for Campus Publications Professionals.* Washington, DC: Council for Advancement and Support of Education, 1991.

Benson, Mary Ellen. "A Jury of Their Peers—Let Focus Groups of High School Students Be the True Judge of Your Recruitment Publications," CURRENTS 25, no. 2 (February 1999): 44-49.

Sevier, Robert A. *Integrated Marketing for Colleges, Universities, and Schools: A Step-by Step Planning Guide.* Washington, DC: Council for Advancement and Support of Education, 1998.

Sevier, Robert A. and Robert E. Johnson, eds. *Integrated Marketing Communication: A Practical Guide to Developing Comprehensive Communication Strategies.* Washington, DC: Council for Advancement and Support of Education, 1999.

Worley, Karen. "Herding Cats—Nine Incentives to Keep Your Publications Team Purring," CURRENTS 25, no. 7 (July/August 1999): 40-44.

Ziegler, Ed. "By Leaps and Bounds; How to Stop Wasting Time, Set Your Priorities, and Soar to Success in the Publications Office," CURRENTS 19, no. 3 (March 1993): 38.

OTHER RESOURCES

Publish: The Magazine for Electronic Publishing Professionals. Subscriber Services, P.O. Box 2002, Skokie, IL 60076-7902. *www.publish.com.*

Fast Company, a magazine on business and marketing trends with a Web focus. Subscriptions available online at *www.fastcompany.com.*

"Cause/Effect," which provides information resources on college and university campuses. Educause, 4772, Walnut Street #206, Boulder, CO 80301-2538. *www.educause.edu.*

A periodical's presence on the Web can show that an institution is technologically progressive and attuned to changes in reader habits. Few editors predict, however, that online periodicals will replace their print counterparts.

Periodicals: Sources of Information and Inspiration

Patricia Ann LaSalle

Associate Vice President and Executive Director of Public Affairs and Editor, *SMU Magazine*

Southern Methodist University

Throughout the history of periodical publishing in higher education, editors have faced two basic challenges: telling the institution's story in a compelling way and appealing to audiences with varying levels of interest in that story. Within those two challenges fall most of the other issues that periodicals editors confront today, from crafting the content of periodicals with freedom and integrity to developing a format that is effective and affordable.

Today, however, any discussion of college and university periodicals also must include consideration of "strategic communication" or "integrated marketing," which attempt to put reason and research behind communication efforts and to implement them consistently throughout the institution.

Discussing periodicals within this context may suggest that integrated marketing themes should direct or control content. But if a periodical lives up to its role effectively, quite the opposite is true. Because effective marketing of complex institutions requires providing not only information but also interpretation, periodicals play a vital role in an institution's efforts to be understood.

Periodicals support an institution's marketing efforts by providing regular communication in a consistent format that helps to build a relationship between reader and institution. To nurture the relationship, the periodical can contain different types of content, ranging from short news articles to longer features. In this way, the periodical offers many avenues of entry into the institution's story, capturing readers who have differing amounts of time and interest to invest. A review of commercial periodicals shows that success on the newsstand depends on this reader-friendly approach. Institutional periodicals must compete for attention in the same crowded marketplace of information and ideas.

The most important way in which periodicals complement marketing efforts is through the quality and range of content presented. Content must be based upon sound journalistic principles and practices of full reporting and excellent writing. Many planners of periodicals mistakenly presume that readers will have an innate interest in their publications simply because the audience has some connection with the institution. To the contrary, familiarity often can breed a lack of interest, simply because constituents may assume they already know the institution. A certain amount of nostalgia among alumni may be desirable, but alumni whose knowledge of the institution is limited to their "good old days" are questionable ambassadors for the institution today. They are unlikely to understand the current realities of higher education.

Because most periodicals use newspaper or commercial magazine formats, they present information in a manner that is familiar to audiences and that conveys a sense of importance. Within these journalistic formats, however, institutional periodicals fail or succeed depending on their substance. Content that is overtly promotional betrays the medium of the periodical and fails, ultimately, to build trust among readers. Periodicals that are balanced and believable advance an institution's credibility. They use both substance and style to show, not merely tell about, the institution's strengths. They build support based upon reality. That is why periodicals—whether produced by an independent alumni association or by the institution's office of public relations—are so essential to an institution's marketing efforts.

THE SEARCH FOR SUBSTANCE

Providing content that is balanced and compelling requires a journalist's curiosity. The periodical editor must be able to look inside and around every corner of the institution to find stories worthy of being told. The search for substance requires avid reading of almost everything the institution publishes, from student newspapers to academic catalogs to every manner of Web site. It requires making personal visits to professors and department heads, as well as top-level administrators and student leaders.

If the institution has a strategic plan, there is abundant material not only about what the institution desires to be, but what changes are taking place toward that end. Visiting classes and attending lectures by faculty not only will uncover provocative topics, but also will identify those who clearly present their subject matter and will make good sources of material. By reviewing reports of new and ongoing research projects, the editor often will find topics with high reader appeal because the subjects provide insights into issues both timely and timeless. No matter what the organizational structure of an institution's advancement function, editors should become fast friends with

those who handle media relations. It is the job of these professionals to find the kind of stories that will appeal to reporters, and by extension the readers of periodicals.

In addition, becoming involved in campus activities can put the editor in touch with the ideas and issues of today's students. The greatest guarantee of a periodical's vitality is the editor's curiosity. The editor is an insider who must maintain the mindset of the outsider—ever inquisitive, even skeptical. The result should be a periodical that becomes a microcosm of the institution—intellectually alive, ever progressing, varied in perspectives—and thus worthy of symbolizing the high calling of education.

A MATTER OF MISSION

An important first step for periodical editors is to write a mission statement, a document that can provide a framework for developing content and making editorial decisions. One university with a strong history of excellence in periodicals includes in its mission statement three little words that are full of meaning: "informed good will."

In their mission statements, the most effective periodicals often reaffirm the traditional roles of periodicals: keeping readers informed about the institution and in touch with each other by sharing news of their achievements. But they do not stop there. What distinguishes the best periodicals—and best advances their institutions—is that they also portray the intellectual vitality of the institution and serve as sources of continuing education to alumni and other readers. By viewing themselves as an extension of the academic enterprise, many periodicals today keep alumni in touch with the institution not merely through news of events but through the exchange of ideas that forms the core of education. In this way, magazines can boost alumni pride, not through blatant promotion, but with the communication of quality through substantive content. In this way, too, a periodical becomes a source of knowledge helping readers to understand the world in which we live.

COVERING CONTROVERSY

A well-developed mission statement can be a valuable tool for maintaining integrity. It can help to obtain buy-in for balanced reporting among chief advancement officials and enable editors to exercise editorial freedom when it is most needed.

The fight for editorial freedom gained its greatest impetus during the 1960s, when protests on campus brought higher education issues to the front pages of newspapers and the top of the evening news. Once the ivory tower stood under the glare of national attention, it was difficult for institutional officials to turn off the light. Instead, wise administrators encouraged campus editors to tell the full story, often covered only partially or sensationally by the media.

Today, editors must continue to remind administrators that once an issue is public, there is no place to hide. If an institution's problem has been reported widely in the media, the institution is best served by presenting the issue in a balanced way—presenting the situation, explaining what is being done to address it, and showing how the issue fits within the larger context of higher education. An important point to remember is that negative news is seldom limited to one institution. Usually problems are part of a broader issue that must be addressed nationally as well as locally. Inviting readers to become partners in that awareness and participants in constructive dialogue serves both them and the institution.

Editors must exercise good judgment, of course, to avoid publicizing transient issues that may well be solved before the periodical even reaches its audience (this is a consideration especially if the periodical comes out only quarterly). What deserve attention are those matters that represent important issues, not petty grievances.

A periodical that covers negative news with balance achieves four important aims:

1. It shows that the institution is strong enough to admit and face its problems, establishing the groundwork for reform.
2. It provides a fuller account of complex dilemmas that the media may cover only superficially. (And in an information void, rumors usually fill the gap.)
3. It places the current situation into a perspective that will enhance reader understanding—and patience—as solutions are sought.

4. It upholds the integrity of the academy, showing alumni and others that it is worthy of their trust and support.

Editorial freedom remains a concern among editors nationwide. In 1998, more than 150 editors and publication managers adopted a "Statement of Professional Standards" aimed at addressing the issue. It reads, "An effective publication balances good news and bad news, popular and unpopular views, as it informs readers about the institution, continues their education, and invites their participation in the life of the institution."

THE CAMPAIGN CHALLENGE

Another issue for editors today is the advent of mega-million and multi-billion-dollar capital campaigns. When the stakes are high, the tension over content tends to rise. During a capital campaign, for example, administrators can become fearful that negative news will derail donor support. Editors respond that campaign time is precisely the time to promote fuller understanding of issues among constituents, especially donors. The academy simply cannot stop being what it is—a place of competing ideas—during capital campaigns. In fact, during such times, enlightened development officers can use balanced reporting as the basis for conversing with donors about issues and controversies. If they are equipped with key points about the institution's position developed by public relations colleagues, they can put issues into perspective for the donor and move on to discuss institutional needs.

Editors and development officers also must find common ground regarding development content in periodicals. There is no question that periodicals have an indirect impact on development. The nature of that relationship, however, requires dialogue between editors and development officers. For example, although periodicals can run ads raising awareness about the annual fund or the campaign, they are not vehicles for raising money. As part of campaign planning, editors and fund raisers should discuss the appropriate role for the campus periodical during campaigns and what other communications vehicles can best serve the campaign's marketing needs.

Many periodicals take a journalistic approach to development—they report on campaign kick-offs and major gifts just as they would any other institutional news. As the campaign funds new academic programs, areas of research, or services for students, the editor can develop feature stories on those topics.

Some periodicals devote a clearly labeled section to reporting campaign news and running donor profiles. This approach enables periodicals to keep alumni and donor audiences up-to-date on the campaign, while retaining the editorial integrity of the overall publication. In all cases, balance is the key. The function of campaign communications in its own right deserves careful planning, staffing, and funding. Effective marketing of campaigns often requires special newsletters to target audiences identified as crucial to the campaign, along with other communications strategies. If this planning occurs and these vehicles are developed, periodicals can publicize campaigns in a manner consistent with their own mission. In this way, they can complement campaign communications and best serve the needs of the entire institution.

Editors commonly use the cultivation metaphor to explain their relationship with the fund-raising function: They prepare the ground for development officers to plant the seeds and harvest the fruit. Communicators spend years cultivating donors by providing information, generating interest, and building trust. Especially during a campaign's "quiet phase," the periodical can be an important tool for creating a climate conducive to fund raising. Out of this fertile ground comes involvement and investment—but not by sacrificing integrity.

FORM AND FUNCTION

When it comes to choosing a medium for our messages, many editors argue that the wrapping on the package sends its own signal. In some ways, the format will determine the periodical's function—whether it will be a quick-read summary or an in-depth examination of the institution's life. And the message must fit the medium.

Because they are the most restrictive of for-mats, newsletters should best be reserved for special-interest audiences—constituents of a particular institute or center within the institution. They offer fast turnaround and flexibility in frequency, but their format is insufficient for comprehensive coverage. Newsletters can, however, serve as effective supplements to longer turnaround periodicals such as magazines.

When one institution became involved in a major national controversy, campus editors knew that the quarterly magazine could not be produced quickly enough to give alumni much-needed updates of information and, in some cases, clarifications of inaccurate reports in the media. To fill this communications need, editors developed an interim newsletter with the latest information. They used the quarterly magazine to summarize developments, to publish different points of view on the controversy and needed reforms, and to talk about the institution's problems within the national context.

In the realm of alumni relations, many institutions have found that reunion newsletters can be a helpful complement to their magazines because the newsletters can contain timelier and more detailed information on specific events for a targeted audience. Few institutions publish newsletters as their major periodical for alumni, donors, and other friends.

Most often, the format of choice for periodical publishing is the magazine or tabloid.

Editors who have adopted a magazine format believe that magazines give their messages both impact and permanence. In the deluge of daily mail, magazines are more likely to be noticed, kept, and displayed. What they lack in timeliness, magazines gain in their ability to cover developments in depth and with perspective.

Magazines also offer higher reproduction quality, with sharp color, slick paper, and more opportunity for creative graphic treatments. Institutional magazines also enjoy prestige by association because most popular consumer periodicals also use a magazine format. In addition, a 1988 study of alumni periodicals by Donna Shoemaker at the University of Maryland found that the magazine format was

● ● ●
Today, editors must continue to remind administrators that once an issue is public, there is no place to hide.

used most frequently by highly competitive institutions.

The magazine format demands, however, that content be able to stand the test of time. Because the magazine format takes more staff and money to produce, its content must be worth the added expense. Some institutions seeking the prestige of publishing a magazine make a common mistake by skimping on content. The versatility of the magazine format accommodates a wide range of copy: regular sections with smaller news items, news features, and longer, provocative articles and essays. If smaller news items dominate the magazine, however, the institution is actually publishing a newsletter under false pretenses. A magazine format does not a magazine make. Some magazines make the added mistake of letting complicated graphic treatments overshadow content, as if visual flash can disguise verbal shallowness. Readers are not fooled, however. Many may think, rightfully, that the institution is wasting its money.

The tabloid format offers versatility at a much lower cost than magazines. The cost factor may enable the institution to publish a tabloid more frequently than it would produce a magazine, giving the institution more opportunities to build reader loyalty. Tabloids may be less likely to be displayed on a coffee table, but they have the advantage of connoting timeliness and immediacy. Although magazines may be kept for later, as the "later pile" grows, chances grow smaller that they ever will be read.

Many editors have made their tabloids as comprehensive as the best magazines by adopting the so-called "magapaper" or "tabzine" approach. The format may be technically a tabloid, and the paper stock may be newsprint, but the content is not limited to small news items. The first page is treated as a cover, with a full-page photo or other graphic treatment, and the tabloid opens to reveal fully developed feature-length articles along with typical tabloid fare. Some of the most compelling and provocative periodicals in education today are tabloids produced by talented editors who enable content to transcend format.

As editors continue to face cost issues, some are publishing tabloids to supplement magazines, using both formats to achieve frequency in their communications. No matter what the format,

however, periodicals must represent the highest professional standards—in planning, writing, editing, and design—to reflect the quality and character of the institutions they represent. Although desktop publishing provides the technical tools for design, it cannot supply the talent. The best periodicals employ a staff of professionals to handle all areas of the publication. The results speak for themselves.

RAISING REVENUE

As postage and printing costs rise, editors today often must become entrepreneurs, developing their own resources to maintain quality and frequency. One way to supplement institutional funds is through a voluntary subscription program, which asks readers to send an established amount as a contribution to the periodical each year. A voluntary subscription program works best with periodicals that are high enough in quality to have established a strong core of loyal readers. The question each institution must ask is whether and how its constituencies will respond to fund raising from the campus periodical along with the annual fund and other development efforts.

At first glance, advertising may seem to be an untapped source of big dollars for periodicals, and some major magazines in particular have mined that source with success. Most editors should, however, proceed with caution. To attract advertising, editors must collect current demographic information on their audiences and prepare a sales kit that makes the case to prospective advertisers. A periodical's circulation and reader characteristics will determine the types of advertisements that might be obtained, from national-brand ads at one end of the spectrum to campus-based ads on the other. Magazines that are a standard size, carry four-color throughout the publication, and are printed on glossy, high-quality paper are more likely to attract advertising, but these factors also add to production costs. In addition, the periodical that is serious about advertising must have adequate staff to handle marketing, sales, and billing. Because of the investment of resources necessary, advertising is not a quick or easy solution for generating revenue.

One of the most vexing advertising issues

confronting editors is how carrying ads for commercial enterprises will affect postal rates for their periodicals. For example, to qualify for some non-profit rates, editors should avoid ads for credit cards, travel services, or in some cases insurance services—all products likely to be offered by a typical alumni association. Because post offices in different regions may not make uniform rulings on what is allowed, editors must conduct careful research before entering the advertising arena. In all cases, editors must consider the character and tone of their periodicals to decide whether advertising fits into that framework.

THE NEXT GENERATION

As online communication becomes more prevalent, many periodicals are appearing on the electronic page. The online periodical offers several advantages: regular updates of content, including class notes; reader interaction; and concise information with hyperlinks for those who want fuller information. In addition, a periodical's presence on the Web can show that an institution is technologically progressive and attuned to changes in reader habits. Few editors predict, however, that online periodicals will replace their print counterparts. Not everyone uses the Internet, and restricting communication to that medium could exclude in particular the oldest (and most loyal) alumni. To many readers, a communications vehicle that can be held and felt, is small and foldable, and is transportable to any room in the house remains a medium not to be abandoned.

With traditional periodicals, the institution reaches out to its constituents, but with online communications, the process is reversed. In using that medium alone, the message could be: "You must come to us for information." Just as radio survived television, and motion picture theaters flourish along with VCR players, online periodicals will co-exist with and complement print versions.

To remain successful, periodicals must change along with the institutions they represent

and the audiences they serve. Continued progress for periodicals will require ongoing audience research and other evaluations of their effectiveness in attracting attention and generating interest. As they compete with commercial enterprises for attention and with nonprofit organizations for support, institutions are becoming more savvy about marketing. Making the institution's case will require a strategic new mix of communications tools. But the basic principles of quality and integrity will continue to separate the winners from the losers in the quest for understanding. Carefully managed and creatively produced, the periodical will remain a major source of information and under the best of editors, even inspiration, whether in print or online.

REFERENCES

College and University Editors, online discussion group: Rachel Morton, Middlebury College; Sally Atwood, Bucknell University; June Davidson, Dalhousie University; Barb Chamberlain, Washington State University; Alfonso Pena, Millersville University; January 1999.

"The Editor and the Fund Raiser: Partners or Adversaries?" CURRENTS 25, no. 4 (April 1999): 42-45.

"Entering the High-Tech Page: Can you Afford to Put Your Alumni Magazine Online?" CURRENTS 23, no. 7 (July/Aug 1998).

"Finding the Perfect Fit: Use These 15 Questions to Determine the Advertising Program That's Just Right for Your Magazine," CURRENTS 23, no. 7 (July/Aug 1998).

LaSalle, Patricia Ann. *College and University Magazines: Building Credibility to Advance Your Institution.* Washington, DC: Council for Advancement and Support of Education, 1991.

McLellan, Jeff. "Moving Mountains—Outsourcing Can Help Even the Smallest Publications Accomplish Great Things," CURRENTS 26, no. 5 (May/June 2000): 32-38.

Proceedings, Panel Discussion: Editorial Independence. CASE meeting, Washington, DC, December 1998.

Shoemaker, Donna, "Alumni Periodical Goals, Resources, and Quality: A Study of the Perceptions of Campus Editors, Alumni Professionals, and Journalism Educators." (Master's Thesis), University of Maryland, 1988.

You can't welcome the media with open arms for good stories and brush them off for the bad ones. If you do, you will suddenly find that there is no more interest in your stories.

Media Relations: Successfully Positioning Your Institution

Dick Jones
Principal
Dick Jones Communications

Years ago, my friend and co-worker, Mike Ramsey, was at his desk at the *Lewistown (Pa.) Sentinel* when the phone rang. On the line was an old man from a rural part of the county.

"Why don't you ever write a story about Lumber City?" the man demanded. "What's going on in Lumber City?" Mike asked. "It's just a wonderful town," the man explained, "full of wonderful people." Pressed for specifics, he could offer none.

We had a flexible definition of news at the *Sentinel* but this failed to meet our modest standards. Of course, the paper ran no story on the wonders of Lumber City.

I think of this when I hear a college president or dean who wants media attention "because this is a fine place with dedicated faculty and good students." I think to myself, "Lumber City." Yes, it's true. When you're pitching stories to news organizations, it helps measurably to be able to offer them news. Fortunately all colleges and universities are loaded with news and opportunities for media coverage. Media attention provides windows through which readers, listeners, and viewers can learn about the institution.

Media attention, however, is an inexact prism. While media coverage shows some part of the institutional story, it rarely reveals it all. That's what frustrates presidents and deans. They want to tell the whole story, preferably in *The New York Times*, on page one, above the fold.

Despite its limitations, media relations is a critically important element of an integrated marketing strategy. Here's why:

■ Media visibility is a third-party endorsement of importance and quality. It is not seen as the institution talking about itself. These are outside validators quoting your expert professors and profiling your innovative financial aid program.

■ Media attention helps develop name recognition. I once heard an admissions dean say, "Students rarely apply if they haven't heard of our school before they receive our publications."

■ Media recognition builds support among key publics. Donors view it as a sign that they are backing a winner. Trustees and alumni leaders feel the same. Employees—faculty and staff— see it as a validator of their choice of employer.

Small schools—those whose football teams do not appear on television on Saturday—particularly need a good media relations program.

Sara Kirkland, vice president for university relations at Susquehanna University, once told me that smaller institutions have to pass the supermarket checkout line test. That's when two mothers are in line with their groceries. One asks the other where her daughter plans to go to college. "When she replies 'Siwash,' she doesn't want to have to explain to her friend that Siwash is a small, private, liberal arts college in Ohio," said Kirkland. "She wants her friend to say, 'Oh, yes, I've heard about that school.'" Media relations can help with that task.

Finding the Stories

In general, there are two categories of news stories. One is where you create an agenda in the media for a story. The second involves plugging your institution into the media's existing agenda. Both are important elements of a media relations plan.

Plugging into the media's agenda is the easier of the two tasks. The requirements include solid news judgment and the ability to find appropriate faculty experts willing to cooperate with journalists on news stories.

Keeping slightly ahead of the news is not difficult. When an election approaches, reporters are in the market for political scientists to comment. When the stock market dips or soars, an economist who can make sense of it can find herself quoted in the newspaper. The calendar yields annual events that never seem to be overdone in the media. Before Christmas, the nutrition professor who tells us how to keep from gaining weight during the holidays suddenly finds herself talking to reporters. The physical therapy prof who can comment on the effects of snow shoveling on the lower back finds his phone ringing on the day of the first six-inch snowfall.

Chase's Calendar of Events is a good investment for a campus PR shop. By consulting this reference, you can learn, for example, that the Great American Smokeout is November 18 and prepare your experts well in advance for media opportunities.

In our office, we say that there are two qualifications for faculty members to be considered experts. First, the professors have to know what they're talking about. Second, they have to be will-

ing to answer their phone (or e-mail). Media relations specialists soon learn that some faculty who are well-qualified to speak on subjects of interest are reluctant to do so. These bashful experts can sometimes be brought on board. Some never can. It's up to the campus media relations professionals to find and encourage those faculty and administrators who will help.

The stories where you have to create an agenda in the media—in other words, convince an editor or broadcast producer that your story is newsworthy—are more difficult to sell. The rewards for placement, however, are often greater. Among these stories are the "reputation-definers" that can set your institution apart in the marketplace. They also include the scholarship and research stories that highlight the substantive achievements of your faculty.

The line is blurring between teaching and research institutions. I know of no college, no matter how small, that does not have a cadre of faculty actively publishing in their disciplines and doing scholarship or research. Media relations professionals will want to review faculty publications for their potential. Those that have news value can be summarized in layman's terms and offered to media. Remember to interview the faculty member as well as to read her paper when preparing such news features. Often questions such as "What surprised you the most about these research results?" or "What did you find that goes against conventional wisdom on this subject?" can yield the angle or hook necessary to make a news story. Always allow the professor to review your draft for errors of fact or interpretation. This is good politics as well as a guarantor of accuracy. Once your media relations office gets a reputation for handling research stories well, the word spreads among the faculty and they are more willing to cooperate with you.

Every institution has, or should seek to have, one or more reputation-defining stories that sets it apart from competitors. The number of such stories is far less important than their quality. In other words, it's better to have one reputation-defining story that you can sell than to have six that cause the public to yawn.

Maybe your reputation-defining story is clear, as was the case for Lebanon Valley College in

Annville, Pa., in the early 1990s. The college designed a then-unique plan whereby high school seniors in the top 10 percent of their class were awarded half-tuition scholarships. Those in the top 20 percent got one-third tuition scholarships. Those from the top 30 percent earned one-quarter scholarships. Parents and prospective students loved it. It was easy to understand. The media liked it too, resulting in national wire stories, CNN coverage, and a favorable *Washington Post* editorial. Applications soared. Enrollment rose significantly along with the academic profile of the student body. Net tuition revenue increased.

More likely, however, the programs that your institution touts are not as easy to describe. In such situations the media relations office needs to do some serious thinking about how to highlight the institutional message. Mythical "Siwash," for example, might consider its core curriculum to be superior to those of its competitors. Your challenge is to tell Siwash's story in the news media, knowing full well that editors consider stories about core curricula to be slightly more effective sleep inducers than Sominex. What to do?

One approach is to position your institution as "advice-giver" to the world. Want to highlight that most of your junior class studies abroad? Then do an advice story aimed at parents and students on "the six essential things students must know before they study abroad" with your study-abroad coordinator as the source. Want to show that your core curriculum hasn't disregarded the western civilization classics as it has increased emphasis on non-western cultures? Try a 700-word newspaper opinion piece from the dean advising parents of prospective students about what they should look for in a college core curriculum for their children.

Few curricula, financial aid programs, internship opportunities, or student life emphases are truly unique. The good news is that they don't have to be unique to be newsworthy. Trend stories are proven vehicles. If you don't think the media will be excited by your institution's off-campus wilderness orientation program, then gather information from other campuses that have similar programs and sell the story to the education editor as a trend.

Be creative in finding angles, bumps, and hooks that will help people grasp whatever the college's reputation-defining stories are. Don't be like the man from Lumber City, laboring to sell a story about a "wonderful town with wonderful people."

Marketing the Stories

You have found the stories. One third of your task is done. The second leg of media relations' three-legged stool is calling the stories to the attention of media gatekeepers.

News Releases

The news release is the traditional vehicle for carrying information from the campus to the media. News releases can be useful. However, they are often misused or used in place of more efficacious communication vehicles. News releases should be employed for disseminating "spot" news such as the announcement of a new president or the fact that classes will be delayed due to a snow emergency. They are also useful for distributing routine information such as the dean's list, the concert and lecture series, and promotions and appointments of mid-level staff.

Many colleges overuse news releases. They develop mailing lists of editors and barrage them with every news release that they produce. Editors and broadcast news directors detest this approach. Anyone who has been in media relations for any length of time can tell tales about editors who throw away news releases unopened simply because, in the past, they have found little useful material in them. Journalists representing national media outlets often receive a daily stack of mail 12 inches tall, much of it news releases for which they have no use.

That's why the trend in media relations is toward personal contacts. It's axiomatic in communications theory that personal contact is the most effective way to achieve results.

Personal Contacts

Personal contact, of course, requires a commitment of time and energy that the simple production of news releases does not. The focus of a campus media relations operation should be on results rather than on production. Results-oriented offices will use visits to reporters and editors, personal letters (either snail mail or e-mail), and judiciously employed phone calls to reach the right people at media outlets.

When we have a story to sell, we ask three questions. What outlets would be interested in this? Who are the right people to contact at those outlets? How should we contact them?

Our own clients are sometimes surprised to find that we have no mailing lists. Instead, we build an individualized contact list for every story we market. When we send information to a journalist it's usually in the form of a personal letter. No mailing labels allowed.

How do you know whom to contact at media outlets? For local media, you can quickly learn the beat writers for the local paper, the TV assignment editors, and the radio news directors.

For media outside your area, there are reference guides that can tell you how to contact the architecture critic at the *Boston Globe*, or the producer for book authors at the "Today Show." Among these are *The News Media Yellow Book* by Leadership Directories, Inc., and *The National PR Pitch Book,* by Infocom Group. Weekly newsletters such as *Partyline, Contacts,* and *Bulldog Reporter* update PR practitioners on beat changes for reporters at national publications and broadcast and cable outlets. These references range in price from about $200 to $500.

You can build your own references, of course, and less expensively, simply by working the phones. In time, your Rolodex and your e-mail address book become your most trustworthy references. They will tell you which reporter prefers a letter before a phone call and vice versa, which ones like to do business by e-mail (a rapidly increasing number), and what the best times of the week, month, or year are to schedule visits with them.

A results orientation for a college media relations shop does not signal that you will be writing less. You simply will be writing smarter. In addition to news releases and their cousins—story tip sheets—you will be writing targeted personal letters to media gatekeepers, and corresponding on e-mail with journalists with fact sheets and situation backgrounders. Words on paper and words in cyberspace remain as important as they ever were.

Op/Eds

Every college should consider starting an op/ed program, if they don't already have one. Op/eds (so named because they traditionally are placed on the newspaper page opposite the editorial page) are short opinion articles. In the early 1990s, 800 words was a standard length for op/eds. Now the norm is 700 words and it is likely to get shorter still. Op/eds offer opportunities for faculty and administrators to lay out a complete argument. The dean of the business school can explain "why companies need more, not fewer, MBA graduates." The president can make his case for "a new model to finance higher education." Op/ed editors judge pieces on how well they are written and how newsworthy the subject seems to be. It's important that op/eds be offered to newspapers as finished products because they will usually be accepted or rejected just as submitted. Only rarely will an op/ed editor suggest changes. Keep in mind that the style of the op/ed is quite different from academic writing. In general, op/ed authors should state their views early in the article and back up opinions with facts, statistics, and anecdotes. Look for op/ed material in papers or books that faculty have written, in speeches by the president, and even among columnists in the student newspaper.

●●●

> I have worked with presidents who loved to talk with reporters and with those who would rather have gum surgery. There are times, however, when the president needs to tell the institution's story to the media face to face.

Face to Face

I have worked with presidents who loved to talk with reporters and with those who would rather have gum surgery. There are times, however, when the president needs to tell the institution's story to the media face to face.

Some institutions make good use of annual breakfast meetings with local journalists to give an informal "state of the college" presentation and to take questions from reporters. Media visits to the offices of journalists can be quite useful provided the president has one or more good stories to talk about. If the leader of the institution can carry some real news with her, she will be received well in the newsroom whether in your hometown or in New York or Washington. You may want to include media visits in the president's travel schedule to see legislators, alumni, or donors. You can often arrange a visit to a newspaper.

Presidents are often fond of news conferences. Reporters usually aren't. News conferences should be held for news of compelling interest and surpassing importance. If those criteria are not met, your president could be at the rostrum addressing one lone sophomore from the student newspaper. Presidents don't enjoy that experience and neither will you.

If the president wishes to ask a newspaper for editorial endorsement of an action or policy, the meeting must be arranged with the publication's editorial board. In such sessions, the president should expect questions from all members of the board, which can range from one or two persons at a small paper to five or six at a large one.

In general, assume that whatever your president says is "on the record" and may well turn up in tomorrow's newspaper or this evening's newscast.

The Internet

Technological innovations have enhanced the options for college media relations practitioners in creating and disseminating information. Use technology wisely, however. As Sam, the piano player in "Casablanca" reminds us, "the fundamental things apply, as time goes by." This means do not bury editors under a blizzard of faxes or e-mails any more than you should snow them under with snail mail. Nonetheless, for handling new sources and story ideas, journalists now rank the Internet second in importance, according to a 1998 Columbia University study. Magazine journalists rank the telephone as number one. Newspaper journalists put in-person contact at the top.

A number of "pay for play" sites have emerged on the World Wide Web and some of them are useful. ProfNet (*www.profnet.com*), a service run by PR Newswire whereby journalists post queries to college and university public relations offices, has proven to be an effective tool when plugging into the media's agenda. Institutions pay PR Newswire for the privilege of belonging to ProfNet and the rates are based on a campus's enrollment. Successful use of ProfNet depends on an institution's ability to monitor it closely and

respond quickly. Newswise (*www.newswise.com*) is another Internet service targeted to benefit beat writers in selected fields such as medicine, science, business, pop culture, and education. Colleges pay Newswise for the privilege of uploading stories that are then made available to journalists who cover those beats. The Darwinian rules of journalism dominate this realm as well, of course. Only interesting stories stand a chance of getting noticed. Dull stories don't. Upload only your most noteworthy stories.

The Internet is already important as a destination for news stories. It will become increasingly so in the future. Most campuses already post their best stories and features on their own Web site. Photos, video, and audio of faculty research, the construction of the new field house, and the homecoming parade will become commonplace in the future. Many institutions already allow grateful alumni to hear their football and basketball games via the Web.

Online publications already have significant reader/viewership, and they should be considered important outlets. Online editions of traditional media, such as newspapers, magazines, television, and cable networks are proliferating. The best way to reach the gatekeepers for these new media is by submitting newsworthy stories via personal contact.

Maximizing Media Relations Successes

You've found the stories and marketed them successfully. The third leg of the stool involves taking full advantage of the positive media visibility you receive. In the age of integrated marketing, this third step is equal in importance to the first two.

The proliferation of media, locally and nationally, means that your constituents and publics hold fewer media experiences in common. In 1970, the average television viewer received seven channels. Now the average is 47, according to a 1998 report by Media Dynamics, Inc. And according to the Radio Advertising Bureau (RAB), the big three television networks, CBS, NBC, and ABC, saw their prime-time audience fall by 42 percent between 1970 and 1997, as viewers fled to cable channels featuring narrow-cast programming on topics such as gardening, the weather, and history. As the century ended, the RAB noted that there were 12,472 radio stations in the United States compared to 6,175 in 1969. While the Newspaper Association of America reports that the number of U.S. daily newspapers declined from 1,748 in 1970 to 1,509 in 1997, most of those papers have developed online editions, effectively adding to the number of information outlets.

Even if *The New York Times* and "ABC World News Tonight" run a story on your college on the same day, many of your constituents will miss it. So you need to call it to their attention. When you do, they will value the story as much as if they had seen it on the day of publication or broadcast.

"Today we are experiencing the end of mass communication," says Larry Lauer, vice chancellor for marketing and communication at Texas Christian University. "The problem with media coverage is that so much of it is never seen by the people whose opinions matter most. Many institutional stories are appearing in the news media but people are still telling you that they believe the place never gets coverage. The strategic answer is to send the clips of the stories directly to the people who matter."

Colleges need to package their media successes and find creative ways to showcase them to donors, admissions prospects and their parents, alumni, faculty, currently enrolled students, and community and legislative leaders.

The president or vice president for development should send favorable stories, perhaps with a personal note attached, to key fund-raising prospects. It's an easy way to keep in touch. Trustees should see clips packets regularly. The government relations office will find reasons why selected state legislators need to see certain clips. Even faculty and current students like to see media coverage, particularly national coverage. It's an indication that their campus is important. Alumni can be reached through a "Siwash in the News" column in the college magazine and by posting something similar on the Web site, a move that also would reach other constituents such as admissions prospects.

Perhaps the greatest untapped area for taking

● ● ●
The president or vice president for development should send favorable stories, perhaps with a personal note attached, to key fund-raising prospects. It's an easy way to keep in touch. Trustees should see clips packets regularly.

advantage of media visibility is admissions. Some admissions offices have media clips in their reception rooms where high school students and their parents await interviews and tours. Few, however, go much beyond that. In the future, enrollment management offices will use clips of print media placements and transcripts of broadcast placements as "yield pieces." An Associated Press article about a Siwash psychology professor's research on peptides that help in weight loss, for example, could be given to applicants interested in majoring in psychology. An article highlighting the care the student life office takes in selecting compatible roommates could be sent—as part of a "yield" package—to all accepted students who have not yet made deposits.

As the marketing of the campus becomes more integrated, media placements will become increasingly useful to showcase the institution's strengths both on campus and elsewhere.

Creating a Climate for Success

To succeed in media relations, a campus public relations office must be able to handle the basics first and then to find, develop, and market the reputation-defining stories. The basics include appointment and promotion announcements; local stories on upcoming concerts, lectures, and plays; the new freshman hometowners and similar stories. These lowest common denominator media relations activities are necessary. If you don't think so, ignore them for a while and see what happens. There won't be enough fire extinguishers on campus to put out the political firestorm. You must find ways to handle the basics and still have enough staff, time, and energy to do the most valuable stories. There is no single answer on how to do this. The successful media relations practitioner will find many combinations of staff and money to get the job done. Student interns and work-study students can be a big help in handling the basics, provided they are adequately supervised. If some money can be found, trusted freelancers can help with more complex stories. Some institutions use outside media relations counsel to help them with national news placement. There are many national media relations firms that focus exclusively on higher education. For a list of some of them, consult the CASE Membership Directory, under Educational Partners.

Another essential element for success in media relations is access to top decision-makers. There is no substitute for hearing first-hand how the president's cabinet decided to respond to a campus crisis when you are the person asked to frame the institution's official response. To merit such access, you must earn it. Keep confidences. Be honest.

Leaders of institutions who actively seek positive coverage from the media need to understand that when they do so, they are opening up the institution to media scrutiny in bad times as well as good times. The same education editor who did such a fine story on your institution's student volunteer service programs will expect you to respond just as quickly when she calls about citizens' complaints to city council about noisy parties in student apartments. You can't welcome the media with open arms for good stories and brush them off for the bad ones. If you do, you will suddenly find that there is no more interest in your stories. To be fair, almost all public relations people understand this maxim. Not all campus leaders do, however.

Whenever you have bad news to tell, the standard public relations prescription is to get it out, as quickly and as comprehensively as possible, and move on. Try to make bad news a one-day story. Remember that responsible people don't expect Siwash to be perfect. They do expect it to be accountable.

One of the structural problems media relations practitioners encounter is the reward system for faculty. Simply put, faculty members don't always perceive incentives to cooperate with you on news stories. Usually there is nothing in the promotion and tenure policy that credits faculty who help the college with its public relations work. You can help to create incentives, however. Ask the president or dean to write a short note to faculty members when they help with projects that result in significant positive visibility for the institution. The professors can use such endorsements in their portfolio for the "service" portion of their tenure and promotion reviews. You can make this relatively painless for the president and dean by drafting the notes for them.

In the age of integrated marketing, a solid media relations program is as important as it ever has been in higher education advancement. Media relations is only one arrow in the quiver carried by university marketers, but it is a remarkable tool. Use it well and you can help set your institution apart from your competitors, boost internal morale, and position your institution for success.

Remember to:

- Plug into the media's agenda when appropriate.
- Create an agenda in the media for your reputation-defining stories.
- Go beyond the news release to reach out to media gatekeepers.
- Maximize media relations successes to reach your key publics.
- Create a climate on campus for media relations success.

FURTHER READINGS

Baker, Lisa. "Big Sell on Campus: How to Persuade Publicity-Shy Professors That Talking to Reporters Can Be a Boon," CURRENTS 23, no. 4 (April 1997): 40.

Finn, Frank. "The Editor's Toolbox: A Guide to Pinpointing Your Market, a Visual That Describes Your Audience, and a Matrix for Planning Editorial—All Here," *Folio: The Magazine for Magazine Management* 24, no. 11 (June 15, 1995): 41-42

Grider, Lisa. "Step Up to the Mike," CURRENTS 25, no. 2 (February 1999): 32-37.

Lauer, Larry D. "More Visibility for Your University? Finding a Strategic Solution," from *Proceedings of the Symposium on Marketing Higher Education*, November 1997, American Marketing Association.

Raley, Nancy and Laura Carter. *The New Guide to Effective Media Relations.* Washington, DC: Council for Advancement and Support of Education, 1988.

Simpson, Kristen. "Technotherapy: Got the Media Relations Blues? Try These High-Tech Tools," CURRENTS 23, no. 3 (March 1997): 22.

Sweet, David E. "Minding Our Own Business," *Presidential Leadership in Advancement Activities: New Directions for Institutional Advancement*, no. 8. San Francisco, CA: Jossey-Bass Publishers, 1980. 37-44.

Volkmann, M. Fredric. "Media Relations, Working Effectively with Print and Electronic Newsletters," from *Excellence in Advancement: Applications for Higher Education and Nonprofit Organizations* by William W. Tromble (ed). Gaithersburg, MD: Aspen Publishers, Inc., 1998.

How do we report education stories to the broadcast media to ensure that we capture the attention of assignment editors or news directors, those decision-makers in television and radio newsrooms? The answer is as simple or as complicated as this: any way they want it.

Broadcast Communications: Getting the Word Out

Annette Hannon Lee
Director of Public Information
Georgia Southwestern State University

For decades, radio was "first with the news," with its capability of hitting the airwaves immediately with the story, relayed from the newsroom as a "rip and read" item right off the wire. After the immediacy of radio came television, with several daily newscasts and the capability of delivering breaking news by interrupting other programming. All-news cable channels, like MSNBC and CNN Headline News, provided increased competition to report the news immediately, just like radio.

Television has changed the way we receive news and information. Television has provided visual and aural home delivery of major national and international events, often as they were happening. It's as though we were there together: the aftermath of President Kennedy's assassination, the first moon landing, the fall of the Berlin Wall, the bombing of the Oklahoma City federal building. Newspapers, magazines, and radio cannot present the immediacy, the combination of sights, sounds, and sensations that make TV news milestones such dynamic recollections for viewers.

Meanwhile, radio news has lost its impact. The number of radio stations reporting the news has steadily declined.

- The National Association of Broadcasters reported 10,300 commercial radio stations in 1997.
- More than 1,000 radio-news operations closed in the 1990s, according to research by Vernon Stone, journalism professor emeritus at the University of Missouri-Columbia.
- By 1999, there were no more than 5,000 commercial radio newsrooms.

What remains of commercial radio news, with condensed "drive-time" headlines and few if any on-the-scene stories, no longer holds the audience it formerly commanded, although National Public Radio continues to provide—to a comparatively small audience—in-depth coverage of selected news and issues.

The Pew Research Center for the People & the Press in 1998 reported that 88 percent of the U.S. population depends on TV as the primary news source about national and international issues, and 50 percent believe that television does the best job of covering the news. The survey found 64 percent of those polled watched local TV news on a regular basis.

Yet education communicators and administrators have been slow to accept the ubiquitous presence of television news. The inclination to aim education stories primarily at newsprint remains the norm on most campuses. We still tend to develop more working relationships with newspaper reporters and editors than with TV correspondents, reporters, news producers, and news directors. And by not targeting TV news specifically, we're excluding the foremost conduit to the largest audience for news and information.

Education news writers have long acknowledged the most direct route to deliver information to either print or broadcast media is via the Associated Press or other wire services. News sent over the wire hits most newsrooms of radio, television, and daily newspapers at the same time. Now those stories also can be carried over the Internet and by satellite to small home receivers. So aiming our most important news and information to the wire services targets the widest possible audience concurrently, including the majority tuned to broadcast news.

However, much of education news is not suited to wire services. We prepare information about student awards and achievements primarily for hometown newspapers. Likewise, we can tailor other information and human-interest stories for periodicals, special publications, speeches, e-mail, campus Web sites, or for radio and television. If we designate news for the broadcast media, it should carry the impact of major breaking news or the audio and visual components of TV reports.

THE LANGUAGE OF BROADCAST NEWS

How do we report education stories to the broadcast media to ensure that we capture the attention of assignment editors or news directors, those decision-makers in television and radio newsrooms? The answer is as simple or as complicated as this: any way they want it.

It's still about building relationships and maintaining communication—and about providing accurate, timely, and useful information of interest to a wide viewing and listening audience in the format preferred by the station or news network we're targeting. Phone calls, e-mail, fact sheets sent by fax, tip sheets incorporating one or more capsules of newsworthy information—with a direct contact telephone number to the news

source—are usually more productive than news releases, which often are written essentially for the benefit of faculty or administrators.

Media specialists in education must be seen as reliable sources of news, ready with ideas for the inevitable slow news day. By maintaining an updated list of newsworthy campus events and projects along with articulate experts to comment, communicators will be considered valuable contacts for broadcast reporters looking for a quick feature when another story didn't pan out, or those aiming to stockpile reports for weekend news or a holiday season.

Clarence Jones, for 30 years an award-winning newspaper and television investigative reporter, teaches print and broadcast "media language" in his book, *Winning with the News Media*. "Once you develop a reputation as someone who understands difficult issues—who can decipher them, so ordinary people understand them—you'll discover reporters come back to you for future stories," Jones writes. "You become an expert they can rely on. If you're skillful, you make their story better. You make them look good."

Jones says there are eight broad categories for news stories. He calls them the "Compelling C's":

- Catastrophe (campus murders, fires, hurricanes);
- Conflict (faculty vs. the president, student protests);
- Crime (drugs, date rape, burglaries on campus);
- Color (human interest, remarkable achievements, students float concrete canoe);
- Crisis (budget crunch, downsizing, measles epidemic on campus);
- Change (new president, new discoveries, economic or weather forecasts, consumer advice);
- Corruption (researchers profit from grant funds, athletics violations);
- Celebrities (Oscar winner, rock star, or U.S. president comes to campus).

Media specialists in education are faced with a diverse variety of choices and decisions in working with broadcast media: Which station gets the first call? Do you pitch the story to other newsrooms? Who is the best campus spokesperson for television sound bites or radio actualities? And how do you prepare that spokesperson for any and all interview questions? Will your informed source be ready and available when the news crew arrives on campus or when the radio reporter calls? What about cutaway footage or ambient sound? Is your story likely to be carried statewide or possibly by a network? Your choices and decisions will be determined by the relationships you develop with contacts in your media market and your working knowledge of that market.

Art Stober, one of the pioneers of higher education communication via the broadcast media, says media-relations offices, particularly at larger institutions, should include specialists who have professional experience in broadcast news. "Those are the ones who recognize good radio and TV stories and who speak the language."

Here are some other good tips for professionals in broadcast communications:

- *Understand the broadcast newsroom.* Targeting education news to the appropriate station or network at the opportune time takes an understanding of the news operation's daily schedule. It requires developing relationships with broadcast reporters who cover the education news beat, no matter how irregular that beat. It takes communication with assignment editors who might welcome your call, particularly on a slow news day, or the delivery of a well-timed tip sheet of "evergreen" (timeless) feature ideas with contact numbers of your campus experts who can handle an interview in front of a microphone or camera.

- *Get acquainted with public affairs directors, producers, and those who book interviews.* They want and need information about your campus experts for talk shows and interview segments. With advance notice, some of them would gladly reschedule studio time or assign a field crew for the opportunity to interview the Nobel Prize winner, U.S. senator, Fortune 500 CEO, Tony Award-winning actor, or other dignitary or celebrity coming to your campus.

- *Know station programming.* To fully grasp the kinds of news stories the local channels cover or the thrust of the talk or interview programs, nothing equals watching and listening to those programs to become familiar with the anchors,

hosts, reporters, format, and style. Tune in to network and cable programs that could serve as the ideal vehicle for your institution's faculty expertise. Your lack of understanding of the programs will be obvious if you try to pitch an inappropriate interview, feature idea, or news story to producers of those shows.

- *Think like a broadcaster.* Targeting news and information to the broadcast media requires communicators to think in sound and pictures and to speak and understand the jargon of broadcasters. Be prepared to describe the ambient sound and the visual aspects of the event or story you're pitching. Instead of just announcing that your institution's largest student population in its history will be coming to campus for the fall semester next week, identify those collegiate events that could draw a TV crew. Find out which residence halls would provide an ideal location for a visit from a video crew; find out about orientation activities that would render unusual visual scenarios—the university president joining in a new-students' game of tug-of-war, students changing class registrations via computer. You may or may not succeed in nabbing an on-camera interview for your president or registrar, but don't be surprised when the microphone is thrust in front of a student and her mom lugging laundry baskets full of clothes to a dorm room. Broadcast interviews often gravitate to the "person in the street" rather than your chosen administrator.

THE LESS SAID THE BETTER

If there is a scheduled interview, most stories you pitch to broadcast news or interview programs call for careful consideration of the campus spokesperson. You may want the faculty member, administrator, or student to go through media training and prepare talking points.

Campus experts can be adept at handling print and broadcast interviews. The challenge, however, is that many academics tend to want to "teach;" this can get in the way of responding concisely to a reporter's question. Long responses are likely to wind up as edited six-to-10-second bites. In the classroom, a professor often spends the first part of class explaining and leading up to the "bottom line" that is delivered just before the students depart for their next class. For media interviews—particularly in the case of radio or TV—the professor must learn to deliver the bottom line right up front. By remaining selective with responses, he or she maintains more control over the direction of the interview and the resulting quotes. Professors also need to remember that many in the audience cannot understand or are turned off by academic or scientific jargon—what he or she says must be understandable to a wide array of listeners and viewers.

Media-training sessions, preferably with practice in front of a video camera, will help a faculty member or administrator better communicate on radio or TV as well as in print. Videotaping practice interviews can also enhance the demeanor, appearance, or body language of the speaker, aspects of communication that can detract from or endorse spoken comments.

Talk shows and consumer-advice programs often provide a venue for an educator's viewpoints, insights, observations, and expertise. However, there are some professors who simply can't make the transition from a didactic approach to succinct response. Don't offer an expert to the broadcast media who cannot hold the interest of listeners or who speaks in never-ending sentences.

Spread the Word

Be aware of all chances to position your institution positively in the news, and make sure when it is in the news, you have it on record.

ProfNet is one way to get your institution and its experts out there. This listserv service offers colleges and universities an opportunity to supply campus experts for broadcast interviews beyond the institution's local area. TV and radio news and talk shows post queries on this listserv, often searching for faculty expertise for breaking news, trend stories, or in-depth feature segments. Subjects that suit your institution's experts are bound to come up occasionally on ProfNet.

News "pegs" or "hooks" are local stories we can connect to larger national or international stories. Campuses offer a variety of academics who can

give insights and viewpoints related to news topics far beyond the local community. You may have faculty members with special knowledge of the stock market or hurricanes or post-traumatic stress disorder. Those professors can become media stars when those topics make the news. Make sure your statewide and regional news networks know the availability of your institution's faculty members who can serve as experts. The satellite feeds shared by regional news organizations also can deliver your expert's comments to the national networks.

To get the most mileage from your "hits" with the electronic media, set up videocassette recorders to capture your institution's TV news stories. Video monitoring services can provide tape or transcripts from beyond your media-market area. Radio news will offer more of a taping challenge, so you might instead compile a list of all campus radio interviews or other radio contacts. Computer news searches will help locate broadcast stories. Use some version of that assortment of "clippings"—tape, transcripts, or abbreviated summaries of either format—to let key campus contacts, alumni, trustees, or other opinion leaders know of your broadcast media successes on a regular basis.

● ● ●

For media interviews—particularly in the case of radio or TV—the professor must learn to deliver the bottom line right up front.

INSTITUTIONAL MISSIONS AND THE NEWS

Many institutions have been successful in communicating their institutional missions through radio and TV broadcasting.

Land-grant colleges and universities have a mission to provide a broad segment of the population with practical education through extension services, and they have done so, efficiently and economically, through radio and television news and public affairs programming. This "consumer friendly" information might be horticulture advice or news of particular interest to a rural community. These land-grant institutions have led the way in delivering "news you can use" in the form of prepared reports packaged for broadcast listeners and viewers. Medical schools and other major research institutions have followed closely in their footsteps.

Pennsylvania State University's College of Agricultural Sciences (*http://aginfo.psu.edu/radio*)

produces a weekly radio newsfeed, with more than 60 stations subscribing to a tip sheet outlining the available news reports. This results in about 25 calls per week from radio newsrooms to the college's telephone newsline. News coordinator Charles Gill says educational and cooperative-extension information reaches a statewide grassroots radio audience. The staff also maintains a digital ISDN (Integrated Services Digital Network) phone line to offer studio-quality audio to stations or news networks interviewing faculty members and researchers by telephone.

Virginia Tech also uses an ISDN line for media interviews. It produces approximately 350 news features annually for about two dozen radio stations in the state and regularly sends "evergreen" video features to in-state TV newsrooms. Tech's "Soundline" offers audio news cuts by telephone. A statewide consortium of public universities in Virginia produces a half-hour program on research and teaching for public radio stations. Tech also has participated in a live feed between the campus and Black Entertainment TV. All of these efforts help overcome the fact that national media find it difficult to come to Virginia Tech.

Auburn University packages radio news features, edited digitally by computer, and posts them to the Web. *(See www.univrel.auburn.edu/ur/ broadcast.html.)* The site has become "a place where students, alumni or anybody can find news about Auburn." See *www.univrel.auburn.edu/ multimedia/videohits* for samples of Auburn's television news. The institution's first media priority is to get a station's news crew to come to campus—insurance that the story will be broadcast. If that's not possible, the Auburn staff shoots and produces the material. Most stories are delivered via satellite uplink to NBC's NewsChannel, based in Charlotte, N.C., a service that feeds news to network affiliate stations, MSNBC, CNBC, and some overseas clients. One of Auburn's most successful video news releases (VNRs) ran on all local area stations and in 19 of the top 50 media markets nationwide.

Frank Ahern, associate director of news and public affairs at the University of Florida, says his primary radio targets are regional or national news networks, not individual stations, unless they rep-

resent a large media market. UF's current method of audio delivery is via Switch 56, a high quality digital phone line and modem preferred by most networks—NPR in particular, where UF lands two or three news stories monthly—and by the BBC. Ahern also has delivered audio to NPR via e-mail in an audio-file format. He predicts that audio will be sent routinely by computer files in the coming years. Only one network TV affiliate is located in Gainesville, Fla., UF's home, and the next closest satellite uplink is about 100 miles away. Ahern says the existence of four in-state satellite news networks is unique in Florida. The situation makes the UF satellite uplink a valuable news commodity and has given the staff uncommon access to daily news feeds of two of those networks on a regular basis and the other two occasionally. This routine participation with regional network news is evidence the UF video production is comparable with other television news operations.

The UF Institute of Food and Agricultural Sciences uses TV as a major component of a public awareness effort. News, PSAs (public service announcements) and "fillers" (segments that occasionally fill the void between PBS programs) tell about the Cooperative Extension programs available in Florida relating to food safety, pesticide information, and other consumer advice.

The UF Health Science Center produces VNRs (edited health news and feature stories) timed for distribution with print-media releases. In 1997, UF's comprehensive coverage of the first embryonic spinal nerve tissue transplant on a paralyzed patient, delivered as an edited tape to UF's News and Public Affairs distribution uplink, resulted in placements on CNN, CBS, ABC, and several international radio and TV stations.

Purdue University's broadcast services produces a half-hour magazine-format show that is aired on five cable outlets around Indiana plus the Indianapolis PBS station. It also produces VNRs, halftime features for sports broadcasts, and recruiting videos; highlights programs for the alumni association; and special videos for promotion, lobbying, fund raising, and other projects. Video production at Purdue is seen as a major resource in getting word out about the university's mission and in helping attract students, staff, and funding.

See examples of Purdue's news services at *www.purdue.edu/UNS/sites.sounds.html* and *www.pur-due.edu/PAA/aboutPAA/sites.html*.

Some universities are investing in selected drive-time radio ads or NPR program sponsorships. At Indiana University in Bloomington, for instance, more than a dozen campus academic units deliver goodwill messages on NPR. During a legislative session, "low level buys" (less expensive time slots) on local radio stations told individual communities specific stories about IU's contribution to that area of the state. A 1996 survey indicated that Indiana residents had strong name recognition of Indiana University, but that nearly a third could not name one strength they associated with IU. These radio announcements were part of the IU administration's statewide effort to reach audiences and to restore the public's awareness of the opportunities IU represents. These broadcast efforts resulted in increased enrollments, a successful capital campaign, and the best legislative session on record.

At Johns Hopkins Medical Institutions, director Tom Haederle produces "Health NewsFeed," a radio program on health and medicine. Five 60-second reports are sent weekly to radio stations and radio news networks around the country. CBS radio distributes the reports to its affiliates, as do UPI and the USA radio network, and Voice of America broadcasts them overseas.

Carolyn Dunlap, manager of broadcast news, produces medical and health video features for the University of Alabama at Birmingham Medical Center and related research areas of the university. Her news packages are routinely delivered to television newsrooms on videotape cassettes. When an "Origin of AIDS" story broke at UAB in early 1999, Dunlap's crew produced a video feature and sent it by satellite. The news landed on 460 broadcast news outlets, including all three national networks and the BBC, among other international news agencies. An entire "Nightline" program was dedicated to the story that originated in the UAB media relations office.

The Duke University staff produced a story

You may have faculty members with special knowledge of the stock market or hurricanes or post-traumatic stress disorder. Those professors can become media stars when those topics make the news.

about the birth of an endangered primate species at the Duke Primate Center. The story went worldwide on CNN and also on other network news. But that wasn't the university's biggest TV "hit." A live broadcast of ABC's "Good Morning America," staged in the center of campus, took months to organize and provided Duke with its most-watched televised campus event.

At the University of Hawaii, five 60-second "University Reports" are distributed weekly to seven Hawaiian radio stations. In addition, 90-second "UH Today" video features are aired twice a week on a television station. Both projects feature people, awards, programs, tips, and research from throughout the UH 10-campus system. The radio spots are broadcast at no charge and the TV stations secure sponsorships for their video features (so there is no charge to the university for broadcast time).

On a regular basis, the University of Alabama-Tuscaloosa's broadcast services crew provides news packages, b-roll (cutaway footage), and interview material to stations and regional news networks via satellite from the campus. They contact assignment editors and producers via phone calls and a weekly "pitch" sheet sent by fax. Their production equipment budget is generated through contract work for a variety of special video projects including student recruiting, alumni, development, and institutional messages for sports broadcasts.

At the University of Queensland in Brisbane, Australia, Tony Murray, director of media and information services, distributes every two weeks broadcast-quality audiotape featuring five interviews with researchers about their work or other topical developments in their fields. "As we are a capital city university serving a large state, this enables regional and community radio stations to run interviews in their chat-style programs," Murray explains. The long-running project is successful, he adds, "because its content is relevant and promotional puff has been strenuously avoided."

The University of South Florida in Tampa uses digital equipment to produce a newsmagazine format audiocassette, mailed twice yearly to 1000 donors, alumni, and government and business leaders. In addition to other campus highlights, the tapes, put together using Pro Tools software, include the "University Beat" features produced by the university's NPR station. Those two-and-one-half minute "positive stories about a student program, research project, or other news" are aired twice weekly following "Morning Edition."

TECHNOLOGY AND THE FUTURE OF BROADCASTING

Broadcast technology is changing as we begin the 21st century. All commercial TV stations in the United States must launch Digital Television (DTV) service by May 1, 2002, and noncommercial stations will start by May 1, 2003. A number of stations initiated DTV in November 1998. The transition to all-DTV should be complete by 2006. Consumers will connect converter boxes to existing TV sets to receive signals, or they will acquire new DTV sets. The new system will permit transmission of high definition television (HDTV), allowing broadcasters to transmit multiple programs via a single TV channel. It will improve audio quality, with up to five channels of sound per program. DTV will make it possible for broadcasters to send electronic publications, program schedules, computer software, and data for downloading to computers, and the flexibility to support new services in the future.

Broadcast media specialists in education are beginning to upgrade to digital-format equipment, while also maintaining communications with broadcast contacts and learning to speak the evolving technical language.

With changing communications technology and the increasing number of households connected to the Internet, online news preference is bound to grow—while the interconnection of broadcast news and the Internet continues its expansion. Sponsored by ABC, CBS, and NBC, a 1997 survey (conducted by the research firm Roper Starch Worldwide) of 2,003 Americans 18 and older found only 2 percent who cited the Internet as their primary news source. Television still provided most news in households with Internet access, with 15 percent of those with access saying they get their news from online services. In those Internet-access households, 36 percent said TV was the most credible news source versus 8 percent for online sources.

The 1996 Telecommunications Act revised the old way of doing business in the industry and brought on more competition in widespread communication. Telephone companies, with the capability of offering as many as 500 different TV channels via fiber-optic lines, now compete with broadcast, cable, and satellite delivery systems. Those same lines can deliver the Internet, interactive shopping, movies, or news. The increased competition among a multitude of news delivery systems presents additional challenges in communicating education news.

REFERENCES

American Journalism Review NewsLink: *www.newslink.org*.

Arbitron: *http://arbitron.com*.

Broadcasting & Cable Yearbook 2000. New Providence, NJ: R.R. Bowker, A Unit of Cahners Business Information, 2000.

Columbia Journalism Review: www.cjr.org.

Digital Television: *www.fcc.gov/dtv*

Jones, Clarence. *Winning with the News Media*. Tampa, FL: Video Consultants, Inc., 1999.

Kalbfeld, Brad. *AP Broadcast News Handbook*. New York, NY: The Associated Press, 1998.

Lee, Annette Hannon. "'Live from the Quad': How to Cope—and Stay Calm—When the TV News Crews Come to Campus," CURRENTS 19, no. 5 (May 1993): 24-30.

Lee, Annette Hannon. "On the Record: An In-House Media Training Program Can Help Faculty Feel Comfortable," CURRENTS 18, no. 3 (March 1992): 14-16.

National Association of Broadcasters: *www.nab.org*.

Neilsen Media Research: *www.nielsenmedia.com*.

The Pew Research Center For The People & the Press: *www.people-press.org*.

ProfNet: *www.profnet.com*.

Project for Excellence in Journalism: *www.journalism.org*.

Stubbee, Melinda. "Broadcast News: Getting Your Message Out Via Radio and TV," CURRENTS 17, no. 1 (January 1991): 38-40.

Stubbee, Melinda. "Making Radio Waves: Tune in to These Tips for Getting Your Campus News on the Air," CURRENTS 19, no. 5 (May 1993): 16-17.

Telecommunications Act of 1996: *www.fcc.gov/mmb*.

Television and Radio News Research:
www.missouri.edu/~jourvs/index.html.

ADDITIONAL RESOURCES

ABC Television: *www.abc.com.*

Ackerman, Helen."On the Air: How I Set up—and Survived—a Broadcast Media Training Session for Top-Level Administrators," CURRENTS 18, no. 3 (March 1992): 10-12.

Audio News-680 News online: www.canoe.com/680news

Barbalich, Andrea. "Voice of Authority: Lillian Brown speaks volumes about appearing in public, working with the media, and projecting your personal best," CURRENTS 20 no. 10 (November/December 1994): 42-47.

Bloomberg Information News Radio: *www.bloomberg.com/wbbt/index.htmlwmbram1130radio.*

Bloomberg Television: *www.bloomberg.com/tv/index.html.*

A broadcast network on the Internet: *www.broadcast.com.*

CBS NewsUptotheMinute: *http://uttm.com.*

CBS Radio: *www.cbsradio.com.*

CBS Television: *www.cbs.com.*

CNN: *www.cnn.com.*

C-Span Networks: *www.c-span.org.*

Fox News: *www.foxnews.com.*

Honnert, Gary T. "Video News Releases: Slick, Newsy Videos are Flooding TV Newsrooms. Will Yours Stand Out?" CURRENTS 15 no. 3 (March 1989): 30-37.

Microsoft® WebTV Network Service: *www.webtv.com.*

MSNBC: *www.msnbc.com.*

National Public Radio: *www.npr.org.*

NBC Television: *www.nbc.com.*

PBS Televison: *www.pbs.org.*

Radio Space-North American Network: *www.RadioSpace.com.*

Rodgers, Joann Ellison and William Adams. *Media Guide for Academics.* Los Angeles, CA: The Foundation for American Communications, 1994.

Simpson, Kristen. "Get Set for Media Training: Prepare your Professors to Master Interviews—Before Reporters Call," CURRENTS 23 no. 4 (April 1997): 43-45.

Soundbites: *www.soundbites.com.*

TV/RadioWorld Directory: *beta.tvradioworld.com.*

Wherever development communications reports, the key to effectiveness is to maintain the perspectives of both the development and public relations operations—to straddle both worlds, and to bring them constantly together.

Development Communications

Roger L. Williams
Associate Vice Chancellor for University Relations
University of Arkansas

A week in early October 1999 foreshadowed just one of the tougher challenges that development communications officers can expect in the years ahead: How to capture public and media attention for your institution's major gifts when the threshold for mega-gifts is rising so quickly?

Georgetown University, in the nation's media capital, chose that week to announce a $30 million gift to its business school. The donation marked the public announcement of its $750 million fundraising campaign. As *The Chronicle of Higher Education* put it:

> Georgetown announced its major gift—from Robert E. McDonough, a 1949 graduate—on October 8. But only two days earlier, the University of Arkansas College of Business Administration had announced an even bigger gift, $50 million, from the Walton Family Charitable Support Foundation. So Georgetown was trumped, and some of the national coverage it might have gained evaporated as the Arkansas news spread.

Those two gifts, coupled with donations of $25 million to Lehigh University and $45 million to Johns Hopkins, made for a total of $150 million to just four institutions in that one October week. And shortly thereafter, the $35 million threshold for *The Chronicle*'s list of "major private gift and grants to higher education since 1967" rose to $50 million.

From a development communications perspective, this rising threshold for big gifts is a problem, but a wonderful problem at that. Giving to education—colleges and universities, elementary and secondary schools, libraries, scholarships funds, nonprofit trade schools, and other educational institutions—totaled $21.5 billion in 1997, a 12.3 percent increase over 1996. Most of this revenue—$16 billion—went to higher education, according to *Giving USA*.

Partly because of the fund-raising success educational institutions have enjoyed over the last 20 years—only religion attracts more fund-raising dollars than education—and partly because of the imperatives that impel institutions to pursue private gift support ever more aggressively, a new area of advancement specialization has come into being. This specialization is development communications, which provides public relations, communications, and marketing programs in support of educational fund raising. Development communications is a subset, or a blend, of both the communications and the educational fund-raising disciplines. It matured as a specialization between 1985-95.

DEVELOPMENT COMMUNICATIONS IN THE LARGER ORGANIZATION

Many colleges, universities, and educational institutions have established formal development communications units, or at least appointed a development communications officer. Reporting arrangements vary. At some institutions, the development communications unit reports to the development office; at others, to communications; and at still others, a dual reporting relationship prevails. In all cases, however, media relations activities are funneled through the news bureau or public information office. To maintain credibility, campaign and fund-raising news must be subject to the same standards that apply to other institutional news.

A development communications unit offers a two-fold advantage: It provides an exclusive focus on fund-raising communications and precludes an "overload" situation that can overwhelm the public relations staff. An overload can impair communications support for development and dilute the effectiveness of institutional communications overall. The chief obstruction to establishing a dedicated unit is cost. In addition, many institutions are reluctant to build up staff for a limited activity such as a campaign because it's hard to reduce staff afterwards. But some research universities in mega-campaigns have established development communications staffs of four to eight persons.

Wherever development communications reports, the key to effectiveness is to maintain the perspectives of both the development and public relations operations—to straddle both worlds, and to bring them constantly together. The obvious role of development communications is to provide total public relations, communications, and marketing support to the fund-raising enterprise. A less obvious, but equally important, role is to look for ways in which the fund-raising program can serve as a communications platform for larger institutional messages. Campaign environments, in particular, offer splendid opportunities for projecting institutional "meta-messages" to key audiences: Who are we? Where are we going? Why are we going there, and what will the result be when we

arrive?" Thus, the strategically-conscious development communications officer always will look for ways to use gift announcements and campaign events to convey larger institutional messages.

THE THREE LEVELS OF DEVELOPMENT COMMUNICATIONS

Development communications, at its best, should think and work on three levels, all of them intertwined.

■ Contextual—creating visibility for the institution and enhancing its reputation with a variety of constituencies so that fund raising can succeed.

■ Strategic—helping to resolve the "what" and "why" issues of educational fund raising and communications: "What are we going to do?" and "Why are we going to do it?"

■ Tactical—determining how to fulfill fund-raising goals with specific communications programs, initiatives, and events.

Contextual Issues

Before development communications officers can put together a fund-raising or campaign communications plan, they need to think about the context in which the institution finds itself.

For example, what is the institution's reputation and image in the eyes of key constituencies and the general public? If this information isn't readily available, it may be time to push for an institutional image or attitude and opinion survey. Additionally, it may be time to commission an attitude and opinion survey of the institution's alumni, or, more to the point, its major gift prospects. What do they think about the institution? What do they like and dislike about it? How do they get their information about it, and how would they prefer to get it? Answers to these questions are fundamental to creating an effective development communications plan. If your major gift prospects feel overwhelmed by the number of letters, brochures, and publications from the institution, you will want to think carefully about adding to the pile.

Other contextual questions have to do with where the institution is going. What is the institution's vision? What are its goals? Does it have a strategic plan in place? Does it have a marketing plan? What are its positioning objectives? Is it working to position itself in the higher education marketplace as "the premier independent institution of higher learning in the Northwest" or "the best private comprehensive university in the United States" or "one of the top five public research universities in the South"? A development or campaign communications plan of necessity will be tied to these larger institutional goals.

Not least, does the institution have a coherent visual identity system? Does it present itself graphically to its various publics in a compelling way—so as to cut through all of the communications clutter in the great "out there" and make a high impact? If not, the development communications officer may want to argue for one.

These contextual questions related to institutional reputation, image, strategic direction, and identity are of extreme importance to development communications. Study after study has shown that the most important variables in fund-raising success are institutional prestige and strategic direction. Development communications officers must work with colleagues in fund raising and public relations to ensure that these issues can be addressed and incorporated so as to create effective fund-raising communications plans and materials.

Strategic Issues: The Fund-Raising or Campaign Communications Plan

The strategic issues for development communications can be addressed in a fund-raising or campaign communications plan. It is here that you address the questions: "What should we do and say?" and "Why should we do and say it?"

The first step is to set goals for the communications plan, taking into account the contextual issues addressed in the previous section. The goals can be broad, such as "to increase awareness, understanding, and support for the institution and the campaign," but they are usually better when more pointed. For example, the overarching goals of a campaign communications plan might be to:

■ Create messages and communications materials that help the institution meet its campaign goal of $100,000,000 in five years.

■ Help position the institution and forge a new identity through campaign communications, as

in the aforesaid "premier independent institution of higher education in the Northwest."

■ Clarify the institution's relationship, through campaign communications, with state government, a religious denomination, the surrounding community, or any other vital constituency.

■ Deliver key messages to key audiences. For example, it may be important to convey a message about "preserving the special sense of place" about the campus to alumni prospects.

■ Provide a high level of visibility among the extended campus family for the campaign's volunteer leadership and major benefactors.

■ Demonstrate to faculty and staff a determination to move the institution to greater heights of achievement.

■ Introduce a new, or strengthen the institution's current, graphic identity system.

The goals of the communications plan should be prioritized in accordance with institutional goals, strategic directions, and needs, and should be worked out with the institution's and advancement division's leadership.

Goals are only one element of the fund-raising or campaign communications plan. Other components will include:

■ *Target audiences.* Fund raising is essentially a marketing process, particularly in audience segmentation. Prospects rated at the $100,000 level and above may require, and respond to, different communications strategies than those prospects rated under $10,000.

■ *Timeline and geography.* The campaign is a continuum of varied phases and activities: the planning and quiet stages, the public launch, the plateau, the climax, and the post-campaign environment. Communications strategies must vary in accordance with this life span. The planning and quiet stages might be the best time to attend to image-building and communications research; the public launch may require some high-end publications and news media activity. Campaign geographical considerations should be treated similarly. Where are the alumni and prospects clustered? Within a 100-mile radius of campus? In a three-state region? In additional pockets around the nation? How do you reach them and when? If the campaign has a regional approach, and it's time for a high-profile volunteer push in, say, Chicago, it may be time to prepare letters, brochures, and other materials tailored to Chicago volunteers, and even try for some media visibility in that region.

■ *Campaign themes.* These generally reflect the institutional positioning statement, institutional strengths and indices of excellence, and campaign goals. They should be incorporated in all communications materials. As with any marketing or advertising campaign, frequency and repetition of message are the bywords here.

■ *Tactics and methods.* These are the "guts" of the communications plan (to be discussed shortly). These are the materials you'll produce and the activities you'll undertake to implement the strategy.

■ *Evaluation.* How do you measure the results of your fund-raising or campaign communications plan? Do you commission a follow-up attitude and opinion survey when the campaign concludes? Do you initiate readership surveys of campaign materials? Be wary of assuming a successful campaign communications effort just because the dollar goal has been met.

The Case Statement

If you're in a campaign, a communications plan is only half of the strategic equation. The other half is the case statement. This should be viewed as a strategic communications activity. It sets the institutional tone for the campaign. It answers key questions about where the institution is going, and why, and how private gift support can help it get there. The case statement has been described as the "single most important document of a capital campaign" and "the communications backbone of any capital campaign." Basically, it is the argument or "case" for why an institution needs and deserves private gift support, and why it needs it now.

The case statement is a product—black marks on white paper—but it is more importantly a process, especially for the internal campus community. Typically, case statements involve interviewing key campus leaders, academic and administrative; testing and refining messages and lines of reasoning; and creating a scenario of a certain future for

the institution. This is serious business, as it gets to the core of what an institution is and where it's going. For that reason, case statements usually go through several iterations, as the campus leadership works through the document to arrive at consensus for what the narrative should say. Such a process can involve some headaches, some argument, and certainly much time. But the result is all-important buy-in for the campaign. For that reason, the case statement is as important for internal audiences as it is external audiences.

Tactical Issues, Methods, and Materials

Given specific goals and a well-defined plan, development communications can then proceed to plan and carry out specific activities to make the larger plan work.

News Media Visibility

Fund-raising activity, especially during a campaign, produces newsworthy opportunities and events. Notwithstanding the opening vignette to this chapter, major gifts for multicultural initiatives, endowments, educational partnerships, novel ways of improving undergraduate education, and research can carry strong potential for media visibility. Gifts made by unusual people under unusual circumstances—the campus janitor who lived frugally and left a bequest of $500,000—will warm a reporter's heart.

When major gifts are announced, encourage the benefactor to send key positioning messages about the institution: "My wife and I are making this gift because we believe this college is on the verge of moving into the ranks of the best liberal arts colleges in the Northeast." As a highly successful, independent third party, a benefactor has enormous credibility.

Media visibility is worth pursuing because it provides objective evidence that your institution needs, deserves, and succeeds at raising private dollars.

Fund-Raising and Campaign Publications

The need for special, carefully-targeted publications to aid fund raising continues to increase. They may be direct mail letters, annual and planned giving brochures, postcards to herald an upcoming telefund appeal, fund-raising advertisements for the alumni magazine or lead brochures for the various schools, colleges, and other units of an institution. The cardinal rule to producing any of these publications is to ask certain marketing questions: What are you trying to accomplish? Why do we need this publication? What is its audience? And what is the publication's intended result?

Periodicals

Fund-raising or campaign newsletters or bulletins are a staple of development communications. These tri-annual or quarterly publications are targeted to the major gift audience. Such a newsletter keeps this audience interested in the fund-raising effort, up-to-date on its progress, and provides examples of giving that they might consider. It can also relate fund raising to academic achievement, or profile benefactors and recipients in ways that might not be convenient or appropriate in the institution's other communications vehicles.

But those "other communications vehicles" certainly should be considered and used. The alumni or university magazine may dedicate a section to campaign news or may be amendable to integrating a compelling fund-raising feature into its main section. The faculty-staff newspaper, president's semi-annual newsletter to internal and external audiences, the research magazine, the vehicles of an institution's sub-units—all should be explored for their receptivity to using fund-raising news. Each of these vehicles contains a measure of credibility and audience penetration that fund-raising-specific communications may not.

Video

Not too many years ago, video was used mainly to add excitement and panache to fund-raising events, such as campaign kick-offs. Now video has become an indispensable part of fund-raising communications. Video is coming to play a larger role in the mix of sophisticated electronic systems that integrate direct mail, telemarketing, and personal solicitation. It is not so much replacing the role of print and people as it is supplementing them.

But video still adds panache to almost any fund-raising event. It is de rigeur at campaign kick-offs and finales. It can be used to great effect as a campaign progress report, conveying emotion and enthusiasm in a way that print cannot. And video clippings and vignettes can be incorporated nicely as part of any power-point presentation.

Indeed, some institutions are using video successfully in telefund appeals for special fund-raising events. Typically, a short video is made and sent to the prospects, along with a cover letter telling them to expect a call from a student volunteer. The prospect, having been forearmed and forewarned, is in a much better position to respond positively to the subsequent telephone solicitation.

The World Wide Web

The Internet and the World Wide Web have opened a new universe of development communications opportunities—and imperatives. Many print pieces can be reworked and posted on the institution's Web site. Information about the advancement operation and the fund-raising program can be posted on a special Web site for viewing by alumni, faculty, staff, and students. E-mail campaign updates can be created and sent as needed to listservs of prospects, volunteers, and supporters. It is both daunting and exciting to think of the as-yet-unimagined ways in which the Web will be used for fund-raising communications in the years ahead.

REFERENCES

Freilicher, Lila, "Getting the Most from Newsletters: Newsletters Can Increase Loyalty, Encourage Donations, and Help Achieve Specific Development and Marketing Goals," *Fund Raising Management* (May 1996): 49-52.

Gayley, Henry T., *How to Write for Development: Better Communication Brings Bigger Dollar Results*. Washington, DC: Council for Advancement and Support of Education, 1991.

Gearhart, G. David, "Public Relations and the Campaign." In *The Capital Campaign in Higher Education: A Practical Guide for College and University Advancement*. Washington, DC: National Association of College and University Business Officers, 1995.

Gilbert, Heather Ricker, "The Winning Combination: When You Put Together Planning and Panache, It Adds Up to a Successful Campaign Special Event," CURRENTS 15, no. 6 (June 1989.)

Jordan, Ronald R., and Katelyn L.Quynn, "Material Benefits: From Basic to Deluxe, the Publications Every Planned Giving Program Needs," CURRENTS 18, no. 3 (March 1992).

Development Communications

King, Roland, "Stating Your Case: The Art, the Science, and the Future of the Quintessential Campaign Document," CURRENTS 15, no. 6 (June 1989).

"Making Movies, Moving Millions: Tips for Creating a Memorable Campaign Video," CURRENTS 24, no. 3 (March 1998).

Mercer, Joye, "The 1990s Bring Colleges a Wealth of Gifts," *The Chronicle of Higher Education* (Oct. 30, 1998): A44-45.

Roehr, Robert J., ed. *Electronic Advancement: Fund Raising.* Washington, DC: Council for Advancement and Support of Education, 1990.

Rose, David. "Seeing and Believing: Many Fund Raisers See Videos as a Jazzy Way to Help Potential Donors Believe in the Cause. In Practice, However, Development Operations Tend to Produce Videos That are Humorless, Predictable, and Boring. It Doesn't Have to Be That Way," *Advancing Philanthropy* 4, no. 3 (Fall 1996): 39-40.

Shoemaker, Donna, "Striking the Campaign Chords: Whether You're Leading the Band or Playing Second Fiddle, Your Campus Periodical Can Play a Special Part," CURRENTS 20, no. 10 (Nov./Dec. 1994).

Tromble, William W., "Marketing the Campaign." In *Excellence in Advancement: Applications for Higher Education and Nonprofit Organizations.* Gaithersburg, MD: Aspen Publishers, Inc., 1998.

Williams, Roger L. "Plan and Deliver: Organize a Campaign Communications Program to Get the Results You Need," CURRENTS 18, no. 9 (October 1992).

Williams, Roger L. "The Role of Public Relations in Fund Raising." In *Educational Fund Raising: Principles and Practices.* Edited by Michael J. Worth. Phoenix, AZ: ACE/Oryx, 1993.

Williams, Roger L., "They Work Hard for the Money: How Public Relations Officers Support Capital Campaigns," CURRENTS 15, no. 6 (June 1989).

Williams, Roger L. and Gearhart, G. David, "Mega Fundraising Campaigns: Do They Make Us Look Greedy?" *AGB Reports* (Jan./Feb. 1991): 16-19.

Special events are akin to inviting guests to your home for dinner. In the same way a dinner guest can gather information about your financial status, eating and drinking habits, reading preferences, and approaches to child rearing, guests at special events can draw conclusions about your institution.

15

Special Events: Creative and Strategic Planning

April L. Harris
Director of Alumni Relations
University of Alabama in Huntsville

Special events are those occasions to which an institution invites outsiders—whether they are alumni, business leaders, parents, donor prospects, potential students, or even members from one department visiting another—for a closer, more personalized look at the facilities, faculty, staff, students, and policies of an institution than is generally afforded on a daily basis.

Special events can include annual events such a homecoming, commencement, convocations, retirement recognitions, or parents' day. They can be unique, one-time events, like the dedication of a new facility, the celebration of an anniversary, or the inauguration of a president, or they can be events planned specifically for a certain audience, such as donor recognitions, legislative relations days, or academic symposia.

Special events also can take place away from your campus. These might include conferences and workshops, planning retreats, alumni meetings in faraway cities, alumni days at places like a museum, a major-league baseball game, an amusement park, or at an off-campus restaurant or hotel.

Sometimes, major special events have many small events tucked under the umbrella of a large theme. On a convocation day, sub-events might include a hospitality reception for the press, a breakfast for visiting dignitaries, a morning program, special displays and tours, a luncheon, a post-convocation reception in a tent for special guests, and a private dinner with the president that evening for a few select individuals.

Whether an event is massive in scope and available to the general public, like a concert, or private, such as dinner for five key alumni at the president's home, special events put an institution on display. They offer the opportunity for people to look at and, indeed, to scrutinize the institution and its programs. Powerful communicators, they send messages that make a far more lasting impression than the most expensive brochure or the slickest alumni magazine money can buy.

Because special events are such powerful communications tools, be sure to use them wisely: Never lose sight of the long-range goals of your advancement program. Do not create your special events in isolation but weave them into your total advancement program so that all activities complement each other.

Each event must be consistent with the spirit and tone of your advancement program and the institutional image you want to communicate. The most brilliantly designed and executed special event will be counterproductive if its message is confusing or inconsistent with your institution's other activities. Plan and implement your special events so that they will add to and not detract from the central themes of your institution.

Special events are akin to inviting guests to your home for dinner. In the same way a dinner guest can gather information about your financial status, eating and drinking habits, reading preferences, and approaches to child rearing, guests at special events can draw conclusions about your institution. Special events reveal more in a few hours' time about institutional priorities, politics, financial condition, management style, and needs than a year's worth of press releases or magazine articles.

A well-planned special event begins with that old journalistic formula, "who, what, when, where, how, why" (and as a professor of mine added, "so what?"). Successful events are rooted in thoughtful, sometimes frustrating, planning. You may be tempted to build a grand event full of razzle-dazzle and hoopla, but if it is not solidly in character with the institution's mission, your efforts—and money—will be wasted.

There is one valid reason to sponsor a special event: It supports and enhances institutional goals and mission, contributing to the accomplishment of objectives in academics, alumni relations, fund raising, student recruitment, or image building. Random events held for the sake of a one-day success or as a diversion from daily routine can send mixed messages to your audiences and sap resources that could be used more effectively in a well-planned public relations program. Therefore, before agreeing to plan and hold a special event, ask yourself these questions. Does the event:

■ support the institution's mission;

■ help achieve specific goals;

■ showcase resources unique to your institution;

■ help raise friends or funds;

■ build goodwill;

■ consistently support the institution's image; and

■ have adequate budget to be executed properly?

Like a holiday, special events serve to bring resources, people, and messages together to accom-

plish specific objectives. With proper research, planning, communications, and implementation, special events can be some of the most effective, creative, and enjoyable components of a comprehensive institutional advancement plan.

PLANNING MAKES IT WORK

Planning is the most crucial, most time-consuming aspect of successful special events. Special events should be developed in the context of your institution's annual public relations plan and in relation to long-range institutional advancement goals. Positioning special events in a "master plan" helps avoid duplication of effort and wasted money. It prevents you from bombarding the same target audience with too many messages and too many invitations. Good planning may help you piggyback on other communications efforts for more meaningful impact. Master planning also helps ensure that events are consistent with institutional goals in public relations, image building, and marketing.

Guided in the long term by the institutional mission and in the short term by institutional goals and objectives, the central university relations office (or its counterpart on your campus) should serve as a clearinghouse for all special events. That is, any time you are considering sponsoring an event designed to attract outside attention from the media, alumni, or the general public, the chief university relations officer of your institution should be consulted before ideas become plans.

From a purely textbook point of view, all special events should be managed from a central office, and today, many larger institutions are creating special events offices for this purpose. In reality, many institutions are too large and are too sparsely staffed to take on such a task. Instead, planners are scattered across campus assigned to specific departments. Nevertheless, the chief university relations officer should have the final approval on all major special events that are planned, particularly if they involve politicians, celebrities, controversial speakers or topics, or encompass a university-wide celebration such as an anniversary.

DO IT BY CAMPUS COMMITTEE

Often, you can learn more about what is happening on your campus by reading the newspaper than you can at work. It is very common for campus departments to work in isolation from each other, resulting in missed opportunities to collaborate or worse yet, resulting in scheduling events that compete with each other. At one university, the athletic department and the library planned fund-raising auctions within two weeks of each other. Both used the same facility, the same volunteer auctioneer, requested donations from the same businesses, and invited essentially the same guest list. Both auctions' fund-raising totals suffered. Guests wondered aloud at the similarities between the two events. The planners were embarrassed. The situation could have been avoided by assembling a committee of people on campus to plan special events. The purpose of this group is to learn what others are doing, consider the list of proposed events, weed out the marginal ones, and schedule the remaining events to avoid duplication, build impact, and maximize the investment of time and money.

A good time for this committee to meet is at the start of the academic year. The first meeting should be very general with the chief university relations officer providing an overview of priorities and goals for the coming year. He or she should sketch the framework of major projects, such as a building dedication, fund drive, or the visit of international dignitaries, within which the committee can plan the year's events.

This is the time to talk about the programs, people, and projects that need to be highlighted. It is the time to confirm the dates for major functions such as commencements, concerts, parents' day, and sports events. It is also an opportunity to gather information that can avert event-planning disasters—such as scheduling a large event at the student union during the time its parking lot will be closed for resurfacing, or planning a scholarship fund-raising concert on the same night that your campus will host the ice hockey championships.

YOUR MASTER PLAN

Armed with a sense of the big picture for the coming year, you can then develop your own office-wide special events master plan. Work your plans around the events already in place. This may mean avoiding a date, dovetailing into a date, or just being aware of other activities and how they could affect availability of space, services, and media coverage as well as your targeted participants.

Refer to the written goals and objectives for your office. What do you want to accomplish? What are the timetables and deadlines?

A good tool to use for this planning exercise is a wall calendar that displays the entire year. Block in the events already scheduled—homecoming, commencements, board meetings, and breaks. Study the calendar. Are several events crowded into a few consecutive weeks? Are they intended for the same audience? Will major events already on the calendar prevent you from having access to a facility or service you need?

Referring to your goals and objectives, make a list of what needs to be accomplished; leave the how until later in the planning process. For example, if you are a member of the development staff, your "what" list might include twice-a-year contact with emeriti faculty, major donor recognition, an announcement for the wrap-up of a successful fund drive, contact with parents of scholarship students, and recognition of volunteers who have helped fund raising throughout the year.

In the public affairs office, your "what" list might contain items such as introducing the president to community business leaders and area media, making key legislators more aware of funding needs, recognizing student leaders, and planning the annual convocation.

Now, match goals and objectives with key dates whenever possible, and, considering your "what needs to be accomplished" list, look for logical tie-ins for your target audiences. For example, you know that the School of Music will sponsor a concert series beginning in February. The afternoon preceding the first concert may be the perfect time to invite select donor prospects to a dinner and present plans to enhance the concert hall.

Pencil in dates that seem attractive and consider the availability of staff and facilities, especially on weekends that are already busy. Will there be enough time to prepare facilities, or are events stacked back-to-back so that one delay means disaster for all that follow? Will your staff be spread too thinly to handle the work effectively? Are so many events planned that caterers and service personnel will be in short supply?

Select the people you want to involve. Will they have just been to campus for another event? For example, if you plan a recent-graduate reunion within a few weeks of homecoming, alumni will probably choose one event or the other but not both. By moving your recent-graduate reunion to a spring weekend, you stand a better chance of having solid attendance at both functions. Or you could package the two events on the same weekend, thereby increasing the incentive for alumni to attend.

Next, get specific and build your special events plan. You've analyzed the big picture; you've zeroed in on probable dates. What should you plan? Think about each project's significance as part of your total master plan and how it will fulfill the specific goals you've decided upon. At this point, decide whether or not to use a committee to develop plans and how much leeway such a committee should have.

PRINCIPLES TO LIVE BY

Follow a few basic principles when you are deciding on the theme or type of event to sponsor:

- *Consider the target audiences.* Are they young, old, students, professional? Are they alumni or parents who are familiar with your campus or are they people who have never been on campus before? Are they affluent or on a shoestring budget? Are they members of a constituency that will have several opportunities to participate in events on your campus during the year, or are they a group for which this special event may be the only firsthand exposure for several years?
- *Be certain the event is consistent with your institution's image and principles.* For example, if alcoholic beverages are not permitted on campus, don't try to skirt the rule in an attempt to incorporate them into an event. Don't merely work within your limitations, but use them to

make a positive statement about your support of your institution's rules and principles.

- *Use events to highlight features unique to your institution.* Or, at the very least, focus on attractions that are not readily available elsewhere in your community. Draw attention to the programs, people, and facilities that set your institution apart. You will increase attendance at your event and make a long-lasting impression on the people you invite.

EVENTS' ROLE IN FUND RAISING

Special events play two main roles in fund raising—cultivation or "friend raising," and making money through the sale of tickets or other means. It sometimes can be difficult to define where friend raising stops and fund raising starts. Both types of events are part of a comprehensive development plan to support institutional fund-raising activities and, as such, become intertwined. While guests at a black-tie dinner to launch a capital campaign may not be asked for contributions that night, they understand that the request is inevitable. The event is a friend raiser and a fund raiser.

On some campuses, glamorous events for which guests pay high prices are the focal points of the fund-raising year. Other institutions never charge current or prospective donors for any event, regardless of how elaborate it becomes.

> *Consider the target audiences. Are they young, old, students, professional? Are they alumni or parents who are familiar with your campus or are they people who have never been on campus before? Are they affluent or on a shoestring budget?*

FINANCING: HOW TO PAY FOR SPECIAL EVENTS

By their very nature, special events fall outside of the traditional budgeting process. Events can appear suddenly, as an answer to a particular problem or as a way to take advantage of an unexpected opportunity. They can grow from modest to grand, seemingly overnight. The number and types of special events vary from year to year. One manager may be more resourceful than another in securing donations to underwrite special events. The projected cost of an event may fluctuate with several different factors, from the size of the audience to the weather. Ticket sales may fall far short of projections or you may discover that the decorating committee has overshot its budget by 50 percent. Budgeting for special events is therefore frequently a process of calculated, educated guesses.

Some planners have an annual budget allocation that includes seed money to invest in events that aim to be self-supporting or to underwrite part of the cost of certain events. More often than not, events are run on a no-budget basis, a concept that every planner is familiar with, but most business people find unimaginable.

Usually, staging a first-class event is a direct reflection of the planner's resourcefulness in borrowing equipment and supplies, making decorations out of available components (the recycled parts of another event's centerpieces), or appealing to donors or sponsors to supply needed components. But while this is true, a seasoned planner should build a preliminary budget based on facts and then decide where to add and subtract.

CONCLUSION

A solid college or university development program cannot rely exclusively on special events to meet its fund-raising goals any more than friend-raising events can meet goals without proper development follow-up. Whatever the present mix of friend-raising and fund-raising events on your campus, finding the right balance is the key to success. In finding that balance, you should select events that make the maximum impact on your target audience. Fund-raising events must be consistent with your institution's image, help to achieve specific goals, showcase resources that are unique to your institution, build goodwill, and match available resources. And remember that all events must have an action follow-up. People want and need to know what you want them to do next. What should they expect? Is a development officer going

to call? Will a pledge card arrive by mail? Do you want them to volunteer their time?

Events aren't newcomers to fund raising; they have been around for a very long time. In days gone by, large fund-raising events called "benefits" or "galas" were, for the most part, the exclusive domain of arts organizations. Today, many fund-raising events jam the social calendars of universities and the communities in which they exist, making it increasingly more difficult to find interesting, relevant events that will raise a significant amount of money. Such a crowded field is also hard on the people who are invited. These days, it's difficult to find anyone of means who hasn't already been invited to several charitable fund-raising events this year. These are important reasons to be certain the fund-raising events you sponsor carry a message, are directly related to supporting your role and mission, and make sense in terms of the big picture on your campus.

FURTHER READINGS

Baldridge, Letitia. *New Complete Guide to Executive Manners*. New York, NY: Macmillan Publishing Company, 1993.

Harris, April L. *Etiquette and Protocol: A Guide for Campus Events*. Washington, DC: Council for Advancement and Support of Education, 1998.

Harris, April L. *Special Events: Planning for Success*. 2nd ed. Washington, DC: Council for Advancement and Support of Education, 1998.

Hunter, Barbara Martin. "Fun For All Ages: Want to Plan a Reunion with Mass Appeal? These Ideas Can Help You Draw Everyone from Babies to Baby Boomers, Young Alumni to Older Graduates," CURRENTS 22, no. 9 (October 1996): 14-18.

Viola, Joy Winkie. *Presidential Inaugurations: Planning for More Than Just Pomp and Circumstance*. Washington, DC: CASE, 1993.

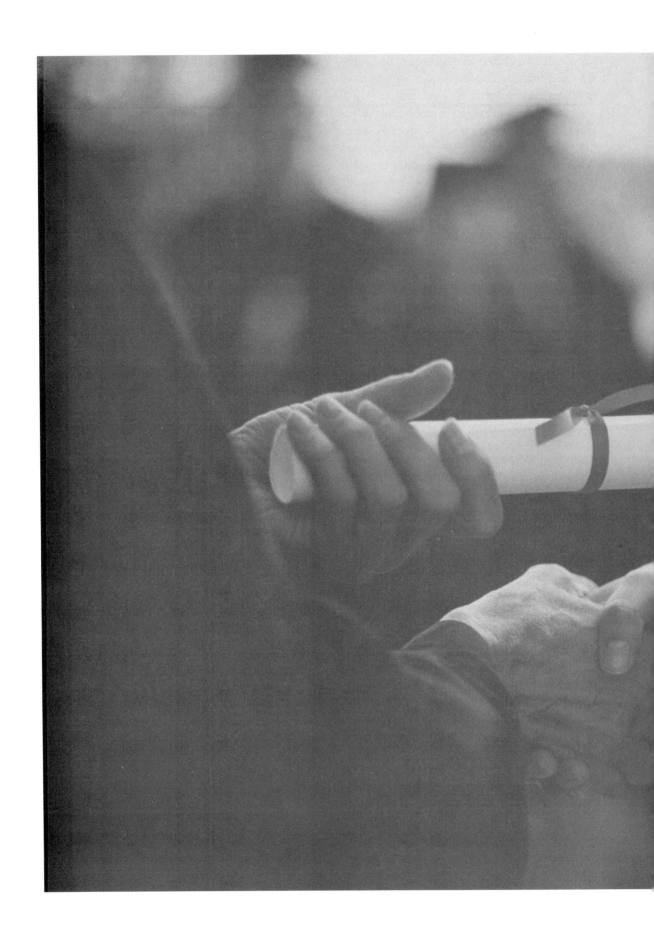

SECTION IV
Alumni Relations

Edited by Steve Grafton

Introduction

Steve Grafton
Executive Director, Alumni Association
University of Michigan

B eing asked to edit this section on alumni relations at the beginning of the 21st century is like being asked to write a chapter on the future of the Soviet Union in 1991, the year it ceased to exist. Who could have predicted how events would unfold in that part of the world? And who can say what unpredictable and lasting changes will reshape our profession in the years ahead?

LOOKING AHEAD

The forces of change—demographic, technological, generational—are creating a new landscape in alumni relations. It is highly possible that much of what we do in alumni relations today will not effectively engage alumni a decade from now, or perhaps even in five years or less. There will inevitably be new ways to engage alumni, new programs, and new services that we have not yet considered.

The authors represented in this section, all well-known and respected alumni relations professionals, are aware of—and at times refer to—these "winds of change." Yet the broad topics they cover are mostly those programs and services that we have been providing for decades. I believe we will continue to provide many of them for decades to come, albeit in some entirely new ways that will require us continually to reinvent the way we do our business.

REINVENTING ALUMNI RELATIONS

And why would we consider reinventing alumni relations? All of us in alumni relations are struggling to prove ourselves. Just look at the growing efforts to develop key success indicators and useful benchmarking tools. All of us endeavor to make the case on our campuses and among our volunteer leaders that we're worthy of respect.

This effort often takes the form of what could be called survival politics—trying to develop ways to convince others that we are doing a good job. And the truth is that we ourselves are not sure we're actually doing a good job! We can attempt to measure our success, or lack of it, by comparing ourselves to peer institutions and grading how we are doing based on how everyone else is doing. Or we can identify "model programs" in alumni relations programming that we all strive to emulate. Or we can establish benchmarks of success—overall or by individual program area—against which we measure our progress. These efforts are designed to move us incrementally toward being better than average.

Let me suggest that being better than the average, or even being the best among all other programs (by whatever measure we use), is not the standard for which we should strive. We need different standards of success and they should have little, if anything, to do with each other. I suggest that we need to measure ourselves against our institution's own particular mission and what our customers (primarily alumni) say they need from us.

The average number of an institution's alumni who are dues-paying members of the alumni association or contribute to the annual fund is between 20 and 30 percent. Rather than focus on such a rate, we should ask ourselves, "What about the 70 to 80 percent who choose not to participate?".

Is it possible to achieve a much higher participation rate—say 50, 75, even 90 percent or more? An officer in our alumni association who works for a national trade association told me his organization has a more than 90 percent penetration rate among potential members. He was also quick to add, "But we are different. Our association provides something the members have to have and can get nowhere else."

Aha! So how can we become like that?

First, we have to find out what our alumni have to have and how we can provide it. Market research, even in alumni relations programs, is not a new concept, but I would argue that we've never really done it right. Some of us have used it, but only to reinforce our current programs or to make incremental changes in them.

I have a theory that current alumni relations programs were designed 40 to 100 years ago for generations that had and have very little in common with the majority of today's alumni. This is why membership in our university's association among mature alumni is at 33 percent, while membership among Baby Boomers is at 20 percent, and membership among Generation Xers is at 22 percent (including a large number of free memberships for last year's graduates). While we might have good programs, we are serving a diminishing percentage of our alumni with those programs. This could have significant ramifications not only for us, but for alumni support of the university in other ways as well.

The future of alumni relations should not be about simply changing programs occasionally as we discover different needs and interests of alumni. Rather, it is about becoming organizations that continually "invent the future" of serving and engaging alumni. Then and only then can we significantly increase not only the percentage that are active participants but, more importantly, the quality of alumni interaction with and support for the university.

Our current approach may no longer allow us to accomplish these goals. While many of us have strong programs today, we may not have in place all the appropriate processes or products to remain that way or to become anything more than slightly better. We must adapt to changes in the way people live their lives—and to the more significant changes ahead—and offer innovative ideas and programs that will accommodate and capitalize on these trends.

WHAT THIS MEANS FOR YOU

As you read the chapters that follow, pay close attention to the suggestions for innovative ways to adapt to your changing constituency. Consider the kinds of changes necessary to engage your alumni, whether it means eliminating long-standing programs, making significant changes in them, or creating entirely new programs and services that create value for your own "customers."

The first chapters in the section focus on services that alumni associations are expanding these days because of keen alumni interest. In Chapter 1, Jeffrey Brenzel, executive director, Association of Yale Alumni, Yale University, discusses alumni education and lifelong learning; in Chapter 2, Douglas Dibbert, president, General Alumni Association, The University of North Carolina, tackles alumni career services; and in Chapter 3, Charles F. Lennon Jr., executive director, alumni association and associate vice president for university relations, University of Notre Dame, writes about community service programs.

In Chapters 4, 5, 7, and 10, the nod goes to more traditional programs. Diane Benninghoff, director, alumni and parent programs, Colorado College, discusses generational issues in programming; Susan Clouse Dolbert, president and executive director, Arizona State University Alumni Association, focuses on alumni awards programs; Todd Coleman, executive director, University of Missouri Alumni Association, writes about chapters and clubs; and Karen Hansen, executive director of the Center for Lifelong Learning (former director of alumni/ae and parent relations), St. Olaf College, explores parents programs. In Chapters 8 and 9, the authors focus on relatively new alumni programs—campus and constituent alumni groups, by Midge Wood Brittingham, executive director, Oberlin College Alumni Association, and student advancement programs, by Paul Chewning, vice president, professional development, CASE. In Chapters 6, 11, 12, 13, 14, and 15, the authors discuss the role of alumni boards (by Amy Button Renz, president, Kansas State University Alumni Association); alumni relations with undergraduate admissions (by Laney Funderburk, associate

vice president, alumni affairs, Duke University); alumni advocacy (by Margaret Sughrue Carlson, executive director, University of Minnesota Alumni Association); alumni role in fund raising (by Jeffrey Todd, director of alumni relations and The Wooster Fund, The College of Wooster); communicating with alumni (by Keith Brant, executive director, UCLA Alumni Association); and international alumni relations (by Reggie Simpson, head of alumni relations, London School of Economics). The final chapters (16, 17, and 18) deal with alumni records and technology, by James H. Melton, president, Florida State University Alumni Association; securing financial resources, by John Carter, president and CEO, Georgia Tech Foundation; and legal issues for alumni administrators, by Dan Heinlen, president, The Ohio State University Alumni Association.

Less than a decade after the breakup of the Soviet Union, that pivotal event continues to reverberate not only within the region, but throughout the world. Those of us in the alumni relations field face changes that, while not as cataclysmic, will surely be unexpected and inescapable. By anticipating and embracing these changes, we can help strengthen and sustain our institutions' vital missions, and serve our alumni in ways we can only now just imagine.

In a consumer society accustomed to continuous quality improvement by enterprises competing for customers, alumni expect (and indeed, assume) that they will receive absolutely first quality programs, service, and response from institutions with which they identify. They therefore expect educational offerings in particular to be first-rate, diverse, and easily accessible.

Alumni Education and Lifelong Learning: Changes in the Wind

Jeffrey Brenzel
Executive Director, Association of Yale Alumni
Yale University

For the immediate future, the watchwords for alumni education programs will be "rapid evolution" and "explosive expansion." Many institutions are experimenting with new delivery technologies and rethinking educational program opportunities. Let's look first at what is driving these changes. Then we can ponder the different directions in which alumni programs could move, as well as the criteria for good decision making in this promising, but challenging area.

WHAT'S DRIVING CHANGE?

1. Motivations. Alumni relations at many institutions used to revolve around alma mater's success in athletic competition and nostalgia for the days of one's youth. While these factors are still significant, they are no longer the key connections for a growing number of alumni. We now see active alumni of every generation seeking engaging relationships with one another and with the intellectual, social, or creative life of the institution. In part, they have adopted a lifelong learning ethic with respect to personal growth and development, and in part they expect their college or university affiliations to reflect their personal identity,

career status, and sense of accomplishment.

2. Expectations. Briefly put, alumni of all eras seem to have higher expectations of their institutions today in almost every respect. In a consumer society accustomed to continuous quality improvement by enterprises competing for customers, alumni expect (and indeed, assume) that they will receive absolutely first quality programs, service, and response from institutions with which they identify. They therefore expect educational offerings in particular to be first-rate, diverse, and easily accessible.

3. Communications. Our alumni audiences are assaulted with an unprecedented variety of media messages. They, too, are themselves using new media and new tools to communicate with one another and with their cultural, business, social, and political institutions. This proliferation of both messages and channels presents us with a significant change in alumni demand for creativity and facility with communications technologies.

IMPLICATIONS FOR ALUMNI EDUCATION PROGRAMS

Three types of education programs have dominated alumni education to date. The first consists of programs offered on campus—stand-alone

Alumni
Education and
Lifelong
Learning:
Changes in
the Wind

seminars and institutes, or programs delivered in conjunction with reunions, athletic contests, or other events that bring alumni to campus. Some alumni organizations have also created traveling seminars that send faculty out to local clubs or associations for speaking engagements or short courses. Finally, many alumni associations have developed travel education programs, sending groups of alumni, with or without university faculty, on customized or packaged trips that usually involve an educational component.

Given the changes we've described, many organizations are experiencing difficulty in meeting alumni expectations with these three traditional types of programs. In short, competition for time, higher expectations for program quality, diversifying interests, and a focus on new communications tools make it harder to satisfy alumni with time-intensive programs of inconsistent quality that take place at a distance from where they live and work.

CRITICAL PATH CRITERIA

Given the factors driving change and the implications for alumni education, how should alumni organizations work to rethink their programs? Here are seven critical questions by which to evaluate your current operations and planning:

1. Are you actively monitoring colleagues at peer institutions that have created online learning centers for alumni? Are you at least experimenting with distance learning projects?
2. Have you allocated or are you seeking serious funds for capital expenditures in areas required by distance learning: delivery systems, course design, faculty engagement, and marketing?
3. Does your education travel program offer a real connection to the institution and substantial educational content? (If not, you will soon face serious competition from increasingly sophisticated for-profit operators and aggressive, non-profit, cultural institutions.)
4. Do your on-campus programs feature the institution's most charismatic faculty, and are you presenting (and promoting) substantive, challenging adult education opportunities?
5. Across all delivery methods, are you adequately segmenting your market? That is, are you offering relevant career, financial, and family-orient-

ed topics and subjects to younger alumni, while recognizing that older alumni often seek reconnection to the humanities or exploration of the sciences? Are you developing programs targeted to special interests ?

6. Are you offering programs at a full range of price points and time commitments? Do you have an integrated marketing strategy for education programs to alert differing age groups and differing income groups to the many ways in which they might participate?
7. Perhaps most importantly, do you understand that most good adult education programs now focus as much on peer-to-peer learning as on delivery by expert faculty? Do your programs both encourage and allow alumni to engage one another, both during and after the program?

A FINAL NOTE ON TECHNOLOGY

After running a company that designed and delivered online education, and then taking on the task of transferring that learning to the alumni association at Yale, I can offer two comments on distance learning and communications technologies. First, there is no way to predict, in this period of rapid evolution, how pedagogical designs, software systems, delivery systems, bandwidth capacities, learner preferences, third-party infrastructure vendors, and a host of other relevant variables are going to work. The critical and difficult challenges are to find the funds, conduct the research, and make the effort to test pilot projects that may or may not prove self-funding or otherwise successful.

The second thing to remember is that, at least so far, multimedia on its own has failed the test of the marketplace. That is, self-paced learning that depends on high production values and focuses exclusively on user interaction with software simply has not proved capable of holding the attention of adult learners. Putting up streaming video and audio on the Web does not constitute education. The missing, and critical, ingredient is other people, including an active and expert instructor. In every successful distance learning initiative with which I am familiar, the incorporation of credible, trained discussion leaders, and substantial peer-to-peer communication, determines the quality of outcomes.

I recognize that most alumni organizations function under severe constraints with respect to capital financing and access to faculty. The truth is that while these challenges will not diminish, the expansion and diversification of alumni education programs will require real capital investments and closer collaboration with an institution's best teachers. At Yale, I have seen a growing recognition among senior administrators that the need to engage alumni more broadly with the core values and programming of the university justifies these investments. My hope is that this recognition will translate into a long-term vision for lifelong learning projects, both here at Yale and at other institutions.

FURTHER READINGS

The Chronicle of Higher Education Web site: *http://chronicle.com*.

Dibbert, Douglas S. "Learning: In It for Life: A CASE Survey Provides an Overview of Alumni Education," CURRENTS 17, no. 5 (May 1991): 20-22.

High, Martha and Alan Dessoff. "Measure Of Success: Continuing Education Programs Can Be Self-Supporting, But They Can't Thrive Unless Your Campus Appreciates Their Intrinsic Value," CURRENTS 20, no. 2 (February 1994): 24-27.

Lefebure, Jane B. "In Search of Adventure: McMaster University Alumni Discover Out-of-the-Ordinary Opportunities for Learning," CURRENTS 17, no. 5 (May 1991): 27-28.

Shaindlin, Andrew. "Alumni Learning Online: Brown's Electronic Continuing Education Course Makes the Grade with Former Students," CURRENTS 21, no. 1 (January 1995): 72.

Todd, Jeffrey S. "Something for Everyone: Young Alumni Can Also Benefit from Continuing Education—If You Use Creative Ways to Catch Their Interest," CURRENTS 20, no. 2 (February 1994): 28-32.

Recognizing that most of us will go through a job search five to eight times in our lifetime, it makes sense to teach people how to assess their skills, do market research, and conduct a job search.

Alumni Career Services: Making a Difference

Douglas S. Dibbert
President, General Alumni Association
The University of North Carolina

Traditionally, alumni associations have focused on alumni clubs, travel programs, athletic events, lifelong learning programs, and reunions to keep alumni informed and connected to their schools, colleges, and universities. However, in the early 1990s, a number of alumni associations started to include alumni career services as an integral part of their programming.

THE CASE FOR ALUMNI CAREER SERVICES

The most compelling reason for alumni associations to get involved in career services is their extraordinary importance to the individual. Career decisions are among the most important decisions we make, and they have an impact on every aspect of our lives. By providing education, guidance, and networking opportunities, alumni career services can help alumni actively manage their careers. In addition, alumni career services are essential when alumni are in a career crisis—when they are unhappy with their career choice or when they are unemployed. At these times, alumni are particularly grateful for what they perceive as a demonstration of support and caring for their well being by their alma mater.

Rapid change, globalization, economic pressures, and corporate restructuring have made it necessary for employees to actively manage their careers. Self-reliance and self-sufficiency have replaced the traditional career paths as the keys to career success and satisfaction. However, most people have not learned to manage their careers. In fact, many seem to have backed into their current careers without much thought about what would make them happy, or what skills and competencies they needed to find the ideal job. As a result of this less-than-thoughtful approach to career management, they are completely unprepared to launch a job search.

Although most colleges and universities offer some career services for alumni, those services frequently reside within the undergraduate career services department and emphasize planning and placement. Resume drops and on-campus recruiting work when large numbers of students eager for entry-level positions need help to gain experience and build resumes. However, these resources are unlikely to serve more experienced alumni who have moved beyond the any-job-at-any-price mentality. Because of their experience, they are frequently looking at careers with more meaning, higher salaries, and greater challenges. They need more than job postings to help them reach their career goals. They may also be poised to entertain a radical career change that better aligns them with their real passion.

A CAREER SERVICES MODEL

The most effective alumni career services focus on education rather than placement. An ancient proverb says, "Give a man a fish and you feed him for a day; teach a man to fish, and you feed him for a lifetime." Recognizing that most of us will go through a job search five to eight times in our lifetime, it is important to teach people how to assess their skills, do market research, and conduct a job search. Helping people understand their personalities, skills, interests, and values gives them the insight needed to select careers that will be meaningful and rewarding. Helping people understand the intricacies of the job search, including writing resumes and cover letters, interviewing, networking, and negotiating, gives them the confidence to create job search strategies that yield results.

SETTING UP A CAREER SERVICES PROGRAM

To create your alumni career services, consider the following steps:

- Determine what your financial objective is. Alumni career services can be provided at very little cost to the association. With the exception of salaries, most programs can generate enough revenue to offset expenses. Depending on the scope of your program, revenue opportunities can come from a variety of services, including counseling, assessment, workshops, job postings, as well as resume matching services.
- Start slowly and do not promise more than you can deliver. Decide on your mission and stick to it.
- Recruit business-savvy career counselors who can provide counseling, coaching, and assessment—as well as a realistic view of the work world—to help alumni define and pursue their career goals.
- Develop an active alumni adviser network made up of alumni volunteers willing to share career

● ● ●
Many people seem to have backed into their current careers without much thought about what would make them happy, or they lack the skills necessary to find the ideal job. As a result, they are completely unprepared to launch a job search.

information, provide support and advice, and generate additional networking leads. The alumni network is one of the most valuable assets of any career services program. In addition to linking alumni to the university and each other, the network helps to warm up "cold calls" to strangers and enables alumni to explore a variety of career options. Alumni advisers can provide inside information about an industry's outlook or a particular profession's salary range. They can also provide an insider's view of a particular company's culture or the day-to-day realities of their chosen career.

- Create a career resource center with self-help and how-to resources, career information, job search materials, newspapers, and magazines.
- Provide computers for creating professional, customized resumes and cover letters.
- Provide Internet access, which is indispensable in researching companies, comparing salaries, and learning about distant cities. (Note: We often make the assumption that the world is computer literate but the reality is that many alumni still do not own computers or have access to the Internet.)
- Establish links to key Internet career sites like the Monster Board (*www.monsterboard.com*) or Career Mosaic (*www.careermosiac.com*) that post available jobs and allow job seekers to submit their resumes online. These Internet connectors simplify the research process for alumni with limited experience navigating the Internet who may become confused or frustrated with the amount of information available. The connectors can also take alumni directly to self-assessment instruments, resume help, interview questions, and annual reports.
- Offer just-in-time counseling—help when you need it. In a world of sound bites and instant replays, we have come to expect immediate results. People are reluctant to wait for a workshop on resume writing when they have identified a job they want in the morning paper. They also want individual help with tough questions as they go to an interview and emotional support when they lose their jobs.

■ Schedule flexible hours and locations—taking services to communities where you have large concentrations of alumni, and outreach to other community organizations to familiarize them with your services. Consider your local library as a convenient meeting place for counseling.

■ Tailor services to the needs of your alumni.

■ Offer some services free or at a reduced rate for association members.

Of all the alumni programs, it can be argued that none offers a better way to connect students with the association in a more lasting way than alumni career services. Increasingly, students come to campus eager to demonstrate to their parents and themselves that their college education will eventually lead to a satisfying and income-producing career. Immediately reassuring those entering students that former students can and will help, and emphasizing that this is a life-long quest, can be important in developing a lasting relationship between students, the alumni association, and alumni.

Alumni career services can create a win-win situation for your association and your alumni. The rewards can be seen in alumni who are flourishing in their careers and who view their alumni association favorably for providing them with the tools they need to do so.

FURTHER READINGS

Carter, Lindy Keane. "Job Descriptions: Alumni Directors Tell How They Share Career Network Responsibilities With the Career Office," CURRENTS 15, no. 2 (February 1989): 36-39.

Carter, Lindy Keane. "Making the Career Connection: Your Alumni Office Can Provide a Link Between Job-Hunting Alumni and the Contacts They Need," CURRENTS 15, no. 2 (February 1989): 30-34.

Conklin, Linda. "Help Wanted: More Than Anything Else, Young Alumni Are Seeking Career Advice. Show You're Qualified to Meet Their Needs by Offering These Four Services," CURRENTS 24, no. 6 (June 1998): 22-23.

Dessoff, Alan L. "Computer Classifieds: Electronic Career Services Link Alumni with Employers," CURRENTS 18, no. 7 (July/August 1992): 10-14, 16.

Larson, Jackson and Comstock, Cheri. *The New Rules of the Job Search Game: Why Today's Managers Hire...And Why They Don't.* Holbrook, MA: Adams Media Corporation, 1994.

Ryan, Robin. "Shaping Alumni Careers: With the Right Planning and Promotion, You Can Create Programming That Helps Your Former Students Find Jobs," CURRENTS 22, no. 1 (January 1996): 34-36, 38.

In delivering service programs, …begin with simple goals and realistic objectives, given your association's size, interest level, available resources, and degree of commitment.

Community Service Programs: Alumni Reaching Out

Charles F. Lennon, Jr.
Executive Director, Alumni Association and Associate Vice President for University Relations
University of Notre Dame

"The best way to get something done is to begin." This message greets, and (we hope) motivates, Notre Dame's alumni club leaders as they open our *Community Service Coordinator Handbook* (*www.alumni.nd.edu*), and this is the advice I offer you as you contemplate designing or improving your association's volunteer program.

As we all know, society today continues to present ever-increasing gaps between the "have's" and "have not's." However, volunteers in America are striving to meet the varying needs of our communities. According to a 1998 national Gallup survey conducted for Independent Sector, an estimated 109.4 million Americans (55 percent of adults 18 years of age or older) volunteered an average of 3.5 hours a week for a total of 19.9 billion hours. With the modest increase in the adult population, these numbers should continue to increase annually. Clearly, it is practical to offer volunteer programs to meet this developing interest of alumni. Don't be surprised when individuals suddenly come out of the woodwork and become active in your clubs after realizing that participating in a service project is a free and social alternative to cocktail parties, banquets, and athletic events.

Sheryl Coon, associate director of the University of Illinois–Chicago Alumni Association, echoes this sentiment. "Community service projects have given us an opportunity to involve a segment of alumni who hadn't been attracted to more traditional alumni programs and activities," she says. With a majority of U of I's graduates living in an urban setting with a bounty of local charitable organizations, Coon recognizes that offering the projects is a win-win. "Obviously, the need for volunteer programming exists and obviously everyone benefits."

RECRUITING VOLUNTEERS

During the last two decades, our campuses have trained young men and women in experiential service learning projects. It is now up to us as alumni administrators to act as institutional stewards by extending this practice through our programming. In the process, an educational element will indirectly emerge as both participants and recipients discover much about each other, including what they have in common as well as the need to eliminate unfounded stereotyping. In addition, by recognizing and stressing the necessity of demonstrating dignity and respect with project recipients, participants and recipients will learn a lesson in diversity.

DELIVERING SERVICE PROGRAMMING

In delivering service programming, you do not have to offer a vast array of initiatives. Begin with simple goals and realistic objectives, given your association's size, interest level, available resources, and degree of commitment. But in doing so, don't cut yourself short. For example, start at the top by asking your president, in conjunction with your governing body, to declare your institution's full-fledged commitment by proclaiming a Humanitarian Week in which your chapters are expected to perform service. This week could serve to kick off your overall community service program. Include both weekends to allow for flexibility; offer a list of sample proven projects (complete with how to's); prepare sample newsletter articles along with promotional clip art; explain the process of acquiring, appreciating, recognizing, and retaining volunteers; and most importantly, display your enthusiasm and encouragement. Finally, remind your leaders that they don't have to reinvent the wheel. Sometimes it's best to piggyback onto proven projects or to work with organizations such as the United Way.

Immediately following the week, ask your clubs to complete an evaluation, send in pictures, and write a report (include a section on sustaining their service project on a regular basis). To encourage them to comply, offer incentives such as alumni merchandise or game ticket giveaways. Use this material in your publications both externally and internally. Brief campus leaders, especially coaches and professors who regularly make presentations to your alumni. Personally recruit them to become advocates of your community service program by asking them to recognize specific club efforts. Don't forget to involve your athletic teams in projects, especially in the off season.

COSTS

Most volunteer projects do not cost much—if anything—to begin and maintain. The major expense is promotion, which can fall under other regular fixed cost categories, such as printing a newsletter, operating a Web site, sending out e-mails, and making personal phone calls. There are, for instance, no real costs associated with asking participants to bring food staples along with them to a club event to donate to a food pantry (and most agencies will pick up the contribution). The same holds true for a roadside cleanup, visiting a nursing home, or serving dinner at a homeless shelter. In addition, your alumni association administrative costs can simply fall under what you normally budget to deliver any other club program.

PARTNERING OPPORTUNITIES

Offer national projects by partnering with established organizations such as Toys for Tots, Habitat for Humanity, or Christmas in April. At Notre Dame, our Family Volunteer Camps in the summer and during mid-term breaks bring alumni from all over the country to campus, Appalachia, or other sites to explore their common interest, volunteering. In order to meet our costs, we charge generally $160 per person, which covers housing in a dormitory and most meals. Much of the food is donated or reduced in price; transportation is the responsibility of each participant; and the partnering agency is responsible for insurance coverage and for supplying the tools and building materials.

Finally, contact your contemporaries within your athletic conference or at sister institutions to join forces to support a designated nonprofit agency such as the Red Cross or a local food pantry. Or work with your admissions office to identify high schools to "adopt." This can involve not only tutoring students but also mentoring them regarding college and the classes required for certain careers, and job shadowing.

Syracuse, Cornell, The Sage Colleges, and the University of Albany, State University of New York are four of the institutions who participate in Party for a Plate. This charity raises money for Albany's regional food bank. The fund raiser, originally conceived by Boston College, attracts about 300 people each year, mostly young alumni, to an evening of sampling donated food from several area restaurants for a reasonable contribution, according to Christine Sarratori, director for constituent and regional programs in the University of

> Remind your leaders that they don't have to reinvent the wheel. Sometimes it's best to piggyback onto proven projects or to work with organizations such as the United Way.

Albany's Office of Alumni Affairs. Each college hosts a table for its respective alumni, who are wearing nametags with campus logos. The program also features a silent auction and raffle. "I think alumni associations across the country are seeking different ways to engage our graduates in activities that are meaningful because we want them to enjoy themselves while reaping some intrinsic rewards," Sarratori says. "In addition, projects such as Party for a Plate are a good component to add to an overall alumni program because, among other things, it casts our institutions in a very favorable light in that we're demonstrating our social consciousness."

It costs little to offer this project. Each alum pays a small entrance fee, and vendors (restaurants, library bookstores) donate their time, services, and products (food, raffle prizes, space) in exchange for visibility.

Why does an alumni relations professional like Sarratori undertake yet another activity for her association when she already has a full plate? "It's easy and fun to organize something worthwhile like this," she says, "and because it helps put food in someone's mouth. That's all the motivation I need."

Now for your motivation. At the end of our *Community Service Handbook* is an inducement by Henry David Thoreau that serves this chapter well: "What I begin by reading, I must finish by acting."

FURTHER READINGS

Kobara, John. "Helping Others, Helping Ourselves," CURRENTS 20, no. 3 (March 1994): 50.

Lennon, Chuck. "Service With a Smile: Helping Alumni Reach Out and Make a Difference in Their Communities," CURRENTS 17, no. 6 (June 1991): 56.

McDaniel, Sheila. "Joint Ventures in Volunteering," CURRENTS 20, No. 3 (March 1994) 52.

Rhoads, Robert A. *Community Service and Higher Education: Explorations of the Caring Self.* Albany, NY: State University of New York Press, 1997.

Sanner, Jennifer Jackson. "At Your Service: Alumni Groups Across the Country are Making a Difference in Their Communities," CURRENTS 16, no. 7 (July/August 1990): 10-14.

Scully, Maura King. "Valuable Volunteers—The Challenges and Benefits of Engaging Alumni in Community-Service Programs," CURRENTS 26, no. 1 (January 2000): 26-33.

Our very survival in difficult times will depend upon the connection our alumni can make between their institution and whatever is most meaningful in their lives.

Generational Issues in Alumni Programming

Diane Benninghoff
Director, Alumni and Parent Programs
Colorado College

Alumni programs have long relied on homecomings, reunions, and other special events to connect and reconnect our alumni with the institution and with each other.

But are we in for "future shock?" Is something happening in the segment of alumni we serve that could change the way we look at these time-honored events? Consider:

■ The World War II generation born between 1901 and 1924 (the classes of 1922–48) is passing out of our active alumni base.

■ The "Silent Generation," born between 1925 and 1942 (the classes of 1946–63), has or is about to retire.

■ "Boomers," born between 1943 and 1960 (the classes of 1964–81) are reaching the height of their influence.

■ Those independent minded GenXer's, born between 1961 and 1981 (the classes of 1982-2002) are becoming our volunteer core.

■ The "millennial" generation, born after 1982 (the classes of 2003 and beyond), is upon us.

When we think about what kind of programming might strike a chord with our alumni, the ideals or ideas particular to each generation, as described in three books by Neil Howe and Bill Strauss, should guide us. We need to think about what matters to these very different generations and how they relate to events in the wider world. What's more, we are reaching the end of a four-generation cycle, so we should expect to see certain characteristics begin to repeat themselves.

EVENTS THROUGH GENERATIONAL EYES

Let's imagine a homecoming, reunion, or special event in the years 2003-2005. What will these various generations expect from us? What kinds of programming will work for them? Recognizing that generalizations about groups are often wrong and inevitably subjective, here's advice based on the generational descriptions presented in the Howe and Strauss books.

World War II Generation

The WWII generation will be coming back to its 55th-70th reunions. As the generation from which we will never take away senior entitlements (they saved the world for us, after all), they are likely to be financially secure and their sense of community will not have dimmed. They'll like our current students, for in them they will see them-

selves: heroes in the making.
- Get them together with current students.
- Create opportunities for them to reminisce.
- Use them as a resource to talk about the value of teamwork, community, and sacrifice.

The Silent Generation

The Silent Generation will be celebrating retirement and 40th-55th reunions. This professional generation, which includes more lawyers, doctors, and others in the "helping professions" per capita than others, brought us civil rights, systems and organizations that focused on making life "fair" to all, and the advent of increasing divorce rates. They will not go gently into retirement, but will stay involved and interested. They will commiserate with one another that the GenXer's are still not concerned enough with others, but they will be impressed with the accomplishments and promise of current students. They will want to reconnect, perhaps even to the college classmates they have ignored.
- Provide even more continuing education. Offer seminars, let them meet faculty (even though "their" faculty might no longer be around).
- Create programs featuring student achievement (singers, actors, seminars featuring students as well as faculty).
- Create inter-generational opportunities: Grandparent days, educational travel that encourages them to bring the grandchildren.
- Schedule estate planning programming, which will allow them a last chance to "set things right."

Boomers

Boomers, who have always known what is best for others, will continue to direct their thinking toward the individual. As leaders of society, they will judge what we do, and what students and others do. Just as alumni directors heard from alumni about the excesses of the Boomers when they were students, we'll be fielding a new raft of complaints from Boomers themselves as they return for their 20th-40th reunions. They will ask much of their alma mater: Are we meeting our moral responsibilities in our treatment of current students? Are our institutions academically and morally tough enough? Are we doing our part to create a more civil society?

But the Boomers will also be in two camps: civil liberals and civil conservatives. Who will win the battle for the soul of our institution and our young people? Expect those 20th reunion folks to bring tiny (perfect) babies, born late, and cherished greatly. These alumni will develop new concepts of community, step back from their workaholic tendencies, and shed their high-tech toys and demand that others do the same.
- Offer children's programs, especially with a moral tone.
- Give them opportunities to gather in focus groups or discussions with the president to tell the college/university how it should operate.
- Develop a seminar on "getting back to basics," or "living the simple life."
- Arrange for alumni panel discussions to advise the current college generation.
- Schedule seminars about why people do what they do, or at least how we feel about things like middle age, retirement, future generations.
- In estate planning seminars, develop ways Boomers can give advice along with their money.

GenXers

Finally, the GenXer's are coming into their own. Celebrating their 5th-20th reunions, they will continue to rely more on personal friendships (which are vast in number) than on institutionally organized gatherings. They'll want to know, "Who else is coming?" while remaining suspicious of traditions and institutions. If you use planning committees in regional groups, GenXers may only want to work with their personal friends. They'll see little need to have other generations—especially Boomers—at the table for planning events. They will continue to "get it done" (whatever "it" is), efficiently and on their own. The most diverse generation ever, they're tired of hearing you talk problems to death. They want you to stop talking and do it! No "spin" on college issues will do, so skip the public relations events. They won't give a hoot about seeing the president,

> ● ● ●
> **Boomers, who have always known what is best for others, will continue to direct their thinking toward the individual.**

unless he or she became a friend during their student years. Likewise, they may only attend a faculty event if there's a chance to see someone who can help get them ahead in a tough world.

Trust and need for institutional identity have been at a minimum, with little loyalty and little team spirit. But, as we near 2004, GenXers will yearn to settle down, with all that goes with that.

■ Offer plenty of children's activities. They will be devoted to their children.

■ No "PR" sessions with the President, but straightforward discussions of budgets, belt tightening, doing less with more. Bring the financial vice president.

■ Professional development seminars show them we really care what happens to them in a tough world.

■ When planning reunions, let them think of ways to hold reunions that will challenge our notions of "how it's done." Electronic, off-site, and special interest groups may hold more appeal than traditional formats.

■ Design events that focus on friends, friends, friends. They know how to get their friends involved; we'd better listen.

■ Introduce community service events that allow them to work one-on-one with individuals.

Millennial Generation

Millennial young adults herald the return to tradition, an *esprit de corps* whose motto is "we're all in this together." This is quite possibly the dream generation for alumni directors. They'll find the selfishness of the boomers bewildering, find the Xer's (who will begin to dominate faculty ranks) competent but sadly cynical. If we ask them to participate in alumni events, they'll see it as their obligation. Homecomings could become bigger than ever. They are likely to be conformist and may depend on others to arrive at decisions. If tradition is what we want, millennial adults will deliver.

CONNECTING IS IMPORTANT

What could be the fly in the ointment? A national crisis in the next five years or so would change things. Alumni programs would seem less meaningful in such a time. But if traveling to a campus is difficult or frivolous, maintaining connections with friends will not be. We may then have to find the way to become a truly electronic community—providing all of the needs of our generations in brand-new ways.

Our very survival in difficult times will depend upon the connection our alumni can make between their institution and whatever is most meaningful in their lives. Our challenge may be to provide an important anchor: an enduring community that can adapt to the times and maintain the lifelong connection of our alumni family.

FURTHER READINGS

Christion, Laura. "Courting Young Alumni: Nine Program Ideas to Help You Ignite the Interest of Recent Graduates," CURRENTS 18, no. 6 (June 1992): 12-13.

Howe, Neil and William Strauss: *Generations: The History of America's Future, 1584 to 2069.* New York, NY: William Morrow and Company, 1991.

Howe, Neil and William Strauss: *13th Gen: Abort, Retry, Ignore, Fail?* New York, NY: Vintage Books, 1993.

Howe, Neil and William Strauss: The Fourth Turning: An American Prophecy: *What the Cycles of History Tell Us About America's Next Rendezvous with Destiny.* New York, NY: Broadway Books, 1997.

Hunter, Barbara Martin. "Fun For All Ages: Want to Plan a Reunion with Mass Appeal? These Ideas Can Help You Draw Everyone from Babies to Baby Boomers, Young Alumni to Older Graduates," CURRENTS 22, no. 9 (October 1996): 14-18.

Kennedy, Marilyn Moats. "X Marks the Spot: Ideas for Targeting Your Alumni Association to Career-Driven, Cash-Strapped Recent Graduates," CURRENTS 24, no. 6 (June 1998): 16-19.

Rochlin, Jay and Sandy Ruhl. "Taking a Hard Look at Homecoming: Has This Major Celebration Become an Unnecessary Habit on Your Campus? Use These Research Techniques to Determine Whether Your Program is Meeting a Real Need," CURRENTS 19, no. 8 (September 1993): 11-15.

Sabo, Sandra R. "Tinkering With Tradition: A Few Adjustments Can Keep the Crowds Cheering Year After Year," CURRENTS 19, no. 8 (September 1993): 17-22.

Associations that develop and maintain strong awards programs recognize their alma mater's strengths while contributing to institutional growth and progress.

Alumni Awards: A Win-Win

Susan Clouse Dolbert
President and Executive Director, Arizona State University Alumni Association
Arizona State University

In alumni relations, we are always looking for situations that are, as popularly phrased by organizational guru Stephen Covey, "win-win." An effective award program can certainly provide a win-win opportunity for the alumni association and for the exceptional individuals and organizations honored by alumni awards.

Awards can also add meaning to events, increase attendance, provide publicity in nontraditional venues (not just the alumni magazine!), and result in increased giving—either from the recipient or from friends and colleagues of the recipient.

Awards presented as part of public events provide the greatest opportunities. Who wouldn't be thrilled to be honored during halftime at a homecoming football game? Similar opportunities exist at broad-based events such as Founders' Day. While a dinner may recognize the institution's founders, it can also be an ideal time to highlight outstanding alumni, faculty, and staff members. Reunions, commencement, and college convocations can also serve as great award venues.

Alumni awards can be presented to individuals or to organizations. Each category has many opportunities for recognition.

INDIVIDUAL AWARDS

Alumni

Awards presented to alumni most often focus on their professional achievements; however, alumni achievement generally involves contributions to community. Many associations determine award recipients based on age or time since graduation (that is, there may be separate categories for graduates younger than 40, or those who have graduated less than 15 years prior to the award).

Other alumni awards may be designed specifically to acknowledge service to the institution or to the alumni association. The award may recognize service as a result of holding a specific office such as president or board member or may simply recognize overall service to the institution by an alumnus.

Most often, alumni awards are symbolic, rather than having any kind of monetary award. More important than the symbol is the enthusiasm displayed by the staff and volunteers during the awards process and ceremony. An opportunity exists for a unique and special remembrance. One association presents its past chairman/chairwoman with a large framed collage of photos from his or her term, along with a letter highlighting the past year's accomplishments. Other associations ensure their awardees receive a plaque or office-related gift so the recipient's affiliation with the college or university can be displayed publicly.

Nonalumni

Most alumni associations provide awards to individuals who did not attend the institution, yet who have demonstrated outstanding service and loyalty to the institution. These supporters are often given recognition through an alumni appreciation award. The recipient may have provided monetary support or may have been a legislator who supported positive student legislation or a retiring member of the institution's governing board whose tenure was exceptional.

Again, a public venue for recognition (Homecoming halftime, or Founders' Day) is appropriate. While a "one-of-a-kind" award is often preferable, a plaque or office-related gift to reinforce the recipient's relationship with the institution is the more standard practice.

Students

Often, alumni associations sponsor awards to graduating seniors. This sponsorship provides great alumni visibility to the senior class. Individual graduating student awards may include man and woman of the year; outstanding male and female scholar; outstanding graduate of a college, department, or program; or highest grade point average.

Many associations recognize accomplishments of students from particular groups or organizations prior to the senior year—from the highest G.P.A. on the football team to the outstanding member of the debate team. Another interesting twist is to recognize students through an alumni award (that is, awarding a book scholarship to a student in the name of an alumnus receiving an award from the association).

It is also common for college and university alumni associations to support scholarship or award programs for high school students, such as providing a scholarship for the outstanding high school junior. Alumni chapters may also recognize high school students based on location or interests. The marching band alumni chapter may rec-

ognize students who plan to participate in college band activities.

Student awards may include money or scholarships, or may be limited to desk sets, plaques, etc.

Faculty

Faculty awards present ideal opportunities to recognize the institution's most outstanding teachers and researchers as well as faculty members who have demonstrated a dedication to university and community service. In academia, where the pressure to produce research is so intense, it is important to develop programs that also recognize exceptional teachers or those who demonstrate a willingness to help students, the institution, or the community. After all, these are alumni awards, and our graduates most remember those faculty members who were excellent instructors or who clearly communicated a caring, supportive attitude toward students.

> ● ● ●
> **In academia, where the pressure to produce research is so intense, it is important to develop programs that also recognize exceptional teachers or those who demonstrate a willingness to help students, the institution, or the community.**

And, since faculty awards generally are part of a larger campus program, they provide an opportunity to educate campus constituents about the alumni association. They also remind constituents of the institution's outstanding graduates—the actual products their hard work produces.

Faculty awards often carry a cash prize or provide an opportunity to fund a student assistant. The award is also generally accompanied by a plaque or certificate (with the alumni association's name prominently displayed) to be hung in the designee's office.

Staff

Many of our graduates tell us their experiences at our institution would not have been as positive had it not been for particular staff members who reached out to them and created a supportive environment for students. Therefore, a number of alumni associations have added staff awards (i.e. achievement, service to students) presented with faculty awards. Again, because these are often presented in all-campus venues, staff awards are excellent reminders to the entire community of the importance of service to students.

As with faculty, staff awards are often monetary in nature with some symbolic memento accompanying the cash award. Generally, a plaque or framed certificate is well received.

GROUP AWARDS

Internal to the Association

Many awards are designed to recognize good work by constituent groups of the association. There are often annual awards for the outstanding chapter, the most improved chapter, the most innovative chapter program, and so on. Each of the award categories can by divided further by type of chapter (such as geographic, special interest, college associations).

Most constituent group awards carry a nominal cash award. However, the most important component is generally the public recognition afforded the chapter by the association. Recognition may be through notations in chapter newsletters or the alumni periodical. Most constituent groups have banners, which are displayed at all events. It is common for an association to provide an attachment to the banner, which recognizes award winners.

External to the Association

Many alumni associations provide recognition for outstanding accomplishments of student groups or clubs. Athletic teams or speech and debate squads that win conference or national championships may be recognized at halftime of a football or basketball game.

You may also want to recognize student groups that demonstrate strong programming. Similar categories used for alumni constituent groups are used for student groups (outstanding group, most improved, most spirited, etc.) These are often presented with the individual student awards at an end-of-the-year banquet or honors ceremony.

Group photos are among the more popular ideas for recognition of these teams or clubs. Another popular gift for student recognition is a T-shirt. Students can never have too many T-shirts, and they love wearing shirts acknowledging accomplishment and involvement with their alma mater.

FUNDING AWARDS

One of the first issues to be addressed with the introduction of any program is funding. Awards programs can be developed on a shoestring budget or can be quite elaborate and expensive. Shoestring programs may use computer-generated certificates, while more expensive programs may have awards as a major budgeted item. Funding sources for awards programs are often the institution's affinity partners, such as credit card companies. Alumni using the association's credit card should be aware they are supporting recognition of outstanding alumni, students, faculty and staff members, and community leaders.

Additional funding may also come from the institution's foundation, recognizing the long-term value of these programs. Another option is an appeal to loyal alumni (perhaps the association's life members or former board members).

SELECTION OF AWARDS

Most alumni associations have a standing committee designated to coordinate the awards program. This committee generally defines criteria (and then reviews and revises criteria at regular intervals), receives nomination and/or application materials, and selects recipients. Faculty, staff, and students may be added for faculty/staff/student award selection. (Oftentimes, former winners of the awards are represented.)

The nomination and application process should be as clear and simple as possible. When the process becomes cumbersome or confusing, the application pool will be greatly reduced (and often become filled with aggressive self-nominators).

Alumni associations must clearly articulate their intention and desire to solicit the broadest and strongest applicant pool possible. The most effective way to create a strong pool is to look at past experience. If the past group of award recipients is diverse, potential nominators and applicants from diverse backgrounds will be encouraged to participate in the process.

NAMING OF AWARDS

Naming an award after an individual who is well known and respected can give added prestige and status to an award and its recipients. It can also provide a "halo effect" for the association, sending a very positive message about the association.

Providing awards can be both exciting and rewarding to the alumni association. The alumni volunteers involved with the program feel productive and enjoy learning about exceptional alumni, students, faculty, staff, and community leaders. The recipients are honored and tied forever to the association and the institution. The association itself enjoys the reflection from the accomplishments of the recipients. Associations that develop and maintain strong awards programs recognize their alma mater's strengths while contributing to institutional growth and progress.

FURTHER READINGS

Carter, Lindy Keane. "Rewarding Experiences: When You're Presenting Alumni Awards, Passion and Creativity Take the Prize," CURRENTS 17, no. 7 (July/August 1991): 22-24, 26.

Fisher, Gillian. "Let's Get Personal: Want a Closer Relationship With Your Alumni? Use These Five Strategies to Make Them Feel Special," CURRENTS 23, no. 7 (July/August 1997): 71-72.

Gupta, Himanee. "May I Have the Envelope, Please?: Ideas for Alumni Awards Programs That Just Can't Lose," CURRENTS 11, no. 3 (March 1985): 20-23.

Hunter, Barbara Martin. "Eyes on the Prizes: Looking for Ways to Improve Your Alumni Awards? Set Your Sights on Solutions to 10 Common Problems," CURRENTS 22, no. 4 (April 1996): 10-14.

One of the most interesting challenges is to help board members feel they are contributing to the advancement of the association without needlessly generating more work for staff members who already put in long work days and travel. There is a balance.

Alumni Board Relations: A Primer for Success

Amy Button Renz
President, Kansas State University Alumni Association
Kansas State University

Alumni boards provide advice and direction for your institution. They often make recommendations on issues like adding more pages and color to the design of your alumni publication or give leadership to projects like building a multi-million dollar alumni center on campus. Most boards fall into one of two categories: advisory or policy-making; some are hybrids.

CATEGORIES OF BOARDS: ADVISORY OR POLICY-MAKING?

An advisory board typically does not set policy or make decisions. Board members make recommendations that do not have to be acted upon by alumni staff and the institution. The membership of these boards often comes from the more prestigious individuals in the alumni body, such as business executives. Direction comes from the institution, not the advisory board.

A policy-making board sets the direction of the alumni association, including budget, staffing, programs, and long-range planning. The alumni volunteers serving on these boards are empowered to make the important decisions about the organi-

zation's future. It is the job of the alumni staff to implement those decisions.

An advisory board offers recommendations to the institution regarding merchandising, electronic commerce, and affinity card programs, while a policy-making board sets guidelines for selecting these programs and even listens to official presentations by the companies.

The important point is that both types of boards provide a link between your alumni and the institution.

At Kansas State University, we have a policy-making board. Its duties range from setting priorities during the budget approval meetings to supporting university initiatives. In the 1980s, for example, student recruitment became a top priority, to boost sagging enrollments. The board appropriated funds to create new association programs and staffing to support student recruitment activities.

Policy-making boards also set long-range goals. For example, our board chose to make construction of an alumni center one of its goals. After careful consideration by the university administration and foundation, the board decided to embark on a building campaign.

REPORTING STRUCTURES FOR
STAFF LEADERSHIP

Staff presidents or the executive directors of alumni boards have a variety of reporting relationships, depending on the type of governance structure of the institution. If independent, the director will report to the board; if interdependent, the director will report to the president and/or the board; if dependent, in most cases, the director will report to a vice president for institutional advancement. The board will hire and fire the association director unless the director reports to a university administrator.

RECRUITING BOARD MEMBERS

Regardless of the form and governance structure of the alumni board, recruiting board members is the key to success. Whether the board is elected or appointed, there are important volunteer selection criteria to consider. Keeping in mind that you want the most able, the most respected, and the most devoted alumni possible on your board to fill seats with specified job descriptions, consider the following:

■ *Gender, geographic location, and ethnicity.* You should have a balance of males, females, and ethnic backgrounds reflecting your alumni population. The geographic distribution of your alumni populations should also be represented. Give consideration to rural areas as well as urban centers, and to in-state and out-of-state alumni. Draw upon your alumni database and make selections matching these various demographic criteria.

■ *Class year.* Look at your class median. Make sure your board has a spectrum of alumni ages to reflect their different interests. Our median class year at K-State is in the 1970s, so we strive to maintain a balance of graduates before and after that median.

■ *Professional background and involvement with the university.* If you need experts or particular college representatives on your board, again use your database to pull a list of graduates to determine the good candidates to fill your needs. For a finance committee, get experts in banking, accounting, and investments. For a publications committee, find experts in communications.

Give careful consideration to selecting board members who have previous experience with the institution, such as alumni volunteers on academic advisory groups. Ask the colleges and departments to submit names of good alumni volunteers. Build a list of potential alumni board members. Use your publications to solicit nominees and ask current board members for potential volunteers.

The essential goal is to create an effective board. Some institutions believe boards should reflect your total alumni base and constituencies. Others believe board members should only be the high-profile alumni. It may be right for your institution to have a mix of both types of individuals. The university administration invariably will view the association's value by the quality of its board members.

NONALUMNI REPRESENTATION ON
THE ALUMNI BOARD

For additional directors, consider recruiting from the following areas:

■ *University administration, faculty, and athletics.* Some associations have their institutional president and athletics director sit on the board. Our university president is a voting member.

■ *Students.* It is extremely important to let students have a voice in your alumni board activities because they are your alumni of the future. This can be achieved by having your student body president, senior class president, or student alumni board president sit on the board.

■ *Development.* At K-State, the chairman of the foundation's executive committee sits on our board, and the alumni association's board chairman sits on their board. Both chairmen are voting members on each board, which fosters close interaction and cooperation. This arrangement is highly recommended.

These board members often serve in an ex-officio capacity. All facets of the university that are integral to the needs of the association should be represented on your board.

POLICIES AND STRUCTURE

Board term limits and membership size will depend on the association's goals. Board sizes vary from as few as 15 members to more than 50 members. For example, Iowa State University's alumni board numbers 15 people, while Oklahoma State University has a 78-member board. At Kansas State, we have 26 members. The average length of service by alumni volunteers is three years, but many associations have five-year terms. Some board members serve in an ongoing capacity, such as the institutional president, while others serve one year, such as the student body president and foundation chairman.

PROVIDE ORIENTATION

We conduct a three-hour orientation for new board members before the June annual meeting. Individuals who participate in the orientation include the association's board chairman, chairman-elect, the association's executive director, and chief financial officer. A board handbook and copy of the by-laws are distributed at orientation.

● ● ●
The essential goal is to create a credible and quality board. The university administration often views the association by the quality of the board.

At the orientation's start, we distribute a loose-leaf notebook of material that board members find useful during their term of office. There is a section giving personal background on each member of the board, a copy of the association's by-laws, budget, and an alumni staff organization chart. Additionally, we include a master calendar of association events, minutes of recent board meetings, and the last annual report.

Retreats are another way to train board members and create a team-building experience. Use retreats to further define your association's mission statement and to conduct SWOT analyses (strengths, weaknesses, opportunities, and threats) of your programs. Retreats have the ability to turn committee work into task forces that will analyze issues important to the association, such as developing the guidelines you will use to select the best revenue-generating affinity card company or guidelines for redesigning your magazine.

Board Position Description

To help an alumni volunteer become an effective and committed board member, provide a job description and a comprehensive orientation process. We developed the following board position description at Kansas State:

Your role as a board member is to insure the continuity of the Alumni Association by planning for the future, establishing and reviewing policies and programs, and making sure the Association is financially sound. The Board meets three times a year: An annual meeting in June, a fall meeting in September, and a winter meeting in February.

The Alumni Association Board of Directors is made up of 26 members. In addition to those elected to serve three-year terms, there are standing directors to include the president of the University, a representative of the KSU Foundation, the KSU student body president, the Student Alumni Board president, the treasurer of the Association, and the past chair of the Board.

The Executive Committee of the board includes its chairman, chairman-elect, past chairman, secretary, treasurer, and an at-large member appointed by the chairman. The Executive Committee exercises administrative responsibilities as directed by the chairman.

Your responsibilities as a new member include the following: 1) attend the orientation session where the Association's by-laws and Board of Directors' policy handbook will be reviewed to assist you in understanding the objectives of the Association; 2) attend all board meetings and become familiar with the agenda items and discussion topics; 3) accept all specific assignments that result from action taken at Board meetings; and 4) serve on at least one of the Association Board committees.

Committee responsibilities. The Chairman appoints each Board member to an Association committee. These committees include: Alumni Events, Constituent Programming, Finance/Long Range Planning, Marketing, Nominating, and Communications. Your specific responsibilities on a committee include: 1) attend all meetings of the committee, 2) carry out individual assignments that are made by the committee chairman; and 3) review all relevant material prior to the committee meeting.

Local community responsibilities. As a Board member, you serve as an important link for the University to alumni in your community. Your responsibilities include: 1) attend meetings of local alumni clubs and 2) consult with local club officers, serving in an advisory manner.

Here is an overview of our board member
orientation:

A. Welcome by the Chairman of the Board
  1. Introductions
  2. Review responsibilities of a Board member
B. Association Review by the executive director
  1. Historical review
  2. Meeting schedule
  3. Deductible expenses form
  4. Board notebook
C. Overview of the Association budget by the financial
   officer
D. Goals and Objectives outlined by the executive director
E. Board Committee Structure presented by the
   Chairman-elect
F. Tour
G. Lunch

BOARD RESPONSIBILITIES

We use board members at K-State on several committees and special task forces to direct their special talents on key issues.

Other committees normally tie into the staff responsibilities for the association, such as member services, publications, and programs. Standing committees of the board almost always include "nominating" and "financial" if the executive committee does not meet that need. Assign staff liaisons to each committee to provide perspective and continuity for the board.

One of the most interesting challenges is to help board members feel they are contributing to the advancement of the association without needlessly generating more work for staff. There is a balance. Perhaps a board member suggests something you're not quite sure will work. Look at the suggestion from all angles—budget, time, and staffing—to see if there is a way to make it work.

At one time, our board wanted the alumni staff to sell merchandise to alumni, items like golf balls and picnic accessories. But when we considered the amount of space to inventory the items, and the cost of goods and staff time, the program didn't match our goals and objectives. We are now out of the inventoried merchandise business. For another institution, a merchandise program may be exactly what its alumni want—and its staff members can provide—and therefore is an appropriate program.

The alumni staff needs to know the limitations of what the association can and cannot do, and work with board members appropriately. While you don't want to say "no" to every board suggestion, you need to balance the desires of the board and the realities of running your association.

BOARD STRUCTURE AND LEADERSHIP

An executive committee with officers helps the ongoing leadership of the board. Titles may vary for the board's leader, but it is most commonly designated as chairman of the board or national president. Officer term lengths also vary nationwide. Ours is one year each for the chairman-elect, chairman, and immediate past chairman. Our chairman also has a job description. And we put that person to work.

Some of our chairman's duties include:

■ Presides at and attends all board and executive committee meetings.
■ Informs the board, executive committee, and officers of the association's conditions and operations after previous consultation with the alumni director.
■ Appoints chairs of association committees.
■ Appoints a search committee upon the vacancy of alumni director.
■ Conducts an annual written evaluation of the alumni director with input from the chairman-elect and past chairman.
■ Participates in the Homecoming Parade, addresses the All-Graduates Banquet during class reunions, and presents Alumni Medallions at spring commencement ceremonies.
■ Serves as a voting member of the KSU Foundation executive committee.

Boards generally meet three to five times a year, usually in conjunction with an existing university function, like cultural and athletic events. The meetings last one to two days. Our board meets three times annually and for two days at each meeting. The officers of the board who comprise the executive committee, along with the association's director, set the agenda for board meetings. It is important that board agendas provide ample time

Here is an agenda for a typical fall or winter board meeting at Kansas State:

FRIDAY

10 a.m.	Executive Committee Meeting
1 p.m.	Board Meeting
	1. Welcome
	2. General items
	a. Approval of minutes
	b. Financial report
	c. Nominating Committee report
1:30 p.m.	Presentation by an alumni staff member
2 p.m.	Updates
	1. Student updates by student body president, student alumni board president
	2. Association update by the alumni director
	3. University update by the president of the university
	4. Foundation update by the chairman of the foundation executive committee
	5. Athletic update by the athletic director
	6. Alumni Center update by the center's campaign director
6 p.m.	Reception and dinner

SATURDAY

8:30 a.m.	Continental breakfast
9 a.m.	Board planning session—committee meetings
	1. Alumni clubs
	2. Constituent programming
	3. Finance/long range planning
	4. External marketing
	5. Communications
11 a.m.	Refreshment break and committee chairs meet with board chairman
11:30 a.m.	Committee reports by the committee chairpersons
12:00	Action items
12:30 p.m.	Wrap-up and closing comments
2:30 p.m.	Athletic event or university activity

for discussing significant issues, usually first in committee and later in full board discussions.

Your association should pay the expenses for meal functions. Either the volunteer or the association bears the travel and lodging expenses. All expenses paid by your volunteers are tax deductible. The U.S. Internal Revenue Service allows volunteers to deduct unreimbursed out-of-pocket expenses directly related to services they give to charitable organizations like the alumni association. We refer our board members to appropriate IRS publications for more information, and our association's CPA firm has prepared a form to help them keep track of expenses. Some of these expenses include:

- Travel, parking fees, tolls, and airfares.
- Meals (limited to 50 percent) and lodging.
- Telephone charges directly associated with rendering the service.

It is important for you to note that expenses paid for a spouse or for another family member to accompany board members are not deductible.

VOLUNTEER STEWARDSHIP

You should establish various ways to show your appreciation to board members for their volunteer efforts, especially at the end of their terms. We invite our board members to sit in the association's stadium suite at football games, offer tickets to attend basketball games, and extend invitations to hospitality events. At the board members' last official meeting, we give them an engraved glass paperweight. The board chairman receives a wrist watch featuring the university seal. Our board chairman serves a total of six years, three more than normal board member terms. After the sixth year, we invite the past chairmen to host an association travel program from one of the international annual alumni tours we sponsor.

KEEPING IN TOUCH

Your staff should provide opportunities for board members to evaluate the meetings and their involvement on the board. Also, provide regular updates to the board highlighting your program and staff successes, university news, and key personnel changes. These updates should serve as a way to keep the board members in contact with and up-to-date on your institution. We do this with a monthly mailing that contains an information-packed letter from the alumni director and news clippings about the university. We provide subscriptions to the campus and town newspapers to the executive committee members. A well-informed board can help staff see beyond the boundaries of the association and enable members to see the big picture. The ability to seek solutions, form new partnerships, and advance the institution directly depends on the degree of board involvement in institutional issues of significance.

Your goal is to have a high-energy board that challenges the association to reach new heights. Extensive board participation and interaction with your staff ensure that your ongoing programs will improve and that your association will be able to help the university advance its mission.

REFERENCES

Bader, Barry S. *Planning Successful Board Retreats: A Guide for Board Members and Chief Executives*. Washington, DC: National Center for Nonprofit Boards, 1990.

Boyd, Thomas. *Ten Basic Responsibilities of Nonprofit Boards*. Washington DC: National Center For Nonprofit Boards, 1997. (Audiotape.)

Brinckerhoff, Peter C. "A User's Guide to Effective Board Retreats: An Interruption Free Environment That Supports Creative Thinking Will Help Directors Focus on Association Issues," *Association Management* 48, no. 6 (1996): 45-46.

Connors, Tracy Daniel. *The Volunteer Management Handbook*. New York, NY: John Wiley and Sons, 1995.

Dunlop, James J. *Leading the Association: Striking the Right Balance Between Staff and Volunteers,* Washington, DC: American Society of Association Executives, 1995.

Howe, Fisher. *Welcome to the Board: Your Guide to Effective Participation*. San Francisco, CA: Jossey-Bass Publishers, 1995.

Lillestol, Jane M. "Blue-Chip Board: Take Stock of Your Alumni Board—And Then Increase Its Value With These Insider Tips," CURRENTS 18, no. 2 (1992): 22-26.

O'Connell, Brian. *The Board Member's Book*. 2nd ed. Washington, DC: Independent Sector, 1993.

Richards, R. R. *How to Build an Effective Board*. Washington, DC: American Society of Association Executives, 1997.

Thiers, Naomi. "Speaking Volumes: A Comprehensive Handbook Can Keep Your Alumni Board on Target and On Schedule," CURRENTS 18, no. 2 (1992): 28-31.

"Toward A Trouble-Free Board: Sure-Fire Solutions to Common Conundrums," CURRENTS 18, no. 2 (1992): 32-36.

Geography is a major means by which to deliver highly focused programs addressing those common interests and needs.

Chapters and Clubs: The Role of Geography in Programming and Delivery

J. Todd Coleman
Executive Director, University of Missouri Alumni Association and Assistant Vice Chancellor
University of Missouri

Since 1853 when Miami of Ohio organized the first local alumni club in the U.S., geographic organizations have been a mainstay of continuing or creating affiliation between alumni and friends and the academy. Geography's role, however, is evolving. Many institutions are finding that marketing to and serving alumni is perhaps best done through niche marketing and affinity group programming. While regional clubs may no longer be as central to program development as they once were, they are still critical to service and delivery of the programs themselves.

As the work and social lives of alumni increasingly leave them little time to go to local alumni "mingling" events, they look for programs that will have specific value to them—gatherings of alumni with similar professional, cultural, social, and family interests and needs. Such focused events may include:

- orientations for freshmen and their families;
- community service projects;
- events to seek advice from the business community about a proposed educational program; or
- career days for graduating students and young alumni.

Geography is one means of delivering highly focused programs addressing those common interests and needs. However, as online technology increasingly allows people who are physically far away to communicate with each other, the need for geography to unite a group of people will change. Online discussion groups or listservs devoted to affinity groups, for example, are becoming a common form of alumni intercommunication.

As alumni look for connections that go deeper than just geographic affiliation, alumni associations have become more creative and sophisticated in capturing data on their alumni's interests and in bringing alumni affinity groups together based on their areas of academic study, race, sexual orientation, and student organization involvement. Still, this data on interest and affinity is often segmented by geography.

Managing Clubs Effectively

In the second edition of the *Handbook of Institutional Advancement*, Stephen Roszell wrote that, "a strong alumni chapter program is a careful balancing act of managing resources and volunteers to achieve certain alumni association goals while, at the same time, meeting the needs of the local alumni groups." Some of the basic challenges Roszell described were how to allocate resources most effectively, how to determine the roles of the alumni association staff and the volunteer leaders, and how to maintain continuity and a sense of the institution's mission among the chapters' activities.

Today's alumni associations also face new and different challenges in effectively managing clubs and chapters. Keeping membership up and engaging active volunteer leaders are two of the basic challenges. Alumni associations are using creativity, niche marketing, and sophisticated business techniques to answer these marketing challenges. Again, though, these marketing techniques are often used within a geographically-segmented structure.

At the University of Missouri Alumni Association we have successfully used budget incentives to increase association membership geographically. Each year, a chartered chapter is allocated funds based on its number of dues-paying members. Each chapter also has the opportunity to obtain additional resources if it recruits new members. We have also delegated as much of the geographical chapters' and clubs' decision making as possible. This has helped to motivate volunteers and give them a sense of ownership; it also relieves an overworked staff of some of its duties. We have developed a detailed honors program by which chapters and clubs earn points that are awarded for conducting certain events that we are promoting and for completing critical administrative responsibilities. We have also provided a worldwide volunteer leadership training program. As a result of these efforts, we have a 25 percent increase in overall association membership, a much more active volunteer base geographically, and more detailed information about our alumni for tracking purposes.

USING TECHNOLOGY IN REGIONAL ALUMNI PROGRAMS

The Council of Alumni Association Executives (CAAE), staffed by CASE in Washington, DC, conducts an annual survey of some 100 of the largest alumni associations (predominantly independent) in the U.S. In the most recent survey, the percentage of resources devoted to alumni clubs and constituent societies had declined, while resources called "other," has increased. We can probably assume that much of this "other" is related to technological resources.

While, in some cases, this increase in spending for technology might accompany a decrease in spending on geographic club and chapter programs, in most cases, technology has been used to build stronger local clubs and chapters and to obtain more information about them. The use of technology will help us discover and respond to powerful common interests and needs of our alumni; this responsiveness, in turn, will lead to their positive affiliation with their alma maters.

There are a growing number of technological tools available that make it easy for clubs and chapters to create their own online presence. Software is now available that actually manages the membership lists, attendance, finances, and special events of local chapters. More and more, local volunteer leaders are finding e-mail a perfect way to reach alumni, remind them of events, collect feedback on past events, and get newsy information to report back to the institution.

Many alumni associations have coordinated, or at least encouraged, the creation of individual Web sites for regional alumni clubs and chapters. These Web sites include schedules of events, photos of past events, information about ongoing community service projects, directories of local alumni in the area, and links to the career center at the institution. For instance, both the Web sites of Harvard and Dartmouth's alumni associations include directories of all the regional and affinity clubs' Web sites; these two alumni associations even provide online instructions and technology tutorials on how to create a new club or class Web site. (See *www.haa.harvard.edu/clubs* and *www.alum.dartmouth.org/clubs*.)

The very use of the Internet will involve many people who have not seen a reason to connect with our chapters and clubs in traditional ways, particularly younger alumni. Technology may give us a new online geography every bit as important and as powerful as any of our face-to-face meetings in the past. Clearly, we have an unprecedented opportunity to make the bond of affiliation stronger than ever.

REFERENCES

Blansfield, Karen C. "High-Tech Communications: Still Relying on Phone and Mail to Communication with Alumni Clubs?" CURRENTS 22, no. 3 (March 1996): 34.

Feudo, John, ed. *Alumni Relations: A Newcomer's Guide to Success.* Washington, DC: CASE Books, 1999.

Romero, Hulda T. "Club Communications: Four Alumni Offices Share Tips on Reaching Regional Audiences," CURRENTS 22, no. 3 (March 1996): 64.

● ● ●

Many alumni have no interest in attending a traditional class reunion or homecoming weekend. They feel no kinship with the wider membership of their class or institution, and they are not comfortable with the typical kinds of social events that occur on these occasions.

Campus and Constituent Alumni Groups: A New Look at Alumni

Midge Wood Brittingham
Executive Director, Oberlin College Alumni Association
Oberlin College

The mission of most alumni relations offices is to involve as many alumni in the life of the institution as possible. This dictates offering a wide range of services and programs, since not all alumni are attracted by all programs. For many years, the typical view of categorizing alumni was by graduation year and by geographical location, thus the importance of class reunions and club and/or chapter events. But as times have changed, our alumni and their needs have also changed. Our job as alumni relations professionals has changed as well. We now must widen our programming and services to suit both our traditional and nontraditional alumni.

ESTABLISHING NEW CONNECTIONS: SPECIAL INTEREST GROUPS

When alumni from large universities recall their undergraduate experience, many recall the personal experience of being part of a particular group or activity. This could mean the university band, an academic department, the basketball team, or the choir. And while they may be interested in the whole university, they're probably much more interested in the ongoing activities of the particular organization to which they belonged.

Although students at smaller institutions perhaps didn't need to find their own special niche because of the *size* of their institution, as alumni they also may find themselves bound together because of particular interests or concerns they shared as students. And it is only natural that their interest in this group or activity would carry on after they graduate. Many alumni have no interest in attending a traditional class reunion or homecoming weekend. They feel no kinship with the wider membership of their class or institution, and they are not comfortable with the typical kinds of social events that occur on these occasions. They are looking for some deeper, or more specific, connection.

Alumni professionals, institution administrators, and faculty agree that promoting the association of alumni who shared a certain activity is part of a good alumni relations program— for instance, a reunion of all former band members. These kinds of events provide many positive results that warrant the staff time and budget expense involved. For example, a reunion of band members from a certain era with other former and current students who have the same interest can lure those alumni back to campus when no other event would. At such a reunion, they can mingle with current student band members, find out about the progress the band has made since their day, or learn about the difficulties the band is now experiencing and ways that they can help. They can dust off their instruments and join with the students in playing the school song. Our students are our best ambassadors on behalf of our institutions, and providing a natural and common interest experience for students and alumni to share is what good alumni relations is all about. Honoring the oldest member, for example, creates a sense of continuity and pride for both alumni and students. Such an event might spark an ongoing, volunteer, special-interest organization that will become a new alumni relations program.

Similar events can be built around a major department or a school within your university. Invite illustrious graduates to give talks about their career paths or their subjects of expertise and include present and retired faculty. Involve students by holding career counseling sessions as part of the event. For alumni professionals, these kinds of events perfectly fulfill the mission of involving alumni in the life of the institution.

CONNECTING COMMUNITIES

Since the 1970s, many institutions have maintained special groups such as black student newspapers, separate black choral or theater groups, and special residential options to represent the growing post-Civil Rights African-American student population. Affinity groups of these alumni was a natural next step—students who had shared the experience of being minorities during an intense period of learning and coping would want to continue those same associations after graduation. Latino and Asian-American affinity groups soon followed the African-American affinity groups.

The desire of alumni for this kind of special interest group posed a difficult question for some alumni programs. How could they create a separate association, based on race or ethnicity, within the alumni association whose only criteria for membership traditionally was attendance at a certain institution? Alumni who attended prior to the

● ● ●

Since the Civil Rights era, alumni relations professionals have been forced to face the question the nation is still trying to figure out: How can we be one nation (or one association) and yet recognize—or better yet, celebrate—the important cultural and racial diversity among us?

1970s would ask, "Aren't we all alumni and therefore don't we share the same interests?" Some called it "segregation" or "separatism."

This attitude ignores the fact that even a liberal school like Oberlin College, with its long history of accepting and educating African Americans, was not in the '50s—and still is not—a comfortable environment for many African-American students. Our older alumni, and even some of our younger ones, still cannot accept or understand the fact that life can be extremely difficult for a minority in a majority setting and that often minority groups find comfort in being with those who share the same race or culture. This leads to a lack of understanding when such alumni see a group of young black alumni sitting together at a reunion picnic or hear about the construction of a new African-American dorm.

Since the Civil Rights era, alumni relations professionals have been forced to face the question the nation is still trying to figure out: How can we be one nation (or one association) and yet recognize—or better yet, celebrate—the important cultural and racial diversity among us?

Institutions and associations have handled the dilemma in different ways. Some institutions with only a handful of minority alumni have ignored the question. Most others have responded with at least a small show of support; some have hired a designated staff person(s), usually a representative of the minority group, and have supplied budget support for affinity groups. Some alumni programs sponsor special reunions and conferences, regional events, a newsletter describing the campus activities of that particular community, community service events, distinguished awards, or an alumni hall of fame. Alumni of these special interest or affinity groups have raised scholarship funds for members of their community, and have helped recruit faculty, staff, and students.

The call for affinity groups based on sexual orientation is newer to the alumni relations field. In many cases, gay alumni, like members of any minority group, have difficult memories of their years as undergraduates. The coming out experience is a painful and frightening one, and in many cases, takes place on campus. If the institution supported that student, he or she as an alum will likely feel very positively toward the institution. On the other hand, if that student found fellow students and the institution to be unaccepting, he or she may decide to disconnect totally from the alma mater. Part of the challenge for alumni relations professionals, and sometimes the joy, in working with a special interest group is to acknowledge, and help reconcile, resentments over negative institutional treatment during student days.

For those institutions that already embrace gay alumni groups, activities are usually the same as for any other special interest group—special reunions and conferences, social gatherings on and off campus. A fund-raising project might support a student cut off from parental funds when he or she "came out." Or it might be used to sponsor a campus lecture series, prize, or student research grant for gay issues.

While these alliances are an alumni relations success in that they clearly offer the opportunity to connect gay alumni and the life of the institution, they also require that each institution make decisions on how to confront this controversial issue and how to balance and respond to the differing beliefs of alumni. This decision must be based on the institution's history, character, and mission. The backlash from older and/or conservative alumni when their institution conducts such alumni and student programs can be considerable, and each institution has to decide what the risks of alienating donors might be, and how much the institution is willing to risk.

The partnership between the institution and minority populations of all kinds, which begins at the undergraduate level, is so important at the alumni relations level. Our institutions educate the leaders of these special communities, and as our nation continues to struggle with issues of plurality, we should embrace the opportunity for alumni relations to help find solutions.

Nevertheless, alumni relations professionals will always receive complaints. Some traditional alumni may threaten to discontinue giving to the institution because of student or alumni programming they find separatist or because they feel their

school isn't what it used to be. It is the job of the school, and the alumni relations office, to continue to educate on the changing needs of alumni without alienating either traditional or nontraditional alumni.

At the same time, minority graduates may have their own set of issues. They may find it very difficult to be in any relationship with an institution that they perceived during their students days as patronizing, and that was reluctant, for instance, to launch a black literary magazine or a Latin-American Studies major. Wooing back disaffected minority alumni is a difficult task, especially if budgets preclude hiring additional staff members or expanding programs. Yet we must persevere and be genuine, not token, in our efforts to involve minority alumni in suitable programming and in volunteer leadership roles. Our efforts must be well thought out and in line with our institutional mission.

AFFILIATE ALUMNI GROUPS

One solution in trying to provide alumni programming and service to an increasingly diverse alumni body is to create a category of affiliate, self-defined groups. This has worked well at Oberlin. Alumni who wish to create an affiliate group apply to the alumni association's executive board, and if the group meets the criteria, which include accepting the mission and goals of the college and the association, it is accepted. As such, these groups plan their own programs and fund all their activities except for one mailing a year. A staff member is assigned as a "liaison," but actual programming is left up to the group. These affiliate groups have representation on the Alumni Council, and even on the Executive Board, so members of those communities are very much a part of the alumni association. These affiliate groups are approached by other segments of the campus—for example, minority students, faculty, and staff—to help support their issues. They can be independent and somewhat autonomous, and yet still are part of the alumni association. The alumni office maintains their mailing list and treasury for them.

Our mission as alumni professionals is to involve alumni in the life of the institution. Knowing the issues and interests with which they identify presents us with an opportunity to help ally them with each other and with the institution. When we do so, we demonstrate how alumni can enhance and strengthen their alma mater, and the institution can, in turn, strengthen alumni.

FURTHER READINGS

Bailey, Archie. "Welcome Back: A Volunteer Tells How to Get Minority Alumni Interested, Inspired, and Involved," CURRENTS 21, no. 3 (March 1995): 56.

Nicklin, Julie L. "Wooing Minority Alumni: Colleges Report Mixed Success in Programs for Black, Asian, and Hispanic Graduates," *Chronicle of Higher Education* 40, no. 25 (February 23, 1994): A29-A30.

Osborn, Kathy. "Leaving the Past Behind: Help Minority Alumni Heal Old Wounds by Focusing Your Programming on the Future," CURRENTS 21, no. 3 (March 1995): 20-24.

Strosnider, Kim. "Gay and Lesbian Alumni Groups Seek a Bigger Role at Their Alma Maters: Some Colleges Welcome the Involvement and Gifts, But Other Institutions are Wary," *Chronicle of Higher Education* 44, no. 2 (September 5, 1997): A59-A60.

Wallach, Van. "A Separate Peace: If Your Affinity Groups Are Sparking Controversy Among Alumni, Don't Despair. Use These Strategic Ideas to Battle Criticism and Build Harmony," CURRENTS 21, no. 3 (March 1995): 14-18.

Financial support of student advancement programs is essential. It may range from less than $1,000 at an independent college with a 15-member student alumni association to programs that receive more than $100,000 at several state universities, whose membership may exceed several hundred students.

Student Advancement Programs

Paul B. Chewning
Vice President, Professional Development
CASE

In 1949, Howard S. "Howdy" Wilcox, the visionary executive director of the Indiana University Foundation, established the first student advancement program, whose purpose was to train current students to become committed and contributing members of the alumni body. Wilcox's successor, William S. "Army" Armstrong, substantially enhanced and developed this program. These student programs began appearing sporadically, and in a variety of forms, at other colleges and universities during the following two decades, but widespread development of such programs did not begin until the mid-1970s. Their growth paralleled that of advancement programs in general, and the need for increased private support of educational institutions. Nearly 50 years later, student advancement programs have matured into three widely-accepted models, each of which is critical to institutional advancement and to the entire campus.

Student alumni associations are sponsored either by the alumni relations office or alumni association. This group is involved primarily with alumni programs such as homecoming and reunions, career assistance and mentoring, student recruitment, family programs, and spirit programs. For example, the University of Missouri, Columbia Alumni Association Student Board (AASB) was given the assignment of recreating traditions at the university and helping to increase alumni attendance at homecoming. AASB researched lost traditions at Mizzou and began introducing them at new student orientation, where a representative showed a power point presentation to incoming freshmen and their parents. AASB also developed a traditions brochure. The program was so successful that the "traditions theme" became a marketing component of homecoming, credited with increasing alumni attendance. Not only has attendance at homecoming events increased, but alumni are helping AASB with identifying other University of Missouri traditions.

Student foundations are sponsored by either the development office or the institutionally related foundation office. They focus on annual giving and phonathon campaigns, senior challenge and gift programs, and other fund-raising activities. Howdy Wilcox originated and Bill Armstrong developed the Little 500, a bicycle race to help raise money for undergraduate scholarships for working students at Indiana University. This program later became the theme of the movie, *Breaking Away*.

Student ambassador programs may be sponsored by the admissions, alumni relations, or president's office. These students are generally identified as ambassadors for their institution and serve as tour guides for prospective students and special guests of the institution, or at reunions or commencement. In *Student Advancement Programs: Shaping Tomorrow's Alumni Leaders Today*, East Carolina University Chancellor Richard R. Eakin described the value of the ECU Ambassadors, a student advancement program on his campus:

> We involve the Ambassadors with all our publics—from major donors to the media— and their confidence and presence send a message of quality and substance. They are good students who are enthusiastic and articulate. The Ambassadors are also among our most committed and loyal volunteers, and we are now seeing more and more of them emerge as local alumni chapter leaders.

Spirit groups are usually affiliated with public relations, residence life, or athletics. They enrich the quality of the institution by engendering pride, loyalty, support, and tradition. Many spirit organizations are the keepers of the campus mascot.

Developing a Student Advancement Program

Regardless of the size of the institution or composition of the student body, a student advancement program has proven to be a valuable asset. These programs have been developed at community and technical colleges, independent colleges and universities, and public institutions. All you need to begin a program are a few dedicated and enthusiastic students, an adviser, and institutional commitment. All three are critical to the program's success.

Mission Statement

The mission statement of a student advancement program should reflect the important link between students and their institution, the need for continued support, and the idea of committed alumni. They are often similar to mission statements of alumni associations, whose connections with alumni, faculty, and students permeate their seminal purpose of existence.

● ● ●
Most student advancement programs have at least one adviser, and many advisers develop lifelong friendships with their students, strengthening the connection between the institution and its graduates.

The Association of Student Advancement Programs (formerly the Student Alumni Association/Student Foundation Network) at CASE represents 350 colleges and universities in the United States, Canada, and England. ASAP developed the following creed for its members more than two decades ago:

> We believe that as students, we have a special relationship with our Alma Mater that represents a lifetime commitment in the fulfillment of our dreams and aspirations. As students, we will represent the result of her mission and the embodiment of her spirit in the world. What she is, we are; what she becomes, we become.
>
> Because we are the emerging essence of our institution, we will strive to enhance this special relationship between students, alumni and others so that the heritage of our Alma Mater will always be a part of our lives, for the present as we follow our dreams, and after graduation as we make them come true.

While the creed was written for student advancement organizations, its philosophy embodies the desired lifetime link between students and their institution, a goal that each and every advancement office strives toward.

Resources

Financial support of student advancement programs is essential. It may range from less than $1,000 at an independent college with a 15-member student alumni association to programs that receive more than $100,000 at several state universities, whose membership may exceed several hundred students. Each student advancement program must determine the resources it needs in such areas as office supplies, printing and postage, telephone and marketing, and promotion of activities. Some programs are line items in the alumni or development office budget, while other programs receive institutional support and generate their own revenue through such activities as silent auctions, raffles, birthday cakes, balloon and candy sales, and survival kits at exam times. Some of these revenue-generating programs also support student scholarships and faculty award funds.

Adequate staffing of student advancement programs is also important. A one-person alumni office can have an active student alumni association. The key is delegation and the involvement of committed and hardworking students, as well as selecting the number of programs and activities you can realistically manage throughout the academic year. Most student advancement programs have at least one adviser who either works exclusively with students or who may also have young alumni programs or constituency programs. Several universities, including Appalachian State University, Clemson University, and the University of Wisconsin, Eau Claire have two advisers. Many advisers develop lifelong friendships with their students, strengthening the connection between the institution and its graduates.

Membership

Student advancement programs have three types of membership—open, closed, and a combination of both.

Open membership is extended to all members of the student body for participation in the student advancement program. Open membership exists at independent colleges like Lebanon Valley College and Claremont McKenna College, to private universities like Drake University and Stanford University, to public universities like the University of New Brunswick and the University of Oregon. The University of Central Florida has one of the largest open membership programs, with 850 students. Many open programs encourage freshman participation as a way of involving new students immediately in campus activities.

Closed membership for student advancement programs involves a competitive process for selecting members. The selection process generally requires an interview, written essay, and letters of recommendation. Current student members or a subcommittee conduct the interviews, review the written material, and make the selections. James Madison University, the Pennsylvania State University, the Ohio State University, and the Iowa State University are examples of closed membership programs. Closed programs may be as small as 12 students or as large as 100 students. Many

closed membership programs require current members to participate in a certain number of activities or hours of service to maintain their membership.

Combination programs involve both open and closed elements. A large number of students may be members of the student advancement program, but a smaller number are elected to the executive committee or student board. These individuals are responsible for managing the student advancement program and working directly with the adviser and other campus administrators. Many combination programs also have participation requirements for their members, both open and closed. Some institutions that have combination membership are the University of Connecticut, the University of North Carolina at Chapel Hill, and Oklahoma State University.

Regardless of the type of membership, student identification, recruitment, and training are crucial to developing strong student advancement programs. The Association of Student Advancement Programs, an alliance of student organizations that provides resources and opportunities for networking and leadership development in order to promote student involvement in educational advancement, is a CASE program. Made up of eight districts, ASAP offers opportunities at the district and international levels for enriching student advancement programs.

ASAP is a wonderful source of information and program ideas about student advancement programs in the United States, Canada, and England.

Student advancement programs have grown in number and focus since 1949. Their importance to their campuses has also increased during these 50 years. Students, who are both the consumers and the products of the educational process, are the lifeblood of the institution and the only permanent members of the academy. Like generations of students, there are generations of alumni, and generational alumni programming is becoming more prevalent.

As ECU's chancellor Eakin said of students involved in advancement programs, "Their confidence and presence send a message of quality and substance." The continued success of our colleges and universities may well rest with how well we engage and involve students through student advancement activities, instilling in them the important responsibility of being committed alumni and supporting their alma mater in a number of ways. As today's student "ambassadors," they will become tomorrow's alumni "ambassadors," which is what Howard Wilcox and Bill Armstrong envisioned half a century ago.

REFERENCES AND FURTHER READINGS

Fisher, Mark A. "Shining Examples: 15 Inspiring Ideas for Student Alumni Programs," CURRENTS 18, no. 5 (May 1992): 20-23.

Lanier, James L., Jr. "Advancing the Institution: The Role of Student Advancement Programs." In *Student Advancement Programs: Shaping Tomorrow's Alumni Leaders Today*. Edited by Barbara Tipsord Todd. Washington, DC: Council for Advancement and Support of Education, 1993: 1-4.

Nuza, Jessica. "A Powerful Network: Student Advancement Programs Are Another Valuable Way to Prepare Your Future Alumni. Here's How They Made a Difference in 1997-98," CURRENTS 24, no. 6 (June 1998): 12-13.

Olson, Beth. "SAAs: The Student's View," CURRENTS 18, no. 5 (May 1992): 8-11.

Todd, Barbara Tipsord, ed. "SAAs: The Adviser's View: For the Alumni Association, Student Programs are Investments With Unbeatable Returns," CURRENTS 18, no. 5 (May 1992): 12-16, 18.

Todd, Barbara Tipsord, ed. *Student Advancement Programs: Shaping Tomorrow's Alumni Leaders Today*. Washington, DC: Council for Advancement and Support of Education, 1993.

Given the wide range of options for engaging parents, the locus of responsibility bedevils many institutional leaders.

Parents Programs: Powerful Strategies for Advancement

Karen K. Hansen
Executive Director of the Center for Lifelong Learning
and Former Director of Alumni/ae and Parent Relations
St. Olaf College

Parents thrill at their child's first steps and first words. Mom and Dad have their hearts in their throats as their child boards the school bus on the first day of school, then, years later, drives off in the family car alone for the first time. Grandparents proudly show off photos of their grandchildren and display their artwork on the refrigerator door. Younger siblings look up to their older brother or sister as he or she heads off to school.

Few ties bind so intensely as those between parent and child, grandparent and grandchild, and siblings. The nature of these relationships makes the investment in parents and/or family programs a natural part of the advancement strategy. The first power of parents programs is the *deeply personal interest* parents have in their children's lives.

The second power of parent programs is the *propensity for participation*, often sparked during the child's early school years or involvement in extracurricular activities.

The third power of parents programs is the *life phase* represented by embarking upon private secondary or college/university schooling. Many parents and grandparents seek appropriate ways to remain involved, even as the young adult achieves greater independence. They yearn to be made welcome by the institution as well.

The fourth power of parents programs is the *desire for positive reinforcement*. For most students and their parents, private secondary and college/university education is a major life decision and financial investment. Parents and grandparents want to know the decision was right and the investment is worth the sacrifice.

The fifth power of parents programs is the *desire to partake* in the educational endeavor from which students benefit—and which parents may have missed earlier in their own lives.

WHERE PARENTS CAN HELP

Personal interest, the propensity for participation, life phase transitions, the desire for positive reinforcement, and the desire for opportunities to partake drive many parents to offer their talents and treasure to aid their child's school. While parents programs demand an institution's time and resources, the potential return is rich indeed. The areas where virtually all institutions need help are precisely those where parents can play a role:

■ Career, internship, and employment resources—influential parents may be just as eager to help their child's fellow students as alumni are to help one another;

- Public relations—what better promoters could the institution have than parents whose children are delighted with their campus;
- Legislative influence;
- Consumer feedback and counsel—parents are "out there," observing your institution with fresh eyes and hearing from their children and school friends. If they have problems or concerns, you want them to tell you;
- Gratitude expressed to faculty and staff—parents' praise can help motivate staff and faculty and boost campus morale;
- Design and implementation of interesting programs for parents and other family members;
- Admissions assistance and representation;
- Direct financial support;
- Identification of and access to prospective major donors and corporate/foundation support;
- Regional representation at chapter events, on advisory councils, in fund raising campaigns, at admissions fairs, and at inaugurations.

CULTIVATING PARENTS

While a parents' day or weekend often is considered the foundation or starting point for parents programming, the repertoire designed to cultivate parents and to elicit their invaluable assistance also includes:

- Weekend programs for parents, grandparents, and/or family members. Once typically called Parents' Day, more broadly oriented "Family Weekend" can serve siblings and grandparents, extending the positive benefits of making family members feel welcome, while remaining sensitive to students whose parents may be deceased, ill, divorced, or far from campus.
- New student and parent orientations offered during the summer before or during move-in days.
- Parents-focused handbooks and newsletters, and receipt of the institution's periodicals.
- Invitations to and warm welcomes at chapter events, "alumni colleges," travel-study programs, and campus celebrations such as inau-

gurations, new building openings, anniversaries, campaign kick-off events, and so forth.

- Parents-only events off-campus with college leaders and/or faculty.
- Parents councils or committees whose advice and feedback is sincerely sought and genuinely considered.
- Representative positions on boards of trustees/regents, campaign councils, and other institutional advisory bodies.

The cycle of parental involvement differs from that of alumni, whom we hope will have lifelong relationships with our institutions. Many parents are most keenly interested while their children are in school, making the timeline for engaging them quite short. Parents' free time and willingness to participate vary according to personal interest, distance, cultural barriers, financial resources, and the "sandwich generation" balancing act of caring for children and aging parents. Yet, while many parents stop volunteering aid or financial support after their child graduates, others remain engaged. Whether the basis for continued engagement is gratitude, relationships formed, or commitment to the institutional mission, these individuals make parents' programs worth the entire effort. Among St. Olaf College's most generous donors are parents cultivated through the Parents Committee who went on to serve as regents, make major gifts, and enthusiastically lead campaigns. Their alumni/ae children are following in their footsteps as leaders and major donors.

> • • •
>
> **Parents' programming should consider distance and differences. Invite distant parents to all alumni chapter events in their area. Or take the institution to parents by sponsoring parents-only events with college leaders.**

ENGAGING PARENTS

Parents' programming should consider distance and differences. Parents who cannot come to campus may be engaged through newsletters, online chat rooms, parents-focused Web pages and publications, and regional associations and events. Invite distant parents to all alumni chapter events in their area. Or take the institution to parents by sponsoring parents-only events with college leaders. Cultural and language differences may dictate the need for printed and online publications in a variety of languages. Solicitations made with cultural and language differences in mind show your institution's sensitivity to multicultural constituencies.

Given the wide range of options for engaging parents, the locus of responsibility bedevils many institutional leaders. For those who can afford it, an office of parent relations clearly demonstrates institutional commitment. Such a model relieves confusion and provides centralized, internal leadership for events planning, advisory committees, publications, and fund raising. Where a separate, designated office is not feasible, candidates for leadership include the offices of student activities, dean of students, alumni (and parent) relations, development, public relations, and admissions. Each can benefit from the involvement of parents. Institutional leaders should determine responsibility for parents programs by first identifying primary needs and objectives.

Collaborative models may work if well coordinated in a cooperative institutional culture. One staff member or department may be charged with primary responsibility and with drawing together staff from other areas for planning, organizing, and staffing programs and communications. Alternatively, a coordinating committee representing departments that will deliver and/or benefit from

parents' involvement may be able to provide greater service than any one department, while keeping internal communication lines open.

Working with the parents of your institution's students can be a joy, bringing the fresh, enthusiastic perspective of newly engaged constituents whose love for their children creates opportunities for lifelong bonds with your institution.

FURTHER READINGS

Halsey, Mary Margaret. "What Parents Want: Princeton's Survey Gave the University Plenty of Parental Guidance," CURRENTS 11, no. 6 (June 1985): 10-13.

Lindemuth, Tim. "A Relative Success: Casting Parents in Leading Roles Can Bring Box-Office Hits to Your Campus," CURRENTS 17, no. 4 (April 1991): 12-13, 15-17.

McNamee, Thomas A. "Ask and Ye Shall Receive: A Survey Helps Hartwick College Find New Ways to Involve Parents in Everything from Internship Programs to Fund Raising," CURRENTS 11, no. 6 (June 1985): 16-18.

Scalzo, Teresa. "The Proof is in the Program: The Best Way to be of Service is to Get Results. Here's How to Create and Evaluate Effective Alumni Activities," CURRENTS 19, no. 1 (January 1993): 30-34.

Weiss, Larry J., ed. Parents Programs: How to Create Lasting Ties. Washington, DC: Council for Advancement and Support of Education, 1989.

Alumni admissions programs require a strong commitment on the part of senior university officials and admissions and alumni affairs staff. Constant communication is essential, and the allocation of duties and responsibilities between admissions and alumni affairs must be fair and precise.

Alumni: Vital Advocates for Undergraduate Admissions

Laney Funderburk
Associate Vice President, Alumni Affairs and Director, Alumni Affairs
Duke University

Alumni are almost always the institution's most numerous, loyal, and dedicated constituency. Directing this resource to accomplish the institution's mission is a serious responsibility. One area in which alumni have a passionate and abiding interest is undergraduate admissions. At many institutions, alumni have translated their loyalty and interest into an invaluable service to the university through activities that include:

- Interviewing applicants;
- Representing the institution at college nights and fairs;
- Hosting accepted student parties; and
- Serving as spokespersons in secondary schools and communities around the world.

PROGRAM ORGANIZATION

In the academic year 1997-98, more than 3,000 alumni were volunteers in the Duke Alumni Association's Alumni Admission Advisory Committee program. Serving on more than 230 committees, alumni volunteers interviewed approximately 10,000 of Duke's 14,000 applications for admission to its two undergraduate colleges. Each local AAAC is autonomous, headed by a chair and is responsible for a finite geographic area.

Duke's AAAC program is organized and directed by the Office of Alumni Affairs. Alumni affairs staff members recruit committee chairs, direct annual training sessions for committee chairs, and generally oversee all aspects of the volunteers' involvement. The program is funded by both the Office of Alumni Affairs and the Alumni Association. Exclusive of salaries and benefits for a full-time professional staff member and half-time support staff members, the annual program budget is $75,000.

Alumni admissions programs require a strong commitment on the part of senior university officials and admissions and alumni affairs staff. Constant communication is essential, and the allocation of duties and responsibilities between admissions and alumni affairs must be fair and precise. Myriad details must be handled effectively between two offices that report to different university divisions and officials.

While the alumni relations staff member responsible for the program usually reports to the alumni director, he or she often attends admissions staff meetings and should confer regularly with the director of undergraduate admissions and admissions officers. This staff member may also be responsible for other admissions-related programs such as alumni legacy and alumni scholarship programs. At Duke, this staff member organizes and coordinates a biennial, on-campus, all-day conference for alumni sons and daughters (ages 15-18) and their families that provides general information about college admissions.

While budgetary responsibilities differ from institution to institution, it is imperative that there be a clear delineation of financial responsibilities between the alumni relations and the admissions offices. It should be clear who is responsible for all costs, including staff, printing and postage, event expenses, and so forth.

WORKING WITH VOLUNTEERS

At Duke, the local AAAC is responsible for determining the number of volunteers on the committee, recruiting them, and training them annually. However, because volunteers often have limited time and knowledge of specific admissions information, the alumni relations staff supports the chair's efforts. Historic admissions patterns determine the number of individual volunteers or the size of the alumni admissions committee required to serve the anticipated applicant pool from an area. In addition to helping with the face-to-face training, the alumni relations staff provides a comprehensive 150-page handbook for the chairperson and committee members, with detailed information about the institution, the admissions process, and the committee members' roles as admissions volunteers.

In addition to recruiting and interviewing prospective students, volunteers help organize accepted student events. Called "capture parties" at Duke, these events are designed to convince recently admitted students to enroll. Planned by the alumni affairs office, these parties include university faculty, administrators, and admissions and alumni staff.

The value of alumni admissions volunteers goes beyond the applicant interview to encompass ambassadorial and public relations roles as well. Contact with the prospective students influences

● ● ●

While budgetary responsibilities differ from institution to institution, it is imperative that there be a clear delineation of financial responsibilities between the alumni relations and the admissions offices.

parents, peers, and others in the community. At many institutions, the national and international applicant pool is such that contact with an alumni volunteer is often the only personal contact an applicant has with the institution. And your trained alumni volunteers, who are extraordinarily well informed about the applicant pool quality and current admissions policies and practices, can interpret and transmit that information to other alumni and friends of the university.

Following the personal interview, alumni volunteers complete an evaluation form for the applicant's file. The admissions office should value alumni volunteer interviews on the same basis as interviews with admissions officers. Therefore, it is important that volunteers thoroughly assess and evaluate the personal qualities of the candidate and report their findings to the admissions office. Volunteers should provide the admissions office with information other than test scores, grades, course listings, and the enumeration of activities, concentrating instead on personal attributes, particular accomplishments, and distinctive characteristics, attractive or unattractive, about the candidate. Interviewers are also asked to probe for any unusual family or school situations, which are often left off the application. These evaluations, when weighed carefully with the factual and quantitative data and recommendations from the school, can be the deciding factors in difficult cases.

A common concern of alumni volunteers in the program is that some of their interviewees are not admitted. The quality of Duke's applicant pool is such that far more deserving candidates apply than can be admitted. Furthermore, alumni volunteers are not provided with grades, test scores, and school recommendations. Alumni see the bright, personable faces of applicants but lack complete information about the applicant's record. When alumni program volunteers inquire about a rejected applicant, the AAAC program director meets with the alumni volunteer and, if necessary, also brings in an admissions counselor to review the case. Discussions cover all but the most confidential information about the candidate.

Volunteers should continue the cultivation process after the interview by phone and letter to congratulate a candidate on some honor or award, for example. They should follow through after the admissions decision, especially to encourage admitted students to matriculate.

THE AAAC LEADERSHIP

Here are lists of responsibilities for the alumni volunteer chairperson and the alumni relations staff member responsible for the Duke program:

AAAC Volunteer Chair

- Updates committee rosters annually;
- Determines size and scope of committee volunteer needs;
- Recruits volunteers;
- Organizes and directs annual training sessions for new members;
- Establishes rapport with area secondary school guidance counselors;
- Maintains liaison with Duke admissions officers responsible for the region;
- Assists Duke admissions officer in arranging visits to the region;
- Assigns candidates to volunteers for interviews;
- Encourages committee volunteers to complete interviews in a timely fashion;
- Reports results of admissions committee decisions to volunteers.

The AAAC Program Director (Staff)

- Updates and distributes the program manual to all volunteers;
- Edits and distributes periodic newsletters to 3,000 AACC volunteers;
- Assists parents of prospective students who have particular questions about legacy matters;
- Leads annual orientation and training sessions for new AAAC chairs;
- Maintains mailing lists and rosters of committee members;
- Assists with the recruitment of new members;
- Monitors the activity of the committees and offers remedial attention, if necessary;
- Acts as liaison with the committees and the office of undergraduate admissions;
- Serves as the sounding board for comments, suggestions, concerns, and complaints.

Duke's Alumni Admission Advisory Committee Program is the Duke Alumni Association's most volunteer-intensive program. Such a program can be one of the most visible and useful activities at any institution.

FURTHER READINGS

Barre, Nancy. "Natural Resources: Your Alumni Can Become One of Your Most Valuable Tools for Recruiting Students," CURRENTS 14, no. 7 (July/August 1988): 34-36, 38, 40.

Christion, Laura. "Critics' Choice: Want to Make Your Campus a Four-Star Hit with Prospective Students? Rave Reviews from Alumni Volunteers Can Boost Your Recruitment Efforts," CURRENTS 20, no. 1 (January 1994): 38-40, 42-43.

Dawson, Harriet. "Views from a Veteran: A Former Volunteer Tells How to Work Best with Alumni Recruiters," CURRENTS 20, no. 1 (January 1994): 41.

Linstrum, Helen. *Taking Your Show on the Road: A Guide for New Student Recruiters.* Washington, DC: Council for Advancement and Support of Education, 1990.

Myers, Judy. "Two-Part Harmony: Alumni and Admissions Offices Learn How to Play the Same Tune When They Run Alumni Student Recruitment Programs Together," CURRENTS 14, no. 7 (July/August 1988): 28-32.

Students and faculty, by their physical proximity to campus, have daily access to the decision-making process. Although the 380,000 alumni are no longer on campus, they, too, should be able to have an impact on the university—through their financial support, ideas, and opinions.

Alumni Advocacy: A Case Study that Worked

Margaret Sughrue Carlson

Executive Director, University of Minnesota Alumni Association and
Associate Vice President
University of Minnesota

This chapter demonstrates the major role alumni associations can play in addressing university policy and issues.

—PMB

The University of Minnesota Alumni Association didn't set out to appear in the *Washington Post* a few years ago. The *Post* publicity came in the middle of a high-profile struggle between the university's board of regents and faculty leaders over proposed tenure code changes. The paper noted that "alumni groups have petitioned the board (of regents) to change its mind, saying the university is being 'ripped apart' by the tenure debate." Because of the critical nature of the debate, our national board of directors implored the board of regents and the university faculty to "mutually explore ways to resolve the tenure dispute immediately because the institution's reputation suffers the longer this dispute continues." In the end, both sides agreed to an amended code that preserved academic freedom while giving the regents more personal flexibility during extreme financial emergencies.

A HISTORY OF ALUMNI ADVOCACY

Alumni association advocacy doesn't always make the national press, but our involvement in university policy and issues has been a tradition since the Minnesota Alumni Association was formed in 1904. In fact, on the day the association came into being, one of its first orders of business was to pass a resolution opposing control of the university by the state board of control and pledging to restore management to the board of regents. In 1906, the alumni association threw its support behind increasing faculty salaries. In 1909, alumni resolved to warn regents not to fill the agriculture deanship as a "mere political convenience." In 1911, the university turned to alumni to help solve student problems caused by proximity to—as historical records note—"a great city with its temptations and lack of home life."

More recently, the association offered alumni perspectives on where the Minnesota Gophers should play football; sought a position on the search committee for the new university president; and surveyed alumni on whether the university should divest itself of its South African investments. We have shared alumni opinion on a variety of issues with administrators, faculty groups, the board of regents, the governor, legislators, and community groups.

As these initiatives unfolded, the seeds of advocacy were sown. We commissioned an alumni survey, the results of which told us that alumni fervently wished for opportunities to make a positive impact upon the university. In 1985, the association's board of directors made the commitment to be involved in the very fabric of the university by establishing a new standing committee: the public policy committee. This group was charged with focusing on university-wide issues, seeking alumni opinion, and reporting to university administrators and key officials.

Among the committee's first-year agenda items was the highly-charged topic of selecting regents. Community concern had been expressed that the current process was too partisan—that only party regulars have access to the regent positions. A decision was made to appoint an independent 23-member task force to study the regent selection process.

The task force, led by a former regent and former Minnesota governor, recommended that a special committee seek qualified applications for regent, screen all candidates, and make recommendations to the legislature and governor, who make the final selections. Such a plan required legislative approval, which did not come to fruition that year due to an extremely short legislative session. However, the following year, thanks to passionate and persistent lobbying by alumni volunteers, the legislature approved a bill that enacted the Regent Candidate Advisory Council, a group whose charge was then and remains today to recruit and recommend regent candidates to the legislature.

These successes became our adrenaline. And when the university was in trouble—whether it was the resignation of the president, the firing of the athletic director, problems with NCAA violations, or criminal accusations against a revered medical school surgeon—the alumni association staff and volunteers were mainstays.

ADVOCACY INITIATIVES

As times have changed, leadership at both the university and association levels have changed, and the thrust of the association has, too. Each year, we have implemented new advocacy initiatives, including:

■ initiating regular meetings between regents and key association volunteers to discuss university issues and ways that we might work together to advance the university's goals;

■ sponsoring an open forum for all regent finalists, who answer questions before an audience of legislators, community leaders, and association members;

■ activating our legislative network, now 2,800 volunteers strong, which helps to carry the university's message to legislators;

■ reporting annually in the association magazine on the university's progress in meeting its diversity goals; and

■ recommending alumni volunteers to serve on major university search committees, including, most recently, two searches that resulted in the hiring of the new university president and vice president for institutional relations.

The alumni association seeks not to set policy but rather to have an impact on policy. Students and faculty, by their physical proximity to campus, have daily access to the decision-making process. Although the 380,000 alumni are no longer on campus, they, too, should be able to have an impact on the university—through their financial support, ideas, and opinions. The outcome of decisions isn't as important as the opportunity to gather information, and to relay the opinions of a concerned university constituency to decision makers to help them set policy. This is what alumni have been telling us they want most from their alma mater.

TACTICS FOR SUCCESS

Over the years, the alumni association has learned how to be successful. Our tactical strategies over the past 10-year period were both planned and evolutionary when it came to governance issues. We know now that it is crucial to:

■ be courageous in facing tough criticism from within and outside the university community;

■ seize one or two major initiatives and hang on to them until the activity is successful—perseverance cannot be underestimated;

■ focus on those things that the association has a direct interest in and can have an impact on;

■ take a behind-the-scenes approach to most of

your activities, but, when appropriate, use the press and community influence;

■ understand that resources may need to be matched with your commitment;

■ protect staff members against fears that their jobs will be on the line if they are affiliated with public policy stances that university or community leaders disagree with.

NEXT STEPS AND GUIDING PRINCIPLES

We continue to make progress because nearly all of the essential ingredients needed to navigate through the thicket of advocacy are now in alignment:

■ mission, vision, goals, objectives, benchmarks, and critical measures that publicly proclaim advocacy as a priority;

■ key alumni volunteers who are deeply and philosophically committed to the association being more than just a fraternal organization;

■ professional staff who can handle complex policy issues and politically-charged situations;

■ operating revenue and endowments that allow adequate funding of the advocacy initiatives;

■ university officials who see the potential of the alumni corps as an incredible asset rather than a threat; and

■ alumni who are listened to and respected because they have unique university experience and because their concern comes from the heart.

Finally, we are guided by these overarching principles:

■ We clarify whether we are speaking as individuals or as representatives of the alumni association's national board;

■ We make sure that we know the facts before we speak;

■ We refrain from making any judgments or comments on personnel issues;

■ We provide extensive advice and counsel behind the scenes, rather than putting our association in the spotlight;

■ If working behind the scenes is not sufficient, we comment publicly if we do not believe the

administration and/or regents are taking responsibility for an issue;

■ We often provide an outside perspective for the university as crises unfold or move to the healing stage.

Has being a leader in the advocacy arena been rewarding? Absolutely. You can imagine the pride in being a fulcrum of institutional change, in being part of an organization that's on the move, in being perceived as an integral part of the university.

There will always be those who strongly caution that the alumni association should not become involved in the weighty or controversial issues facing the university. However, our bylaws, written in 1904, command a global charge to "do all lawful things for the welfare, benefit, and betterment of the University." Indeed, the people who guided the alumni association in its infancy saw themselves as champions of a strong and vibrant university—the key to a better life and a better state. They understood that betterment sometimes means disagreeing with the status quo.

It is true that it would be more pleasant to take the middle ground on tough issues, or ignore these issues altogether. But it is important to remember that discomfort is the price that an association must pay for maturity and relevancy. Again, we look to the wisdom of the early leaders of our association and university.

"University graduates should stand united, as an organized body representing and advocating all that is best in education, purest in civil government, and noblest in human life," said the dean of the Law School to those attending the first alumni annual meeting. "Only by focusing the intellectual light of the whole body of alumni can the wisest plans for university advancement be discovered, and only by unifying all their moral, social, and political influences can those plans be effectively consummated."

The key to the University of Minnesota Alumni Association's advocacy success are our alumni volunteers, who are deeply and philosophically committed to the association's being about more than class reunions, a magazine, special

> ● ● ●
> **Take a behind-the-scenes approach to most of your activities, but, when appropriate, use the press and community influence.**

events, and travel programs. We are all of those things, but so much more. University administrators have learned that, occasionally, we may not see eye to eye on every issue, but alumni offer a unique and heartfelt perspective on university issues and concerns.

FURTHER READINGS

Cook, Constance Ewing. *Lobbying for Higher Education: How Colleges and Universities Influence Federal Policy.* Nashville, TN: Vanderbilt University Press, 1998.

Hooper, Mark S. "The Alumni Lobby: How Alumni Clout Can Strengthen a Government Relations Program," CURRENTS 10, no. 7 (July/August 1984): 36-39.

Koral, Mimi. "Political Performance: If You Want Campus Support From Legislators, Alumni Volunteers are Instrumental to Your Success. Here's How to Fine-Tune Your Advocacy Efforts," CURRENTS 24, no. 1 (January 1998): 46-52.

Scalzo, Teresa. "The Power of Politics: How to Turn Supportive Alumni Into Political Capital for Alma Mater," CURRENTS 18, no. 3 (March 1992): 20-24.

Institutions with dynamic advancement programs do seem to have one trait—the close coordination of alumni relations, communications, and development programs.

Alumni Involvement in Fund Raising: A Tie That Binds

Jeffrey S. Todd
Director of Alumni Relations and The Wooster Fund
College of Wooster

The role of any productive alumni association and alumni relations office is to promote a meaningful and, we hope, life-long relationship between alumni and their alma mater. To accomplish this mission of actively engaging alumni in the life of the academy, we offer a wide variety of programs and services. But this is not an entirely benevolent act on the part of colleges, universities, and schools. In addition to fulfilling the institution's commitment to the alumni community, we have the clear anticipation of a return on our investment. Universities, colleges, and schools want to translate the positive feelings and loyalty of their alumni into active advocacy.

HISTORICAL ROOTS

While advocacy can take numerous forms, philanthropic support is what most of us think of first. Alumni financial support dates back to the origins of many alumni associations but regular, systematic alumni fund raising didn't begin until the late 1800s. In their infancy, alumni organizations provided alumni with opportunities not only to stay connected with one another, but also to stay in touch with their alma maters. In some cases, the first alumni fund-raising project was raising money to pay for the salary of the alumni professional, often titled alumni secretary, as well as for the alumni program. When formal alumni associations first began appearing on the landscape, so too did alumni annual funds. Other forms of alumni fund-raising activities soon followed.

STRUCTURE

Institutional advancement today provides no single standard model or practice for involving the alumni office in fund-raising activities. Instead, this involvement varies by the culture, tradition, and philosophy of each institution. At some campuses, the alumni relations and development programs are completely separate entities, while at others, the two programs fall under the same management umbrella. Institutions with dynamic advancement programs do seem to have one trait, however: the close coordination of alumni relations, communications, and development programs. Whatever the structure, the alumni relations program can play a pivotal role in helping the institution meet its fund-raising objectives.

Alumni professionals can have direct responsibility for both fund-raising activities and alumni programming. One of the most common ways alumni offices may be involved is through the annual fund.

At some campuses, the alumni relations office manages both the alumni program and the annual fund. The arrangement works because alumni relations and the annual fund share calendars and the need to coordinate alumni volunteers. When well managed and executed, linking alumni relations and the annual fund makes both programs more effective.

Reunion gift programs are another fund-raising initiative for alumni offices. These can be designated for annual fund, capital projects, or endowment, but they have one common trait: they are organized around the occasion of a class reunion at the institution. Alumni offices may either work cooperatively with the development office, involving the reunion committee in event planning and networking as well as fund raising, or the office may actually take responsibility for working with the class on both projects. Alumni offices also help regional or affinity groups interested in supporting the institution financially. These groups may sponsor projects or special events to raise funds for scholarships, academic programs, athletics, buildings, or general institutional support.

INDIRECT FUND RAISING

If alumni offices are not engaged in "direct" fund-raising activities, they are involved indirectly. Alumni offices play a major role in nurturing relationships between alumni and their alma mater. A future donor's engagement with the institution often begins with involvement through alumni programs such as regional meetings, reunions, travel programs, or volunteer assignments.

To cultivate alumni relationships, alumni and development offices must communicate frequently and accurately. Alumni professionals should share information about alumni who demonstrate interest in the institution and have the financial ability to support it. They should also identify alumni who have connections to other key individuals or organizations. The alumni office can also help identify prospective volunteers for development efforts such as phonathons, campaigns, or special projects.

At the same time, development officers should share their knowledge about alumni with the alumni office. Often, prospective donors are

● ● ●
It behooves everyone to see that development and alumni programs communicate and collaborate because they best serve the needs of both the institution and alumni.

not only interested in fund-raising projects but would be enthusiastic volunteers for alumni office activities in admissions, reunions, or regional events. Development officers also meet alumni who could be engaging speakers for alumni programs or clubs, or who have access to facilities suitable for alumni activities, such as museums, performing arts centers, offices, or clubs.

As advocates for development office programs, alumni offices can sponsor regional and campus forums to provide information about fund-raising projects, especially during major capital campaigns. Alumni clubs and chapters can have one or more volunteers assigned to work with development on fund-raising activities. Members of the alumni office staff should be fully conversant with institutional needs and be aware of opportunities for alumni to provide financial support.

The average alumnus or alumna doesn't naturally distinguish between an institution's alumni and development offices. He or she assumes the two are coordinated or perhaps even one and the same. At smaller institutions, coordinating alumni and development programs may be relatively easy, while larger, more complex universities face significant challenges to integrate those distinctly separate entities. But it behooves everyone to see that development and alumni programs communicate and collaborate because in working together, they best serve the needs of both the institution and alumni.

REFERENCES AND FURTHER READINGS

Guarino, Mike. "Blurring the Lines: Why Do We Focus on Differences Between Fund Raising and Alumni Relations?," CURRENTS 24, no. 7 (July/August 1998): 72.

Jackson, Laura Christion. "Concentrated Efforts: For Alumni Offices That Don't Manage Annual Giving, the Focus Is On Friend Raising, Not Fund Raising," CURRENTS 23, no. 5 (May 1997): 14.

Lucy Lillian Notestein, *Wooster of the Middlewest*. New Haven, CT: Yale University Press, 1937.

Walker, Mary Margaret. "Balancing Act: Managing Alumni Relations and the Annual Fund Is No Easy Feat. To Master the Art, Begin with These Five Lessons," CURRENTS 23, no. 5 (May 1997): 10-14.

Worth, Michael J., ed. *Educational Fund Raising: Principles and Practice*. Phoenix, AZ: ACE/Oryx Press, 1993.

Who is your audience? That should always be the first question. It's far too easy to focus on the medium and fail to fully understand the audience.

Communicating with Alumni: Your Route to Success

Keith E. Brant
Executive Director, UCLA Alumni Association
University of California, Los Angeles

Just about everything we do in alumni relations involves communicating messages to audiences using a variety of media. If our objective is to generate support for our institution, then our strategies are the ways in which we communicate in order to garner that support. It's difficult to look at communication without thinking in terms of marketing. In other words, communication to what end? If our intention is to move the audience toward some action (that is, join the alumni association, give to the annual fund, attend a lecture, support the team), we're really talking about marketing. Communicating with alumni is fundamentally tied to your success. In fact, next to having good records of alumni, communicating with them regularly is the heart of what you do.

BREADTH VERSUS DEPTH

The economics of communication is fundamentally the trade-off between breadth and depth. Breadth, or reach, refers to the number of people who receive the message. Depth refers to the quality of the message received. There are several dimensions to depth, including "band width" (the amount of information), customization, and interactivity. In general, when the reach is vast, the depth is weak. When the reach is small, the depth can be strong.

To illustrate this point, compare the difference of approaches between major gift fund raising and annual giving. The first relies on one-on-one meetings where the conversation is built around the interests of the individual donor. In this case, breadth is at its smallest but depth is at its richest. In contrast, annual giving often depends on direct mail campaigns to thousands of alumni. The reach is vast but the depth is rather shallow.

As you prepare to communicate with alumni, consider the audience, message, and the vehicles. Be clear with yourself on the trade-off between breadth and depth and the impact on your immediate objective. Of course, cost is always a factor as well. For example, if you set out to market a reunion program, you could design one marketing piece for the entire program or you could design one customized piece for each class member. The former will be less expensive while the latter will allow for greater depth. Breadth remains constant, although customization should provide a greater return.

AUDIENCE

Who is your audience? That should always be the first question. It's far too easy to focus on the medium and fail to fully understand the audience. Begin by sketching out a demographic profile of your audience. For example, when we market alumni travel programs, we believe that the likely participants tend to be over age 55. Immediately, we consider some fundamental factors in designing a brochure: Make the print larger! We also know that people born before the television age generally tend to think linearly and enjoy reading in depth. Avoid trendy design and make certain the forms are easily understood.

When we market membership in the alumni association, we segment the audience and tailor a message to them. A good database and a productive mail house will allow you to segment an alumni list into many parts. For example, if your segments are membership type (annual, lapsed annual, paying life), region (local, out-of-the-area, international), and age or class (one for each the last eight decades), you have created 72 segments (3x3x8). We then utilize a mail house to insert various messages in the marketing pieces so they are customized for each segment. When you use segmentation, be sure to measure the results to be sure it's worth future effort and expense. Inserting segmented messages using laser technology at a local letter shop will generally cost from 5 cents to 15 cents per piece (in addition to other expenses such as printing, handling, and mailing). Smaller segments (under 2,000 pieces) cost more per piece than larger segments (50,000 plus pieces).

How might you speak to students differently than alumni? To donors differently than non-donors? Volunteer leaders versus the general alumni population? Consider the demographics and life cycles of your audience and tailor the message accordingly.

MESSAGE

Take time to carefully consider and craft the message you wish to communicate and stay focused on that message. After an event (yours or someone else's), have you ever thought, "Well, that was nice, but what's the point?" That is not the impression you want to leave on your audience. Instead you want the audience to leave thinking, "That was great!" and have it respond appropriately.

Delivery of the message may be multi-dimensional. Take an alumni career program, for example. You may have several opportunities to reinforce your messages: the initial marketing brochure, a confirmation letter, a packet or folder of materials at check-in, event signage, the host's personalized words, the speaker's remarks, and follow-up correspondence.

Don't miss the chance to cross-market your products. For example, we make certain that our committee chairs promote various association programs throughout the year at committee meetings.

Crafting a message for a single marketing piece, event, or publication is not difficult. The real challenge is to create an integrated marketing program in which a consistent message is delivered throughout the organization over the course of a year or several years. At some point, you may want to delve into the issue of branding and identity for your institution or association.

MEDIA

Once you have determined the audience and the message, select the medium or vehicle for delivery. An alumni magazine may serve to showcase the best aspects of your institution and help to cultivate alumni affinity over the long run. But don't expect it to produce results independently. It's important to understand, as thoroughly as possible, the characteristics of each medium you use. For example, several years ago we conducted market research on our alumni magazine and discovered that it was not a good tool to market our products and services. Alumni treated it more as a "coffee table" periodical, a magazine to flip through when they had a chance, but not something to read cover-to-cover.

The cost of conducting market research can vary greatly, depending on how much you can do in-house versus outsourcing. If you hire a graduate student to handle survey design, statistical analysis, or focus group moderating, you might only spend a few thousand dollars. If you hire a market research firm or research consultant, you can spend tens of thousands of dollars or more. In early 1999, we hired a local research consultant to do a series of four focus groups. The whole project cost about $16,000.

Smaller, more targeted correspondence can often produce desired results. A letter from the dean updating alumni on accomplishments of their school or department might be viewed as more personal. A newsletter from the alumni director to current and past alumni leadership may help keep people in touch with the events of the alumni office. A newsletter to people in a particular region or with an interest in a specific issue can be particularly relevant. For example, we co-produce with our office of government relations a quarterly newsletter for alumni advocates, alerting them of future legislation that may affect the university.

Electronic communication offers exciting possibilities. What are the messages on your World Wide Web site? It is essential that your home page is succinct and interactive. Subsequent pages may contain greater detail. How can you use the Web to communicate your message and create dialogue? Instant feedback combined with database technology make it perfect for such applications as a searchable alumni directory, chat or discussion rooms, surveys, career services, and networking. Left alone, however, the Web is passive. You have to market your Web site address aggressively through other vehicles.

E-mail is emerging as perhaps the most powerful, fast, and cost-effective vehicle for communicating with alumni with their permission. For alumni committees, our association routinely employs e-mail for agendas, minutes, and messages from the chair. For association members, we inform them monthly of timely programs and services. E-mail messages should be succinct and refer readers to your Web site for greater detail. If you send widespread e-mails, set up a mechanism to respond to feedback and record incorrect addresses.

Don't overlook the mainstream media. Issue press releases to local newspapers and magazines. For example, when our association awards scholarships to students, we send a press release to each student's hometown newspaper announcing his or her accomplishment. Contact radio and television stations about creating public service announce-

● ● ●
What are the messages on your World Wide Web site? It is essential that your home page is succinct and interactive.

ments for events. If you have video facilities, produce programs for broadcast. Many communities require their cable companies to reserve air time for community and educational broadcasts. Videotape your alumni awards program for local broadcast and promote the air time and station in your print and electronic communications.

When looking for the best vehicles, brainstorm the possibilities. If you have an alumni credit card, ask the company to include your messages on bill statements. Or ask the athletic department to promote alumni homecoming events when it mails football tickets. And what's the message on your stationery and business cards? The possibilities are endless.

What you spend on communicating to alumni varies greatly depending on the resources available to you on campus. For larger projects that you might need to outsource, such as for designing a Web page or creating a video, get bids from several vendors. Don't forget to consult alumni volunteers who may be able to negotiate deals or *pro bono* work.

FINAL ADVICE

Let me offer two more pieces of advice. First, once you have considered breadth versus depth, audience, message and media, and begin communicating, don't forget to design mechanisms to collect feedback from your audiences. They will help you benchmark your success. And finally, the art of communicating with alumni is a perfect opportunity for professionals in alumni relations and communications to work collaboratively. Both sides of the advancement profession are critical to your success.

FURTHER READINGS

McKim, Robert. "Choosing the Right Media for Your Message," *Target Marketing* 20, no. 10 (October 1997): 86.

"The Right Tools for the Right Jobs: A Chart Showing the Best Uses for 17 Different Communication Strategies," CURRENTS 21, no. 5 (May 1995): 25.

Sevier, Robert A. and Robert E. Johnson, eds. *Integrated Marketing Communication: A Practical Guide to Developing Comprehensive Communication Strategies.* Washington, DC: Council for Advancement and Support of Education, 1999.

Stoner, Michael and Phillip Cartwright. "Alumni, Public Relations, Admissions—And Technology," *Change: The Magazine of Higher Learning* 29, no. 3 (May/June 1997): 50-52.

Tromble, William W. *Excellence in Advancement: Applications for Higher Education and Nonprofit Organizations.* Frederick, MD: Aspen Publishers, 1998.

*The advancement profession is no longer
the exclusive domain of North America, nor
has it been for some time.*

Global Alumni Relations:
A UK/US Perspective

Reggie Simpson
Head of Alumni Relations
London School of Economics

The British are coming! And the Dutch, the French, and the Swedes. The advancement profession is no longer the exclusive domain of North America, nor has it been for some time.

The CASE Europe office in London recently marked the fifth anniversary of its opening (1995). Increasingly, North American advancement professionals are finding themselves at British and European institutions.

As one of the first to have crossed the Atlantic, I have reached an interesting career milestone—I have now worked more years in alumni relations in the United Kingdom (seven) than in the United States (five).

Looking back to my arrival in the UK in 1991, the alumni relations profession was still very much in its infancy. Today, the CASE Europe office counts more than 900 European individuals who work in, or have expressed interest in, starting an alumni program at their institutions. The bulk of the established alumni programs are in the UK; however, interest on continental Europe is spreading rapidly.

What has attracted me to work in alumni relations in the UK is being at the cutting edge of a profession that is really growing outside North America. It's taking my preconceived notions of what makes for successful alumni programming in North America and shaping them to fit different contexts and cultures. It's about the global dimension within which universities here increasingly operate.

A CASE STUDY

Few universities can claim to be more international than the London School of Economics and Political Science (LSE). The school enrolls more than 6,000 students from 140 countries and supports a network of more than 60 international alumni groups.

LSE has long nurtured a relationship with its international groups, although mainly from afar. Of course, in today's information age, distance is not a problem, but telephone and e-mail communication doesn't replace meeting face-to-face either.

Recently, we have seen a much more dynamic, 'on the ground' approach to cultivating our international alumni. Four factors in particular that have contributed to our recent success in this area include:

1. Bringing our international alumni leaders back to the school for the first-ever Alumni Leadership Forum. Forty leaders from 23 countries returned to

LSE for a highly intensive three-day forum in September 1998, which combined updates on the school's strategic initiatives with practical sessions—and, of course, some fun activities! They came from as far afield as Australia, Brazil, Africa, and Japan, each paying his or her own airfare—a strong indicator of their commitment. In time, we plan to take the forum "on the road," and eventually get the groups to take turns hosting.

2. *Involving LSE's Director, Anthony Giddons, in visits to alumni groups.* World renowned as a sociologist and prolific author of more than 30 books, he has been dubbed British Prime Minister Tony Blair's favorite intellectual. His most recent works, *Globalisation, The Third Way, The Third Way and Its Critics,* and *Runaway World* have inspired discussion and debate, leading to hundreds of invitations to share his views with political leaders, the media, academia—and of course, LSE alumni—around the world.

In recent months, Giddens has criss-crossed Europe and circled the globe, visiting alumni groups in Germany, Switzerland, Spain, France, Greece, India, Hong Kong, the United States, Mexico, and Iceland. The opportunity to meet with alumni on their home turf and the presence of the director have made an enormous difference to our international alumni relations program, boosting alumni pride in LSE. As the president of our Delhi Alumni Society, Ashwajit Singh, said following his visit to India:

> The much awaited visit of the director acted as a catalyst for revitalising and reactivating the alumni group in Delhi and strengthened alumni feelings about the school. This in turn has helped renew the ties that LSE has had with India. The net result will be an increased flow of new students to the school and opportunities for generating income.

3. *The school's student recruitment program.* International (non-UK/Europe) student fees account for 25 million pounds sterling—one third of the school's annual income. The school's student recruitment manager, Tim Rogers, and I have developed a strategy that uses alumni in recruitment activities and in helping increase the visibility

of LSE. On a recent trip to Mexico, the alumni leaders proved invaluable in giving local advice about appropriate 'feeder' institutions, opportunities for collaborative agreements, cultural nuances, and what subjects or academic programs would most attract Mexicans to LSE.

● ● ●

Concentrate on areas where there are significant numbers of alumni and look at where your institution's strategic interests lie. Then act accordingly.

4. *Collaboration with the school's Press and Public Relations Office.* Our international alumni groups place LSE press releases in local media. The groups also monitor local press for LSE mentions and reviews about the state of British higher education. I remember being in Singapore once when the annual rankings for British universities were published. The British press was particularly negative about British higher education. Singaporeans take serious note of such rankings, so it is no wonder that Australian and North American universities are taking an increasing share of Singaporean students away from British universities.

L SE may well have a much larger international population than your institution. Yet, all institutions presumably face the issues presented by distance learning. Consider the wisdom of LSE Professor of International Relations, Fred Halliday, who said in a lecture on 'The International University':

> The debate on the international character of universities has . . . been transformed in the 1990s by a set of changes in context and direction. Anyone reading the education press will be familiar with the terms 'world class status,' 'global' campuses, plans for world-wide distance learning . . . *The Economist* speculated [in 'The Knowledge Factory', 4 October 1997] . . . on the university of the future, with a restricted physical campus and a network of computer-linked outlets and students, a 'virtual' or 'cyber-university' . . .

My advice for anyone looking to start or increase international alumni activity is to follow the same rules you apply to your domestic alumni chapter relations: Concentrate on areas where there are significant numbers of alumni and look at where your institution's strategic interests lie. Then act accordingly.

FURTHER READINGS

Fitzgerald, Nancy. "All Roads Lead Back to Alma Mater: How Campuses Stay Connected with Alumni Around the Globe," CURRENTS 25, no. 9 (October 1999): 30-35.

Gearhart, G. David and Roger L. Williams. "The British are Coming: Fund Raising in the United Kingdom is Catching Up Fast—And That Means Competition," CURRENTS 16, no. 9 (October 1990): 72.

Ryan, Ellen. "Common Bonds: Three Experts Offer Tried-and-True Tenets of International Fund Raising," CURRENTS 20, no. 8 (September 1994): 18-22.

Trimarco, Paola. "Taking on the World: International Alumni Programming Needn't be a Daunting Task. Use These World-Class Strategies to Reach Your Overseas Audiences," CURRENTS 20, no. 8 (September 1994): 32-37.

Global Alumni
Relations:
A UK/US
Perspective

● ● ●

Alumni associations are taking a leadership role in developing user-friendly, customized Web portals that can be used as windows to the Internet.

Alumni Records and Technology: New Tools for Keeping in Touch

James H. Melton
President, Florida State University Alumni Association
Florida State University

Our alumni associations provide the most important communications link to our worldwide network of alumni and friends. For decades, alumni records have been a consolidated mix of management information computer systems on mainframe hardware. To support that network, most of us have relied on various computer systems to integrate and manage alumni records. As we cross into the new millennium, each member of the advancement profession is challenged by the need to maintain and provide accurate information on our graduates, while supporting the various constituencies of the university. We need systems that are both easy to use and capable of handling complicated layers of information.

TODAY

Since the late 1960s, our alumni/advancement systems have evolved from single application modules that produced lists and labels of our graduates by class year and major, to complex systems that serve all areas of the university. The elements of data that we collect and manage continue to expand from basic demographic information to wealth indicators, imported from outside commercial vendors; additional addresses; business and personal preferences and interests; lifetime giving histories; membership information; and now, e-mail addresses.

As we place the batch systems of the early 1960s and the online terminal access applications of the 1980s into the pages of history, we now have the opportunity to develop and use our new database management systems to improve the efficiency of our advancement programs. Most of our systems will be purchased from firms and companies providing comprehensive systems with unlimited options. The new advancement system will include the alumni, foundation, and athletic booster modules in an integrated format, on either the campus mainframe unit or more likely, local mainframe hardware. Systems integration will interweave the expanding databases, alleviating the problem of data duplication.

How does one address the cost to the institution of installing such a high-end system? Commercial advancement systems do have significant front-end acquisition costs and continuing maintenance charges. However, the hardware costs for these systems continue to decline, with corresponding increases in operating capacity. Desktop computers that access the main system have multiple uses beyond simple connectivity to include data uploading and downloading. Depending on the system's design, most areas of the university will have access depending on need. The concept of waiting for a list should be a thing of the past. The efficiency and usefulness of such a sophisticated system will quickly justify its initial cost to the institution.

TOMORROW

Even now, alumni associations are planning, designing, and implementing new techniques of interacting with our worldwide alumni. We must exploit the new technologies that are becoming commonplace—the Internet and the World Wide Web.

It has been reported in various media that more than 80 percent of college graduates have access to the Web either at home or at work. This ubiquitous medium can be used both to enhance alumni relationships and maintain advancement system data.

Many schools and most colleges and universities and their alumni associations have developed customized and informative Web sites. Alumni now expect instant access to up-to-date information on their institution's activities and issues and links to other informational sites like enrollment and sports. The university's Web environment is well-suited to such features as travel coordination, reunions, club programming, alumni "chat" clubs, and the release of important information.

Alumni associations are taking a leadership role in developing user-friendly, customized Web portals that can be used as windows to the Internet. These portals will channel alumni, friends, and students to existing Web initiatives that detail the current university daily operation. They will offer content, tools, and services that offer merchandise and e-commerce opportunities. Our constituents are using portals every day to get what they want and need from the Internet and this initiative can channel daily connects back to the university.

How many times have we wondered how we could remain connected to our alumni and have

correct data? Each of our current students has an e-mail address. As these students become alumni, their record should include their collegiate e-mail address. By maintaining this address and providing an opportunity to attach a forwarding address, we can stay connected to our alumni as never before. Alumni associations have developed weekly news reports that are e-mailed to a selected database or placed on the Web to be accessed anytime. Instant information, once only a dream, is now commonplace.

BEYOND TOMORROW

There are many unknowns. How sophisticated must staff members become to operate new systems and technologies? How will we "limit" data collection—what information has value and what is just clutter? With increased accessibility to information, what kind of privacy issues will arise? How do we decide who should have access? In planning strategically, how can we predict what new technology applications will exist?

As changes in hardware and software continue at a rapid pace, universities must invest in advancement systems that can serve future needs. We can expect performance of systems to improve and costs to decrease, and we must continue to educate our staff members to ensure they are at the forefront of developing and using technology. Regardless of technological breakthroughs, we must honor and respect the confidentiality of our alumni records, and provide safeguards throughout our operational environment. We must use technology to more broadly serve our core mission of education, research, and service to our global alumni community. Alumni should expect nothing less from their link back to alma mater.

● ● ●

More than 80 percent of college graduates have access to the Web either at home or at work. This ubiquitous medium can be used both to enhance alumni relationships and maintain advancement system data.

FURTHER READINGS

Blansfield, Karen C. "High-Tech Connections: Still Relying on Phone and Mail to Communicate with Alumni Clubs? The World Wide Web, E-Mail, and Even Video and Satellites Can Help You Reach Regional Audiences Faster," CURRENTS 22, no. 3 (March 1996): 34-38.

Dolbert, Susan Clouse. "Entering A New Domain: Alumni

Associations Launch Web Portals to Capture Daily User Traffic and E-Commerce Revenue," CURRENTS 26, No. 2 (February 2000): 18-23.

"Ideas Online: Click On These Creative Suggestions for Using the Internet in All Areas of Advancement," CURRENTS 22, no. 4 (April 1996): 32-38.

Macy, Heidi. "High-Tech Tactics: Three Ways You Can Use Computers To Reach Members," CURRENTS 22, no. 10 (November/December 1996): 38.

Strange, Diana Tilley. "The MIT Way: How One Alumni Association Keeps its Web Strategy Grounded in its Original Alumni Relations Mission," CURRENTS 26, no. 2 (February 2000): 24-29.

Stoner, Michael. "Coming Up Next: If You Manage Your Alumni Office Web Site, Watch for These Trends: More Valuable Features, More Outside Expertise, and More Evaluation," CURRENTS 24, no. 3 (March 1998): 10-15.

Woodbeck, Dean. "Making the Web Work for You: An Alumni Office Home Page on the Internet's World Wide Web Can Be a Benefit—If You Use It Properly. These Ideas Can Help You Manage This Tool," CURRENTS 21, no. 10 (November/December 1995): 40.

Alumni Records and Technology: New Tools for Keeping in Touch

●　●　●

Believe it or not, you can identify additional revenue for your association budget without ever picking up a phone or leaving your desk. Simply cut your expenses.

Securing Financial Resources: Membership, Fund Raising, Program Fees, Self-Generated Income

John B. Carter, Jr.
President and CEO, Georgia Tech Foundation and
Former Vice President and Executive Director, Georgia Tech Alumni Association
Georgia Institute of Technology

Budget shrinking? Want to add new programs or services? Want to expand your publications, your clubs? Want up-to-date technology? Want your alumni relations program to be the best of the best?

As professionals in higher education, we all want to maximize our efforts to engage alumni with our institutions. That is the premise of our profession. In today's fast-paced, ever-changing world, it is increasingly difficult to involve our alumni in a meaningful way. What makes it even more difficult is the scarcity of funds.

Whether your institution is public or private, an independent school, a two- or four-year college or university, or a research university, the demand for funds is becoming more competitive than ever. And priorities for funding are shifting. In most states, financial support for public higher education as a percentage of the state budget has declined in recent years, and the future isn't promising. So how do you continue providing a viable alumni relations program in the face of these funding woes?

Believe it or not, you can identify additional revenue for your association budget without ever picking up a phone or leaving your desk. Simply cut your expenses. Most association professionals agree that they could probably cut 10 percent of their budget without a negative impact on the services they provide to their constituents. So why not give it a try? It may not be an easy process, but it gives you an opportunity to review your programming and sends a message to your staff and association board that you want to run an efficient operation.

SIX RULES TO LIVE BY

Now that you have just increased your budget by cutting expenses by 10 percent, let's look at other ways to identify additional revenue and what to keep in mind during the search. But first, let's review the six rules to live by.

1) Know your mission.

Before you decide to provide a product or a service to your constituencies—including not only alumni, but also faculty, staff, students, parents, and friends of your institution—you must first determine if what you want to do is consistent with and supports your mission. You may be able to generate significant revenue, but the cost may be more than it is worth. Selling your alumni list to a listing service for magazines, for example, will upset your alumni. The result will be decreased support

Securing Financial
Resources:
Membership,
Fund Raising,
Program Fees,
Self-Generated
Income

of your programs and those of the institution.

2) Know the benefits.

Ask yourself whether the product or service you wish to provide actually benefits your constituency. If not, the project is doomed from the start. A benefit may be in the form of discounts from vendors that only your constituents may receive, or something that they can acquire only through your association. Be wary of the possibility that the benefit may be renegotiated and offered at a greater discount by another organization.

3) Know your vendor.

If you decide to offer a product or service in order to generate additional revenue, you will most likely partner with an outside vendor. Selecting this vendor is crucial to the success of your program. Consider preparing a request for proposal (RFP) and making it available to any vendor who might have an interest. This is essential because you may have constituents who want to bid on the project. Make sure your selection process is open and fair.

Choosing a reputable vendor is a must. Check references and credit history. Ask your colleagues at other institutions about their experiences with a vendor. Require guaranteed revenue and signed contracts. Use legal counsel to help with the contract and to address issues of liability should the vendor default. Have the vendor provide sample products, and beware of those who take 10 to 12 weeks to ship orders. Your constituents won't be happy with the delay.

4) Know your income.

Determine whether the revenue received will be treated as related or unrelated business income. The Internal Revenue Service is always looking for possible tax revenues. As a general rule, royalties are not considered taxable, but revenue from advertising is. Use legal counsel because you don't want anything to jeopardize your tax status as a nonprofit organization.

5) Know your campus.

Make sure products or services you're offering don't conflict with or duplicate the efforts of other campus organizations. Competing with your campus colleagues is a lose-lose situation. However, be prepared to partner with campus organizations to support their causes. An example would be providing ad space in your publications for the bookstore catalog in return for a percentage of sales.

And you need to be aware of what your development office is doing, including development activities in the athletic association. You want to make sure what you're offering doesn't adversely affect their ability to raise money. For instance, you wouldn't want to mail your membership information the week before the annual fund solicitation is mailed. Also—to the extent you can—try to identify new sources of revenue. It only causes hard feelings when you capture revenue that used to flow to a colleague's budget.

6) Know the traps.

Once you have developed a revenue stream, be careful how you allocate it. Most associations use the revenue to fund new programs for their constituencies. It is easy to fall in the trap of creating a much-needed program or expanding an existing one, only to find out that in a year or two the revenue that funded it is no longer available. Exercise extreme caution when budgeting this revenue. Use the revenue from programs that generate consistent revenue flow over time.

DUES AND DON'TS

Many alumni associations receive revenue from membership dues, which generally range from $25 to $50 a year. Life memberships beginning at $500 are a popular way to build an endowment. Be careful, however, to spend only the interest from the life memberships and preserve the principal. Keep in mind that alumni will expect certain benefits as members of your association.

Some associations are responsible for the annual fund. Where this is the case, the associations usually do not have membership dues, but consider all alumni members of the association. Alumni clubs and chapters may have annual dues to help offset expenses of the club. Clubs may also raise money from their members for scholarships for local students.

OTHER SOURCES OF INCOME

Regardless of your institution's structure, there are certain intellectual rights that provide you opportunities to generate funding from external sources. These rights may be as simple as your trademarks and licensed logos, or as complex as the intellectual property rights derived from research on your campus. Regardless of what opportunities there are, you must first decide if what you want to do is in the best interest of your institution. This is a vitally important and often difficult task and may involve consensus from a diverse group of administrators who have differing agendas.

Career services is not only an excellent program for alumni, but can provide a steady stream of revenue. Corporations are most willing to pay for access to your alumni who may be searching for a new position. Job bulletins, career conferences, and electronic databases are the most commonly used services. There are companies that provide electronic databases if you are unable to provide the service yourself. The financial arrangement for this service varies from company to company.

Comprehensive alumni directories are an excellent way to provide a service to alumni at virtually no financial risk to your association. The types of directories provided in today's market offer a variety of choices, from hardbound and soft-bound printed directories to those on compact discs or online. Each has its advantages and disadvantages, and the financial return to your association varies by what type of directory you choose and how much you charge for it.

While a number of programs offered by alumni associations are free, it is totally acceptable to charge for certain programs and events. Reunion parties, homecoming meetings and dinners, career seminars, and club dinner meetings are a few examples. Corporations are an excellent source for sponsoring events. They usually ask only to receive publicity in your promotional material and signage at the event.

Tours are an additional source of revenue. However, most associations provide this service to alumni with the expectation that the revenue received will fund the program expenses, including staff costs. Only a few associations with established travel programs have revenues that exceed those expenses.

Advertising is an excellent source of revenue. Generally it consists of advertisements in your alumni publications. The expenses associated with advertisements are minimal. Some associations take advertisements a step further, offering sponsorships to advertisers who sign contracts of a year or longer. These sponsorships generally offer the advertiser some additional benefit, such as tickets to events or an on-campus presence at special activities. Keep in mind, though, that working with advertisers may initially take staff time and add to the production costs.

Merchandising is an excellent opportunity to generate revenue, but it will require you to assume more risk than other revenue-producing opportunities. Some larger associations have an association store that sells university and association merchandise ranging from pens, mugs, and key chains to high-quality sweatshirts, golf shirts, and embroidered jackets. The risk involved is knowing what merchandise will sell and managing your inventory. Most associations prefer to partner with the campus bookstore to sell the low-priced items and soft goods while focusing their efforts on specialty mail-order items such as class rings, clocks, watches, lamps, and chairs. The risk is much lower for mail-order items because you can contract with a vendor to provide the products and pay for all marketing costs.

AFFINITY PROGRAMS

Affinity programs are typically revenue-generating marketing efforts by for-profit companies in partnership with institutions. Common examples are credit cards and insurance. The nonprofit affinity partner usually benefits from a royalty from the contract, and the position of the nonprofit is usually a passive one.

The insurance industry offers a wide range of products to alumni through associations. The most

> ● ● ●
> **Regardless of your institution's structure, there are certain intellectual rights that provide you opportunities to generate funding from external sources. These rights may be as simple as your trademarks and licensed logos, or as complex as the intellectual property rights derived from research on your campus.**

Securing Financial
Resources:
Membership,
Fund Raising,
Program Fees,
Self-Generated
Income

popular products over the years have been term life, short-term, and major medical coverage. More recently, disability, property and casualty, whole-life, and extended-care policies have been offered. The insurance companies offering these products incur the marketing expense and provide a royalty to the association usually based on a percentage of premiums paid by your alumni.

In the past 10 years or so, bank, credit card, and telephone affinity programs have generated the most revenue. In today's market, the number of vendors offering these programs seems to be decreasing because of mergers and acquisitions, but that shouldn't be cause for concern. Banks and investment firms are beginning to offer new affinity programs that will provide alumni opportunities to invest in private-label funds sponsored by the association. These programs are so new that there is no data on revenue returned to the association, but the projections are impressive. E-commerce brings to market a number of additional affinity possibilities, such as online banking, investment trading, and shopping malls. Some Internet service providers are willing to share revenue with associations whose members sign up for their services.

PARTNERS PAY OFF

There are any number of companies that will partner with your association to offer products and services to your alumni. You can expect to receive revenue every time a purchase is made by one of your alumni. These initiatives are different from affinity programs in that they usually don't require you to endorse the product or service. The utility industry is a good example of how this might work. With the deregulation of utilities in most states, utility companies are becoming very aggressive marketers. They may offer your association a percentage of their customer's bill if the customer designates your association as the recipient. Again, this particular program is new and has no data to support revenue expectations.

On occasion, companies may enter into a grant or contract with your association. This can be very beneficial to you because it might underwrite an important project for which you have no funding. Examples would be a market research project to determine why alumni become members of your association, a readership survey of your publications, or an image survey of your association. These are usually one-time projects that are important to the success of your alumni programs but are not budgeted.

THE BOTTOM LINE

Determining what revenue-producing programs are viable for your particular association is not easy. Think carefully about the quality of the products and services being offered, and the ability of the company or vendor to perform up to your association's standards and the expectations of your alumni. Consider also the impact all these activities might have on your nonprofit status. Most alumni relations professionals will agree that the primary considerations of whether or not to enter into a revenue-producing activity are: does it add value to the service you provide your alumni and your institution and is the activity consistent with the mission of your alumni association? If you choose your activities carefully, you can indeed generate substantial revenue that will go a long way to providing a comprehensive alumni relations program of which your alumni and institution can be proud.

FURTHER READINGS

"And Now, a Word from Our Sponsor...: How Corporate Gifts Can Boost Your Alumni Programming," CURRENTS 33, No. 6. (June 1997): 8.

Arsenault, Jane. *Forging Nonprofit Alliances: A Comprehensive Guide to Enhancing Your Mission Through Joint Ventures and Partnerships: Management Services Organizations, Parent Corporations, and Mergers.* San Francisco, CA: Jossey-Bass Publishers, 1998.

Blasius, Chip, Bill Frauhiger, and Ralfie Blasius. *Earning More Funds: Effective, Proven Fundraising Strategies for All Non-Profit Groups.* 3rd ed. Fort Wayne, IN: B C Creations, 1995.

Block, Deborah, Ivan Levison, and Mal Warwick. *999 Tips, Trends and Guidelines For Successful Direct Mail and Telephone Fundraising.* Berkeley, CA: Strathmoor Press, 1995.

Blumenstyk, Goldie. "Alumni Associations Seek Corporate Ties: More Associations Seek Corporate to Provide New Services to Their Members," *Chronicle of Higher Education* 40, (April 20, 1994): A42, A45.

Carley, David. "Enter the Entrepreneur: How Institutions Can Engage in Large-Scale Business Development,"

CURRENTS 14, No. 3 (March 1988): 26.

Detweiler, Gerri. "Banking on Alma Mater: Alumni Credit Cards, Mortgages and Other Financial Services Can Benefit Graduates and Boost Revenues," CURRENTS 21, No. 9. (October 1995): 18.

Hodgkinson, Harold L. "Resource Raising: Putting Your Campus Assets to Work Full Time," CURRENTS 19, No. 8 (September 1983): 14.

Lengsfelder, Peter, Robin Simons, and Richard Steckel. *Filthy Rich & Other Nonprofit Fantasies: Changing the Way Nonprofits Do Business in the 90's.* Berkeley, CA: Ten Speed Press, 1989.

Marketing Loyalty: High-Quality Merchandise Can Be a Valuable Service to Alumni If You Know What They Want," CURRENTS 23, No. 6 (June 1997): 41.

Muehrcke, Jill, ed. *Enterprise (For Profit) Endeavors, Leadership Series.* Madison, WI: The Society For Nonprofit Organizations, 1993.

Nicklin, Judy. "Some Colleges' Alumni Giving Comes in Form of Muscle and Sweat: Former Students Return to Berry and Oral Roberts to Spruce Up the Campus," *Chronicle of Higher Education* 42 (July 19, 1996): A33-34.

Rolnick, Joshua. "Some Colleges See Fund-Raising Potential in Commercially Designed Web Sites for Alumni," *Chronicle of Higher Education* 45 (Dec. 4, 1998).

Sabo, Sandra R. "Taxing Situations: Do Your Merchandising Efforts 'Substantially Relate' to Your Association's Mission?" CURRENTS 21, No. 6 (June 1995): 24.

Scalzo, Teresa. "Beyond the Bottom Line: There's More to Alumni Merchandising Than Just Raising Revenue." CURRENTS 21, No. 6 (June 1995): 10.

"Shawnee State U. Alumni Raffle Off Cash Prize to Raise Funds," *Chronicle of Higher Education* 42 (Aug. 16, 1996): A33.

Taylor, Karla. "Campus Capitalism: Ten Ways That Institutions Are Raising New Resources," CURRENTS 9, No. 8 (September 1983): 18-21.

Teagno, Gary C. *Profiting Through Association Marketing.* Blue Ridge, IL: Irwin Professional Publications, 1994.

"What Works and What Doesn't: Alumni Directors Share Details on Their Most- and Least-Successful Merchandising Efforts," CURRENTS 21, No. 6 (June 1995): 21.

Wolfson, Leslie J. "From Neckties to Nikes: Starting an Alumni Merchandising Program Demands More Than Just Business Sense," CURRENTS 17, No. 8 (September 1990): 30.

Young, Joyce, and Ken Wyman. *Fundraising For Nonprofit Groups: How To Get Money From Corporations, Foundations and Government.* Seattle, WA: Self-Counsel Press, 2000.

The desire is for a favorable outcome for your organization. It is almost always less expensive to get it right the first time through proper selection of legal representation, whether choosing a firm or an individual.

Legal Issues for Alumni Administrators: Worth a Second Look

Dan L. Heinlen
President/CEO, The Ohio State University Alumni Association, Inc.
The Ohio State University

Risk. It's an element to consider in undertaking any activity and is magnified with the complexity and number of participants. It is present in every decision made by you, your staff, and your volunteer leaders. Minimizing risk possibilities is a priority and while you can never be assured of total immunity, knowing where issues may arise should help provide preemptive protection. Likewise, determining when you need legal expertise and selecting appropriate counsel adds another layer of confidence.

Many alumni relations offices are organized as a wholly-owned subsidiary, department, or agency of a college or university. The institution's policies and procedures would then usually govern the program's operation just as they would cover the chemistry or English department. Associations that operate as self-governed entities may choose to adopt different methods to conduct business using resources in the private sector. But in either case, wise administrators use additional networks and information pipelines to keep up with ever-changing rules, regulations, and compliance codes that may affect their operations. CASE is often an excellent source of information through its conferences, books, and Information Center, as are personal contacts with other professionals through listservs and various Internet sites.

LOWERING LEGAL LIABILITY

What issues should administrators of alumni programs and services consider to lower the potential for legal liability? Without attempting to assign rank order, knowing the importance of when to engage legal counsel—and which one—should appear near the top of the list. Just as physicians often specialize and only treat problems fitting their area of study, lawyers (both individuals and firms) may do the same. Identify those whose expertise covers the area needed to address your specific issue. When facing a dilemma dealing with the hiring, dismissal, or discipline of an employee, it makes most sense to find legal support from one whose specialty encompasses human resource issues. Would it be better to have a broken leg tended by an orthopedic surgeon or a plastic surgeon? A general practitioner may do the job in an emergency but, given the circumstances and desire for a superior outcome, a GP would most likely refer such a case to the specialist. Know the choices open to you and carefully analyze the problem as you see it. In any case, the goal is a favorable outcome for your organization. It is almost always less expensive to get it right the first time through proper selection of legal representation, whether choosing a firm or an individual.

LEGAL ISSUES TO WATCH

In the United States, federal requirements have mushroomed during the past several years in so many areas of significance to alumni administrators that I surveyed a number of colleagues, including past presidents and board members from the Council of Alumni Association Executives, to get their thoughts on legal issues affecting alumni relations. Here is a compilation (by no means exhaustive) of those to which an alert professional should be sensitive. These are simply examples; volumes have been written about each item.

■ *Fiduciary responsibility of staff and volunteers.* Where assets have been placed in trust, they must be treated with the same care an ordinarily prudent person would provide in similar circumstances.

■ *Constitutions, by-laws, articles of incorporation, codes of regulations.* These govern the way in which an organization is run and offer guidance to its decision makers.

■ *Contracts.* Words are powerful and contracts, once signed, mean exactly what they say. When appropriate, do not be reluctant to seek competent outside help when drawing up contracts.

■ *Tax exempt status.* Organizations receiving a tax exempt designation from the Internal Revenue Service under any of the 501(c) sections assume certain unrelated business income tax (UBIT) liabilities and restrictions. Auditors and attorneys specializing in the nonprofit sector are good sources for current information and should be asked for guidance.

■ *Protection for leaders.* Protect your elected leadership through directors' and officers' liability insurance, indemnification, and good corporate governance practice and policies. Many leaders now require such protection before agreeing to serve on volunteer policy-level boards.

● ● ●

Words are powerful and contracts, once signed, mean exactly what they say. When appropriate, do not be reluctant to seek competent outside help.

■ *Liability insurance.* Are you adequately insured with general liability or other coverage on staff/volunteer business travel? Ditto on exposure for you and your volunteers when liquor is served at your functions? For sponsored tours, does your travel agent list the association as an additional insured on its policy?

■ *Employment law.* Areas of interest include policy development for benefits, interview and hiring protocols, grievance, harassment, discrimination, and wrongful termination. Some other issues to investigate: personnel files (what information should be where), sexual harassment (terminology is changing to anti-harassment to more broadly cover the issue), and the wisdom of annually reviewing this with staff to alleviate employer liability. The Family Medical Leave Act (FMLA) requires proper tracking and notification of staff rights and obligations. Termination issues often revolve around performance appraisals (note: written records of such meetings with employees should be a requirement). EEO and Affirmative Action job posting requirements: what are they?

■ Other items of interest include use and sale of mailing lists, *quid pro quo* and conflicts of interest, implications of the Americans with Disabilities Act for alumni events and travel, agreements between separate 501's and the university, and association-owned for-profit enterprises, such as dining clubs and retirement centers. Consider related issues with advertising income, publications, postal regulations, deduction of life membership dues, Web/e-mail offerings by association online directories, and investment services or mortgage sales (what about your liability in the event the financial institution fails?).

This list could continue with additional topics and greater detail. Seek the counsel and wisdom available to you from professionals and colleagues on specific issues of concern and understand your responsibilities are great because of the trust placed in you.

FURTHER READINGS

American Society of Association Executives. *Association Insurance Program Guide and Survey Report.* Washington, DC: American Society of Association Executives, 1996.

DeLizia, James. *The National-Chapter Partnership: A Guide for the Chapter Relations Professional.* Washington, DC: American Society of Association Executives, 1993.

Jacobs, Jerald A. "Weighing the Benefits of 501(c)(6) Tax Exemption: Tax Exemption Has Become a Mixed Blessing, But Think Carefully Before Giving It Up," *Association Management* 49, no. 8 (August 1997): 113-114, 116, 118, 120.

Jacobs, Jerald A. *Association Law Handbook.* 3rd. ed. Washington, DC: American Society of Association Executives, August 1996.

Sabo, Sandra R. "Taxing Situations: Do Your Merchandising Efforts 'Substantially Relate' to Your Association's Mission? The Answer Means A Lot to the IRS and Postal Service Rule Makers," CURRENTS 21, no. 6 (June 1995): 24-28.

Legal Issues for Alumni Administrators: Worth a Second look

SECTION V
**Educational Fund
Raising**

Edited by Michael J. Worth

Introduction

Michael J. Worth
Vice President for Development and Alumni Affairs
The George Washington University

Philanthropy has played a key role in the advancement of colleges and universities since the earliest days of American higher education. With today's competitive environment limiting the growth of other sources of revenue, fund raising has a central place in the advancement strategies of all institutions. Once important primarily to private colleges and universities, philanthropy is now vital to both public and private four-year institutions as well as to two-year colleges and private schools.

Fund-raising staffs and budgets have grown concomitantly with the increased importance of private support. Nearly all higher education institutions employ at least some fund-raising professionals, and staff at large universities number in the hundreds. Multi-year comprehensive campaigns with goals in the tens or hundreds of millions have become commonplace, with some setting—and achieving—goals in the billions of dollars. Educational fund raising in the United States has become a sophisticated enterprise, using specialized techniques and requiring highly-trained professional staff. As many nations have "privatized" their higher education systems, colleges and universities across the world have sought to implement fund-raising programs on the American model, making educational philanthropy an international phenomenon.

The chapters in this section describe the major components of a comprehensive fund-raising program, consider issues facing the field today, and look ahead to possible changes in the educational fund-raising environment of the 21st century. The discussion begins with my own chapter on positioning the institution for successful fund raising. Drawing on the lessons of research as well as the experience of practitioners, this chapter identifies some of the key preconditions that a college or university must consider before setting its fund-raising goals and designing its program.

The annual giving program remains the bedrock of the entire effort and Fritz Schroeder's chapter provides a review of the principles and practice of annual fund programs today. Some donors will eventually give major gifts, but the cultivation of such support requires a careful and thoughtful process. David Dunlop's chapter discusses its principal elements and defines basic concepts. While some consider major gifts and planned gifts to be distinct elements of the overall fund-raising program, Jonathan Heintzelman describes an approach that integrates major gifts and planned gifts, both in concept and in the organization of the development office.

Support from corporations and foundations represents an important component of overall philanthropy at many colleges and universities, especially those with a strong research mission or academic programs that relate closely to the interests of business. Carolyn Sanzone's chapter on corporate support and Patricia Gregory's chapter on foundations describe the principal considerations in seeking gifts and grants from these sources.

The campaign pulls it all together. An intensive effort to increase support from all sources within a defined period of time, generally encompassing gifts for both operating and capital needs of the institution, the campaign has become a primary vehicle for achieving the strategic goals of colleges and universities and broadening their base of ongoing support. Terry Holcombe's chapter on the campaign reflects the state of the art in the planning and management of such an all-out effort.

In Chapter 8, Kenneth Dayton provides a perspective that is in contrast to the intensive and time-limited nature of a campaign. The former chairman of Hudson Corporation and a philanthropist himself, Dayton describes nine stages of giving that identify an individual's evolving approach to philanthropy. It reminds us that donors have their own needs and priorities that may or may not coincide with our short-term goals. Achieving campaign goals is important, but it is equally important to nurture life long relationships

between our institutions and their donors.

The next four chapters explore important aspects of organizing, managing, and supporting the development program. Tracy Savage discusses what happens after the gift is made, and how campuses can continue their communications with donors in order to develop long-term relationships. Thomas Kelly describes models for organizing the development function within different types of institutions, and Richard Boardman reports on research to help guide the selection and management of fund-raising staff. Eric Wentworth's chapter discusses special considerations for institutionally related foundations at public colleges and universities.

In today's age of open communications and access to information, the need for ethical behavior is of practical as well as moral importance. In his chapter on ethics in fund raising, Gary Evans discusses some choices that development officers may face and how their decisions can be made to protect both their own integrity and the reputations of their institutions.

Bruce McClintock, as a fund-raising consultant with a national perspective spanning various types of institutions, looks ahead to some of the trends that will affect higher education philanthropy in the decades ahead.

The American system of higher education is acknowledged as the finest in the world and our colleges and universities have been essential to our success as a nation. Now we are living in a new world economy, one that emphasizes ideas over products and the life of the mind over work with the hands. In this environment, higher education is more central than ever to the economic and social progress of all nations. Philanthropy provides the means to assure the future of our colleges and universities, and the advancement professionals' mission to seek and facilitate support for higher education will be of vital importance.

A close relationship between institutional plans and fund-raising objectives is essential to make fund raising both purposeful and possible.

Positioning the Institution for Successful Fund Raising

Michael J. Worth
Vice President for Development and Alumni Affairs
The George Washington University

To some people, the term "fund raising" is synonymous with the solicitation of gifts or simply "asking for money." But in successful programs, solicitation is the penultimate step in a sophisticated process of development that is directly tied to the academic mission and is fully integrated with the overall management and growth of the college, university, or school.

The process begins at the core of the institution itself, by determining its academic priorities and strategic directions, from which come its fund-raising needs and goals. The next step includes identifying prospects for gifts who have both financial capacity and interests that can be matched with the institution's needs. Once donor prospects have been identified, programs must be established to involve them in the life of the college or university in substantive and meaningful ways in order to build their understanding of, and commitment to, its goals. Only then is it time for soliciting gifts.

The process continues once a gift has been made, including the institution's responsibility to carry out gift purposes faithfully and effectively, and to keep donors informed of what their support has helped accomplish. This stewardship is in itself a form of cultivation for the next gift, making the development process truly a cycle, in which the donor's relationship with the institution expands and deepens over time.

When properly executed, this process is mutually rewarding to the donor and the institution, a far cry from the negative images often associated with the term "fund raising." As Henry Rosso wrote in *Achieving Excellence in Fund Raising: A Comprehensive Guide to Principles, Strategies, and Methods,* "The process is justified when it is used as a responsible invitation, guiding contributors to make the kind of gifts that will meet their own special needs and add greater meaning to their lives."

THE ACADEMIC PLAN

A close relationship between institutional plans and fund-raising objectives is essential to make fund raising both purposeful and possible. Harold J. Seymour once wrote, "Nobody buys a Buick because General Motors needs the money" (*Designs for Fund-Raising: Principles, Patterns, Techniques*) and surely donors do not make gifts to colleges and universities simply to relieve themselves of excess wealth. Donors, whether individuals or organizations, make significant gifts to advance educational, research, and service programs that are consistent with their own values and philanthropic goals. As Thomas Broce observed in *Fund Raising: The Guide to Raising Money From Private Sources,* "An organization that hires someone to 'go out and raise money' cannot expect impressive results. The person may get 'donations,' but he [or she] will not be able to attract substantial funds." The effort to secure significant support cannot be presented as an end in itself, but rather as the means to accomplish important and well-considered academic objectives.

The need to relate fund raising to substantive institutional goals is perhaps more important than ever before. If ever there was a time in the past when donors responded to emotional appeals to loyalty and obligation, today's sophisticated donors approach giving with the same care they would apply to evaluating an investment. An increasing number of major donors have accumulated their wealth in entrepreneurial businesses and some say they comprise a breed of new and more rational philanthropists. They are skeptical of requests for general support and expect colleges and universities to meet the same standards of good planning and management they would apply to their own companies. This includes a clear set of objectives and a credible plan for their achievement.

Basing fund-raising goals on the academic plan is also essential to assure that gifts bring real value to the college or university. Writing in *Educational Fund Raising: Principles and Practice* (edited by Michael Worth) in 1993, Rick Nahm and Robert Zemsky saw educational fund raising "at a crossroads," with "the character and purpose of fund raising [and] also the institutional role of development professionals" at stake. They cited critics who claim that many gifts are "donor-driven" and that colleges and universities too often respond to what donors are willing to support rather than the institution's own priorities. This can turn gifts into burdens rather than benefits, as the institution takes on the continuing costs of new projects that gifts do not fully fund. It also can breed cynicism about the fund-raising program, since real institutional needs may go unmet although dollar goals have been achieved.

Nahm and Zemsky propose as the alternative

to donor-driven gifts an institutional planning process that ". . .examines an institution's mission within the external environment, defines the institution's current position, develops a set of goals and objectives. . . [and] then becomes the road map for developing an effective fund-raising program. . . ."

PREREQUISITES OF SUCCESS

An academic plan that includes the expectation of significant philanthropy must reflect the institution's true fund-raising potential. Plans based on hopes rather than reality can only lead to disappointment and failure. The basic prerequisites of successful fund raising are well established, by experience and research. An intelligent planning process will include an evaluation of the institution's fund-raising "market" based on this body of professional knowledge.

In *Conducting a Successful Capital Campaign: A Comprehensive Fund-Raising Guide for Nonprofit Organizations* (edited by Kent Dove), consultant Martin Grenzebach identifies five key prerequisites to a successful development campaign. If these prerequisites do not exist, then the college or university must either develop a plan to improve its situation or scale back its ambitions:

- a positive image with the institution's constituency and the community;
- a clearly perceived need, well defined in the minds of those who know the institution best;
- the presence of available funds in the institution's constituency to meet the institution's goal;
- capable leadership, holding the respect of the community and willing to devote time and talent to the institution;
- a favorable economic climate and the absence of competing campaigns or enterprises.

A number of academic studies have examined the variables related to the fund-raising performance of colleges and universities and the research findings are generally consistent with the observations of practitioners. (See studies by Pickett, Loessin and Duronio, and CASE referenced at the end of this chapter). Some of these variables may be "givens" for the institution, over which it has no control, but others can be changed in order to position the institution for success. For example, a college that traditionally has recruited students from wealthy families likely will have greater potential for gifts than one that serves first-generation college students. A college located in a growing urban region near many corporate offices may have greater access to support than one located in an isolated small town. A university with professional degree programs in law, medicine, and business may find greater wealth among its graduates than will an institution focused on the preparation of teachers and public servants. These environmental conditions cannot be altered. History cannot be reversed and campuses are not easily moved. The institution must strive to maximize its fund-raising potential within its natural constraints and to set ambitious but realistic goals.

Other essential variables are within the control of the institution's leaders and must be addressed before ambitious goals can be achieved. For example, the commitment and leadership of the president and the board are high on every list of prerequisites to effective fund raising. The responsibility for fund-raising leadership cannot be delegated, and a half-hearted effort by those who govern and manage the institution will not call forth the sacrifice of others on its behalf. Not all presidents will be born as inspirational leaders or natural fund raisers, but some skills can be acquired with effort, and sincerity is more important than polished sales skills.

The willingness to commit budget and staff resources commensurate with the institution's potential and goals has been identified as one of the most consistent predictors of fund-raising success. In the social science language of research studies, there is a strong and positive correlation between the resources devoted to fund raising and achievement of the institution's fund-raising potential. In more ordinary terms, colleges and universities will get what they pay for in the quality of fund-raising staff and programs. The setting of ambitious goals without the commitment of resources necessary to acquiring them is an exercise in fantasy.

● ● ●

The willingness to commit budget and staff resources commensurate with the institution's potential and goals has been identified as one of the most consistent predictors of fund-raising success.

MATCHING PROGRAMS TO THE GOALS

The development "program" of a college or university is more accurately a collection of programs, selected from a tool kit of available strategies and techniques. The design needs to reflect the specific needs of the institution or, as architects say, form follows function.

For example, a struggling college in need of support to augment current operating budgets might emphasize its annual giving program. It should encourage bequests but it might not be wise to invest significant resources in a sophisticated planned giving program. On the other hand, a university with diverse sources of operating revenue might focus its fund-raising efforts on building its endowment and obtaining foundation support for research programs. A small college with a long tradition of class loyalty and volunteer involvement might develop a strong reunion class gifts program, while an urban, public university might find it more appropriate to build effective programs of mail and phone solicitation. An institution raising funds for its endowment would actively seek planned gifts, but such commitments might be less useful if the need is for funds to build new facilities.

While comprehensive campaigns with multi-million-dollar goals gain the most attention and publicity, a campaign is but one strategy a college or university might adopt in order to meet its needs for philanthropic support. While a campaign offers many advantages and benefits, it should not be undertaken unless or until the college or university has developed its academic plan, identified its needs for support, determined that it has in place the necessary prerequisites to success, and decided that a campaign is indeed the best strategy for obtaining the resources it needs.

There is often a temptation to observe the practices of other colleges and universities and to try and replicate all of them on our own campuses. Board members, presidents, deans, and others may feed this temptation by pointing to successful strategies at their own undergraduate and graduate institutions or by advocating something that may have worked for them in previous positions elsewhere. But, just as a physician cannot use the same prescription for every patient, development strategies and programs must be designed to reflect the institution's own environment and goals. They should not be adopted merely to imitate those of some other college or university, which may face very different circumstances and needs.

TOWARD AN INTEGRATED UNDERSTANDING

Educational fund raising or development today must be much more than "asking for money." It must be rooted in the institution's history and mission, its traditions and values, its inherent strengths and its aspirations for the future. As Frank H.T. Rhodes, the distinguished former president of Cornell University, noted in *Successful Fund Raising for Higher Education: The Advancement of Learning*, "Fund raising is not a convenient source of extra revenue to be tapped by smart tactics. It is an integral part of the larger mission of the institution. . . . [It] is neither an optional extra nor a distraction from the core business of the university. The core business of a university is learning, in its most expansive sense. Fund raising is an exercise in extended learning, an effort to create wider familiarity and a greater support for the most basic activity of our society."

REFERENCES

Broce, Thomas E. *Fund Raising: The Guide to Raising Money From Private Sources.* Norman, OK: University of Oklahoma Press, 1979.

Council for Advancement and Support of Education and National Association of College and University Business Officers. *Expenditures in Fund Raising, Alumni Relations, and other Constituent (Public) Relations.* Washington, DC: Council for Advancement and Support of Education, 1990.

Dove, Kent E. *Conducting a Successful Capital Campaign: A Comprehensive Fundraising Guide for Nonprofit Organizations.* San Francisco, CA: Jossey-Bass Publishers, 1988.

Loessin, Bruce A. and Margaret A. Duronio. "Characteristics of Successful Fund-Raising Programs." In *Educational Fund Raising: Principles and Practice.* Edited by Michael J. Worth. Phoenix, AZ: American Council on Education/Oryx Press, 1993.

Nahm, Rick and Robert M. Zemsky. "The Role of Institutional Fund Raising." In *Educational Fund Raising: Principles and Practice.* Edited by Michael J. Worth. Phoenix, AZ: ACE/Oryx Press, 1993.

Pickett, William L. "An Assessment of the Effectiveness of Fund-Raising Policies on Private Undergraduate Colleges," Ph.D. dissertation. University of Denver, 1977.

Rhodes, Frank H.T., ed. *Successful Fund Raising for Higher Education: The Advancement of Learning.* Phoenix, AZ: ACE/Oryx Press, 1997.

Rosso, Henry A. *Achieving Excellence in Fund Raising: A Comprehensive Guide to Principles, Strategies, and Methods.* San Francisco, CA: Jossey-Bass Publishers, 1991.

Seymour, Harold J. *Designs for Fund-Raising: Principles, Patterns, Techniques.* New York, NY: Fund Raising Institute, 1988.

To the institution, the annual fund is a reliable, consistent source of money for immediate investment, an effective communications tool, and a connection point for its constituency.

Annual Giving: The Front Door to Your Development Program

Fritz W. Schroeder
Executive Director of Annual Programs and Alumni Relations
The Johns Hopkins University

Twenty-three years ago, in the first edition of this handbook, Stanley McAnally began the annual giving chapter with the sentence, "Annual giving is based on the theory that people give to people." While many of the specifics of annual giving have changed dramatically, this principle is as true today as it was in 1977. Annual fund efforts represent the broad-based, regular solicitation of an institution's largest constituency, including alumni, friends, parents, grateful patients, and others. Annual fund revenue typically involves "current use" funds—monies that are raised today and spent tomorrow. Efforts are cyclical, with a very clear beginning, end, and next beginning. However, the annual fund plays many different roles:

■ To the donor, the annual fund is a communication vehicle, a way to "give back," and the public face of fund raising for the institution;

■ To the development office, the annual fund is the front door of the development program, an identification program for major donors, and a great way to involve volunteers;

■ To the institution, the annual fund is a reliable, consistent source of money for immediate investment, an effective communications tool, and a connection point for its constituency.

It is safe to say that at every institution, there is a slightly different way to look at annual giving. Each of us manages a program that involves different constituencies, focuses on different aspects of our institution, or has a slightly different strategy from that of our peers. For purposes of this discussion, we will divide annual giving into three distinct sections: planning, solicitation techniques, and evaluation. While there are volumes of information about annual funds and annual giving, these sections will present an overview of each stage of the process and specific points for success.

PLANNING

Behind every successful annual fund, there is a strong plan. Behind every *really* successful annual fund, there is a strong plan that has a great deal of flexibility. Murphy's law is alive and well in annual giving, and it is almost certain that in any annual fund effort, a mailing will be delayed, a phonathon will underperform, or a volunteer will neglect his or her donor list. But the plan will succeed if it has four things:

1) *A clear sense of purpose and mission.* Annual

fund programs that don't know where they want to go will never get there. You should work very hard to help your institution determine what your annual fund should be. Is it primarily a source of flexible dollars or a feeder for your major gift program? (Yes, it can do both.) Is your highest priority raising purely unrestricted dollars or broad-based participation? How about the double-ask decision for your major gift donors—do they give to the annual fund in addition to their larger commitment? All of these issues must be addressed in order to organize your team and your resources in pursuit of this goal. While some programs are strong enough to pursue multiple goals, these programs are well supported by years of tradition, healthy budgets, a strong and experienced staff, and a culture of philanthropy. Most younger programs should identify a central mission and structure their efforts accordingly.

2) *Accurate projections for programs, solicitations, and people.* Each of us has faced the imperative, "We need to double the annual fund this year!" Occasionally, annual funds can double in a year, but only if you make very accurate projections for where that increase will be found. For example, you might project that 30 percent of the growth will come through increasing alumni participation, 20 percent through increasing gifts from parents, and 50 percent through doubling the membership in your high-end gift society. This provides you with the framework for your plan to double the annual fund, and gives you the "hot buttons" to watch throughout the year.

Keep in mind that the annual fund "cost-to-raise-a-dollar" typically ranges between $.10 and $.25, although younger programs may spend as much as $.40 or even $.50 on the dollar. Part of establishing accurate projections includes establishing realistic budgets to support your efforts. The annual fund dollar is the most expensive dollar to raise in any development program.

3) *Goals that are both quantifiable and qualifiable.* Our performance numbers (total dollars raised, average gifts, participation rates, and so forth) are the heart of the goal-setting process. These are the numbers that we work for and that

> ● ● ●
>
> **Clearly, personal solicitations can be the most rewarding and exciting part of any annual giving program. It reminds us that the heart of any program lies with people, not numbers or percentages.**

give us a sense of how we perform from year to year. However, qualifiable goals are equally important for a well developed program. Is your senior class gift program positioned to educate students about the importance of lifelong philanthropy? Even if your corporate volunteer program hasn't raised more matching gifts, has it created a cadre of introductory-level volunteers who are being cultivated for their next step in your organization? Are your solicitation materials creating a tangible understanding of the importance of annual gifts? While these goals are not necessarily tracked in dollars and cents, they are important in creating a comprehensive effort that is both capable of and positioned for long-term growth.

4) *Back up plans.* There will be some years when nothing seems to go right. However, one of the exciting parts of annual giving is that we have multiple opportunities to correct errors or respond to changes. Remember, a good annual fund plan allows for this flexibility. For example, assume you launch a really creative October direct-mail campaign expected to increase your participation. It flops—not just a little, but more like a .001 percent response rate and an average gift of $1.17. The key is to use the two months left in the calendar year (and possibly eight months in the fiscal year, for those on a July-June cycle) to recover. Consider a targeted mailing in December or a special phone campaign in February that may not have been a part of your original plan, but will allow you to compensate for the under-performing solicitation.

In general, the annual giving planning function is an 18-month cycle. If your fiscal year begins on July 1, you should begin the planning process on January 1. You should begin this 18-month process by examining your program, and in the broadest of terms, outlining growth opportunities and changes for the next year. Incorporate in your plan how to improve programs that are underperforming and programs that have further growth potential. Begin to replace program segments that are in need of a complete overhaul.

SOLICITATION TECHNIQUES

Annual giving efforts combine two important components: Solicitation *tools,* like phonathons, direct mail, Web home pages, and personal visits; and *programs,* such as the young alumni fund, parents fund, class agents, reunion gift program, leadership gift clubs, and matching gift programs. The "art" of annual giving involves developing strong volunteer teams and creative programs for young alumni and parents, aggressive marketing of leadership societies, and the exploration of new programs and opportunities. The "science" of annual giving implies using the solicitation techniques in the most effective, cost-efficient manner to bring in the largest possible number of donors and dollars. The principles of our solicitation tools have remained fairly consistent for many years. However, the application of different techniques has changed rather dramatically.

Direct Mail

Although there are exceptions, direct mail is typically the least expensive approach with the lowest response rate. While response rates, or yield, can vary significantly, a 2 to 5 percent response rate on a large mailing is considered successful. In contrast, a smaller, targeted mailing to high-end or consistent donors may produce a 50 or even 75 percent response rate. There are several important reasons why we incorporate direct mail into our program:

■ It creates a visual image of the annual fund and helps to make the program tangible to donors.

■ It has a long-term reminder effect—donors can keep a direct mail response card in their bill pile for days, weeks, or even months, allowing them to make the gift according to their timetable.

■ With the growth in answering machines, caller I.D. machines, and other screening tactics for telemarketing, direct mail letters are often the only contact with a donor.

■ Direct mail allows us a level of creativity and innovation that is harder to accomplish with telemarketing scripts.

Phonathons

Phonathon programs, whether volunteer-based or employing salaried callers, allow for high volume with a modest amount of personal interaction. In a three-to-five minute telephone call, your caller can connect with a donor on several levels that are not possible in direct mail. Most importantly:

■ Phonathons allow for two-way conversations, the exchange of information, and reminders of important dates and upcoming events. They allow a caller to more thoroughly build a case for support by responding to objections and offering clarification where needed.

■ Phonathons allow the caller to negotiate the dollar amount of the pledge, the payment schedule, and other details that help to encourage a pledge.

■ We can tailor phonathon solicitations to individual donors and prospects—each script can incorporate certain messages, activities, and references to giving habits and affiliations in a way that targets the specific appeal to a level that is not possible with direct mail.

Personal Solicitations

Personal solicitations are the final component of a strong annual giving program. Personal solicitations provide an opportunity to meet with donors face-to-face, talk about the importance of their involvement in our organization, react to verbal and nonverbal cues, and make a very personal appeal for support. We typically use personal solicitations in annual giving as a means to: 1) increase the gift of a current donor, 2) solicit a VIP donor for a large annual gift, or 3) solicit the first gift from a nondonor with excellent future potential.

The principles that apply to annual gift solicitation techniques parallel those for major gift solicitations. The significant difference lies in the fact that the multiple steps in major gift solicitation (identification, interest, cultivation, solicitation, and stewardship) are condensed into two steps. In many cases, the first four steps are accomplished in one visit, whereas the major gift process may take three, four, or more visits. Clearly, personal solicitations can be the most rewarding and exciting part of any annual giving program. It reminds us that the heart of any program lies with people, not numbers or percentages.

Programming and Involving Volunteers

The art of annual giving is found in the creation of effective programs to address the special needs of certain constituencies within our programs. These programs include parents' funds, young alumni efforts, the senior class giving program, faculty-staff campaigns, class agents, reunions, and others. The applicability of these programs to a particular institution is determined by how well the program fits the culture and demographics of that institution. For example, a school of continuing studies with many part-time and returning adult students may not be the appropriate place to launch a parents program. Continuing education programs attract nontraditional, older students, whose parents are less likely to be involved in their education. However, this same continuing studies school may be an excellent candidate for a faculty-staff campaign given the large, and mainly adjunct, faculty constituency.

Regardless of which programs best fit each institution, the most important aspect of these special efforts is their ability to involve volunteers. Without question, a peer volunteer can be a stronger solicitor than a paid staff member can. Involving volunteers as class agents, reunion gift chairs, parents fund chairs, and as gift society leaders provides your potential donors with a strong endorsement from their peers.

The most important principles for enlisting annual giving volunteers (or any other volunteers, for that matter) are:

- Providing potential volunteers with a clear understanding of their duties and responsibilities during the recruitment process, and reinforcing them throughout their involvement.
- Giving volunteers the tools and the opportunities to be successful. There is no greater mistake than placing volunteers in a position to fail.
- Training your volunteers for their task. This includes educating them about your organization, your case for support, and the "art" of fund raising.
- Investing the proper amount of staff time and money to support fully your volunteer leadership.

EVALUATION

The process of evaluating annual giving efforts must be an integral part of the planning process. Comparing goals of total dollars raised, number of donors, number of personal solicitations, and number of volunteer solicitations against results is your first step. Then you must identify the underlying reasons why you did or did not make each goal. If you fell short of your target for alumni participation, determine whether a certain decade, school, or demographic fell short of its potential. If you only made one-half of your personal solicitations, can you account for your time in a way that will illustrate why? In addition, you should examine external benchmarks from your peers. Remember you make these comparisons not for the sake of competition, but to check the reality of your goals and to find areas of untapped potential in your program.

Annual giving efforts are not insulated programs unaffected by the outside world. Programs can be helped or hindered by the economy, leadership changes at the institution, technology changes in the market, competition for the fund-raising dollar, and yes, even an NCAA tournament win (or loss). A thorough evaluation will pinpoint which achievements or failures we can control, and those that stem from other influences. The most important thing an evaluation provides is the answer to what can or should be changed next year to improve the overall result.

FUTURE CHALLENGES

Our greatest future challenge will be convincing people that making annual gifts to their alma mater is as important as gifts to their church or synagogue, health agencies, disaster relief funds, children's issues, and others.

Phonathons may continue to drive our mass solicitation programs in the short run, but the World Wide Web will eventually change our mainstream solicitation techniques. Personal solicitation of annual donors, at all levels, is becoming a mainstay of our programs. Often, it is the face-to-face ask of a staff member or a volunteer that helps to make the case for, or encourages, continued annual gifts, as well as increased dollars.

Our international constituencies (alumni living abroad, foreign students who attended our U.S. institution, foreign parents of current students, etc.) will play a more prominent role in our programs in the future.

Annual giving is no longer an entry point to a development career. Clearly, the annual fund continues to be not only the foundation of a strong institutional development program but also a highly specialized area of fund raising requiring skills in marketing, personnel management, quantitative analysis, personal solicitation, special events, fiscal management, and strategic planning.

FURTHER READINGS

Christ, Rick. "Put Your Direct Mail to the Test: Try Out New Annual-Fund Stratifies—One at a Time—to Increase Your Returns with Less Risk," CURRENTS 24, no. 5 (May 1998): 20.

Council for Advancement and Support of Education. *Clasic Currents: Annual Giving: 14 Articles on Planning, Mail and Phone Solicitations, Closing the Year Successfully, Tips from the Experts, and More*. Compiled by Lindy Keane Carter. Washington, DC: CASE Books, 1998.

Gee, Ann D. *Annual Giving Strategies: A Comprehensive Guide to Better Results*. Washington, DC: Council for Advancement and Support of Education, 1990.

Greenfield, James M. *Fund Raising Fundamentals: A Guide to Annual Giving for Professionals and Volunteers*. New York, NY: John Wiley and Sons, Inc, 1994.

Hauk, Jeff and Robert A. Burdenski. "Is Direct Mail Dead?" CURRENTS 24, no. 9 (October 1998): 44-51.

Johnson, Jeffrey W. and Peter D. Eckel. "Preparing Seniors for Roles as Active Alumni," In *The Senior Year Experience*. San Francisco, CA: Jossey-Bass Publishers, 1997.

Nichols, Judith. *Changing Demographics: Fundraising in the 1990's*. Chicago, IL: Bonus Books Inc., 1990.

Pollack, Rachel H. "Divide and Conquer: Get More From Your Annual Fund by Targeting Your Appeals to Special Groups," CURRENTS 24, no.5 (May 1998): 12.

Schroeder, Fritz. *Annual Giving: A Practical Approach*. Washington, DC: CASE Books, 2000.

Walker, Mary Margaret. "Balancing Act: Managing Alumni Relations and the Annual Fund is No Easy Feat." To Master the Art, Begin with These Fine Lessons," CURRENTS 23, no. 5 (May 1997): 10.

When considering the gifts your institution seeks, or the fund-raising activities to encourage them, it is the giver's perspective more than the institution's perspective that will help the fund raiser choose the right things to do and to avoid doing the wrong things.

Fund Raising for the Largest Gifts: Concepts and Principles

David R. Dunlop
Former Senior Development Officer
Cornell University

I t takes a special kind of fund raising to encourage the largest gift of a lifetime to your institution. Your effectiveness in this special kind of fund raising requires an understanding of three kinds of gifts, three methods of fund raising, and two different bases for fund-raising decision making. You must also understand how to conduct the three methods of fund raising simultaneously in an integrated, coordinated, and complementary manner. From this understanding comes not only an ability to substantially increase the size of gifts given to your institution's annual fund and to campaigns to meet its special needs, but also to effectively encourage some individuals' largest gifts of their lifetimes to be made to your institution.

To be effective in encouraging individuals to make part or all of their largest gifts to your institution involves attention to two things:

■ Disciplined attention to your institution's procedures for relating to a limited number of individuals—potential major donors.

■ Attention to building an institutional culture with sensitive attitudes that will have a positive effect on all who encounter the institution.

KINDS OF GIFTS

When considering the gifts your institution seeks, or the fund-raising activities to encourage them, it is the giver's perspective more than the institution's perspective that will help the fund raiser choose the right things to do and avoid doing the wrong things. For this reason, it is more helpful in this chapter to look at the concepts of *regular, special,* and *ultimate* gifts rather than traditional gift definitions that are based on the amount of the gift (major, principal, leadership, etc.) or to the method of expression (current, deferred, planned, testamentary, etc.).

Regular Gifts

Regular gifts are made repeatedly and at regular intervals. The gift placed in the church collection plate every week, the check written to support the public television station every quarter, and the gift made once every year to the United Way, the Cancer Crusade, the United Jewish Appeal, or an institution's annual fund are examples of regular giving. The timing of these gifts is largely a function of the calendar. Regular gifts are usually the smallest gifts the individual will make. Nevertheless, a person with great wealth may make fairly large gifts regularly. For comparison with a person's other types of giving, let us ascribe a unit value of one to the regular gift.

Regular Gift: (1-X)
(timed to the calendar)

Special Gifts

Special gifts are gifts a person makes to help an institution meet a special need. They are usually made to an organization that the giver also supports with regular gifts. The three-year pledge to help pay for the new roof of the church, the two-year pledge in support of the community center building fund, and the five-year pledge to support a school's campaign for a new library are typical special gifts. The timing of special gifts is influenced by the needs of the institution receiving them. Special gifts are often five- to 10-times larger than the regular gift the person makes to the same institution.

Special Gift: (5-X to 10-X)
(timed to the needs of the institution)

Ultimate Gifts

Ultimate gifts are an exercise of the full giving capacity of the giver. They are the largest philanthropic commitment the giver is capable of making. Most ultimate gifts are made by trust or bequest. Some individuals, however, have sufficient resources to make their ultimate gift during their lifetime. In contrast to regular gifts and special gifts, the timing of ultimate gifts is most influenced by factors in the life of the giver. Ultimate gifts are often 1,000 or more times larger than the giver's regular gift to the same institution. They may be given to one institution or divided among several.

Ultimate Gift: (1,000-X or more)
(timed to the life circumstance of the giver)

METHODS OF FUND RAISING

Just as there are three kinds of gifts, there are three methods of fund raising to encourage these kinds of gifts.

Speculative Fund Raising

Speculative fund raising, which has nothing to do with gambling and everything to do with the law

of averages, focuses heavily on asking for many gifts very often. It is based on the speculation that, if you ask enough people for gifts, a sufficient number will respond favorably to make the effort worthwhile.

Direct mail appeals, phonathons, telethons, and even some personal solicitations are typical of speculative fund raising. The time and resources invested in this kind of fund raising are directed primarily toward asking, with a much smaller proportion of time and resources invested in developing the individual giver's sense of commitment. In speculative fund raising, the proportion of effort devoted to nurturing the giver's readiness to give before he or she is asked, versus the effort invested in asking, might look like this:

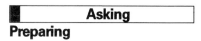

Speculative fund raising is most often used in soliciting regular gifts and occasionally soliciting special gifts.

Campaign/Project Fund Raising

Campaign/project fund raising also primarily focuses on the process of asking but, before the actual solicitation, more time and resources are invested in preparing the prospective giver for the request. This increased attention to the prospective giver, before he or she is solicited, is undertaken to anticipate the solicitation. For example, you invite a prospect to campus to meet the institution's curator of rare books before a classmate calls her to consider a special commitment to that institution's library campaign. The initiatives undertaken before the solicitation to prepare the giver before the ask, versus the effort invested in asking, might look something like this:

Preparing   Asking

This method of more individualized fund raising is used to solicit special gifts and to increase the size of regular gifts. Some refer to it as a "cultivate-solicit" approach to fund raising.

Nurturing Fund Raising

Nurturing fund raising focuses on building the

prospective giver's sense of commitment to the institution over time so that the institution becomes one of the giver's priorities for all types of giving, including the giver's ultimate gift. Much more effort and resources are invested in initiatives to build that sense of commitment than in asking. In contrast to campaign fund raising's cultivation in anticipation of asking for a gift, nurturing fund raising invests in initiatives to develop an individual's commitment to the institution, its values, its mission, and its plans, without a specific gift in mind. Nurturing fund raising is based on the belief that the values and interests an individual shares with your institution, and his or her capacity to respond to those values and interests, will result in your working out together over time many increased regular and special gifts and perhaps an ultimate gift. However, neither you nor the individual will know what they will be when you start. The proportion of effort put into building the individual giver's sense of commitment before asking looks something like this:

Preparing	
	Asking

EXPERIENCES THAT ENCOURAGE ULTIMATE GIFTS

While the experiences of each ultimate gift giver will be unique to the giver and to the institution receiving his or her gift, every ultimate gift giver has identical types of experiences that developed their:

■ Awareness,
■ Knowledge and understanding,
■ Interest and caring,
■ Involvement,
■ Sense of commitment, and
■ Expressions of commitment.

Individuals who have made ultimate gifts have not only had experiences that developed their awareness, understanding, caring, involvement, and commitment to the institution; but also to its values, its mission, the strategic plans for accomplishing its mission; to the people carrying out those plans; and to the specific objectives their gift supported. The wise fund raiser works to duplicate

these types of experiences among other individuals to encourage the giving of ultimate or other substantial gifts.

DECISION MAKING

In individual fund raising, the decisions of what to do, how to do it, when to do it, who should do it, and even how we evaluate it are typically based on one or the other of two factors: (1) a transaction to be accomplished, or (2) a relationship with an individual.

In speculative and campaign/project fund raising for regular gifts and special gifts, decisions are primarily based on transactions to be accomplished. For example, in these two kinds of fund raising, the creation of a direct mail piece, a campaign event, the solicitation of a gift, or a gift acknowledgment provides the basis for deciding what to do, when to do it, how to do it, who should do it, and so on.

In nurturing fund raising for ultimate gifts, decisions are primarily based on the relationship with an individual. The relationship determines just what should be done, who should do it, and when and how it should be done. In both speculative fund raising for regular gifts and in campaign fund raising for special gifts, a transaction to be accomplished usually leads in the decision making. Relationships are also considered, but secondarily. In nurturing fund raising for ultimate gifts, a relationship usually leads in the decision making.

Transactionally based and relationally-based fund raising are not mutually exclusive, but interdependent. You must consider the requirements of both as you integrate and coordinate transactionally-based and relationally-based fund-raising activities. This integration and coordination are not simple. At times, they may even appear to be at odds with one another. A sophisticated understanding of relationally-based nurturing fund raising will often change how some aspects of the more transactionally-based speculative and campaign fund raising are conducted and vice versa. For example, in campaign fund raising the focus is on soliciting prospective givers as effectively and efficiently as possible. When someone you were counting on for a lead gift to a campaign declines to give, after thanking them for their consideration, you would turn your attention to the next person to be solicited. When nurturing fund raising is factored into the campaign, considering the relationship with that individual would result in your taking several more initiatives to make sure he or she felt no less a friend of the institution because the time was not right to make the special lead gift for which you were hoping.

SIX-STEP DISCIPLINE

The core of relationally-based nurturing fund raising consists of creating a stream of the initiatives discussed above. These are initiatives tailored to each individual that builds awareness, understanding, caring, involvement, and welcomes expressions of commitment in the full range of each individual's unique capacity to express a growing sense of commitment. To create this stream of initiatives, someone must periodically:

1. Review (what has transpired in the relationship).
2. Plan (what is appropriate to do next to advance the relationship).
3. Coordinate (with those you need to involve in the next initiative).
4. Execute (the initiative).
5. Evaluate (were the objectives accomplished? what to do next?).
6. Report and record (the results of the initiative).

Plan on each person requiring at least one initiative a month, and even more if you can manage it.

FOREGROUND AND BACKGROUND INITIATIVES

The types of initiatives that advance a person's awareness, knowledge, interest, involvement, and commitment fall into two categories.

1. Foreground Initiatives

Foreground initiatives are conceived, planned, and executed with a specific individual in mind. For example:

■ Request to borrow art for display on campus.
■ Invite the person to dinner with the dean.
■ Request advice in an area of special competence.
■ Invite the person to meet with a trustee.
■ Name a garden, room, or building.

■ Set up a phone call from a faculty member or student to say thanks.
■ Send a message of congratulations about a business promotion.
■ Mail a letter reporting on the impact of a gift the friend made previously.

2. Background Initiatives

Background initiatives are conceived, planned, and executed with a group in mind that may include one or more prospective givers. These initiatives include:

■ Class reunions;
■ Newsletters and alumni magazines;
■ Films and video tapes;
■ Alumni events and functions;
■ Annual report of the institution;
■ Musical, theatrical, or athletic events;
■ Campus tours;
■ Advisory councils; and
■ Seminars and institutes of special interest.

NATURAL PARTNERS

In speculative fund raising for regular gifts, and in campaign or project fund raising for special gifts, the work is usually done by someone who is either assigned or has volunteered. This works well for an annual fund or in a campaign, but this approach is not appropriate when engaged in nurturing fund raising for an ultimate gift. Nurturing fund raising requires a far greater familiarity and understanding of the individual and his or her values, interests, responsibilities, capacities, apprehensions, state of mind, feelings, etc., than is required to simply ask for a regular or special gift. In relational fund raising for ultimate gifts, it is important to discover the individuals who are naturally involved in the prospective giver's relationship with the institution. These natural partners are in the best position to determine, direct, and help execute the types of initiatives that need to be taken.

Many years ago, G. Taylor (Buck) Smith described natural partners in terms of "primes and secondaries" to help use natural partners more effectively. The prime and secondaries for an individual are the people who care about both the individual and the institution, and who are willing to work with you to draw the two closer together for the benefit of both.

Prime

The prime is the natural partner in the best position to have his or her finger on the pulse of the friend's relationship with your institution. The prime can be anyone—a faculty or staff member, trustee, or some other volunteer. Rarely will a development officer fit this role.

Secondaries

Secondaries are other natural partners in a position to help guide and execute initiatives with the prospective giver. Like the prime, the secondaries can be persons who, by virtue of their relationship with the prospective giver and the institution, are in a good position to help. Occasionally, development officers are secondaries.

Staffing

A problem with primes and secondaries is that their lives are often so full that they don't bound out of bed in the morning thinking of what they will do with the person they are helping to connect with your institution. In fact, even weeks and months may pass before they might get around to fulfilling their good intentions with that individual. This requires a member of the institution's development staff to facilitate, coordinate, and stimulate the work of the primes and secondaries.

There are many qualities that contribute to a staff member's success in nurturing fund raising. Sensitivity, hard work, devotion to the cause, maturity, integrity, and enthusiasm are certainly valuable assets. The quality I would rate right at the top, along with integrity, is a kind and forgiving nature. Over time, a staff member will become familiar with the individuals they are addressing with nurturing fund raising. They will see their virtues, but they will also see their faults. This work is not to be approached from a posture of judging others, but rather a posture of seeing the best that others may become and helping them to become that.

GETTING STARTED

The nurturing of relationships from which ultimate gifts arise is so time-consuming and cost-

ly that nurturing fund raising must be limited to relatively few individuals. You should start with one or two and increase the number as you and your institution gain experience. For staff highly experienced in nurturing fund raising, a practical maximum number is around 50-70 individuals and/or families. The ratio for true nurturing fund raising should never exceed 70 to 1. Three criteria should be considered in the selection of the friends you address with nurturing fund raising:
1. Financial capacity,
2. Interest or potential interest, and
3. Charitable nature

When selecting someone to be addressed with relationally-based nurturing fund raising, the failure to take into account any one of these criteria can disastrously reduce your effectiveness.

Limitations

Considering that an ultimate gift is often a thousand times larger than the same gift an individual gives to the same institution on a regular basis, institutions are tempted to develop more such relationships than they can sustain. Just as Aristotle taught that the very nature of true friendship limits the number of personal friendships an individual can sustain, there are also real limits to the number of friendships an institution can sustain. Genuine relationships require the kind of familiarity and attention that you cannot mass-produce. Even an institution with substantial experience in nurturing fund raising can still only address a small proportion of its constituency with this type of organized, managed effort.

Culture and Attitudes

A very important dimension of nurturing fund raising is cultural and must rely on the understanding, attitudes, and actions of people across the length and breadth of the institution. For example, the vice president for institutional advancement and the person who answers the phone in the admissions office must have the same understanding and attitude toward working with constituents. It may be the grace and patience of the admissions officer who deals with a giver irate over the handling of his grandson's application that makes the difference between keeping or losing the institution's relationship with someone who may some day make an ultimate gift to your institution.

ESSENTIALS FOR SUCCESS: QUALITY, FREQUENCY, AND CONTINUITY OF INITIATIVES

Those who would take initiatives to develop a friend's awareness, knowledge, interest, involvement, and commitment to your college, university, or school must do so in a way that assures quality, frequency, and continuity or run the risk of much wasted effort. Unless your institution enters the life of the friend every few weeks, it is likely that her ultimate gift will go to other charitable institutions with which she is more closely involved.

The great thing about fund raising for the largest gift of a lifetime is that it requires you to relate to people as individuals. When you do, you start to understand their values, interests, and capacities. And when their values and interests are the same as your institution's, you can help them do greater good through your institution and at the same time add new meaning to their own lives.

FURTHER READINGS

Dunlop, David R. (with Ellen Ryan) "Thirty Years of Fund Raising: Master Fund Raiser David Dunlop Tells What He's Learned About the Staff's Role in Dealing with Donors," CURRENTS 16, no. 10 (November/December 1990): 32.

Hartsook, Robert F. "Gifts That Go Out of the Box: When You are Considering Gift Levels of $100,000 or More, High Levels of Tension and Anxiety Occur with Both the Solicitor and the Donor. Too Often, We Do Not Consider Every Alternative of How the Gift Can Be Made," *Fund Raising Management* 28, no. 2 (April 1997): 16-17.

McNamee, Mike. "Can There be a Transforming Gift in Your Future?: Yes—If You Help Create and Communicate a Vision for Your Campus," CURRENTS 19, no. 2 (February 1993): 18-22, 24.

McNamee, Mike. "The Transforming Gift: To Inspire Great Gifts, Campuses Must Build a Compelling Case For Remaking Education," CURRENTS 19, no. 2 (February 1993): 6-8.

Jerold Panas, Born to Raise: *What Makes a Great Fundraiser: What Makes a Fundraiser Great.* Chicago: Bonus Books, Inc., 1988.

Pelnar-Zaiko, Ivana. "The Greenhouse Effect: Care and Attention to Your Principal Prospects Can Blossom into Principal Gifts," CURRENTS 19, no. 3 (March 1993): 21-24.

Ryan, Ellen. "Courtship Rituals: Chats, Visits, Long Walks Around Campus...How Two Institutions Wooed and Won Top Donors," CURRENTS 22, no. 10 (November/December 1996).

In this business, there are no universal road maps for marketing effectiveness; each institution must use every available technique to promote its major and planned gifts and to identify new prospects.

Major Gifts: Up Close and Personal

Jonathan R. Heintzelman
Assistant Vice President for University Development
and Director of Planned and Major Gifts
Northwestern University

The process of securing large, periodic gifts from individuals is a fascinating and sometimes frustrating adventure; it is a journey that can lead to deep valleys of disappointment and failure or to the very pinnacle of euphoria and fund-raising success. Those who are chosen for the journey should bring ample supplies of patience, perseverance, and good humor, not to mention comfortable shoes and a good map! But for the hardy and bold, there is no more exhilarating pursuit in all of advancement than the pursuit of the big individual gift. The goal of this chapter is to provide you with some basic signposts for establishing and maintaining a flourishing and successful major gift program.

Many development offices have separately designated major gift and planned gift functions. A discussion of some pros and cons of each structure under "To Merge or Not to Merge" appears later in this chapter. Otherwise, this chapter treats major gifts and planned gifts as a single function.

"Major" and "planned" should no longer be considered appropriately separate or parallel adjectives when applied to large gifts because every large gift, whether outright or deferred, should be "planned."

WHAT IS A MAJOR GIFT?

The precise definition of a major gift will vary from institution to institution, but everyone agrees that major gifts are high-end gifts, outright and or deferred, not given annually, from individual and institutional donors. Generally, the entry level for this category is $25,000 for small institutions and $50,000 to $100,000 for larger ones. Some institutions will create a "presidential" level or "leadership" level for super-sized gifts at $1 million or $5 million and above. While these levels will increase over time, they must be tailored to the institutions' experience, ambition, and realistic expectations. Major gifts, therefore, are very broad in scope. They may involve the transfer of *any* kind of asset, from cash to cows, and may be structured with the intricacy and delicacy of a spider's web.

For most of us in fund raising, these gifts offer the greatest potential reward because we have the responsibility and the privilege of working with individuals who own the vast bulk of disposable wealth in society. Beyond the obvious technical complexities, major gift fund raising is the only endeavor in which we seek to obtain significant assets from the person who acquired and accumulated these assets. It is the most intensely personal form of fund raising; its success is heavily dependent upon the people doing the actual fund raising.

CHARACTERIZING DONOR PROSPECTS

Until quite recently, some believed that success in securing major gifts through trusts and bequests actually came at the expense of major outright gifts to the institution. The fear was that deferred gifts gave many prospects an easy way out, reducing the gift dollars needed for current use. Some institutions actually went so far as to exclude all planned gifts from major comprehensive campaigns. We know today that such exclusionary practices were ill advised. The relegation of such donors to an underclass status failed to recognize the rich diversity among those capable of making large gifts, whether outright or deferred.

While broad generalizations about donors are suspect, many outright gift donors have a different profile than their deferred giving counterparts, especially the donor whose gift is a bequest rather than a life income plan. Outright donors tend to follow the traditional pyramidal pattern of giving; at Northwestern, for example, more than 90 percent of donors who make an outright gift of $50,000 or more are already giving well in excess of $1,000 annually. For most major gift donors, their gifts are extensions of earlier, smaller outright gifts, part of a habitual lifestyle of giving.

Whereas many major outright gift donors begin their philanthropic association with an institution via modest but increasing annual gifts, many planned gift donors actually begin their giving to the institution with a planned gift. A closer examination of these donors often reveals a lifestyle of asset accumulation (rather than disposition), and an inclination for saving (rather than spending). Understanding this dynamic is important to the success of any major gift program, as well as to the broader initiatives of the advancement office.

Here are a few basic theories to remember when planning your strategy to approach different types of donor prospects:

1) Since deferred gift donors tend to have a different profile from major outright gift donors, planned gifts will be made, for the most part, in addition to major outright gifts, not instead of them. Provided that it begins with an outright ask, major gift solicitation should never exclude deferred gifts.

2) Since deferred gift prospects generally will not have a history of regular or even sporadic giving, these prospects cannot be identified through traditional giving patterns. Moreover, since these prospects tend to save their money rather than spend it, they will also not show up on traditional demographic radar screens. This relative invisibility of planned gift prospects places a premium on creating and maintaining a robust and diverse marketing program that will provide forums for prospect self-identification along with an aggressive prospect visitation program. Since most planned gifts are incremental to outright gifts, a mature major and planned gift effort will pursue both outright and deferred gifts with utmost vigor.

THE "CORNERSTONE" OF MAJOR GIFT SOLICITATION

The process of securing major and planned gifts from individuals is the most intensely personal form of fund raising, as well as the most challenging and rewarding. Success and failure are often measured by high-dollar yardsticks and, in some cases, a transformational impact on the institution. The very personal nature of these gifts places a high premium on the effectiveness of the major gift fund raiser.

A good major gift fund raiser must identify with the mission of the institution, have highly honed interpersonal skills, and possess both intelligence and a flair for entrepreneurship. Moreover, in an arena where establishing and developing effective interpersonal relationships with prospects and donors is paramount, continuity of major gift staff is essential.

The personal relationship between the fund raiser and donor is a very labor-intensive one. Like fine wine, effective relationships take time to mature and ripen, as trust and confidence build. Since many major gifts involve the transfer and commitment of a significant portion of a donor's assets, such decisions often occur only after long gestation periods of consideration and cultivation.

● ● ●

All major and planned gift officers should have an assigned pool of prospects who are to be asked for a gift within a limited time period.

Several months ago, we were able to finally close on a gift of a Nebraska farm—this took "only" 17 years after we had first discussed this possible gift with the donor! The key fact here is not that the gift took 17 years to develop but that we were able to maintain a strong relationship with the donor throughout this period. Major gift staff retention and development are the most important priorities. A realistic goal for retention is a minimum of five years, a period of time within which most major gifts can be developed and closed.

There is no responsibility more important for a major gift fund raiser than meeting with prospects and donors. Accordingly, we have found that the most important individual nonmonetary goal for fund raisers is the number of personal visits. Major gifts are not raised from behind a desk! We believe a goal for personal visits is mandatory. We use an annual goal (or minimum) of 120 visits. The typical range is 100-200 per year)—what is important is that the development manager has a goal, counts the visits, and that the development officer understands that a major factor in his or her evaluation is achieving those goals.

All major and planned gift officers should have an assigned pool of prospects who are to be asked for a gift within a limited time period. At Northwestern, our officers have prospect lists in the range of 150 to 200 and a time horizon for gift development of 18 to 24 months. This creates both a monetary and non-monetary measurement of the fund raiser's effectiveness. Many of these assigned prospects will be among the officer's annual visits for each year, but it is also important that the officer continue to see new prospects beyond the assigned list. In this way, the roster becomes dynamic as it is refreshed with the addition of new prospects.

MARKETING TOOLS

A robust major gift program will use a variety of techniques to market the program and identify new prospects and donors. These may include:

■ *Major gift recognition publication.* This piece would publicize and highlight major gift donors and highly personalize the process. This gives you an opportunity to thank your best donors in a classy way and also hold them up as role models for others to follow. It is also an effective means for stimulating further gifts from some of your best prospects. At Northwestern, we have found that more than 90 percent of major donors make an additional major gift within 24 months of being featured in the major gift newsletter.

■ *Planned gift newsletter.* Since most planned gift prospects will not be in your current donor pool, it is imperative that you publish a regular direct mail piece that will enable prospects to identify themselves through a qualified response, and that the mailing list for this newsletter not be based on prior giving. Over time, you should expect a qualified response in the range of 5 percent of the total mailing. These respondents will be some of your very best planned gift prospects. A "qualified" response would indicate interest in a life income plan or bequest, not some general interest in income or estate planning information.

■ *Related publications and mailings.* Most institutions have a variety of publications and mailings to different audiences that lend themselves to an inexpensive marketing "piggyback." This can be as simple as adding a line with a check-off box on an annual fund direct mail response card or a partial page in your alumni newsletter. In this business, there are no universal road maps for marketing effectiveness; each institution must use every available technique to promote its major and planned gifts and to identify new prospects. Diversity and saturation are the goals, since we never know which prospect will respond to which message. Years ago, we had a sign outside our building that read "Office of Estate Planning Services." One year we closed on a $300,000 and a $400,000 bequest to the university from two persons who were nonalums but who merely walked into our office to talk about estate planning after seeing the sign.

■ *Planned gift recognition society.* Creating a recognition society for planned gift donors is a must for every institution. We initially created one of these at Northwestern years ago with the intent of thanking those planned gift donors whom we knew. To our surprise, more than half of the responses to our announcement came from new prospects. Thus, the planned gift recognition society is not only a great way to thank your current donors; it is also effective in identifying new planned gift prospects and donors. The recognition society should be open to anyone making a planned gift of any type and of any amount. We want to make it as easy as we can for them to join.

TRENDS

We live in a golden age for major and planned gifts from individuals, an age that is likely to continue unabated, absent a major economic depression. At the same time, there are subtle currents beneath the surface that may dramatically influence the focus of major and planned gifts in the years to come, including:

- *Tax planning.* Gift and estate tax planning in charitable giving is increasing as we focus more on the impact of wealth transfer. This is a stimulus to charitable giving because planning alternatives with gift and estate taxes are more severely limited than with income taxes.

- *For-profits.* The for-profit world has discovered charitable gift planning since other tax-savings devices have been curtailed. Good news: more prospects are exposed to charitable giving techniques; bad news: for-profit advisers may oversell and over-promise the benefits of charitable giving.

- *Appreciated assets.* Large gifts of appreciated assets, especially securities, from individuals should continue to be a very significant source of support for most institutions. At Northwestern last year, gifts of appreciated securities represented only one percent of total gifts and yet accounted for 50 percent of the total gift dollars for the year. This type of dramatic impact only increases with gains in the stock market and other assets such as real estate.

- *Intergenerational gifts.* As prospects live longer and acquire more wealth in the process, many proposed gifts now involve a discussion about, or with, the next generation. This trend will continue to intensify in the coming years as longevity and personal wealth grow.

- *Integrating major and planned gifts.* Despite

the disparity in profiles between major and planned gift prospects (the "spenders" vs. the "savers"), the line between the two groups is blurring. More discussions and gifts today involve a combination of outright and deferred gift techniques and options, rather than exclusively one or the other.

TO MERGE OR NOT TO MERGE

Most major gift offices developed before their planned gift siblings. Planned giving is generally the new kid on the development block, and in most shops, the planned giving office has been added to, rather than integrated with, the major gifts office. Both separate and combined offices can work; the critical element is that each structure encourages and allows for an integrated approach to prospects and donors.

My own experience at Northwestern strongly favors a merged major and planned gift operation that makes no distinction between outright and deferred gifts for the following reasons:

1) A merged system allows for a "cleaner" assignment of responsibility by the officers.

2) The merged system allows the fund raiser to stay with the prospect regardless of the gift type; there is no need to hand someone off to the "expert" since all of the fund raisers are "full service" representatives. As the lines between major gifts and planned gifts continue to blur, an integrated or merged system is better able to respond to "blended" inquiries.

3) The merged system gives each fund raiser more prospect diversity, which creates a greater variety of calls, and a more interesting and fulfilling job. For example, many major gift prospects may be quite a bit younger than their planned gift counterparts.

4) The merged system creates greater challenge for the fund raisers since each is expected to close on planned gifts as well as major gifts. The planned gift component carries with it at least a two-year learning curve and continuing education thereafter. But for the right people, greater challenge is what they want.

5) Greater prospect diversity and technical difficulty act as a stimulant. People who are challenged to stretch are generally more productive and

happy; this helps retention, which enhances performance.

Arguments favoring a split staff include:

1) With a merged system, it is too easy for the fund raiser to "fall back" on a planned gift option at the expense of a potential major gift.

2) It is much easier to have one or two planned gift experts to handle all of the technical matters than to train an entire major and planned gift staff on the technical aspects of planned giving and estate planning.

3) Since much of planned giving is of a legal nature, it is important to maintain control of what is being presented to donors. This is easier done with fewer planned gift staff members.

But while the training and control with a merged system takes a major commitment, I believe the merged system offers the greatest opportunity to attract, develop, and retain an outstanding major gift staff. This gives us the greatest chance for success.

REACHING YOUR GOALS

If you follow a few simple guidelines with your major and planned gift program, you will achieve success.

1) *Hire good people.* At Northwestern, we have always asked our major and planned gift colleagues to choose new hires since they understand the job and have an incentive to choose effective team members. Don't feel that you need to "purchase" someone's expertise—all that we do technically is learnable. The quality of the person is paramount.

2) *Keep the job "pure."* A very common mistake is to add non-major and non-planned gift responsibilities to this job. For example, one local organization defined a job as 50 percent major and planned gifts and 50 percent events planning. This just doesn't work. Keep the job pure so that none of the officers has anything to divert him or her from the personal contact with prospects and donors.

3) *Build a team.* Obviously in a one-person shop, this won't apply. But major and planned gifts occur best where the officers are all part of a greater organism. You want to hear laughter as they share tales from the road and to see the sparks of imagination flash around the table as the group solves a problem. This can be an incredibly lonely, yet exhilarating, job and it helps to feel part of a group of colleagues and friends who can support, instruct, and inspire.

4) *Support your people.* Once you hire the right people, you need to focus on giving them all of the support that they need to succeed. If you are their manager, this is your primary responsibility. If you do this well, your people and your program will flourish.

REFERENCES

Barth, Steve. "Globetrotting for Gifts: How to Identify, Research, and Solicit Major Gifts Around the World Without Causing an International Incident," CURRENTS 24, no. 4, p. 32.

Barrett, Richard D. and Molly E. Ware. *Planned Giving Essentials: A Step by Step Guide to Success.* Frederick, MD: Aspen Publishers, 1997.

Burlingame, Dwight F., Timothy L. Seiler, and Eugene R. Tempel, eds. *Developing Major Gifts: New Directions for Philanthropic Fundraising,* no. 16. San Francisco, CA: Jossey-Bass Publishers, 1997.

Gough, Samuel N. Jr. *Major Gift Programs: Practical Implementation.* Frederick, MD: Aspen Publishers, 1997.

Heintzelman, Jonathan, Harrie M. Hughes, and Wes Lindahl, "Lions and Tigers and Bears, Oh My!" *Planned Giving Today* IV, no 5 (May 1993): 3-4.

Schoenhals, G. Roger, ed. *Getting Going in Planned Giving.* Seattle, WA: Planned Giving Today, 1997.

Stanley, Thomas J., Ph.D., and William D. Dank, Ph.D. *The Millionaire Next Door: The Surprising Secrets of America's Wealthy.* Marietta, GA: Longstreet Press, 1998.

Teitell, Conrad. *Planned Giving: Starting, Marketing, Administering.* Old Greenwich, CT: Taxwise Giving, 1996.

Act collaboratively. Create consortia with other institutions. Build alliances to extend the impact of the corporate support you seek.

Securing Corporate Support: The Business of Corporate Relations

Carolyn S. Sanzone
Assistant Vice Chancellor Science & Technology Advancement, Corporate & Foundation Relations
University of Massachusetts, Amherst

During the 1980s, corporate philanthropy, as an overall component of institutional fund raising, reached record highs and netted millions of dollars in the favored areas of giving: endowments, unrestricted grants for students and faculty support, institutional campaigns, and capital projects. An analysis of the decade of the '90s, however, yields a different picture.

Corporate support for institutions continued to grow, but the nature of that support changed substantially. As companies downsized, outsourced, restructured, and redefined themselves in an increasingly complex and competitive marketplace, unrestricted corporate gifts and unrestricted gifts to endowment have been replaced by more restricted gifts and more spendable gifts for targeted, defined purposes, aligned with corporate objectives. Ronald Kraus, president of the New England Colleges Fund, wrote in a 1998 CURRENTS article, "Several changes have caused corporations to focus their giving more on their goals and less on your needs. Businesses are applying benchmarking and quantitative productivity analysis to every aspect of their operations, including investment in education." A chart that accompanied the CURRENTS article, pro-

vided by the Foundation for Independent Higher Education, shows a steady increase in the amount of restricted donations in the 1990's and a steady decrease of unrestricted dollars.

THE CHANGING CORPORATE MARKETPLACE

Profound changes in the marketplace have shaped a new and different framework for corporate philanthropy. Competition has increased. The focus is global rather than national or local. Costs are higher. Resources are fewer. The marketplace is governed by customer-driven, value-added, bottom-line results. Companies seldom give resources out of altruistic motivations. Support for higher education is a strategic investment. *Quid pro quo* is the watchphrase of this era. More than one Fortune 100 CEO has noted that companies will give a gift, as long as it is in their business interest to do so. It must be a justifiable strategic investment guaranteed to yield a concrete benefit for the company and its shareholders.

And how is that benefit defined? What do corporations want from their relationships with educational institutions? Two main goals appear to be *workforce recruitment* and *education and technology development*.

Recruitment of students is certainly a central

Securing
Corporate
Support: The
Business of
Corporate
Relations

reason why companies want to connect with educational institutions. Companies use their resources to gain access to top students pursuing studies in areas of strategic importance to them. Providing corporations ways to increase their visibility, become involved with key programs, influence curriculum development, and find well-trained students will enhance the ability of an institution to compete for corporate support. And, while higher education remains a key focus of corporate activities, in an ironic twist of fate, some corporate giving programs have reduced their support of higher education because of pipeline concerns. The increasing support for targeted populations in K-12 and science and technology education may reduce support for higher education.

The second, and growing, workforce development interest is continued educational and technological development. Business is willing to invest heavily to retool, retrain, and retain top talent. Institutions that can design cost-effective, targeted opportunities to assist in this effort—with innovative curricula, distance education offerings, faculty exchange, and onsite advanced degree and certification opportunities—will gain an advantage with the companies they approach. Technology is the other major development area for corporate relations—one that has major ramifications for the research enterprise at institutions of higher education. Corporate support inevitably will be stronger for an institution whose research strengths match corporate priorities than for those whose research strengths do not. This kind of support is less unrestricted, more targeted, more aligned to strategic business objectives, and more likely to be viewed as an investment rather than an outright gift (even if it is a gift).

Increasingly, corporate dollars focus on strategic initiatives and comprehensive partnerships. These are interactive, ongoing, dynamic relationships that evolve and change over time. Because a growing number of corporations view university support as part of a larger, comprehensive relationship, they have generated "short lists" of those universities with whom they seek to develop such rela-

tionships. Although criteria and emphases vary, "short list" opportunities are generally grounded in several variables. These include current number and executive strength of alumni employees; current recruitment targets; successful corporate recruitment; and available research and academic programs producing personnel who meet technology and diversity objectives. The corporate agenda for support of educational institutions has moved away from senior executives' personal interests and affiliations toward their business interests and objectives.

THE UNIVERSITY RESPONSE TO MARKETPLACE CHALLENGES: SETTING THE STAGE

Developing a response to this dynamic and challenging environment for corporate fund raising often involves a creative restructuring of the institution's corporate relations management. Here are some suggestions that can help campuses respond to this changing corporate environment.

▪ *Think locally, act globally.* Do a critical self-analysis to identify the specific niche strengths your institution offers the corporate sector in the arenas mentioned previously—workforce development, workforce education, and technology development. The most significant opportunities will be local. Because many local corporate initiatives are motivated by common national and global concerns—whether diversity in the workforce or emerging technology discovery areas—they offer an opportunity to approach national corporate prospects.

▪ *Build a corporate relations program, not a corporate fund-raising program.* Widen the focus of attention of your institution to the entire corporate relationship. Adopt goals to generate support from varied corporate venues, including research contracts. Because corporations link their philanthropic goals with recruiting priorities and technology development agendas, institutions must be able to facilitate relationships between admissions, career services, sponsored research, technology transfer, and development offices. At some research uni-

> ▪ ▪ ▪
>
> **Invite institutional CEOs and corporate executives to serve as advisers to key academic areas and thank them. Cultivate alumni networks within companies and thank them. Solicit aggressively matching gifts, and thank the company and its CEO.**

Securing
Corporate
Support: The
Business of
Corporate
Relations

versities, for example, corporate relations staff have double reporting lines to development/ advancement and academic research administration. At some institutions, 50 percent or more of the corporate relations agenda is directed at non-philanthropic interactions with companies. As the corporate trend towards more strategically deployed philanthropy continues and expands, those institutions able to achieve greater internal flexibility and cooperation will be most successful .

■ *Build strategic new internal alignments.* Build a comprehensive and effective internal team. The corporate relations office needs strong and effective links with all areas in the institution that directly interact with companies, including grants and contracts offices, student placement services, and offices that deal with vendors. The direct involvement of senior academic administration (provost and deans) in strategic planning of the corporate relations program will be very important. The corporate relations officer should seek and develop strong faculty liaison relationships across academic disciplines.

■ *Be proactive, not reactive.* Companies are not experts in working with educational institutions. Take a bold approach, proposing a well thought-out plan and providing specific ways the corporation can work with the institution These new internal relationships reflect the kind of knowledgeable and flexible institutional behavior highly valued by industry.

■ *Act collaboratively.* Create consortia with other institutions. Build alliances to extend the impact of the corporate support you seek. Although creating a mutually beneficial working relationship with other institutions can be difficult and time consuming, Elizabeth Loudon in *Corporate and Foundation Support: Strategies for Funding Education in the 21st Century* emphasizes several benefits to working in a consortium. These arrangements can save individual institutions money in the long run; they may appeal to corporations and foundations; and they can bring unlikely people together and can accomplish goals the individual institutions couldn't have accomplished individually.

STRATEGIES FOR SECURING CORPORATE SUPPORT

The successful approach for seeking corporate support will require a strong strategic plan, opportunities, a prospect pool, a history of giving, and good stewardship over time. Here are some basics to remember when seeking corporate support.

■ *Establish strategic directions and advertise them.* Companies have gone through strategic redesign. A lot of them don't think educational institutions understand this. An institution that establishes, promotes, and acts to implement a strategic plan is an attractive corporate partner.

■ *Create partnership opportunities.* Restructure your own organization to promote greater flexibility, a more welcoming enterprise, and greater involvement of internal players, and varied vehicles to engage the corporate partner. Remember, there are multiple sources of support from companies. In addition to philanthropy, there are opportunities to secure support from the marketing or public relations arena, from human resources, from business divisions for technology-relevant projects and programs, and from other venues within the company that need to look to external resources to achieve goals. In addition to money, there are personnel resources, equipment donations, and infrastructure development support.

■ *Establish a prospect pool.* Variables that make a good corporate prospect include:

- Geography. Companies in your own backyard are likely prospects.
- People. Alumni executives, significant numbers of alumni, and faculty contacts (research) are important factors.
- Strategic alignments. Complimentary research priorities, workforce education potential, and diversity workforce pipelines are key values for companies.
- Organizational giving frameworks. Corporate foundations, corporate contributions units, and publicized priorities open doors to corporate resources. The more variables in place, the more likely your suc-

Securing
Corporate
Support: The
Business of
Corporate
Relations

cess with the prospect. Look at small and mid-size companies as important long-term prospects.

■ *Establish a history of giving.* Look for strategic matches of institutional strengths to corporate interests and needs. Consider a corporate annual fund to inaugurate new corporate prospects. As with foundations and major donors, pay attention to what the company will and will not support.

■ *Steward, steward, steward!* Invite institutional CEOs and corporate executives to serve as advisers to key academic areas and thank them. Cultivate alumni networks within companies and thank them. Solicit aggressively matching gifts, and thank the company and its CEO. Never take corporate prospects for granted!

In the complex and professionalized environment in which educational fund raisers compete for corporate support, success will depend not just on the state of the economy. Increasingly, success will depend on the commitment to build strategic relations with companies and a holistic corporate relations program. The institution must work hard and creatively to seek out new and appropriate opportunities for corporate support; the institution must demonstrate how a relationship with its institution will benefit the company; and the institution must prove its ability to consistently use and manage gifts

and other corporate revenue responsibly. A strategic, broad-based, interactive agenda for corporate relations will yield solid support over a longer time period for the institution ready to take on the challenges of restructuring, reinventing, and refocusing its approach to corporate relations.

FURTHER READINGS

Johnson, David C. "The Changing Face of Corporate Giving: In a Dramatically Altered Corporate Funding Landscape, How Can Not-for-Profits Attract Corporate Support? They Must Never Forget That Corporate Philanthropists Expect a Return on Their Investment," *Advancing Philanthropy* 5, no. 1 (Spring 1997): 35-37.

Kraus, Ronald J. "The Changing Face of Corporate Giving: Although Businesses Are Looking Harder at the Effects of Their Gifts, You Can Still Make the Case for Both Unrestricted and Restricted Support," CURRENTS 24, no. 2 (February 1998): 10-14.

Murphy, Mary Kay. *Corporate and Foundation Support: Strategies for Funding Education in the 21st Century.* Washington, DC: CASE Books, 2000.

Newman, M. W. "Getting Through the Door: Typically, Corporations Fund Only One in 10 Grant Applications. You Can Increase Your Own Odds by Knowing Your Donor, Fine-Tuning Your Funding Requests and Heeding the Advice of Some High-Powered Corporate Grant Makers," *Advancing Philanthropy* 4, no. 4 (Winter 1996-1997): 19-23.

Pollack, Rachel H. "Give and Take: Create a Mutually Beneficial Relationship to Bring Corporate Support to Your Campus," CURRENTS 24, no. 2 (February 1998): 16-22.

Rather than addressing your institution's immediate needs, think of foundation grants as partnerships. The first question to ask is: "Can your institution provide the means to achieve the foundation's goals?"

Seeking Foundation Support

Patricia Gregory
Senior Director of Corporate and Foundation Relations
Washington University School of Medicine in St. Louis

With foundation assets now approaching $300 billion, foundations are becoming an increasingly prominent feature on the philanthropic landscape. All the information needed to target foundations is readily available. The rewards—both personal and institutional—make foundation grant-seeking a worthwhile pursuit. But it isn't easy.

"Foundation grants are the most challenging form of educational fund raising," says Mark W. Jones, vice president for advancement at Goucher College. With recent trends toward funding K-12 education, public health, social welfare, and global issues, Jones sees institutions of higher education struggling to find foundations still receptive to their needs. The long process of proposal development and review adds to the challenge. Although today's information-intensive environment has leveled the playing field, the field is crowded as more institutions enter the foundation grant-seeking arena. Competition has never been more intense.

But with a quarter of the nearly $15 billion distributed annually by foundations going to education and new foundations being formed that will substantially increase this amount, every institution,

if patient and willing to take a long-term approach, can benefit from foundation support.

Launching a foundation fund-raising program should start with a thorough review of the foundation's principal areas of interest and the academic strengths of your institution. This will help you identify which foundations are likely prospects and the programs at your institution that fit their funding priorities.

IDENTIFYING FOUNDATION PROSPECTS

At the heart of a solid foundation fund-raising plan is thorough research of potential funders. Abundant sources of information are available on foundations. Directories, annual reports and other foundation publications, IRS 990-PF tax returns, and periodicals are the staples. The recent explosion of resources available on the World Wide Web has transformed the way prospect research is carried out. The downside, of course, is that everyone else has access to the same information, intensifying the competition.

A database on your personal computer is an essential tool for organizing this wealth of information, keeping track of deadlines, and planning your moves. The best way to get started is to search a comprehensive directory of foundations, such as

The Foundation Directory, published annually by The Foundation Center. Many directories also are available through libraries and regional collections, making foundation research accessible to organizations that can't afford to purchase directories. Some directories now are available in searchable CD-ROM or Web versions, significantly reducing the time you'll need to identify and research funders. You'll pick up other leads by reading about recent grants in *The Chronicle of Philanthropy* and other periodicals, or by subscribing to a listserv discussion group on the Internet. *CFRnet,* for example, is focused on corporate and foundation fund raising for educational institutions. Traffic is light, so subscribing shouldn't flood your e-mail inbox.

The other half of the research you'll need is institutional information. Be sure you understand the unique characteristics of your institution. Read everything you can to become familiar with your institution's academic mission and other areas of strength, including community service. As your institution's spokesperson to the foundation, you'll be called upon to answer questions and cite statistics. Work with the president, deans, provost, head, chancellor, and other administrators to stay abreast of institutional priorities. They will expect you to represent them well.

The history of foundation relations at your institution is key. Review your files for any previous grants from a foundation you intend to solicit. Consult with faculty grantees if files are insufficient. Don't forget the individual prospect files to explore relationships with board members, especially when dealing with local or family foundations. Build strong ties with your sponsored research office and exchange information regularly about faculty-generated proposals. Though foundations will be less responsive than individual donors to a capital campaign will, the strategic plan used to set your institution's campaign objectives will be one of your most important guides in working with foundations.

PROJECTS APPROPRIATE FOR FOUNDATION FUNDING

Despite the increasing wealth of private foundations, not all projects are suitable for foundation funding. Some are best funded by individual gifts or federal grants. For others, institutional funds may be the only source. When top priorities don't mesh with foundation interests, grants for projects of lower priority that do match foundation interests sometimes can free up funds for other needs. "Don't send in a proposal that falls outside a foundation's interests because you believe your project is so good the foundation will be moved to fund it anyway," cautions Susan M. Fitzpatrick, program officer for the James S. McDonnell Foundation.

Educational fund-raising consultant William P. McGoldrick notes, "Few of our proposals demonstrate real imagination." Most foundations seek to fund innovative projects with the potential to break new ground. Don't send them a project for which other funding has ceased. Make sure there is a plan in place for funding when the foundation's support ends. Be careful not to let the tail wag the dog. Foundations easily can weed out projects that are pieced together just to secure a grant.

Foundations often will help you determine the likelihood of funding a project. This can save you the effort of writing a lengthy proposal that has little chance of being funded. Some program officers will review a brief menu of potential projects. When seeking guidance, be sure to do your homework first. Don't call to ask what they fund unless you have thoroughly reviewed their published guidelines. You only have one chance to make that first impression for your institution.

CULTIVATING FOUNDATION SUPPORT

Since most foundations are set up to make grants in perpetuity, a long-term relationship is key to securing future grants. Rather than addressing your institution's immediate needs, think of foundation grants as partnerships. The first question to ask is: "Can your institution provide the means to achieve the foundation's goals?"

The relationship can be initiated with a letter, a phone call, or a visit. Today, some foundations with limited staff prefer e-mail inquiries, providing hot links on their Web sites to encourage this approach. Visits are less common these days because foundations simply cannot accommodate the increasing number of institutions seeking grants. For this reason, it doesn't make sense to set call quotas for foundation relations staff. Without leaving the office, the foundation relations officer already knows how much prospects are inclined to give and for what purpose, the best time to approach them for a gift, and the organizations they have supported in the past. "Let's get acquainted" visits are rarely entertained these days.

With visits harder to come by, you'll rely more on the written word when starting a relationship. Use your connections. Trustees who know foundation board members, for example, can introduce your institution, but the guidelines still must be followed. Be careful not to do an "end run" around the program officer. Philanthropy consultant Sandra A. Glass, vice president emerita of the W. M. Keck Foundation, reminds us that program officers "can't say 'yes' without board approval, but they can say 'no.'"

Send a brief letter of inquiry that introduces your institution and outlines how the project fits the foundation's guidelines. If time is short and you need to start with a phone call, precede your call with a fax concisely outlining your inquiry. This will prepare the program officer for your call and prevent a knee-jerk response. Glass advises foundation relations staff to be thoroughly familiar with the project and prepared to discuss alternative projects. "Keep your desk full of projects," she says.

"Never assume that just because a foundation has a great deal of money, they will give it to your institution," cautions Glass. There is no easy money out there, and certainly no shortage of grant seekers. In fact, competition will be especially keen at foundations with substantial assets, because so many organizations target them.

Since foundations are often repeat donors to an institution, good stewardship is vital. Remedy any lapses in reporting on recent grants. Share the impact of previous grants, even if they were made a decade ago. Provide selected information about your institution at regular intervals to familiarize the foundation with your institution. Send short notes about major grants and awards received, new appointments, and other news. This is a simple and effective cultivation technique that will solidify your institution's relationship with a foundation.

WRITING THE PROPOSAL

Good writing is at the core of successful foundation fund raising. Aim for a lively tone rather than the passive voice. The most common errors are proposals that are too long, too technical, or fail to adhere to foundation guidelines. While a few faculty may resist conforming to the style of development writing, most welcome editing that will improve their chances of securing a grant.

The executive summary is the most important part of the proposal. If a program officer has only a few minutes to scan your proposal, this may be the only part that is read thoroughly. Let your colleagues in public relations read it first and offer suggestions. Don't leave it to the reader to draw important connections. Foundations today are much more directive in their giving. Even if it seems obvious, show how the project ties in with their objectives. You are offering the foundation an opportunity to turn its vision into practice. Emphasize how the grant would achieve the foundation's objectives.

> ● ● ●
> **The executive summary is the most important part of the proposal. If a program officer has only a few minutes to scan your proposal, this may be the only part that is read thoroughly.**

When using a letter format, be sure it's clear that you're requesting funding. State up front how much you're seeking. Tell why your institution is in an ideal position to undertake the project. McGoldrick urges grant seekers to differentiate their institutions from the rest of the pack, noting that "most of us look very much alike" to foundations. He suggests using bullets, headings, and charts to make it easier for an overworked program officer to get the point.

Glass says always include a budget, as well as the plan for supporting the project after the grant ends. Finally, she advises, mention any past grants from the foundation and their impact. Express appreciation for the foundation's willingness to consider the proposal.

Once the proposal is sent, call to make sure it was received or enclose a stamped return postcard for the program officer to sign. Ask if any other information is needed. Invite the foundation to visit your campus or offer to visit the foundation, perhaps with your president or the faculty member directing the project. Find out when it would be appropriate to check on the proposal's status. Be prepared to supply audited financial statements; foundations prefer to invest in institutions with a balanced budget over those that need their funding for survival. McGoldrick says, "People give money to opportunities, not to needs."

If the grant is funded, send a thank-you note and draft one from the president, dean, or other appropriate officer. Make sure the project director sends a note. Always provide an accounting of expenditures on the grant. Submit all required progress reports on time. Explain any unanticipated circumstances or delays in the project timetable and continue to leave the door open for a site visit.

If the proposal is declined, thank the foundation for considering it and ask for honest feedback. "Listen between the lines," says Glass. Learn everything you can from a rejection, but don't be a pest if the foundation says "no.' If there's insufficient money, even the worthiest proposals will be declined. Priorities may change or the focus may narrow. Glass notes that foundations talk among themselves. Don't grouse to colleagues about unfair treatment or criticize a foundation's goals when they differ from your institution's needs. We are a very small community of professionals. If you get an abrupt response from an overworked program officer, remember that the reason foundations are short-staffed is to reserve most of their money for grantmaking.

QUALITIES OF A SUCCESSFUL FOUNDATION RELATIONS PROFESSIONAL

What does it take to be a successful foundation relations officer? First, the personal qualities required of all advancement professionals also apply to foundation relations. While it's true that you're soliciting organizations, McGoldrick reminds us that "people give to people."

You'll need the ability to translate complex, often highly sophisticated, academic projects into lay language while retaining sufficient detail to pass muster with technical reviewers. Jones believes that a sharp intellect, broad interests, and the facility to work with a wide range of demanding constituents are crucial qualities. "Patience and persistence are essential," he notes.

Also essential are superior analytical and planning skills, the capacity to process extensive infor-

mation and identify potential matches, and the organizational skills to manage multiple deadlines, most of which rely on faculty for proposal development. Much of this work is behind the scenes, so you'll need to be willing to take a back seat.

Years of service are another asset. The high turnover that characterizes the fund-raising profession can be costly in foundation relations. Foundation staff may be in place for a decade or more, and their files store your institution's past interactions.

In addition to your external role with foundations, the foundation relations professional is the in-house expert on foundations. Faculty and administrators will look to you for advice on which foundations might be approached for a particular need and the best method for approaching a particular foundation. You'll be called upon to serve as an honest broker when more than one project fits a foundation that only accepts one. You'll need to be diplomatic, discerning, assertive, credible, fair, and sincere.

PARTNER WITH FOUNDATIONS

Foundations are a tremendous, but not untapped, resource for funding educational institutions. With patience and a few simple rules, your institution can experience the rich rewards of partnerships with foundations, and pave the way for future support. First, "Know your institution: past, present, and future," advises McGoldrick. Then:
- Research foundations thoroughly.
- Understand and adhere to foundation grant guidelines.
- Write clear and concise proposals.
- Follow up with good stewardship.
- Learn from rejection.
- Be honest and straightforward.
- Be patient.
- Say "thank you."

Historian Arnold Toynbee observed that "Civilization is a process, not a condition, a voyage and not a harbor." Few organizations last as long as educational institutions. Former Washington University Chancellor William H. Danforth says, "Universities endure, I believe, because they promise hope and renewal, two perennial human needs." Education is civilization's best hope for improving the human condition. Seeking foundation support for the advancement of education is a goal worthy of our commitment. Few investments offer foundations the promise of such lasting impact on society.

REFERENCES AND FURTHER READINGS

Geever, Jane C. "Spin Control: Move Your Grant Request to the Top of the Pile by Learning Grantmakers' Preferences and Pet Peeves," CURRENTS 23, no. 7 (July/August 1997): 38-42, 44.

Geever, Jane C. and Patricia McNeill. *The Foundation Center' Guide to Proposal Writing.* 2nd ed. New York, NY: Foundation Center, February 1997.

Gershon, Gail Levitt. "Three Pieces of the Puzzle: What are the Steps of the Proposal Process? Each Foundation Has Its Own Variation on the Same Theme. One Regional Association Workshop Offered a Good Overview of the Key Elements of the Proposal Review Process," *Foundation News and Commentary* 37, no. 3 (May/June 1996): 32-35.

Gooch, Judith Mirick. *Writing Winning Proposals.* Washington, DC: Council for Advancement and Support of Education, 1987.

Locke, Elizabeth H. "The Foundations of a Relationship: Foundations are Fickle, Unpredictable and Require Frequent, Burdensome Reports. So Why Bother With Them? For a Simple Reason: They Fund Great Projects and Stimulate Creativity Throughout the Not-for-Profit Sector," *Advancing Philanthropy* 4, no. 3 (Fall 1996): 20-23.

Murphy, Mary Kay, ed. *Corporate and Foundation Support: Strategies for Funding Education in the 21st Century.* Washington, DC: CASE Books, 2000.

Scanlan, Eugene A. *Corporate and Foundation Fund Raising: A Complete Guide from the Inside.* Frederick, MD: Aspen Publishers, June 1997.

HELPFUL REFERENCE TEXTS AND ONLINE RESOURCES

The Foundation Directory, produced by the Foundation Center (New York, New York). (*www.fdncenter.org*)

The Foundation Grants Index, produced by the Foundation Center (New York, New York).

FC Search: The Foundation Center's Database on CD-ROM, produced by the Foundation Center (New York, New York).

The Foundation Reporter, produced by The Taft Group. (Detroit, Michigan).

Foundation News and Commentary, a bi-monthly magazine produced by the Council on Foundations, Inc. (*www.cof.org*)

CFRnet, a listserve of corporate and foundation fund raising for educational institutions. To subscribe, send the message <subscribe cfrnet> to *listproc@medicine.wustl.edu*

Seeking
Foundation
Support

● ● ●

The early campaigns sought a once-in-a-lifetime gift. By the end of the century, the emphasis was on developing a solid and sophisticated relationship that would lead to many substantial gifts throughout the donor's lifetime.

Capital Campaigns: Making the Goal and Working Within the Total Fund-Raising Effort

Terry M. Holcombe
Former Vice President for Development
Yale University

The word "campaign" connotes an effort dedicated to the achievement of specific goals within a limited period of time. Familiar examples are military and political campaigns. In the world of development, goals are usually stated in terms of dollars to be raised in cash and pledges. By definition, campaigns have publicly-announced start and end dates, and many are of five years or less in duration, although the CASE management reporting standards permit campaigns of up to seven years, including both "silent" and "public" phases.

With all the drama and energy called up by the word "campaign," it is easy to lose sight of the fact that campaigns are usually just focused periods in a larger, longer-term effort. A political party, for example, must cement its long-term positioning, accumulate power, and win particular elections if it wants to ensure its continued existence and achieve its objectives. In the same way, military campaigns move toward the ultimate objective of winning the war. Fund-raising campaigns, particularly as they appear at the beginning of the 21st century, are but one limited part of an institution's continuing, overall effort to secure the necessary resources to achieve its goals.

THE EVOLUTION OF CAPITAL CAMPAIGNS

Over time, the role of campaigns has changed, as have the strategies and tactics employed in them. The earliest "development" efforts were probably as simple as the first military engagements, wherein two champions squared off in single combat. The president of the institution engaged with one or two major donors, his efforts unsupported by staff. In due course, countries developed volunteer and then standing armies; charitable entities moved from volunteer-driven solicitations to fully staffed fund-raising organizations. Just as the 20th century brought "total war," in a geopolitical sense, it also saw the onset of the "comprehensive capital campaign," where virtually every individual with any relationship to the institution is solicited by anyone else with that relationship—from student telemarketers at dinnertime to faculty and administrators in less intrusive settings.

Although campaigns have existed since the origin of academic institutions in America, their essential form has evolved. Harvard, William and Mary, and Yale began as financially insecure institutions, dependent on local charity, lotteries, and other *ad hoc* devices for support. In the 1640s, Harvard sent a fund-raising delegation back to England. Its quest for support was successful. The

Capital
Campaigns:
Making the Goal
and Working
Within the Total
Fund-Raising
Effort

"Collegiate School" in New Haven followed suit in the early 1770's with the result that Elihu Yale, a merchant whose fortune originated in India, made what would now be called a "naming gift." The distinguished solicitors sent on these missions were armed with the contemporary version of case statements, and no doubt employed other familiar campaign techniques as well.

By the early 19th century, alumni began to be more active, coming forward with support and organizing themselves into gift-giving entities based on classes and degree affiliations. (It is likely that they also began, at this time, to write the president with pithy advice about admissions, curriculum concerns, and financial management.) "Annual funds" began to emerge as formal entities following the Civil War. These funds had largely volunteer staff members to generate broad-based support; presidents still tended to concentrate on a few major prospects at the top of the giving pyramid, or "principal prospects," as they came to be known a century later.

Capital campaigns as we understand them began early in the 20th century, with the leadership role taken by the Young Men's Christian Association movement and later, the Red Cross. Educational institutions followed suit, initially with narrowly targeted programs, such as funding the renovation of "Founder's Hall."

With the explosive growth of educational institutions in the 1950s, campaigning entered a new phase. As needs increased and prospects became more affluent, campaigns were mounted with greater frequency and with more ambitious goals. These efforts sought support for facilities or endowment on a "once in a lifetime" gift basis and annual, expendable support for programs was not included. The immediate objective of a traditional campaign was short term, to cause a temporary upward blip in gift revenue rather than to engender a permanent change in gift totals and in the behavior of donors. Institutions tended to "staff up" (with volunteers or paid staff members) for campaigns, and to reduce the expenditures back to "peacetime" levels when the effort was completed.

Several difficulties, as well as some new opportunities, emerged as this mode was tested by major campaigns in the 1960s and 1970s. There were real costs to the stop-and-start nature of the model: staff members were dislocated; budgets fluctuated with changing revenue, making planning problematic; long-term prospect relationships were disrupted. Furthermore, as aggressive capital solicitations began to run into equally aggressive annual or expendable giving programs, donors became confused if not overtly alienated.

By the 1980s, a new model had emerged as the standard: the comprehensive campaign. All gift revenue and pledges to the institution, including both annual and capital support, were counted in setting the goal and toward its achievement. Solicitations across the board were carefully managed and coordinated to avoid conflict between annual giving and capital giving goals. Approaches such as planned giving and telemarketing were given full play. The campaign period was more or less fixed at five years, preceded by one or two years of a "quiet phase" during which initial, nucleus fund commitments approaching one-third of the total goal were secured.

During the 1990s, comprehensive campaigns had become virtually continuous as well. Several factors contributed to this change. It became increasingly clear that prospects' ability and willingness to make significant gifts was determined more by a number of highly personal factors, such as estate planning, family and business issues, and tax exposure, rather than whether or not the institution happened to be in the midst of a campaign. As the size of individual gifts increased, so did the cultivation period required to consummate them. It takes far longer to negotiate and close a gift to endow a chair or to set up a program than it does to solicit a small, unrestricted reunion gift. The early campaigns sought a once-in-a-lifetime gift. By the end of the century, the emphasis was on developing a solid and sophisticated relationship that would lead to many substantial gifts throughout the donor's lifetime.

To maintain lifelong and complex relationships with donors, long-term staffing is a necessity. It takes a great deal of time to get to know and respond to a donor's needs. In addition, donors prefer to deal with the same people they have in the past. As a result, the staff-up and staff-down cycle attendant with the earlier campaign model is untenable in today's environment. Institutions now rely on steady (and steadily increasing) flows of cash into the annual operating and capital budgets, rather than peaks and valleys caused by campaign activity. In turn, because institutions engage in more sophisticated strategic planning, fund raisers garner major budgetary support on a regular basis. Today's long and large campaigns thus reflect the realities of higher education and economic conditions of the early 21st century.

THE STAGES OF THE TYPICAL MODERN CAMPAIGN

With considerable room for local variations and tailoring, most campaigns go through several sequential stages and are comprised of certain elements outlined below.

Planning and Preparing

Well before a campaign begins to take shape, two steps are essential. First, the institution needs to develop and review its strategic plans and commit them to writing. This exercise will clarify the organization's mission, a timeframe and budget, what it hopes to accomplish, and where resources will come from. Separately, those responsible for fund raising need to assess the potential of corporate, individual, and foundation prospects to provide support toward these objectives. The assessment may be done internally through rating and screening sessions, where alumni and other knowledgeable informants help the staff in a name-by-name review of actual prospect gift potential and inclination. Or it may be done as a feasibility study with the assistance of outside counsel. This process will produce a table of needed gifts, showing various giving levels and the number of donors and prospects required at each level to reach the goal. Preparing a gift chart can be a sobering experience, for it inevitably points up the critical importance of a few very large gifts to the success of the enterprise. It shows the virtual impossibility of relying on gifts in $10,000 increments to make up for a $1 million major gift that does not materialize.

Determining potential must take into account the institution's recent gift history. Aggressive campaigning does increase giving, but only within limits set by the base. In other words, it is unlikely that an institution raising $20 million a year can raise $100 million simply by having a campaign. The campaign's preliminary goal, used at this stage for internal and planning purposes, should be a reasonable compromise between the market potential and the institutional needs. A draft campaign plan should also be prepared, showing staffing, structure, governance, and timing.

Nucleus Fund Phase

Most campaigns then move into a "quiet" or nucleus fund phase, lasting up to two years preceding a five-year campaign. This period is used to make key advance solicitations, recruit volunteers, prepare a communications plan and materials, and plan for special events. It is a final test of the campaign plan. Ideally, the nucleus fund solicitations will result in commitments representing 30 to 40 percent of the planning goal. If gifts and pledges fall far short, it may be time to lower the goal before making it public or raise it if the variation is in that direction.

Two crucial documents should appear in the nucleus fund phase, the *case statement* and *final campaign plan*. The case statement needs to be a persuasive presentation of what sums are needed and why. It illustrates how the institution will be different if funds are committed. While most solicitations for larger gifts are done with individualized proposals or special materials, the case statement sets the context and serves as evidence that the institution is publicly committed to the stated plans. Many donors and all volunteers need to be persuaded not just that their own gift will make a difference, but also that the enterprise as a whole will succeed. A final campaign plan must be specific, with amounts and dates, including a formal goal set after confirmation or adjustment by the nucleus fund solicitations, and must demonstrate a reasonable chance of success.

Public Campaign Period

Next comes the public campaign period. This usually begins with a formal launching or kickoff event.

> ● ● ●
> **Preparing a gift chart can be a sobering experience, for it inevitably points up the critical importance of a few very large gifts to the success of the enterprise.**

Capital
Campaigns:
Making the Goal
and Working
Within the Total
Fund-Raising
Effort

The event is an opportunity to showcase the institution and its plans, recognize nucleus fund donors and key volunteers, and generate a sense of excitement about the campaign. During the next five years, the prospects originally identified are solicited and closed, and new potential donors are identified and asked for support. Five years is a long time in the history of an institution, and it may be necessary to modify some of the campaign assumptions in response to opportunities and problems. The progress of the campaign will dictate end-game strategies, such as resolicitation of key donors (or not). Well before the final year of the campaign, plan how ongoing development activities will continue following its conclusion.

Wrap up

Campaigns represent an opportunity not just to generate incremental gift revenue for a period of years, but to raise annual gift revenues to new highs and sustain them there. Despite the fact that many participants may be tired of the campaign as it approaches its conclusion, it is essential to consolidate the gains achieved. New gifts require careful attention to stewardship requirements. New prospects will have been uncovered, and those who gave early may be ready for resolicitation. Reward and re-engage effective volunteers. Revise and update materials and fund-raising plans.

THE FUTURE

As we begin the new century, the effective fund-raising program will be highly professional and fully integrated into the financial and academic planning of the institution it serves. It will generate ever-increasing revenue, year in and year out. Campaigns, in this context, will become both less and more important. The successful development program's day-to-day operational activities will be much the same, whether the institution is in a campaign mode or not. Long-term strategies and tactics will have smoothed the peaks and valleys of both expenses and revenues.

It would be easy to conclude that modern campaigns are mere "packaging devices," tacked onto ongoing development programs for a few years to gain attention or generate excitement. Yet they are clearly more than that. They have retained the ability to galvanize the attention of all elements of an educational community, and to focus them on the fund-raising tasks at hand. What's new, however, is the understanding that a campaign's short-term focus and energies can translate into permanent enhancements for an institution's advancement program.

Conceptualize the new campaign environment by distinguishing between goals and objectives. Every campaign has well-articulated goals, expressed quite simply as certain amounts of cash and pledges to be amassed over the campaign period. These goals are easy to explain and track, and they form the basis for a public understanding of the campaign's mission and progress. Accordingly, a campaign goal might be presented as $100 million, with $50 million of that for endowment, and $25 million each for facilities and ongoing programs.

But an effective campaign should also be a key part of a longer-term institutional fund-raising plan and strategy. Attaining the plan's objectives will have a lasting impact on gift flows. Campaign objectives might include:

- increasing the number of major gift prospects identified from 2,000 to 5,000;
- increasing the percentage of alumni giving each year from 30 to 35 percent;
- upgrading all computer support systems;
- reorganizing the volunteer support structure and replacing ineffective solicitors;
- enhancing stewardship activities;
- introducing a reunion giving program;
- identifying a new generation of volunteer leaders; and
- enhancing the institution's academic reputation.

The campaign thus becomes a vehicle not just for raising the $100 million, but for moving the entire program forward to a higher level and sustaining it there. The campaign concept is important in other ways as well. Ideally, regular institutional planning produces a campaign and the fund-raising agenda. Often, however, the institution must articulate its mission and make necessary decisions in order to produce a case statement and a list of specific needs. The campaign itself has an almost magic quality in a bureaucratic setting: budgets are increased, reorganizations proceed, and personnel issues are resolved. The governing board takes a much deeper interest in development than at any other time.

If there is one major change in development activity over the last century, it is the increasing competition for the charitable dollar. Whereas 100 years ago, there were but a few private colleges and universities seeking support, now there are many hundreds of institutions in both the public and private sectors doing so. These are joined by thousands of other charitable entities. Virtually all have important roles and ongoing development programs. In this competitive environment, donors will increasingly have to make tough choices with their charitable dollars. In this context, the campaign will be crucial as a means to convey with urgency, clarity, and commitment the unique contribution a particular educational institution can make to society. Campaigns will be no less important in this new century, but their contributions will be more as communication vehicles than as ways of organizing fund-raising activity.

FURTHER READINGS

Dessoff, Alan L. "Capital Offenses: Leaving Alumni Leaders Out of Your Capital Campaign Plans Can Be a Major Blunder. To Avoid Bad Feelings and Poor Results, Get Everyone Involved," CURRENTS 19, no. 10 (November/December 1993): 11-16.

Gearhart, G. David. *The Capital Campaign in Higher Education: A Practical Guide for College and University Advancement.* Washington, DC: National Association of College and University Business Officers, 1995.

Grossnickle, Ted R. "Are You Ready? Before You Shell Out Big Bucks for a Campaign Feasibility Study, Make Sure You've Completed These Eight Steps," currents 23, no. 10 (November/December 1997): 34.

Pollack, Rachel H. "Starting on the Right Foot: Answers to Campaign Questions That May Have You Stopped in Your Tracks," CURRENTS 23, no. 10 (November/December 1997): 31.

Quigg, H. Gerald, ed. *The Successful Capital Campaign: From Planning to Victory Celebration.* Washington, DC: Council for Advancement and Support of Education, 1986.

Ryan, Ellen. "Setting the Standards: After Lengthy Study, CASE Releases New Ground Rules to Ensure Apples-To-Apples Fund-Raising Campaigns," CURRENTS 20, no. 5 (May 1994): 8-10.

Wise, Charles B. "Ready Or Not?: A Top 10 List of Questions To Ask—of Yourself and Your Institution— Before Plunging into a Campaign," CURRENTS 20, no. 10 (November/December 1994): 19-22.

Planned giving—and thoughtful giving—can be a lifetime endeavor. It should command the same kind of dedication and energy as accumulating wealth.

The Stages of Giving

Kenneth N. Dayton
President
Oak Leaf Foundation (Minneapolis, MN)

Having spent many years making money and accumulating wealth, my wife and I have decided to spend this phase of our lives giving our money away—hopefully with standards and goals similar to those we used in making it. Back in 1945, the first year for which I have a record of my personal contributions to charitable organizations, I donated $1,250. This was not an inconsiderable amount for someone on sergeant's pay just discharged from the Army. I suspect the money was divided more or less equally between the Community Chest (as we then called it), Westminster Church, and the Orchestral Association of Minneapolis (as it was then known).

Last year, Judy and I passed a significant milestone in our lifetime giving. Over those 50-plus years, we have steadily increased our giving from the $1,250 in 1954 to the present level. The absolute amount of our giving is unimportant because giving is relative to income and other factors. What is important is the trend of one's giving and the way individuals determine and measure their own giving. Furthermore, who are we to brag? After all, the poor give a much higher percentage of their income than do the rich.

As we have grown older and wealthier, our giving has evolved from being responsive (and even responsible) to being proactive (and perhaps innovative). More significantly, we have moved through seven of nine identifiable stages of giving. Because we have thought a lot about these stages, I would like to identify and comment on them in the hope we can help others struggling with the question, "How much should we give?" So here are the seven stages of giving through which we have passed and the two additional ones we now are contemplating:

1. Minimal Response
2. Involvement and Interest
3. As Much as Possible
4. Maximum Allowable
5. Beyond the Max
6. Percentage of Wealth
7. Capping Wealth
8. Reducing the Cap
9. Bequests

Minimal Response. Most people start their giving by responding to a knock on the door by a Boy Scout or Girl Scout or a child raising money for some equivalent cause in the neighborhood. We all give to such causes and usually just enough to satisfy the solicitors and send them away with a smile on their faces.

But giving became more involved and difficult when major institutions began to solicit us. In all cases, they undoubtedly asked for what they thought I could give, and I gave as much as I felt I should. I call this phase Minimal Response not because we responded with the least amount we could get away with but because it was purely responsive giving—giving because we were asked and only because we were asked. There's no shame in this; I suspect every donor starts this way. It's a good way to start, but no place to stop. The trick is to evolve out of this phase as soon as possible.

Involvement and Interest. Becoming a volunteer in a nonprofit organization changes one's perspective on giving dramatically. You believe in the cause of your choice, and you want to make it better. So your giving to that institution changes and grows and becomes more thoughtful. You give not only dollars but also time and energy. Giving takes on a new and far more joyful approach. It becomes meaningful and purposeful. As your giving grows, so do you.

As Much as Possible. The joy of involvement in an important cause leads to Stage 3, where one no longer gives as little as possible but as much as possible. This applies both to individual drives and to total annual giving as well. I'll never forget our joy the first time we told a solicitor we would give more than we were asked. We thought we *should* give more and felt the organization needed us to give more if the drive was to be successful. What a breakthrough for any concerned and thoughtful citizen: Giving in response to a request is easy. Giving as much as possible is hard. It requires thinking about total giving and the share of that total to each drive or area of interest. It requires a plan and a budget; it forces priorities.

The transformation from *Minimal Response* to *As Much as Possible* changes one's entire outlook on giving. It moves giving from a neutral act to a positive one. It frees the spirit and raises one's self-esteem. It is a mind-boggling experience. It's a shame so many givers never make it to this third stage.

Maximum Allowable. Of course the law allows us to give as much as we want, but the law only allows us to deduct on our income taxes a certain percentage of income given in cash, a smaller percentage in stock, an even smaller percentage to personal foundations, and so forth. In 1986, the alternative minimum tax further restricted the amount allowable for income-tax deduction.

For most of the last 30 years or so, we used this formula—maximum allowable by the IRS—to determine our level of giving for each year. Some years we gave more than the allowable, but then we took advantage of the five-year carry-forward provision of the tax law, thereby reducing our giving in the out years. We found that *Maximum Allowable* was a marvelous discipline. For the first time, it gave us a budget for giving, which gave us an opportunity to plan our giving. We worked hard to determine the relative size of gifts to major drives and important institutions, and we began to think creatively about our philanthropy.

Beyond the Max. There was one fly in the ointment of *Maximum Allowable*—the alternative minimum tax enacted in 1986. This new law really put a crimp not only in our giving but also in our ability to plan. It severely restricted our flexibility and our ability to initiate meaningful giving programs.

One day, while despairing over the IRS's strictures, we decided to ignore the maximum allowable deduction and give what we wanted to give. I'll never quite understand how or why we made this decision, but we did. What a breakthrough! No longer would we let the IRS tell us how much (or how little) we could give. We immediately began to build up more carryover than we could possibly use up in the five-year grace period. This sum just kept getting larger and larger, and after five years, we began to see bigger and bigger chunks of so-called deductibility just disappear off our tax returns.

On the one hand, that is not a happy situation. But on the other hand, we felt great about giving as much as we wanted and could afford. The only problem was that now we no longer had a benchmark—*Maximum Allowable*—against which to measure our giving. We needed to invent one.

Percentage of Wealth. If one no longer measures giving against income (or income-tax deductibility), logic soon leads to using total wealth as the measure. After using this measure for several years, we have found it is a far better tool than income for determining a giving budget. Investing wisely and avoiding overspending on personal consumption has left us with adequate money to give generously and to reinvest to accumulate additional wealth. The trick is to determine the right percent-to-wealth standard for giving. Until we started to measure our giving against our wealth, we did not fully realize how much we could give away and still live very comfortably and well.

Capping Wealth. Giving away a percentage of your wealth each year forces you to consider some fundamental questions: How wealthy do you want to be? How much money do you want to have when you die? Reflecting on such questions leads inevitably to the concept of capping one's wealth—setting a limit on what you accumulate and giving away everything above that figure. Several years ago, we decided to do just that. The decision has forced us to consider our personal and philanthropic priorities and has given us many giving options. At the end of each year, the last line of our financial report lists the amount we are "open to give" during the coming year. Find this figure: It is gratifying to know that you can live well and still afford to give generously.

So many people are fearful of giving large sums because they cannot foresee future economic conditions. The exercise I have described can help alleviate such fears. We can't foresee the future either, but we feel comfortable we have provided adequately for our well-being. Because the future is uncertain, we someday may find it necessary to curtail our giving. So be it—the open-to-give figure may drop to zero. But with ideal economic and market conditions over the last several years, we have been able to share our wealth and see it at work.

Reducing the Cap. We are at Stage Seven of the nine stages of giving, but we long ago started to think about the next two stages. Who is to say whether we set the right cap for our own wealth? Only time will tell. We think it is right for us now because it provides a large enough base for good earning power—enough to eat well and give well.

Although we are not at all ready to reduce the cap, we can visualize the possibility of doing so as

we get older, as perhaps we spend less, and as we face our inevitable deaths. Whether we ever will have the courage, fortitude, and intelligence to lower the cap we cannot say. But thinking about the nine stages of giving and our current place on the continuum have at least put the subject on our table. We are comfortable discussing the subject.

The ideal, of course, would be to give away your last dollar just before you die. Who wants to die rich or turn over $1.10 to Uncle Sam for every dollar you bequeath your heirs? That is an expensive and inefficient way to transfer wealth. Of course, it's near impossible to achieve the ideal; after all, no one wants to go broke too soon. Therefore, continuing our giving plan has become the focus of our wills. This focus has made estate planning an exciting adventure, not a gruesome task.

Bequests. We decided long ago that we had transferred enough of our assets to our heirs. Consequently, we see no need to provide for them in our wills (at horrendous cost). Accordingly, we are able to leave almost all of our assets to the nonprofit organizations we have selected—mainly cultural institutions in Minneapolis. Doing so avoids taxes and enhances the giving program we developed over the years. It gives us great satisfaction to know that our bequests will fortify the programs we have helped construct for the past half-century.

We did not consciously move from one stage to the next, of course. Rather, we did what we wanted and what we thought was the responsible thing. In retrospect, we now can identify those steps as the nine stages of giving. By so doing, we hope to help others recognize where they are on this exciting course and to make the steps to the next stage of giving more thoughtfully and purposefully than we were able to do on our own. Planned giving—and thoughtful giving—can be a lifetime endeavor. It should command the same kind of dedication and energy as accumulating wealth.

Reprinted with permission from Trusteeship, *the magazine of the Association of Governing Boards of Universities and Colleges, March/April 1999, pp. 14-17 and from the booklet,* The Stages of Giving, *by Kenneth N. Dayton, published by Independent Sector, Washington, DC, 1999.*

The most sophisticated fund-raising techniques are almost never as effective as the careful attention we give, one by one, to our long-term relationships with donors.

Donor Relations: Achieving Effective Donor-Centered Stewardship

Tracy Savage
Assistant Head of School for Development and Public Relations
National Cathedral School

Stewardship is the process whereby an institution cares for and protects its philanthropic support—its gifts and those who give them—in a way that both responds to the donor's expectations and respects the act of giving. Many colleges and schools use the term "donor relations" interchangeably with "stewardship." I like to think of stewardship as an idea, a standard of behavior, and I use donor relations more often to mean those activities in our development offices that further the standards of stewardship. Whatever distinction you make, both terms usually refer to the same components of advancement practice:

1. Gift acknowledgment;
2. Donor recognition (including gift societies, special events, and publicity); and
3. Supervision and reporting of restricted and named funds.

In addition, another key aspect of a good donor relations program (which we'll discuss later) is the successful use of creativity, technology, and innovation. Most importantly, good stewardship is a donor-centered process. In the last decade, one of the most dramatic changes in the advancement world has been our shift from a program-centered

profession to a donor-centered profession. We have learned that the most sophisticated fund-raising techniques are *almost never* as effective as the careful attention we give, one by one, to our long-term relationships with donors.

GIFT ACKNOWLEDGMENT

The first tenet of good stewardship is good response to a donor's gift. Different gifts and different donors call for different responses, but all effective acknowledgments have four things in common:

1) an accurate and timely confirmation of all of the gift "facts," such as who, exactly, made the gift; what, exactly, the gift was for; what was the form or type of gift; what was the value and duration of the gift; and sometimes even why the gift was made;
2) an expression of gratitude, whether it be formal, institutional, personal, or even in the receipt record of the gift transaction;
3) a blueprint for future interaction between donor and institution, such as when we will next report to the donor, what kind of information is to be forthcoming, when the results of the gift will be public, etc.;
4) a reinforcement of the institution's case for sup-

port, however simple or grand that may be, affirming the reasons why the gift was a good idea in the first place.

What We Include in an Acknowledgment

Most of us use many different forms of acknowledgment, depending on the nature of the gift. In this diversity of options, we often neglect one or more of the components listed above. For example, in an annual fund acknowledgement, we know we must be accurate and timely (component 1), so we are usually careful to include data about donor and gift. But we might forget the blueprint for future interaction (component 3), making an assumption that with an annual gift there IS no future interaction. What an opportunity we miss when we don't include a warm sentence about how the class agent will also be sending along his thanks. Or in a letter acknowledging a pledge payment to an endowed fund, how much we reinforce our institution's case when we describe how payments made to date have played a role on campus already.

No, we cannot personalize every word in every piece of mail that leaves our offices. But, we can develop a broader menu of boilerplate options that are thoughtful and personal. We can segment our responses as well as we do our solicitations. And we can remember that the first thing a donor sees in writing after making a gift can have a lasting impact on his or her relationship with the school.

How We Acknowledge

What we include in our gift acknowledgments is the easy part. *How* we accomplish our acknowledgment objectives is the challenge, and the fun. We start by agreeing that every acknowledgment should be tailored to the nature of the gift, the allocation of the gift, the amount of the gift, and to the identity of the donor. It is in the tremendous variety of gift responses that we have the best openings for the stewardship of our donors.

For example, most of us pair certain gifts and/or donors with the most appropriate signatory. The vice president for development writes to members of gift society X, the president writes to

gift society Y donors, and the chair of society Z signs letters to Z donors. Many of us also arrange for adjunct signatories, or seconding "thank you's" from key volunteers. The best of us ask, in the instance of every significant donor, whom else should we invite to send a note of gratitude to our donor? Perhaps that trustee who met her at last fall's convocation? Perhaps next year's annual fund chair, with thanks for "setting the stage"?

> ● ● ●
> We must remember that neither altruism nor requests for anonymity preclude recognition; they simply challenge us to recognize such donors with greater sensitivity.

In addition to identifying the ideal signatory(ies), we should also be thoughtful about the timing of gift acknowledgments. Immediate responses are essential for acknowledging primary gift data. Second communications, expressing special or personal gratitude should follow in short order. But what about additional correspondence a month later, or three months later? A supplemental "thank you" more distant in time can sometimes prolong the warm sensations of a gift.

By What Means We Acknowledge

And, of course, the actual means of acknowledgment can vary as well, often to our stewardship advantage. Many advancement professionals worry that our increased technology will depersonalize our relationships. The spur-of-the-moment telephone call, the handshake and heartfelt spoken words of gratitude in the quadrangle or the campus art gallery, these methods of acknowledging gifts have acquired new stature. They are not substitutes for the written response, but they play a role that no letter or gift receipt can ever play. And without the barrier of paper, such impromptu, donor-centered gratitude solidifies a very human connection. As Jeanne McKown at Georgia Tech says in *Donor Relations: The Essential Guide*, ". . .the warmer the approach, the more intense the impact."

DONOR RECOGNITION

Let us agree that recognition is universally desirable. Of course we all have donors who seek nothing but the good impact of their gifts, and we all have donors who request anonymity. Even so, we must remember that neither altruism nor requests for anonymity preclude recognition; they simply challenge us to recognize such donors with greater sensitivity.

Gift Societies

Gift societies increase giving levels. They do so in two ways: 1) they encourage larger gifts by setting "giving bars" at strategically higher levels, and 2) they discourage gift decreases by emphasizing the distinction between different gift levels. In the end, gift societies are most effective when each gift club, or "giving bar," symbolizes or suggests something attractive or compelling to the donor. When we enhance the distinctiveness of our gift societies, we make them more effective. Does each club have a special insignia? Do written solicitations and invitations come on special society stationery or with special brochures? Does the name of the gift club make a clear statement? ("Patrons" and "Benefactors" are wonderful gift club names, but they do not seem to mean very much.) Tammie Ruda at Brown University reminds us in *Donor Relations: The Essential Guide*, ". . .think about (whether it is) easy. . .for your audience to understand the value of each level."

Many of our institutions offer premiums to donors as a form of recognition for gift club membership. A lapel pin, a mug with the school seal, or perhaps an invitation to dinner with the president, all can be very popular. Certainly such premiums help enhance the distinctiveness of the club and reward the donor. They also, however, can be logistically cumbersome to manage, and sometimes can even provoke ill will. And we must always be mindful of tax deductibility issues when valuable premiums are offered to the donor as an incentive to join a gift club. Hence, those of us in small offices sometimes avoid using premiums altogether.

If gift society premiums need to be part of your program, consider four rules:

■ *The cost of the premium must not exceed the "token" nature of the premium.* Cost here means more than just the price of the item itself: high risk with tax deductibility is a cost; donors who hate seeing their charitable gifts spent on premiums are another cost.

■ *Premiums need to be desirable, not a nuisance* (something functional, or if purely ornamental, something that can be displayed easily).

■ *Premiums need to be chosen strategically, with foresight.* For example, if a donor stays at the same gift club level for several years, the premium must be one that is appealing to the donor year after year.

■ *The item used for a gift society premium can only be acquired by the gift club membership* (you can't buy it in the campus book store).

Gift societies are standard practice in most institutional advancement programs. Even so, they need careful planning. Changing a gift club level or establishing a new society requires thoughtful marketing, with lots of advance PR. Your membership policies also warrant attention. For example, do spouses have membership rights? How about matching gift companies? Is the membership for life, for a year, for a certain term?

Gift societies are an advancement program. And we should remember our guiding principle—to think about donors instead of programs. However your gift clubs are set up, seek ways to personalize the membership benefits for your leading philanthropic supporters. Add the hand-written note to the premium that comes in the mail. Make a telephone call to the new member for that first invitation to dinner with the vice president. Ask a life member to preview and critique the new gift society logo. Think very carefully about what your most significant donors really want, as you revise and improve your club programs.

Events

Most donors (except those who truly desire anonymity) feel good about public recognition of some kind. Beyond that, there is no reliable rule about what kinds of events best recognize our donors. The truth is, special recognition events are labor intensive, often expensive, and their effectiveness is hard to measure concretely. Since public accolades and celebrations can be the best form of stewardship for some donors, most of us include events in our donor relations repertoire.

Whether you produce large-scale events for a big group of donors, or a special event for an individual philanthropist, here are some essential guidelines for successful recognition events:

■ *Match the style of the event to the style of the*

donor(s). Some of the best recognition moments are those events that are atypical, but which are tailored to match a donor's special interest or area of enjoyment, i.e. a group of benefactors, who have just endowed a faculty chair in music, is invited to sing with the school's graduate chorale at a concert held in honor of the donors.

■ *Take special care with the guest list.* Perhaps it is the donor's mentor whose presence will be meaningful, or the donor's family, or professional colleagues. Without the right audience, the right community of peers, recognition is wasted.

■ *Attend to every detail of the event with care.* Invitations sent well in advance, minimal use of recycled decorations or favors, and extreme care in consulting with the donor ahead of time all help the event signal the value of the donor's gift. Anything less is self-defeating.

As if it hasn't been said enough, try not to overlook opportunities to recognize major benefactors with small donor-centered activities that are personal, sometimes purely social, and relatively intimate. The weekend invitation to the trustee's summer cabin, the gathering of a handful of VIP's for coffee before the track meet, such simple connections bring real meaning to donor recognition.

Publications

Our magazines and newsletters can help recognize donors in a way no other vehicle can, because, in print, the recognition moment lasts forever. That moment can be shared *ad infinitum*, re-used in new displays, on Web sites and in reprints, even retrieved from the archives for new recognition events as the relationship continues. Also, special printed programs and commemorative invitations or any printed records of recognition have lasting value. A surprising number of donors cherish such records greatly.

There are two key issues with printed recognition:

1) Can we ensure accuracy and donor approval, so that we *don't offend* the donor in perpetuity *rather than honor* him or her?

2) Can we sustain an effective enough *working*

relationship with our publications/PR professionals so we can use the campus publications for our stewardship purposes?

Neither of these challenges is easily met, but both warrant our best efforts.

In addition, we must use as much creativity in our printed recognition as we do in our gift societies and our special events. An accurate annual report of donors is but the starting point. Feature articles on the powerful work of a donor's gift, profiles of faculty that are beloved to a long-time supporter, donors who are themselves invited to write for our publications—the options are endless, and wonderfully donor-centered.

A word about anonymity and donor recognition: It is easy to assume that the donor who asks for his or her identity to be kept secret has therefore asked for no recognition. That is rarely the case. The individual on campus who *does* know about the donor's gift and identity, be it the provost, the major gifts officer, or the board chairman, has a responsibility to execute whatever recognition is appropriate, *depending on the donor.* The institution officer "in the know" might invite the donor to join her for a walk through the new observatory (that the donor funded); or perhaps she might privately send the donor a copy of the first admission ticket printed for the new concert hall (that the donor funded). Recognition need not be public, but it does need to happen.

NAMED AND RESTRICTED FUNDS

Many institutions are blessed with gifts that establish endowed or restricted funds. Such gifts support ongoing aspects of campus life, be they endowed professorships, financial aid funds, library acquisition endowments, research fellowships, or other purposes. These funds are gateways to continuing relationships between schools and donors, and they expand the role of the institution in the donor's life. Thirty years ago, Harold Seymour wrote in his book *Designs for Fund-Raising,* our task is to let " . . . the interested person know that his support . . . is paying rich dividends." That is our long-term role as stewards.

In carrying out that important role with

named and restricted funds, we have two primary responsibilities:

- Determine, and then adhere to, the restrictions and allocations intended by the donor.
- Report to the donor regularly on the work of the fund, the status of the fund balance, and pertinent investment or expense information.

We cannot carry out these responsibilities well unless we have a few things in place. For example, we need to maintain a working knowledge of the complex regulations and guidelines imposed on us by outside agencies, such as FASB (Financial Accounting Standards Board) and NACUBO (National Association of College and University Business Officers). We need to establish well-oriented gift committees that will review named and restricted funds regularly, and well-designed donor report formats that will help us handle the reporting details easily and accurately.

In addition, we need to develop a named fund protocol, equally endorsed by the advancement office *and* the business/accounting offices, for accessing and reporting fund information. We also need an effective avenue of communication between the donor relations staff and those faculty or students whose personal testimonials or grant summaries we need for our reports to the donors.

Perhaps most importantly, we must establish clear guidelines for donors when the gift is initiated. We should have on hand documented policies on minimums for establishing a named fund, endowment spending policies, pledge period parameters, and gift agreement procedures and details. Institutions often struggle with what to do when funds become outdated. Clear guidelines at the outset help us avoid later dilemmas with outdated funds.

TECHNOLOGY, INFORMATION MANAGEMENT, AND INNOVATION

A discussion of stewardship is incomplete without some mention of technology and information systems. We need to be vigilant in focusing our miraculous electronic capabilities on donor-centered activities. Technology must serve our efforts to personalize and customize our acknowledgments, our donor recognition, and our reporting.

More importantly, we need to be creative in the way in we use technology to help us in stewardship.

A sufficient segment of our nonprofit world now operates in a fully electronic environment, and we, as a result, must maintain this community standard if we are to remain meritorious in the eyes of our donors. We cannot fail to:

- use sophisticated database managers and advanced fund-raising software to track our donors and funds;
- recognize and steward our donors on our Web sites; and
- use every available technology to communicate (e-mail, video-conferencing, list-serves, etc.).

As we strive to stay on the cutting edge of technology, we must always remember that electronic innovations are not about new scientific miracles, but about new routes to achieving effective, donor-centered stewardship.

REFERENCES

Borentstein, Henry P. "Recognition: The Stepchild of Fundraising: In Creating Donor Recognition Programs, There Are Several Points to Consider Along With Some Areas of Concern," *Fund Raising Management* 23, no.2 (April 1992): 18-

Bunin, Irene M. et al. *Donor Relations: The Essential Guide to Stewardship Policies, Procedures and Protocol.* Washington, DC: CASE Books, 1999.

Burnett, Ken. *Relationship Fundraising.* Chicago, IL: Precept Press, 1995.

Collins, Walton R. "The Subtleties of Stewardship: Some Fund Raisers Regard Stewardship Only as a Buzz Word. Others Define the Concept Narrowly, as Finding Ways to Say 'Thank You' for Gifts. At Its Most Effective, Though, Stewardship is the Focused Application of Recognition," *Advancing Philanthropy* 4, no.3 (Fall 1996): 12-16.

Dessoff, Alan L. "Put It in Writing," CURRENTS 23, no.2 (February 1997): 30-35.

Fey, Don. "The Stewardship Report: Keeping in Touch with Friends," *Fund Raising Management* 26, no.9 (November 1995): 42-43.

Gerber, Richard. "Pay Attention to 'Small Touches': In Life It's the Little Things That Count. And in Fund Raising Too, It's the Small Touches That Transform Small Donors into Major Donors," *Fund Raising Management* 26, no.2 (April 1995): 28-29.

Greenfield, James M. "Gift Size vs. Amount of Recognition: Balancing Your Donor Club Budget," *FRI Monthly Portfolio* 35, no.6 (June 1996).

Donor Relations: Achieving Effective Donor-Centered Stewardship

Harrison, Bill. "When a Plaque Isn't Enough: How Do You Thank Major Donors? Planning What To Do After Receipt of a Gift Begins Long Before the Actual Event. Recognition of Major Donors is One of the Most Important and Critical Aspects of a Development Program," *Fund Raising Management* 27, no.5 (July 1996): 36-39.

Kirkman, Kay. "Thanks Again—And Again: Seven Simple Steps to a Successful Donor Recognition Program," CURRENTS 21, no.8 (September 1995): 38-40.

Lewis, Herschell Gordon. "Hello, Good Donor. Uh— What's Your Name?: Honor Your Donors. Treat Them Like Friends and Make Them Feel Like Insiders. Otherwise You May Lose Them," *Fund Raising Management* 22, no.11 (January 1992): 44.

Logan, Frank A. "Starting a Donor Recognition Society," *Give and Take* 27, no.4 (April 1995): 5-6.

McLelland, R. Jane. "Essentials of Endowment Stewardship," CURRENTS 23, no.8 (September 1997): 28-33.

Muir, Roy and Jerry May, eds. *Developing an Effective Major Gift Program: From Managing Staff to Soliciting Gifts.* Washington, DC: Council for Advancement and Support of Education, 1993.

Nichols, Judith E. "Growing From Good to Great: By Focusing on Renewal Rather Than Acquisition, You Don't Have to Work as Hard to Replace Large Numbers of Donors and You Have the Opportunity to Concentrate on Upgrading Current Donors," *Fund Raising Management* 26, no.1 (March 1995): 24.

Ostrom, Jacquelyn B. "After the Major Gift, Then What?" In *Establishing the Major Gifts Program: A Workbook for Independent Schools.* Seattle, WA: PNAIS.

Pierce, Susan P. *Gift Club Programs: A Survey of How 44 Institutions Raise Money.* Washington, DC: Council for Advancement and Support of Education, 1992.

Philanthropic Services for Institutions. *Accent on Recognition: Saying Thank You to Donors and Volunteers.* Philanthropic Services for Institutions, 1991.

Purcell, Philip, M. "Eternal Gratitude—Show Donors You Value Their Planned Gifts with Continuous Recognition and Stewardship Efforts," CURRENTS 25, no. 3 (March 1999): 34-38.

Ruda, Tammie L. "Up Where They Belong—Here's How to Create Prestigious Clubs That Meet Your Goals," CURRENTS 25, no. 1 (January 1999): 40-46.

Scott, Michael P. "Building Strong Relationships: Developing Good Relationships is Your Key to Fund-Raising Success. Make Contacts in Person, Don't Forget to Follow Up—And Be Sure to Focus to Keeping Your Current Donors Happy," *Advancing Philanthropy* 4, no.1 (Spring 1996): 47-48.

"Screen Saver Used to Thank Donors," *Chronicle of Philanthropy* 7, no.22 (September 7, 1995): 46.

Seymour, Harold J. *Designs for Fund-Raising: Principles, Patterns, Techniques.* Rockville, MD: Fund Raising Institute, 1988.

Shaw, Sondra C. and Martha A. Taylor. *Reinventing Fundraising.* San Francisco, CA: Jossey-Bass Publishers, 1995.

Struck, Richard C. "Confirming the Major Gift: It's Essential to Discuss and Document Gift Arrangements to Tune Into and Clarify Donor Intent," *Fund Raising Management* 24, no.3 (May 1993): 37-

Taylor, John H. "The Morning After: You Finally Got That Big Gift. Here's What to Do Next," CURRENTS 22, no.10 (November/December 1996): 30-32.

Williams, M. Jane. *Big Gifts.* Rockville, MD: Fund Raising Institute, 1991.

Regardless of the model employed, it is essential to establish an effective system for prospect management and clearance.

Organization of the Development Program

Thomas F. Kelly
Vice President for External Affairs and Professor of Management
Binghamton University, State University of New York

Like a finely prepared orchestra, an effectively-functioning development program can be a work of art. Just as every note of a symphony is carefully planned and organized, development officers perform various tasks in cooperation with each other; their goal is to build relationships with prospective donors for the purpose of transferring wealth to the university. Gifts from donors may support buildings, programs, endowments, faculty, or students, but the end result is to facilitate learning and send forth educated minds into the world. It is a worthwhile purpose, and one that, if done right, can be very rewarding for the donor, the beneficiaries, and the development officers who orchestrate the process.

THE FOUR KEY PROCESSES

A development program is comprised of four key processes:
1) Prospect identification
2) Engagement
3) Solicitation
4) Stewardship

Prospect Identification

Prospect identification is the way in which a development program systematically selects and prioritizes individuals or organizations (i.e., foundations and corporations) on which it will focus strategic attention. This process has become extremely sophisticated in recent years with the development of specialized software programs and systems specifically designed for development and alumni offices. Given the level of available technology, the profession of prospect researcher has begun to grow and many institutions seek individuals with database management skills. However, there is no substitute for development officers, particularly senior development officers, to continue the old-fashioned process of "scoping the environment" through involvement in campus and community events, and by actively listening when conversing with alumni and friends to learn about prospective leads.

Engagement

Engagement describes the way development officers communicate with and seek the involvement of high-priority prospects. Strategic communication should lead to personal interaction with the donor and to that donor becoming involved in the life of the institution. This involvement might include attendance at special events and, perhaps later, appointment to advisory committees, boards, or other similar groups. The aim of engagement is to build solid relationships between the donor prospect and key individuals at the institution.

Solicitation

Solicitation means asking for the gift. It is this process that sets development officers apart from others in the institution who also work at developing relationships on behalf of the college or university. The pinnacle of the development program is when a development officer directly asks for support or arranges for a senior official or volunteer to do so. This is the *raison d'etre* of the development process. Solicitation takes place through direct mail appeals, annual phonathons, or face-to-face interaction, and includes asking for an annual gift, a major gift, or a planned gift.

Stewardship

Stewardship incorporates the acts of receiving and recording the gift, expressing appreciation, and ensuring that the gift is spent for its intended purpose. As part of expressing appreciation for a gift, stewardship often includes holding a public recognition event, providing the donor has not requested anonymity. The act of stewardship engenders trust on the part of donors and creates a situation for them to be acknowledged, engaged, and solicited for additional support.

ORGANIZATION OF THE DEVELOPMENT OFFICE

Managing each of these four processes requires placing development professionals into specific jobs and placing those job titles into organizational charts. Development charts are as idiosyncratic to an institution as are the people who hold the positions in various development offices. Often an office's organizational chart is structured based on the talents and abilities held by the specific persons in the development office. The chart reflects the size of the institution and the level of maturity of the development program itself.

For example, at small colleges with fewer development professionals, each person is often assigned several responsibilities. In such offices, it is common to find a chief development officer who also handles major giving. This individual generally has an assistant development officer to manage the annual giving program and another officer to handle relationship building and special events. The support staff of this development office provides both secretarial and advancement services. One example of a small development operation would have the directors of annual giving, advancement services, alumni relations, and special events reporting to the vice president for (or director of) development. In addition, the advancement services and alumni relations offices would work closely with one another. See Figure 10-1.

In a medium-sized development operation, a chief development officer might have four to six officers reporting to him or her. As employees assume more responsibility and duties, we now see "lean" organizational charts with larger numbers of individuals reporting to one manager. This model can work, providing the chief development officer has a delegating style of leadership and appoints individuals who display a high level of maturity, that is, both the ability and the willingness to fulfill responsibilities. Figure 10-2 is provided as an example of one typical organizational chart for a medium-sized operation, but there are many variations on this theme.

In a large development office, the officers who

● ● ●

Advantages of [a decentralized structure] include independence, motivation, and responsibility— tied to the deans— from development officers who report to them.

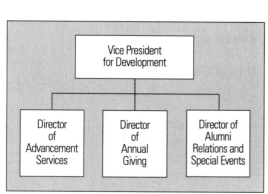

Figure 10-1. Sample Organizational Chart for a Small Operation

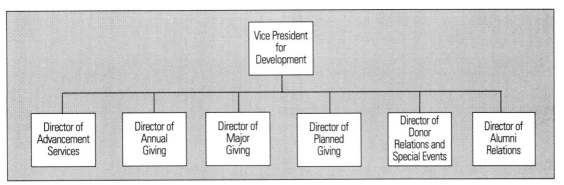

Figure 10-2. Sample Organizational Chart for a Medium-Sized Operation

report to the chief advancement officer will have more narrowly-defined responsibilities. For example, the staff who perform the following duties may all report to the head of advancement services: receiving gifts and recording them, database management, financial management and analysis of resources, and prospect identification and research. There is some debate concerning the reporting line for prospect research. Some argue that the line should lead to advancement services due to its heavy orientation toward systems and database management. Others believe that prospect research should report to a major gift officer in order to have a full appreciation of a development officer's needs. Additional administrators who report to the advancement services coordinator include the director of special events and possibly an associate vice president for annual giving. The latter may have individuals reporting to her who include, for example, the director of the alumni fund, the director of the parents fund, the director of the community campaign, and the director of phonathons.

The associate vice president for major giving often manages development officers who are assigned to serve units of the university (i.e, schools, colleges, athletics programs). This associate vice president may also have individuals reporting to him that include, for example, a planned giving officer and a director of corporate and foundation giving. An organization chart reflective of this type of operation is provided in Figure 10-3. In this example, we show an institutional advancement vice president, who is responsible for development, alumni relations, and public relations. Not all vice presidents have this entire portfolio.

Centralization/Decentralization

The mention of unit-based development officers leads to the issue of whether or not the development operation at a university should be organized centrally. There are three possible configurations:

1) *Centralized.* The term "centralized" relates to the notion that all development officers ultimately report to the chief advancement officer. Under this structure, for example at a university, the central office staff would conduct an annual alumni campaign on behalf of each of the various schools and colleges. A charge for this service might be levied to the school and typically deducted from funds raised for that particular unit. Furthermore, a major gift officer in a centrally organized operation would be assigned to serve a particular school. In such a system, the chief advancement officer retains total control and responsibility for fund raising and simply provides services to the various deans or directors of units. The focus in such a structure is primarily on the overall needs and strengths of the university. One disadvantage of this system is that the development officers may not identify fully with their assigned unit and may not have an understanding of the substance and nuances of the unit's core activities. The structure also creates the concept of serving two masters, as the development officer is required to report to the central office and serve a dean or a unit director.

2) *Decentralized.* The converse of this model is the "decentralized" development program. In this structure, each major unit directly hires development officers. For example, the dean of arts

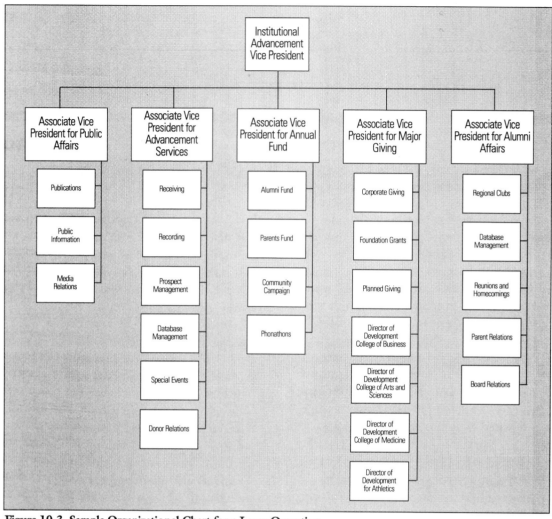

Figure 10-3. Sample Organizational Chart for a Large Operation

and sciences will have her own director of the annual fund and a director of major giving. Advantages of this structure include independence, motivation, and responsibility—tied to the deans—from development officers who report to them. Disadvantages of this system include a heightened level of competition for prospects among the units, a lack of coordination that can create embarrassment for the university, less understanding of the university's overall goals and mission, and the temptation to assign non-development duties to the development officer.

3) *Coordinated decentralized.* In a "coordinated decentralized" system, annual fund raising is conducted for the major units of the university

through a centralized office. However, major gifts officers, who report to the chief advancement officer or his or her associate, and who have all or most of their salary paid through the CAO, work on a daily basis with the dean or director of a unit. The development officer has a solid line to the chief advancement officer or her designee, and has a dashed line to the dean or director of the unit that he serves. The advantages of this system include identification with the unit, coordination with the central development office, and a heightened level of understanding of both the university and the unit. Disadvantages include the notion that the development officer is serving two masters, the temptation for the dean to assign non-development duties to the development officer, and competition among the various units for the same university prospects.

Margarete Hall, in *The Dean's Role in Fund Raising*, discusses the advantages and disadvantages of the three models in greater detail and reports on the results of a study she conducted.

Regardless of the model employed, it is essential to establish an effective system for prospect management and clearance. For example, a senior officer needs to prepare and implement carefully-written policies that determine how decisions are made to assign prospects to particular units (i.e., the business school, the athletics department) or to particular individuals (i.e., the president, the chair of the board). This is necessary to avoid the embarrassment of unplanned, duplicate solicitation. The prospect management system creates a productive tracking process to ensure that effective cultivation and solicitation occurs in a timely manner.

Institutionally Related Foundations

A discussion of development program structures would not be complete without mentioning independent foundations such as those found at most public institutions and at some private institutions. Public institutions often create a separately incorporated, nonprofit organization, recognized by the Internal Revenue Service as a bona fide 501 (c) (3) organization. Such a foundation has its own self-perpetuating board of directors. The foundation exists to receive gifts on behalf of the university and to channel or invest them according to the purpose intended by the donor. The chief advancement officer of the institution is sometimes designated as the president or the executive director of the foundation, and reports to its board of trustees as well as to the president of the university or college.

Advantages of this model include:
1) The foundation can serve as a buffer for the development program from both internal and external forces.
2) By having the foundation own and manage the endowment, funds are legally separated from the hand of any state agency that controls and/or audits the university.

3) Trustees of the foundation are solely focused on fund raising and management of the endowment.
4) For those donors concerned that their gift may end up in a state agency or may reduce state support for their alma mater, the foundation provides independence from the state.

Disadvantages of having an independent foundation include:
1) The trustees or directors of the foundation do not set institutional policy and, therefore, sometimes feel removed from the operation of the university.
2) The trustees or directors of the foundation can also exert independence and take issue with the way in which a president wants to allocate gifts and earned income.
3) The creation of a foundation board adds another governance group to be managed and motivated by the president and the chief advancement officer.

In this chapter, I have identified some of the common organizational and structural patterns for organizing a development program. However, for any one of the structures to work, the chief advancement officer needs to develop his or her leadership and communication skills to a high level. There is no substitute for a leader who can inspire those within any organizational structure to work hard, to grow as individuals and professionals, and to perform beyond expectations for the institution.

REFERENCES AND FURTHER READINGS

Bass, Bernard and Ralph M. Stogdill. *Bass & Stogdill's Handbook of Leadership*. 3rd ed. New York, NY: Free Press, 1990.

Hall, Margarete Rooney. *The Dean's Role in Fund Raising*. Baltimore, MD: Johns Hopkins Press, 1993.

Estey, Gretta P. and Steve Wilkerson. "Harmonious Arrangements: Your Institution's Character May Set the Tone for a Centralized Ensemble—Or a Decentralized Collection of Soloists," CURRENTS 20, no. 6 (June 1994): 22-26.

Phair, Judith and Roland King. *Sample File: Organizational Charts and Job Descriptions for the Advancement Office*. Washington, DC: Council for Advancement and Support of Education, 1998.

Organization
of the
Development
Program

Phelan, Joseph F., ed. *College and University Foundations: Serving America's Public Higher Education.* Washington, DC: Association of Governing Boards of Universities and Colleges, 1997.

Ryan, Ellen. "Too Many Hooks: Don't Spoil Your Chances with Donors by Allowing Uncoordinated Solicitations. Here, Some Ideas on Prospect Management in Any Kind of Development System," CURRENTS 20, no. 6 (June 1994): 34-39.

Sabo, Sandra R. "A Fertile Climate: Essential Elements for Raising the Green," CURRENTS 20, no. 6 (June 1994): 31.

Sabo, Sandra R. "Hybrids in Bloom: Taking One Cutting from the Centralized Model and Another from the Decentralized Has Blossomed into Fund-Raising Success for Some Institutions," CURRENTS 20, no. 6 (June 1994): 28-33.

Worth, Michael J. ed. *Educational Fund Raising: Principles and Practice.* Phoenix, AZ: ACE/Oryx Press, 1993.

The best fund raisers are confident, active self-starters with healthy egos that never get in the way of relationships with co-workers, donors, or others with whom they interact.

Selecting Staff and Managing for Results

Richard B. Boardman
Executive Director of the Harvard College Fund
Harvard University

A successful development operation reflects good hiring decisions. Your office's ability to raise money depends largely on the competencies of your employees. So start with this question: What skills and characteristics must my fund-raising staff have?

STUDY RESULTS

In 1985, Harvard asked 25 professional fund raisers to rank the importance of 70 competencies commonly associated with development work. Ten skills were rated as essential, and in contrast, 10 skills came out on the bottom.

Ten MOST Important Competencies for Successful Development Officers

1. Being committed to the organization and its mission
2. Developing teamwork and cooperation
3. Being a good listener and understanding people well
4. Following up on assignments
5. Communicating effectively
6. Thinking logically
7. Writing clearly

8. Conducting meetings and interviews efficiently
9. Making good first impressions
10. Making concise presentations

Ten LEAST Important Competencies for Successful Development Officers

1. Adjusting to priorities of supervisor
2. Achieving results within budget
3. Improving work procedures and systems
4. Helping supervisor gain support for his or her plans
5. Dealing with difficult personalities
6. Seeking new learning experiences on the job
7. Initiating changes to make work more satisfying
8. Communicating with other people on behalf of his or her supervisor
9. Being aware of and adept at organizational policies
10. Working on task force groups

The 10 most important qualities provide us with a good beginning and should offer no surprises. Those deemed "least important," however, suggest that fund raisers are a rather independent lot!

Do effective fund raisers disregard work procedures, shun difficult people, go over budget, and ignore organizational policies? Probably not.

However, today's development officers are more directly involved in making solicitations than ever before. Given this reality, individuals who rate poorly in the "least important skills" categories may nonetheless be superb fund raisers.

In 1988, Daniel B. Hogan of The Apollo Group, with Richard L. Dowell of Management Consulting Services, conducted a study for the Harvard Development Office. One hundred and eleven senior development officers from Stanford, MIT, and the Ivy League schools were asked to rate "the best/most effective frontline senior development officer" they have ever known against "the average/typical development officer." The evaluators were given a defined list of 25 competencies needed by effective fund raisers and were asked to prioritize those competencies. (They also ranked the current and future importance of each.) Study results are as follows.

Top 10 "Differentiating" Competencies: Most Effective vs. Typical Fund Raisers

1. Proactivity
2. Integrity
3. Commitment to and knowledge of the institution
4. Good judgment and intuition
5. Knowledge of constituency
6. Fund-raising expertise
7. Oral communications
8. Positive, optimistic, can-do attitude
9. Empathy/listening
10. Strategic thinking

Might development officers differ in their perspectives from one college to the next? Do major gift, annual giving, and planned giving officers have different opinions about skills effective fund raisers need? The answers provided by this study were amazingly consistent, regardless of the respondent's gender, function (major gifts, annual giving, or planned giving), years of experience in the field, or institution.

In short, the results suggest that as development has matured as a profession, a consistent set of values has emerged. There is a feeling that individuals of high integrity who are knowledgeable, active,

and committed to their institution will enjoy successful careers as fund raisers. Hire them with these thoughts in mind and manage them accordingly.

MAKING THE HIRING DECISION

The next time you hire a development officer, consider rating each candidate against the list of qualities that you believe effective fund raisers must have. Immediately after conducting each interview, complete an interview report (see Table 11-1, "Interview Report" at the end of this chapter) that will help you evaluate candidates consistently. Remember that the most successful candidates will demonstrate a sincere commitment to the institution they serve. The best are confident, active self-starters with healthy egos that never get in the way of relationships with co-workers, donors, or others with whom they interact. They enjoy building teams and laugh with ease. As a hiring manager, you should seek individuals who will initiate action and ask prospects for specific support face-to-face, all with a passion for what your school or college is about. The ideal staff member will express affection for alumni and friends while demonstrating good judgment and maturity. Look for these essential characteristics whenever you hire a new development officer.

SETTING PERFORMANCE STANDARDS

Guided by sound intuition and an understanding of the skills required for success, you can hire the right people. But how do you measure their success once they are on the job? The key here is to hold regularly scheduled individual meetings to set goals and appraise progress. A formal, written annual performance evaluation is also essential. (See Table 11-2, "Performance Assessment" at the end of this chapter.)

Keep handy the list of top qualities for effective fund raisers. Use it to help you set goals for your staff and to evaluate their performance and growth over time. Officers relatively new to the profession should be evaluated on their use of basic tools and their progress in honing the essential skills. More experienced fund raisers should have mastered those attributes; their evaluations should focus on evidence of leadership and overall fund-raising effectiveness.

Treat goal setting and performance evaluation meetings with flexibility and warmth, and conduct them in a relaxed atmosphere. Anyone gravitating to this business wants to do well. Your staff members' questions are likely to include: How can I do better? How can I grow? In what ways can you help me improve my contribution to the team? As a supervisor, your job is to support strengths and provide perspective in whatever performance areas need work.

APPLYING COMPETENCIES ON THE INSIDE

Your most successful fund raisers actively build internal relationships, use strategic thinking to prepare budgets and plans, and listen carefully to their president. Your most important prospect is not your biggest past donor. Rather it is your president and your chief financial officer. Why? Because they approve your budget and you recognize that, if given additional budget support, your return on investment will increase. Therefore, maintain strong, close relationships with anyone who has a say in your budget request. Provide these individuals with easy-to-understand reports regarding gifts, pledges, and return on investment.

Make sure that reports issued by the development office reconcile with those produced by your institution's financial office. Credibility is essential. Financial officers frequently fail to see the long-term benefits of development because they seek quick results within 12-month intervals. As development managers, we understand that gift decisions may take years to fall into place and may involve planned gifts, for example. Educating your institutional leadership about the long-term nature of successful fund-raising programs must be an ongoing priority.

Institutions differ in their approach to reporting results. To create your own approach, begin with those already in use and consult with colleagues at other institutions that are similar to your own. However you decide to go forward, consider incorporating the following ideas:

- *Report real money.* Always start with cash: report how much you raised in actual dollars. Show exactly where the money came from: alumni, alumnae, parents, friends, corporations, foundations, fund-raising events, or auctions.

Document where the gifts will be felt: unrestricted annual support, buildings, endowment, special programs, etc. Highlight what was raised against the year's or the campaign's specific goals and note what was collected in dollars for areas and programs falling outside those objectives. However, be careful about how you handle the latter. For example, gifts for a new program or initiative seldom cover the entire expense, so your president may actually have to divert unrestricted money to pay the balance or you may have to direct donors to designate gifts to low priority areas.

- *Maintain baseline figures.* Be careful about making major changes in your accounting process or crediting guidelines. While enhancing the quality and perspectives of your reports annually is important, it is dangerous to drop entirely any previously established formats or methodology. Since you are conveying the long-term impact of development, reporting individual and institutional giving histories over time in a consistent manner is critical. Your next president will appreciate your attention to detail and documentation.

- *Track donor activity.* Beyond gifts and pledges, it always helps to maintain records of prospect activity and attendance. Commonly, visits by major gift and other officers are reported monthly or quarterly. The same should be done for visits made by presidents or headmasters to ensure that their personal investment in development is balanced and does not just mean showing up at events.

- *Use the gift scale as a management tool.* A gift scale projects the number and size of gifts or pledges needed to meet a fund-raising goal. Construct gift scales based on your institution's giving history or from the results of previous campaigns. Experienced fund-raising managers can share with you the well-known rules and formulas for gift-scale development. One cautionary note: different formulas exist for various kinds of drives. Annual giving campaigns, for example, depend less on large gifts. On the other hand, capital campaigns with a narrow focus may depend more on a few very large gifts. In capital giving, years ago it could have been said that 20 percent of the donors would provide 80 percent of any campaign's total. Today, you more commonly hear that 10 percent of the donors will provide 90 percent or more of the total. The reason for this trend is the increasing importance (and size) of major gifts, and the trend itself most likely reflects the distribution of liquid assets (and wealth) among households. The top-heavy distribution of gift scales is often one of the first things that newcomers to the fund-raising profession learn— and usually with some surprise. So the rules and formulas may vary depending on many factors.

Good fund raisers are independent thinkers who believe that a hard day on the road is better than a good day in the office. Without being oppressive, give discipline to your hiring guidelines, carry out regular performance appraisals, and measure your success. Campaign with an appreciation for entrepreneurship and attention to detail, and good results will follow.

REFERENCES AND FURTHER READINGS

Henderson, Nancy. "Motivating Your Development Staff: From Praise to Pay to Parking Perks—Build a Structure to Keep Fund Raisers Peppy and Productive," CURRENTS 22, no. 2 (February 1996): 31-34.

Kaplan, Gary. "Opportunities Were Never Better for Fund Raisers—But Are They Qualified? The Job Specifications for Development Management are Basically the Same as Those Used to Fill a Top-Level Position in Corporate America: Diversity, Creativity and a Strong Bottom-Line Orientation," *Fund Raising Management* 26, no. 7 (September 1995): 20-22.

Jerold Panas, *Born to Raise: What Makes a Great Fundraiser: What Makes a Fundraiser Great*. Chicago, IL: Bonus Books, Inc., 1988.

Michael J. Worth, ed. *Educational Fund Raising: Principles and Practice*. Phoenix, AZ: ACE/Oryx Press, 1993.

TABLE 11-1 INTERVIEW REPORT

Personal & Confidential

Interview Report

Candidate _____ Interviewer _____ Date _____

(please print)   (please print)

Competencies Evaluation

Knowledge and Experience	low high	Comments
• Fundraising	1 2 3 4 5 N/A	_____
• Institutional knowledge	1 2 3 4 5 N/A	_____
• Relationship building	1 2 3 4 5 N/A	_____
• Management	1 2 3 4 5 N/A	_____

Skills
- Speaking — 1 2 3 4 5 N/A
- Writing — 1 2 3 4 5 N/A
- Listening — 1 2 3 4 5 N/A
- Planning and organizing — 1 2 3 4 5 N/A
- Strategic thinking — 1 2 3 4 5 N/A
- Attention to detail — 1 2 3 4 5 N/A

Personal Attributes
- Integrity — 1 2 3 4 5 N/A
- Initiative — 1 2 3 4 5 N/A
- Maturity/judgment — 1 2 3 4 5 N/A
- Sensitivity/empathy — 1 2 3 4 5 N/A
- Flexibility/tolerance — 1 2 3 4 5 N/A
- Confidence — 1 2 3 4 5 N/A
- Humor — 1 2 3 4 5 N/A

General Evaluation
- Will relate to office and institution — 1 2 3 4 5 N/A
- Proactive/goal-oriented — 1 2 3 4 5 N/A
- Positive attitude — 1 2 3 4 5 N/A
- Will work well with alumni — 1 2 3 4 5 N/A
- Capacity for independence — 1 2 3 4 5 N/A

General comments/follow-up recommendations

_____

_____

_____

_____

Conclusion

- Position match
  Division: ☐ Major gifts ☐ Planned giving ☐ Special gifts ☐ Annual giving ☐ Administration
  Level: ☐ Senior officer or/manager ☐ Officer ☐ Associate ☐ Assistant
- Recommendation
  ☐ Refer ☐ Review ☐ Possible finalist ☐ Definite finalist

TABLE 11-2 PERFORMANCE ASSESSMENT

Personal & Confidential

Performance Assessment

Name   Supervisor   Date

Use specific examples wherever possible. Avoid generalizations.

Evaluate Competencies

1.	**Personality Traits**	**integrity • initiative • positive attitude** competitiveness • modesty • sincerity • flexibility • confidence • humor
2.	**People Skills**	**ability to listen** sensitivity • desire for collaboration and teamwork • makes good first impression
3.	**Cognitive Capability**	**judgment • intuition • strategic thinking** intellectual curiosity • productivity • capacity for independence
4.	**Professional Competencies**	**oral communication • fundraising expertise** written communication • attention to detail and documentation • planning • organizing • industry and market awareness • specific expertise
5.	**Institutional Commitment**	**commitment to institution • institutional knowledge** connection with culture • professional standards • knowledge of constituency
6.	**Personal and Management Skills**	training and mentoring others • generates ideas • gains consensus • delegates tasks • supervises progress
7.	**General Effectiveness**	**meets or exceeds objectives** • establishes challenging goals

Performance Review (attach or use reverse side)

8. **Record Strengths**

9. **Set Goals**

10. **General Comments**

Note: Research suggests high performance in competencies indicated in bold face predicts long-term success in development.

In general, institutionally related foundations have become the corollary in public institutions for the large fund-raising staffs and investment officers and investment board committees of private institutions.

A Primer on Institutionally Related Foundations

Eric B. Wentworth
Former Director of the National Center for Institutionally Related Foundations
CASE

Institutionally related foundations are playing increasingly important roles in securing and managing private resources for public colleges and universities throughout the United States. The roles these foundations perform, and how they perform them, are as varied as the institutions themselves—which range from flagship universities to community colleges. Moreover, foundations' roles today are constantly evolving as they move from the wings toward center stage to support public institutions' surging quest for the resources to support excellence.

WHAT ARE INSTITUTIONALLY RELATED FOUNDATIONS?

Institutionally related foundations are separately incorporated 501(c)(3) organizations, with separate boards of directors, whose purposes are to raise, invest, and steward funds and other assets for the benefit of public institutions. They are officially designated as public charities and have been created to support a wide variety of institutions, including hospitals, public schools, public museums, and public libraries as well as public colleges and universities throughout the United States.

While most prominent public universities have foundations, there are notable exceptions, including the University of Michigan and Penn State University. There are more than 1,000 institutionally related foundations in higher education, and new ones continue to be established. The oldest institutionally related foundation in American higher education, the Kansas University Endowment Association, was established in 1891.

These foundations were initially created to serve as custodians of a public institution's private assets—such as a parcel of real estate or endowments for scholarships or professorships—or to administer government or corporate research grants. Historically, many of the smaller four-year and two-year public institutions did little, if any, organized fund raising. Especially in recent years, public institutions have been under severe pressure to expand the sources of fiscal support, and fund raising has provided part of the answer.

Today, especially among the large publicly supported research universities, institutionally related foundations direct some of the most sophisticated fund-raising programs in the nation, and serve as investment managers for billions of dollars of total assets. In general, they have become the corollary in public institutions for the large fund-raising staffs and investment officers and investment board committees of private institutions.

Even though they are called 'foundations,' institutionally related foundations bear little resemblance to large grant-making foundations, such as Ford or Kresge, or to smaller family-run foundations. They are often described as 'private' to distinguish them from the public institutions they support, but in the eyes of the Internal Revenue Service, they are a form of public charity.

While many foundations serve the dual purpose of conducting all fund-raising activity for the institutions and providing investment management of their assets, there are many specialized foundations. For example, 'pass through' foundations receive gifts but don't retain them. There are also foundations created to meet special programs such as athletics, to help support specific professional schools, or to generate revenues from leases, or royalty payments from licensees of patents from faculty research. Some foundations are engaged in entrepreneurial activity on behalf of the institution, which may include non-tax-exempt initiatives.

Structure and Leadership

While institutionally related foundations may share generic language in their articles of incorporation and by-laws, they come in a wide variety of structures, sizes, and relationships with their institutions. The largest among them will be led by a president and chief executive officer who reports to the foundation's self-perpetuating board of directors, which typically includes a number of very wealthy and influential individuals. Examples of this model include the foundations serving most, but not all, of the large public state institutions.

Other foundations may be responsible only for soliciting and administering planned gifts, or non-cash gifts or other assets, while the institution's own advancement staff runs the annual fund and solicits major outright cash commitments. Still others have far less autonomy and a dual reporting relationship to the foundation's board and chief campus executive. There are still numerous cases where the sponsoring institution's staff conducts the fund raising and the foundation serves as steward and asset manager.

Benefits of Institutionally Related Foundations

Institutionally related foundations provide the following principal benefits:

1) *Preservation of privacy for their donors and for their investment and investment-related activity.* Foundations' exemption from state freedom of information and 'open meetings' laws and regulations applying to state agencies, means that donors who prefer to contribute anonymously are assured that their privacy will be preserved. Donors and their personal advisers who share sensitive information with fund raisers about their personal wealth or estate plans in contemplation of making major gifts can be certain that all such information will be zealously guarded from outside scrutiny.

   The ability to share and discuss sensitive information in confidence is essential for other foundation activities as well, among them: determining investment strategies for endowments, selecting and evaluating investment managers and their performance, acquiring or developing real estate, and doing business with for-profit entities.

2) *Stability and continuity during times of political and fiscal uncertainty.* Autonomous and apolitical, foundations can provide long-term, stable stewardship for the institution's private assets and protect them from diversion, expropriation or other unwanted intrusion by the state. This protection is also a powerful incentive for major donors to support the institution with large assets in perpetuity. They are assured that those gifts will be devoted in perpetuity to the intended purpose for which they were given regardless of any demands or pressures that may arise for their expedient diversion to other needs.

3) *Flexibility in the investment and use of assets.* Provided they follow prudent investment principles, independent foundations can usually choose investment strategies and invest in classes of securities otherwise unavailable to state agencies. This flexibility can bolster donors' confidence in the quality of investment management of their endowment gifts. Moreover, a foundation can disburse unrestricted funds to the institution for purposes that public funds

will not underwrite, such as funds for travel and entertainment by the president and senior academic officers of the institution.

4) *Flexibility in procurement, and in acceptance of new assets, especially real estate.* Foundations can usually purchase real estate, or accept real estate gifts, far more quickly than the college or university, as a state agency, can. Examples include the purchase of buildings, laboratories, and land that, if subjected to normal state procurement policies, could not have been purchased on the open market for the benefit of the institution unless purchased by the foundation on its behalf.

5) *Involvement of volunteers.* The independent, self-perpetuating board of directors of a foundation provides an opportunity to recognize and empower volunteers and donors to support the institution through their services and gifts. Since most public institutions' governing boards comprise politically appointed or elected members, they often have little desire or capacity to raise and/or invest money. Furthermore, they are usually limited to the residents of a particular local or state jurisdiction. Foundations are free to recruit their members from anywhere. As a result, they can enjoy a level of member commitment and sophistication comparable to any private institution's board, and often greater than that of the public institution's board.

Autonomy of an Institutionally Related Foundation

Because of the wide variety of functions carried out by foundations, the degree of autonomy can vary from one institution to another. However, the following criteria are useful indicators of the truly autonomous foundation:

1. A separate nonprofit corporation with a separate self-perpetuating board that files its own informational tax returns (990s) and other required reports.

2. While its board may include representatives of the institution, its membership has sufficient numbers to ensure the exercise of independent judgment as warranted.

3. Has its own bank accounts, adopts and controls its own operating budget, and generates from fees and other sources the necessary funds to cover its expenses; maintains foundation funds separately from institutional funds and any state funds.

4. Hires and fires its own staff and has clear hiring and firing policies in place governing any of its employees jointly supported by the institution and the foundation.

5. Has independent auditors and access to independent legal counsel.

6. Has its own physical facilities, equipment, and supplies—or, to the extent it uses those of the institution, it reimburses the institution for their use.

7. Maintains an arms-length relationship with the institution, which is documented in an agreement spelling out the respective expectations and responsibilities of both parties.

THE RELATIONSHIP BETWEEN A FOUNDATION AND THE INSTITUTION

Typically, the institution authorizes the foundation to operate in its name to raise funds and/or manage endowments and other assets for its benefit, and the foundation agrees to perform those services in accord with the institution's policies and priorities in a written agreement.

The nature of this agreement will be dictated by many factors, among them history, maturity, size, the political and economic environment of the jurisdiction or state, the interests of various stakeholders, the fiscal realities of the situation, and applicable laws and regulations. The ideal agreement reinforces trust and a cooperative relationship between partners working to advance the mission of the institution and the interest of those it serves. It is comprehensive in character, detailing all forms of in-kind support that the foundation receives from the institution and specifying similarly the service outcomes provided by the foundation. Accountability and effective management are absolutely essential.

Compliance with both the letter and the spirit of policies established by the institution, of principles of fiduciary behavior, of financial reporting

● ● ●
There appears no limit to the future potential of these foundations other than the limitations of the institutions they serve.

standards, and of all jurisdictional state and federal regulations is the foundation of every strong foundation's relationship with its institutional partner.

FUTURE PROSPECTS FOR THE INSTITUTIONALLY RELATED FOUNDATION?

There appears no limit to the future potential of these foundations other than the limitations of the institutions they serve. They are increasingly asked to develop and implement longterm strategic plans for the responsibilities they undertake. They are irreplaceable partners in public higher education, the privatization of which appears to be a longterm phenomenon, and, internationally, is growing exponentially. If this trend continues, the institutionally related foundation of the future may dwarf in size, complexity, and sophistication any foundations we know today.

FURTHER READINGS

Hedgepeth, Royster C. *How Public Colleges and University Foundations Pay for Fund-Raising.* Washington, DC: AGB and CASE, 2000.

Orcutt, Amos E. "Foundations for Excellence—The Importance of Institutionally Related Foundations," CURRENTS 25, no. 3 (March 1999): 11-12

Szabo, Joan. "Funding the Foundation with Fees: Endowment Fees May Seem Like a Painless Way to Increase the Foundation Budget. But Implement Them Carefully to Prevent Major-Donor Headaches," CURRENTS 23, no. 8 (September 1997): 34.

While the settlement of my father's estate may be a matter of public record, is it really right—ethical—for my college to probe that information and use it to assess my giving potential?

Ethical Issues in Fund Raising

Gary A. Evans
Vice President, Development and College Relations
Lafayette College

Twenty to 30 years ago, the topic of ethics was rarely presented at fund-raising conferences. Any reference to ethics, in oral presentations or in the literature, usually occurred when describing the qualities of a good development officer—ambitious, thorough, articulate, organized, persuasive—oh yes, and ethical. Perhaps as the profession has grown, so has the interest in ethics. Operating norms and generally accepted conventions, often passed by word-of-mouth, begin to lose their influence in a profession that is expanding rapidly. New people challenge old ways. Standards dissipate. Eventually, professionals begin to talk about and write about issues that at one time had been commonly understood but now need discussion, clarification, and consensus. The ethics of fund raising is among those issues.

The pressure to raise money—more and more each year—can create practices and behaviors acceptable to some and questioned by others. Development officers may occasionally find humor in the funny-money accounting sometimes used in campaign reporting, but such distortion, and even fabrication, poses a variety of problems—including ethical problems—for the profession.

The example of prospect research clearly illustrates the need for ethical discussion in our evolving profession. In days past, a development officer knew a number of things about prospects. Little of what was known was written down. It was stored in the memory file. Development officers cultivated and solicited donors based on what they personally knew and what they inferred from that knowledge. The development officer's behavior could hardly be considered intrusive or unethical.

Today, we have access to court records on the settlement of estates and divorces, public records on property value, and resources in cyberspace providing considerable information, both financial and personal, on our donors. While the settlement of my father's estate may be a matter of public record, is it really right—ethical—for my college to probe that information and use it to assess my giving potential?

Keep it Legal, Keep it Reasonable

Although it is proper for development professionals to turn their attention to ethical issues, is it possible we have made the subject more complex than necessary, looking for evil where it does not exist? Some might say there are really only two standards for judging ethical behavior.

1) *Obey the law.* It is illegal, and therefore unethical, to give a person credit and a receipt for a gift not made. It is illegal to inflate the value of a gift in order to increase a donor's tax deduction. It is illegal to give gift credit for payment of a bill that is not a tax deductible contribution, such as tuition. Some might say that if we simply obey the law, ethical questions do not arise.

2) *Avoid excessive and egregious behavior.* Do not accord blatant favoritism for a gift received. Do not participate in matching gift fraud such as accepting corporate matching gifts for individual contributions that were given for purposes not approved under corporate policy (athletics, fraternities, etc.). Those who apply this guideline believe that if we avoid behaviors that any reasonable person would recognize as questionable, the likelihood of encountering ethical dilemmas is nearly eliminated. The simplest guide to ethical behavior is clear: keep it legal; keep it reasonable.

The Dilemmas Continue

Even with the admonition to do nothing illegal and to avoid practices that are clearly excessive, we still encounter ethical dilemmas. I doubt any officer would falsify the evaluation of a gift of stock or would backdate to December a receipt for a gift made in February. However, how would you deal with this: a donor consistently and generously sends a check to the annual fund on December 30; but this donor was hospitalized at year's end and did not send a check, which was dated December 30, until January 15. The check was not processed until after the institution had closed its books for the year. The donor is not asking for an inflated evaluation. The donor is not asking for a receipt for a gift not made. The donor is simply asking for a little consideration because she was ill at year's end and is now doing two weeks late what she always did in December.

"What is the problem?" she asks, "My local library will treat my gift to them as a year-end contribution." We all know that the envelope in which the check was mailed must be postmarked no later than December 31. In this case, it was not. Is it really so bad to give her credit for a year-end gift? Is anyone hurt in doing so? Can we actually break (a harsh word—try "bend") the law and still have

not done something unethical about which we should be embarrassed?

Although some thoughtful development officers might think otherwise, this is a time when I would hold the line. While it is unfortunate that the donor failed to make a gift before year's end and will miss the tax deduction she sought, I would explain to her that it is in her interest that we abide by IRS regulations. If, for some reason—even a reason unrelated to her charitable contributions—her income tax return were audited, she would not want to have to explain why she took a charitable deduction in a year when the contribution was not made. That discovery would open her to an audit of her tax returns from prior years. She certainly would not want that aggravation. Furthermore, she will simply have larger charitable contributions in the new year than she was able to take in the previous year.

What about influence? Without much debate, development officers would consider it unethical to accept a gift from a donor and promise, in return, the admission of a child. But suppose the donor is a trustee. He has recently chaired a fund-raising campaign and repeatedly uses his "influence" to obtain gifts from corporations with whom he does business, and from alumni and friends with whom he has leverage. Now he approaches the development office, and without promising any additional gifts, asks favorable admissions consideration for his neighbor's child whom he likes very much. Under normal selection standards, the young man is marginal. Offering him admission may not be in his best interest and it will certainly raise questions in the high school guidance office. And yet, the institution owes much to this trustee. The admissions office will go along if the development officer insists. Since we often ask our volunteers to use their influence to help secure gifts for the institution, is it unethical to use our influence to return a favor?

In this case, I believe one's judgment may be guided by the willingness of the admissions office to accept the applicant. Such willingness suggests that the applicant is deemed capable of doing satisfactory work at the college level, even though his credentials are not up to the usual standard for admission. I would explain to the trustee that the applicant is being accepted because he meets the minimum requirements, and that if the admissions office thought he was below those requirements, he would not be accepted even with the expressed interest from a trustee.

Guidelines for Decision Making

There are many reasons we face ethical choices. In some cases, such as issues of tax deductibility and influence, we are under pressure to please our donors. In other cases, we face ethical decisions because of institutional need. Is it unethical or just unfair to ask several donors to give $100,000 each to name rooms in a new library and then reduce the gift level to $50,000 for the last few donors because we need the money? In the *CASE Management Reporting Standards,* are there standards that an institution can choose not to follow without being considered unethical, and are there other standards that, if breached, throw doubt on the ethical posture of an institution?

It is not the purpose of this chapter to propose ethical solutions to these questions. However, perhaps I can propose guidelines to help professionals make the right decisions.

The Conventions of the Profession

When a development officer encounters what appears to be an ethical issue, it is always valuable to try to determine the conventions and standards that have been followed in the profession over the years. While a situation may raise questions not previously faced by a development officer, it is unlikely that the situation has never been encountered before by others. Serious people in the development profession want to encourage ethical behavior. Therefore, they are ready to help one another. Development officers should feel encouraged to call others whose opinions they respect to share their ethical dilemmas and seek advice. The very nature of an ethical dilemma means that the answer is not clear. Other development professionals may offer conflicting points of view. Nonetheless, input from colleagues can help a development officer decide how to proceed.

The Test of Full Disclosure

One convenient, though perhaps simplistic, test is to ask, "What would (fill in the blank) say?" When a development officer makes a decision with ethical implications, how would she defend that decision if it appeared on the front page of the newspaper?

U.S. News & World Report, in developing its college and university ratings, uses the percent of alumni giving as an indicator of alumni satisfaction with the education they received. The instructions are clear that the percentage is determined by dividing the number of donors by the total number of alumni. For some institutions, this is not fair. Many of their alumni may have received their degrees by attending on a part-time basis and are not likely to be donors. It may not even be cost-effective for the institution to solicit some alumni. Such an institution may believe it is fairer and more accurate to calculate the percentage by dividing the number of alumni donors by the number of alumni who were actually solicited. If an institution submitted this data, could it defend its decision if that decision were publicly known? Could "enlightened self-interest" be sufficient justification for departing from the directions when submitting data, or is that just a rationalization for trying to look good?

When promoting your institution appears to be in conflict with the integrity of a public process, you must make a choice—often an ethical choice. A development officer may find guidance in making a decision by considering what would be best for the institution if the decision were made with full public awareness.

Others find guidance in their ethical choices by asking, "Would I be happy to have my family know the decision I made?" While those who are closest to us are the most forgiving, they also want to believe the best about us. If a development officer faces an ethical dilemma and finally makes a decision, uncomfortable though it may be, he would hope that those closest to him would respect the decision and, more importantly, respect the individual for having made that decision. If the decision requires rationalization to appear to be justified, then perhaps the decision is wrong.

> **Amoral people face no ethical dilemmas because they raise no ethical questions. But even among moral people, there are different ethical sensitivities.**

The Personal Barometer

While it is useful to ask other professionals what they would do, or to wonder how the public or one's family would react, it is interesting to note that an ethical choice does not exist unless the individual development officer first raises the question, "Is this an ethical issue?" Amoral people face no ethical dilemmas because they raise no ethical questions. But even among moral people, there are different ethical sensitivities. Some development officers would find it painfully unethical to report campaign gifts that fall outside CASE's reporting standards. They would ponder long and hard and perhaps consult others about whether to report a pledge if the payment period extends two or three years beyond the recommended reporting period. Others would find no ethical issue at all in making a decision they believe best serves the donor and the institution. For them, the ethical question would never arise; therefore, there would be no ethical dilemma. Guidelines, standards, and conventions, while helpful, do not replace the personal ethical barometer each development officer brings to the job.

By raising ethical questions and by dealing with ethical matters in conferences and in literature, the development profession can help to sensitize individual practitioners. Ultimately, ethical choices begin and end with the individual. As we heighten our ethical sensitivity and raise the personal ethical barometer, we will make better decisions.

FURTHER READINGS

Anderson, Albert. *Ethics for Fundraisers*. Bloomington, IN: Indiana University Press, 1996.

CASE Advisory Committee Volunteers. *CASE Management Reporting Standards: Standards for Annual Giving and Campaigns in Educational Fund Raising.* Washington, DC: Council for Advancement and Support of Education, 1996.

O'Neill, Michael. "A Spare Literature: Fund Raisers Have Practiced and Violated Ethical Principles for Millennia. Yet Almost No Research Exists on the Ethics of This Key Profession. Here's a Review of What is Available and Suggestions for Further Scholarship," *Advancing Philanthropy* 5, no. 2 (Summer 1997): 26-30.

Pastin, Mark. "Bright Lines, Big Deals: Is It Wrong for Fund Raisers to 'Transport' Donors From One Job to Another? Or to Conveniently Forget a Donor's Wishes? Or to Accept a $100 Gift? What is the Big Deal, and What Isn't? A Plea for Fluorescent Ethical Lines," *Advancing Philanthropy* 5, no. 2 (Summer 1997): 21-25.

Ryan, Ellen. "You Made the Call: Readers' Responses to Five Ethical Dilemmas in Development," CURRENTS 22, no. 1 (January 1996): 46-50.

Szabo, Joan. "The Perils of Philanthropy: A Questionable Gift Can Undermine Your Entire Operation. Use Ethics Training to Help Your Staff Identify and Address Potential Problems Before They Occur," CURRENTS 24, no. 1 (January 1998): 40-44.

While campaign size and focus are of constant concern, and should be, institutions are increasingly aware that the focus of campaigns must be on the institution's purposes.

SECTION V
Educational
Fund Raising

14

Trends in Educational Fund Raising

Bruce R. McClintock
Chairman
Marts & Lundy, Inc.

The decade of the 1990s was marked by stark contrasts. The economy sustained remarkable levels of growth; the country witnessed an unprecedented accumulation of individual wealth; and philanthropic support for education increased at impressive rates.

Yet most educational institutions struggled mightily throughout the decade to adjust to a new set of realities in planning, financing, and marketing their educational programs and priorities. With few exceptions, educational institutions across the spectrum (both public and private) had to reduce costs, reallocate resources, and adapt to a changing market place.

Because of these contrasting trends, the dynamics of philanthropic support are undergoing significant transition. Most schools, colleges, and universities view charitable giving in a different context now than in past decades. Philanthropic support has become a much higher priority at publicly-supported colleges and universities as state appropriations have decreased. At private institutions, the fact that net tuition revenues are not keeping pace with educational costs translates into greater need for endowment and current operating gifts.

To understand what the future holds, Marts & Lundy reviewed philanthropic results at 275 educational institutions for each of the 10 years from 1988-1997 reported to the Council for Aid to Education (CAE). They represent three broad categories of educational institutions: independent schools; private liberal arts colleges; and both public and private research universities. The following statistical data have been supplied through the CAE's Voluntary Support of Education (VSE) Data Miner online service.

PHILANTHROPIC PATTERNS AND TRENDS

Between 1988 and 1997, total philanthropic support to the 275 institutions studied increased at an average annual rate of 16.3 percent. That was an extraordinary accomplishment, made even more remarkable by the modest increases in inflation experienced throughout the decade. In addition, philanthropic support increased at a faster pace than did educational costs at these institutions (which increased at a 13 percent annual growth rate). The net effect is that, by the mid-1990s, these educational institutions had come to view philanthropic support as an increasing source of revenue at a time when other key revenue streams were (and continue to be) less robust.

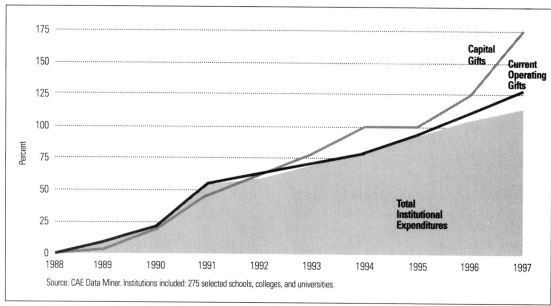

**Figure 14-1. Current Operating Gifts and Capital Gifts Compared to
Total Institutional Expenditures (Cumulative Growth Rate since 1988)**

As you read the following paragraphs, also see the graphic representations of these statistics in Figures 14-1 through 14-4, all prepared by Marts & Lundy, Inc.

Current Operating Support

The good news is that total current operating gift dollars kept pace with educational expenditures between 1988 and 1997, each having an annual growth rate in the 13 to 14 percent range. See Figure 14-1. The less good news is while unrestricted gifts (the top priority at most private institutions) grew by an average of 10.6 percent over the past decade, that rate was well below the increases in institutional expenditures. The net result is that unrestricted gifts were (and probably will continue to be) on a downward trend in terms of their impact on an institution's current operating budget.

Capital Gifts

Gifts for capital purposes increased at an average annual rate of nearly 20 percent over the decade. Sustained growth in the economy and the stock market were clearly the engines behind this unprecedented period in capital gift giving.

There was also a decided shift in the purposes for which donors designated their capital support. In 1988, endowment accounted for 66 percent of all capital gift dollars contributed; by 1997, the percentage had increased to 76 percent. Gift support for facilities and equipment, on the other hand, decreased from 34 percent in 1988 to 24 percent in 1997.

Individuals, corporations, and foundations are the primary sources of philanthropic support to educational institutions. From 1988 to 1991, the growth patterns for gifts from individuals and from institutions (corporations and foundations) were similar. Since 1994, the momentum has shifted to individual giving. See Figure 14-2.

Corporate and Foundation Support

Corporate and foundation gifts/grants have declined as a percentage of total gift dollars, especially since 1994. The impact has been greatest at independent schools and colleges, where the cumulative decrease during the decade was 30 percent at independent schools and 20 percent at liberal arts colleges. The least impact was at major research universities, down from 47 percent of total gift dollars in 1988 to 42 percent in 1997.

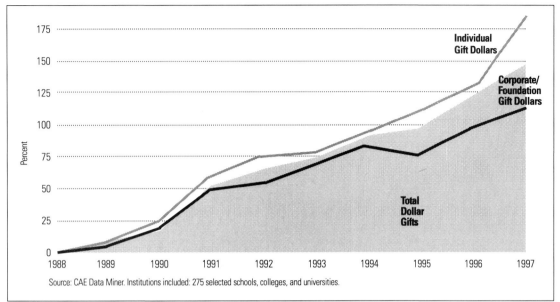

Figure 14-2. Individual and Corporate/Foundation Support Compared to
Total Gift Dollars (Cumulative Growth Rate since 1988)

Individual Gifts

Gifts from individuals grew at an average annual rate of 15.8 percent from 1988 to 1994. Between 1994 and 1997, the annual growth rate averaged a robust 29.3 percent. While it is unlikely that individual giving can sustain the extraordinary growth rate experienced during the most recent three-year period, the gap in growth rates between individual giving and institutional giving is likely to continue.

Planned giving has been a growth area in philanthropic support for the past several decades. Refer to Figure 14-3. Between 1988 and 1993, the average annual rate of growth was 16.6 percent. During the period 1993 to 1997, increases in planned gifts averaged an astonishing 40.5 percent increase annually. Most of the growth occurred in the area of deferred gifts (life income agreements). These gifts (counted at face value) grew by more than 550 percent over the decade. In 1988, deferred gifts accounted for 19 percent of total planned gift dollars; in 1997, they accounted for 44 percent.

The pyramid of giving has become steeper over the past decade at colleges and universities (complete data was not available for independent schools). As noted earlier, the growth in total gift dollars to the institutions we analyzed was, on average, 16.3 percent annually. The corresponding

growth in the total dollar value of the top three gifts to these institutions rose by 26.9 percent annually. The growth rate for individual gifts totaling $5,000 and above grew by 20.1 percent annually. See Figure 14-4.

ISSUES TO CONSIDER

The trends in educational fund raising that will influence future results cannot be measured only through quantifiable, statistical analysis. There are also qualitative issues that will have a profound impact on philanthropic support in the next decade.

Donor Attitudes and Expectations

As dramatic as some of the dollar trends have been, an equally important change revolves around the attitudes and expectations of donors. I have found that donors and prospective donors have increased the standards by which they measure the institutions they support.

Feasibility studies at Marts & Lundy suggest that constituents want to be reassured, often in specific ways, that their institution is living within its financial means; reallocating existing resources to fund new priorities; making tough choices; and targeting resources to address specific, measurable priorities.

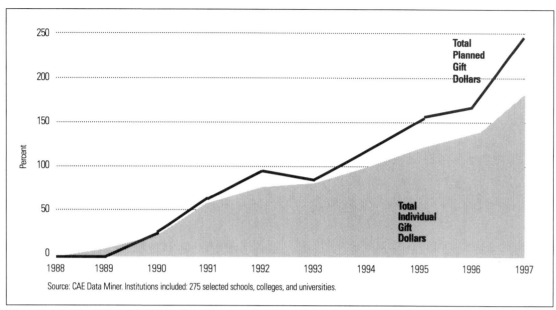

Figure 14-3. Total Planned Gift Dollars Compared to Total Individual Gift Dollars
(Cumulative Growth Rate since 1988)

Advancement professionals generally are sensitive to these changing donor expectations. If there is a particularly vulnerable part of the donor constituency, it is young alumni. They have not yet established a clear sense of their philanthropic priorities. I sense that younger alumni clearly place the burden of responsibility on the institution to make a compelling case for their involvement and their financial support.

Technology

Technology has helped to create an environment where we have instantaneous access to almost anything. The challenge technology poses is how we use (or abuse) it. Technology offers the opportunity to engage people in interactive relationships at any time that is convenient to all parties, and without the constraints of travel. In this way, technology can enhance communication. An institution can also use technology to communicate with constituents quickly and efficiently through e-mail, home pages, and teleconferencing.

There are some potential hazards associated with this new technology. First, the convenience of remote communications between an individual and his or her alma mater may lead to less emphasis on face-to-face meetings. Second, the ability to transfer information electronically, quickly, and cheaply may result in institutions overwhelming constituents with messages, surveys, requests, and other information.

Voluntarism

In the 1950s and 1960s, alumni generally had time to give to their alma mater, but not much in the way of monetary support. Today, overall philanthropic support has grown dramatically, but there is a serious decline in time volunteers can, and will, contribute. Too little is being done at educational institutions to address this changing situation. Volunteer roles, responsibilities, and expectations need to be revisited and redefined to meet the time constraints of busy volunteers.

For example, if volunteers and advancement officers work together as partners, the staff member can often relieve the volunteer of time-consuming tasks. Or perhaps the volunteer can be most effective in "opening the door" for a personal visit by an advancement officer (or someone else) with a prospective donor—rather than having to juggle schedules so that he or she can be present at the meeting. Or the volunteer can perhaps be most effective by conducting a telephone follow-up call to a prospective donor after a visit by a staff member.

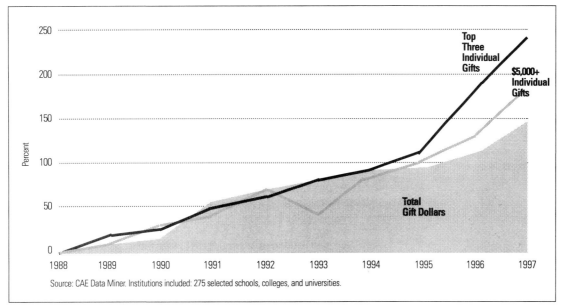

Figure 14-4. Total of Top Individual Gift Dollars Compared to Total Gift Dollars
(Cumulative Growth Rate since 1988)

Competition

There is more competition for philanthropic support today than there was 10 years ago. First, the sheer number of nonprofit institutions increased by 19 percent from 1987 to 1996. Second, as public funding for nonprofit organizations has steadily decreased during the past 15 years (especially for public colleges and universities), these institutions have increasingly turned their attention to private, philanthropic support as an alternative source of revenue. According to a recent article in *The American Benefactor*, community foundations are now the fastest growing segment of philanthropic support. And many younger philanthropists are finding it attractive to set up their own private foundations to control their giving themselves.

Increased competition translates into more choices for prospective donors; the bar has been raised for those seeking charitable gifts to articulate more clearly, and document more thoroughly, their case for private support.

At a time when most private institutions are placing top priority on unrestricted current operating gifts, donor giving patterns are moving in a different direction. Many donors have a specific maximum unrestricted gift in mind. For requests that exceed that level, these donors want to be able to specifically designate those gifts.

Donor-designated gifts for capital purposes have long been acknowledged as a key factor in successful campaigns. Because of the increasing desire of donors to give restricted gifts, most institutions will need to become more creative in translating current, budgeted educational commitments into opportunities for donor-designated annual fund gifts.

Alumni Participation

Overall alumni giving rates held up reasonably well during the 1990s—remaining virtually unchanged since 1988. For some institutions, however, participation rates rise and fall depending upon whether or not the institution is in a major, comprehensive campaign. Rates often fall during campaigns and increase after the campaign. Why? Campaigns tend to focus on the top end of the gift pyramid in order to succeed. The campaign events and promotional materials also highlight the impact that large, capital gifts have on an institution. The annual fund suffers by comparison—if not in dollars, then certainly in its perceived importance to the institution. Donors of more modest gifts may feel less valued by the institution and so may opt not to give.

What of the Future?

Here are some possible trends we see for the first decade of the 21st century:

■ *Rising Importance of Stewardship.* The extraordinary increases in gifts from individuals in the past 10 years in outright, deferred, and testamentary form places enormous pressure on institutions to properly steward those individuals, or be accused of institutional indifference. The sharp incline in the gift pyramid exacerbates this need; in their efforts to fully steward large donors, institutions may not properly steward the more modest donors. The result could be a growing loss of the large body of institutional supporters, and especially young alumni.

Technology has the capacity to improve or hinder an effective stewardship operation. In the absence of face-to-face contact, e-mail correspondence may strengthen institution-donor relationships, if skillfully employed. We must learn, however, how not to overuse technology, so as to overwhelm donors with information, or become too reliant on it. Technology can also provide information on donors that will help institutions more appropriately steward them.

■ *Fund-Raising Participation Rates Unchanged.* Because alumni participation rates have not changed materially in the past 20 years, the unresponsive 30 percent to 80 percent of alumni populations may not change regardless of new ways of communicating with them. So, participation rates will likely hold at current levels in the future. Similarly, technology will be employed to produce better stewardship, and hence today's pool of donors will not be diminished tomorrow.

■ *Decline in Voluntarism Levels Off.* Voluntarism in education has declined in the past 10 years as a direct result of changes in society. The major culprit has been the two wage-earner family. Competition among nonprofit institutions for volunteers and the increasing pace of modern life have also contributed to the decline. Technology could be an enormous asset in this struggle to regain the volunteer strength of the past. Creatively approached, staff can work with volunteers in much more efficient and effective ways. With an affirmative view of technology, I believe that the decline in voluntarism will plateau in the next 10 years, remaining no worse than it is today.

■ *More Campaigns, Better Targeted.* Comprehensive campaigns will survive every assault on them and the billion dollar programs will continue to increase in number and size. While campaign size and focus are of constant concern, and should be, institutions are increasingly aware that the focus of campaigns must be on the institution's purposes. A wider lens on campaigns will become more the rule than the exception. The public demand for educational accountability in the years ahead will help ensure that campaigns are conducted accordingly.

■ *Fund-Raising Focus Shifts.* Greater competition for philanthropic support and the changing expectations of institutional accountability are shifting the focus of fund raising from an institutionally based perspective to a donor-based perspective. This shift is likely to strengthen the relationships between the donor and the institution, and to lead to increased philanthropy.

FURTHER READINGS

Flessner, Bruce. "The Next Generation: How Economic and Philanthropic Trends Will Affect Your Next Campaign's Goals, Length, and Focus," CURRENTS 23, no. 10 (November/December 1997): 14-18, 20.

Goodale, Toni K. "Changes in Giving and Volunteering," *Fund Raising Management* 27, no. 12 (February 1997): 28-29.

Pollack, Rachel H. "Which Way Is the Wind Blowing?—Trends in Corporate and Foundation Giving," CURRENTS 26, no. 4 (April 2000): 42-48.

Schervish, Paul G. and John J. Havens. "Embarking on a Republic of Benevolence? New Survey Findings on Charitable Giving," *Nonprofit and Voluntary Sector Quarterly* 27, no. 2 (June 1998): 237-242.

"What's Up? Giving to Education: Two Reports Show Strong Increases in Education-Related Philanthropy," CURRENTS 24, no. 8 (September 1998): 7.

"What Will the Future Bring?: Better Data Collection, More Sophisticated Technology, and a More Prominent Role. That's What Experts Predict for Advancement Services in the Year 2002," CURRENTS 23, no. 6 (June 1997): 12-15.

Whitley, Frank V. and Penny Staples. "Womenpower: The Growing Factor in Gifts Fund Raising in the Decade Ahead:

Women are Gaining a Growing Importance in Campaign Leadership and as a Source of Big Gifts. Professional Fund Raisers Must be Alert to This Emerging Vast Potential of Women and Learn How to Utilize This Power for Their Causes," *Fund Raising Management* 28, no. 6 (August 1997): 14-18.

● ● ●

University of Central Florida, Orlando, Florida

374

SECTION VI
Marketing and
Advancement

Edited by Larry D. Lauer

Marketing is really a way of thinking, not a way of commercializing. Commercialization comes from the way marketing is carried out, and there is no need to commercialize the academy. But there is a need to market it.

Introduction

Larry D. Lauer
Vice Chancellor, Marketing and Communication
Texas Christian University

Competition for students and dollars intensified significantly in the last decade, and colleges and universities now face prospective students and parents who are "shopping" them differently. These increasingly intelligent consumers are comparing institutions more carefully, expecting personal service in every corner of the campus, and defining quality more in terms of teaching effectiveness and earning potential than test scores required for admission. At the same time, fund-raising campaigns are launched in environments where donors and trustees are frequently involved in other campaigns, often in the same community. In this competitive marketplace, many colleges and universities are taking a closer look at how to maintain a distinct advantage. One of the ways they are doing that is through marketing.

MARKETING IN THE PAST

In most of the academy, the word "marketing" has been verbotin. Students are recruited by admissions "counselors" and money is raised by "development" or "advancement" officers. Using these terms seems to "soften" the nature of the work, which is mostly decentralized.

The admission office is seen as an academic unit; adult and graduate education programs are promoted out of separate offices; and the athletics department often is a completely different world. In fact, all of these areas of "marketing" activities usually report to different academic officers and their work is rarely coordinated or even strategically planned. In the past, this was seen as no problem. Appearing to be "hard to get in" actually seemed enough to make many institutions attractive and successful.

But, now, competition is changing all that.

In the 1990s, many secure institutions began to experience enrollment declines. Standard predictors of final matriculation figures—number of applications and deposits received, for example—no longer seemed reliable. The marketplace appeared unstable. In some cases, the demographics of a region simply changed. But in most cases, the reason was intensifying competition stimulated by a more intelligent "shopper." While enrollment soared in some places, it declined in others. And so, even healthy institutions began to feel they needed to launch new initiatives to protect themselves.

At the same time, museums, theaters, symphonies, operas, and ballets all began launching sophisticated fund-raising campaigns. Past loyalty was no longer a guarantee of continued support and there was a growing need to find new ways to retain past donors as well as attract new ones.

THE SOPHISTICATED CONSUMER

Students and parents were becoming sophisticated consumers. More parents had been to college and knew the ropes. Experienced high school guidance counselors were coaching students to ask the right questions and compare financial aid packages. Indeed, many began to play one financial aid offer against another. Families found that if they were willing to lose some deposit money, they could wait longer to decide, even attending new student orientations for multiple colleges.

Changing state and local priorities reduced financial support for many publicly supported institutions. They launched major fund-raising programs to supplement their shrinking tax support, competing effectively for private gifts. More and more parents also began seriously to consider public institutions with their low tuition rates. Gone were the days when many families decided in advance that they wanted a private school education for their children. Privately supported institutions sought to prove the benefits of a higher-priced education as never before.

All of this price talk led inevitably to the subject of "quality." The truth is that many institutions define their quality by how high their admissions standards are set, and the average or median SAT scores of entering freshman class. "Difficult to get in" means "valuable." Increasingly, parents and prospective students wanted to know who was teaching the courses, how many were in the classes, how many senior professors would be having contact with their son or daughter, and what could be expected in terms of job placement at graduation. Quality was redefined by the consumer. Cost-benefit, special strengths, creative programming, and customer service became important considerations.

Today, cost versus perceived value has become the focal point for parental decisions. Just as consumers stretch to pay more for the car they really want when they come to "feel" its value, prospective students and their families are doing the same thing. The few top-tier schools will always be able to demonstrate that value. Institutions just below that top tier, the ones that have a high price but can't quite deliver the very top prestige, face daunting challenges.

Technology is also changing educational delivery. Most institutions enroll residential and/or commuter students. That's changing with the Internet and virtual classrooms. How many students of the future will choose these alternatives? What will they be willing to pay for an education largely delivered on their own computer? The fact is, no one knows. Many will still choose a campus experience with technology enhancements. The biggest virtual education market will be nontraditional age groups. No matter what the final outcome, some will choose distance learning and, as a result, campus-based education's growth will slow or decline. Whether new institutions offering distance learning will negatively impact traditional ones will depend on how the latter can offer both opportunities and how quickly they do it.

(In Chapter 1 of this section, Charles S.

Madden, vice president for university relations at Baylor University and a leader in the American Marketing Association, elaborates on how education has gradually adapted marketing principles to make them work in academe.)

THE NEED TO INTEGRATE

In order to compete effectively, institutions that traditionally have been decentralized in their marketing-related functions will need to find a way to coordinate their planning. College and university leaders traditionally developed knowledge and skill in fund raising and coordinated the institution's approach to it. Even where fund-raising staffs are decentralized, the overall campaign strategy is usually coordinated from the president's office. This same kind of overall coordination can maximize marketing initiatives in undergraduate student recruitment, graduate admissions, public relations, internal communications, athletics marketing, bookstore merchandising, and student and academic program development. Marketing higher education requires an integrated effort, not unlike that of major fund-raising campaigns.

Marketing is really a way of thinking, not a way of commercializing. Commercialization comes from the way marketing is carried out, and there is no need to commercialize the academy. But there is a need to market it. Faculty, staff, students, and others will get used to the "m" word when they can understand it clearly. Integrated marketing, then, coordinates the planning and implementation of marketing initiatives, and depends on participation across the institution. Its aim is to mobilize the total institution, from locating talent and resources to fostering an environment where everyone has a stake in making the strategy a success.

Integrated marketing also requires coordinating all advertising and public relations work—such as media relations, special events, publications, and advertising—around common goals with similar design elements and slogans and one central institutional message. Institutional priorities must be identified. Over time, these goals broaden and change, but usually, integrated marketing comes to an institution because a president or the senior staff develops a concern about the marketplace. Often, that concern comes from a fear of declining enrollment or in response to alumni criticism of insufficient institutional visibility. Or the concern may come from a desire to raise money in a town with competing campaigns. Initial goals are often direct extensions of these initial concerns.

This raises an important point: The president and executive staffs are crucial to the success of integrated marketing. However the project is organized, the president should announce it and operate it out of his or her office. The entire executive staff should "walk the talk" in supporting the marketing concept and reinforcing its themes.

Marketing as a way of thinking focuses on the "customer," which leads to market segmentation—grouping prospective students and parents into "market segments" based on their academic abilities, personal interests, life styles, leadership potential, geographic location, and more. This way of thinking produces the most significant change in what communications, admissions, and other people do with their time.

When the marketplace is seen in terms of separate audiences or segments, then strategies can be put into place that will build relationships. And with those relationships, comes the bonding loyalty that provides the real competitive advantage the institution is seeking.

(To read more about developing an integrated marketing plan, see Chapter 3 in this section, by Robert A. Sevier, vice president for research and marketing, Stamats Communications, Inc.)

Thinking About the Whole

Marketing professors tell us that the four P's of marketing are product, place, promotion, and price. In higher education, it is sometimes difficult to identify the product or products. Is it the institution itself? Or are they the academic and student affairs programs? Research suggests that students and parents are shopping more for career-oriented academic programs, but that their perception of the overall institution can provide an emotional reason to make a final choice.

For example, there may be a difference between the physical place and the "experienced" place. The physical place is what is seen first, such as the buildings, landscaping, and overall appearance. But the experienced place quickly has the larger influence. This is the lasting impression the person has after meeting people and developing relationships. The perception of academic quality is extremely important in making sure an institution is considered, but the actual choice is more often based on emotional feelings related to services, convenience, or lifestyle preference, or to meaningful relationships formed in the process of communicating with the institution.

Incidentally, this does not mean that easy academics are attractive. On the contrary, a challenging world of ideas appeals conceptually to most prospective students and parents. But strong academics today must be accompanied by convenient personal services, a safe campus environment, and an educational experience that appears to provide the individual a personal advantage in life.

The Need for Research

As with strategic planning, many administrators prepare costly research for a report that ends up on a shelf, not implemented. Or the report confirms what you already knew.

Market segmentation leads to more precise research design. It focuses on a particular category that helps clarify the questions you need answers to in order to make decisions. Usually, segmentation not only makes research projects smaller and less expensive but it also makes a significant contribution.

Begin with the students you are currently recruiting. Analyze and profile them thoroughly. This is sometimes called "data mining" and it is the first kind of research you should do. You quickly learn in services marketing that it is easier and less expensive to find more customers, clients, or students like you already have, and it is more difficult and a lot more expensive to find and attract those who are different from what you have. Identify where they come from, their academic abilities, what they like to do, the services they use, and their satisfaction with their experience.

Now identify potential new markets—by geography, academic ability, leadership behaviors, and lifestyle preferences. Base this on an analysis of your current programs and their potential for distinction. By targeting potential market segments carefully, you can target your research activities. Therefore, you will ask better questions and get back useful information. Do your research one segment at a time.

One of the hard lessons of marketing, especially higher education, is that your product really exists only in the minds of your consumer and you can't change that quickly. If you try, you will only confuse them. And so, going after students like you already have, at least as a first step to secure your enrollment base, is very important.

(Read more about marketing research in Chapter 4 by Donna A. Van De Water of Lipman Hearne Inc.)

Additional Lessons About Admissions

Because your product exists only in the minds of

your consumers, it is essential to position your institution by defining a market niche that differentiates you from your competition. This requires developing a written institutional message (no more than a page) and making sure all marketing communications in one way or another convey and reinforce this message. This is sometimes called a positioning statement. It should follow from your missions statement, which is what your institution came into existence to do, and your vision statement, which is what it wants to become. The positioning statement should list distinction-defining strengths, character traits and institutional values, and basic facts that describe the institution's size and nature. You should audit current materials in light of this central message, and make necessary changes in design, content, flow, and timing. Often, fine-tuning your total communication program process—how your materials work with other interactive personal contacts—will bring a new measure of stability to your recruitment program.

Your ultimate aim is building relationships. To diversify your student population, for example, you need to be certain that the effort you make is comprehensive and intense enough to do the job. The problem with most minority student recruitment programs is the lack of a total, long-term marketing effort. Hiring a minority student recruiter is not enough. Success requires building meaningful relationships between minority communities on and off campus, and that requires integrated communications and an interactive, long-term commitment.

Institutional Visibility

Integrated marketing teaches that getting more visibility is a strategic problem with a strategic solution. Indeed, most institutions cannot afford to make their name a household word. And so the key question is: visibility with whom at what cost?

If you are able to identify the people who control the future health and success of your institution and you bring them to believe you are visible, then for all practical purposes you are. That is the strategic solution. So build your public relations program around identifying publics or segments and communicating directly with their key leaders.

It is important to identify stakeholders and opinion leaders with each identified market segment. Communicating effectively with them will influence others. When you send a news release to the media, send it also to appropriate stakeholders and opinion leaders. When you place an ad, send a reprint directly to them as well. When you get good press coverage, send them the clips. Invite them to events. Call them on the phone. Send them e-mails and faxes. Integrated marketing sends a mix of coordinated messages directly and interactively to your target audiences.

Integrated marketing also teaches that impressions of executive behaviors count more than pictures or publications. Developing a favorable image and reputation involves getting the whole town talking: generating word-of-mouth comments such as "they are really doing exciting things there." The strategy then is to get the right people saying the right things to the right people at the right time. This is accomplished by getting your executives to speak to key associations and to serve on key boards. It is done by orchestrating visible events that demonstrate your institution's involvement in economic development or in the arts. It involves designing projects with corporate or nonprofit partners that demonstrate your organization's vitality and interest in the community.

Name recognition, or "branding," is impor-

> ● ● ●
> **The problem with most minority student recruitment programs is the lack of a total, long-term marketing effort.**

tant. If your name is already known when your admissions counselor arrives in a high school, your success rate will be much higher than if your name is unknown. Use institutional advertising to establish name and presence in places were you need it. These places might include the printed programs of arts organizations in your community if you want to establish presence there, or in a well-read business magazine if you want to influence parents of prospective students. Other ads can be a waste of money. Also, if you need real presence in a place, one ad is also a waste of money. You need to be careful about where you think you need presence and then you need to commit enough to get it. To use advertising effectively, you must identify your market segments clearly and place ads only in publications that influence them. Don't buy an advertisement because a salesman calls on you or because other schools are in the publications; buy it because it achieves a strategic purpose as part of a larger strategically designed initiative.

IMPLEMENTING INTEGRATED MARKETING

In an academic setting, integrated marketing can be implemented through an administrative marketing division, a task force, or a team. In the first instance, this could mean bringing student recruiting, public relations, publications, athletics marketing, and other marketing related areas under one administrative officer. Alumni relations divisions could benefit from this arrangement, or even the campus police, as they are often the first contact visitors have with the university. One institution is considering putting student programs in the marketing department because of their critical "after the sale" role in the total integrated process. This approach serves the institution well by making a major public statement to remain aggressively competitive in the future.

But even where such a division is estab-

lished, it's difficult to include every unit that should be involved in marketing planning and follow-through. That's where an integrated marketing group of some kind can be helpful. Many institutions are forming such groups as a way to launch an intensive program. Some call them task forces; others call them teams. They exist at all sizes and types of institutions. They usually include most everyone on campus who has a stake in marketing and they are usually appointed by and report to the president.

Membership may include undergraduate admissions, financial aid, graduate admissions, public relations, publications, athletics marketing, continuing education, bookstore management, student programs, development, alumni relations, the business office, institutional research, an academic dean, a faculty member or two, a student or two, and so forth. Other members might include such off-campus representatives as the president of the chamber of commerce, local public relations or marketing professionals, or several trustees.

To coordinate so many people, one university has established several subcommittees. A marketing advisory board, comprised of 30 or so people from on and off campus, meets several times a year to brainstorm marketing problems and solutions. This group is advisory only and its primary purpose is widespread participation. The second group, known as the marketing management committee, is comprised of 10 internal professionals who receive input from the advisory board and are responsible for developing the plan of action. Then there are five action groups, which are responsible for implementing the initiatives. Each action group chair serves on the management committee, and each action group is made up of professionals with specific skills to bring to the work.

The chair of the whole project must be a champion of marketing. This person can come from any administrative discipline. The primary requirement is that he or she sees how to adapt marketing principles to the higher education environment and is effective at explaining how it works. This person must also have the ability to see the project through what can be a frustrating early phase.

Anticipate at least three barriers:

- The biggest problem will be from those who see marketing as cheapening the academy. This can only be dealt with through patience and persistence. Go to meetings, listen to ideas, and avoid being defensive. Visit with the academic deans and the faculty senate, attend administrative staff meetings to answer questions, and meet with serious critics one-on-one.

- A second barrier will come from those who think the marketing champion is more concerned about his or her career advancement than the institution. In other words, launching a total institutional marketing initiative can be perceived by some as a power move on the part of its advocate. Again, only time and results will solve this difficulty.

- And the third one has to do with budget. Don't worry about finding new money at first. Pool talent and available resources first. New money will come once your creative ideas and early successes begin to prosper. And some new funding sources can be found outside normal budgeting cycles. One group member might say "I can find some money in my budget if several more of you will match it." Or, "I know a business off campus that might be interested in sponsoring that."

Planning must be ongoing and produce multiple plans. As soon as a single plan is published, people will protest that they weren't included. A continuous process that produces periodic reports or action blueprints in which new ideas can be incorporated quickly works best.

Supporting the Work

When an institution begins to see the world in terms of market segments, it no longer makes sense to put too much emphasis on news media placement. News organizations are in business to advance their goals, not yours. And many institutions are reorganizing their communications offices to adjust to this reality. (In Chapter 2, Sandra Conn, director of marketing at Indiana University, talks specifically about how her institution has successfully used marketing principles in the news and information arena.)

News placement is still important, but now more effort is put on placing fewer stories. Press releases are no longer written for every campus event. Rather, identify reputation-defining stories as well as a comprehensive approach for telling them. The news or information office becomes an office of strategic and integrated communication, comprised of strategic planners, writers, designers, events managers, media buyers, Web masters, and media relations people. Staff members relate to university departments more as account executives, assessing the potential for advancing university goals and designing comprehensive communication initiatives. In short, it helps the marketing group or groups mobilize the total organization while it helps produce the necessary materials and events.

(Note the major role the Web plays in campus marketing in Chapter 5 by Robert E. Johnson, vice president for enrollment, Albion College and author of his own marketing online newsletter.)

Marketing Inside

Every successful marketing initiative includes aggressive internal initiatives. This includes a comprehensive campaign of media, personal calls, and presentations to reinforce key values and traditions. Some institutions initiate customer service training for offices that have direct contact with students or other members of the public. Others broaden a "service to others" campaign to include student groups and faculty members. Many find it effective to add a motivational "Help Tell Our Story" component in new staff and faculty orientation programs.

Using Trustees

Trustees are accustomed to helping plan and implement fund-raising programs.

But most institutions keep them away from getting involved in other day-to-day management problem-solving. For the most part, this is as it should be. But marketing, like fund raising, is another place where trustees can bring real expertise. When involved with a marketing team or group projects, many are able to contribute ideas, offer advice from experience, and suggest resources for implementation. And when the time comes, those trustees who have helped build the institution's visibility will have a natural commitment to making any fund-raising initiatives succeed.

MAKING YOUR INSTITUTION MORE COMPETITIVE

Integrated marketing is a way of thinking. It is not a way of commercializing the academy. It can mobilize entire colleges and universities to tell their stories with one voice, raise their visibility, and meet the challenges of an increasingly competitive marketplace. You can achieve this by taking several important steps. Locate and use the institution's creative talent. Maximize the use of resources. Coordinate marketing and communications, and integrate all advertising and public relations. Set priority goals and make them the responsibility of everyone on campus. By doing so, your institution can not only survive the competition, but it can achieve a whole new level of distinction and recognition.

Over the past three decades, marketing goals have broadened from delivering tangible products to delivering intangible services, and more recently, ideas, opportunities, and ideals. Marketing can embrace the diversity of lifestyles on campuses.

Adapting Marketing Principles for Use in Education

Charles S. Madden
Vice President for University Relations and
Ben H. Williams Professor of Marketing
Baylor University

Marketing has become a hot topic in higher education in recent years. Over the past three decades, nonprofit organizations, social causes, and other non-product or service-related applications gradually realized the benefits of strategic marketing. Education was one of the last nontraditional areas to embrace marketing as a tool for growth and success.

Why the delay? One of the barriers was certainly the belief that marketing was only for products and services, and had little or nothing to do with the way in which choices were made by those managing educational institutions. And many in academia believed that properly run institutions did not need marketing.

WHAT MARKETING IS AND ISN'T

Marketing has been defined many ways—how goods and services flow from producers to consumers, for example, or the way products and services are promoted to a consuming public. Marketing is used frequently to describe the exchange of goods for money. Contemporary views include the process through which ideas are distributed. For the purposes of this discussion,

marketing is about the theory and practice of creating and sustaining exchange relationships. This move from focusing on exchange transactions to exchange relationships more easily accommodates the highly-involved and complex decision making of educational recruiting and fund raising.

Developmental Phases of Marketing

In the early days of marketing, if a good product were produced, then it was assumed that a market would be receptive. That idea has some residual impact on education: If a really great job is done teaching classes or creating programs, demand will materialize. In reality, you must still do a number of other things—in addition to having great products—to be successful.

In the 1920s and 1930s, the concept of marketing moved from a focus on making great products to emphasizing effective selling techniques. Much of the residual resentment toward high-pressure sales tactics, at least in the United States, comes from that era. That tactic brought short-run success, but over time, customers lost trust. For years, educational leaders feared that campus marketing would take the form of high-pressure selling.

An effort began to take shape in the 1950s and 1960s that let market demand determine what products and services would be offered, and for many years, that emphasis defined the way in which marketing was practiced. Research determined customer needs and products were then constructed to meet those demands. While this is still a relatively effective marketing strategy, education has largely not been driven by demand, nor has it benefited from a market focus as an origin for service ideas.

More recently, marketing has focused on long-term relationships formed between potential buyers and sellers. Instead of single sales transactions between buyers and sellers, the emphasis is on developing trust and exploring mutual needs and interests. Education has benefited from this evolution through relationships that are formed and managed with students, alumni, faculty, and staff. For certain marketing applications in education such as recruiting, fund raising, and developing audiences for athletics and arts on the campus, relationships may take precedence over individual games, events, or other singular decisions. When intentionally managed, targeted, and nurtured, relationships make the education community work successfully.

Evolution of the Object of Marketing

Over the past three decades, marketing goals have broadened from delivering tangible products to delivering intangible services, and more recently, ideas, opportunities, and ideals. While higher education offers a variety of products and services, the focus on ideas, opportunities, and ideals makes marketing very appealing to education now. Marketing can embrace the diversity of campus lifestyles, products, and opportunities.

Managerial Marketing Paradigm

Those who manage education marketing must assess the strengths, weaknesses, opportunities, and threats to their institution while determining the differential advantage it has over competing peer institutions. The only variables that are generally under the control of an education marketing manager are the product (programs, courses, and other services), price (tuition, discount rates, etc.), promotion (public relations, communications, etc.), and place (location of educational products delivery, campus, etc.).

Why Marketing Is Essential to Education

As campus administrators discovered marketing, they appropriated its principles primarily in four areas:

1) Fund raising. For many years, private schools have been funded, at least partially, by gifts and later, endowments. Public institutions have had to follow that lead in recent decades as state and federal governments have reduced financial support in real terms.

2) Athletics. There is an increasing pressure on campuses to provide large event ticket sales, promotional sponsorships, and other types of relationship inducements to fund both revenue and non-revenue-producing sports.

3) Enrollment management. In recent years, schools began to realize that sophisticated marketing could bring very positive results in quality and quantity of students, enhancing tuition and fee revenues, especially at private institutions.

4) Public image management. At many campuses, this has become an active process as alumni and other institutional supporters press for more positive stories in media outlets about their alma mater.

Each of these marketing efforts has been a response to identified needs. The view that institutions would run "on their own" without a deliberate, managed constituency relationship-based effort has virtually disappeared.

Organizational Fragmentation

Very few colleges and universities, at least in the United States, have fully organized or integrated their marketing efforts because most developed in an era when there was very little competition for students or donated funds. Education marketing grew incrementally as departments were created for fund raising, public relations, and enrollment management. These areas were thought of as singular efforts and were added as a result of constituent group suggestions or by administrators responding to problem areas.

As these marketing efforts were added to the existing structure of education institutions, they were expected to conform to the existing organizational structures. In many cases, marketing efforts were scattered across student services, development, alumni relations, public relations, and other areas.

Need for Strategic Framework

This process of ad hoc and incremental additions of marketing for educational institutions has a downside. Not only is there an organizational crisis when the "parts" of marketing do not effectively cooperate, but there is also a need for a more comprehensive strategic framework to coordinate them. Many campuses have a strategic plan but it is often unrelated to constituency efforts. Setting measurable goals for public image management efforts, enrollment management, fund raising, and even governmental relations is still foreign to many institutions.

To test the strategic orientation and organizational synergy of your campus marketing, answer the following questions:

1) Is your marketing effort as strategically aligned and managed as well as the campus financial and budgetary system?

2) Do the specific goals of the marketing effort tie back to the mission and overall objectives of your institution in a measurable way?

If these questions are difficult to answer, there is probably little if any alignment of marketing with the overall strategic efforts of your institution.

WHERE IS EDUCATION MARKETING TODAY?

The following market-related areas are frequently not made part of the organizational or strategic plan of many institutions today:

- recruiting (finding customers)
- admissions (selecting customers and closing the sale)
- financial aid (credit, discounting, customer service)
- public relations (image building, advertising, product positioning)
- institutional research (understanding customer choice and service evaluation)
- governmental relations (monitoring and relat-

ing to legal and regulatory environments)
- alumni relations (relating to and serving mature customers throughout their lives)
- institutional advancement (relating to and serving donor customers)

Each of these areas exists in one form or another on most campuses today. A good test of a school's overall marketing effectiveness is the frequency with which each of these areas cooperates with all the other areas. If the dialogue is not constant and if the objectives are not interrelated, there is a good chance that some departments are working at cross purposes.

● ● ●
Windows of change occur infrequently. Institutions should take advantage of leadership transitions and/or the availability of financial resources in order to integrate marketing functions.

Campus Activities That Need a Marketing Approach

Many campuses make decisions without serious thought being given to the strength of demand or market consequences. Each of the following policies needs to have some type of marketing discussion before a decision is finally made. At most institutions, these decisions are made either by the academic division or the financial affairs division with little consideration:

Pricing
- tuition setting
- financial aid discounting
- fee setting
- housing, parking fees, food service prices, etc.

Product
- demand measurement for new programs
- service bundling (meal plans, athletic season tickets, cross-selling of arts and public events, etc.)
- copy cards, phone cards, etc.

Promotion
- athletic logos, licensing, etc.
- public event planning
- athletic event promotion

Place
- distance learning, competitive positioning
- off-site or continuing education courses
- event venue for activities on campus

Relationship Marketing in the Future of Higher Education

Each institution that looks at integrating its marketing must also look at the type of relationships it is developing with individual constituents. Education has begun to invest heavily in students, alumni, and other constituent supporters, resulting in lifetime partnerships rather than individual transactions. These relationships have to be initiated and sustained with a perspective on constituent rather than on institutional, needs.

Relationship marketing also relies on extensive information about its constituents. Knowing their needs enables the institution to engage in strategic relationship-building activities. For example, young alumni are often uninterested in traditional activities, but may have career development or family finance needs that could be addressed by courses, conferences, or professional certification on the Internet. Using information to strengthen these relationships and create reciprocal activities will encourage constituents to take part in campus activities.

Interaction between the campus and the individual constituent is imperative. Simply informing constituents about the activities of the school has limited impact. What is being created could be described as a "virtual limited friendship." Through the use of regular interaction (the Internet, mail, telephone, etc.), an institution can approach potential students; engage current students, their parents, and their friends; and remind alumni of relationship-building activities. In addition, internal audiences can provide relationship-building opportunities. Whether it be faculty or staff, the campus represents a diverse community of needs and interests. Relationship marketing, which is ultimately based on knowledge, trust, and mutual interest, can enhance the quality of that community. Integrating the overall marketing function enables those relationships to flourish.

As with any successful innovation, marketing—both integrated and relationship oriented—can contribute to an ever stronger education environment.

FURTHER READING

Hanson, John H. "Let the Marketer Beware: For Not-for-Profit Organizations, It is a Powerful Agent of Change. Thus, Mistakes in Marketing Strategies Can Lead to Organizational Disasters. Here's How to Avoid Stumbling in the Marketplace," *Advancing Philanthropy* 5, no. 3 (Fall 1997): 22-26.

Roy, Robin J. "In Defense of Real Marketing in Advancement Literature Has Been Filled With Stories on Marketing: Integrated Marketing Here; the Differences Between Marketing and Development There; the Good, the Bad and the Ugly of Marketing Everywhere," *Advancing Philanthropy* 6, no. 2 (Summer 1998): 18-20.

Sevier, Robert A. *Integrated Marketing for Colleges, Universities, and Schools: A Step-by Step Planning Guide.* Washington, DC: Council for Advancement and Support of Education, 1998.

Sevier, Robert A. and Robert Johnson, eds. *Integrated Marketing Communication: A Practical Guide to Developing Comprehensive Communication Strategies.* Washington, DC: Council for Advancement and Support of Education, 1999.

Integrated marketing communications uses the broad range of traditional communications disciplines commonly found in higher education. What's new is the way they are planned and deployed.

Marketing and
Advancement

Making the Move to Marketing:

How One University Realigned its Communications Strategies Away from the News Bureau and Toward Today's Realities

Sandra Conn
Director of Communications and Marketing
Indiana University

A few years ago, we at Indiana University conducted an experiment. We asked selected members of our Hoosiers for Higher Education grassroots advocacy organization—many with family members representing nearly every audience we communicate with—to save everything they received from Indiana University for one month and send it to us. A month later, we received big envelopes and boxes filled with up to 100 pieces, ranging widely in quality, look, and message. All were sent by a variety of campus units that had no idea what other units were sending the same families.

The image presented to our most valued audiences? Cacophony. Waste.

Their response? Too much information. Does your right hand know what your left hand is doing? Get your act together. Stop!

For years, we had been hearing rumblings along these lines and disregarding them. From this experiment and others, we suddenly got the picture about what a confusing image we were projecting, and we had the tangible evidence to share with others.

This evidence was just one of many findings that have prompted us to make enormous changes

in the ways we get the message out about Indiana University. Many of these changes involve moving from a news-bureau-centered approach to an audience-centered approach, building relationships that we carefully evaluate. Although this process of change is still in its early phases, it is delivering dramatic results. After less than two years of following our new course, Indiana University experienced enrollment increases at seven of its eight campuses. The increase at Indiana University Bloomington alone was 10 percent. And follow-up survey work shows statewide awareness of Indiana University's quality factors and career-development prospects has increased significantly.

These are not just happy outcomes, but the exact results we planned. How we got the results presents a case study in how a campus can shift away from the usual media relations approach and offers a step-by-step guide that other campuses can apply to improve their results through the carefully reasoned, measurable use of integrated marketing communications (IMC).

A PR EVOLUTION, NOT A REVOLUTION

First, let's review the rationale behind the traditional news bureau approach that many colleges and universities, including Indiana University,

SECTION VI: MARKETING AND ADVANCEMENT   **389**

have long used to promote themselves. These campuses rely on placing stories in the news media about accomplishments of their faculty and students, assuming that these stories will build awareness of their institutions, convey an image of excellence, and differentiate them from their competitors. This approach made sense when we lived in a world of fewer media outlets. Then we could count on our target audiences to glean their information from the relatively few mass-media sources: national and area newscasts on the three major networks; a national, metropolitan, or local newspaper; and a handful of national newsmagazines.

The explosion in technology and media has changed all that. Today, campuses have the ability to customize not only the information we offer but also the media channels we use to target the specific interests of smaller and smaller audience niches. And, just as our targeting ability has grown, so has our audiences' expectation that we will use this ability to direct our communications through their self-selected niches and address them as unique individuals.

All these forces challenge higher education to enlarge its concept of promotion. As we at IU see it, we must move from communicating on the averages (mass communication calculated to reach an average percentage of a mass audience) to marketing on the differences. This means using research and segmentation strategies to define audiences and their interests; distributing relationship-building as well as "newsmaker" messages; and monitoring results to ensure we get a return on our information-outreach investment.

This call to change is typically greeted by two responses: hostility or denial. Those who are hostile passionately defend the status quo. For them, the traditional way of promoting their institution—through a news bureau—is the right way, the true way, the only way, and those seeking to change this paradigm are infidels and hucksters. These defenders can't see that the move from promotion to marketing is simply the next step in the evolution of university public relations and external affairs.

The traditional tactics of a news bureau—news releases, op-eds, video news releases and satel-

lite feeds, radio actualities and tip sheets—remain an important part of IMC. But before using these tactics, we now conduct substantial research and communications planning to help media relations professionals better understand their target audiences. This includes understanding who they are; what information and messages they find compelling; where and when they get their information; and how we can expect them to act on that information, once encountered. In fact, there are some examples of where this approach is being taken in the traditional news bureau model.

On the other hand, those who deny the need for change simply, for whatever reason—anxiety, complacency, habit—overlook the benefits of the IMC approach. When faced with IMC concepts, they dismissively reply, "That's nothing new," or "That's what we already do."

In one way, they are right. Integrated marketing communications uses the broad range of traditional communications disciplines commonly found in higher education. What's new is the way they are planned and deployed.

Integrated marketing communications is based on the comprehensive planning of cohesive campaigns that integrate and apply the strategic advantages of a variety of communication disciplines—for example, advertising, publications, direct response, the Internet, media relations, personal contact, and more. Then, IMC combines these disciplines to produce clarity, consistency, and maximum communications impact on the attitudes and behavior of selected audiences.

Most institutions of higher education have multiple barriers blocking any move toward comprehensive, cooperative communications strategies.

BREAKING FROM TRADITION: MORE IS NOT ALWAYS BETTER

Indeed, most campuses have been using all of these disciplines in abundance. What they have not been doing is planning integrated, cohesive campaigns. In fact, most educational institutions have multiple barriers blocking any move toward comprehensive, cooperative communications strategies.

First, most are organized to reinforce separation of powers, including powers of communicating to audiences. These barriers begin to multiply if each power or unit has generous, autonomous financial ability to pursue its audience. And the barriers to cooperation are further intensified if the communications staff in each unit subscribes to the academic/artistic notion that, in order to be creative (even ethical), each communication message must be new, unique, without reference to others' messages.

Thus, admissions talks to 17-year-old high school students. Athletics talks to sports fans. Graduate recruiting talks to college graduates. Alumni affairs talks to graduates of the institution. Development talks to donors and prospective donors, usually also alumni of the institution, and corporate friends. And so on. Since each unit's target segment presents a different profile, with different interests and different levels of commitment to and understanding of the institution, the various units use this as justification for pursuing their own independent communications campaigns without reference to one another. Charted out, the process looks something like Figure 2-1.

This was the situation at Indiana University when we asked our supporters to show us the many and varied things we were sending them. Seeing that we had to orchestrate our media and messages in order to transform cacophony into

harmony, from that point on, we began working toward integrated marketing communications. That is not easy in a campus environment, where units have traditionally disregarded, in some cases even disdained, other units' communications programs. It takes time to build cooperation and trust and to arrive at an understanding that all interests—the units', the institution's, and the recipients'—are best served by planning together and working toward the following model.

In corporate marketing environments, the goal of this model is to gain control of the message, recognizing that today's consumer must be presented with a clear, consistent message on behalf of the product or service, no matter where it comes from within the organization. The recipient simply will not acknowledge or process conflicting messages.

A more workable goal for education marketers is to balance, rather than control, the message. This means, as suggested in Figure 2-2, that the institution's marketing communications professionals operate like a hub. They review each unit's needs and plans for communication with its audiences. They help each unit develop its communications with awareness of what those audiences are receiving from other units in the institu-

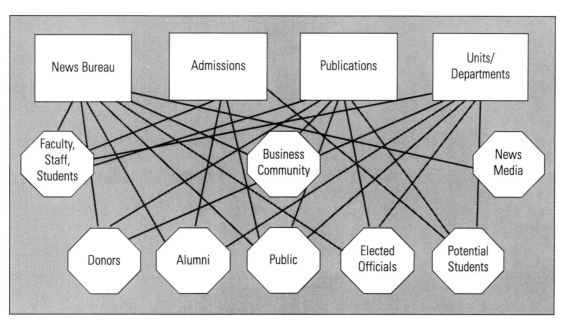

Figure 2-1. Evolution to Integrated Marketing (Before)

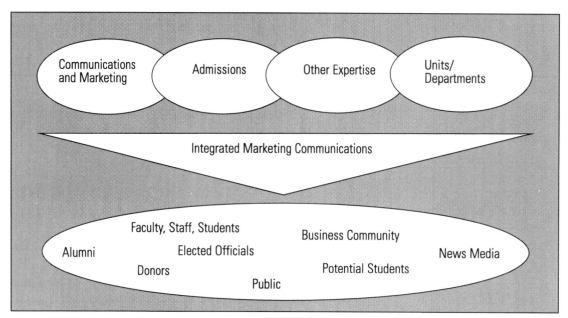

Communications
and Marketing

Admissions

Other Expertise

Units/
Departments

Integrated Marketing Communications

Faculty, Staff, Students

Business Community

Alumni

Elected Officials

News Media

Donors

Potential Students

Public

Figure 2-2. Evolution to Integrated Marketing (After)

tion. And they ensure that each unit uses and benefits from the unifying elements of the over-arching institutional message. Not surprisingly, this approach often helps a unit realize its own unique appeal and the specific audiences to target for maximum impact.

The creative role of the institution's marketing communications professionals is to develop, test, and implement the over-arching message, media, and strategy that communicate why recipients should believe in the institution. When incorporated into a unit's communications, this message provides recipients with the familiar, unifying reason why they should heed and believe the unit's more specific messages to its target audiences.

RESEARCH: LEARNING WHAT TO SAY, WHERE TO SAY IT

At Indiana University, we refer to this over-arching message and strategy as our university-wide umbrella campaign. Since 1997, the campaign has been based on the theme "Indiana University. Quality Education. Lifetime Opportunities." It relies heavily on TV advertising and billboards to carry it throughout the state, and the visual message that unifies three sequential creative iterations of the message might be summarized, as one IU student said after viewing the three families

of TV commercials: "Indiana University. It's about people."

We didn't just think up this message or randomly choose TV advertising as our primary medium. Nor were these decisions delivered to us by an agency. We arrived at them after months of intensive quantitative and qualitative research with both external and internal audiences. This process taught us what to say and how and where to say it.

Here is a summary of what we learned from a statewide quantitative survey:

1. When selecting a college or university to attend, our audiences look for quality (defined as a combination of accessibility, caring teachers, and reputation) and job opportunity.

2 Compared to our competitors, Indiana University ranked high on quality, our audiences thought—but they weren't quite sure why. This is where the cacophony of communications from units, multiplied across eight campuses, was leading to confusion and indifference.

3. Finally, the medium they get most of their information from is television.

Using this information as background for discussion, we conducted 18 focus groups involving several hundred representatives from the following audiences: top administrators, faculty, professional and clerical staff, prospective students, current students, alumni, donors, and the general public in different regions of the state. In the focus groups, we tested the validity of the survey results and worked together with the groups to review and refine a developing set of creative concepts.

From these sessions, we learned that Hoosiers like commercials that evoke Main Street rather than Madison Avenue and feature real people, not actors. While they appreciate more lyrical positioning like "Dream Big" or "Quality Means Everything," they like straightforward positioning of the type that characterizes the theme we chose, "Quality Education. Lifetime Opportunities." And they like verbal messages that back up the positioning with verifiable statements of fact. Both the external and internal audiences, younger and more mature, repeatedly used the word "authentic." They wanted authentic communications—communications they could believe.

These findings guided our umbrella campaign's creative efforts. We run TV commercials, primarily, throughout the state to generate awareness and establish a unifying image. Under this umbrella, each campus and unit can leverage off this awareness, targeting its audiences with appropriate supplemental media campaigns and leading them into its own specific messages.

PLANNING FOR IMPACT: BEGIN WITH THE END IN MIND

At the heart of every successful integrated marketing communications effort, including ours, is a carefully reasoned, measurable communications plan. The effort begins by asking: With whom do we want to communicate? And what effect do we want our communications to have on them? The following planning steps that we used can also guide all communications campaigns, from institution-wide to the smallest unit.

Step 1. Audience Considerations

It goes without saying that all campuses must communicate with a variety of audiences or market segments. Each segment has a different level of understanding of its relationship to the institution, and within each segment, different individuals play dif-

ferent roles. So, to begin, you must identify the audience(s), the role being targeted, and the decision to be affected by the communication. Ask the following questions.

- Who is the audience for the communications plan? There may be many.
- What is the priority audience? Again, you may have several. One way to identify priorities is to perform this exercise: If you had $100 to spend on reaching these audiences, how would you divide it up to reach each one?
- What is their current interest in or understanding of your institution? Prospective students have very different interests and understanding from alumni. Sports fans' interest and understanding are quite different from funding agencies. And so on.
- What communications effect do you want to achieve? Establish a need? Build awareness? Develop "brand" attitude or motivation? Create commitment to buy? Facilitate buying process? Enhance "brand" loyalty? Deepen core loyalty?

Step 2. Competitor Considerations

All institutions and units within them have competition for their target audiences' attention. Too often, units simply respond that they are, for example, "the top honors program in the state" or the "No. 1-ranked religious studies program." The trap of "talking to ourselves" finds easy prey in academic units with little experience in marketing. Every entity in the institution has competition— whether it comes from another institution, another top-ranked department on campus wooing the same top students as majors, or another nonprofit seeking the same charitable dollar. To understand the competition, you must ask these questions:

- What alternatives does your audience have for taking the action you are seeking? Among the possible answers: The audience can be looking to other institutions, doing nothing, or doing something outside the realm of education.
- Historically, who are your competitors? Be precise. Don't just answer "other departments," for example, or "other Big Ten schools." If you don't know, some research is in order.
- How are your competitors communicating

with the audience? Again, be exact. How close can you get to finding out how many times they contact the audience? What media do they use? Look at examples of their communications vehicles. Do a competitive audit.

■ What do their communications look like and say? Carefully examine your competitors' publications and other communications in a competitive audit.

■ What success are they having with their communications? Try to assess objectively the impact on yourself, your client, and sample members of the intended audience. Try to get evidence of the effectiveness of competitors' campaigns.

Step 3. Decision-Making Considerations

As a representative of higher education, you need to apply the best practices of instructional design in developing communications, understanding, and relationships with audiences. As part of this, you need to identify where individual audiences are when you approach them: Where do they start from when they step down the communications path with you? From this common ground, you need to plan the sequence of messages that will take them from where they are to where you want them to be. This is a far smarter tactic than heaping on them all the messages you want them to hear without regard to their background knowledge, attention span, or ability to absorb, comprehend, and synthesize. Here are the questions to ask:

■ What decision stage is your audience in? These can range from the decision-to-consider stage to the decision-to-commit stage to the decision-to-act-on-the-commitment stage.

■ What role does your target audience have in the decision? This includes acknowledging that there may be several role players—students, parents, spouses—present during the receipt and review of a message. Are you communicating with an individual or a group?

■ What is the timing of the stages? Knowing this helps you understand how to roll out the corresponding sequence of messages and how to schedule the media arrival.

■ Where does each stage occur? This allows you to match the media arrival and the message to the location where the stage is most likely to occur, and where it will encounter the least distraction by other communications or competitors for attention.

Step 4. Media Considerations

The practice of integrated marketing communications assumes the use of a mix of media that "touches" the target audience in different ways at different stages in the decision process, and that guides the audience toward the understanding required to take the action you desire. It relies on the orchestration of media and message, including repetition of key messages and building of sequential messages across the stages. This is done using the most appropriate medium—what the audience will be most receptive to at each stage—including advertising, direct mail, editorial coverage, telephone, personal presentations, displays, literature, recycling of media coverage, Webcasting (driving the audience to your Web site), and more. You'll uncover the right media by asking these questions.

■ What media are appropriate for the audience? There are many factors to consider here, including the size of the audience, the value of the response of that audience, your budget for reaching it, what media it favors, and more.

■ What media is this audience receiving—not only from competitors but from within your own institution? For example, if your target audience is receiving substantial amounts of direct mail letters and literature from various units, you might deliver your message on an audiotape. This would differentiate it and heighten the likelihood it will be selected out, and carefully attended to, by the audience.

■ How will the mix of media integrate from the view of the recipient? It must be planned from the recipient's perspective to present a purposeful, planned variety, not appear as a hodgepodge "trying out" of different media.

Step 5. Creative Considerations

As you answer many of the above questions, the creative possibilities will begin to become evident. Some final questions can guide you and your client unit to the actual execution.

■ What should the visual presentation and verbal weight and tone of each piece in the communication chain be? Key factors include repetition, diversification, sequencing of information, and build of persuasive message.

■ What are the "mandatories"? These include relating each piece back to the unifying institutional message, as well as the creative, legal, or institutional elements, like logo treatments, affirmative action statements, etc.

When you go through the integrated marketing communications planning process with internal clients group by group—from top administrators (for institution-wide programs) to the smallest units—you accomplish a number of goals. You involve them in their own communications and set the stage for sharing responsibilities. You also demystify the process, demonstrating that there is a very deliberate, research-driven method behind marketing communications. You show that the process involves neither smoke and mirrors nor light bulbs suddenly lighting up in people's minds.

From the standpoint of institutional accountability and efficiency, you build relationships through interactive communication not only between your marketing communications professionals and units, but also among units. It can be remarkable to observe units taking interest in what others are doing and finding appropriate ways to collaborate for greater effectiveness and cost savings.

Of course, the development of any integrated marketing communications campaign returns you and your client unit full circle to research. Ideally, you will have the opportunity to test your messages, media mix, and creative execution elements as you develop the campaign. In real life, timing issues often press you to launch the campaign without prior testing. Yet testing should begin as soon as reasonably possible, and the client should be involved in planning and conducting this research.

INTEGRATING MEDIA RELATIONS: BACK TO THE NEWS BUREAU

Bringing media relations into the IMC mix is one of the greatest challenges. No higher education institution can afford literally to close its

news bureau function. Rather, you may change its name, realign its priorities, and assign its staff to working teams with marketing communications professionals. Initially, this may offend professionals in media relations, who maintain journalistic assumptions of independence, objectivity, and separation from "commercial" interests. It helps to discuss with them the ways journalism practice has also changed over the last two decades, and how these changes parallel the ways marketing communication has changed as a result of growing competition and what author Don E. Schultz calls "demassification" of the media.

For example, in the days of mass communication, topics such as "women's fitness" might earn, at best, an article a week in the women's section of a major daily paper. Now, as mass communication has given way to myriad special interest niches, that topic is represented by at least a dozen national-circulation monthly magazines. The editorial in these magazines is, by necessity, a mix of original articles developed by the publications' staff members and marketing-related messages supplied by major vendors to that market. This combination of journalism and marketing communications is what their audience—and the audiences of the majority of niche-market media—wants and expects.

Nevertheless, it takes more than persuasive examples to bring media relations into the mix. There are few models to follow. Even mergers between advertising and public relations firms aimed at creating IMC firms have stumbled—and many have fallen apart—on the attempt to unify marketing and media relations cultures. It takes time for each side to understand and respect the other's expertise, and time is in short supply in an increasingly fast-paced, multidisciplinary environment.

At Indiana University, we began to make progress when we took a very rational approach. We worked with our media relations professionals to compile an informal time study. We looked at the proportions of their time spent on the indispensable media relations tasks; responding to media requests; researching, writing, editing, and distributing media releases; developing and cultivating media contacts and specific placements; and damage control and crisis management. To this set of tasks we suggested adding two more: serving on marketing communications teams and advancing their objectives; and publishing a blend of "news" and marketing messages using e-mail and the Web.

We found we could make time for these two added responsibilities by doing two things:

1. Reducing our news-release activities significantly. This has required altering our internal clients' expectations so that they generate many of their own releases, which we then edit and distribute.

2. Directing a portion of our media contact time toward the objectives of marketing teams. This means focusing heavily on developing media relationships and placements targeted to media venues or geographic markets specified in our university-wide, out-of-state marketing plans and in our individual units' marketing plans.

At this writing, we have just defined this course and reorganized our media relations staff to pursue it. We are not far enough down the path to recommend what we are doing with certainty, but we are pursuing it with new confidence and energy and it is delivering quick results. The test will be in our ability to perform consistently and creatively—qualities, in fact, that are central to thinking and working in the integrated marketing communications model.

BUILDING AN INTERNAL AGENCY: IMC, INC

In short, at Indiana University we have been moving toward developing an internal marketing communications agency. Our services include marketing and marketing communications consulting and strategic planning; creative consulting and selected assistance; selected marketing publications development and production; media relations consulting, editing, and distribution; selected broadcast and electronic media consulting, development, and production; and Web consulting and selected development work.

All of our activities focus on extending the influence and objectives of our university-wide unifying image and messages. At the same time, we help our client units benefit from these and coordinate with other university-generated communications activities to enhance the success of their communications. (This approach probably comes as a surprise to those who falsely assume that a "corporate" marketing approach undermines institutional values like academic freedom and school autonomy.)

Like any agency, we are a service organization. We live daily with the same pressures as any mid-sized agency in the private sector: deadlines, production schedules, and issues with client relationships, client reporting, and financial management. Looking up the hierarchy, our clients include top administration. Our other clients are potentially every campus, school, department, institute, and administrative office within Indiana University. It's a big, challenging marketplace, with both a singular communications mission and hundreds of unique communications missions that must look seamless— integrated—in the minds of our audiences. Our goal is to earn our reputation as the most responsive, knowledgeable, and creative agency our clients can find to serve them.

REFERENCES AND FURTHER READING

Belch, George E. and Michael A. Belch. *Advertising and Promotion: An Integrated Marketing Communications Perspective*. Fourth Edition. Boston: Irwin McGraw Hill, 1997.

Lauer, Larry D. "Marketing Across the Board," CURRENTS 24, no. 1 (Jan 1999): 19-24.

Percy, Larry. *Strategies for Implementing Integrated Marketing Communications*. Chicago, IL: NTC Business Books, 1997.

Schultz, Don E., Stanley I. Tannenbaum, and Robert F. Lauterborn. *The New Marketing Paradigm: Integrated Marketing Communications*. Chicago, IL: NTC Business Books, 1994.

Schultz, Don E. "Integrated Marketing Communications: Maybe Definition Is in the Point of View," *Marketing News* (January 18, 1993): 17.

Schultz, Don E. "Integration and the Media: Maybe Your Approach Is Wrong," *Marketing News* (June 21, 1993): 15.

Sevier, Robert A. and Robert E. Johnson, eds. *Integrated Marketing Communication: A Practical Guide to Developing Comprhensive Communication Strategies*. Washington, DC: Council for Advancement and Support of Education, 1999.

Simpson, Christopher. "The Day We Closed the News Bureau," CURRENTS 24, no. 1 (January 1998): 26-32.

Before you can begin, you must have the active commitment of the president, or a very senior administrator with the backing of the president, to write a marketing plan.

Developing an Integrated Marketing Plan

Robert A. Sevier
Vice President for Research and Marketing
Stamats Communications, Inc.

The decision to proceed with an integrated marketing plan is an important one. And while plans almost always improve performance and help achieve greater efficiencies, a handful of questions asked—and answered—early in the planning process can help make the plan even more effective and easier to write.

1. *Why are you interested in writing a plan at this time?* To what opportunities are you trying to respond? What problems are you trying to solve? Is the plan designed to help increase enrollment, raise dollars, or enhance an image? Is the need for a plan widely felt on campus? Is everyone defining marketing the same way? How closely is the marketing plan tied to the strategic plan? How will you determine whether or not the planning—and resulting plan—was successful? Often, the answers to questions like these will help determine the broad outline and shape of the plan and help you clarify the overall marketing mandate, your plan's raison d'être.

2. *Are you writing an integrated marketing plan or an integrated marketing communication plan (IMC)?* While these two plans have different foci and goals, they are closely related and often confused. By definition, integrated marketing involves coordinating such p/c strategic assets as product/customer, price/cost, and place/convenience to meet strategic goals. The outcomes of decisions involving the mixing of these assets are promoted or communicated (the fourth p/c) to target audiences.

The integrated marketing communication plan, however, is more narrowly focused. It tends to emphasize the coordination or integration of messages rather than strategic assets. More than promotion, integrated marketing communication focuses on communication that presupposes active and ongoing listening.

For the sake of this chapter, I will assume that you are writing a more comprehensive integrated marketing plan rather than an integrated marketing communication plan.

Integrated marketing is distinguished by its commitment to strategic, organizational, and message integration:

■ Strategic integration involves the assessment and meeting of target-audience needs through the allocation of key resources within the constraints of your institutional mission. This includes a willingness to make data-based decisions, and a desire to segment and mix such strategic assets as product, price, and place (or if you prefer, customer/consumer, cost, and convenience). Finally, it relies on feedback to help assure that strategic decisions are on track.

■ Organizational integration allows or encourages (from a systems perspective) complete strategic and message integration. At its most basic, organizational integration involves coordinating resources and sharing goals.

■ Message integration, the last component of strategic communication, means that messages are consistent, coordinated, and driven by strategic decisions. Integrated messages have a common look, sound, and feel across various media and over time.

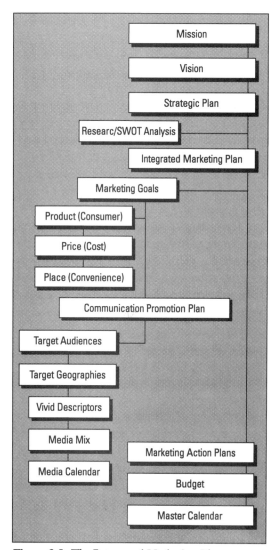

Figure 3-1. The Integrated Marketing Plan

Integrated Marketing Plan

1. Marketing goals
   - Consumer (product)
   - Cost (price)
   - Convenience (place)
2. Communication (promotion) component
   - Target audiences
   - Target geographies
   - Vivid descriptors
   - Media mix
   - Media calendar
3. Marketing action plans
4. Budget
5. Master calendar

Figure 3-2. Outline of an Integrated Marketing Plan

As you can see from Figure 3-1, the integrated marketing plan is nestled under the strategic plan. In an ideal world, the strategic plan develops from solid research and a legitimate analysis of strengths, weaknesses, opportunities, and threats—also known as a SWOT analysis—and flows directly from the institutional mission and vision. It is also worth noting that there is a fuzzy boundary between a well-conceived strategic plan and the integrated marketing plan.

As you can see from Figure 3-2, the integrated marketing plan has five major components.

In their most elegant form, marketing goals are what you hope to accomplish through the integrated marketing plan. Not surprisingly, most integrated marketing goals tend to be strategic and involve the first three Cs and Ps: consumer/product, cost/price, and convenience/place. In addition, marketing goals often include image-related activities.

The next element of the integrated marketing plan is the communication component, which is responsible for coordinating communication with both internal and external audiences. Target audiences include the people—the daring among us may even call them customers—whom you wish to inform or influence. Surprisingly, the list of target audiences in an integrated marketing plan is generally small, usually no more than half a dozen or so. That's because the plan must focus on meeting the needs of the relatively few people who will truly, quickly, and significantly have an impact on your institution's future.

Understanding your target geographies—where people live—is extremely important in order to coordinate media buys, purchase mailing lists, schedule visits, and generally steward resources. Many plans founder or cannot be sustained because they try to reach target audiences spread out over too large a geographic area.

Vivid descriptors, or as some call them, points of pride, are the institutional core values expressed as words and phrases that you want to communicate aggressively to your target audiences. Like your target audiences, the number of vivid descriptors is usually relatively small, and must also be strategic. Vivid descriptors are very important because they form the backbone of the integrated marketing plan's communication component.

The media mix is the array of media incorporated into the overall integrated marketing plan. The media mix is heavily influenced by the media habits of the target audience, the budget, the sophistication and competitiveness of the media market, the complexity of your vivid descriptors, and other variables.

The media calendar keeps track of messages, media, and deadlines. Readers with a planning bent may find similarity between a media calendar and master calendar. Both feature GANTT charts (chronological overviews of a series of activities in which each is represented as a bar or symbol on a calendar) and are designed to help keep the plan on schedule and to increase accountability and control.

Marketing action plans outline individual activities that, when completed, will help accomplish the marketing goals. Action plans detail how the activity will support the marketing goal, who will be responsible for its implementation, and note how the activity will be evaluated. Action plans also often include a budget and timeline for completion.

An overall budget reflects a compilation of the budgets established for each marketing action plan and other resources such as those required for the media plan.

Finally, the timeline or master calendar is a management tool. As such, it includes all the action plans, as well as the media calendar, so that you

have an exact understanding of what is happening when.

GETTING STARTED

Like any planning activity, creating an integrated marketing plan is multi-step and sequential. In an ideal world, the integrated marketing plan flows from the strategic plan, which is founded on legitimate research and a comprehensive SWOT analysis. However, experience has taught me that many overlook this research and environmental diligence. To address this problem, I have included a basic SWOT analysis and research scenario.

Before you begin, you must have the active commitment of the president, or a very senior administrator with the backing of the president, to write a marketing plan. This commitment takes several forms.

- A commitment to affirm the viability of the institution's mission and a willingness to create and communicate a strong, compelling institutional vision.

- A commitment to spend time, money, talent, and political capital on marketing. You simply cannot proceed in creating a marketing plan without this commitment.

- A commitment to make tough decisions—to change institutional priorities and remove organizational stumbling blocks and territorial imperatives that hinder the marketing-planning process.

- A commitment to choose a champion and empower both the team leader and the overall team.

Though the president may or may not be involved in actually writing the marketing plan, his or her role is still pivotal. The president is involved in all key decisions beginning with deciding to proceed with marketing; committing the dollars; selecting the marketing champion and team; and establishing the marketing goals, target audiences, and action plans.

The president should designate a "champion," the single person responsible for the overall planning process. She or he must have the respect of the campus community, have both a theoretical and an experiential understanding of marketing, have power and clout (or access to power and clout), and be able to lead and motivate people.

Next, it's time to begin assembling the planning team. Note that we're calling this a marketing *team* rather than a marketing *committee*. This word choice is not accidental because creating a marketing plan involves a true team effort—individuals working together with a unified goal in mind. While the exact composition of the marketing team will change depending on the president's mandate, most include one or more people from the following areas:

- Public relations
- Recruiting and admissions
- Academics/faculty
- Student services
- Fund raising
- Athletics
- Institutional research
- Finance

As you set about selecting people for the team, keep in mind that its two most important functions are to gather insight and information from internal constituencies and the larger campus community, and to spread ownership of the planning process and the resulting plan.

Unless there is a compelling reason, I do not generally recommend that the integrated marketing planning team include the following audiences:

- Current students
- Alumni
- Trustees
- Community residents
- Business leaders
- Donors
- The president

Rather than having them on the team, I believe that their needs and the institution's needs are best served by having other team members aggressively solicit their input, especially at the situational-analysis stage.

It is important to note the tension between having input from various internal and external stakeholders and the need to keep the team as small as possible. Jon Katzenbach and Douglas Smith indicate that while it is theoretically possible to have

a team of any size, critical interaction is often lost as the team size expands: "Large numbers of people —by virtue of their size—have trouble interacting constructively as a group, much less agreeing on actionable specifics. Ten people are far more likely than 50 to successfully work through their individual, functional, and hierarchical differences toward a common plan and hold themselves jointly accountable for the results."

UNDERTAKE A SITUATIONAL ANALYSIS

Marketing plans begin with a thorough understanding of the institution and its marketplace. This process is called a situational or institutional analysis and includes a careful, systematic evaluation, from a marketing perspective, of your institution and its environment. The most important outcome is the gathering of data that will help guide the overall planning process. However, a properly conducted situational analysis is also a powerful way to help generate campus support for the planning process and the resulting plan.

If you have recently completed a strategic plan, you likely completed a situational analysis as part of it. If this is the case, examine the SWOT developed then and evaluate its completeness and currency before deciding to proceed with another one for the marketing plan.

Generally, the situational analysis is divided into two broad areas: internal/institutional and external/environmental. Depending on the degree of sophistication sought and the mandate from the president, the internal/institutional analysis may include the following activities:

- Evaluate current leadership.
- Review existing planning documents:
  - Strategic plan
  - Academic plan
  - Marketing plan
  - Recruiting plan
  - Fund-raising plan
  - Capital-improvement plan
  - Technology plan
- Review current market research.
- Review quality and currency of the institution's general core and overall curriculum.
- Evaluate faculty competencies.
- Evaluate success of current recruiting and fund-

raising strategies and activities.

■ Determine how such internal audiences as students, faculty, staff, administrators, and trustees perceive the institution. (Some may consider trustees an external constituency, and that's all right. The important thing is to make sure they are queried.)

■ Examine current product, price, place, and promotion strategies.

■ Review facilities and the physical plant.

■ Evaluate deferred-maintenance schedule.

■ Audit internal communication strategies.

A comprehensive external/environmental analysis, which in many cases parallels the internal one, would include the following:

■ Review linkages and exchange relationships with such key external publics as business leaders, community leaders, local government officials, and area religious institutions (if applicable).

■ Determine how such external publics as these perceive the institution:
  • Prospective students
  • Parents
  • High school influencers
  • Regional employers
  • Business leaders
  • Alumni
  • Community residents
  • Community leaders
  • Legislators and legislative staffs
  • Donors
  • Foundations

■ Examine local, regional, national, and even international economic, demographic, and employment trends.

■ Determine unmet educational needs in primary service areas.

■ Complete an analysis/comparison of the institutions with which you compete for students, gifts, or media attention.

■ Complete an audit of your external communication strategies.

As part of the situational analysis, you will ask different constituents their opinions on various aspects of the educational institution. These queries may occur one-on-one, in groups, or through sur-

vey research. Your interviews or surveys should begin with a basic explanation of why you are seeking opinions and how you'll use them. Because many of the questions and answers are sensitive, you should, where appropriate and possible, offer respondents both anonymity and confidentiality.

With each group of stakeholders, ask the following general questions:

1) From your perspective, what are the institution's major strengths?

2) What do you believe are its major weaknesses?

3) What do you believe are the major opportunities in our marketplace?

4) What are the major threats or challenges in our marketplace?

5) If you could change one aspect of the institution, what would it be?

6) If you had a reasonable budget, what marketing activity would you undertake?

7) I'd like to see the institution . . .

8) I choose to work here (or go to school here) because . . .

9) I think the institution can better respond to the future by . . .

10) I believe institutional quality entails . . .

11) For what should this institution be known? When people hear our name, what images would you like to have pop into their minds?

ORGANIZE THE DATA

During a situational analysis, you will quickly find yourself under an avalanche of data. It will help to begin organizing your findings into four broad categories, known collectively as a SWOT analysis.

■ *Strengths*. These are comparative advantages over competitors and resources that establish the institution's desired position, or something on which you can capitalize.

■ *Weaknesses*. These are problems, deficiencies, shortcomings, or flaws that detract from the institution's desired position. Weaknesses often consume resources that are better used elsewhere.

■ *Opportunities*. An opportunity is an attractive, sometimes fleeting, occurrence or trend where action is likely to produce a positive, competitive advantage. Responding to opportunities can propel the institution forward.

■ *Threats* are unfavorable trends or specific events that would lead to stagnation, decline, or demise of the institution or one of its programs.

As you gather and organize your data, it is very likely that you will soon have a grid like Fig 3-3, prepared by a client in the West as it worked through its strengths, weaknesses, opportunities, and threats.

Note that the grid in Figure 3-3 contains summary statements that often represent more complex issues. Don't worry; the marketing-team secretary will capture the exact wording. Also, the grid contains several characteristics that are labeled as both strengths and weaknesses or opportunities

Strengths	Weaknesses	Opportunities	Threats
Faculty credentials and emphasis on teaching	Value vs. cost	College/business links	Increased competition from publics and privates
Graduation rate	High cost to attend	Internships	Tuition gap between publics and privates
Presidential leadership	Dated, often antiquated facilities	Service/community relations	Uncertain government policies
Location	Low endowment	Leadership opportunities for students	Private college competition with more name recognition and financial aid
Current student research	Campus climate: anger and apathy	Summer school	Declining student pools
Commitment to customer service	Location	New recruiting markets	
Campus ambiance/ environment	Little institutional image, especially in emerging recruiting markets	Transfer market	
Many credible alumni	Poor retention rate	Experiential learning	
	Low level of student involvement in campus activities	Employer needs	
	Low annual fund participation	Summer camps/ conferences	
	Meager fund-raising ability		
	Lost alumni		
	Inability to make decisions in a timely manner		
	Too much faculty involvement in governance process		
	No common vision		
	Few noteworthy cultural events		

Figure 3-3. SWOT Analysis

and threats. Finally, note that these characteristics are marketing-oriented. The purpose of this grid is not to outline every ill and option your institution faces but to focus on those variables that might affect its ability to market itself more aggressively.

MAKE A DECISION ON MARKET RESEARCH

The situational analysis will often lead to a realization that you don't know enough about a particular issue. For example, the campus may not have recent data on how various internal or external audiences perceive it. Perhaps the institution has never examined unmet educational needs in its target geography. Maybe no one has undertaken a systematic evaluation of its curriculum.

At this point, the college must make a decision on whether it should undertake formal market research to gather the data it needs. This is often a tough decision. On the pro side, good data will provide extraordinarily valuable insight. On the con side, research requires time and money.

There is no simple rule that will help you determine whether you need to undertake research. But, if you need perspective, work in a politically charged environment, need data to help you make major or difficult decisions, plan to spend significant dollars over a number of years implementing your marketing plan, or politically simply cannot afford to be wrong, then undertake market research. You won't regret it.

PRIORITIZE AND FINALIZE SWOT

At this stage, your SWOT list is probably very long and cumbersome—and you probably do not have the institutional resources to address every item. To solve this problem, use the list as a ballot and let team members vote on which items are most important.

The voting process works like this. Every team member gets a number of votes, say 12. The member can use three for each SWOT category. Members can give all three of their votes to one item, give one item two votes and another just one vote, or give one vote to three different items. This voting accomplishes several important tasks. First, it sets priorities. Second, because some additions to the list were not unanimous, the voting allows a final group evaluation. And third, because the vot-

ing is done in secret, individuals are protected from group dynamics and pressure.

The SWOT is then retabulated on the basis of the votes. This new, prioritized list reflects the strengths, weaknesses, opportunities, and threats of most significance to the marketing team.

ESTABLISH YOUR MARKETING GOALS

Next, coalesce the SWOT grid into a cogent set of manageable marketing goals. You may prefer to create a list of target audiences and then outline the marketing goals. It really doesn't matter which you do first. Marketing goals and target audiences are a chicken-and-egg kind of issue. It's hard to know which comes first, but you need both before you can write marketing action plans.

As we learned in the introduction to this chapter, a marketing goal is something you wish to accomplish. Sometimes called an objective, a good marketing goal builds on a strength, addresses a weakness, realizes an opportunity, or neutralizes a threat. It is perfectly acceptable to include in your new marketing plan goals you are already working on, as long as they survive the critical light of the SWOT.

Good marketing goals have specific characteristics that make them easier to conceptualize, achieve, and evaluate. Good marketing goals are:

- important, usually based on your institution's mission and vision;
- derived from your prioritized situational analysis;
- founded on research;
- realistic and achievable;
- as quantifiable as possible;
- unambiguous and narrowly focused;
- usually directed at one or more clearly defined target audiences.

As you assemble the goals, remember to keep the number of goals as small as possible, ideally no more than five or six. Any more and you run the risk of too large and cumbersome a plan. The only time to consider more goals is if you already have some experience with marketing plans and/or your SWOT analysis clearly indicates that you need more goals.

Second, try to keep the goals straightforward

and universally accepted. If you can, begin with goals that most campus constituents believe should be accomplished. Not only will this help win initial acceptance of the plan, but it will allow you to gain experience and credibility you can use later as you seek to address more complex, perhaps controversial, goals.

And finally, consider the timing. It is sometimes wise to implement some goals earlier in the plan and hold some until later. A good marketing plan is designed to run for five or more years. During the first couple of years, focus on goals that most constituents feel positive about. This will help you gain both credibility and momentum.

SAMPLE MARKETING GOALS

Let's look at some sample marketing goals:

1. We will raise undergraduate enrollment by 20 percent, from 3,800 to 4,560, over the next six years.
2. We will increase freshman-to-sophomore retention from 63 percent to 75 percent over five years.
3. We will establish a campus culture that stresses the following qualities:
   - outstanding academic quality;
   - programs and instruction that lead to jobs and graduate school;
   - a friendly, safe, fun, and nurturing campus that stresses participation;
   - individual responsibility and accountability;
   - the economic, cultural, and social impact our institution has made and will continue to make in the region.
4. We will establish a strong institutional image that focuses on a 150-mile radius. This image will stress the qualities outlined in Goal 3.
5. We will develop a comprehensive customer-service program that embraces prospective and current students, faculty, staff, administrators, and visitors to the campus.
6. We will increase annual-fund participation from 39 percent to 50 percent over three years, and we will increase the average contribution from $22 to $45.

These goals have some subtle distinctions that are worth noting. First, they all begin with "we." This is a small but significant point. The institution is stating from the beginning that these are our goals—not merely the goals of the marketing team. Second, the tone of these goals is invigorating. There is a sense of mission and vision here. These goals are strategic and far-reaching. Third, as much as is reasonably possible, these goals are built on baseline data. Enrollment growth, annual-fund growth, and participation levels are clearly documented. The radius of the institutional image is clearly outlined. Fourth, these goals are both internal and external. Goal 3 outlines campus values, while Goal 4 stresses the marketing of these values to external audiences.

THE COMMUNICATION COMPONENT OF THE INTEGRATED MARKETING PLAN

Once you have established the marketing goals, it is time to begin working on the communication subset of the overall integrated marketing plan. Remember, it is this portion of the plan that is charged with communicating the decisions you made about your three Cs and three Ps to target audiences.

Target Audiences

In higher education, there are some oft-targeted audiences. See Figure 3-4.

Take the time to define your target audiences carefully. For example, if you include faculty, are you including part-timers as well as full-timers? If you are going to focus on alumni, do you include those alumni who didn't earn a degree as well as those who did?

You may quickly find yourself with 15 to 20 likely candidates. Ask yourself which of these audiences:

- have you defined as critically as possible?
- were consistently highlighted in the situational analysis?
- have the most potential to advance the vision significantly?
- are you able to realistically serve?
- reside in your primary recruiting region?
- are most advanced on the six-stage behavioral matrix?
- are merely loud and persistent rather than truly important?

Students	College or University	External: Fund Raising	External: Other
Current students	Faculty	Current donors: major	Parents
Prospective undergraduate, graduate, and continuing education students	Staff	Current donors: minor	Legislators
Inquiring students	Administrators	Former donors	Church leaders
Applicants	Alumni	Prospective donors	Community residents
Matriculants	Trustees	Foundations	Community leaders
Nonmatriculants			Business leaders
Withdrawing students			High school contacts
Students of color			Media
International students			

Figure 3-4. Target Audiences

As an example of target audiences, a large public institution in Ohio created this list:

■ prospective undergraduate, graduate, and continuing-education students;

■ parents of traditional-age prospective students;

■ high school influencers—guidance counselors, teachers, club advisers;

■ community residents within 75 miles of the institution;

■ the education, business, sports, and science press;

■ alumni;

■ donors.

Target Geographies

Your target geography is the physical landscape in which your target audiences live. One of the biggest mistakes that planners make is to overestimate the size of their target geography. A useful way to get a clear sense of where your most important target audiences live, in numbers that are sufficiently dense, is to use a mapping software such as Microsoft ACCESS for Windows 97 or MapLinx.

Consider, for example, a college that attracts students from 42 different states, the majority of which come from the upper Midwest. A map diagram would be an extremely helpful demonstration as the institution develops an advertising campaign or seeks to establish alumni clubs where they would have the most impact on student recruiting.

As you attempt to get a better handle on your target geography, consider plotting—on a single map—the following seven databases:

1. Current students
2. Prospective students
3. Alumni
4. Alumni clubs
5. Feeder high schools
6. Feeder churches
7. Two- and four-year competitors (both public and private)

If resources are tight, for example, you might want to focus on areas and regions where these databases overlap because it is these target geographies that offer the greatest synergy.

Based on our experience, many integrated marketing plans and their communication components fail, or are not sustainable budgetarily, because they try to address geographies that are too large, too distant, or too disparate. All things considered, it is more efficient and effective to work in a smaller area than a larger one. We realize that this may not be as glamorous, but we are convinced it is a better stewardship of dollars and time.

Vivid Descriptors

Now that the situational analysis has been approved, it is time to begin clarifying your vivid descriptors and points of pride. A vivid descriptor is something for which you want to be known. It is the answer to the question, "When people hear your institution's name, what image do you want to pop into their minds?"

Initial answers to this question were gathered as part of the SWOT analysis. However, it is also useful to consider answers to this question in light of your primary competition, the nature of your marketplace, and even your target audiences.

Vivid descriptors must represent core institutional values. Second, they must be widely shared and appreciated by key campus and external constituencies. And third, they must be enduring—things to which the institution can commit for a long period of time.

Many people feel that vivid descriptors should be unique, and if they are, that's certainly helpful. But more important, the descriptors should be mission-critical and of value to your target audiences. Your vivid descriptors may well be "mixed," much like your four Ps. For example, donors may be more interested in some of the descriptors than students are.

Let's look at a list of vivid descriptors developed by a public four-year institution in Texas. In response to the question "For what do we want to be known?" the institution settled on the following vivid descriptors:

■ A caring, supportive campus culture;
■ High-quality faculty, facilities, programs, and graduates;
■ A valuable economic, cultural, and intellectual asset to the region.

A private institution in Ohio wanted to be known for:

■ Respect of individual students, faculty, staff, alumni, donors, and the community;
■ Service to students;
■ Timely graduation;
■ Academic programs that lead to jobs.

As you gather and evaluate potential vivid descriptors, keep their number as small as possible. Five or six descriptors are usually more than adequate. Any more and the list becomes unmanageable. It is also important that the list serves the entire institution, not just recruiting. Good descriptors and points of

pride can also have a catalytic effect on fund-raising and alumni relations.

Media Mix

For the most part, developing a media mix involves answering a series of questions. You have already discovered who your target audiences are and where they live. The other questions are:

■ What is their awareness of or attitude toward your institution?
■ What are their media habits?
■ What media are prevalent within your target geography?
■ What media can you afford to use over time?
■ What are your communication goals? Create initial awareness? Persuade? Motivate?
■ What is the character and complexity of your message?

Some of these can only be answered with audience research. This is especially true for questions dealing with audience awareness and media habits.

As you will see from the Table 3-1, we encourage a very rich definition of "media." This expanded definition is intentional for two reasons. First, many plans falter because they focus on a media array that is too narrow. And second, the media plan should embrace all communication and outreach, not merely print or broadcast.

Media relations: PSAs	Outdoor/transit advertising
Media relations: Feature stories	Specialty advertising
Media relations: Hometowners	Environmentals/signage
Media relations: Wild art	Web/Internet/Intranet
Media relations: Tip sheets	Video/audio
Media news	Compact discs
Alumni relations	Publications
High school relations	Direct mail
Public relations	Special events
TV/cable advertising	Telemarketing
Radio advertising	Word of mouth
Newspaper advertising	
Magazine advertising	

Table 3-1. Media Mix Options

As you develop your media mix, it is extremely important to assess initial audience awareness. For example, if you are developing a message strategy for prospective students that have never heard of you, it is relatively ineffective to focus on highly personalized telemarketing or direct mail. Rather, you should consider media-mix options that seek to establish an initial awareness before developing customized, and often more expensive, messages.

We should emphasize that different media, used in conjunction with different audiences, will not require different messages, but variations on message themes. For example, a radio spot that stresses academic quality has to be less sophisticated and less detailed than an editorial in the op-ed page of the local newspaper or even a print ad in a regional magazine. While all three messages may focus on academic quality, they are intended for different audiences and respond to the characteristics of different mediums. In some respects, the need to customize and modify will force you to be more creative than usual. In addition, all these variations on the same theme will help reinforce that theme in your marketplace.

To help you develop an effective media mix, make a simple grid with three columns. In the left column, list your primary target audiences. In the middle column, based on the audience research you have completed, list how the particular target audience defines and interprets your vivid descriptors. And in the right column, list the media habits, once again based on audience research, of the individual target audiences. This grid will help you keep track of the essential elements of the integrated marketing communication plan. (Table 3-2.)

Make sure the media mix you adopt is sustainable over time. Big splashes are just that—splashes—and seldom have any long-term impact. Second, avoid the temptation to automatically turn to mass advertising. Unless you have substantial dollars at your disposal and have carefully matched different media buys to the media habits of your target audiences, it's seldom a good first choice. Keep in mind, too, that even mass advertising should be supported by other media such as direct mail, special events, etc.

Third, try to develop a media mix that serves more than one audience. It is very confusing and

Communication Grid		
Target Audience	Vivid Descriptors	Media Habits
1.	a. b. c. d.	a. b. c. d.
2.	a. b. c. d.	a. b. c. d.
3.	a. b. c. d.	a. b. c. d.
4.	a. b. c. d.	a. b. c. d.

Table 3-2. Communication Grid

time consuming to develop overly segmented mixes. Fourth, don't overlook "low-end" but incredibly powerful media such as word-of-mouth or special events. They are not particularly sexy, but are often highly effective. Fifth, take the time to test your messages and media on smaller subsets of your target audience before the big rollout. You will almost always be glad that you pretested because this will give you one last chance to catch any mistakes and to refine your concepts.

Finally, and perhaps most importantly, make sure the media you choose and the messages you craft focus on the needs and expectations of your target audiences, not simply those of your president, faculty, or major donors.

Media Calendar

The media calendar is a management tool that helps you coordinate all your communication activities. Typically, this calendar can be accommodated in the larger master calendar, but because media are often expensive and deadlines tight, some prefer a separate media calendar.

MARKETING ACTION PLANS

If goals are what you want done and target audiences are the people to whom goals are directed, then the marketing action plan is the means by which goals are accomplished. In essence, the marketing action plan, or MAP, is a simple device that tells who will be doing what as you execute strategies. Consider, for example, the following goal:

Increase freshman-to-sophomore retention from 66 percent to 75 percent over five years.

Let's outline a handful of action-plan topics that will help accomplish the marketing goal:

■ Define retention appropriately for each type of student—traditional, nontraditional, and graduate—and use this definition consistently.

■ Conduct extensive research of current students' needs and expectations and of why students withdraw.

■ Develop a more effective freshman orientation program.

■ Target at-risk students.

■ Implement a mentoring program.

■ Create a profile of students who are more likely to enroll and graduate.

■ Document to faculty the dollar and non-dollar cost of each lost student.

■ Offer an honors college with special orientation, advising, programs, scholarships, and privileges.

■ Develop aggressive residence-life programs; use residence assistants as part of an early-warning system.

■ Implement a campus ombudsman program.

■ Discount tuition by five percent for sophomores, juniors, and seniors.

■ Offer "one-stop shopping," a place where students can register, pay fees, and deal with financial aid.

■ Increase quality of residence life.

■ Train, motivate, and reward advisers and make them accountable for their mistakes.

Each of these strategies would be accomplished through the creation of one or more marketing action plans.

Marketing Action Plan Template

Develop a standard template for all your marketing action plans. Some templates are fairly simple; oth-

ers present the MAP in more detail. At a minimum, a MAP template needs to describe the activity, when it will begin and end, who will be responsible, and how much it will cost. I have used variations of the template in Table 3-3 with great success.

Earlier, when discussing creation of the list of marketing goals, I suggested you work with general goals and leave details and wordsmithing for later. I make this same recommendation here. Creation of your MAPs will proceed much more quickly if you work with MAP titles and avoid detail until later. Once the marketing team has assembled the complete range of MAP topics, it can make preliminary decisions about which to flesh out.

ESTABLISH BUDGET

You must reconcile two variables as part of the budgeting process: the rough budget established by your president at the outset, and the dollars required to accomplish the assembled MAPs. With luck, these two amounts won't be too different. Chances are, though, that your MAPs require more money than your president anticipated. If this is the case, you must begin to make your case for more dollars. Thankfully, you will enter this discussion with two important assets: Your chief finance officer has been involved in the planning process and the president has approved, as the plan progressed, the SWOT, goals, and target audiences.

> ● ● ●
> **Remember one of the fundamental rules of budgeting: Put a little extra in earlier so you can take a little more out later.**

Before discussing the actual budget, work carefully with the president through the SWOT, marketing goals, and target audiences that he or she previously approved. Show how the MAPs are designed to accomplish the marketing goals and, by extension, help achieve the president's vision. If some of the goals and action plans will help increase revenue through the annual fund, a capital campaign, or tuition, give some reasonable projections. Remind the president that although the plan represents a multiyear commitment, chances are that plan expenditures will decrease once it takes effect. It is generally less expensive to maintain marketing efforts than to start them.

Even with the most ardent support of your president, you will probably have to go back and

Title of marketing action plan	
Description of the MAP	
Which goal(s) the plan supports	1.
	2.
	3.
	4.
	5.
Target audiences	1.
	2.
	3.
	4.
	5.
Action plan step-by-step	1.
	2.
	3.
	4.
	5.
Timeline	Begin date:
	End date:
Budget	$
	$
	$
	$
	$
MAP assigned to	
Evaluation mechanisms	
When to evaluate	
Who evaluates	
Report results to	

Table 3-3. Marketing Action Plan Template

trim the budget. As you do so, focus on the prioritized marketing goals. Make every effort to preserve dollars, and the activities they represent, in the areas that matter most to the institution. Remember one of the fundamental rules of budgeting: Put a little extra in earlier so you can take a little more out later.

MASTER CALENDAR

Like the media calendar, the master calendar is a management tool that helps you keep track of your integrated marketing action plans. Use FastTrack or some other software to create your master calendar. It should depict a series of activities for a three-month period of a theoretical integrated marketing plan. The calendar should indicate the activity name, the cost, the start date, and

then present a series of diamonds and bars to show how the different activities relate to one another.

The final step is to debug the plan. Review each component. Make sure the SWOT is complete. Clarify that the goals are well conceived and important. Working from the individual and collective MAPs and the assembled GANTT charts, evaluate the following:

- Are you spending 80 percent of your time and resources on the 20 most important activities?
- Is every MAP clearly supporting a goal? If it isn't, take it out, or at least highlight it for cutting if a budget crunch occurs.
- Is the viability of each MAP clearly borne out in the SWOT?
- Has enough time been allocated for each MAP? Remember, things take longer the first

time through.

■ Are the budgeted dollars realistic? If not, costs will cartwheel out of control.

■ Are too few people doing too many things? All major administrative departments should be involved in executing action plans.

■ Are first things being done first? Do what needs to be done now so that other things can be done later.

■ Are early MAPs primed for success? For morale and political reasons, make sure some of your early MAPs are highly successful and highly visible.

If your MAPs survive after you ask and answer these questions, you have gone a long way to developing a sound plan. Because you have used planning software, you can also run a total budget and timeline. When these are done, add them to the marketing-planning notebook. Congratulations, you've written a marketing plan. Now it's time to put it into action.

EXECUTE THE PLAN

As you look at your completed plan, you will probably feel anxious about implementing it. Before you panic, reconsider the master calendar you have just assembled. The master calendar is more than a summary of all your marketing activities; it is a chronological guide of what should be done and when. By following your calendar, you keep the execution of the plan on time and on target.

EVALUATE AND MODIFY THE PLAN

As you begin to execute the marketing plan, you are also beginning to evaluate and modify it. Evaluation occurs along two dimensions. First, you might evaluate whether a MAP is on schedule or completed and whether it ran on, under, or over budget. This is evaluation at its most basic. However, you must also be prepared to determine whether the MAP helped accomplish the overarching goal or goals and even whether the goals themselves have been accomplished. This is a more complex type of evaluation.

As in the completion of a single MAP, you might assume that if all the MAPs are completed, the goal was accomplished. However, even if you accomplish all your MAPs, you may or may not have accomplished your goal. This requires a different level of evaluation. If your marketing goals are quantifiable and built on baseline data, it is relatively easy to measure progress.

Also keep in mind that ongoing evaluation may lead you to add or modify action plans. The odds are great that you, someone from the marketing planning team, or someone else on campus will have a great idea for a new plan or plans long after the original plan is complete. This is ok. Remember, the written plan is less important than the planning process that accommodates this kind of modification.

One final thought about evaluation. You will find that the best goals are always a little bit beyond your reach. For example, let's say your goal is to increase retention from 45 percent to 60 percent over three years. After executing a number of MAPs, you find you've accomplished that. However, it is never a good strategy to rest on this accomplishment. Instead, after a period, raise the goal.

Although achieving quantifiable goals is extraordinarily important, you can evaluate the overall success of your marketing plan, in part, by answering the question: Has the financial condition of the college or university improved since it began marketing? Some people will find this question overly simplistic, even crass. But think about it. Most marketing goals have as their logical end the improvement of the institution's financial condition. You recruit more students because of the revenue they bring. You attract excellent faculty members because they will attract better students and more grant money. Stronger images attract more students and donors. Satisfied students stay longer. Happy alumni contribute more. Tightening bonds with a local community will help preserve the flow of resources.

Is this oversimplified? Sure. But the point is an important one. One way to measure the overall effectiveness of your marketing plan is to see whether the institution is better off afterward than before.

HOLD A PLANNING POSTMORTEM

Once the plan is under way and you have had a chance to reflect on the progress of individual MAPs and the overall planning process, it is time to hold a planning postmortem. The postmortem is designed to help you evaluate the process you just completed so your next planning cycle will be more effective and efficient. There is no prescribed postmortem process. The goal is to gather as much insight and information as possible.

To this end, it is often best to begin with the president, the senior administrators, or both. After the plan has been under way for a period, ask the president how she feels about the planning process and the resulting plan. Was the president comfortable with her role? Was the budgeting method sensitive to other campus needs? Was the approval process well-engineered? Did the overall process live up to the president's expectations? What would she like done differently the next time around? Ask good questions. Listen closely. And probe.

It's also a good idea to spend time with the planning team. What did they like and not like? What would they do differently? What do they wish they could undo? What was their favorite part of the planning process? What part surpassed their expectations? What part did they like least? Was enough time spent on each step; was too much time spent? How did the process affect their interaction with colleagues not directly involved? And don't forget to ask whether the planning process was a good use of their time.

It is also useful to talk to campus constituents. Perhaps working through the team and its liaisons with different groups, ask the following questions:

- Do constituents feel that they were listened to?
- Do they feel sufficiently involved in the process?
- Do they understand the need for planning?
- Do they think their involvement was a good use of their time?
- Do they feel a sense of ownership with the plan?
- Are they committed to the plan and its success?
- Do they feel that things have improved?

And finally:

- Do they feel that marketing is a good use of campus resources?

Integrated marketing is much more than communication and promotion, and deals with larger issues than institutional images. It is more strategic in nature than more traditional marketing and emphasizes the stewarding of strategic assets to meet mission-critical goals. In addition, it is much more outward-looking and listening-oriented because it is keenly interested in meeting the needs of customers and not just stakeholders. It is not a panacea. But for institutions confronted with difficult times—or great opportunities—integrated marketing can be a highly effective and efficient way to realize your mission and vision.

Author's note: Some of the material in this chapter is condensed from my book, Integrated Marketing for Colleges, Universities, and Schools, *published by CASE Books in 1998.*

REFERENCES

Beckwith, Harry. *Selling the Invisible: A Field Guide to Modern Marketing.* New York, NY: Warner Books, 1997.

Brooks, L. and J. Hammond. "Has Higher Education Been Using the Wrong Marketing Approach?" *Journal of Marketing for Higher Education,* 1993.

Dolence, Michael G., Daniel James Rowley and Herman D. Lujan. *Working Toward Strategic Change: A Step-by-Step Guide to the Planning Process.* San Francisco, CA: Jossey-Bass, 1997.

Hall, Cindy, "Demystifying Marketing: Campuses Use and Confuse This Concept. To Understand It, Start by Cutting through the Fog," CURRENTS 18, no. 2 (Feb 1993).

Katzenbach, Jon R. and Douglas K. Smith. *The Wisdom of Teams.* New York, NY: Harper & Row, 1994.

Kriegel, Robert and David Brandt. *Sacred Cows Make the Best Burgers: Developing Change-Ready People and Organizations.* New York, NY: Warner Books, 1997

Nanus, Burt. *Visionary Leadership.* San Francisco, CA: Jossey-Bass Publishers, 1992.

Peppers, Don and Martha Rogers. *Enterprise One to One: Tools for Competing in the Interactive Age.* New York, NY: Doubleday, 1997.

Percy, Larry. *Strategies for Implementing Integrated Marketing Communications.* Chicago, IL: NTC Publishing Group, 1998.

Roman, Erman. *Integrated Direct Marketing.* Chicago, IL: NTC Publishing Group, 1998.

Schultz, Don E., Stanley Tannenbaum, and Robert F. Lauterborn. *Integrated Marketing Communications:*

Developing
an Integrated
Marketing Plan

Putting It Together and Making it Work. Chicago, IL: NTC Business Books, 1993.

Schultz, Don E., Stanley Tannenbaum and Robert F. Lauterborn *The New Marketing Paradigm: Integrated Marketing Communications.* Chicago, IL: NTC Publishing, 1997.

Sevier, Robert A.: "Why Marketing Plans Fail: Nine Reasons Student Recruitment Efforts Break Down—And How to Avoid Them." CURRENTS 19, no. 10 (November/December, 1994.)

Sevier, Robert A. *Integrated Marketing for Colleges, Universities, and Schools.* Washington, DC: CASE Books, 1998.

● ● ●

Marketing research is the process by which information is specified, gathered, analyzed, and interpreted to help an organization understand its marketing environment.

SECTION VI
Marketing and
Advancement

4

Marketing Research for Advancement Professionals

Donna A. Van De Water
Vice President for Research
Lipman Hearne, Inc.

Marketing research can be an extremely useful and effective tool for advancing the institution. It's surprising, then, that it's so often given short shrift by marketing professionals. That's because research is also one of the most misunderstood of marketing tools. Changing that misconception is what this chapter is all about.

As an educator and marketing research professional, I work with two distinct groups of people who need to know something about research. The first is my graduate students— individuals who need an in-depth and theoretical understanding of the work. The second group is institutional leaders who must identify and articulate research objectives, manage the process, then use the data to solve institutional challenges. This chapter is for that group.

WHAT REALLY *IS* RESEARCH—AND WHAT IS IT *NOT*?

Marketing research is the process by which information is specified, gathered, analyzed, and interpreted to help an organization understand its marketing environment. In a nonprofit institu-

tion, marketing research can help development professionals to identify problems and opportunities, and to develop and evaluate courses of marketing action. Marketers can use research to:

- **Identify opportunities:** How should the institution be positioned in the eyes of its constituents? How can those constituents be segmented into meaningfully distinct groups? What messages should be *targeted* to various segments?

- **Understand constituents:** What are the motivations of our prospective and current students, alumni, friends, and other supportive publics? What are the trends in their decision making? In the future, what are they likely to demand from an educational institution, and how might we better serve those needs?

- **Develop the marketing and communication plan:** How do we communicate key messages to our target audiences to position the institution? How can we highlight programs and services to attract constituents?

- **Develop advertising:** What creative concepts are most effective in reaching our audiences? Where should advertising be placed, and what's the best use of our budget?

But before you become too strong a convert to the cult of marketing research, take a step back. Marketing research is not a silver bullet: miraculous revelations are few, and rarely will obvious answers to institutional quandaries come leaping out of columns of numbers. To tell the truth, research usually *raises* more questions than it answers. Confronting those questions—and using the research to answer them—is your task as a manager. Research is a valuable aid to decision-making, but it does not replace your experience and sound judgment.

THE RESEARCH PROCESS

Any research project includes a number of distinct but interrelated tasks:

1. Specify objectives.
2. Establish research design.
3. Determine data collection method.
4. Select the sample.
5. Collect the data.
6. Analyze the results.
7. Report the results.

Any manager who's going to make effective use of research needs to take a role in deciding among the many choices and options present at each stage of the project.

Specify Objectives

At the outset, you have to understand thoroughly your objectives for research. Which of these three sounds most like your situation?

1. We need fresh insights into a challenge facing the institution. We need to define the problem better, to identify an appropriate course of action, or to develop more focused research. (Indicated: *Exploratory research*)

Examples:

■ Decline in the annual fund.
■ Chronically low rate of matriculation by admitted students.

2. We understand the questions facing us, and now we just need data to help us decide among possible responses. (Indicated: *Descriptive* research)

Examples:

■ We're confident our annual fund decline can be tied to the audience's lack of awareness. Now we need to measure what messages constituents will find most compelling.

Criteria That Predict Effective Research

It's important to consider the cost and benefits of research before you begin. Effective research requires real commitment. Insightful, actionable research fits these criteria:

■ **Research must be planned by marketing research professionals and decision-makers working in concert.** Careful dialogue is needed if researchers are to design research that yields the answers leaders really want. Institutional leaders and researchers must establish and work toward mutually agreed-upon goals and objectives. (Designing effective research is rarely as simple as managers think it ought to be!)

■ **Research must begin with an end in mind.** Researchers need to understand not just the information that's sought but how it's to be used and by whom. Having clear objectives is the only way to

develop an effective research instrument.

■ **Research must be relevant to current or future decisions.** If the research isn't of strategic or tactical importance, skip it.

■ **Research must be timely.** If the research will not be used to answer questions that are immediately on the horizon, it's better to wait for key issues to clarify themselves—because time can invalidate research results. Conversely, if there isn't time to do the research correctly, don't do it—because lack of time can also yield poor results.

■ **Research must be cost effective.** If the value of the research doesn't exceed the costs, don't do it.

■ **Research must be accurate.** As we'll see in the next section, accuracy is a matter of choosing the right kind of research for the job at hand.

■ We believe our follow-up with admitted students is too unfocused. We need to discover what follow-up measures will be most effective.

3. We believe we understand our challenge and what's causing it. Now we need to prove that causal relationship without any doubt, so we can have the utmost confidence in our response. (Indicated: *Experimental* research)

Examples:

■ We intend to shift some resources from direct mail to phone solicitation and want to predict our return on investment.

■ What increase in enrollment can we anticipate if we reduce tuition by 10 percent?

Establish Research Design

The description that sounds most like your situation will dictate which research design you should choose. There are three major research designs.

1) Exploratory Research

This is the least structured and most flexible of the three basic designs. Usually, the number of survey participants will be small and only partially representative of your constituency.

Exploratory research usually focuses on these data-gathering methods:

■ Secondary data, including literature searches, census data, industry reports, papers and talks from conferences, and previously conducted research (which must be reviewed carefully for hidden bias);

■ Individual *interviews* with knowledgeable people;

■ Case studies;

■ Pilot surveys;

■ Focus groups.

Focus groups are a widely used—and misused—method for gathering data in exploratory research. As such, they're worth some discussion. Everyone has a mental image of a focus group: a small number of people discussing a topic of interest to the institution. In an open-ended discussion led by a moderator, each individual is exposed to the ideas of others. The interplay of perspectives helps gen-

erate new, creative ideas, uncovering basic constituent needs and attitudes, and testing new products and services. Focus groups truly are exploratory, as you uncover underlying reasons and motivations for people's attitudes, preferences, and behavior.

Focus groups are very useful in understanding and defining problems, specifying information needs, or planning further, more rigorous research. They can also be used at the back end of a research process, to help amplify quantitative conclusions and make recommendations from research data.

Focus groups offer a number of advantages for research designers:

■ *Quick*—They can be executed quickly, and the information is immediately available.

■ *Cost effective*—They're fairly inexpensive (though travel, reporting, and participant recruiting costs can be considerable).

■ *Flexible*—From session to session, or even within sessions, you have the opportunity to observe and react to findings—or even change your study design as data is being collected.

■ *Secure*—You can expose sensitive concepts or prototypes to a limited number of respondents in a tightly controlled environment. (The moderator should be made aware of any security concerns and be advised about information that should not be shared.)

■ *Immediate and personal*—Focus groups allow staff members to perceive issues from the constituents' point of view.

Apart from choosing the type and number of participants, a good moderator is the most important key to successful focus groups. An engaging, skilled, thinking-on-one's-feet moderator can make all the difference when it comes to putting participants at ease and collecting excellent feedback. Yet even for the most talented moderators, preparation is essential. Educate your moderator so that he or she is thoroughly familiar with the topic under study. Provide a site visit and background information, including current market conditions, your institutional positioning, competitor profiles, examples of your advertising, etc.

Moderator's guides—the list of questions and issues to be explored—should be thoughtfully prepared. The guide should include enough questions to cover your information needs, but not so many that respondents become bored, tired, or disinterested. Sequence the discussion in an orderly fashion to avoid conversations that jump from topic to topic with no apparent connection and with exhausting effect.

Here's a typical sequence:

■ *Introduction*—Explain the reason for the focus group. Preview the discussion and any ground rules. The goal is to relax respondents, develop rapport, and encourage interaction.

■ *Warmup*—Begin with low-anxiety questions. It's important to have all participants introduce themselves briefly. This jumpstarts self-disclosure and builds the respondents' confidence in their ability to participate.

■ *In-depth discussion*—Transition to critical issues. The skillful moderator will shift gradually from eliciting descriptive, concrete input to a more abstract, thoughtful discussion that plumbs respondents' imaginations and attitudes.

■ *Closure*—Sift notes to check moderator's interpretations; send up trial balloons to identify group consensus on issues. Ask for additional comments or suggestions.

2) Descriptive Research

Descriptive research is appropriate in situations where, because of previous research or a strong hunch, you understand the questions facing the institution and need to decide among possible responses or quantify some particular factor. In general terms, descriptive research attempts to determine the frequency with which something occurs, or to discover the relationship between two variables. You might want to describe the characteristics of certain audiences, determine their perceptions of products or services, or measure and predict the behavior of the target population. Basically, you're trying to understand subject characteristics and their likelihood of acting or feeling a certain way.

Obviously, this model is a little more scientific and less flexible than exploratory research. There

are two main types: cross-sectional and longitudinal. Cross-sectional research measures a sample of the population at one time, providing a snapshot of attitudes at that particular point. In a longitudinal study, a sample of the population is measured repeatedly over time so you get a series of snapshots. These snapshots provide a clear understanding of the changes that are taking place in a situation. For example, a university that is considering eliminating certain programs may want to survey alumni of those programs repeatedly to understand how the changes affect their attitudes and behavior toward the institution.

3) Experimental Research

Do you need to find out whether an alumni yield calling program will result in more students with higher GPAs matriculating at your university? In such a situation, researchers might conduct experimental research to establish a reliable cause and effect relationship between such variables.

To establish a causal relationship, it's necessary to learn how changing the independent variable (in this case, the calling program), produces a change in the dependent variable (matriculation). Your research must measure the extent to which the cause and effect occur together (a concomitant variation or association) and the time order of the occurrence (cause must precede effect), and must eliminate other possible causal factors.

If you suspected that phrases like scientific causality, independent variable, and concomitant variation probably describe the most scientifically exacting of the general research models, you'd be right. And this complexity only scratches the surface. In-depth research resources encompass four categories of experimental designs (for the record, pre-experimental, true experimental, quasi-experimental, and statistical). They'll also introduce you to more detailed designs including Randomized Blocks, the Solomon Four Group, the Latin Square, and other techniques that are beyond the scope of this chapter.

I'll spare you this discussion because, to be honest, such scientific exactitude (read: expense) is

● ● ●
Bottom line: for the purposes of college and university marketers, nonprobability samples (where respondents are chosen because they satisfy certain criteria) usually suffice.

rarely necessary for the kind of marketing research pursued by colleges, universities, and schools. However, managers who use research should understand one aspect of experimental research: scientific validity.

Generally, validity expresses the confidence we have in the results of a research project. To create valid experimental research, you have two goals:

■ To construct the study so that the data clearly show a cause and effect relationship between one variable and another (*internal validity*); and

■ To be able to generalize the effect reliably to the real world (where *most* of our institutions operate) (*external validity*).

There's an inevitable tension between internal and external validity. To increase internal validity, we want to eliminate as many outside variables as possible. But if we do that, we create an extremely artificial situation that may not be applicable to reality. Because of this tension, managers should be aware of possible threats to validity. You want to make sure that the changes in the dependent variable are attributable only to the independent variable. To probe validity, ask these questions:

1) Could any outside events influence the independent variable? (*history*)

2) Will the passage of time affect biological or psychological processes that yielded the results? (*maturation*)

3) Will the measurement instrument change over time (different measurement scales or interviewer)? (*instrument variation*)

4) Will the groups studied lose members at different rates over time? (*experimental mortality*)

5) Will the very taking of a measurement have an effect on subsequent measurements? (*premeasurement effect*)

6) Could a premeasurement alter respondents' sensitivity to the independent variable? (*interaction effect*)

7) Are the groups being formed for the experiment unequal in their inclination to respond to any variables? (*selection bias*)

8) Have individuals been assigned to different groups because of extreme scores on some

premeasure? People with extreme attitudes have more room for change, so greater variation is likelier. (*statistical regression*)

9) Does the experimental environment or sample differ significantly from what will be encountered in reality? (*surrogate situation effect*)

10) Will pre- or post-measurements be made at a time that will not allow for full effect of the independent variable? (*measurement timing*)

Determine Data Collection Method

The electronic age continues to multiply the survey tools we have available. Today, survey methods include the following:

■ Telephone
  • traditional telephone interviewing
  • computer-assisted telephone interviewing
■ Personal
  • in-home/at place of business
  • mall intercept
  • computer-assisted personal interviewing
■ Mail/Fax
  • mail/fax survey
  • mail panel
■ Electronic
  • Web site survey
  • Internet survey

To select among these methods, begin by considering those to be surveyed. From whom do we need data? How accessible are they? How much time are they willing to spend as research participants?

If the participant group cares about the institution or issue, they'll respond well to a mail survey (responding well means a response rate of about 20 to 40 percent for the average college alumni survey). But people can look ahead at a mail survey; if you need unbiased, off-the-cuff answers, then a phone survey is best. It's not unusual, though, for telephone interviewers to spend one hour trying to make calls for every half hour of actual interviewing. Face-to-face interviews are appropriate for high-level, strategic questions and for less structured topics or when the respondent needs to look at stimulus materials. Computer-assisted interviews (such as those conducted at a walk-up kiosk on campus) are appropriate when the survey is quick and most responses are close-ended. Fax and e-mail surveys work well when you are surveying people at work. Mail and telephone techniques are best if you need to preserve anonymity in order to collect sensitive information.

No matter what survey tools are used, response rates can be increased through various techniques, including monetary incentives, advance contacts, follow-ups (postcard reminders, etc.), and sponsorship (such as when a well-known alumnus encourages participation in the survey). Obviously, you can also increase response through the use of salience—surveying on issues of great importance to the survey targets.

Developing a questionnaire

Your questionnaire must be appropriate to the data collection method you've selected. It should translate your information needs into a set of questions your respondents can and will answer. The questionnaire should inspire their involvement and minimize response error. A general guide:

a. List your overall information needs.
b. Decide the survey type or types.
c. Identify the content of individual questions.
  • Do you address all the facts and/or attitudes?
  • Is every question necessary? (Can you achieve the research objective without some?)
  • Will respondents have the information needed to answer all questions?
d. Determine the question structure.
  • Are your response categories mutually exclusive and exhaustive?
e. Determine the wording of questions.
  • Will respondents interpret questions the way you intend?
  • Is your question leading or loaded?
f. Arrange questions in a logical sequence, such as:
  • *Qualifiers*, to identify target respondents;
  • *Warm-ups*, to show respondents the survey is easy to answer;
  • *Transitions*, somewhat more difficult, to-the-point questions;
  • *Challengers*, questions requiring insightful judgments, careful or time-consuming

thought, and so on.
  • *Classifiers*, information that allows respondents to be grouped for study purposes. (Caution: Respondents may resist overly personal questions.)
g. Pretest and revise questionnaire as appropriate.

Select the Sample

Selecting the study sample involves five steps:

1. Define the population: population means the entire group of subjects of interest to you. Definitions need to be precise and inclusive if data is to be reliable.
2. Identify the sampling frame that's the source of your survey participants, such as the alumni directory, local phone book, random digit dialing, and so on.
3. Determine the sampling plan (either probability or nonprobability, which will be discussed shortly).
4. Determine the sample size.
5. Select those to be included in the survey.

The trick in sampling is to select a group of respondents that will be appropriately representative of the larger population. There's a trade off: truly random samples are more likely to be representative, but often require proportionally larger resources to survey. You'll want to expand the sample size if the decision at hand is critically important, if the analysis is to be very sophisticated, if you're studying lots of variables, or if you expect a low completion rate among respondents. You want a smaller sample if you are conducting a pilot survey or if time and money are key constraints.

The most ambitious (and potentially expensive) sample is the census—a survey of every member of the population. It's appropriate when the population is small, when the cost of error is high, or when the range of responses is expected to be extremely variable.

Most institutions recognize they don't need a census, so they consider two types of sampling procedures: probability and nonprobability samples. There's a lot of complex math involved, but the succinct difference is this: With probability samples, you can pinpoint the accuracy level of your results much more precisely. That's because in probability samples, respondents are chosen with scientific randomness—that is, for every person in your population, you have accounted for the exact probability they will be included in the research. However, determining this probability requires you to identify every single person and every potential segment in the affected population, requiring a tremendous amount of work and expense for very little increase in accuracy. The bottom line: for the purposes of college and university marketers, nonprobability samples (where respondents are chosen because they satisfy certain criteria) usually suffice. Unless you're looking for very precise market forecasts, researching new pharmaceuticals or other literally life-or-death issues, nonprobability sampling should do nicely.

Collect the Data

This is where you need to sit back and stay calm. Telephone surveys typically require trying 10 (sometimes more) people before completing an interview. Mail surveys take weeks (six or so) to reach the respondent, be filled out, and returned in the mail. It's a good idea to pretest your survey to ensure your respondents are completing it the way you intended. After it's received, all data should be carefully coded and cleaned (proofed to remove processing errors) to ensure reliable analysis.

Analyze the Results

The first step in analyzing the results actually comes before you've collected any data: you should design the tables and charts for your final report up front. Ask yourself what you need to learn and in what form the data will be most useful. That process will help you frame questions that fit your eventual information needs. At the same time, you'll create an organizational template that's all ready for the data when it arrives.

To discuss all the various analytical materials and techniques available is clearly beyond the scope of this chapter. I'd encourage you to spend some time with your institution's statistics or marketing faculty, professionals who are experienced in institutional research, or other research professionals.

Report the Results

If you're going to tell the future, it's not enough to make some tea, you also have to read the leaves. The same is true of research. Assembling lots of data will get you nowhere until you tease out their meaning and recognize the opportunities they represent.

Your research report should not simply report findings. Rather, you should spend some time thinking about initial project objectives and how the findings can help. In other words, the report should tell readers what they need to know. In some cases, readers will simply want a summary, without discussion of how the data were obtained. Others want lots of detail. Take time at the start of the project to talk about expectations. In any case, the report should be complete, accurate, clear, and concise. There should be a conclusion for each study objective.

There are two styles from which to choose: a reporting or an analytical style. In the reporting style, you simply relate the salient data that may be relevant to the objectives of the research, with no attempt to interpret it:

- 26.7 percent of minority respondents said they would consider taking a continuing education course.

The analytical report, on the other hand, *creates meaning* for the numbers and suggests courses of action:

- Recommended: an advertising campaign featuring nontraditional minority students and focusing on the most popular majors for continuing education.

Obviously, the analytical recommendation report draws on intelligence that extends well beyond the reported research, tapping into your own professional instincts and experiences. The report links research findings to institutional objectives, and creates a springboard for new ideas and approaches to those issues. This type of report is where human interpretation comes into play—where the art of leadership finally catches up with the science of research.

WRAPPING IT UP

Marketing research differs significantly from scientific research and even from institutional research. Marketing research recognizes the role of systematic information gathering and analysis in making marketing decisions. Individuals or organizations specializing in marketing research are best equipped to handle the statistical tools and survey methods appropriate for marketing research projects. In addition, educational advancement programs have unique and complex strategic goals and objectives not easily understood by those without experience in the field. Look to work with marketing research professionals who can draw from previous experience with like institutions. It can keep you from reinventing the wheel and you'll learn from the work conducted for your peers.

FURTHER READINGS

Alreck, P.L. and Robert B. Settle. *The Survey Research Handbook: Guidelines and Strategies for Conducting a Survey*. Homewood, IL: Richard D. Irwin, 1994.

Andreasen, A. R. "Backward Marketing Research," *Harvard Business Review*. (May-June 1985): 176-182.

Andreasen, A.R. *Cheap but Good Marketing Research*. Homewood, IL: Dow Jones-Irwin, 1988.

Churchill, G.A. *Marketing Research: Methodological Foundations*. New York: Dryden Press, 1999.

Gallagher, W.J. *Report Writing for Management*. Reading, MA: Addison-Wesley, 1969

Kalton, G. *Introduction to Survey Sampling*. Beverly Hills, CA: Sage Publications, 1982.

Kotler, P. and A.F.A. Fox. *Strategic Marketing for Educational Institutions*. Englewood Cliffs, NJ: Prentice-Hall, Inc., 1995.

Malhotra, N.K.. *Marketing Research: An Applied Orientation*. Upper Saddle River, NJ: Prentice Hall, Inc., 1996

Sageev, P. *Helping Researchers Write, So Managers Can Understand*. Columbus, OH: Batelle Press, 1995.

Templeton, J.F. *The Focus Group: A Strategic Guide to Organizing, Conducting, and Analyzing the Focus Group Interview*. Chicago, IL: Probus Publishing Co., 1994.

A unique feature of a collaboration-marketing communications program is that the participants themselves create and update much of the content of the Web site. This is a difficult premise for any organization, and especially for educational institutions, to accept.

Transforming Your Web Site into a Collaboration Marketing Tool

Robert E. Johnson
Vice President for Enrollment
Albion College

You are no doubt familiar with mass marketing. It's based on the pre-mise that if you communicate often with enough people via such broad media as newspapers and network TV, over time you will sell more products or change their opinion of you. Since you don't need to sell to everyone who hears your message to achieve success, you don't need to be especially concerned about the specific individuals you reach.

Although mass marketing may never disappear completely, its importance has been diminished by the popularity of traditional direct marketing. You probably know quite a bit about direct marketing as well. The idea here is that marketers can identify specific target audience segments and what products they're interested in. Marketers then design communication programs accordingly, especially via mail, phone, and specialized magazine and radio campaigns.

What you may not be as familiar with is collaboration marketing, a new trend that has emerged along with the Internet. Thanks to e-mail and the World Wide Web, virtual communities spring up through which people of similar interests share a continuing involvement with one anoth-er—and with the organization offering a product or service. Collaboration marketing is designed to help, as well as to sell to, those people. It's based on the premise that if an organization helps people to know more about a product or service that interests them, sales will increase.

Collaboration marketing is ideal for schools, colleges, and universities. That's because as a marketer, you're in the business of building strong communities for specific audiences, including prospective students, current parents, and alumni who are willing to provide continuing financial support to alma mater.

Like direct marketing, collaboration marketing can succeed if the desired customers share a common interest. For prospective students and alumni, this is most likely the academic program and the other faculty, students, and graduates involved in it. An appealing, well-targeted campus Web site then becomes the source for learning and sharing information about the common interest. Chat rooms, discussion threads, and e-mail newsletters with links back to a Web site are all examples of interactive communications that build continuing involvement and therefore a sense of community.

A unique feature of a collaboration-marketing

communications program is that the participants themselves create and update much of the content of the Web site. This is a difficult premise for any organization, and especially for educational institutions, to accept. By definition, community members themselves decide what they want to know and discuss, rather than what the organization thinks they should know and discuss. You as the sponsor lose control of the communication message. But in return, you gain continuous involvement with people, which makes them more likely to enroll, give dollars, refer students, and support your institution in general.

Even as you lose control over some aspects of the Web site, you retain the ability to influence your community members. You can, for instance, advertise annual fund gift opportunities to a prospective donor who is using the Web site to talk with fellow pre-med alumni. A small pop-up "ad" can let visitors know that the biology department needs to upgrade its microscopes and that each new piece of equipment will have the donor's name clearly engraved where students can see it. "Click here" will bring more information, including the ability to immediately make a donation via credit card. Making the donation will automatically add the donor to the "most current" supporters list that's maintained on the biology Web site. The donor will instantly receive an e-mail thank-you, followed later by a more personal conventional letter. None of this is difficult to do with the current state of technology.

Just as Dell Computer does for special customers, you can even allow alumni or prospective students to customize the front page of your Web site to feature the areas that are of most interest to them. For an example of how one institution is doing this for prospective students, visit the sites created by the University of Dayton (*www.udayton.edu*), and customize it for yourself. What you will find there can easily be adapted for your alumni as well.

To succeed at collaboration marketing, first you must get over that feeling that you must remain in control of the message sent. On the Web, visitors want to go where their interests take them rather than where you want them to go. Don't try to stand in their way. Instead, help them.

Second, you need Web and e-mail strategies that work well in many ways, including attracting, serving, and persuading your visitors. Some of the principles are the same as for direct marketing. Others require using new tools in new ways. But all of them will help you succeed with a new kind of marketing for our electronic age.

THREE VITAL BASICS OF EFFECTIVE WEB MARKETING

To attract and serve those visitors, your Web site must be three things: easy to navigate, enriched with new information on a regular basis, and interactive.

1. Making your site easy to navigate. From a marketing communications perspective, a Web site is not just a place to post as much information about your institution as you possibly can. People have to be able to find what interests them quickly and to avoid what is of no interest. This means you need an organizational structure that's easy to use and a design that's attractive as well as functional. Plan the organization first. Do research with the people you expect to visit the site and ask them what they are most interested in finding. Then do whatever you must do to help them find that in no more than three clicks from where they enter the site. Fewer clicks is even better. Once the organization is planned, then complete the design last. That will ensure that creative design doesn't get in the way of a clear path to what the visitor wants to know or do. Finally, plan the use of graphics very carefully to be consistent with the download speed of your guests. Despite an increase in access to the Web, the most common complaint of users remains slow download times. That's because too many of us add fancy interactive graphics that keep access slow. Web users hate "slow," so be careful here.

Yet another essential is an effective "search" feature at the beginning of the site. A good search engine allows visitors to do the following:

- Type in the name of anyone who works or studies on your campus and send that person an e-mail.
- Type in the name of any academic program you offer and go directly to a relevant Web page. For example, prospective students (or potential

corporate donors) can type the word "pre-med" or "medicine" and get where they want to be. Don't make them scroll through an entire list of academic programs. (Actually, a recent search for pre-med information was in most cases a failure. Despite the great interest in this pre-professional program, it is lost on many college Web sites because it is not a formal academic major. Type "pre-med" or "medicine" on your college site and see what you find.)

■ Type in the name of any generic key word and obtain a list of Web site locations addressing that topic.

2. *Providing fresh information constantly.* Your Web site must be so interesting that after the first visit, people tell themselves, "I've got to bookmark this and come back again or I'll miss something important." Exactly what attracts them depends on their specific interests. Your goal is to build relationships with your regular visitors so that they feel they belong to a community of like-minded people. When you have done that, you are poised for effective collaboration marketing.

What features are likely to inspire bookmarking for return visits? Consider these five examples, to which you can no doubt add more. An added benefit: Someone else is already creating each of these. This keeps your Web site supplied with constant sources of new content.

■ Student newspapers, which alumni, parents, and prospective students will all likely want to review regularly. You shouldn't worry about articles that treat some aspects of your institution unfavorably. People expect this of student newspapers. They also know that nearly every campus has one—and if you don't provide access to yours, people will wonder why you don't.

■ Alumni notes. Encourage alumni to provide new information on a regular basis, including automatic e-mail links if they wish. Then make sure these notes are integrated with your search engine so visitors can readily find specific things they're looking for. An addition you can make: updates on class contributions to your annual fund or capital campaign.

■ Links to favorite alumni Web sites, complete with mini-reviews. For instance, your graduates might enjoy posting links to sites for financial planning, wine, food, cars, health care, and home renovation. And people might also want to share "professional development" tips that relate to their academic majors—the favorite technical sites of your engineering graduates, for instance, or outstanding examples of literary criticism or creative writing for your English majors. Group these alumni favorites by topic so they're easy to locate.

■ Press releases. Post each and every one to your Web site. The news media are your obvious audience for these, but other people may find them useful as well. For example, if you link these releases to your search engine, a pre-med scan might turn up biology professors with new grants, alumni with new medical appointments, and students with new scholarships. Whether or not these releases are ever printed in the media, visitors interested in the topics will see them.

■ Sports news. Whether you are a major NCAA Division I university or a small Division III college, provide regular access to news about your teams. Ideally, your sports information director will post news of every sporting event on your Web site as soon as it's over. Such an up-to-the-minute site provides results more quickly than the next morning's paper and in more detail than the local TV station.

A final note about what sorts of content draw visitors back: You need to realize that course listings, faculty names and credentials, degree requirements, mission statements, maps, and visitor instructions—items regularly found on college Web sites—will not prompt return visits. Static features that aren't updated often simply don't. This sort of unchanging information is still useful, but it won't give you what you need to foster community and collaboration.

3. *Building in interactivity.* To figure out the best ways to make a site interactive, it's useful to step back and think about the essential components of how a good Web site works. Let's start by looking at a Web version of the "five Ws" that journalists use to write a news story. These come from J.D.

Mosley-Matchett, a regular Web marketing columnist for the American Marketing Association's *Marketing News*.

■ *Who are the people you want to visit?* Though this question may seem basic, it is very important and too often overlooked. For our purposes, it means defining who you think the most important visitors are.

I assume that readers of this book are primarily concerned with prospective students, current and prospective corporate and foundation donors, alumni, and the parents of current students. To start, each of these groups should have their own "front page," which reflects what you know about visitors' general interests before you allow them to tailor the page to their personal interests.

Consider this example from Wellesley College. The college has a standard front page (*www.wellesley.edu*) and another front page to which prospective students are directed (*www.wellesley.edu/admission*). Visit each and you will immediately see the point in designing different pages for different groups. There is yet another front page for the alumni association (*www.wellesley.edu/alum/alumnae.html*), which includes a series of sites for different graduating classes.

■ *What do visitors want to find?* If you want to keep the tracking simple and interactive at the same time, ask people to send you an e-mail about things they wanted and could not find. Tracking software grows more sophisticated all the time and you don't have to be an expert on it. But you should expect that your Web site developer stays up-to-date with what is available and can give you "information" that you can use rather than "data." Pay special attention not only to which Web pages people visit, but to how long they stay there. Lots of quick visits is often a sign that people are not finding what they need. If you want to keep up with what's new in tracking software and make suggestions to your Web developer, regularly visit the *DM News* site (*www.dmnews.com*) for regular ads and reviews of what's new.

■ *When do you update your site?* You should update it regularly and make sure people know what's new. Hope College (*www.hope.edu*) does this by regularly changing its front page. If you decide to include when the last update occurred, make sure the date never gets to be months (even years!) old. Check your entire Web site and try to eliminate old dates. Ask yourself why a section is even on the site if it hasn't been updated in the last 12 months.

■ *Where do you place promotions?* This is tricky. Promotions shouldn't prevent people from finding what they came to see on a Web site, but neither should you avoid them. You do want to remind people of homecoming, a student visit day, an opportunity to sign up for a newsletter. You'll get ideas on how to do this by visiting sites recognized for their marketing expertise at (*www.webbyawards.com*).

■ *Why should anyone care?* If you don't give people what they want, they won't care what you do give them. Don't assume that just because your campus has important faculty, a great mission, and the most wonderful core curriculum in the world that people are going to want to visit your site. To build traffic on your site, put visitors in interactive communication with the people and things that interest them. It's that simple—and that complicated.

> ● ● ●
> **Check your entire Web site and try to eliminate old dates. Ask yourself why a section is even on the site if it hasn't been updated in the last 12 months.**

Do your alumni like to talk to one another? How about your new, deposit-paid, first-year students? Of course they do. And that's why your Web site should feature chatrooms and discussion threads that allow a visitor to sort comments by topic as well as date. Many sites do this well, but none better than the site for the popular NPR show, Car Talk (*www.cartalk.com*). Visit this site and explore the varied opportunities for interaction among visitors. Then ask your Web developers to do the same for you.

You'll need a monitor to make sure that discussion stays "on topic" within whatever rules you set. And you'll need to accept the fact that you'll have less "message control" of the content than you'd like. If you can't accept open discussion, chatrooms and discussion threads are not for you. People who use them expect minimal restrictions on what they can say as long as it is "on topic."

Of course, one of the best and easiest ways to make a Web site interactive is to equip it with e-mail links. But e-mail is only as good as the response it generates. In "Time to Redirect Your Thinking," a 1996 article for *DM News*, Robert Brueckner urges marketers to respond to e-mail inquiries with a message "that blows the recipient's doors off." He went on to note that most responses (when they exist at all) go out late and don't say much. This makes for a missed opportunity.

Needless to say, personal responses are best. Within 24 hours of contacting the University of Michigan site for graduate nursing programs, I received an e-mail that thanked me by name, included information about an upcoming open house, and had the name of a real person (and her e-mail address) at the end. Very impressive. Your prospective students, alumni, and parents deserve no less.

Even so, most short-staffed campuses rely on an automated system for the first response. And that's OK; even an impersonal response is better than none, since it at least tells visitors that their e-mail was received. Just make sure your automated responses are as useful as possible. At a minimum, they should be addressed by name to the person who sent it, tell how long it will take to send any information requested, include a real person's name and e-mail address in case more help is needed, and say thank you.

If you are responding to something more than basic requests for information, someone must monitor your e-mail and send a response of some type within 24 hours. If you delay any longer than that, you are failing to meet the expectations of people who use e-mail regularly. If, for example, your alumni and parent relations office can't respond that quickly, then the staff should set up an automatic response system that tells the sender when to expect something more personal.

Another way to make your e-mail useful: Let's say you receive an inquiry about your pre-med program. The response should include the URL (or better yet, an embedded link) that will take the person directly to the relevant section of your site. This will be especially helpful to your inquirer if your site is difficult to navigate.

COMMUNICATING EFFECTIVELY: WORDS THAT WORK FOR THE WEB

Let's face it: The Web is not the right vehicle for a literary masterpiece. Even so, you need to pay special attention to how you write for your site. If you regularly read *USA Today* and *Atlantic Monthly*, you have an idea of how—and how not—to write for the Web. Consider this advice from two masters of direct marketing copywriting, Hershell Gordon Lewis and Robert E. Lewis, in their book *Selling on the Net*.

■ *Remember that long copy isn't necessarily bad.* Visitors to the Web will read long copy if the topic interests them. But you do need to present the copy in short, easy-to-read steps. Long stretches of continuous copy will drive people away.

■ *Make sure your copy concentrates on benefits to the reader and seeks an emotional connection.* An annual fund campaign, for instance, can emphasize that donations help buy improved equipment in biology labs, providing better educational opportunities for a higher caliber of student. These students will be better prepared for medical school, further enhancing their reputations and yours.

■ *Don't be afraid to sell.* In essence, your Web site is selling community and membership in a collaborative environment. Be sure to ask people to join. Ask parents to "click here" to receive updated information on government financial aid policies. Ask alumni to "click here" to receive a free e-mail newsletter on athletics, or to charge their annual fund gift to their credit card.

■ *Keep it interesting.* As you write or review every headline and every sentence, ask yourself if they maintain your interest in the subject. Writing in the language of an academic discipline is appropriate for an academic meeting. It is not appropriate when presenting academic information to prospective students, parents, and most alumni. Know your audience and write for it.

■ *Allow for response on the Web.* Some people will want to receive admissions materials or donate by phone or mail after they finish reading your Web copy. But not everyone. Many will find it strange that you are forcing them to use a telephone rather than simply clicking on an automatic e-mail reply form. Choice is the key here.

The next important key to effective marketing communications on your Web site is to select key words that capture people's attention and motivate them to act. Direct marketing research shows that some words are almost impossible to ignore. Consider these recommended by Ted Nichols in his 1995 book, *Magic Words:*

- Discover
- Amazing
- Announcing
- Do you?
- You
- Free
- New
- Breakthrough
- Secrets of
- Yes,
- Only
- How will?
- Protect
- Now
- True
- At last

Here are some brief examples of how these words can enliven your Web page and appeal to different audiences:

1. For parents:
   - Weak phrasing: "Send me information about financial aid at TipTop College."
   - Strong phrasing: "Yes, I want to discover how to lower college costs."
2. For alumni:
   - Weak phrasing: "Send your annual fund contribution to Tip Top College."
   - Strong phrasing: "Yes, I want to protect the reputation of my Tip Top College degree."
3. For prospective students:
   - Weak phrasing: "Send for information about the excellent faculty at Tip Top College."
   - Strong phrasing: "Discover the secret to your success in college."

Motivating words are not appropriate for every place on your Web site, but you should pay constant attention to the locations where they do fit. These include the pop-up or banner ads that motivate people to take a desired action. They might also include headlines that introduce text sections. Consider this headline that came up after a pre-med

search at the SUNY-Buffalo site (*www.buffalo.edu*): "How do you make Harvard Medical beg for you?" If you're a prospective student wondering how SUNY-Buffalo would prepare you for medical school, that's certainly an attention-grabber.

With these notes in mind on powerful words for the Web, here are nine caveats published in "From Boring to Brilliant," an article by marketing expert Pat Frieson in the August 1997 *Target Marketing* magazine. The examples really are from higher education; only the names have been changed.

- *Avoid presumptuous openings.* When answering an e-mail inquiry, don't overstate your case. Telling a recent graduate "I know you care about the reputation of Tip Top in the next *U.S. News & World Report* ratings" is only valid if the alumna has actually told you that she cares.
- *Write in language the reader understands.* Academic jargon such as "core curriculum," "modes of inquiry," "co-curricular," and "liberal arts tradition" should seldom be used with alumni, prospective students, or parents.
- *Avoid overstatements.* If you write that "Tip Top College's campus is now one of the most scenic in the United States," I will expect an awesome sight when I return for my 25-year reunion. Can you deliver? Many campuses are attractive and some are scenic. Few can be "one of the most scenic." Make sure your statements are believable and do not create false expectations.
- *Use real, not rounded, numbers.* Stating your endowment as $53,763,000 as of June 30, 2000, shows you cared enough to be accurate and sets you apart from those who say "about $54 million." Your credibility will increase.
- *Know your reader's possible objections and address them in your copy.* This may seem scary, but if you have good research that tells you why people don't do what you want them to do, address those problems directly.

Assume, for instance, that your alumni survey reveals that recent graduates don't give to the annual fund because they believe your campus doesn't appreciate small contributions. To counter this, begin your alumni association Web page or e-mail solicitation with this: "You're wrong if you think that we don't value a $10 gift as much as a $100 gift. Each counts equally in the *U.S. News & World Report* ratings." (Of course, if you say that in the solicitation, you have to send donors who give even small amounts a personal letter of thanks for their gift.)

■ *Be appropriately personal.* Don't use "we" unless you are referring to two or more people. In most communications from one person, "I" is more appropriate and believable. Leave the imperial "we" to monarchs and politicians. Similarly, use "you" to heighten the fact that you are communicating one-to-one with a prospective student, alumnus, or parent.

■ *Repeat key features and benefits.* The direct marketing adage that "if it's worth saying once, it's worth saying twice—or three times" applies to your Web and e-mail writing. Say it in the headline, say it in the introduction, and say it again before you close: "If 45 percent of our alumni give to the annual fund at Tip Top College each year, our reputation will grow and so will the value of your degree."

■ *Give your reader a reason to respond.* Explain how your college lags in giving compared to your presumed peers and note the negative impact this has on the *U. S. News* ratings. Surely your alumni want to help correct that situation. True, most alumni probably don't know that your annual giving rate influences the ratings. (If you don't know either, go to the *U.S. News* Web site and review the rating criteria: *www.usnews.com/usnews/edu/college.*)

■ *Use an occasional parenthetical comment.* See the last sentence above. Parenthetical statements relax the severity of your writing, adding an element of informality that will increase the personal nature of what you are saying.

A SEPARATE SPECIALTY: WRITING FOR THE E-MAIL NEWSLETTER

Assuming that e-mail newsletters have become part of your communications toolkit, capturing new subscribers should be a primary purpose of your Web site's marketing plan. When visitors subscribe to newsletters, they automatically separate themselves from the visitors who do not.

Subscribers are telling you that their interest level is high. They are joining your community. They are giving you a continuing opportunity to build strong relationships and deliver your messages to people who want to receive them. Here are the key points to remember as you develop your e-mail newsletter marketing plan:

■ Remember that e-mail newsletters are simple to write. Use standard newsletter copywriting techniques. Examples are readily available on the Web; also note the e-mail newsletters in the resource section at the end of this chapter. Most of the copywriting guidelines already covered here will work for your e-mail newsletters as well.

■ Remember that newsletters are simple to tailor to different audiences. You can use some of the same copy in newsletters to different audiences, but match the specific interests of the people subscribing to them as well. You could, for instance, include general news about your college in a series of newsletters built around your graduates' professional interests. Similarly, parents and students can subscribe to career-interest newsletters that contain information about the accomplishments of your graduates in similar academic areas.

■ Build subscriptions with "opt-in" lists. Never automatically send newsletters to groups of people you think might want to receive them. But always give visitors a clear, easy opportunity to subscribe. Direct people to a sample copy on your Web site, with a subscription opportunity at the end. A special note: Direct marketers are slowly accepting that an "opt-out" option (you present visitors with a pre-checked box and hope they don't delete the checkmark) are not as good as an "opt-in" option where visitors have to make a choice. Remember that you are seeking interactivity and involvement on the part of your visitors. The community you are building will be stronger if members make a conscious choice to join it.

■ Give subscribers an "opt-out" option. At the end of each newsletter, clearly tell people how to end their subscription. And pay attention to who uses it. Consider a brief, automatic survey that simply asks them why they are leaving. If it doesn't take much time to complete, you are likely to get useful information. After subscribers leave, send them an automatic "thank you for being with us" note.

■ Archive your newsletters. Because you'll always be adding new subscribers, give them an opportunity to catch up to past news by reviewing the old issues. Keeping newsletters accessible for 12 months is long enough.

■ Link your newsletter to your Web site. Don't miss the opportunity to bring people directly back to your Web site via URLs embedded in the newsletter. Your athletics newsletter, for instance, can take people directly to pictures of the most recent game. Your announcement that a biology professor will be featured on the Discovery Channel can take people right back to news and pictures of her search for the Loch Ness monster.

■ Keep it simple. Technology allows you to add pictures and video to your newsletters. But for the moment, don't do it. An important feature of e-mail is that it is quick to send and receive because it is only text. Direct marketing research indicates that newsletter readership decreases sharply when anything is added that increases reading time.

■ Keep a database of your subscribers. As marketers, we want to take advantage of a primary function of offering e-mail subscriptions: learning more about the subscribers. Most people will complete a brief form with basic information about who they are and what they're interested in. But always give people the option not to include personal information they might not want to send. (Recently, for instance, I attempted to subscribe to a newsletter. I received a return e-mail asking for phone and mailing address information to "confirm" my biographical information. It seemed like a not-so-subtle effort to solicit further business. I didn't send the information back.)

E-mail newsletters are obvious vehicles for long-term cultivation of alumni. And as student recruitment moves into the early high school years, the cultivation concept can be used for enrollment development as well. Here are sample newsletter topics of interest to advancement professionals cultivating increased annual fund participation:

■ Moving Ahead: Your Classmates in the News
■ Viking Athletics: Coach Tom's Weekly Update
■ Inside the Leadership Club: Monthly Updates from President Peabody

THE FUTURE OF WEB TECHNOLOGY

We have barely begun to explore the impact that Web technology has on marketing communications today. Nevertheless, we need to stretch our imaginations to consider the possibilities that new technology holds in store for us tomorrow. Here are three examples.

1. Joining the power of digital printing with the Web

Nothing has the potential for more revolutionary change than combining digital printing, or "printing on demand," and databases built on information supplied by people visiting your Web site. Consider this step-by-step example of how it will work as reported in "SmartSite Automates Fulfillment with Web, Database, Digital Printing," an October 19, 1998, *DM News* article by Mark McLaughlin. The examples have been changed to fit higher education.

■ Alumni and parents visit your Web site and enter information into a text file about themselves and the things that interest them most about your campus. You also capture their mailing address. The visitor could also, of course, be a corporate or foundation grant officer.

The alumnus is searching for giving opportunities in the just-introduced capital campaign. He's most interested in information that relates to his academic area and extracurricular interests when he was a student. That information is located deep within the material assembled for the university's case statement. The parent and the foundation representative are searching for similar information.

■ The text file is transferred automatically to a database that first transforms the information into a profile of the visitor and his interests and then sends this profile to a digital printing system. The digital printing system creates a personal publication that addresses the visitor's most important interests.

- The publication is mailed directly to your visitor from your fulfillment house within 24 to 48 hours. A personalized cover letter can be included if you wish.

This technology portends a rapid expansion of the one-to-one marketing concept in campus marketing communications. It will make publications of greater interest and give them more of an impact than anything that's been published in the past.

Digital printing is a reality now. Whirlpool Corporation, for one, uses this technology to prepare different responses to inquiries about its products. However, the process faces two hurdles before it's widely adopted—although neither of these is insurmountable.

First, and most significant, digital printing is now more expensive than traditional printing. If you plan your publications based on the cost per piece, your costs will increase over the short run. On the other hand, digital printing will increase your publications' yield. Your annual fund contributions will increase as your literature becomes more valuable and interesting to the people you send it to. So if, as a good marketing person, you measure the value of your dollars by the dollars raised rather than the marketing tools purchased, you will find that digital printing improves your yield at every stage of the fund-raising process.

The second objection is the publication quality. To the trained observer (especially when equipped with a loupe), the photographic quality in a digital publication is not equivalent to traditional printing. I do not consider this a serious objection. When given the "eyes of a normal human being" test, the digitally printed publications from Whirlpool will more than serve their purpose. A small loss of printing quality doesn't outweigh the impact of more personal information.

I can make one prediction with confidence. In the competition for charitable dollars, you don't want to be the last person to combine digital printing with Web site capabilities. To review what's being offered in this area now, visit the Web site of

● ● ●

I can make one prediction with confidence. In the competition for charitable dollars, you don't want to be the last person to combine digital printing with Web site capabilities.

a printing company featured in McLaughlin's *DM News* article (*www.webcraft.com*). Finally, to remove any doubt that substantial sums of money are being invested to promote this approach, learn what IBM is doing by visiting its site for digital printing (*www.printers.ibm.com*).

Adopting this approach to publications response makes an important first impression on visitors to your Web site. Your printed response will signal visitors that you care enough about their interests to tailor what you do for them. That level of attention will pay important dividends as you attract members to your virtual community and develop long-term relationships.

2. Creating alternatives to banner advertising as we know it

Have you been thinking about developing banner advertising? Think again.

Right now, banner ads are common at the beginning of many Web sites. Visit the Yahoo college and university section, for instance, and you may see a banner ad from the University of Phoenix for its online MBA program. Banner ads are similar to teasers on the outside of envelopes. Just as the content of the teaser is supposed to get someone to open the envelope, the banner ad is designed to get people to "click here" and open the way to another Web site. When visitors finish their business at the banner ad site, they can return to the original site—sometimes easily, sometimes not.

Banner ads can also take people to different places within your Web page. Colleges use them to announce big sports victories, special campaign results, or upcoming special events. But are they effective?

Banner ads developed as a spin-off from conventional print advertising. In the words of Sean Carton, managing partner at Carton Donofrio Interactive, "They seemed like a good idea at the time." They appear to be an easy way to segment Web advertising to the interests of people visiting different Web locations. Unfortunately, in 1998, Web advertisers began noticing a special problem: Fewer and fewer people actually clicked on them. Why was this happening?

According to Donofrio in "Here's What Will Save the Web," a Web article at the Click Network site (*www.searchz.com/clickz102898.html*), fewer people are using banner ads because they don't want to leave the site where they are to go to another. In other words, following the link on a banner ad is more complicated than opening an envelope. Donofrio uses this analogy: "Can you imagine if advertising in magazines required you to drop the magazine you were reading and pick up another to read more about the product you were interested in?"

Web marketers have devised an alternative approach that allows the visitor to remain at the original Web site while receiving new information. Consider how it will work:

■ After seeing a banner ad with a message of interest, you click on it, just as you do now.

■ The banner expands to about one-third the size of your normal viewing page. That larger section contains the equivalent of a full ad for the University of Phoenix's online MBA or the special biology department giving opportunity for Tip Top College's annual fund. You can click on a button for more information or just click to close and continue with what you were reading.

■ If you click for more information, you receive instructions relevant to the ad itself. Tip Top College, for instance, presents additional information about how a donation helps pre-med students and includes a form for people to use in making a credit card donation. The University of Phoenix includes testimonials about its MBA program, details of how long it takes to complete the program, and a form requesting that a U of P staffer contact the visitor by phone, e-mail, or regular mail. (Note, of course, the ability to tie this back into the digital printing described above.)

■ When you finish, just click to close and return to your original Web page. As Donofrio describes the experience, "You've never left the page you were on, never had to worry about hitting the 'back' button, never got confused about where you were in cyberspace."

A company called 9th Square has a patent pending on the technology described above. Called E*Banner, the technology works from a simple principle: The advertiser brings content to the Web site where you happen to be, rather than requiring you to visit a different Web site. Whether or not this exact format takes hold in Web marketing, something similar is likely to happen.

The message is clear: Stay alert, visit Web marketing sites regularly, and never assume that the new approach you adopted yesterday will still be effective tomorrow. Things are changing far too quickly to make that dangerous assumption. In the meantime, reconsider very seriously any plans you have for traditional banner advertising.

3. Tracking e-mail's growing importance

"The hot new medium is e-mail." So wrote David S. Bennahum in an April 1998 article in *Wired* magazine. I repeat the statement here to remind us that despite technological innovations, e-mail remains one of the most rapidly growing areas of the Internet. The ability to send and receive e-mail is greatly improved over the pioneer days, but it's still the main reason people come to the Internet in the first place. Bennahum's perceptive comment: "During all this hype about videostreaming, people have been e-mailing each other. There's been a denial about what's going on. E-mail works and people like it."

People of all ages like it, too. Teenagers use e-mail to replace phone conversations. A November 3, 1998, *New York Times* article called "From Yakety-Yak to Clackety-Clack" recounts in detail how high school students use AOL features such as Instant Messenger system and Buddy Groups to "talk" with one another regularly. More daily time is spent on this basic use of the Web than on surfing for topics of interest or visiting previous Web sites.

At a higher age level, Bennahum's article recounts the rapid growth in both for-profit and "virtuous," or free, e-mail lists compiled by authors of e-mail newsletters. (My own free e-mail newsletter on higher education marketing increased from 400 subscribers to more than 1,100 in five months in 1998.) Most of these lists grew from simple e-mail exchanges between people interested in a common topic to more formal e-mail publications prepared by a single person who reviews material in many different sources and combines the best into a newsletter. Most also take contributions from subscribers. Note that these are not the traditional listservs, which allow communication among members similar to what the teenagers in the *Times* article are doing. Instead, many of these evolved from listservs that overwhelmed the participants with too many messages. A monitor arose, screened and edited the messages for the most useful content, and began writing a newsletter.

Compare this with the rapid demise of several 1995 and 1996 Web magazine publishing ventures as reported on the front page of the January 14, 1997, *Wall Street Journal*. According to that article, called "Facing Early Losses, Some Web Publishers Begin to Pull the Plug," elaborate publications were not what most Web users were looking for when they went online. E-mail newsletters, on the other hand, are much easier to receive and read, and appear to be prospering for reasons similar to the virtual community concept introduced earlier.

FINAL OBSERVATIONS

Marketing on the Web is different—but not completely different. Anyone familiar with the principles and practices of direct marketing will be at home in the Web marketing world. People who are not may feel a bit lost at first. But nobody, especially not today's direct marketers, know what is really going to work in Web marketing five years from now. Between now and then, here's some advice.

■ *Realize that Web marketing is very different from mass marketing, with its emphasis on frequency and reach.* Don't be concerned about reaching the millions of people who visit the Web every day. For example, most schools, colleges, and universities should not consider placing banner ads on Yahoo and AOL. The exception might be institutions promoting distance education programs.

■ *Be concerned with what visitors will (or won't) find when they visit your site.* Know what your visitors expect and help them find it. Most campuses are not yet doing a good job of this. See for yourself by taking the pre-med test.

■ *Don't forget that Web marketing is an adaptation and evolution of direct marketing.* Visit the *DM News* Web site, and the sites listed in the index for this chapter, on a regular basis. In effect, you need to become a good direct marketer before you can become a good Web marketer.

■ *Keep in mind that Web marketing is the perfect medium for the continued personalization of marketing.* It may someday bring the concept of one-to-one marketing very close to reality. The technology is here. We simply have not yet learned how to use it in effective marketing communications.

■ *Finally, always remember that collaboration marketing is a concept that should work well for campuses.* Many alumni, for instance, are gregarious people who enjoy talking with one another—which makes them perfect candidates for regular participation at a site promoting a virtual community. But to encourage this, we administrators have to first give up control and let our alumni create the content of the parts of our Web sites they inhabit. Are we willing to do that?

We advancement professionals, whether we work with prospective students, alumni, parents, or corporate and foundation staff, are in the relationship business. In that context, Web marketing is an important part of an overall mix of marketing communication activities designed to create and sustain relationships. Web marketing will not replace human contact at reunions or a personal visit from the president to ask for a major capital gift. It can, however, create an easily accessible means of communication among like-minded people apart from those relatively infrequent personal meetings. In that role, it is indeed powerful.

FURTHER READINGS

Books

Bayne, Kim M. *The Internet Marketing Plan: A Practical Handbook for Creating, Implementing, and Assessing your Online Presence*. Somerset, NJ: John Wiley & Sons, 1997.

Hagel III, John. *Net Gain: Expanding Markets Through Virtual Communities*. Cambridge, MA: Harvard Business Review Press, 1997.

Lewis, Hershell Gordon, and Robert E. Lewis. *Selling on the Net*. Chicago, IL: NTC Business Books, 1997.

Stern, Jim. *Advertising on the Web*. Que Education & Training, 1997.

Stern, Jim: *Customer Service on the Internet: Building Relationships, Increasing Loyalty, and Staying Competitive*. Somerset, NJ: John Wiley & Sons, 1996.

Web Sites

Car Talk: *www.cartalk.com*. The same two guys you may listen to on National Public Radio have a Web site, and it's the best example of collaboration marketing I've found. Pay special attention to the various ways you can communicate with fellow car fans on this site.

DM News: www.dmnews.com. The weekly newspaper for direct marketing professionals included regular updates on Web and Internet marketing.

Don Peppers and Martha Rogers: *www.marketing1to1.com*. The people who have built an international career on one-to-one marketing regularly review practical applications on the Web. Subscribe to their free e-mail newsletter.

Georgia Tech University: *www.cc.gatech.edu/gvu/user_surveys/*. Visit this site to review regular research on how people use their Web sites.

Guerilla Marketing: www.gmarketing.com. If you liked the book, you'll like the Web site. Frequently features innovative examples of Web marketing for people without enormous resources.

Wilson Internet Services: *www.wilsonweb.com*. Strong emphasis on Web marketing. Subscribe (for a fee) to a Web marketing newsletter. Be sure to check the list of Wilson's marketing articles.

Advancement Services

Edited by John H. Taylor

Introduction

John H. Taylor
Director of Alumni and Development Records
Duke University

At the time of the *Handbook*'s last publication in 1986, no institution of higher education was engaged in a fund-raising campaign exceeding $1 billion. Now, the first multi-billion-dollar campaign has been conducted by Harvard University as this third edition goes to press. As the amounts of money being raised, both in campaigns and annually are ever greater, so, too, are the rules, regulations, systems, and procedures necessary to ensure that those contributions are properly handled.

In 1986, it was rare to hear anyone use the phrase "advancement services" in any kind of fund-raising context. Now, advancement services is not only a professional field but also one of the largest components, in numbers and expense, of any advancement operation. For those interested in a more comprehensive review of advancement services topics, you may wish to read the book *Advancement Services: Research and Technology Support for Fund Raising* (CASE Books, 1999). For the *Handbook*, we feel it is important to address those advancement ser-vices topics that permeate the business of fund raising at all institutions.

No area in advancement services has seen more change than fund-raising technology. Robert Weiner of MyPersonal.Com addresses the issues of selecting and implementing the proper system for your institution. Tom Chaves, from Systems and Computer Technology Corp. (SCT), discusses the optimum department structure to support these systems. Jonathan Lindsey of Baylor University covers prospect research, an increasingly dominant topic in fund-raising operations. Alison Paul, a noted attorney specializing in nonprofit law, discusses IRS rules and regulations, particularly the numerous and frequently changing rules that govern charitable giving. This segues into a discussion of the importance of simple, yet functional, gift and pledge agreements by Kathy Stanford from the University of California, Irvine. Finally, Lynne Becker from the University of Washington concludes with a review of donor relations systems.

As education underwent a transformation from being a privilege to a right of citizenship, advancement officers realized the need to make the social and civic relationships of influential persons explicit.

Prospect Research: An Introduction

Jonathan Lindsey

Director, Donor Information Services, University Development,
Baylor University

Art?
Science?
Combination?
Playing hunches?
Educated guesses?

Prospect research is all of the above, but no two research units are organized or integrated into the advancement process in the same manner. There are similarities, but each fund-raising operation is discrete, thus the research functions are related directly to the institution.

In this chapter, we'll first address conceptual issues, the development/advancement profile, and changing procedures. Then we will move to the development of APRA (Association of Professional Researchers in Advancement, formerly Association of Professional Researchers in America), which provides a distinct professional identification for those directly involved in producing research for fund-raising activities or those who manage that activity as part of advancement services.

A discussion of demographic and biodata, whether on four-by-six cards in a shoe box or on the most sophisticated computer system, will lead us to issues associated with prospect research. We'll also look at the current electronic data deluge and prospect tracking/moves management and screening. Finally, we'll explore what's to come in the next century, including analysis versus research, data and data source reliability, and the essential quality of the researchers.

TWO DECADES OF CHANGE

As a professional subgroup of advancement services, research has grown dramatically in the last two decades of the 20th century. Before the 1980s, only a few major educational institutions had formal research units as part of their advancement efforts. Progressive development officers and fund raisers were beginning to recognize the impact of market research in direct mail and telemarketing efforts and the need for information about the net worth, expendable income, potential inheritance, and other financial characteristics of their best donor prospects

In the mid 1980s, large educational institutions, with connections on Wall Street, began to develop an appreciation for what research could produce about well-known individuals. Development officers who had carefully read newspapers, clipped material, and put it into files, began to use, compare, and evaluate that information more astutely.

Enterprising and entrepreneurial development officers saw an opportunity to focus an area that had a new feel to it—research. This could range from discovering relationships between individuals or families, to determining how a person's interests coincided with the interests and needs of the campus.

Thus the development/advancement profile was born. One of the first books to benchmark these practices was *Prospect Research: A How-to Guide* by Bobby J. Strand and Susan Hunt (CASE 1986). (It's interesting to note that there's been little change since 1986, except for the introduction of online data resources.) Although institutions adapted the profile to suit their particular idiosyncrasies, a standardized profile began to appear. Common to the profiles were name, residence and business addresses and phones, personal history, educational history, special interests, gift history, significant relationships, family history, indications of affinity, philanthropic interests, and other special items deemed necessary at each institution. One institution had a place on its profile for emotional valence, which was translated by one development officer as "hot buttons."

The development of these profiles required painstaking bibliographic and documentary research conducted in development offices and university libraries. Of course, each time the profile changed slightly, the whole document had to be redone. Soon word processing technology provided a "cut and paste" environment for creating "instantaneous profiles" to be used ad lib.

Advancements in information delivery systems had an effect on advancement research in many more ways. Dialog, an online database with a complex search strategy, originally developed for science, was just one of the databases that began to be used in fund-raising research for its biographical capabilities. Newspaper indexes went from print to microfilm to digital. Today, easily accessible online data is almost taken for granted.

APRA: A PROFESSIONAL ORGANIZATION FOR ADVANCEMENT RESEARCHERS

In the early 1980s, through the leadership of researchers in the Minneapolis-St. Paul area, a professional group was formed to deal with questions specific to advancement research. By 1983, this group had changed its name to the Minnesota Prospect Research Association (MPRA), and by 1986, the group had developed a guiding document that dealt with the rights and responsibilities of researchers.

In 1987, the group adopted the name of American Prospect Research Association (APRA), and on January 11, 1988, APRA was incorporated in Minnesota. APRA has since grown to an organization of more than 1,600 members led by a board of directors; the group has also adopted a statement of professional ethics.

APRA's annual conference program topics provide a clear indication of the changes in technology; in methodology of research; and in the growth of research as an infrastructure for fund raising, particularly in higher education and medical centers. In the mid-1990s, the board considered the question of certification of researchers, and a study committee recommended delaying this action until the association matured. Recognizing the developing internationalization of research with members in Canada and Europe, in 1995, the membership adopted a name change: Association of Prospect Researchers in Advancement.

At the end of its first decade, APRA is a growing professional group within the broader areas of fund raising. It has helped gain respect for the services these professionals provide to their organization's fund-raising efforts, while grappling with the impact of a membership that is sizable enough to warrant multiple training tracks at conferences. In 1997, APRA published a skills set necessary for effective prospect research, which was a major step toward confirming researchers' professional identity in educational advancement. APRA publishes a professional journal, *Connections,* and a newsletter, and has strong connections with other professional fund-raising groups.

DEMOGRAPHIC AND BIODATA

Demographic data in fund raising is agency specific. Social service nonprofits, for example, need one set of specific demographic data, while in higher education, the constituent focus is alumni and nonalumni populations. Institutions may have other classifications of donors within these two groups, including parents, students, governing boards, and advisory boards. Sometimes, although less frequently, institutions break alumni into two groups: those who have degrees from the institution, and those who attended but who have no degree from the institution. But at the most basic level, we deal with alumni and nonalumni. Nonperson constituents are businesses and corporations, foundations, and other organizations.

Whether the record-keeping system is a shoebox of four-by-six cards or the most recent software system offered on the market, there are certain requirements for demographic data. Electronic data systems for advancement are best analyzed and chosen according to the size of the institution and its operations, its levels of technological support, the reporting structures of the institution, and the hardware/software combinations already in place. The best current source for information about the variety of systems available is in the vendor section of *The Chronicle of Philanthropy*. Regardless of the system used, the following list contains data that effective higher education fund-raising programs should have on prospective donors.

- Prefix
- First name
- Middle initial/name
- Last name
- Suffix

- Business name
- Title
- Business street/PO address
- City/state/zip
- Telephone
- E-mail
- Fax

- Residence street/PO address

- City/state/zip
- Telephone
- E-mail
- Fax

- Household mail name
- Recognition name 1 (individual)
- Recognition name 2 (household)

- Degree
- Date
- School (if multiple schools in institution)
- Major
- Minor
- Concentration
- Honors
- Scholarships received
- Student activities

- Spouse name
- Title
- Business name
- Business street/PO address
- City/state/zip
- Telephone
- E-mail
- Fax

- Date of birth
- Date of death
- Gender
- Ethnicity
- Religious preference

- Child name 1/gender
- Child name 2/gender (etc.)

You can obtain this information in a variety of ways. The alumni record is created at the time of graduation. Thereafter, it is a matter of obtaining and maintaining updated data. Collect information at the time of address changes and through alumni surveys. The real costs here are for data input and maintenance.

Some may call the data above biodata rather than demographic data. Regardless, this is the data that is most often needed by an advancement office to communicate effectively and on a personal level with its primary constituency: alumni. To relate effectively to alumni, institutions must include a great deal more in their databases than this basic information.

This leads us into the question of what role prospect research plays in advancement efforts.

PROSPECT RESEARCH

Prospect research provides the advancement team with basic and detailed information about a donor or potential donor. This information comes from publicly available resources in print and digital media. (When it is recorded in the constituent's record, it is important to attribute the source of the information.) The research office may record information such as:
- wealth indicators;
- real estate tax value assessment information;
- luxury registrations: cars, planes, and boats;
- stock holdings;
- company reports;
- newspaper indices and articles;
- philanthropic listings/interests;
- social and professional memberships;
- board memberships; and
- institutional relationships.

Good research is a cooperative endeavor of the major gifts officers and the research staff. The major gifts officer obtains information relevant to the advancement process from the potential donor, and from contacts knowledgeable about the potential donor. This information may include:
- family history;
- health issues;
- personal financial information;
- bequests and legacies;
- unique relationships;
- emotional valences (hot buttons); and
- personal interests.

There is a major discussion among prospect researchers about the viability of estimating net worth. Net worth is the difference between assets and liabilities. Some people may know their net worth only on April 15 when their accountant advises them of it. If the donor shares information about his or her liabilities, and the development

team identifies assets, you can estimate net worth. Awareness of net worth is important in predicting the donor's philanthropic potential. But even more important is information that deals with affinity and ability.

The Electronic Data Deluge

Technology has brought on significant advancements in managing information. Massive mainframe computers gave way to desktop units with networking configurations. Soon business information management systems and software was being used in advancement services. Anticipating this shift, many institutions created homemade systems to maintain gift records in a digital environment, and to keep prospect records that were connected with the institution's financial records.

As American industry developed electronic solutions for controlling inventory and tracking sales and customers, these same systems were applied to the needs of advancement offices. Complex data, such as securities holdings, that had previously only been available in government depositories and that required laborious manual research, are now being collected in digital formats. When these became available with search strategies that allowed faster access, obtaining financial data got easier. These data, coupled with census data (in digital format after 1990), and other information collected by enterprising entrepreneurs opened another technological door: electronic screening.

Since 1995, the Internet has revolutionized attitudes about information and access to information. Researchers have begun to rely primarily on electronic data, turning to paper resources only when necessary. Accessing information still takes time, though, even though each researcher and development officer has developed a private list of favorite sites. Effective use of the Internet and print resources—don't underestimate the resource of the daily newspaper—can help you gather information about an individual, particularly if he or she is wealthy, sits on corporate boards, is newsworthy, or owns real estate. Add the sophisticated computer information systems currently used by many colleges and universities for both information storage and management purposes and you have an advancement revolution. At the vortex of this revolution is the advancement researcher, who is normally a college graduate, computer literate, "likes the chase as much as the answer," has an analytical mind, and finds that the human side of the advancement infrastructure is immensely important.

Prospect and Donor Tracking and Management

In many advancement operations, prospect management includes two other research activities. Contact history records the essence of each contact with a donor/potential donor, thereby creating an institutional memory of the relationship. This information is immensely important to the institution as donor relationships mature. As a collegial courtesy, development officers should record information on any interaction with a donor or prospect as accurately as possible for future use.

The final research activity is prospect tracking, which involves recording a series of prescribed activities before, during, and after the solicitation process. For instance, a development officer may plan a varied series of contacts with a donor or prospect leading up to his or her solicitation. Each activity or move is calculated to lead to an "ask" for a gift. Prospect tracking, or moves management, provides a means to identify the progress being made in the donor relationship.

All of today's computer-based data management systems share one common philosophical approach: to carefully anticipate that particular donor's interest and appropriate timing for an "ask." In the end, prospect or donor tracking and moves management are aimed at the same objective: a stronger relationship with, and a gift to, the institution.

Screening

Data obtained from formal research and personal contacts can collectively identify the affinity and ability of a prospect. Affinity is the level and quality of relationship, and ability is an estimate of philanthropic potential and action. Effective research and analysis by the development staff leads to a determination of whether or not the constituent is "ready, willing, and able." Without all three, asks are futile.

> ● ● ●
> **Whether the record keeping system is a shoebox of four-by-six cards or the most recent software system offered on the market, there are certain requirements for demographic data.**

In some advancement operations there is a weekly meeting of development officers, researchers, and administrators to discuss new prospects. These prospects are assigned to development officers for cultivation toward a specific gift or project. Other advancement operations do this in a less formal matter. In both instances, the prospective donor is being screened on the basis of information that has come from a variety of sources to establish affinity and ability.

Another form of screening is performed during large campaigns, when volunteers are asked to review lists of prospects and identify those whom they feel have an affinity for a prescribed project, as well as the means to make gifts at certain levels. Information from volunteers is carefully reviewed, collated, and fed into formal and informal staff screening processes, which an advancement staff manages.

Most advancement operations now take advantage of consulting companies that specialize in electronic screening. This process of data analysis matches names and addresses with publicly available, and some proprietary, data resources. Electronic screening identifies individuals with similar demographic characteristics, interests, luxury item registrations, memberships, and a variety of other data. Note, though, that advancement staff members should always exercise care when checking information returned from electronic data analyses.

ISSUES FOR THE 21ST CENTURY

As the twenty-first century ensues, constituent research will most likely move its emphasis from providing information to analyzing information. Achieving this change will require some intellectual retooling for many of us. We will need to develop skills in interpreting complex financial data. We will have to become close followers of business activities, not just of principal or potential donors, but of international markets where ownership is multinational. We may need to apply several languages in the process of filtering and assessing information.

In the old days, data reliability was often a

phenomenon of timeliness; by the time data became available to us, it was outdated. Today, we find the data in a variety of electronic sources, some more reliable than others. Home pages, business profiles, industry directories, real estate records, political gifts, auto and luxury item registrations, professional membership directories, census records—all provide such a quantity of information that analysis has become an essential skill. We will need to synthesize information, spot relationships, look for intersections of data, detect dissonance, and assertively review constituents' data in order to make suggestions to major gifts officers.

More significantly, advancement researchers must become critical questioners. Each research activity will lead to a new set of questions to ask of the data, to find out what characteristics are necessary to make the match between a constituent and a particular project. By carefully reviewing contact reports and questioning the content of those reports, research staff may discover information concerning affinity and ability that has been overlooked via external research. The research staff should review such important internal information as each new project develops.

The challenge for constituent research in the coming decade will be to question critically. Achieving the task will require our art, science, hunch playing, educated guesses, and strongly inquisitive minds.

RESOURCES

Dunlop, David. "Major Gift Programs." In *Educational Fund Raising*. Edited by Michael J. Worth. Phoenix, AZ: ACE/Oryx Press, 1993.

Dunlop, David. "The Ultimate Gift," CURRENTS 13, no. 5 (May 1987): 8.

Grant, Andrew J. and Emily S. Berkowitz. "Knowledge is power," CURRENTS 14, no. 9 (October 1988).

McDonald, Kathleen. "Uncommon Knowledge," CURRENTS 23, no. 7 (July/August 1977).

McNamee, Mike. "Privacy and the Prospect Researcher," CURRENTS 16, no. 6 (June 1990).

Millar III, Robert G. "How Much is that Donor in Your Records?" CURRENTS 21, no. 7 (July/August 1995): 38.

Rowland, A. Westley, ed. *Handbook of Institutional Advancement*. 2nd ed. San Francisco, CA: Jossey-Bass Publishers, 1986.

Samuel, Tess. "Coming attractions: Five Trends that Will Affect Prospect Research on the World Wide Web," CURRENTS 23, no. 6 (June 1997): 24.

Smith, G. T. " The Chief Executive and Advancement." In *Handbook of Institutional Advancement*. 2nd ed. Edited by A. Westley Rowland. San Francisco, CA: Jossey-Bass Publishers, 1986.

Strand, Bobby J. and Susan Hunt. *Prospect Research: A How-to Guide*. Washington, DC: Council for Advancement and Support of Education, 1986.

Taylor, John, ed. *Advancement Services: Research and Technology Support for Fund Raising*. Washington, DC: CASE Books, 1999.

Walker, Margaret. "The Dirt on Donors: Decide Now Who Can See Your Most Sensitive Fund-Raising Files—and What Those Files Should Show," CURRENTS 22, no. 1 (January 1996): p. 10.

Worth, Michael J., ed. *Educational Fund Raising: Principles and Practice*. Phoenix, AZ: ACE/Oryx Press, 1993.

Also see:

APRA's Web site: *www.aprahome.org*

CASE's Web site: *www.case.org*

Because of the many different forms that a charitable gift can take, determining when a charitable gift takes place can actually become quite complicated.

IRS Rules and Regulations

Alison Paul
Attorney
Montana Legal Services Association

Nearly every Section 501(c)(3) organization in the United States uses a fund-raising program of some form or another. These programs range from soliciting relatively small donations from a large number of contributors in a direct mail campaign, to fund-raising banquets and auctions, to soliciting large donations through a complex planned giving and bequest program. In order to successfully operate all of these fund-raising programs, a nonprofit organization and its development professionals must understand the restrictions that a Section 501(c)(3) organization must follow in order to protect the tax deductible nature of the donations, and to shield itself and its donors from various penalties that the IRS may impose.

WHAT IS A CHARITABLE GIFT?

This chapter will explore the basic IRS rules regarding what makes a charitable gift by an individual, or a corporation, a tax-deductible charitable contribution. The three key aspects to a charitable contribution for income tax purposes are:

■ *The contribution.* Only certain types of "contributions" qualify as tax-deductible charitable contributions.

■ *The donee.* A tax-deductible charitable contribution must be made to a qualified donee.

■ *The receipt.* The donor must be able to substantiate the charitable contribution with a receipt from the charity that is required by the IRS.

In order to be a successful fund raiser, a development professional should be familiar with all three of these components.

The Contribution

In order for a charitable gift to be considered a "contribution" for income tax purposes, the gift must involve the transfer of money or property to a qualified charitable organization. Gifts of cash or stock are obvious examples of this type of gift. A development professional working for an organization that only receives cash gifts is lucky enough to be able to stop reading here and skip to the next section.

It is important for development professionals to be able to identify what types of transfers to charity do not qualify as tax-deductible charitable contributions. A development professional who inadvertently gives a donor inaccurate information about the tax deductibility of a charitable contribution is risking invoking the wrath of the IRS, both upon the charitable organization that gave the erroneous information and upon the donor that claimed an inaccurate tax deduction.

The following list identifies common types of "contributions" by donors that do not qualify as tax-deductible charitable contributions:

- a payment by a donor for a raffle ticket;
- payment to a charity that is earmarked for an individual, regardless of the charitable nature of the payment;
- volunteer time; (A volunteer who provides services to a charitable organization may not take the value of those services as a tax deduction. For example, an attorney that gives your organization *pro bono* legal advice may not take a charitable contribution for the billable value of his or her time. Just to confuse things, however, a volunteer's out-of-pocket expenses, such as mileage, parking or supplies, are deductible.)
- a payment to a charity that is earmarked for use by the organization for lobbying activities;
- a gift that is conditional on a future event; (The gift is not considered a charitable gift for income tax purposes until the future event occurs. For example, if a donor gives a valuable painting to a university but retains the painting in his or her home for three months before moving the painting to the university, then the gift does not occur until the painting is actually transferred to the university. Another example is if a donor transfers stock to a charitable organization, but retains the voting rights over the stock until the end of the year. The gift would not be complete until the charitable organization has total control and ownership of the stock.)
- the use of a donor's property by a charitable organization; (For example, if a donor allows a charity to use office space without paying rent, the donor is not allowed to deduct the fair market value of the rent as a contribution to the charity.)
- a *quid pro quo* contribution; (if a donor receives something back in return for his or her contribution, then only part of the amount paid is tax deductible. The most common example is a fund-raising dinner where in return for the donor's contribution to the organization, he or

she receives the right to attend a social event. The only part of this "contribution" considered tax deductible by the IRS is the excess amount paid over the fair market value of attending the event. Another example of a *quid pro quo* contribution is a payment for an item at a charitable auction. The disclosure requirements imposed on charities with respect to *quid pro quo* contributions are discussed later. Under certain circumstances, when a small item or a benefit of token value is received in exchange for the contribution, the entire amount of the contribution is fully deductible.

A benefit received in connection with a contribution will be considered a token if: (a) the payment occurs in the context of a fund-raising campaign in which the charity informs the contributors what amount constitutes a deductible contribution; and (b) the fair market value of the benefits received is not more than 2 percent of the payment or $74, whichever is less, or the payment is $37 or more and the only benefits received are token items bearing the organization's name (such as a mug or t-shirts). The cost—not fair market value—of all of the items received must be less than $7.40. These amounts are indexed each year for inflation and are current for Year 2000 contributions. The IRS releases the updated amounts in December of each year.)

- a portion of the payment by a donor for the right to purchase tickets to athletic events; (Under IRS regulations, 80 percent of the payment is treated as a charitable contribution and 20 percent as a payment for the right to purchase the tickets. For example, if a donor makes a payment of $300 to a university for the right to purchase basketball tickets, the substantiation receipt furnished by the university must show that the taxpayer received a benefit of $60 for the right to purchase the tickets. You may treat $240 of the payment by the taxpayer as a deductible charitable contribution.)
- a contribution by a corporation to a foreign organization; (However, a contribution by a corporation to a charitable corporation organized in the United States, but where the funds are to be used abroad, is tax deductible as a

charitable contribution. The organization must be formally organized as a corporation, and not another type of legal entity for this rule to apply.)

■ an acknowledgment of a contribution that includes an endorsement or other comparative language concerning a donor's products or services; (The payment is not considered a charitable contribution, but rather a payment for advertising. Under IRS regulations effective December 31, 1997, if a payment by a corporation qualifies as a "qualified corporate sponsorship payment," the corporation will consider it a charitable contribution. To qualify, the corporate contributor can receive an acknowledgment of the contribution from the charity, but any further language will be considered advertising. A single payment by a corporate sponsor may be divided between a qualified sponsorship payment and a payment for advertising services.)

Another issue that must be considered is when the charitable gift arrives. Although this seems like an easy question, because of the many different forms that a charitable gift can take, determining when a charitable gift takes place can actually become quite complicated. The basic rule is that a charitable gift is complete when the charity receives the cash or property. However, the IRS has stated that a charitable gift made by check is made at the time the check is delivered or mailed, provided that the bank eventually honors the check. For example, a check that is mailed on December 30, 1999, would be considered a 1999 charitable contribution by the donor, even though the check was not received by the charity and the funds did not clear the bank until 2000.

A gift of securities or stock is made at the time the certificate is delivered or mailed to the charity with a transferring document, such as a signed stock power. If a stock broker completes the transaction, the gift is considered to be made when the stocks are re-registered in the charity's name. Accordingly, if a charity receives a letter stating that

the donor has transferred 50 shares of stock to a charity on December 29 of one year, but the securities are not actually re-registered until February of the next year, the transfer did not actually occur until the second year.

The Donee

A development professional who is soliciting donations from individual or corporate contributors should understand which organizations are considered "qualified donees" by the IRS. If you are working for a university or an established charity, then it is unlikely that you need to be concerned about whether your organization is a qualified donee. However, in order to address the tax deductibility of contributions to other organizations, such as independent auxiliaries, programs of your charitable organization or payments under a matching gift program operated by your organization, it is important that you understand what organizations the IRS considers to be qualified donees.

An individual or corporation may deduct contributions to organizations described in Internal Revenue Code Section 170(c). For practical purposes, most organizations described in Internal Revenue Code Section 501(c)(3) will also qualify under Internal Revenue Code Section 170(c). In addition, organizations like hospitals, universities, and churches generally qualify to receive tax deductible charitable contributions, even though they are not Section 501(c)(3) organizations. Other types of tax-exempt organizations are not recognized recipients of tax-deductible charitable contributions. For example, deductions under Section 170(c) are not allowed for contributions to social welfare organizations exempt under Section 501(c)(4), business leagues exempt under Section 501(c)(6), and social clubs exempt under Section 501(c)(7).

To be described in section 501(c)(3) of the Internal Revenue Code, an organization must be organized and operated exclusively for religious, charitable, scientific, literary, or educational purposes. Further, no part of its net earnings may inure to the benefit of any private individual and no sub-

> ● ● ●
> **A development professional who inadvertently gives a donor inaccurate information about the tax deductibility of a charitable contribution is risking invoking the wrath of the IRS, both upon the charitable organization that gave the erroneous information and upon the donor that claimed an inaccurate tax deduction.**

stantial part of its activities may be carrying on propaganda or otherwise attempting to influence legislation. Finally, the organization may not intervene or participate in any campaign on behalf of or in opposition to any candidate for public office. Every charitable organization described in Section 501(c)(3) is presumed to be a private foundation unless it establishes otherwise to the satisfaction of the IRS. However, whether a Section 501(c)(3) organization is considered a public charity or a private foundation is only important if the contribution is to be made by a private foundation. Individual and corporate donors can make tax-deductible charitable contributions to either type of organization.

Verification of a Donee's Tax-Exempt Status

A donor may want verification that your organization is a qualified donee. The most reliable way to verify an organization's tax status is to give the donor a copy of the organization's IRS determination letter. This letter will state the type of 501(c) organization and, if the organization is a 501(c)(3) organization, whether or not the organization is a private foundation or a public charity. If this letter is more than five years old (as it often is), you also may want to request a signed statement from the organization that there have been no material changes in its tax status since the letter was issued. If an organization is unable to find its IRS determination letter, the organization can write to the IRS for confirmation or verification that it is a Section 501(c)(3) organization and give you a copy of that letter.

Hospitals and universities may not have an IRS determination letter because they are not required to apply for Section 501(c)(3) status. Accordingly, many donors will not require verification of the tax status of these types of organizations. If required, a corporate officer of the organization can verify the tax status by signing a statement that the organization is qualified to receive tax-deductible contributions under Internal Revenue Code Section 170(c).

The second most reliable way to check an

• • •

Although thank-you notes and other tokens of donor appreciation are a common practice within the development field, the interaction of these IRS rules with your standard donor recognition practices may present difficulties.

organization's tax status is to confirm that the organization is listed in IRS Publication 78 (the renowned "Cumulative List"). This publication is updated annually by the IRS (as of October 31) and lists organizations to which gifts are deductible for income tax purposes. Revocation of tax-exempt status between updates of the list is published weekly in the *Internal Revenue Bulletin*. You may obtain IRS Publication 78 from the Superintendent of Documents, U.S. Government Printing Office, Washington, D.C., 20402. Publication 78 is also available on the IRS Web site, *www.irs. ustreas.gov/plain/bus_info/eo/index.htm*. This is a rather unwieldy, yet searchable, database, which purports to list all organizations covered by Publication 78. Be aware that the absence of an organization's name from Publication 78 does not necessarily mean that the organization is not qualified as a Section 501(c)(3) organization. Often, the organization is qualified but for some reason was not included on the list. For example, the organization could be a local chapter or an affiliate of a national organization without its own Section 501(c)(3) determination. In these cases, you will need to verify the organization's tax status by some other means. Other publications that list potential donees are included at the end of this chapter. While these directories do not guarantee the tax status of an organization, you may find them helpful in locating an organization.

The Receipt—Documentation of Tax-Deductible Contributions

Several years ago, the IRS adopted a set of requirements for the documentation of tax-deductible charitable contributions. These rules govern the type of documentation that an individual or corporation is required to keep in order to substantiate a gift to a charitable organization. In fact, individuals making charitable contributions of more than $250 to an organization may not claim a tax deduction for the contribution unless they have the required receipt by the time the tax return is filed.

Although thank-you notes and other tokens of donor appreciation are a common practice within the development field, the interaction of these IRS rules with your standard donor recognition practices may present difficulties. With good intentions, you may issue a thank-you letter to a donor that is beautifully worded, yet does not contain the "magic" language required by the IRS. While the donor may appreciate your eloquence, the donor is unlikely to make another gift if your oversight means that he or she is not able to deduct the charitable contribution.

What should an individual or corporation collect or use as documentation to prove that a gift to a charitable organization is a deductible contribution? If a contribution is $250 or more, the individual or corporation is required to obtain a receipt stating that the charity received the contribution, the amount of the contribution or a description of property that was contributed, and a statement regarding whether or not any goods or services were received by the donor in exchange for the contribution. The following is an example of language that may be used to meet this requirement. While you are not required to use this exact language, each part must appear in your thank-you letter.

1. Receipt of contribution
   Thank you for your contribution on [insert date] *of* [insert amount of cash contribution or description of property] [Do Not Value Property].

2. Amount of description
   [Use One of the Following Statements]
   ■ *We estimate that the fair market value of the [describe goods or services] you have received from* [insert name of institution] *is $*[insert FMV]. *The amount of your contribution that is deductible as a charitable contribution for federal income tax purposes is $* [insert deductible amount], *the excess of the amount of your contribution over the value of the goods or services we provided to you.*

3. Statement that nothing was given in exchange
   ■ *As no goods or services were provided to you in return for your charitable contribution, the entire amount of your contri bution is tax deductible to the full extent otherwise allowed by law.*

Note that under IRS rules, it is critical that the gift acknowledgement indicate whether or not the donor received goods or services in return for the gift. The receipt should be signed by an individual authorized by the organization to issue tax receipts. The donor must have the receipt by the time he or she files a tax return for the year in which the gift was made (including any extensions).

Substantiation of Gifts from Private Foundations

As a development professional, it is likely that you also will be soliciting gifts from private foundations. Or, you may work for a corporation that manages its matching gift program through its corporate foundation. A foundation is not required to substantiate gifts to donees under the substantiation rules discussed above. Because a foundation does not pay income tax, it is not required to prove that its contributions are tax deductible.

Instead, a different set of rules applies and a foundation must prove that any distribution by the foundation is a qualified distribution for purposes of complying with the foundation tax rules. At a minimum, the foundation will want to verify that the donee you represent is a Section 501(c)(3) organization and a public charity. A foundation may ask for a copy of your organization's determination letter from the IRS, showing that it is described in Section 501(c)(3) and that it qualifies as a public charity. In addition, for particularly large grants, a foundation may require a signed copy of the grant letter and program information about the charitable organization, such as a copy of the organization's latest budget, annual report, or most recent tax return.

Substantiation of Noncash Contributions

Increasingly, donors are willing to donate property as opposed to solely making cash gifts. Accordingly, it is important for development professionals to understand how the IRS expects these donations to be valued and reported. There is potential for abuse by donors who overvalue property in order ultimately to reduce the amount of tax that must be paid to the government. In order to keep track of property that is donated to charities, the IRS uses a series of reporting forms that are required to be submitted by the donor, the tax-exempt organization, or both.

Form 8283. An individual or corporate donor must file Form 8283 if the amount of the donor's deduction for all noncash gifts made to charitable organizations is greater than $500. The primary function of Form 8283 is for the donor to set forth the value of the donated property for which the deduction is claimed, and for the charitable organization to acknowledge receipt of the gift. If your organization receives property for which the donor is claiming a charitable deduction in excess of $5,000, the name, address, and employer identification number of the organization must be included on the Form 8283. In addition, an authorized official of your organization must acknowledge the gift and state that it will file Form 8282 (see below) in the event that the organization sells, exchanges, or otherwise disposes of the donated property within two years after the date the organization receives the property. The person acknowledging the gift to the charity must be an official authorized to sign the tax returns of the organization or a person specifically designated to sign Form 8283. Note that a person in the organization's development office is not likely to qualify as an authorized individual unless the ability to sign the form has been specifically designated to that individual by an officer or the board of directors.

By signing the donor's Form 8283, the Section 501(c)(3) organization is not indicating that it agrees with the claimed fair market value of the donated property. Therefore, simply by signing the form, your organization should not be liable for an overvaluation of the property. The donor is required to furnish you with a copy of the signed Form 8283.

Form 8282. If your organization disposes of property for which it signed a Form 8283 within two years after receiving a contribution, you are required to file Form 8282 with the IRS. There are, however, two important exceptions in which Form 8282 does not need to be filed. (1) If the original donee provided on its appraisal summary a statement that the appraised value of a donated item was not worth more than $500 at the time of the contribution; and (2) The property received by

the charitable organization is consumed or distributed without consideration, in fulfilling its charitable purpose or function. In all other cases, Form 8282 must be filed within 125 days after the date of disposition of the property by your organization, and a copy of the form must be provided to the original donor.

It is important to note that the requirement to file Form 8282 applies to successor donee organizations if the property is transferred to another charitable organization. If you fail to file Form 8282, fail to include all of the required information, or include incorrect information on the form, you may be subject to IRS penalties. The penalty for each violation is generally $50, with an annual limit not to exceed $250,000.

Disclosure Requirements Imposed on Charities

As stated above, when a "contribution" involves the receipt of something of value by the contributor (a *quid pro quo* contribution), it will not be considered a gift for charitable contribution purposes. The tax-deductible amount of a *quid pro quo* contribution is the excess of the amount of the contribution over the value of any benefits received in return. If a donor makes a payment in excess of $75 to a charity, and the charity provides any goods or services to the donor in exchange for the gift, the charity must provide a written disclosure statement to the donor stating that the amount of the deductible contribution is limited to the excess of the amount contributed by the donor over the value of the goods or services provided by the charity to the donor. Further, the statement must include a good faith estimate of the fair market value of the goods or services that the donor received. The charity is not required to value the contribution made by the donor.

The IRS rules and regulations discussed in this chapter were developed to guard against income tax fraud by donors. Unfortunately, the complexity of these rules can also trap the unwary. If you take the time to master the tax rules with respect to the three key parts of a charitable contribution—the contribution, the donee, and the receipt—you should be able to comply with the IRS requirements.

FURTHER READINGS

For Colleges and Universities:

HEP Higher Education Directory. Available from Higher Education Publications, Inc. 6400 Arlington Boulevard, Suite 648, Falls Church, VA 22042.

Taylor, John. *Advancement Services: Research and Technology Support for Fund Raising.* Washington, DC: CASE Books, 1999.

For Hospitals:

Guide to the Health Care Field. Available from the American Hospital Association, One North Franklin, Chicago, IL 60606; (312) 422-3000.

For Museums:

Official Museum Directory. Available from Reed Reference Publishing, P.O. Box 31, New Providence, NJ 07974; (800) 521-8110.

For Associations:

The Encyclopedia of Associations, Volume 1, National Organizations of the United States. Available from Gale Research Inc., 835 Penebscot Bldg., 645 Grinswold St., Detroit, MI 48276-4094; (800) 877-GALE.

Above all, the purpose of a donor relations operation is to enhance relationships between the institution and donors.

The Anatomy of a Donor Relations System

Lynne D. Becker
Assistant Vice President for Development, Development Services
University of Washington

Donor relations in our institutions represents a new way of doing business. Managers, supervisors, and workers in education are challenged today to change their fundamental approach and beliefs about how to perform effective donor relations. Philanthropy is more and more about relationship building, and donor relations professionals are expected to respond promptly and in a personalized manner to the needs of donors in new ways. This new approach benefits the frontline worker, the open-minded manager, and introduces a new age for relationship building in the advancement enterprise. Its emphasis on crosstraining and employee initiative makes for a dynamic program.

COMPONENTS AND CHARACTERISTICS OF A PROTOTYPE DONOR RELATIONS PROGRAM

Donor relations responsibilities include:

- acknowledgments: Receipts (IRS compliant) and thank you's (highly personalized).
- stewardship: A range of services from maintaining prospect tracking systems and donor databases to proper coding for events attendance and recognition ceremonies.

- coordination of events: Opportunities to keep donors connected through recognition, education, and entertainment.
- coordination of publications: Communicating priorities and providing recognition in internal and external media.
- participation in marketing and communications strategies: Relaying our institutional values, priorities, and messages through philanthropic programs, market research strategies, product brand development, and electronic media.

THE HEART OF THE MATTER—A DONOR RELATIONS PLAN

Above all, the purpose of a donor relations operation is to enhance relationships between the institution and donors. A thoughtfully crafted donor relations plan provides a standardized recognition strategy for the advancement office to use with all donors—individuals, corporations, foundations, and associations. It can also respond to changing needs of the institution by creating tailored recognition for donors who support endowment, scholarship, capital projects, and unrestricted funds. The system is flexible enough to match the level and type of recognition to the donor's age, gift level, and giving interests, as well as to the donor's preference for public recognition and inclusion in exclusive groups.

BENEFITS OF AN EFFICIENT DONOR RELATIONS PROGRAM

A responsive donor relations program ideally:

- contributes to the positive experience that the donor feels from giving to the institution;
- increases familiarity with the donor's area of interest;
- prepares donors and prospects to consider giving to institutional priorities;
- provides stewardship by giving donors opportunities to meet recipients of their support;
- supports key development strategies as outlined by the institutional leadership for advancement;
- supplements cultivation and solicitation strategies undertaken by decentralized efforts of schools, colleges, and program advancement officers;
- inspires increased gifts over a lifetime; and
- honors donors who make extraordinarily generous commitments to the institution.

RECOGNITION

Recognition of donors is the underlying reason for many of the activities the donor relations office undertakes. Not only is recognizing donors the right thing to do; it also encourages a long-term philanthropic relationship. There are many types of gifts to recognize, many kinds of donors to recognize, and many ways to recognize both.

Annual Recognition

Gift societies recognize annual gifts that are over a certain level. Members of these societies often receive gifts such as personalized identification cards, auto window decals, reduced-rate coupons for parking, and library borrowing privileges. The donor relations staff prepares a recognition package, which includes a letter signed by a senior level advancement officer. That staff may also organize an annual event to recognize such donors.

Revocable and Irrevocable Gift Recognition

The donor relations office also recognizes donors who have made deferred gift commitments in the form of bequests, life insurance, or trusts. A packet of information, including an invitation to an annual luncheon and a recognition letter signed by the highest leadership, is developed in concert with gift planning. Recognition activities are tailored for donors' age group, gift level, and giving interests, and may include an annual reception/luncheon with special presentations on campus, individualized outreach efforts, stewardship, and gift planning publications.

Major Gift Recognition

The donor relations system supports *ad hoc* efforts to cultivate and provide recognition and stewardship to major gift donors. The donor relations system pays strategic attention to major gift level donors to endowment, unrestricted funds, as well as to those priorities that change from year to year.

The system also seeks to identify the next generation of leaders. It is not necessary to be an alumnus or past donor to the institution to qualify for this attention. Each year donor relations helps in planning an event that provides the institution an opportunity to establish contact with these individuals. In addition to recognizing the professional achievements of emerging leaders, the event serves as a springboard to more significant involvement in institutional activities through contributions of time, expertise, and money. These efforts also target young alumni and nonalumni donor prospects.

> ● ● ●
> **Naming a room, building, facility, or physical object—or placing a commemorative plaque—takes time and involves an extensive review process.**

Highest Gift Society Recognition

The highest gift society includes individuals who have achieved a cumulative giving level of a certain amount within a designated amount of time; those whose deferred gifts have a present value of this cut-off amount; or those who make pledges at a certain designated level. These donors may be offered an opportunity to accept or decline a special gift, the value of which they must declare for tax purposes.

Donor relations is responsible for maintaining and publishing the definitive list of these donors (living, deceased, and anonymous), coordinating the notification of donors and advancement directors, producing the identification cards and gifts, and coordinating recognition events.

Strategic Stewardship

The donor relations office produces and distributes an annual, consolidated endowment-fund unit report as well as a stewardship letter signed by the advancement administrator for all current endowment donors. Financial management provides a report on the earnings an each endowment with a detailed summary of its historical growth, which is included in the mailing.

Publications and Marketing

Donor relations coordinates the advancement office's recognition and stewardship publications. This might include an annual report to contributors, a series of brochures on gift planning, an annual fund advertisement in each publication of the alumni magazine, and other advancement publications including the schools, colleges, and programs publications, magazines, and newsletters as needed.

Donor relations coordinates marketing for advancement, including advertising in the alumni magazine, local business journals, and the (alumni-targeted) annual giving newsletter. As a marketing device, the newsletter is designed to appeal to the interests and giving potential of a large audience and inspire it to make gifts. Articles may feature the achievements of students and faculty, recognize donors and volunteers, provide stewardship for gifts received, or inform donors about school and college programs.

Events

Donor relations plans events for donors at most, but not all, giving levels. This audience includes donors who give to an annual institution priority; corporate, foundation and association donors; major donors; the foundation board donors; and many donors from the governing body. Annual events include gift society recognition receptions, cultural events, ground-breaking ceremonies, and/or special recognition of endowed scholarship/professorship funds.

Recognition through Naming

Naming a room, building, facility, or physical object—or placing a commemorative plaque—takes time and involves an extensive review process. Institutions generally have a policy for naming physical facilities. When naming is gift-related, the size and visibility of the space or object named must be consistent with that policy.

A campus committee usually reviews all names proposed for campus buildings, rooms, laboratories, atriums, or physical objects and spaces. And it recommends them to the institution's governing board for approval.

Donor walls and plaques to recognize individuals, corporations, foundations, and associations whose cumulative gifts and pledges total a designated amount are now common at most institutions. The donor relations staff is responsible for coordinating the nomination and approval process for these donors, ordering the inscription, and determining an appropriate date for installation.

Such permanent recognition requires careful planning that must include answers to the following questions:

- Why is a plaque proposed for this type of gift?
- Who will be honored? How many people? What giving levels?
- What wording will be used?
- Where will it be installed?
- When will it be installed (include timeline) and announced to donors?
- How will it be funded and maintained?
- Who is paying for it?
- Which members of the staff (the advancement officer, senior advancement officer, facilities manager, campus names committee, and donor relations designated personnel) will be doing what during the implementation of this plan?

Other Forms of Recognition

Within the overall acknowledgment process, donor relations is responsible for: 1) thanking donors for gifts 2) acknowledging donors who qualify for recognition 3) composing and generating letters for gifts that qualify for personalized response.

The donor relations staff that is responsible for gift processing and records management generates and sends receipts (with dollar amount, fund name, donor name, and address) to every donor for every gift, with some exceptions. Several agencies in the institutions may have their own 501(c)3 tax-deductible status and acknowledge gifts independently. Receipts are sent for deferred gifts to gift planning for handling and receipts for company and foundation support are sent to the office of corporate and foundation relations.

The donor relations office tracks acknowledgments of all levels and types and coordinates this information institution-wide, including those made by officers of various schools and colleges in a large institution.

GETTING THE MOST FROM YOUR DONOR RELATIONS PROGRAM

The best donor relations program will bring together employees from across the university. They will work in project teams on assignments that include recognition events for donors, publications, market research, and product development, among others, to ensure a common message throughout advancement. Designing and implementing a donor relations system of this nature is a stellar opportunity to bring under one umbrella the varied and extensive ways we communicate with our donors and build ever-stronger relationships with them.

FURTHER READINGS

Bunin, Irene et al. *Donor Relations: The Essential Guide to Stewardship Policies, Procedures, and Protocol.* Washington, DC: CASE Books, 1998.

Dessoff, Alan L. "Put It in Writing: Don't Let Donor Thanks Fall by the Wayside. Create a Written Recognition Policy to Make Thank-Yous a Part of Your Development Office Routine," CURRENTS 23, no. 2 (February 1997): 30-34.

Greenfield, James M. "Gift Size vs. Amount of Recognition: Balancing Your Donor Club Budget," *FRI Monthly Portfolio* 35, no. 6 (June 1996).

Harrison, Bill. "When a Plaque Isn't Enough: How Do You Thank Major Donors? Planning What to Do After Receipt of a Gift Begins Long Before the Actual Event. Recognition of Major Donors is One of the Most Important and Critical Aspects of a Development Program," *Fund Raising Management* 27, no. 5 (July 1996):36-39.

Hart, Theodore R. "Putting the Donor First," *Fund Raising Management* 27, no. 10 (December 1996): 20-24.

House, Michael L. "Structured Stewardship: How One Campus Plugged In a System to Thank, Inform, and Remember Its Top Donors—All Year, Every Year," CURRENTS 22, no. 4 (April 1996): 40-42, 44.

Keep in mind that each case is unique; be clear,
concise and detailed, but be careful not to make any
promises that you cannot keep.

SECTION VII
Advancement
Services

Gift and Pledge Agreements

Kathy Stanford
Director, Gift Policy and Administration
University of California, Irvine

This chapter is designed for individuals responsible for drafting gift/pledge agreements, sometimes referred to as "Memorandums of Understanding" between donors and educational institutions. They serve as a "contract," so to speak, between the donor and the institution.

I strongly recommended using gift/pledge agreements to clarify the intentions of the donor and to clarify the mutual duties and expectations of all the parties. Gift/pledge agreements are of critical importance when the donor is providing funds for an endowment, capital projects, and multi-year pledges. In rare cases, the document may be used in a legal action.

This chapter provides basic principles for the creation of gift/pledge agreements. These principles should not be interpreted as legal, tax, or financial advice. Always consult your institution's attorney, tax adviser, and chief financial officer for specific advice relating to gift agreements. Keep in mind that each case is unique; be clear, concise and detailed, but be careful not to make promises that you cannot keep.

Components of a Gift Agreement:
1. Title
2. Introduction
3. Description of the gift
4. Exempt status
5. Purpose and administration of the gift (or fund)
6. Recognition
7. Binding obligation
8. Unforeseeable circumstances
9. Miscellaneous
10. Signatures

1. *Title.* Title your document; it can be as simple as the words "gift agreement." You may want to elaborate depending on the type of gift. For example, if the gift is to establish a scholarship fund in the name of the donor, you might title the document "Gift Agreement to Establish the 'Doe Endowed Scholarship Fund in Music.'"

2. *Introduction.* The introduction provides a brief summary of the understanding between the parties. Include exact legal names of the donors and the institution in this paragraph; you may use another name in this paragraph (in parentheses) that indicates how you will refer to the entities throughout the remainder of the document. You

should consult with legal counsel in cases where there is more than one entity entering into the agreement with the institution, such as an individual wishing to include as donors himself or herself and a family foundation or trust. Here is an example of a gift/pledge agreement introduction:

> The purpose of this agreement is to summarize the mutual understanding of John and Jane Doe (Donors) and the University of Learning (University) regarding the establishment of an endowed scholarship fund. This agreement will be made a part of the University's permanent records, and is intended to serve as a guide to those who administer the fund in the future.

3. *Description of the gift.* This section describes the type of gift or pledge. It includes the value of the gift or pledge and outlines how and when the donor intends to satisfy the gift or pledge. Here are a few examples:

Example A [Pledge]:
The donors irrevocably pledge $1,000,000 (one million dollars) to establish the John and Jane Doe Endowed Scholarship Fund as described by this document. Pledge payments will be made as follows: $500,000 due and payable on June 30, 1999 and $500,000 due and payable on June 30, 2000."

Example B [Outright Gift]:
The Donors intend to gift, outright and concurrently with this Agreement, to the University, $1,000,000—or—the following assets, with an (estimated/appraised/ established) aggregate fair market value of $1,000,000.

Asset: _____ Value: _____

Asset: _____ Value: _____

Example C [Charitable Remainder Unitrust]:
The Donors intend to establish a charitable remainder trust, designed to pay ____ percent (___%) to Donors for their lifetime, with _____ percent (___%) of the remainder interest passing irrevocably to the University. The (estimated/appraised/ established) fair market value of the asset to fund the Unitrust is $_____.

Example D [Bequest]:
The Donors intend to provide a bequest in their (will/living trust) naming the University as a beneficiary of ($_____ / _____%) of the estate.

Example E [Insurance or Pension Beneficiary Designation]:

The Donors intend to designate the University as a beneficiary of
($_____/___%)

in the following (insurance policy/ IRA/pension/Keogh/profit sharing/ 401(k) account) :

Name of (Policy/Account):

_____

(Policy/Account) number:

_____

Name of (Agent/Broker):

_____

Address of (Agent/Broker):

_____

4. *Exempt status.* Use this section to reference your organization's tax status. Here's an example:

> The University of Learning represents that it is qualified as a charitable organization (federal ID 95-254XXX), for which the Donor is or will be entitled to charitable contribution tax deductions, under Internal Revenue Code sections 170(b)(1)(A), 170(c), 2055 or 2522.

5. *Purpose and administration of the gift (or fund).* Describe the purpose and use of the gift in detail. Be specific to ensure that all parties are clear as to the intended use of the funds. Also use this section to indicate your campus's policy on investments and spending policy. Example:

> [The income from the endowment or the gift] will be used to provide scholarships to undergraduate students enrolled in the School of the Arts Music Program. The principal criteria to be used for the award shall be academic excellence. In addition, the Dean may consider financial need and/or other factors; scholarships may be awarded on a single or multi-year basis, as determined by the Dean.

This endowment will be managed by the Regents of the University in accordance with the campus' investment and disbursement policies. The fund may be combined with the University's other assets for investments purposes. The President may authorize the addition of income to principal to the fund to mitigate the effects of inflation. If funds are not distributed in any year, the Dean may direct the income earnings to be added to the principal of the endowment.

6. *Recognition*. Use this section to clarify any consideration, appreciation, and public disclosure of the gift. Here's an example:

In recognition of this gift and subject to Presidential approval, the University agrees to name the music building in the School of the Arts "The Jane and John Doe Music Hall." The commonly used name will be "Doe Hall." The naming will be handled consistent with University policy, including identification of the building as Doe Hall on maps and through appropriate signage. The University [shall/shall not] have the right to disclose the names of the donors in its publications and press releases."

7. *Binding obligation clause*. This section protects the university in cases where the donor dies before fulfilling the pledge. It should be included in multi-year pledge agreements, especially when your institution is allocating its resources for a particular project. This clause should also be used in an outright gift agreement that is being signed prior to the actual transfer of the asset from the donor to the university. Example:

This agreement shall be binding upon and inure to the benefit of the Donors and the University, and their respective successors, heirs, assigns, administrators, and executors. The Donors intend the Gift Agreement to be fully enforceable against the Donors' estate, to the extent that the obligation has not been satisfied by gifts completed following the date of this agreement. The Donors agree to insert incontestable provisions in their will or living trust that will be consistent with this Agreement. If any portion of this Gift is to be paid by an organization or entity other than the donors individually, the

● ● ●

This is a "just in case" clause that protects the university from not being able to fulfill the obligations of the agreement some time in the future. Of course, every effort should be made to comply with the terms of the agreement, but institutional needs and priorities may change.

Donors represent that they have the legal authority to bind such organization or entity.

8. *Unforeseeable circumstances*. This is a "just in case" clause that protects the university from not being able to fulfill the obligations of the agreement some time in the future. Of course, every effort should be made to comply with the terms of the agreement, but institutional needs and priorities may change. It is especially important to include this clause for gifts to establish endowment funds, since they exist in perpetuity, and for deferred gifts or bequest expectancies. Example:

Notwithstanding the above, in the unlikely event that at some future time it becomes impossible for this fund to serve the specific purpose for which it was created, the President shall direct that its principal and income be devoted to purposes that are most consistent with the wishes of the Donor. If not possible, the funds should be assigned through consultation with the Donor's heirs.

9. *Miscellaneous*. This section may be used for miscellaneous items such as situs, amendment, irrevocability, and effective date. Example:

Situs: This Agreement is executed in and shall be governed by the laws of the state of _____.

Amendment: This Agreement may be amended at any time by written agreement signed by each party.

Irrevocable: Except as otherwise provided, this Agreement shall be irrevocable.

Effective Date: The effective date of this Agreement shall be _____.

10. *Signatures*. Provide a space for each required signature and date. Be sure to include both husband and wife for married couples, especially important in community property states. Know your institution's policy on gift acceptance and be sure to include all required and appropriate signatures. It is recommended that the institution's parties sign before the donor to ensure that all final changes are made internally before presenting the agreement to the donor for his or her sig-

nature. Finally, be sure to properly indicate the exact titles of all parties signing. Your institution's signers may have more than one title because they may serve in more than one capacity. For example, the gift may come into a university foundation where the vice president of the institution is also the foundation's president or executive director. Whoever is the appropriate chief executive officer of the foundation should sign the agreement.

FURTHER READINGS

Britz, Jennifer Delahunty. "Promises to Keep: After the Annual Fund Proposal, Encourage Alumni to Fulfill Their Pledge to Alma Mater," CURRENTS 22, no. 7 (July/Aug 1996): 34.

Culligan, Tom. "Gift Acceptance Policies: Don't Go Out Without Them," *Planned Giving Today* 7, no. 1 (January 1996): 5-6.

McLelland, R. Jane. "Essentials of Endowment Stewardship: Meet Campus and Donor Endowment Needs With Good Agreements, Well-Managed Money, and Regular Reporting," CURRENTS 23, no. 8 (September 1997): 28-33.

Shehane, John A. "Development Policies: Protect Your Image: Without Development Policies, Many Otherwise Sophisticated and Successful Non-Profits Expose Themselves to Aggravation, Public Relations Nightmares and Even Lawsuits," *Fund Raising Management* 26, no. 5 (July 1995): 18-20.

Smith, Francis S. *Looking a Gift Horse in the Mouth.* Washington, DC: National Association of College and University Attorneys, 1993.

No system is going to do everything you need, so know which requirements are most important.

Buying and Implementing a Development System

Robert L. Weiner
Director of Product Strategies
MyPersonal.com, Inc.

Software selection is like shopping for clothes. You can buy something you'll love for years, or something you'll be ashamed to admit owning one month from now. Technicians often select alumni/development systems, since it is their job to develop applications and keep them running. But buying and implementing software is a critical business decision for you in the alumni or development office. While technical considerations are crucial, the system must also meet your business requirements. This chapter discusses the major steps involved in selecting and implementing packaged software.

THE SELECTION PROCESS

Before You Start: Decide How You Will Decide

Who will make the selection—one person or a team? Technical staff or users? If you include both groups, whose needs take precedence? Will this be a consensus decision? Will you issue a Request for Proposals (RFP)? Who will be in charge of managing the process?

A decision document that outlines how you intend to resolve differences helps to build consen-

sus and can be a lifesaver later if problems arise. The document should include the roles and responsibilities of decision makers, their limits of authority, and the process to be used if appeals are needed. Agreeing to these rules before you begin will help you avoid charges of "stonewalling" or "railroading" later if factions develop in the selection process.

Plan Ahead For Buy-In

If you get buy-in from users during the selection process, they're more likely to support you during the implementation. If stakeholders believe a software package was forced on them, it's difficult to change their minds later. This is not to say that software selection is a consensus decision. But users need to understand how the system was selected and that their interests were taken into account. If you don't get buy-in from the start, all subsequent decisions are likely to be questioned. Be consistent in your communications to interested parties; if your process is honest, fair, and reasonable, you should find support.

Assemble the Team

Assuming that you're using a selection team, who will be on it? Who will be in charge? What constraints will they work under? Does anyone else need to approve the decision? Will they need any assistance?

Selection teams usually have at least three members and no more than 12. While the team should be broadly representative of the user community, it needs to be small enough to work efficiently.

The team's role will be to understand thoroughly your requirements (and the RFP if you use one), understand your selection criteria and rating and weighting schemes (if you use them), read and rank any RFP responses, and attend and rate the product demonstrations. Team members may be required to visit institutions that use your selected system. This will require a significant time commitment.

One member of the team should be the project leader. The leader is responsible for keeping the team on track, making sure it has a consistent understanding of the selection criteria and process, taking care of logistical details, checking references on the finalists, and addressing any questions or problems. The project leader will also play a key role in communicating the status of the selection process to interested parties.

Develop Detailed Requirements: What Are You Looking For?

Why are you looking for a new system? What's going to make it better than what you're using today? The first step in the selection process should be an assessment of your needs.

The needs assessment should start with the "big picture." The software should allow you to achieve your strategic vision of how your operation should run and where it needs to go.

The needs assessment can be the most time-consuming part of the selection process, particularly at a large university. Obviously, you'll want to meet the needs of the units in your office. And you might want to establish "best practice" goals based on what other development operations are doing. You might also need to consult with other departments (such as finance, registrar, internal audit, and the computer center) to determine the full set of requirements.

At the end of this process you should have a

list of functional and technical requirements for the new system. The requirements document can easily be turned into an RFP, and can be used as a scorecard for rating systems.

Know Your Limits

Your selection might be limited by your budget, the time available for implementation, your staffing resources or technical talent, required or prohibited technologies, or your need to interface with other systems. You need to answer questions such as:

■ Are you looking for a "best of breed" solution or are you buying into a campus-wide, integrated system?

■ Will you pay to customize the system to meet unique requirements or should the system meet your needs without modifications?

■ Does your fund-raising strategy require leading-edge technologies?

■ Are you limited to a system that runs on specific computer hardware or operating systems?

■ Does the software have to run on a specific database management system?

■ Does the system have to work with both Macintoshes and PCs?

■ Does it have to have a graphical or Web interface?

■ Does it have to be a client/server system?

The selection team needs to know (or determine) these constraints.

How Do You Rate Requirements?

No system is going to do everything you need, so you need to know which requirements are most important. One way of doing this is to document mandatory requirements and screen out any system that can't meet them. You can also assign points to each requirement based on how critical it is in meeting your goals for the system. You can use a simple point system (i.e., 15 points for mandatory, 10 points for "nice to have" and five points for "wish list" items). You can give extra points for features that aren't mandatory but are important for your long-term vision of how you'll operate.

You might assign a weighting factor to an entire category (i.e., technical requirements equal

20 percent of the total score, donor management/gift processing features equal 25 percent, alumni/membership features equal 25 percent, references equal 30 percent, etc.). You can also create ratings for the demonstrations, particularly if you're asking all the vendors to demonstrate certain features or scenarios. Ratings and weightings help take the subjectivity out of evaluating RFP responses and demos.

Be cautious about designating mandatory requirements, however. If you use the term too loosely, you might inadvertently exclude most or even all potential vendors. But if you don't use it enough, you might wind up with a system that lacks critical features. And remember your strategic goals. Mandatory requirements are often purely technical; don't lose sight of your business needs amid the sea of technical details.

It's often helpful to place a limit on the total points that can be assigned to your set of requirements. For instance, if you have 50 requirements, you might limit total points to 400 to prevent everything from being assigned 15 points. You might even limit the total mandatory points to 75, so only 10 percent of your 50 requirements could be designated mandatory. This will force your committee to prioritize. It is often helpful to have someone who is not invested in the outcome to help your team set priorities. This can be an analyst or facilitator from another unit on campus or an external consultant.

Write and Send Out the RFP

Even if you're not required to write an RFP, you might find it helpful to have one. Circulating the RFP draft internally can help you identify missing requirements and clarify the requirements' priority. And vendors will be forced to give you a written response stating whether they can meet your requirements. This forms the basis for a contract between you and the vendor. If you've documented your requirements, the RFP should be easy to develop.

It's often helpful to review sample RFPs from comparable institutions or from several vendors. You may see features or ways of describing requirements that you hadn't thought of. But resist the temptation to simply stick your name on someone else's RFP. The RFP needs to describe your needs, not theirs.

Review RFP Responses

The selection team will need to read each of the RFP responses, discarding those that fail to meet mandatory requirements and rating the rest. They need to understand each requirement in the RFP so they can rate the responses uniformly. If you use a numerical rating scheme, the team needs to apply it consistently. And they need to understand the selection process, timeline, and their responsibilities. The project leader is responsible for making sure the team is prepared for its role.

When the team reviews the RFP responses, it can assign points to each requirement, as described above. Or each item can be rated based on how well it meets your requirements, using categories like "met," "partly met," "is expected to meet in next release," or "didn't meet." These categories can have point values—e.g., if the requirement is worth 10 points, then "met" is worth 10 points, "partly met" might equal five, "next release" might equal two, and "didn't meet" gets no points. After the points are assigned, any weights are applied. Each vendor who met the mandatory requirements would be ranked based on its score, and the top vendors, perhaps three to five, would be invited to demonstrate their products.

Note that price isn't necessarily a screening factor at this point. Some RFPs instruct vendors to submit prices separately, or at a later date, so the first review can be based solely on features.

Schedule Product Demonstrations

The selection team must attend all demos. But you should also invite a wider audience and ask for feedback. The selection team might want to have the audience fill out a survey so it can get opinions on specific features. The team should also have its own rating scheme so it can score the demos consistently.

Vendors will have "canned" presentations that they are prepared to give. You might also want to request "scripted demos." In scripted demos, the selection team creates scenarios for the vendors to demonstrate. For instance, you might have vendors create some user accounts and set up their security profiles. Next, they might create profiles for some alumni, donors, and parents. Then they might show you how to enter a variety of gifts that match different scenarios (e.g., hard versus soft credit, matching gifts, joint gifts, split gifts, multi-year pledges, campaign gifts, and so on). They might "marry" some alumni and show what happens to their donor histories. Then they might divorce some of them.

Be sure to allow time for the vendor to do a canned presentation to show features you're not asking about. And allow plenty of time for questions. Demos usually last two to four hours and can easily take a full day. You might want to schedule separate demos for different groups: the computer staff will want to see how the system is configured and test the security, while the fund raisers will want to see the donor and prospect management features.

Do Your Homework

After the demos, you should have narrowed your choice of vendors to two or three. Now you need to verify your impressions.

Check References

Each vendor should provide you with several references. The selection team leader should contact each reference, ask the same set of questions, and try to contact other clients.

Visit Client Sites

Once you've narrowed your choice to one or at most two products, consider sending the selection team to visit comparably sized offices that have the software running. These sites have survived the conversion and can show you how the product works in real life. They can point out the hazards you're going to face and offer survival tips. The team can see how the software performs with a real user at the keyboard. And, as a side benefit, the team will meet people who are likely to be valuable resources during your conversion.

You need to view site visits and reference checks with a critical eye, however. It's important to distinguish between a poor software implementation and weak software. On the other hand, just because one college loves a product doesn't mean you will.

Make Sure you Understand the Full Price

The price of the software is just one piece of the "total cost of ownership." You're likely to need to upgrade your server and may need to upgrade your desktop computers and office automation software. You might need consulting help to implement the software. There will be annual maintenance costs for your software and hardware. You might need to invest in additional training or enhance your technical support organization. You may initially see these as one-time capital expenses, but many will become ongoing operating costs.

Ask Lots of Questions

The following questions can get you started when you check references or visit other clients. If possible, send the questions you'd like to ask ahead of time.

About Their Implementation Project:

- How long did it take for you to "go live" on the software?
- How many of your staff worked on the implementation?
- What were their skills, roles, and job titles?
- Did you dedicate any staff to the project full time? Did you have to hire temporary staff?
- What did the vendor do to help you with the implementation?
- How did you organize the implementation team(s)? How many teams did you have; how many people were on each; and what were the teams' roles?
- Did you use consultants? If so, for what? How much did it cost? Was it worth it?
- Did you contract with the vendor for additional implementation support?
- Did you try to improve operations as part of your implementation? If so, how extensive was the process improvement project, and at what stage did you do it?

About the Data Conversion:

- Who handled your conversion programming?
- What weren't you able to convert?
- Were you happy with the vendor's support during the conversion? If not, why not?

About the Software and Vendor Support:

- Have you required any customization of the system?
- How many software upgrades (patches, bug fixes, new releases) do you usually get each year? How much time does it usually take to install them? Do you usually have to shut the system down to install upgrades? Do upgrades tend to introduce new bugs?
- How quickly does the vendor respond to technical support questions? Are problems resolved to your satisfaction?
- Were you happy with the training provided by the vendor? If not, why not?
- Did you have to buy more training than you'd anticipated?

About the Ongoing Support of the System:

- How many technical staff members support the system? Where do they report? What are their titles and roles? Did they have to learn new skills in order to implement or support the system? Did you have to hire new staff to support the system? Did you have to reclassify your technical positions to retain or recruit staff?
- How many functional staff members support the system in each unit? Did you have to create any new positions or change job descriptions or classifications?
- Did you have a help desk before the implementation? Do you have one now? If you do, how is it staffed? If you don't, who answers users' questions about the system and troubleshoots problems?
- What other investments did you have to make as a result of the implementation (hardware, software, networking, training, etc.)?
- How are you handling ongoing training?
- Did you experience unusual staff turnover during the implementation or after you went live?

About the Daily Use of the System:

- Are fund raisers, alumni officers, and other senior administrators able to do their own research in the system?

- Can administrative staff members write their own reports? If so, what tools do they use?

About Your Operations Generally, and What You've Learned:

- What would you do differently if you had it to do over?
- What would you do the same way?

Negotiate

Based on your requirements analysis, the RFP responses and demos, reference checks, and site visits, you may identify gaps in the software or areas where you'll need additional support. You may be able to negotiate with the vendor over costs such as additional training, conversion support, or software modifications. If you're buying based on the expectation that the next product release will include new features, or that the vendor will meet specific deadlines during the implementation, you might build performance incentives into the contract.

You'll want a legal opinion on the proposed contract. You might also want an opinion from a consultant who is experienced with software contracts. He or she can provide assurance that safeguards are in place and pitfalls are avoided. For example, the consultant can help you define what it means to accept the software or help define what type of problems might be found and the vendor response time that would be appropriate to address them.

Take a Deep Breath

The hard work—implementing the new system—is about to begin. Before you start, complete the selection process by documenting why you selected this system, how the selection process occurred, and who was involved. Then communicate your message broadly. If you've started your implementation planning, include as much as you know about the schedule and project team. Be sure to thank everyone who was involved in the selection process. Progress reports such as this will help you gain buy-in and support.

> ● ● ●
> **Be cautious about designating mandatory requirements. If you use the term too loosely, you might inadvertently exclude most or even all potential vendors. But if you don't use it enough, you might wind up with a system that lacks critical features.**

IT'S TIME TO IMPLEMENT

Congratulations! You've bought a new alumni/donor database. No matter how simple or complex your selection process was, you should mark this important milestone. A small celebration will help build enthusiasm and energy for the implementation—which is likely to be long and grueling.

Implementations are complex projects. You'll need strong project management, a focused team, lots of communication, and a plan.

Determine the Scope

Most software packages have more functionality than you will be able to implement immediately. Some may contain features that your institution is not interested in at all. To keep the implementation on track, ask yourself these questions:

- What are you trying to accomplish?
- What will success look like?
- How much time do you have?
- What's your budget?
- Are you planning to reengineer processes as you implement? If not, should the team spend any time trying to improve operations?
- When do you move from implementing the system to operating it?

Beware of "scope creep." For instance, will upgrading your department's desktop computers fall within the project's scope? What about computers for other campus departments that will be using the system? Would a network upgrade for your office be within scope? What about upgrading the network between you and the campus computer center? Scope creep can undermine your timeline, your budget, your confidence in the project, and your staff's morale.

Think About Process Improvement

Implementing a new system will invariably require changes in the way your office operates. This can be a great opportunity for process improvement. Encourage staff members to question the way they've always done things and to use the new system to its fullest.

Process improvement often takes the form of a process-reengineering project to diagram work-

flows; trace handoffs of paper and responsibilities; and eliminate inefficiencies, unnecessary steps, and redundancies. Large organizations usually require formal meetings and the help of a facilitator. But your project team can often identify simple process improvements as they determine the codes and steps necessary to run the system.

Assemble the Implementation Team

You need to identify the people who are going to get the job done. The staffing of an implementation project will vary considerably depending on the size of your institution and the complexity of your project. Minimally, you will need a project sponsor, who provides executive-level support, and a project manager. You might also need a steering committee to provide broad participation in decision-making, and multiple project teams.

Once you appoint the team, you need to make sure they understand the goals and scope of the project and their own roles and responsibilities. If your college is small, all these roles might have to be filled by one or two people.

The primary tasks to accomplish during implementation are:

- determining how the system will integrate with your business processes (i.e., how will work get done using the new system?);
- preparing the technical environment;
- defining all necessary tables and values used by the system;
- setting security and access parameters for use;
- building reports and queries;
- converting data from existing systems;
- developing documentation for operating procedures;
- preparing and delivering training for users; and
- establishing maintenance procedures for the system after you go live.

Here are descriptions of the major roles of the implementation team:

Project Sponsor
This person:
- is often the least involved in the details of an implementation but most critical to its success.
- should be a member of upper or executive

management, and, in most cases, should not come from the technical side of the house.

- champions the project from cradle to grave. She sends the message that this project is critical and is worth the effort and disruption. The sponsor makes sure the project manager has the resources she needs, and keeps other executives informed about the project.
- is the ultimate authority for removing road-blocks and resolving conflicts.
- is the project's cheerleader and patron. When implementation projects falter or fail, it is often due to poor stewardship by the sponsor. Very little that the project manager can do will over-come a lack of leadership in this critical role.

Steering Committee

In a small office, the project leadership might con-sist of one or two people. But larger institutions generally require a steering committee, particularly when the project involves multiple departments. The steering committee will:

- guide the project and make sure affected parties are consulted;
- make high-level decisions about the project's direction and goals;
- provide advice to the project manager and team; and
- help resolve conflicts.

The major stakeholders should be represented on the steering committee. The project sponsor is often a member of the steering committee.

Project Manager

The project manager is the day-to-day leader of the project. This person:

- works with the steering committee, imple-mentation team, software vendor, and any consultants to assemble and manage the implementation timeline, budget, and project team;
- determines and tracks key milestones and deliv-erables. She needs to monitor the project's schedule and keep the steering committee and sponsor informed of progress and problems;
- is often a member of the steering committee, at least in an *ex officio* capacity; at a minimum, she

should give the committee frequent status reports on the project.

Ideally, the project manager will not be responsible for the hands-on work involved in the project. Nor should she have routine operational responsibili-ties. It is nearly impossible to stay focused on a complex project amid the distractions and daily crises of the office. Lack of time for the project (on the part of the manager, team leaders, or team members) is one of the most common causes of missed deadlines.

Team Leader

In a large university environment, you might have teams representing each department and profes-sional school, while a small college might not need a team. If you do have teams, each requires a leader. This person:

- is responsible for making sure each team mem-ber understands her role, responsibilities, and where her work fits within the overall project.
- must keep the team's part of the project on track and resolve any problems that arise.
- is responsible for communication with all other team leaders and the project manager, and for keeping the team informed of any changes in the project.
- must also support the team by keeping it moti-vated and helping it get resources.

Like the project manager, team leaders will be most productive if they are relieved of their regular duties. If you can't get by without them, try to reassign half of their duties.

Team Members

Team members are the most critical part of the team, yet often the least visible. Team members:

- help translate day-to-day needs into the codes and business rules that drive the system.
- may also need to have duties shifted in order to have time for the project.

Think About "Buy-In"

The people who will implement the system need to be committed to its success. They're going to go through a lot of hard work and inconvenience, and therefore need to know that it will be worthwhile. They need to feel that they are stakeholders in the project and that there is a decision-making structure to address their concerns. If they don't buy into the project, they're likely to fight it, overtly or covertly, and may continue to do so long after the conversion is finished. The project will be much easier to lead if the troops are supporting you.

Create the Project Structure

Everyone involved in the project will benefit from a well-articulated decision-making process, clearly identified resources, ongoing communication, and good planning.

Decision-Making Process

Colleges and universities are often unaccustomed to making the kinds of quick decisions needed to keep an implementation moving. Getting decisions made can be the hardest, most time-consuming, and most expensive part of the project. The larger and more complex the institution, the more difficult it becomes. Implementations can take years if you have to get consensus from dozens (or hundreds) of departments on every code in your system. You need to devise a decision-making process that allows you to reach agreements quickly, and decide how you'll break logjams.

You need to decide what's open for debate and what's not. The project manager, implementation team, steering committee, and project sponsor must take responsibility for keeping the project moving. If your project will involve consultants, this is often a place where they can be helpful. They may be able to help you design objective criteria and a process for making and vetting decisions that are not tainted with an "insiders' agenda."

Communication

Regardless of the size of your project team, communication is critical to the success of the project. Communication sets expectations for the outcomes and conduct of the project, creates buy-in, maintains momentum, and minimizes rumors and misunderstandings. Communication should be two-way, allowing you to keep stakeholders informed about the project and to receive their input.

Good project communication is seldom *ad hoc*; it requires a plan. Your communication plan might be as simple as regular updates at staff meetings. Or it might involve a schedule of town hall meetings, reports at other departments' staff meetings, newsletters, surveys, e-mail bulletins, Web page postings, suggestion boxes, and other ways of informing the campus and learning about their concerns.

It's a good idea to select a member of the project team to lead the communications effort. This person should prepare materials for release. The project manager or sponsor should review the materials for accuracy and consistency. The more active your project team is regarding communications, the more effectively you can manage the grapevine.

Timeline

Your software vendor and/or implementation partner or consultant, working closely with the project manager, usually outlines the project timeline for packaged system implementations. The vendor or implementation partner should know the major steps involved in the project and how long they normally take. The project manager needs to adjust for special circumstances such as the complexity of the environment; the decision-making process; budget; availability of the project team; university culture; dependence on other projects, decisions, or funding allocations; and other issues that might affect the implementation. The timeline is only a guidebook. It needs to be edited continually to match reality.

Budget

Obviously, the project budget will have to cover the cost of your new software. And you probably thought about a new or upgraded server. Other expenses that are often covered within project budgets include new forms or letterhead; licenses for applications like Word or Lotus; and report writing software, scanners, and document management systems. You may want to include funds to cover training and attendance at user group meetings. You may need additional staffing during the implementation. Depending on the software's degree of fit with your unique requirements, there may be significant costs for software customization. You may also need to budget for programming assistance for data conversion. If your organization will use consultants during the project, you'll need to add another budget line for them. And don't forget to build the annual maintenance costs of your new software and hardware, as well as ongoing training, into your annual operating budget.

Contingency Plans

Of course, nothing will go wrong on your project. But what if it does? What if your new system is so popular that you need more user licenses? What if the server you bought isn't fast enough to support all those new users? What if the network can't handle the traffic? Or your project manager finds another job? Some of these contingencies can be anticipated; for instance, you might create incentives for key staff to stay with you at least until the project ends. But you also need to have contingency reserves and creativity on tap in case something unforeseen occurs.

Prepare the Technical Environment

Minimally, you need to install and configure your software. Depending on the current state of your technology environment, you might also need to install network cabling, networking equipment and security, servers, desktop computers, e-mail software, applications software, scanners, printers, or Web servers. Each will take time to install, configure, and test. Many institutions begin the implementation process with a technical assessment so that they can include time (and funding) for any necessary purchases, installations, or upgrades in the project plan.

Configure the Software

This sounds like a purely technical step, but don't be deceived. This is where your decision-making process comes fully into play. The project team needs to decide everything from how you'll code addresses to what the rules are for managing donor stewardship. If your new software is complex, the team may have to make thousands of decisions. If

your environment is complex, you might have hundreds of departments whose needs must be addressed. The project team needs to communicate with stakeholders, make the decisions that fall within their authority, request decisions on questions that are outside their area, and get disagreements resolved expeditiously.

Develop Interfaces

If you're implementing stand-alone software, you'll probably need to link it to other campus systems and to external systems (e.g., a telemarketing system). But you might need interfaces even if your system is part of a campuswide software package. Not every module will go live at once; you might need temporary interfaces (e.g., to the general ledger, admissions, or student systems).

● ● ●

Regardless of the size of your project team, communication is critical to the success of the project. Communication sets expectations for the outcomes and conduct of the project, creates buy-in, maintains momentum, and minimizes rumors and misunderstandings.

Develop Reports

Your new system will come with "canned" reports. In the best of all worlds, these reports will give you all the information you need in just the way you want to see it. But don't count on it. You need to look at your current reports and decide which ones you really use. Then make sure you can get the same information from the new system—either in hard copy or through on-line inquiries. Many institutions find that the information available through inquiry screens makes many of their former reports obsolete.

You're also likely to need a way for end-users to run their own reports. This often requires an additional report writer or an interface with commercial spreadsheets or databases. And users will need training on both the reporting software and the techniques for creating *ad hoc* reports that balance with the canned reports.

Train the Staff

Even the best development software won't run itself. You need to invest in the staff members who will use the system. And you're likely to spend more on training than you'd planned.

Obviously, you need to train the team when you begin the project. But six months or three years later, when you finally go live with the new system, they might need a refresher course. You're also likely to lose and/or add staff, and the new staff will need training. And upgrades to the system might be extensive enough to require still more training. A "train the trainer" approach can help you bring training in-house and contain costs. But not everyone is an effective trainer, so you need to make sure you have a staff member with the skills and patience to do a good job. And even with a train the trainer approach, your technical staff and "power users" are likely to require more in-depth training than you can deliver in-house.

Don't forget the population of casual users who may need training on inquiry and data searches. They may not have direct responsibility for using the system in your department, but they will benefit greatly from understanding how to use the information the system provides.

Develop Documentation

One frequently overlooked aspect of the training phase is preparation of a documented set of administrative procedures. It's important, as the business processes are being applied to the system (and vice-versa), that you capture the flow of work with clear, concise procedures documentation. This will become the basis of your training program and help ensure that information about how the system works and how the development enterprise operates is available for reference. A good set of procedure documentation is your insurance against loss of institutional memory, which can occur with frightening speed if you lose key individuals in your department.

Convert your Data

Data conversion has two major steps: mapping and programming.

Data Mapping

In this step, you are trying to translate all the fields in your old system into corresponding fields in the new system. This is a time-consuming process that requires communication among several parties: a staff member who knows your data, technical staff members who know the new system, technical staff members who know the old system, and the programmer(s) who will do the translating.

Identify a staff person who knows your data and assign him or her to this project. The people who handle data entry or report generation are probably your best resources. If you don't have anyone who knows your data, find and assign a person who is familiar with your old system, preferably from a functional perspective. This person might be from another college or a consultant recommended (or provided) by the vendor of your old system. They won't know the idiosyncrasies of your data, however, so they will need to ask lots of questions.

If your only choice is to use technical staff members, you must work closely with them. They probably won't know your data, are unlikely to know a LYBUNT from a nondonor, and might not know what questions to ask.

This step will be more complicated if you have used fields in your current systems in varying ways (e.g., spouse name was used to store children's names if there was no spouse). To the extent that you are aware of such practices, you should arm your conversion team with everything you know. This is no time to be coy about the condition of your data.

Programming

In this step, your old data is massaged to match the format of the new system. The complexity of this step varies tremendously. In the best case, the data comes out of your old system just the way the new system expects it to look. In the worst case, you will need a lot of technical help.

The problems that you might face in this step include:

■ The new system can store all of the data that was in your old system (this is rarely the case, but let's fantasize). But some fields are too short. What do you do with the last five characters of long addresses?

■ Your data has been forced into fields in irregular ways over time.

■ You don't have a (good enough) programmer on staff and can't afford (or find) anyone else.

■ The programmer hasn't done this type of work and doesn't anticipate the hazards.

■ The documentation for the new (or old) system is so bad that no outsider can figure out how the data is organized.

- The conversion requires the use of special tools that only the software vendor can use.
- The programmer doesn't ask enough questions.

A do-it-yourself approach at this step can get you into trouble. And accepting a cut-rate bid from a hired gun will frequently backfire. If you bought a simple system, any programmer (and perhaps a talented amateur) might be able to program the conversion. But if your new system is (or your old system was) complicated, the programming is probably equally complex. Get multiple bids, and be prepared to invest in this critical step.

In many cases, the vendor who wrote your new system has a huge advantage in handling the conversion programming. The vendor knows how the new system stores and organizes data. And some systems are so complicated and/or so poorly documented that only an insider can figure them out. But the vendor is often the most expensive option and isn't always the best. Some vendors routinely fail to meet their conversion schedules. Other vendors simply don't do conversions.

If you didn't ask about conversions when you checked references on your software vendor, locate its user group and start asking. If someone wasn't happy, investigate. Was it the vendor's fault? If so, was it symptomatic or an isolated problem?

If you decide to look elsewhere for programming help, try to find a consultant with experience handling conversions to your new system. Some software vendors are happy to recommend consultants. If they're not, try asking through their user group. You may also want to look into firms that provide "data scrubbing" that can, at the least, remove duplicate records and prepare your current data for importing to the new system.

Since development operations are so data-dependent, it is critical that you use the implementation conversion to "get it right." After cleaning the data and preparing the conversion plan, be certain that your standards and formats are documented and added to your operating procedures. This will help ensure that your new system's data stays clean and usable.

Test Everything

Now you're ready to make sure the previous steps were done properly. Do the dollars add up? Are dead donors still coded "deceased"? Are alumni couples still linked? Do the new reports balance with the old? Can you read them? Are the screens laid out logically? Can users move around the system in ways that make sense? Do reports come out on the right printer? Is the system security working?

Remember, of course, that any garbage from the old system is still garbage in the new system. Data cleanup is another project altogether. If you didn't attend to it during the conversion, you should plan to devote significant resources to it during or immediately after your conversion.

Who should do the testing? Everyone. The programmers should have been testing all along. Now the people who did the data mapping should look at sample screens and reports. So should fund raisers, alumni officers, researchers, data entry staff, and receptionists— anyone who knows your data or constituents. Look up your own record and anyone else's whose information you're familiar with. Run the same reports on the old and new systems and compare the results. If something looks wrong, ask lots of questions, get problems fixed, and test again.

Consider running parallel systems for some period of time. This means entering the same data on your old and new systems and making sure everything balances on both. This can be a good training exercise before cutting over to the new system. The duration of parallel testing can range from one gift batch to a full year, but few development offices run parallel for more than a month. You probably won't want to run parallel during a busy time of year, but you should try to test a range of scenarios.

Flip the Switch

Be prepared for minor upsets. Most people take a great deal of pride in their work, and having new systems to work with can disrupt their sense of accomplishment. Under pressure to perform, it's easy to feel overwhelmed. The transition will go more smoothly if everyone allows a little more time in the first week or so.

Celebrate!

Your staff has been through a long, difficult project. You need to acknowledge staff members' hard work, and let them know it was worthwhile. Plan to end the first week with a party to celebrate the cut over and publicly thank your team members. Invite your sponsor and other officers to join you and be sure that they also take time to thank the team.

Take Stock

Going live on a new system doesn't mean your implementation is over. The project team will have a long list of details that aren't finished. And the technical staff members are about to be deluged by requests for new reports, screens, codes, alumni regions, honor rolls, labels, tapes, pledge rosters, receipt programs, and so on. They're going to need a process for prioritizing requests, communicating with users, fighting fires, working on long-term projects, and balancing ongoing implementation with their daily workload.

As these mechanisms are worked out, it's a great time to make the transition from the project manager to the systems support team. Schedule regular meetings to make assignments, report progress, and continue the integration of your new system into the daily operations of your office.

Kathryn E. Behrens, senior manager, KPMG Consulting, Inc., provided advice on this chapter. The views and opinions expressed are those of the author and do not necessarily represent the views of MyPersonal.com, Inc. or KPMG Consultiing, Inc. The information provided here is of a general nature and is not intended to address the specific circumstances of any individual or entity. In specific circumstances, the services of a professional should be sought.

FURTHER READINGS

Barth, Steve. "Finding a Needle in the Haystack: Use Computer Screening and Database Analysis to Discover the Hidden Major-Gift Prospects Among Your Alumni," CURRENTS 24, no. 6 (June 1998): 32-34, 36-38.

Miller, James D. and Deborah Strauss, eds. *Improving Fundraising with Technology: New Directions for Philanthropic Fundraising*, no. 11. San Francisco, CA: Jossey-Bass Publishers, 1996.

Pollack, Rachel H. "The Road to Software-Buying Success: Computer Pros Who've Both Bought and Sold Alumni-Development Software Tell How to Make an Informed Purchase," CURRENTS 23, no. 5 (May 1997): 36-40.

"Software Update—CURRENTS guide to vendors of alumni-development software," CURRENTS 26, no. 3 (March 2000): 44-51.

Combining information support for advancement areas promotes efficiency, accuracy, and appropriate division of responsibility.

Department Structures to Support Advancement/Development Information Systems

Tom Chaves
General Manager
SCT Global Education Solutions

Who enters gifts? Address changes? New employment updates? Who is responsible for getting information out of your advancement/development system? Who makes sure that the system is meeting your institution's and your user's needs?

In 1998, a survey was conducted that attempted to answer some of these questions. Results showed that these questions and more are being addressed differently in the many institutions across the United States and Canada. (Only U.S. and Canadian schools responded, which is not to say that international institutions are necessarily dissimilar in structure and needs—we simply were not able to collect enough data to analyze them.)

There can be many ways to analyze the management of advancement/development systems information—by type of school (e.g. private, public); size; Carnegie class (e.g. community college, private liberal arts); dollars raised; and so forth. However, there are similar characteristics and trends among all these types of institutions that strive to best support the "information needs" of their advancement and development and alumni offices. Arguably, "best" is a somewhat subjective

term and technology is pushing the envelope on how we define our "information needs."

The only assumption I will make in this discussion is that your institution is using a computer system to manage its alumni and development records. If you are not using a computer system, then you can skip this chapter because the manual approach to record keeping involves a whole different set of issues.

As computer systems become more intuitive with their graphical and Web front ends, more users can perform their jobs (or at least part of their jobs) independently without having to rely on computer center staff to perform all computer input and output. In order to make decisions and get work done, people now expect instant access to information. But how does that information get managed—i.e., found, entered, validated, analyzed, reported—so that people (and the institution) can feel good and confident that it is useful? We all know what bad information can do to decision making.

IMPORTANCE OF ACCURATE INFORMATION

How important is accurate information in alumni and development operations? Well, you probably want to report the right campaign totals at the board meeting, and give the president

Departmental
Structures to
Support
Advancement/
Development
Information
Systems

an up-to-date and correct biographic profile of that top prospect he or she is meeting with for lunch. How about making sure you report to your volunteers who are asking others for pledges and gifts the progress of their contacts—who gave and didn't give? Don't forget that big alumni event you are planning in California—you want to make sure you have the most recent address changes for all the people who live and/or work there. No doubt, without correct and complete information, alumni and development operations would be crippled.

INFORMATION SUPPORT FOR ADVANCEMENT OPERATIONS

In this chapter, my definition of "advancement" is all areas that include and support alumni relations, development, public relations, external affairs, and similar areas. I am not suggesting that all of these functions *should* be under one umbrella, as different institutions group these functions differently to meet their individual missions. However, I am suggesting that *information support* for these areas should be considered under combined management.

Combining information support for advancement areas promotes efficiency, accuracy, and appropriate division of responsibility. It allows people to concentrate and focus on a primary task—for example, development officers can concentrate on "getting the gift" while the foundation can focus on "investing the gift." (Taken from one survey response.) Added or changed addresses, revised employment status, updated degrees, and notices of marriage are important information for all advancement professionals; at an institution, there should be a centralized and standardized way of recording and validating that information.

What is needed for information support in the advancement fields? Many institutions recognize the advantage of having a distinct group of individuals to support and use an advancement computer system. Departments of advancement services or development services are becoming more prevalent these days, and while these divisions vary in size depending on the institution, they have common responsibilities:

■ perform all data entry and reporting needs of the system (address updates, gift receipts and

acknowledgments, weekly gift reports, etc). This includes performing appropriate measures for ensuring data integrity.

■ provide training to advancement staff and others who need access to, and information from, the system.

■ extend technology to advancement staff (e.g. Web access for internal and external [alumni] use, bar-coding, imaging).

■ serve as a liaison to other institutional system needs (e.g. importing new graduates, payroll deduction pledges).

Also common to most institutions is the fact that most of these managers report to a vice president, which implies that they support the *entire* area and not one distinct area (like development or alumni).

THE SURVEY RESULTS

In 1998, SCT distributed a survey electronically to over 300 customers who use SCT's advancement software and to all subscribed members of the fundsvcs listserv. Fifty-six people responded. The goal of the survey was to determine how information that supports advancement operations is managed. In writing this chapter, I also relied on other sources of information, such as informal correspondence with SCT customers and research on the RI Arlington Web site, *www.riarlington.com*. Following are analysis and comments based on all information I gathered on this topic.

Major Job Functions and Deliverables of an Advancement Services Group

With or without the support of an advancement services group, survey respondents said they must perform the following functions to manage their information systems:

■ data entry of all biographical information received (including maintaining data integrity);

■ data entry of all pledge and gift information (including maintaining data integrity);

■ produce acknowledgments and receipts;

■ produce monthly, weekly, and annual reports (including *Voluntary Support of Education* [VSE] report, pledge reminders, phonathon pledge cards);

■ support donor recognition and stewardship

(including producing honor rolls, planning donor recognition events);

■ produce profiles of major donors and prospects (including prospect research, contact reports, and screened prospect lists);

■ produce *ad hoc* reports (including labels, data extracts);

■ offer computer support and training;

■ provide key contact for integration with other institution systems;

■ improve institution's use of advancement system;

■ know emerging technologies and how advancement can benefit from their use.

In addition to these common functions, other respondents indicated that they managed or coordinated scholarship and endowment tracking; materials for mass mailings; centralized annual fund tracking (telefund, direct mail, and faculty-staff campaign). Whether or not respondents included these functions seemed based on experience, as well as on the type of institution (e.g. in some cases, a separate foundation handles the advancement function that exists apart from the university).

Whether an institution has an integrated institutional system or not, it is important for development offices to be able to take advantage of the information other offices on campus have (e.g. students' graduation records) and have timely updates when appropriate (e.g. gifts being sent to the finance system).

Learning about emerging technologies (Web, bar-coding, imaging) and planning how to incorporate them into your advancement operations are important duties for the advancement services personnel. This could mean sitting in on a campus "technology" committee as well as keeping abreast of new technologies through colleagues, conferences, and trade journals.

The function of "improving your institution's use of its advancement system" is a very important one and a topic most institutions wish they spent more time doing. Most advancement systems contain an excessive amount of functionality, and most advancement programs would manage informa-

tion better if they spent concerted and continuous effort understanding how those processes work.

Institutions recognize the importance of managing this information under one organization; the need for this information can easily cross multiple divisions. The interdependent relationship between the different functions is evident when, for example, in order to perform appropriate donor recognition, you need:

1. accurate data entry standards and processes for capturing the information;

2. acknowledgments and receipts produced in a timely manner; and

3. the ability to identify whom should be recognized and for what.

Needless to say, unless the upfront homework was done (prospect identification and research), there wouldn't be any donors to recognize.

Staff Roles in an Advancement Services Group

What are the typical roles in an advancement services group? Varying titles abound, but I have classified five distinct types of roles.

1. *Director:* This person is responsible for the entire advancement services operations. He or she coordinates all work that is being done and assures that future needs will be addressed (e.g. moving into a capital campaign). This person also needs to be attuned to the technology available and how it can be used for advancement purposes. He or she should attend conferences, network, and attain a good understanding of the advancement business. This person also is responsible for budgeting and personnel within the group. Directors are key in making decisions about whether to outsource or perform certain functions within their areas (like creating an alumni directory, producing Web sites for alumni access, or building intranet sites for internal access). The director also needs to be involved with institutional system decisions, especially if an integrated system exists. Typical titles for this position include director of advancement services, director of development services, director of advancement (or

●●●
Improve your institution's use of its advancement system. Most systems abound in functionality, and you'll manage information better if you spend concerted and continuous effort understanding how those processes work.

Departmental
Structures to
Support
Advancement/
Development
Information
Systems

development) operations.

2. *Coordinator:* This person enters the data into the system, whether it is biographical or financial in nature, and is responsible for assuring data integrity—developing standards and procedures for validating information going into the system. Coordinators also help find lost alumni by working with a researcher. Specific titles in this group include gift record clerk, accountant, manager of gift processing, manager of constituent records, data control specialist, and data processor. If there are student workers, a coordinator usually manages their work.

3. *Researcher:* Typically, a researcher is heavily involved in such prospect activities as researching individuals and corporations/foundations, screening prospect lists, and managing prospect solicitation strategies. Researchers also direct efforts to find lost alumni by working with a coordinator. Common titles for this position include director of prospect research and director of prospect management. They are not always found in the advancement services area; sometimes they report to a director of development.

4. *Programmer/Technician:* This person provides the technical support of the advancement services group. The programmer can perform functions like creating reports, data extracts, labels, and other output needed from the system. They also help clean up data integrity issues, support hardware and software, and provide training. For those institutions that are "pushing out" the generation of reports to more end users (e.g. institutions relying on end users to generate their own reports), programmers are setting up the menu-driven systems for these people to use. This person is also a key contact for other system interfaces that might exist (e.g. bringing over student graduate records, and for implementing new technologies such as Web enhancements). Common titles for these people are database information specialist, database maintenance clerk, and PC support.

5. *Administrator:* This person performs administrative work within the division. This includes sorting mail (gifts, pledges, bio updates), copying, filing, and ordering supplies. He or she is also the group's contact person for external people (development officers, faculty, and so on).

Depending on the size of the institution and staff, there could be different numbers of people in the five categories, and varying reporting structures. Some people in director roles also have direct fund-raising goals as well. However, the key point is that there are major job functions that need to be carried out.

Another variable is the size of the advancement services staff in relation to the entire advancement area. The survey showed that the range was significant, from as low as 10 percent to as high as 50 percent, with an average ratio of 28 percent. This information could be further analyzed based on different criteria—size of institution, type, for example. However, the important point is that there should be a correlation between the two sizes; when an overall advancement program grows, so should the advancement services staff.

Does it Work Today?

When survey respondents were asked to comment on the benefits of their current advancement services structure, the message was consistent. Most of their responses were in comparison to a previous structure that did not have a centralized advancement services area:

■ "Advancement services has more control over what goes out to our customers. We apply a customer service attitude towards our work and the people we deal with."

■ "Our institution now has better control of the information in the database and updates that occur to it."

■ "Centralization, better donor relations, and a stronger tie between information services and the annual fund."

■ "Allows full service to all external affairs [advancement]."

■ "Advancement services is key to our role in a total enterprise [institution] system."

■ "There is now consistency, accuracy, accountability, and easier training."

■ "Gift processing and constituent records are now under one director, which allows us to combine similar tasks and eliminate duplicate ones. We can now support ALL development and external affairs."

■ "We are now able to provide cross training and

Departmental
Structures to
Support
Advancement/
Development
Information
Systems

better integrate the information systems management—there is one place to go."

- "There is now efficiency of operations, better supervision, better coordination of efforts between offices, accurate reporting."

- "It has elevated the perception and treatment of staff within our organization. It has also enhanced the college's overall image in maintaining alumni loyalty."

- "We have become the necessary support group for effective fund raising."

In addition to these very positive observations, respondents also indicated tasks that are not being accomplished (or not accomplished well). However, they don't necessarily attribute these shortcomings to the advancement services structure. Weaknesses include:

- prospect research during a capital campaign;
- staff to support emerging technologies (Web, bar-coding, imaging);
- stewardship activities;
- attracting and retaining qualified and dedicated people;
- not all reporting needs are met on time;
- timely updates to records (e.g. phone numbers, address changes, student activities, finding lost alums);
- more personalization of correspondence (solicitations, acknowledgments);
- matching gift follow-up;
- better use of system functionality; and
- better documentation of institutional standards/policy review.

These are all very important areas. Obviously, staff size has a lot to do with what projects can be addressed, and staff is not an unlimited resource. However, sharing information with colleagues at other institutions, focusing on projects at key opportunities, and identifying priorities can help establish what can (and what does) get done.

Furthermore, some institutions strive to accomplish these tasks by being creative and analyzing needs to see how they align with the institution's goals and mission. They cross-train personnel, research the automation of mass database updates, outsource data entry, focus on campus

technology needs, add new systems-analyst positions, and investigate technology uses. At a higher level, they are involved with strategic planning, which is essential to being able to adjust to changes that occur in technology, higher education, the institution, and the advancement division itself. Dealing with such issues in a focused manner is easier when advancement services is a distinct component of an institution.

Will It Work Tomorrow?

One of the survey questions asked what changes to the current structure could better support existing or anticipated situations. As would be expected, many commented on adding new staff for the specific functions described above. However, there were also a number of more creative and forward-thinking suggestions, such as:

- "Need to better define our organization as a services function."
- "Position advancement services to have its own budget for training and technology."
- "Change our name from 'Development and External Affairs Services' to 'Advancement Services.'"
- "Plan to focus on integrating with the rest of the college systems."
- "Put stewardship and research under advancement services."
- "Decentralize some data entry functions—like volunteer and prospect tracking."
- "When hiring for staff, require more technical knowledge/aptitude."
- "Concentrate [prioritize] on technology changes and utilizing them to the fullest."
- "Push out [decentralize to those who need to perform the task] report generation to end users utilizing intuitive reporting tools."

A common thread throughout the survey was the need to take advantage of emerging technologies (and sometimes just to keep up!). With the pace that technology is evolving, this becomes a critical management issue. Simply put, technology affects the way we work and live. Unless we plan, manage, and use it properly, we will not be as effective and efficient as we could be.

Departmental
Structures to
Support
Advancement/
Development
Information
Systems

When Your Institution Doesn't Have an Advancement Services Group

A small percentage of institutions responding to the survey did not have a centralized advancement services group. In these institutions, job functions were spread out across the advancement area. For example, a person responsible for constituent records might report to a director of alumni relations, while a person responsible for donor records (pledges and gifts) might report to a director of annual giving. Reporting support might come from a centralized computer center.

Common issues among these institutions are:

■ lack of consistency in data entry;

■ limited options and productivity;

■ time-consuming and redundant tasks; and

■ receipts and acknowledgments not centralized.

Overall, there was no coordination of the job functions that is necessary to manage the advancement system. As a result, some basic functions weren't even being accomplished—bio updates, certain reporting needs, prospect research, and using the advancement software functionality. Offices were not taking advantage of the many software applications available. On the positive side, many of these institutions were performing strategic planning to assess their current structure and to improve it.

FINAL ANALYSIS AND COMMENTS

Every institution is unique in its mission, fund-raising goals, and organizational structure. Institutions are made up of people who differ in style, approach, and beliefs. Each institution has to assess its position in the higher education market and structure itself accordingly.

Having a coordinated support group for managing the information needs of higher education advancement can provide a concerted focus. This centralized effort is not meant to restrict the use of the system or the information from anyone who needs to use it. Rather, it should promote a better opportunity to "push-out" the use of systems such as reporting and online access because it provides a method for delivering a consistent message as well as training on how to use valuable information to enhance people's effectiveness.

FURTHER READINGS

Phair, Judith T. and Roland King. *Sample File: Organizational Charts and Job Descriptions for the Advancement Office*. Washington, DC: Council for Advancement and Support of Education, 1998.

"What Will the Future Bring?: Better Data Collection, More Sophisticated Technology, and a More Prominent Role. That's What Experts Predict for Advancement Services in the Year 2002," CURRENTS 23, no. 6 (June 1997): 12-15.

Worth, Michael J. and James W. Asp II. *The Development Officer in Higher Education: Toward an Understanding of the Role: ASHE-ERIC Higher Education Report*, no. 94-4. Washington, DC: George Washington University, School of Education and Development, 1994.

Taylor, John, ed. *Advancement Services: Research and Technology Support for Fund Raising*. Washington, DC: CASE Books, 1999.

● ● ●

The Clarke School for the Deaf, Northampton, Massachusetts
Photography by Jim Gipe, Pivotmedia, Inc.

480

SECTION VIII

Advancement in Special Sectors of Education

Edited by Patricia King Jackson

Introduction

Patricia King Jackson
Assistant Head of School for Development and Alumni Relations
Sidwell Friends School

Areassuring trend in educational advancement is the increased movement of professionals among the various sectors of educational institutions. No longer are individuals "typed" as, say, medical development director or college advancement officer or independent school fund raiser. Rather, the professional moves freely among all sectors. This trend is not only healthy as a means of equalizing employment opportunities in educational advancement, but it also helps to define us as a single profession: the profession of educational advancement.

This section of the *Handbook for Institutional Advancement* is dedicated to those who feel outside of the mainstream of educational advancement. It is for those of us who, for one reason or another, feel that our institutions and the way we go about pursuing our advancement function require a slightly different set of advancement perspectives, rules, or guidelines. It is for those who, from time to time, sit in large conferences sponsored by the Council for

Advancement and Support of Education (CASE) and wonder what the lessons of Harvard, Princeton, and Yale say to us. Or whether the wisdom in this book can really apply to all of us.

How many of us have started a new job recently (and the statistics of our profession suggest that that may be most of us) and been inordinately struck by the "differences" between our new institution and our old one? This tendency to view ourselves and our circumstance as "unique" or *sui generis* is both understandable and very human. Celebrating one's differences—in education and in life—can be a useful attribute and one that can expand opportunities and achievements. Our differences, however, should never become an excuse for lower aspirations or productivity or for not understanding the fundamental rules of our profession. Bruce Stewart, current Head of Sidwell Friends School, has said: "People don't invest in excuses; they invest in promise."

Within the next chapters, we highlight the unique differences of specialized sectors of education and how advancement works in them. In Chapter 1, Karen MacArthur, executive director of institutional advancement at Delta College Foundation, tells you about advancement in community colleges, an important and growing sector of higher education. Similarly, in Chapter 2, CASE's Director of International Programs Janet Sailian and Susan Montague, director of public relations and development at the University of New Brunswick, outline the impact of advancement internationally, especially in Great Britain, Europe, and the Far East. In Chapter 3, Lynn Hogan, executive director, Medical Affairs Development at the University of Washington, tackles advancement, especially fund raising, at academic medical centers. Helen Colson, president of her own development firm, focuses Chapter 4 on advancement at independent schools and what the future holds for that constituency. Finally, in Chapter 5, Peg Hall, former vice president of advancement at Gallaudet University and currently associate professor of public relations, College of Journalism and Communications, University of Florida, writes about such niche institutions as Gallaudet University and Berea College and how advancement serves their interests.

In these chapters, we guide you in the application of fundamental rules of advancement in each of these cases. We acknowledge the different applications and institutional nuances in each case, yet we start with the assumption that we are all more the same than we are different. We are all nonprofit, educational institutions with relatively defined constituencies and missions that extend well beyond the advancement function. Once we understand the ways in which we are all the same, then we can truly celebrate—and exploit—our differences. Here are three strategies to help us better appreciate and

Once we understand the ways in which we are all the same, then we can truly celebrate —and exploit —our differences.

exploit the ways in which we are different.

1. Understand and value the common attributes of an educational advancement program.

In contrast to other fund-raising and public relations professionals, we in educational advancement are blessed with a core of defined constituencies on which to target our fund-raising, communications, and public relations activities. Our students, alumni, and parents are the major constituencies whom we try to influence and from whom we try to raise funds. Yes, there are differences here among us. Public universities also target state legislatures. Independent schools claim a tie to grandparents. Academic medical centers have patients. And some "niche" schools can claim many "friends" because of the special populations they serve. But the key professional advantage we share is that our institutions all have a core of unique constituents who care about us, who will open our mail and read our publications, and who will come relatively easily (at least in comparison to the "man in the street") to the decision to support us. Most of us are strangers to direct mail marketing, the brokering of lists, and the costs and perils of donor acquisition.

In terms of fund raising, our strong and defined constituencies give us an advantage over our cousins in other development operations because, since donor acquisition is less of an issue, we can devote relatively fewer resources to our annual giving programs. Annual giving in our institutions relies more heavily on four- and five-figure gifts; it is usually integrated closely with major and planned giving and becomes a vehicle for donor identification and cultivation as well as a program for raising annual support.

2. Examine the factors that make you different from the prototype educational advancement office and perhaps even different from the peer institutions occupying the same sector of education.

Your institution's mission is of primary importance. It defines both your case for support and the nature of the relationship your institution will likely have with those who will support you. Your institution's mission is not only important to the development officers. If you are in communications, your institution's mission will likely define your media outlets. An alumni relations program will likewise be defined—and sometimes constrained—by an institutional mission that depends on transferring its students to other institutions rather than granting them terminal degrees, as is the case with community colleges and elementary schools.

The institution's mission also defines the peer group—or institutional sector of education—to which it belongs. Identifying peers is a fundamental aspect of sound professional advancement practice. Knowledge of peer groups provides both networking opportunities and comparative profiling, both of which can help us avoid endlessly reinventing the wheel—a useful service to the novice and the seasoned professional alike. Peer groups may be rooted in Carnegie classifications or in other less formal groupings, such as schools or colleges with which you compete for students. Generally, peers are of similar size, have consonant missions, and celebrate similar institutional cultures. Often, for independent day schools, at least one set of peers is local.

Many of us will find our peer schools profiled in the Council for Aid to Education (CAE) *Voluntary Support of Education.* This is a useful tool for professionals seeking to compare profiles of their fund-raising support with the achievements of other "like" institutions. Enough institutional data is provided so that some comparisons may be leveled out on a per student, per alumnus, or per dollar of operating budget basis, thus eliminating variations based solely on size or age of program. CAE has also recently made available an online service, called DataMiner, which enables universities, colleges, and schools to compare themselves online with various peer groups, either selected for them or of their own selection. This database includes CAE surveys since 1989, and makes it very easy to profile your own progress over time, comparing it with others to analyze strengths and weaknesses and target where your own program's next generation of growth should be. To lift the tide of professionalism for everyone in our field, I hope that all who have the opportunity will participate in the CAE annual surveys. I also hope that the opportunity might be given in the near future for new sectors of education (such as non-U.S. institutions and professional schools affiliated with large universities) to share in the wealth of resource represented by the CAE database.

Networking is also a fundamental outgrowth of institutional peer identification. Whenever you see—whether by CAE profiling or in an awards program or assembly sponsored by CASE or another group—a program similar to your own, only better, pick up the telephone and ask your counterpart about his or her achievement. All of us in the advancement field are, by definition, communicators. In 30 years of asking colleagues for advice and guidance, I have never found advancement professionals unwilling to share their secrets!

3. Use fundamental advancement principles to capitalize on your institution's unique character.

One of the greatest points of differentiation among our institutions is the size of our institutional advancement budgets. The wisest allocation of scarce budget resources requires a basic understanding of how successful advancement programs are structured, as well as where the potential lies for your particular program. For example, you would not likely begin a development program with a planned giving effort or major gifts program; usually, annual giving forms the base for both of these larger gift efforts. Likewise, an independent day school would not likely allocate many resources to a corporate solicitation effort, whereas a community college or medical school may well take the opposite tack. An understanding of basic fund-raising rules, combined with knowledge of where your particular institution's potential is strongest, should drive the decisions about where to allocate budgets and energy.

The successful advancement officer usually drives an institution-wide process of setting ambitious but realistic goals for the program. The chief executive officer of your institution, as well as key members of the board of trustees (if not the whole board), should understand and support these goals; such goals should include not only bottom-line fund-raising achievement but also anticipated activity for publications, public relations, and alumni activities. Present these goals in the context of a multi-year plan and tie them to your own analysis of your institution's mission and its competitive advantages relative to your peer institutions. As an integral part of the goal-setting process, establish institutional policies, particularly policies governing gift acceptance, which support the institution's goals.

The small advancement office, the university with a special niche, the independent day school, and the academic medical center trying to cope with special constituencies and a central development office all face special challenges. But with knowledge of basic advancement principles, understanding how our institutions relate to their peers and competitors, and disciplined planning and resource allocation, these challenges can be turned into competitive advantages for our institutions. Every one of us is *sui generis,* but we are also all part of the evolving profession of educational advancement.

REFERENCES

Morgan, David R. *Voluntary Support of Education.* New York, NY: Council for Aid to Education. *Co-sponsored by CASE and the National Association of Independent Schools. Published Annually.*

Community colleges have given those who need it a second chance at education. They have brought people into the mainstream and have served people hindered by problems of cost and transportation. And they have provided options for students who can only attend college on a part-time basis.

Advancement in Community Colleges

Karen M. MacArthur
Executive Director of Institutional Advancement
Delta College Foundation

Community colleges across America have an important story to tell. Since the 1960s, they have become the fastest growing sector of American higher education. In fact, recent reports indicate that over 50 percent of graduating high school students choose community colleges as their entry into higher education. According to the American Association of Community Colleges (AACC), more than 10.5 million students (or 45 percent of all U.S. undergraduates) are enrolled in the more than 1,100 community colleges across the country.

Community colleges, which can be traced back to the 1920s, award associate degrees at the completion of two years of full-time study, and prepare "transfer" students who choose a community college for their first two years of bachelor's degree programs. They also offer technical study programs and certificate programs that prepare students for immediate entry into the job market. And they provide lifelong learning educational opportunities for anyone who chooses to take advantage of the service.

Community colleges have a mission very different from and yet similar to other institutions advancing higher education. Community colleges are learning-centered compared to four-year research-focused institutions. Faculty members often teach students in smaller classes. While the curriculum in community colleges mirrors the formal course work in traditional institutions of higher education, community colleges also design programs and services to fit the needs of the people they serve—*the community*. They consult "customer needs" and ask what educational services the citizens want to buy. Their curriculum responds to the ever-changing civic, social, and vocational needs of the local community.

The original mandate of community colleges stipulated that they be close to home and low cost, offer open enrollment, and make available a broad variety of educational programs. These charges have resulted in a diverse student body in the community college setting. The typical community college classroom may include a dual-enrolled high school student, a recent high school graduate or one who has just completed a GED, a middle-aged or older student, and students of different ethnic and socioeconomic backgrounds.

Community colleges have given those who need it a second chance at education. They have brought people into the mainstream and have served people hindered by problems of cost and transportation. And they have provided options for students who can only attend college on a part-time basis. According to the AACC, 64 percent of community college students attend part-time.

INSTITUTIONAL ADVANCEMENT: A FOCUS ON INTERNAL COMMUNICATIONS

The goals of the community college institutional advancement office are similar to those in other higher education settings. They include conveying a positive public image to produce confidence in the institution; fostering public interest and participation in activities; recruiting students—in conjunction with the office of admissions; generating financial support from public and private sources—in conjunction with the governmental relations office and the development office; and helping attract top-level faculty, staff and students.

However, the case for institutional advancement in community colleges rests on their unique mission. By their very nature, community colleges are an extension of the communities they serve.

The institutional advancement staff has no monopoly on contact with internal and external constituencies. The stakeholders in a community college—the taxpayers—are, in fact, the neighbors of its faculty, staff, administrators, and students. A considerable amount of communication takes place every hour of every day between the stakeholders and the community college's representatives. Therefore, one of the greatest single factors affecting the college's advancement is campus morale. The institutional advancement staff in a community college sees internal communications as a crucial piece of what it does, and must be concerned with internal staff and faculty morale to perhaps a much greater degree than other institutions.

Along with communications (internal and external), the institutional advancement staff is also responsible for fund-raising activities and alumni relations. Staff must consider how all programs might affect the attitudes and behavior of selected audiences – the faculty and staff, the potential student, the legislator, the donor, and the taxpayer.

■ ■ ■
The average community college endowment more than doubled between fiscal years 1989 and 1996. And three community colleges hold endowments exceeding $100 million, ranking them among the country's largest 275 endowments.

COMMUNICATIONS: THE LOCAL ANGLE

A successful institutional advancement program for community colleges should include a number of components that communicate with a large and varied audience.

First, develop a strong marketing and recruitment plan, based on solid market research of the community and the college's constituents. The college's mission statement, strategic planning documents, and budget and planning procedures must reflect this research. Create a marketable statement or slogan, clearly distinguishing the community college from other educational opportunities. The Delta College slogan is, "The Delta Difference: Quality, Affordability, and Personal Attention."

Develop targeted recruitment publications to appeal to the diverse audience community colleges serve—high school students, adult business and community leaders, and the general public. In addition, disseminate current information on a regular basis to the community college's internal audience—faculty, staff, and students.

Because the whole community is a stakeholder, it is sometimes easier for community colleges to command the community's media attention. Therefore, a solid local media relations program is extremely important. Develop and maintain daily communication with print and electronic media. Make sure a group of employees (the community college president, chief officers, faculty, and other staff members) are readily available to respond to the local media on issues and events, and schedule regular media training sessions for board members, college administrators, and faculty members.

As in any higher education advancement office, handle controversial issues with honesty and integrity. A professional relationship with local media outlets has many short- and long-term benefits.

GOVERNMENT RELATIONS AND FUND RAISING

Government relations has remained a primary focus in the field of institutional advancement for community colleges. It is crucial to maintain a liaison with key governmental leaders—state legislators, politicians, and other executives throughout the community—who may play influential roles in the future. The strength of institutional advancement in a community college setting relies on governmental relations, in order to deal with complex programs of assistance and regulation, and to attempt to shape newly emerging legislation and regulation into the most favorable form possible.

Unfortunately, since 1980, community colleges have seen state governmental support drop from one-half to one-third. And, there has been little increase in governmental support from federal and local sources. To continue operating, community colleges have raised their tuition rates while searching for other sources of money. The single biggest growth area in community colleges has been in private-sector fund raising.

Private-sector donations to community colleges supplement operating budgets and provide a "margin of excellence" for faculty, staff, and students. Approximately 90 percent of community colleges currently have foundations in various stages of development.

According to a recent AACC survey, 50 percent of the foundations are valued at more than $1 million. And, the 1997 Council for Aid to Education's *Voluntary Support of Education Survey* reported 30 of the nation's community colleges received contributions ranging from $1 million to $32 million. (Never has it been truer that "success breeds success." Research indicates that gifts of this magnitude are usually replicated in a very short period of time.)

Endowment building is one result of successful fund-raising and large contributions. According to the AACC, in fiscal year 1996, the average community college endowment had a market value of $2.1 million. Compared with the average four-year college and university endowment of $350 million, that seems small. However, community colleges are surprising even themselves with their successes.

The average community college endowment more than doubled between fiscal years 1989 and 1996, according to U.S. Department of Education statistics. And three community colleges hold endowments exceeding $100 million, ranking them among the country's largest 275 endowments.

The first place a community college goes to gain private support is obviously the community, since every person who lives or works in the community directly or indirectly benefits from the institution's presence and is therefore a prospect. Often, donor prospects get acquainted with community colleges through special events, which are planned for "friend-raising" and fund-raising purposes. With this involvement, prospects are frequently moved up the "donor pyramid" from their initial investment to more significant gift levels.

Each community college would do well to appraise their "environments" when initiating fund-raising programs. Generally, community colleges have limited resources (that is, staff and money to raise funds) and must determine where best to invest the development staff's energies. As an example, a community college in an area where constituent wealth is primarily held in appreciated property (stock, real estate, etc.) might focus on planned gifts. Another community college might identify a local private foundation with significant assets as a prime prospect for capital projects.

The harsh reality of fund raising, though, is that there are *countless* institutions, causes, and efforts worthy of support in community college localities. In order to keep up with the pace of fund raising, community colleges are becoming more sophisticated in their appeals. They are emphasizing their ties to the business community. They are soliciting sources other than the traditional alumni base. Community college faculty and staff members are proving to be a reliable source of donations. They can also point out the economies of scale inherent in community college education, where the dollar is stretched further than in other sectors of higher education.

Businesses are strong supporters of community colleges. Statistics show that corporate sector donations to community colleges (45 percent) far exceed those given to four-year colleges and universities (20 percent), excluding research universities. And, because many community colleges also establish training programs for large employers in their community, the businesses are often approached to donate equipment used during the training sessions. This is another source of benefit to the community college, assuring that the latest and most up-to-date technology will be available to the college's students.

ALUMNI: A GROWING RESOURCE

Don't overlook alumni relations as a strong part of institutional advancement in the community college. This is extremely important, yet very challenging. Because of their new found mobility, alumni are difficult to track after they leave the community college environment. However, many remain in the communities where they are educated, are supportive of the institution, and are one of its most important sources of support.

Community college alumni may provide a number of services and benefits to the institution. They can:

- financially support a variety of programs;
- influence their employers or employees to donate equipment and dollars;
- help in special event fund raising;
- assist in lobbying state legislators for support;
- foster local community support for tax referenda;
- help market the community college's programs and serve as potential continuing education students;
- provide a broad base of support and a pool of volunteers;
- serve as curriculum advisory committee members; and
- help with fund raising and capital campaigns by contacting and/or soliciting potential donors.

MOVING THE INSTITUTION FORWARD

In order for a community college to advance the institution effectively, it must have a strong, organized, and focused plan for success; and a clear and concise mission statement. Active involvement from the community college president is of vital importance, along with a strong public relations program and a healthy foundation, which provides a source of student aid. All of these components work together to move the institution forward and establish it as a strong part of the higher education process.

REFERENCES AND FURTHER READINGS

DeWees, Deborah. "Traditions for Nontraditional Campuses: Homecomings Can Also Benefit Community Colleges," CURRENTS 19, no. 8 (September 1993): 18-19.

Kerns, Jennifer R. and Richard Witter. *Alumni Programs at Two-Year Colleges: 1997 Report of a National Survey.* Washington, DC: Junior and Community College Institute, 1998.

Larson, Wendy Ann. "Mr. Community College: A Longtime Advocate For Two-Year Institutions Reflects on Advances Already Made and Progress Yet to Come," CURRENTS 17, no. 7 (July/August 1991): 8-12.

Manzo, Kathleen Kennedy. "Comprehensive Fundraising Programs Breathe New Life into Community College Coffers," *Community College Week* 8, no. 47 (September 25, 1995): 8,11.

Morgan, David R. *Voluntary Support of Education.* New York, NY: Council for Aid to Education. *Co-sponsored by CASE and the National Association of Independent Schools. Published Annually.*

Patnode, Darwin. "New Territory in Educational Fund Raising: Community Colleges: Today Fund Raising for Two-Year Colleges Is Coming into Its Own. In Fact, It's One of the Fastest Growing Areas in the Fund-Raising Field," *Fund Raising Management* 22, no. 5 (July 1991): 32-34, 36.

International work requires an especially long-term view; any "hit-and-run" temptation must yield to the reality that everything takes longer and costs more, in dollars and effort, than within your country's borders.

Globalization of Advancement

Janet Sailian
Director of International Programs
CASE

Susan G. Montague
Director of Development and Public Relations
University of New Brunswick

Internationalization, the global village, world-class: are these just buzzwords, or do they represent a sea change in how educational advancement professionals think and do business? Look at the number and diversity of international programs at universities, colleges, and schools worldwide, plus the increase in advancement position titles that include the word "international," and you'll sense a major trend afoot. Educational institutions and the advancement professionals who guide their outreach efforts, increasingly venture beyond their national borders to connect with alumni, offer study-abroad programs and academic exchanges, recruit students, and raise funds.

The potential benefits of internationalization have attracted the attention of world leaders. Great Britain's government announced in 1999 a major program to promote its higher-education system overseas and to attract more international students. Prime Minister Tony Blair launched the three-year, 5 million pound initiative, which aims to bring 75,000 more international students to the United Kingdom by 2005.

CASE is an active participant in this growing globalization trend, as well as such organizations as the National Society of Fund Raising Executives (*www.nsfre.org*) and Civicus (*www.civicus.org*), an international alliance dedicated to strengthening citizen action and civil society throughout the world.

In 1995, CASE established a European office in London, England, and in 1998 hired its first director of international programs. CASE is holding more and more workshops and conferences in Canada, the U.K., and Continental Europe, and by 1999 had offered its first conference in Mexico. Its publications focus increasingly on global realities and perspectives in advancement, with the October 1999 issue of CURRENTS devoted entirely to "advancement's global marketplace." CASE Books has published compilations of CURRENTS articles in both French and Spanish. CASE's International Committee developed an international protocol that provides 20 scholarships annually to enable members to attend major conferences outside their home country, to build international awareness, and share ideas across borders. It is also actively pursuing collaborations with like-minded international organizations.

PRINCIPLES AND PRACTICES

Attend an international advancement conference and you're likely to hear some variation on the theme: "We are more alike than different." All alumni directors aim to maintain graduates' affinity to their alma mater; all fund raisers nurture relationships with past and potential donors with the goal of gaining financial support for their institutions.

Building personal relationships, conducting research about alumni and donor interests, stewarding donors, and engaging past and potential supporters in the ongoing life of the institution are essential to successful advancement programs in any context. Culture and language modulate how these activities are carried out, yet the underlying principles apply everywhere.

International work requires an especially long-term view; any "hit-and-run" temptation must yield to the reality that everything takes longer and costs more, in dollars and work, than within your own country's borders. Media and public relations efforts—unless linked to student recruitment or major donations or spearheaded by a local supporter—are difficult to do from a distance. So, the first principle of international advancement work is that success depends upon long-term staying power.

Another principle supported by Colin Boswell, former executive director of CASE Europe, is: "Research, research, research!" Learn about the culture of education and philanthropy in countries where your institution has decided, for reasons of strategic importance, to develop its advancement program. Respect for and sensitivity towards other ways and norms is essential. Europe, Asia, and Latin America are not monoliths; each country has its own traditions and culture. Most important, each institution has its own unique culture, its own special way of doing things. Differences can be striking.

For example, universities in Germany and Sweden have traditionally been funded entirely by their governments. Boswell notes: "Students see higher education as a right rather than a privilege that comes with a price tag." Nostalgia for alma mater is not generally a feature of these cultures. A Swedish alumni officer once told Boswell that from

the viewpoint of his alumni, getting together with fellow graduates "makes as much sense as forming a group of those who frequent the same dentist."

Remember that language skills are a valuable asset. Learning even a few phrases and some key advancement terms in the local language creates good will; staff with foreign-language abilities and cultural sensitivity have a great advantage.

Equally important are the understanding and long-term commitment of the home campus. International advancement officers need to educate their institutions about the value, principles, and reality of international outreach, and instill realistic expectations.

Start with a strategically selected, modest number of international markets. Success and buy-in are more likely if you start with just a couple of key targets. Analyze enrollment and alumni data to pinpoint where a critical mass of alumni, parents, or potential students exists. Get faculty to help identify alumni of influence in target countries with continuing ties to their alma mater. Ask selected, properly briefed faculty, administrators, and board members who travel overseas to visit alumni, donors, and families, and to make presentations about campus news and events.

There is no substitute for "on-the-ground" intelligence, says Krista Slade, executive director, University of Toronto Hong Kong Foundation and head of U of T's Hong Kong office. Slade's presence in one of her university's key overseas markets helps maintain contact with Hong Kong alumni and donors, and facilitates event planning. While not every institution can open an overseas office, reliance on committed, informed volunteers can also get the job done.

Trish Duff, alumni relations officer at McGill University in Montreal, advises keeping a diverse volunteer pool. To capture cultural nuances when planning events and materials, don't rely only on expatriate grads who live abroad, but also cultivate alumni volunteers native to that country. International students currently on your campus can be a valuable resource, too, advising you on the best way to build relationships in their countries and

> ● ● ●
> **Educational institutions, and the advancement professionals who guide their outreach efforts, increasingly venture beyond their national borders to connect with alumni, offer study-abroad programs and academic exchanges, recruit students, and raise funds.**

serving as representatives during their visits home.

Local alumni leaders can play many vital roles: organize events, identify and arrange contact with potential donors and students, edit or even write letters and solicitation materials, and mail campus publications (bulk-shipped from your institution) to others in their country. It's vital to keep these overseas "ambassadors" up-to-date and to thank them often. Consider electronic communication venues: an e-mail newsletter or country-specific updates on your institution's Web site.

Personal relationships are critical to successful international advancement programs. Visiting key countries on a regular basis, at least annually, improves communication and the sense of belonging for distant volunteers, alumni, and donors. Bring the president, vice-chancellor, or school head whenever possible. In some countries, it's best if the CEO makes the ask for all major donations, and can reinforce the prestige of local volunteer leaders by hosting events in their honor.

International Web sites and e-mail are an excellent way to keep alumni, particularly those who live far away, in touch with their alma mater and each other. Some campuses provide alumni chapter or branch Web sites within the main Internet site. Electronic newsletters, permanent e-mail addresses, listservs, and alumni chat rooms are used by an increasing number of institutions to maintain contact quickly and cost-effectively with far-flung graduates.

International fund-raising efforts must be sensitive to widely differing tax and privacy laws. Local legal and tax advice are important at the outset.

Careful prospect research and cultivation are even more important when working in cultures other than your own. Understanding historic patterns of philanthropy will also be helpful. In Mexico, according to Adalberto Viesca, vice president for institutional advancement at the Universidad de Monterrey and CASE District IV Board member, the philanthropic culture is underdeveloped and a small pool of donors is solicited repeatedly by all kinds of charitable organizations. While capital campaigns have been the traditional fund-raising vehicle in Mexico, institutions are starting to understand the importance of annual funds and alumni support. Campaigns have tended to focus on facilities and buildings, but endowment fund-raising has begun.

Systematic alumni relations programs are developing in Mexico and are often in the vanguard of advancement programs. In a country where direct mail is rarely successful, alumni programs are finding innovative, often labor-intensive ways to reach alumni (for example, by personal delivery of materials by bicycle squads).

TREND-SPOTTING

Advancement is growing and evolving rapidly around the world, albeit in different ways and at varying rates. Here's a brief synopsis of some emerging trends:

- Privatization of higher education appears to be a worldwide trend.
- Government support of educational institutions is on a downward trend in many countries, from Hong Kong to Brazil to Germany, leading to growing interest in fund raising.
- As tuition fees rise (or are imposed for the first time in decades), students and parents demand more accountability and more of a voice in governance.
- CASE is receiving more and more inquiries from developing former Soviet countries, indicating the emergence of advancement in these areas.
- International study programs are proliferating, as are individually-arranged advancement job exchanges across borders.

WHAT DOES THE FUTURE HOLD?

In a world where technology has virtually eradicated the concept of borders and intellectual inquiry and discovery are global in nature, advancement professionals must reach out to their most influential and important constituencies—no matter where they are around the world. More and more of these most influential and important constituents will be found beyond the institution's home country.

The most successful advancement professionals recognize that countries, like people, have to be treated as different from one another, and relationships will only prosper when their unique characteristics are valued and respected.

FURTHER READINGS:

Barth, Steve. "Globetrotting for Gifts: How to Identify, Research, and Solicit Major Gifts Around the World Without Causing an International Incident," CURRENTS 24, no. 4 (April 1998): 32-39.

Bernstein, Steven. "Exploring Philanthropy: Democracy, Voluntarism and Community Organization in Post-Communist Society," *Fund Raising Management* 26, no. 2 (April 1995): 34-37.

Directory of Grant Making Trusts 1997-98. Kent, United Kingdom: Charities Aid Foundation, 1997.

Directory of Grant Making Trusts Focus Series: Education. Kent, United Kingdom: Charities Aid Foundation, October 1997.

Directory of International Corporate Giving in America and Abroad 1997. 8th ed. Detroit, MI: Taft Group, 1996.

Dundjerski, Marina. "Giving Abroad: The Spread of Democracy Has Led to a Tidal Wave of Overseas Grants From U.S. Funds; Now Some Reconsider International Gifts," *Chronicle of Philanthropy* 10, no. 6 (January 15, 1998): 9-12.

Hall, Holly. "Spreading U.S.-Style Philanthropy to Eastern Europe May Be Mistaken, Fund Raisers Are Told," *Chronicle of Philanthropy* 6, no. 11 (March 22, 1994): 24-25.

Hall, Holly. "The Struggle of Russia's Charities: To Survive, They Must Overcome Poverty, Loss of a Philanthropic Tradition, and Organized Crime," *Chronicle of Philanthropy* 8, no. 14 (May 2, 1996): 1, 14-19.

Henderson, Bruce E. *Philanthropy in the Americas: New Directions and Partnerships.* Coral Gables, FL: University of Miami, North/South Center Press, January 1992.

Jung, Ku-Hyun, ed. *Evolving Patterns of Asia-Pacific Philanthropy.* Seoul, Korea: Seoul Press, 1994.

Kidd, Harry. *The Voluntary Sector in the European Union: The Legal and Fiscal Framework.* Kent, United Kingdom: Charities Aid Foundation, 1996.

Lambrakis, George B. "Looking Overseas for Funds: Colleges and Universities Have Been Turning Out International Graduates for Years. They Represent an Untapped Source of Funds Which Some Institutions Are Beginning to Tap," *Fund Raising Management* 21, no. 1 (June 1990): 50-

Legendre, Paul. *The Non-Profit Sector in Russia.* Kent, United Kingdom: Charities Aid Foundation, 1997.

Peebles, Jane. *The Handbook of International Philanthropy.* Chicago, IL: Bonus Books, 1998.

Pharaoh, Cathy, ed. *Dimensions of the Voluntary Sector 1997.* Kent, United Kingdom; Charities Aid Foundation, June 1997.

Rittinger, Mark. "Who Are Your Undergraduates? Your Donors Want to Know," *Ensemble* 6, no. 3 (Winter 1997): 1-2.

Ryan, Ellen. "Common Bonds: Three Experts Offer Tried-and-True Tenets of International Fund Raising," CURRENTS 20, no. 8 (September 1994): 18-22.

Soloman, Lester and Helmut K. Anheier, eds. *Defining the Nonprofit Sector: Germany.* Working Papers of the Johns Hopkins University Comparative Nonprofit Sector Project no. 6. Baltimore, MD: Johns Hopkins University, Institute for Policy Studies, 1993.

Zyla, Melana K. "No Small Change: Foreign Groups Learn Charity Begins inHong Kong," *Far Eastern Economic Review* 158, no. 34 (August 24, 1995): 52.

We contend with potential donors and families who are grieving or facing uncertain futures and sometimes imminent death. Those skills found in all good development officers of empathy, sensitivity, and intuition are doubly critical for those working in academic medical centers.

Fund Raising at Academic Medical Centers

Lynn K. Hogan
Executive Director, Medical Affairs Development
University of Washington

Those of us raising private support for one of this country's 125 academic medical centers face circumstances that set us somewhat apart from our fund-raising colleagues in other areas of academia. By virtue of the services that our faculty provide, we can lay claim to a pool of prospective donors only dreamed of by our counterparts in engineering or the liberal arts ("No one ever died of English," ruefully claims one colleague in the humanities). At the same time, most of us operate as part of a larger university development program, with all of the attendant advantages and constraints conferred by being a constituent program. Furthermore, most of our programs represent the largest share of business transacted by the development office at our universities. We are "team players," but typically, to carry out the metaphor, we are the hulking 300-pounders on the starting 11, who want to make all the plays. Fundamentally, we raise funds the way everyone else does, by building relationships over time.

The distinguishing feature of most medical school fund raising is, in a word, patients. We not only educate and train and do research, a common mission throughout a university setting, but we also apply that research and training in treating illness and disease. While any number of alumni can say they owe their livelihoods to their former professors, our prospective donors frequently owe their lives to our faculty. Anyone and everyone, at any stage of life, is our potential prospect, we can argue. Almost every family, at some point, faces a crisis in health and has a compelling stake in our successfully carrying out our mission. However, turning this universe of the chronically or temporarily ailing into donors involves a process that rarely is straightforward. Here are nine of the circumstances that complicate and enliven the job of the academic medical center fund raiser:

1. The Number of Institutions/ Facilities/Programs that We Represent

The recent upheavals created by the way we pay for health care in the United States have irrevocably separated some of our medical schools from their teaching hospitals; others of us, after a merger or acquisition, find ourselves dealing with confused, disaffected donors and new institutional partners. Typically, however, each of us covers a distinct combination of school/hospital/clinical network. At the University of Washington, for example, my territory includes the only medical school for five states (Washington, Wyoming, Alaska, Montana, and Idaho), two teaching hospitals (one the county hospital and regional trauma center), and a burgeoning network of primary care clinics. Often, each entity we serve has its own governing board and its own agenda. Ideally, there is one person in charge to whom each of us reports. The reality in many situations is that lines of authority are ambiguous, making the fund-raising task infinitely more difficult.

2. The Complexity of the Educational Environment

While our colleagues across campus contend with undergraduate, master's, and Ph.D. programs, we in academic medical centers additionally deal with M.D. students, those in residencies, fellows, and post-doctoral students. Filling the pipeline of potential donors entails recognition of these varied constituencies and a tailoring of messages and appeals to each distinct audience. We must customize our fund-raising programs department by department.

3. The Divergent Strategies for Patient Versus Alumni Fund Raising

With patient fund raising, the stakes—life and death—can be high, the timeframe often is more condensed, and the relationships potentially more intense, than those relationships that most development officers cultivate with their alumni. In traditional academic fund raising, it may take 18 to 24 months to close a major gift, but, typically, that major gift is the culmination of years of annual giving and relationship building. With grateful patients, six months may well be too late to secure a gift. Academic medical center fund raisers often are dealing with both patient and alumni major gift prospects simultaneously, demanding nimble changes in focus. There is the short view, of quickly identifying patient prospects whose gratitude for successful treatment understandably tends to fade over time as health returns. There is the traditional long view of involving our alumni and friends and, ideally, former patients in the annual fund and the life of the institution over their lifetimes.

4. Our Dependence on Physician/Partners

While the involvement of the president, the dean, and/or a faculty member is generally essential for the full development of alumni prospects, development officers in most areas of academia easily can work alone. They think nothing of making a "cold call" to an alumnus to seek an appointment. This is rarely the case with patient prospects. In the academic medical center, we are careful to preserve the patient-physician relationship and refrain from acting without the physician's knowledge and approval. Often, we depend solely upon the physician to identify patients who may be prospective donors. This dependence demands considerable time on our part to persuade individual faculty physicians to be attuned to patients' potential interest in supporting the physician's work. Many of our physicians find fund raising distasteful, but some believe it unethical, subverting the patient/physician relationship. Often, an unsolicited gift for their work is enough to enlighten a reluctant faculty member to the potential. We attempt to assuage the reluctant, offering assurances that we will take no action without their approval. We offer help at every step in the process. However, even in a culture where philanthropy is valued and celebrated, we can never make fund-raising converts of all faculty members.

5. The Empathy Element

More than most of our development counterparts across a university campus, we encounter as a matter of course potential donors and families who are grieving or facing uncertain futures and sometimes imminent death. The characteristic empathy, sensitivity, and intuition of all good development officers are doubly critical for those working in academic medical centers. Knowing when to listen is every bit as important as knowing when to ask. A recent letter from parents mourning their son's death praises one of my colleagues for being professional, intelligent, and personable and a good listener: "It seemed natural to have our son the topic of conversation." All of us in development talk daily with prospective donors about one of our culture's great conversational taboos: money. Those of us in academic medical centers deal regularly and directly with another of those taboos: death.

6. The Faculty "Bonus" Factor

The bottom line for private support in many of our programs is greatly augmented by the entrepreneurial brilliance of our faculty. Singlehandedly, with little or no help from the development office, these scientists manage to generate major dollars for their research from corporate and foundation sources and make the development office look good. This "bonus" factor also should help keep us humble. It is our job to figure out how to capitalize on faculty research relationships to generate a gift for endowment or another institutional priority. We have much greater opportunities for success than do many of our development colleagues elsewhere in academia.

7. The Faculty Donor Factor

A number of our academic medical center faculty are the highest paid individuals in the university. While they may not be as well compensated as their counterparts in private practice, they are significant potential donors. They are a constituency that is informed, involved, committed, and are, on average, of greater giving potential than faculty in other areas of our institutions.

8. Competition with Our Alumni

As many academic medical centers create or acquire primary care networks or affiliates, our institutions increasingly compete in the marketplace with our graduates. This can have a chilling effect on alumni giving. Institutions focused mainly on tertiary care, a boon to our general practitioner-graduates and their patients in our region, now increasingly offer primary care. Once partners in providing a full range of services, academic medical centers and their graduates now often are rivals in enrolling new patients. Focusing our efforts on the teaching/training/research functions that we uniquely provide rather than the treatment services may help decrease this competition between these two "rivals."

9. Donor Acquisition

Academia uses the annual fund to reach out regularly to alumni and to other friends who have identified themselves by making a gift. Rarely will a college or university send a fund-raising mailing to the "general public" or segments thereof; the miniscule return would never justify it. Because of the universality of many health issues—cancer and heart disease, for example—academic medical centers, depending on their resources and reputations, may successfully build a base of donors through direct mail.

Because of the research we conduct to seek cures for the major scourges of disease and illness, many of our institutions attract volunteers and donors who have no previous affiliation with us as graduates or patients. We in academic medical centers have an inherent advantage over our academic colleagues because we can appeal to a broad base of the population for support.

The complexity and great potential of academic medical center fund raising pose special challenges. My counterpart at one of this country's leading medical schools, in discussing the challenges of hiring good development officers, said that her institution had zero tolerance for error or misstep. Thank goodness that isn't universally true, or we would all find ourselves at some point unemployed. For most of us, this medical world, as consuming as it can be, is only part of our environment. We also are part of a constituent program of a larger university development effort. I see this state of affairs as having more advantages than disadvantages. At the University of Washington, I look to central development for prospect research, planned giving, much of gift processing, information management, a portion of stewardship and publication services, a large piece of corporate and foundation fund raising, and the alumni annual fund and telepledge. By being a part of this collaborative team of development professionals, our medical center development program benefits by receiving many of the basic services essential for running a development operation. Therefore we can concentrate, for the most part, on major gift fund raising.

● ● ●

While any number of alumni can say they owe their livelihoods to their former professors, our prospective donors frequently owe their lives to our faculty.

Occasionally, we become impatient with a prospect management system that places us second or third in line with a prospective donor, but that is more than compensated for by the large pool of prospective donors interested in health issues that are ours alone. One of the joys of fund raising is working collaboratively to help generous people accomplish what they wish while benefiting worthwhile programs and institutions. The process of trust building, among colleagues, faculty, and donors, is fundamentally the same, I've found, whether at a small liberal arts college, a research university, or an academic medical center. My pride in representing brilliant physician/scientists, clinician/teachers, and researchers is far exceeded by the gratification of our donors who are helping our institutions address important questions for sustaining and improving life.

FURTHER READINGS

Academic Health Care Fund Raising: Planning and Operating a Successful Development Program. Falls Church, VA: Association for Healthcare Philanthropy, 1996.

Evans, Gail. "Paving the Way for Life One Brick at a Time: The Lehigh Valley Hospital's Memorial Brick Campaign Not Only Raised Money for a New Cancer Center, But It Touched Lives by Offering Donors a Way to Honor and Remember Loved Ones," *Fund Raising Management* 26, no. 11 (January 1996): 26-29.

Reckseen, Donna M. and Thomas R. Poole. "The Anatomy of an Endowment/Capital Campaign: The Right Campaign Leadership Can Overcome the Most Difficult Set of Circumstances—Even War, Recession and Unprecedented Change in the Health-Care Field. Long Beach Memorial Medical Center is a Case in Point," *Fund Raising Management* 27, no. 6 (August 1996): 14-18.

Reid, Gregor. "Engaging the Faculty: A University Science Professor Recommends Getting His Colleagues in Deep With Fund-Raising Programs: Now, More Than Ever, It Is Essential That Alternative, and Increasingly More Often Non-Traditional, Funding Sources Be Obtained to Advance Scientific and Medical Inquiry," *Fund Raising Management* 29, no. 5 (July 1998): 32-33, 42

Stanfield, Doug. "Doctors Don't Give: Penn State's Milton S. Hershey Medical Center Found That Doctors Do Give Generously When Approached Like Any Other Major Donor-Namely With Concern for Their Interests," *Fund Raising Management* 24, no. 2 (April 1993): 23-27, 44.

Major gifts to independent schools have grown in size and number. Thanks to a legion of baby boomers inheriting significant sums and young entrepreneurs earning astounding sums in high-tech industries, the million-dollar gift is no longer rare.

Development at Independent Schools: The Challenges and the Assets

Helen A. Colson
President
Helen Colson Development Associates

Independent schools vary significantly in age, size, mission, location, culture, history, and fund-raising sophistication. However, at almost all schools, development has become an important, indeed an essential, portfolio. The typical fund-raising program is far better planned and evaluated, and far more comprehensive than a decade ago.

Recent progress reflects not only good economic times but also improved fund-raising expertise. Seven areas are noteworthy:

1. *Focus on Donors.* Throughout the independent school community, it is well understood that the most successful fund raising is donor focused. Major gift solicitation is ongoing, timed to meet the donor's needs as well as the institution's. Prospect research is continuous and more often done in-house. Cultivation and stewardship of major prospects and donors is continuous and creative.

2. *Major gifts.* Major gifts to independent schools have grown in size and number. Thanks to well-known and widely-praised philanthropists like Walter Annenberg, Ted Turner, and Bill Gates, independent school fund raisers know that the ultimate gift is possible. And thanks to a legion of baby boomers inheriting significant sums and

young entrepreneurs earning astounding amounts in high-tech industries, the million-dollar gift is no longer rare.

3. *Capital campaigns.* More carefully organized and better run, capital campaigns set new records every year. New England boarding schools with long-established development programs and loyal multi-generation donors now launch campaigns in the $100,000,000 to $200,000,000 range. Urban day schools are regularly achieving $25,000,000 to $50,000,000 results. Even elementary schools with very small staffs are reaching for $10,000,000 and $15,000,000 goals.

4. *Planned Gifts.* In the 1980s, independent school planned giving programs were high in quality but few in number. Two decades later, it is the rare school that does not market some planned gift options. Each year, more schools add full-time planned giving development officers. Written gift acceptance policies and gift acceptance committees are the norm. The charitable lead trust, a fine way both to pass assets on to the next generation and to make a generous charitable gift, appeals to top donors at even the smallest schools.

5. *Boards of Trustees.* Trustees are becoming more

sophisticated fund raisers. More schools are drafting trustee job descriptions in order to make it clear during the recruitment process that all trustees are expected:

    a) to play an active role in development,

    b) to make the school a philanthropic priority during their trustee term,

    c) to help identify, cultivate, and solicit prospects, and

    d) to oversee and evaluate the development program.

6. *The Fund-Raising School Head.* Many independent school heads have been fund-raising pros for decades. In fact, it is their personal relationships with key prospects that have led to major gifts for their schools. It is now well understood throughout the independent school community that all school heads must raise funds and they must do it with knowledge and skill. Search committees are making this requirement clear.

7. *The Development Plan.* It is the rare independent school that does not support its development program with three documents:

    a) the mission statement, which tells what the school is trying to do, why, and for whom;

    b) the strategic plan, which tells how the school plans to implement its mission during the upcoming years, and

    c) the development plan, which tells how and when the school will raise the money it needs to achieve its goals.

As a result, campaign goals more frequently reflect fund-raising potential in contrast to institutional need. Development officers frequently focus on fund-raising concepts (the relationship between the actions taken and the results achieved) rather than on timetables and mailings.

SPECIAL REWARDS

The independent school development director has a particularly interesting and satisfying job. Absent is the competition and territoriality that can characterize advancement in higher education.

At most independent schools, the chief advancement officer:

■ *Oversees all institutional fund raising.* Fund raising is centralized; requests for gifts are coordinated. Competition between divisions of the school is minimal or nonexistent.

■ *Plays a leadership role on the school administrative team.* Serving as a senior administrator gives the independent school development director in-depth and up-to-date knowledge about the school as well as a context within which to make fund-raising plans.

■ *Becomes an expert in all areas of advancement,* including annual, capital, and planned giving; alumni relations; publications; and special events. With this comprehensive base of knowledge, the chief advancement officer can set appropriate priorities and coordinate fund-raising initiatives.

■ *Participates in fund raising.* Independent school development officers are not only administrators, but major gifts officers as well. They are able both to plan and to participate in fund-raising. They have personal relationships with prospects; the most experienced have the ability to solicit major and planned gifts.

SPECIAL CHALLENGES

On the other hand, independent school development directors sometimes look enviously at their colleagues in higher education, because most independent schools must cope with limitations of size:

■ *The major donor pool is smaller.* Although some schools are as large as small colleges, many independent schools are very small. In 1997-98, the average enrollment at the approximately 1,000 schools that are members of the National Association of Independent Schools (NAIS) was 485. Furthermore, increasing numbers of students receive financial aid. And even affluent parents who are providing an independent school education for several children from pre-kindergarten through grade 12 often find it difficult to provide generous voluntary support as well.

■ *Resources are scarce.* Many independent schools have only recently come to terms with the need to spend more money in order to achieve their fund-raising potential. The development director salaries at NAIS schools vary significantly—ranging in 1997-98 from a low of $19,000 to a high of $182,000. Development budgets cover the same extraordinary range.

■ *Elementary schools must work hard to attract alumni support.* There are elementary schools that have kept in close touch with their alumni and achieve significant alumni annual giving goals. However, at most elementary schools, alumni relations is in its infancy. There is no alumni association and few alumni reunions; the alumni mailing list has been poorly maintained.

■ *Corporate and foundation support is limited.* Foundations and corporations do provide important seed money and appealing challenge grants to independent schools. However, compared to the large research university, foundations and corporations provide a tiny portion of the total raised.

■ D*evelopment is often poorly understood within the school.* Although trustees and major prospects have a far more sophisticated understanding of philanthropy, at many independent schools, development is still poorly understood by the faculty and staff. Unlike their peers in higher education, relatively few school deans or teachers help to write proposals or solicit gifts. The work of the development office is often underrated; its key role in the future welfare of the school is unacclaimed.

THE ROAD TO SUCCESS

What empowers development success at independent schools? It always begins with the well-researched and well-cultivated major prospect, and the well-solicited major gift. It focuses first on building close individual relationships with those whose generosity can empower a school.

Beyond that, several other factors are key:

■ *Development director tenure matters.* Those schools with the best programs are almost always those at which the chief advancement officers stay 10 years or more in that position. These development directors are appropriately compensated and much appreciated. They care

● ● ●

Although trustees and major prospects have a far more sophisticated understanding of philanthropy, at many independent schools, development is poorly understood by the faculty and staff.

deeply about the school.

■ *The school head must be intimately involved.* There can be no exceptions to this rule if a school is to achieve its fund-raising potential. Unlike many institutions of higher education where there are multiple leaders, typically a school has only one. This makes his or her development role at once more challenging and more important. It is the school head who must communicate the school's mission, cultivate major prospects, solicit major gifts, and evaluate the development program and its chief.

■ *Donor education is essential.* Because independent schools are attracting increasing numbers of first-generation private school families, education about the economics of independent education has become an essential prerequisite to fund-raising success. Too many parents and even alumni misperceive their schools as rich institutions because the tuition is high and the campus is impressive. Too many believe erroneously that independent school teachers are better paid than their public school peers and that school endowments and savings are ample. Before they can be successfully solicited, these potential donors must clearly perceive the fiscal need.

■ *The board of trustees sets the fund-raising tone.* Although the responsibility of trustees to give is now well understood, the quality (as distinguished from the amount) of those gifts still varies. At many independent schools, particularly day schools, trustees are well-known community members; their fund-raising leadership and philanthropic generosity is visible. In a real and personal way, these trustees set the fund-raising tone and raise the sights of many other donors. Those schools whose trustees can claim that the institution is a number one priority have far more success attracting major gifts.

LOOKING AHEAD

Although development programs will surely continue to expand and thrive in the new millennium, there are four particular concerns for independent school planners who look ahead:

■ *Debt.* The need for expanded facilities to

accommodate increasing enrollments and the ease of borrowing have encouraged many schools to incur substantial long-term debt. For some trustees, debt, particularly in the form of tax-free bonds, has appeal. For fund raisers, however, a large institutional debt for a school with a small endowment can provide a significant development challenge.

■ *Turnover.* Schools that change heads frequently—an increasing number in recent years—find it far more difficult to sustain meaningful long-term relationships with their best prospects. It takes a new head several years to get to know prospects. It's a clear fund-raising disadvantage when a succession of heads remain only two to five years.

■ *Underinvolved alumni.* Some day schools are far too reliant upon current parents for fund-raising success. Their challenge in the new millennium is to reach out more effectively to their alumni, the one constituency with a lifetime relationship to the school. Often, independent school alumni have spent many years at one institution—far more than they have spent at one college. Furthermore, families often send many generations of students to a single school. Both the potential and the need for increased alumni support are leading the most savvy schools to send their fund raisers on the road, to establish regional alumni associations, and to host alumni reunions in an expanding number of cities.

■ *Overinvolved parents.* Today's parents sometimes behave more like demanding consumers than loyal constituents. They characterize their gifts as investments and they are interested in the nature and quantity of the return. They sometimes direct their philanthropy to special projects that are their personal priority rather than the school's. Those schools with clear gift acceptance and counting policies deal best with these consumer parents. Fortunately, few schools let the manipulative donor prevail.

GOALS FOR THE FUTURE

It can no longer be said that independent school development programs are a decade behind those in higher education. Today, independent school development directors, particularly those with long years of experience, are among the most knowledgeable and creative fund-raising professionals in the educational fund-raising field.

In years to come, all schools are likely to rely increasingly on the skilled and talented development professional. As leading fund-raising professionals in the independent community demonstrate that larger and larger sums can be raised, they will raise the sights of their peers. In the 1990s, independent school development programs expanded and thrived. In the new millennium, the important and obvious benefits of a professional development effort will lead even the smallest and youngest schools to establish even more professional programs and to set even more ambitious goals.

FURTHER READINGS

Brown, Charles D. Jr. "Lawrenceville Redux: In 1992, the Lawrenceville School Embarked on a $125-Million Capital Campaign. Now Three Years Later, the Campaign Has Realized 84 Percent of Its Goal—Two Years Ahead of Schedule—With $105-Million in Gifts and Pledges. Here's How It Was Done," *Fund Raising Management* 27, no. 2 (April 1996): 20-24.

Burnett, Jefferson and Donna M. Orem. *Questions and Answers on Gift Substantiation and Quid Pro Quo Disclosure Statement Requirements for Private Schools.* Washington, DC: Council for Advancement and Support of Education, National Association of Independent Schools, and the United States Catholic Conference, 1994.

Colson, Helen A. *Philanthropy at Independent Schools.* Washington, DC: National Association of Independent Schools, 1995.

Jones, Jeremy. A *Development Handbook: Promoting Philanthropy at Independent Schools.* Washington, DC: Council for Advancement and Support of Education, 1992.

Ryan, Ellen. "The Nonstop Shop: Potomac School's Advancement Team Does a Lot with a Little—And Does It Very Well. Its Secret: Lists, Loyalty, and Laughter," CURRENTS 20, no. 2 (February 1994): 10-14.

Having a clear niche doesn't necessarily mean that the case for philanthropic support is clear. As advancement professionals, we know that the case for support must be bigger than the institution.

Schools Filling an Educational Niche

Margarete (Peg) Rooney Hall
Associate Professor of Public Relations, College of Journalism and Communications
University of Florida and

Former Vice President of Advancement
Gallaudet University

"Every president you've ever met probably told you that his or her university is the center of the universe, right? Well, they are all wrong . . . except me." The president of Gallaudet University greeted a national group of leaders from corporate philanthropy last year with these words and got a laugh of recognition.

Gallaudet fascinates people because of its clear niche in the universe of American higher education. It is the only university in the world where all the undergraduates are deaf or hard of hearing and where all graduate programs focus on deafness and deaf people. Many remember the student protest in 1988, *Deaf President Now!,* that resulted in the appointment of the university's, and the world's, first deaf president. Despite its traditional, comprehensive, undergraduate curriculum and programs, it is really easy to see that Gallaudet is different. There are numerous advantages to having such a clear niche.

As advancement professionals, we spend a lot of our time and energy defining what is distinctive about our institutions. The differences may relate to history, size, or demographics, as at historically black or women's institutions. They may relate to location, governance, or mission, like schools with a value-centered, or a conservative educational program. A niche school, like Gallaudet, comes with a unique mission and a distinctive student population that sets it apart from the several thousand other institutions in higher education. These distinctions shape the school's case, and they influence the way institutional advancement is practiced.

The differences influence the way in which we apply institutional advancement practices. They don't change what we know about good practices, but they enrich our application of these practices and help to set priorities among our programs.

Institutional advancement practice is rooted in the theories of public relations. The research and writings of Kathleen S. Kelly in this area are particularly useful. We know that successful advancement creates a two-way communication between the university and its various publics and that this communication seeks results that are mutually beneficial. The process requires a clear identification of the institution's role and goals; a clear statement of the needs and the case for supporting the institution; the identification and involvement of potential supporters; and the stewardship of support received to assure that the desired results accrue. This chapter discusses the effect that having a clearly defined institutional niche has on advancement practices.

THE INSTITUTIONAL NICHE AND THE CASE FOR GIVING

Having a clear niche doesn't necessarily mean that the case for philanthropic support is clear. As advancement professionals, we know that the case for support must be bigger than the institution. It ought to position the university strongly in the society it serves. For those of us whose schools have a clear institutional niche, the case can reflect the role of people like our students in the broader society.

For example, Gallaudet's case for support is *not* that the students are deaf. Rather, it is that Gallaudet provides society with educated and skilled deaf citizens who have had every opportunity to fully develop their intellectual and interpersonal talents. Recent changes in access and attitude have greatly improved opportunities for deaf students at all universities. Nevertheless, because all the undergraduates are deaf, the Gallaudet experience is different. The students take the same courses as students in any good university. But the classes are taught visually, not aurally. Students and professors communicate directly, using sign language, without having to go through an interpreter. Because everyone on campus can use sign language, students can participate in late-night bull sessions, make dates, resolve problems in student accounts—all without using interpreters. A deaf student will be the lead in the theatrical performance, the quarterback of the football team, the resident adviser in the dorm, the intern in PR, and the student government president. The case for support of Gallaudet is that it offers a level playing field for practicing all the skills an educated person needs to learn in order to make a full contribution to the broad spectrum of American life.

As another example, the case for support at Mount Saint Mary's College in Maryland is not just that it is value-centered, or that it is Catholic. Rather, it is that at Mount Saint Mary's, students learn to integrate their values with the knowledge and skills they will carry into the broader society as educated citizens. The curriculum is highly structured; students take a number of courses "in com-

mon" each of their four years. The courses held in common develop knowledge and skills within the framework of life values. Mount Saint Mary's provides society with educated citizens with strong analytical and critical thinking skills and a broad view of the interconnectedness of human history and knowledge. That's the idea that attracts the particular students and that differentiates them from students at other colleges. It's not a physical difference, but it is a real difference. It is a key to the case for support.

Centering the case statement on the institutional niche is powerful. It helps to motivate donors to support institutions that produce graduates with shared characteristics that the donors believe will make the world a better place.

THE INSTITUTIONAL NICHE AND POTENTIAL DONORS

Students bring diverse educational, cultural, and economic backgrounds to college. Despite those variables, in a niche school, the characteristic that the students share defines how teaching and learning happen. Fund-raising priorities clearly reflect the niche, especially the differences in learning and teaching that the niche demands. The niche helps to attract and motivate donors. It is central to the communication with donors.

Alumni

Understanding the student body and the characteristics they share with each other should affect the way we involve them later in alumni activities and cultivate their support as donors. This is true of all institutions, and especially important at niche schools. Niche school alumni often share experiences from growing up that affect the way they think about philanthropy.

For example, research published in 1995 by Sandra Shaw Hardy and Martha Taylor showed that women tend to be more motivated to give when they work together to achieve a goal rather than when they are encouraged to compete with each other to achieve it. With this in mind, as advancement professionals at institutions with demographically distinctive student bodies, we need to tailor our interactions with alumni to their experiences. If students tend to be more collaborative and less competitive in how they give, this may mean that we should involve potential alumni donors more in planning and enhancing programs through permanent advisory boards or short-term task forces.

If the school does not yet have a tradition of strong alumni support, we may need to build a core group of influential alumni who become major donors and are willing to talk to others about giving. With these volunteers, we could design and implement a program to change thinking among other alumni and instill a stronger willingness to give, a stronger sense of responsibility for assuring educational opportunity for future students like themselves.

If the students are more value-centered, advancement officers may need to design activities that reinforce those values and encourage alumni to support giving that continues the cycle of education and community involvement.

For most schools, students do not arrive imbued with a sense of responsibility for future giving. Few smaller universities believe they have the resources for a formal student-alumni program that begins the education about giving. Even without a separate student alumni program, students can often be pulled into alumni programs that are designed by institutional advancement professionals and alumni volunteers. This involvement improves the alumni program by keeping the alumni focused on helping students rather than serving alumni. As a side benefit, student leaders who meet with, speak to, and work with alumni to improve resources for learning and teaching learn the value of alumni support with little additional cost in programming for the alumni relations staff.

Parents

Unlike alumni, the parents' involvement with a university tends to have a shorter life span. Issues related to communication, teaching and learning, and career preparation provide excellent opportunities to pull parents into the community and interact with them in mutually beneficial programs.

For example, parents tend to have a lively interest in knowing and participating in the students' learning environment through Parents' Weekend and similar involvement opportunities.

They are particularly interested in the issues related to transition from college to careers or graduate school. At a niche school, these programs can focus on issues appropriate to the niche, such as value-centered careers, or the increasing opportunities for deaf professionals.

The fact that the students share a significant characteristic offers the opportunity to design parent programs around a shared experience. It allows institutional advancement professionals to build a relationship with parents that can lead to more lasting support.

Friends

"Friends" are individual donors who are not alumni. Although at many institutions, some friends became involved through a business, artistic, or professional interest in a program or service, most traditional schools have little opportunity to attract friends, particularly ones who are not trustees, parents, faculty, or staff, and who are willing to become major donors. This is an area where niche schools have a high potential, because the niche can provide a philosophical and philanthropic link with the donor, even when there is no academic or professional tie to the school.

For example, Berea College accepts high-ability, low-income students primarily from southern Appalachia and Kentucky. Each student receives a full scholarship. As part of the scholarship agreement, the students work on-campus at least 10 hours a week. Because of the work ethic and the special population the college serves, it attracts support nationally from people who believe in the basic premise of "paying one's own way." According to data from the Council for Aid to Education, in 1999, friends contributed 61 percent of the total gift amount received by Berea. This compares to 29 percent received from friends by the 189 other schools in the Carnegie classification Private Liberal Arts I category.

Historically black colleges and universities attract friends from among all people who are interested in providing a learning environment where race is not a barrier. Women's colleges attract friends who feel the same about a learning environment where gender is not a barrier.

Public relations officers play a major role in

attracting friends to a university by segmenting constituencies that are likely to have potential friends and targeting those constituencies for interactive communications.

CORPORATIONS AND FOUNDATIONS

For smaller institutions with broad curricula, corporations and foundations often are not strong prospective donors. An institution's niche can sometimes change the dynamic.

Where a foundation has an expressed program interest, the overlay of the student demographic can compensate for the relatively small number of students who will be affected by the program. For example, after the passage of the Americans With Disabilities Act opened new career opportunities to deaf people, the W. K. Kellogg Foundation supported the establishment of a conference center at Gallaudet to increase access to life-long learning and professional development for deaf people. Although the foundation has long provided support in these areas, Gallaudet's small size and broad, traditional curriculum probably would not have attracted Kellogg's attention without the university's niche.

Similarly, student demographics can make a campus more attractive to a corporate donor, especially if the corporation seeks to increase the diversity of its workforce and customer base. On average, other universities in CAE's Private Master's I category, like Gallaudet, received 34 percent of their gifts in 1998 from corporations and foundations. But Gallaudet received 64 percent of its gifts from this source.

THE INSTITUTIONAL NICHE AND THE GOVERNING BOARD

Niche schools have both opportunities and challenges in building an effective governing board. We know that trustees must understand, cherish, and enrich the mission that distinguishes the institution.

We know that they also must be major donors. But often, the trustees and potential trustees who are most committed to the demographic group that a niche school serves either are

not wealthy or do not have the strong link to the institution that causes them to put it first among their philanthropic priorities. In selecting trustees, a basic conflict can occur between the need to have individuals who know the niche and trustees who can provide substantial philanthropic support.

Trustee decisions advance or diminish the institution's capability to be what it claims to be. Trustees set policy; they govern; they select the president; they assure financial and legal stability. In an institution where the students share a primary differentiating characteristic, most of the trustees need to share it, too. Otherwise, the message is conveyed that people like the students cannot become the decision makers.

One of the tenets of demographically differentiated education is that the broader society presents barriers that are best set aside in an optimal learning environment. If the trustees are not like the students, they have not shared the barriers. They do not have the same life experiences and will never have them. They know the barriers intellectually, but not experientially. If most of the trustees are outside the students' niche, their governance decisions are very likely to reflect the experience of the majority, not of the students. They can help the students, but they can't lead the students.

Therefore, when niche schools select trustees, they usually give great weight to trustees' demographic characteristics, even more than to their ability to be major donors. As a result, the reality often is that the trustees cannot be major donors. Advancement officers need to help identify potential trustees who are influential, affluent, wise, and members of the student demographic group. In working with less wealthy trustees, the challenge is to assure that their gifts are major, given their wealth level. For alumni and parents, this conveys the message that philanthropic support is the community's responsibility and that community leaders will make sacrificial gifts because it is important, necessary, and personally fulfilling to be part of the university's success in this influential way.

In addition to their governing boards, most universities have non-governing boards that are set

> ● ● ●
> **In a school where the students share a primary differentiating characteristic, most of the trustees need to share it, too. Otherwise, the message is conveyed that people like the students cannot become the decision makers.**

up to advise and to provide support for advancement efforts. At niche schools, these are particularly helpful. They can be formally linked to the governing board by a trustee resolution establishing them with a specific mission, like enlarging the circle of people of influence and affluence who know the university and its students. Leaders can be recruited to these boards who can provide some of the wealth that the trustees don't provide.

A non-governing board at a niche school can provide a good, alternative way to cultivate alumni, leaders of influence and affluence, and other major donors. It can also be an attractive service option for busy executives who want to give back to the community but don't have the time that a governing board requires. They get a whole new perspective on a demographic group that they have not had a lot of contact with in the past. The cultural experience is intellectually and professionally interesting. The board members can provide valuable service as guest lecturers, as advocates for internship and employment for students, and as intermediaries between the school and other influential executives. If carefully set in a supportive juxtaposition to the governing board, an alternative board can be very productive as a means to establish two-way communication between the university and a group of powerful advocates who were previously outside the university's circle of influence.

THE INSTITUTIONAL NICHE AND STEWARDSHIP

Philanthropic support is a blending of a donor's financial resources with the university's professional resources to achieve an outcome that is important to both of them. Neither the donor not the university can achieve the results as well working alone as they can working together. Stewardship is a way of sharing with donors the results that their gifts produce.

Niche schools have wonderful opportunities for stewardship. Donors are eager to meet students and participate in the unique, barrier-free environment that the university builds with their participation. Stewardship events and communications can reflect the uniqueness of the campus and provide donors with insights that encourage continuing involvement. Time spent visiting classes can be particularly rewarding for the donors because it allows them first-hand experience with the environment they have helped create or perpetuate.

APPLYING THE LESSONS FROM NICHE SCHOOLS

All college and university advancement officers strive to define a meaningful differentiation between their institutions and others. Building on the successful practices of special-mission colleges, institutions with a broader student base also can adapt institutional advancement practices to better meet their unique situations. The adaptations will help institutions segment their constituent groups and enhance ongoing programs by giving them more focus. The result will be an increase in the number of people and organizations that become part of the educational community, be supported by it, and provide it support. By adapting to the niche interests of our key publics, we may help them better understand the value that our students bring to their universe as their future employees, neighbors, and leaders.

REFERENCES

Kelly, Kathleen S. *Effective Fund-Raising Management.* Mahwah, NJ: Lawrence Erlbaum, 1998.

Shaw, Sondra C. and Martha Taylor. *Reinventing Fund Raising.* San Francisco, CA: Jossey-Bass Publishers, 1995.

The Role of Key Institutional Leaders in Advancement

Edited by Linda Weimer

Introduction

Linda Weimer
Vice President for University Relations
University of Wisconsin System

I t was a dark and stormy night. A late November squall churned the waves on Lake Superior and visibility was worsening by the minute. The captain, a veteran of many frightful Great Lakes storms, took the bridge of his huge ore carrier as it heaved slowly through icy waters.

In the distance, he could see the light of a ship approaching dead on. He had the right of way and ordered his crew to send the signal: "Turn 10 degrees to port." Back came the signal: "Turn 10 degrees to starboard."

He ordered another signal: "Turn 10 degrees to port. We have the right of way." Back came the signal: "Turn 10 degrees to starboard."

Annoyed now, the captain signaled: "Turn 10 degrees to port. I am a captain." Back came the signal: "Turn 10 degrees to starboard. I am a seaman, second class."

Concerned now as the light was drawing nearer and cursing under his breath, the captain sent the signal: "Turn 10 degrees to port. We are an ore carrier."

The reply: "Turn 10 degrees to starboard. We are a lighthouse."

When Donna Shalala was chancellor of the University of Wisconsin-Madison in the early 1990's, she often told that joke. She compared navigating a large and complex research university to navigating a Great Lakes ore carrier.

Indeed, schools, colleges, and universities of any size are hard to steer. Charting a course is challenging. The fates throw walloping storms in their paths; and shallow shoals lie just beneath the surface threatening to run aground even the most skillful captain.

But teamwork brings the ship safely to port—teamwork throughout the organization. No matter how good the captain and officers, they will not succeed without a good engineer, a good communications officer, or a good cook, for that matter.

By the same token, an educational institution—no matter how great the leader—will falter if the enterprise is not built on teamwork, and if the team doesn't understand both the institution's goals and the role that advancement plays in helping to achieve them.

This handbook contains a wealth of information on the basic tools, skills, and tricks-of-the-trade that contribute to a successful advancement program with all of its elements. But those outside the immediate advancement "family" often have just as great an impact on an educational institution's relationships with its donors, alumni, students, faculty, parents, neighbors, government officials, the media, and others who are vital to the organization's well-being.

This section deals with the impact that those institutional leaders have on advancement. A primary focus of this section is on the institutional leader—be it a president, chancellor, vice chancellor, or head of school. The first two chapters speak to the leader's role in fund raising and in friend raising. Both are written by university presidents. The institution's chief executive has the vision, sets the tone, and embodies the institution's values and aspirations. He or she must be, at once, an able governor, politician, fund raiser, celebrity, mentor, communicator, and leader. And, this person is also ultimately responsible for the success or failure of the advancement function.

Edward G. Coll, president of Alfred University, writes very specifically about the president's role in fund raising. His colleague, Harry Peterson, is president of Western State College of Colorado. Peterson provides a perspective on the president's role in working with government and community leaders. Both offer tips for presidents but those tips are equally valuable for advancement professionals.

Academic leaders also play an important role in advancement. Deans, department chairs, and faculty opinion leaders are all, to some degree, friend raisers and fund raisers—perhaps more so than ever before. Mary Kay Murphy of

Morris Brown College gives some special insight into the relationship between the institution's academic priorities and the advancement function, reminding us all that the purpose of advancement is to further the academic agenda—and bottom line—to educate students.

There are other leaders in the institution who play a role in advancement—the athletic director, the vice president of finance, the admissions director, the vice chancellor of legal affairs, the assistant head of school, and many others. Though they can and do play some role in fund raising and alumni relations, they often play their largest role, sometimes reluctantly, in media relations. Sharon Kha of the University of Arizona offers her insight into how best to work with and support academic leaders in this arena. Terry Shepard and Debra Thomas of Rice University follow up in a chapter that offers a perspective on the importance of internal communication among institutional leaders.

Though not always thought of as institutional leaders, students and alumni play critical roles in that regard. They often serve on governance boards and have their own governance structures that can have a huge influence on public relations, alumni development, and fund raising. They are considered together in one chapter, written by Bruce Darling of the University of California and me. They are on the same spectrum; student leaders very often become alumni leaders. There is increasing awareness that time spent cultivating and engaging student leaders in the advancement function can pay big future dividends for advancement. Finally, there are parents who are enormously invested in the institution during the time that their children are enrolled. Parents play a particularly large role in the operations and advancement programs of independent schools, as Deirdre Ling notes. She shares her insights and experiences as head of school for Middlesex School.

Each chapter in this section is written from the special vantage point of the author(s) and so each offers a fresh take, based on his or her own experience. This is not meant to be a comprehensive guide to all the roles that all institutional leaders play in advancement. Indeed, that topic could justify its own handbook. But from these chapters, you will glean insights as they pertain to your own particular institution, insights that will help you join your colleagues at the helm of your institution as you sail safely into the future.

The president personifies the institution's goals. Like it or not, he or she is the chief spokesperson for the campus.

The Role of the President in Fund Raising

Edward G. Coll
President
Alfred University

Twenty years ago, newly elected presidents needed only to have on their resume an impressive background in teaching and academic administration. Search committees and governing boards looked primarily at scholarly distinction in selecting a new CEO. But state and federal deficits, inflation, and recessions signaled a need for change. New types of searches were mounted—for individuals with strong skills in management, vision in planning, and enthusiasm for fund raising. The fund-raising pressures on the president have increased dramatically in recent decades and there is no sign that they will diminish.

As a survivor of nearly two decades as a university president, I can testify to the increased need for outside resources to finance the ambitions of campus scholars, researchers, and students. When I retire, I will have completed three capital campaigns and after my departure, my successor and our governing board will move immediately to plan for a new capital campaign. The beat will go on. My successor will have no doubt about the president's role in resource development. And I believe Alfred University is more the norm than the exception.

THE PRESIDENT AND PLANNING

People everywhere want and need to be part of something larger—something more lasting and meaningful than themselves. Educational institutions must embody their hopes and dreams for the future. Our institutions aren't perfect; they always face challenges. Yet the people who care about our colleges and universities—faculties, students, alumni, parents, and friends—yearn for continued progress and improvement. Presidents must provide the inspiration those constituents need and encourage others to dream.

The first condition for presidential success is to build a compelling plan for future institutional prosperity. The term "vision" is overworked today but, still, it expresses the kind of plan required—one that will inspire others to action. The president must listen carefully to the hopes and aspirations of those serving the institution, and meld these into a coherent plan that will make for a better future. Out of the many individual views of the future, the president must forge a meaningful agenda for progress and change that is at once compelling, challenging, and achievable.

The president must share that view with others who will help make it real. Those who doubt must be inspired. Those who criticize must be heard and allowed to shape and improve the vision. Those who believe must be promoted and enlisted to recruit others to the cause. Having observed hundreds of presidential colleagues over the years, I can say without reservation that those who articulate a clear and compelling case for the future of their institutions, regardless of their individual personalities or temperaments, will succeed as fund raisers. Those who cannot will struggle, regardless of charm, intelligence, or other qualifications.

The president personifies the institution's goals. Like it or not, he or she is the chief spokesperson for the campus. When money is involved, major donors always insist on "speaking to the boss." Others on campus can help "sell the project." But the reality of successful fund raising is that the CEO is the chief salesperson while others are supporting characters in cultivating and persuading donors. Attempting to delegate this responsibility wastes time.

Capital campaigns support the critical needs of an ambitious institution. They flow from the planning process and usually involve buildings, endowment, financial aid, strengthening of the annual fund, and a variety of specialized projects designed to enhance the university's reputation and reward productive faculty, deans, and staff for their hard work and accomplishments. Multiple project campaigns have proven successful since campuses usually have multiple audiences interested in supporting them. Multiple project campaigns also expand the donor base. This is very healthy because previous donors tend to be "repeat" contributors, usually at a level higher than their earlier gift. So be bold and imaginative in constructing campaign goals. The more varied the project menu, the broader the audience, thus expanding the donor base for both current and future campaigns.

Nothing is more important than direct presidential involvement in capital campaign planning. Time must be spent in meeting with each vital campus constituency to share the president's vision and to secure commitments toward the goals and objectives of the fund-raising effort. The governing board—or in public institutions, the foundation board—should be the first source of input for the

campaign structure and goals. Nothing creates greater enthusiasm for a campaign than being involved in planning and understanding the consequences of a successful campaign effort. Involving key trustees early and then continuing those discussions with the full board energizes members and helps raise their sights regarding their individual gifts. Once the board buys into the campaign objectives and initial leadership gifts are secured, the remaining board members are quick to follow. Once trustees have made their commitment, they become able and successful solicitors of their peers for both the silent and public phase of the new campaign.

THE PRESIDENT AND THE ADVANCEMENT TEAM

A new president should immediately gauge the strength of the institution's advancement program and its staff. Unless the new president was selected to address a crisis in the academic, finance, or student affairs areas, his or her first step should be in the direction of making the advancement team an active partner with these areas. This is especially true if the campus is in the midst of a capital campaign. Expect to make a heavy commitment of time and energy.

Meetings with your senior advancement officer should take place at least once each week, beyond which you will spend a considerable amount of time travelling together. There must be total candor between you, and you must honestly evaluate each other. You may leave a visit to a prospect feeling that you did a great job when, in fact, you failed to present the case. A good advancement professional will always tell you the truth. A candid suggestion to change focus on the solicitation or a tip regarding some personal idiosyncrasy might be sufficient to salvage the gift and better prepare you for future solicitations. Your advancement executive should expect no less from you. Suggesting improvement in your partner's participation in the solicitation will make both of you more effective.

If, as a new president, you inherit a proven senior advancement officer with whom you can enjoy such a relationship and who has an established track record of success, count your blessings

> ● ● ●
> **Nothing is more important than direct presidential involvement in capital campaign planning.**

and do your best to retain that person. If your administration needs such a talent, spare no resources in the recruitment process. Successful advancement professionals always understand the need for talented staff and will, in turn, recruit and train a productive team.

Like all good organizations, advancement programs reflect the quality of their leader. Every advancement director should have the most senior title you can bestow on the position, reflecting the critical nature of the position to campus constituencies, alumni, foundations, and corporations so that the officer can speak with acknowledged authority in fund-raising efforts. The senior advancement executive must be a key officer of the administration and have his or her authority reinforced by the CEO on public occasions, in board meetings, and with alumni associations.

Many institutions rely on professional search firms who specialize in recruiting senior advancement executives. Most are good and do a reasonably thorough job. However, never base your evaluation solely on the search firm's recommendation. It is always helpful to check secondary sources. These include the prospect's colleagues, trustees at other institutions, business and industry leaders, and other advancement professionals.

The annual institutional reports on giving filed with the Council for Aid to Education (CAE) can also help assess a candidate's effectiveness. Many campuses complete the extensive gift report requested by CAE and individual reports are available to public scrutiny. In addition, the *Chronicle of Higher Education* and *Chronicle of Philanthropy* carry major stories on individual advancement programs, providing national and regional comparisons with regard to fund-raising effectiveness. These reports not only help you scout out talent, but also may give you good ideas for your own fund-raising programs.

The most effective measure of a candidate's potential is found in personal evaluations by their peers or the volunteers they serve. As a president, one important aspect you will want to probe is how your candidate uses the strengths of his or her current president and, more importantly, works around the weaknesses of the current boss. Spare no expense in your search for, and support of, good

advancement personnel. They will pay off your investment many times over. Pouring resources into a development staff and advancement operation is not as sensitive on campuses as it was a decade ago. However, departments and administrative units seeing scarce resources go toward the advancement program need to be consulted and apprised of the rewards that such an investment could bring to the campus family.

Just as you spend a lot of time with your chief advancement officer, so, too, should you meet frequently with the advancement staff. Nothing energizes people more than working sessions with the president and feeling his or her commitment to their efforts. The president can provide feedback on the strengths and weaknesses of advancement staff. Staff meetings also provide a focus on the goals of fund-raising and friend-raising projects and serve as a learning experience for the CEO.

Contemporary fund raising—indeed, all areas of advancement—for any institution is a team effort. There is no substitute for a staff of talented, trained, imaginative, and dedicated people. Fund raising, in particular, is no longer an art form but a rapidly developing science. Nothing is more important than the CEO's support and personal encouragement of the advancement staff. Recruiting good people is always a problem but keeping them is even more difficult. Advancement departments are never cheap; limited resources guarantee diminishing results. Moving an annoying dean or unproductive colleague from his or her current position to the advancement staff is usually a failure regardless of good intentions. Learning "on the job" is also a proven prescription for failure and frustration for the parties involved.

With a talented leader and a capable support staff, you need an operations budget that provides adequate funds to support fund-raising programs, publications and videos, cultivation gatherings, travel, and lodging. Skimping on the operations budget guarantees growing frustrations among your development staff. Never save nickels and dimes by leaving dollars for others to pluck and enjoy.

A special word about travel. It is a major component to successful fund raising. Telephone solicitations and appeal letters are seldom successful in soliciting major gifts. One-on-one meetings with prospects are now common and expected. Campuses in major metropolitan areas may not need extensive travel budgets, but travel to alumni and prospect cities is a fact of life. Never fund travel or lodging "on the cheap." Travel is a hardship and an inconvenience, regardless of the style of transportation or quality of housing. Send your advancement staff off in the most comfortable settings you can provide and encourage upgrades to first class through the use of frequent flyer mileage that rapidly accumulates for you and your staff. Generosity in travel, housing, and meal allowances is a modest investment for keeping talented staff.

THE PRESIDENT AND THE DONOR

Fund raising is a major component of presidential responsibilities on virtually all campuses, and it is expected that the president will personally solicit major gifts. The job requires a great deal of enthusiasm. The president, as solicitor, must project the vitality of a salesman, visionary, and leader. Your ability to convince prospects of your leadership capability, the soundness of your planning, and the eventual rewards of their investment is paramount to success.

The mere thought of fund raising is usually uncomfortable to most mortals. Asking people for huge sums of money while giving nothing tangible in return is a challenging concept. Regardless of how often any of us ask for six-, seven-, or eight-figure gifts, it is accompanied by damp palms and the nagging thought that the prospective donor might be offended and never again speak to you. Don't blame yourself for having these normal feelings. Enthusiasm is contagious and I make every effort to convey my sense of excitement and enthusiasm for a project to a prospective donor.

Describe the merits and rewards of a meaningful project and it will not be long before the prospect sends signals to you about comfort, or reluctance, in being a partner in the venture. Once the prospective donor buys into all or part of the venture, the enthusiasm is shared. However, achieving participation by the prospect in the project is seldom an isolated incident involving just the CEO.

A long-time trustee of Alfred University has a philosophy, developed over more than 50 years as a volunteer fund raiser, about people and their giving habits. He notes that one-third of the people you meet will not give, regardless of how worthy they believe your cause is. Such people simply do not have a generous spirit, and they cannot be moved, so don't even try. Another third will make only token gifts to your cause. They have some charitable inclinations, but they have other more pressing priorities. Accept their gifts graciously, thank them, and move on. The final third are those with truly generous spirits. They know the real joy that comes with helping a valuable cause, and they will be the source of most of the money that you raise. These are the people whom the successful fund raiser will find and cultivate. Grateful for what they have achieved, they are usually humble and want to give something back to society.

I have often been moved by the comments of top donors to our university. They often thank me, sometimes with great emotion, for the opportunity to give. Here are three of the most powerful motivations for giving that I have encountered over the years:

- *A belief in the power of education to change lives:* Virtually every major donor I have ever met has been a "true believer" in our cause. They have experienced the full power of education in their own lives and recognize that their achievements are due in large part to what they learned as young people on the campuses they support.

- *Gratitude:* Many of the most generous people I have ever met have made their gifts to honor another person, perhaps a selfless adviser, a wise teacher or a beloved spouse, parent, or child. They want to repay kindness given at a crucial moment in their lives by helping students themselves.

- *The desire to make the world a better place:* Generous people are by nature optimistic people who believe in progress and improvement of society. They become involved in our campuses, see the good that we do, and want to help us to achieve even more. We become the instruments of their optimism.

I am awed by the people who give to higher education. They are among the brightest and most interesting people on this planet. It is a continual joy to know them and to work with them.

However, if you find yourself pursuing a gift from someone who is looking for personal advantage, regardless of how much money is at stake, beware! A brilliant fund raiser said it concisely: "Beware of nondonors bearing gifts!"

Really meaningful gifts almost always come from individuals. I have great respect for the contributions of the organized philanthropic sector that has done so much for higher education in America. But the gifts of generous individuals who believe in education have made the real difference for our colleges and universities.

Such people rarely arrive with checkbook in hand, asking how much you need. You must find and cultivate them, sometimes for many years. Knowing where to look for them is one key to success in fund raising. Almost invariably, your top donors will have become more and more involved with your institution over time, so look for those who have served the cause.

How do people get involved at your institution? Do they serve on an alumni council, community advisory board, or in a parents group? Do they volunteer to recruit students, raise funds from classmates and friends, or help your graduates find their way into the world of work? Do they lend their advice and support to teaching and research on your campus? The list of places to look is as long as you want to make it. But looking among your most active volunteers is one place to find your best prospective donors.

You also can better your odds for future fundraising success by creating new avenues for volunteer service and involvement. The greater the number of people working for the betterment of your institution, the greater your chance of raising serious sums of money. Almost without exception, the most successful fund-raising programs are at institutions that provide the most avenues for volunteer service.

Beware of disingenuous attempts to build volunteer involvement on your campus. The truth is that working through and with volunteers is very hard work—a good deal harder than simply doing it yourself or paying someone to do it for you. Many people on your campus will resist attempts to

● ● ●

Your ability to convince prospects of your leadership capability, the soundness of your planning, and the eventual rewards of their investment is paramount to success.

truly empower and engage alumni and friends in the essential work of the institution. It's not because they aren't sympathetic, but because they will have to work harder with few visible results in the short run and they already are going flat out for your school. Your volunteers will quickly sense whether they are welcomed at your organization's grassroots level and if not, they will soon become disaffected.

Another place to look for top prospects is among your current supporters. We have all heard stories about complete strangers who suddenly endow a chair or give an entire building. Such occurrences are rare. The odds are great that the person who will make the biggest gift your institution will ever receive is already one of your donors—and a regular donor, too. So tell your prospect researcher to start looking for wealth among the people who already give, and make it a practice to visit your most regular donors whenever you travel.

Previous donors always make the best future donors but each case needs a new appeal that again creates a sense of partnership between the institution and the donor. Never take a major donor's interest for granted. Major donors deserve a "fresh approach" that conveys the president's vision and dreams for the continuing success of the first project. Doing your homework on the second gift will make the third gift much easier.

By the same token, don't expect to be successful with every donor. Not everyone will like you or respect your vision and style. Don't become flustered or defensive. Some people will dislike you and others will find a lack of comfortable "chemistry." Don't take it personally. The president's job is a difficult one; critics, even enemies, go with the territory. And some of those critics will be major donors or prospects for your institution.

Abandoning people who are unfriendly to you is not good policy. When you read body language that suggests displeasure with your company, cut your losses and start planning alternate approaches to the prospect. Perhaps a dean, a trustee, or your chief advancement officer will be a more effective representative for your cause.

Remember that people give to people. Take advantage of the strengths you have on your campus and pull out one or two people who have chemistry that is more in line with the prospect's personality. You will both be relieved by the switch and be able to greet each other warmly for the celebration marking the gift.

Perhaps the most frustrating part of prospect cultivation is the "slow no"—endless hours spent with major gift prospects who tantalize with occasional interest in your cultivation, then defer the ultimate decision of making the gift to "the next meeting." Never kid yourself that you are going to turn this prospect's head or heart to your interest area regardless of how mesmerizing the gift potential might be. The "slow no" prospect drains your energy and raises your level of frustration and that of your advancement team and volunteers. Cut your losses and move on.

Much has been written on the role of the president and institutional fund raising. This role will remain important as resources at our educational institutions become more strained. Raising tuition and fees beyond inflation is no longer a viable option considering the political and media climate. And cutting costs is difficult in our competitive environment with rising demands for service from students and parents. To continue to develop and expand education's contribution to society, presidents will play a central role in institutional advancement. They are and always will be their institutions' chief advancement officer.

FURTHER READINGS

Costello, Kathryn R. "What I Expect of My CEO: A Chief Advancement Officer Outlines the Qualities That Make a President or Head an Ally in Fund Raising," CURRENTS 19, no. 10 (November/December 1993): 24-28.

Fisher, Mark A. "Seasoned CEOs: Now That They've Reached the Top Spot, Former Fund Raisers Tell What They Know Now—And Wish They'd Known Then," CURRENTS 19, no. 10 (November/December 1993): 38-40, 42.

McNamee, Mike. "The Joy of Asking: The Best Fund-Raising Programs Take Root When the CEO and CDO Cultivate a Sense of Fun Together," CURRENTS 23, no. 1 (January 1997): 16-20.

Murray, Dennis J. "The CEO's Role in Fund Raising: It's No Secret That Not-for-Profit CEOs Must Cultivate Major Gift Prospects. But That's Not Where an Executive's Development Responsibilities Should Begin—Or End. The CEO Must Communicate the Organization's Vision and Build an Effective Board. A College President Offers His Views of the CEO's Role," *Advancing Philanthropy* 2, no. 5 (Spring 1995): 19-23.

"The Public Perspective: What CEOs at 40 Public Universities Think About Fund Raising," CURRENTS 24, no. 4 (April 1998): 6.

A president who does not provide effective leadership within the organization will not be an effective advocate to outside constituents.

The Role of the President in External Relations

Harry L. Peterson
President
Western State College of Colorado

To what degree legislators, alumni, donors, and others support a specific school, college, or university greatly depends on how well the president has articulated a vision for the institution. The advancement team can then help promote that vision. Often, this involves overcoming a certain skepticism about higher education in general. Part of this skepticism is due to a lack of understanding of our enterprise. The more that influential people know about us, the more helpful they will be when it is time to ask for their support.

CHANGING PUBLIC VIEWS OF HIGHER EDUCATION

This century has seen the role of colleges and universities in the United States evolve from serving as "finishing schools" for the leisure classes to becoming essential contributors to a democratic society and economy. The public attitude toward our enterprise has ranged from unquestioned support, beginning with the end of World War II, to one of increasing skepticism and scrutiny, particularly on the part of state and federal legislators.

Although most of us did not participate in the period of enormous growth in funding and enrollment immediately after World War II, we are perhaps too often affected by that history. We may misinterpret the current public mood of skepticism and conditional support for higher education as greediness and anti-intellectualism. For colleges and universities to thrive and obtain the public and private support they deserve, we must understand current public attitudes toward higher education. We must skillfully mobilize support for our enterprise, using the concepts and skills we teach our students in government, marketing, and communications classes.

THE ROLE OF THE PRESIDENT

The role of the president in this activity is crucial. Just as there are tasks that only the president can undertake inside a college or university, only the president can successfully carry out certain responsibilities in governmental and community relations.

Often, these assignments are difficult for presidents. Typically, presidents have experienced their professional lives inside colleges and universities. They have started as professors and become department chairs, deans, and academic vice presidents. Although many new presidents have a natural aptitude for external relations work, others find it alien and "political." To presidents with such concerns, I would suggest they reconsider their experience within colleges and universities. They might be surprised to find they have had good and relevant training.

Institutions of higher education are loosely organized. They consist of constituent groups, faculty, staff, and students who often disagree among themselves about goals, priorities, and allocation of resources. Successful administration within such organizations requires skills in communication, listening, consensus building, and making conceptual sense out of what at times may appear to be chaos. These are political skills. Not surprisingly, the study of college and university presidents by Cohen and March, in their book *Leadership and Ambiguity*, reported that "mayor" was the metaphor for a college or university presidency chosen most frequently by the presidents they studied. A successful president must relate effectively to external constituents.

While there are many important strategies and techniques to successfully accomplish these tasks, I make two fundamental assumptions about the role of the president and the relationship between a college or university and its community.

The first assumption is that the primary job of the president is leadership. This includes creating a long-term vision and setting clear and achievable goals, consulting closely with faculty and staff and, where appropriate, board members, and working to achieve those goals. Although every presidency includes a certain number of management responsibilities, a president who does not provide effective leadership within the organization will not be an effective advocate to outside constituents.

The message must be understandable and achievable, consisting of no more than three or four elements. It must be a set of goals that make sense to community members, alumni, donors, and legislators. The goals must be consistent with their view of reality and address issues they believe important.

The second assumption is that there is no clear and simple differentiation between the college or university and the larger community. Our insti-

● ● ●
A president communicating mostly about changes in parking regulations, snow removal, and building management is not going to inspire internal support, donations from alumni, or legislative appropriations.

tutions of higher education interact with, and are shaped by, external forces, including community and national public opinion and priorities. College and university goals must reflect the concerns of the larger society and those goals must be described in ways that respond to those concerns.

Former Yale President Bart Giamatti once commented: "I have always been amused by people who thought the university was some kind of cloister. That's a myth academics promote in order to keep other people away from them. I have said over and over that the university is not a sanctuary from the rest of society but a tributary to it, because the worst thing that can happen is that you begin to believe your own mythology."

A president and the advancement team can only be successful for an extended period of time in government and community relations by being successful in leading the college or university. The president is working to enlist support from people who do not get their information about the college or university solely from the president. Legislators, local community leaders, and alumni interact with other members of the college or university who provide their own views of how the college is doing. If there is a lack of congruence between the president's version of how the organization is doing and where it is headed, the alternative version is most likely believed. The relationships that supporters have with others are likely to be more informal, of longer standing and, hence, be more credible.

Advancement staff members may be part of that informal network. They may have been at the institution much longer than the president has been. They may be graduates or have been employed in the community. As such, they can serve as useful conduits for the president.

ELEMENTS OF A SUCCESSFUL PROGRAM

In my experience, a successful government and community relations program features the following elements:

■ *Effective Communication.* I have already emphasized the need for clear and understandable goals. The president should not assume the faculty, staff, and students—or external constituents—understand these goals. The goals must be repeated again and again in internal newsletters, speeches, and alumni publications. The best way for a president to determine if he or she is communicating effectively is to review comments made in newsletters, alumni publications, speeches, and internal memos for the past year. Do they address important goals of the organization, or are they primarily about management issues? A president communicating mostly about changes in parking regulations, snow removal, and building management is not going to inspire internal support, donations from alumni, or legislative appropriations.

■ *Ability to Listen.* Communication goes both ways. Most people who want to talk to you about your institution care about it, often deeply. In fact, the commitment of community members or alumni to their college or university is often for life. These individuals may be seeking confirmation that the president, and members of the advancement team—most of whom probably came from somewhere else— are as committed. They want to tell you about their experiences, good and bad, and about the unique history of the place they love. Get a dozen people who know about the college or university in a room and ask them to tell you about their institution. Confine your role to asking questions and soliciting more information. The results will be helpful and can be surprising. The participants also will be pleased they were asked for their insights and advice. And don't forget staff. If a president does not encourage staff to give blunt advice, that president will fail.

At institutions with a troubled history of external relations, new presidents and institutional advancement staff members may interpret the deep unhappiness and occasional bitterness as permanent disillusionment with the college or university. This would be a mistake. Most alumni, legislators, and community members are prepared to support the institution again. As in all relationships, however, they must be convinced that things will be different

and that they will be listened to. It takes special patience of the president and the advancement staff to repair these relationships, but it is worth the time. Often supporters will renew their support with greater enthusiasm than ever, wanting to make up for the lost time.

■ *Ability to Develop Allies.* It is common for a president to feel beleaguered and alone when dealing with a problem or trying to achieve a goal. You are not alone. There are people prepared to help if you seek their help and will be flattered you asked. Community leaders have an important stake in your institution's success. Successful alumni are proud of their institution. Newspaper editors are key leaders, particularly in smaller communities. Properly informed, they can inform and shape public opinion.

There are unlikely allies who can help as well. Constituents of higher education often have specific interest in programs offered by campuses. This fact is often overlooked, because presidents understandably tend to focus on the entire organization. Athletic boosters, agribusiness leaders, accountants, media professionals, and others who graduated from your institution can be enormously helpful in specific ways. Some of them have relationships with legislators and donors—and credibility in those relationships—that a president will never have. For this reason, it is very important to think not only of the larger college or university when seeking help, but also of specific programs and the people who care about those programs.

■ *A Program Built on Strengths.* The organization you lead has probably existed for a long time. An important job of an institutional leader is identifying its strengths and history and building on those elements. There are reasons why the college or university has that unique history and those strengths. The people you will be asking for help understand that history and they want you to honor it. It is why they care about the place.

Vartan Gregorian, president of the Carnegie Foundation and former president of Brown University, served as president of the New York Public Library in the 1980s. He said that he carefully reflected on the history and character of

New York City before choosing goals for the library. He realized that the people of New York City liked things that were big and ambitious, consistent with the history of that city. He chose a fund-raising goal for the library that some thought was far too ambitious for what seemed to be a declining institution. He believes he was successful because he chose a goal that was congruent with the history of New York and challenged the city to live up to that history.

BUILDING A SUCCESSFUL PROGRAM

Here is advice to remember in executing a successful program of governmental and community relations.

■ *Thank helpers.* This may seem obvious. Maybe because institutional leaders believe their projects are so important, and their merits so obvious, that accomplishing the goal is sufficient without thanking those who helped. However, legislators need to be thanked because they stand for election every few years. Alumni and other supporters are enormously flattered by private and public expressions of thanks from their college or university, particularly when expressed by the president. College and university presidents have the respect and admiration of the public, particularly among people who care about the institution.

■ *Work with people beyond the obvious leaders.* Younger, more junior individuals may have more time to devote to your cause than more senior people. Also, annual donors become major donors. Back benchers in the legislature become leaders. Newspaper reporters become editors. Young professionals in organizations become senior managers of those organizations.

■ *Don't whine.* People want to work for something important. They want to help make your institution better, not just fix problems. They want to be a part of something bigger than themselves. Convey a vision for your college or university with which they can identify. Focus on opportunities, not problems.

■ *Start locally.* When people consider running for public office, they first seek support from their friends and then work to expand their base.

Before you develop projects and firm ideas, spend time with local community members, alumni, and legislators. Ask them to help shape your ideas and the plans will be stronger as a result. If the people who are close to the institution can understand your idea, you may be able to explain it to people who are not as close or involved. If these people tell you your proposal is not a good one, maybe it isn't!

■ *Don't burn bridges.* It has been said that, in politics, there are no permanent friends and no permanent allies. While some view this statement cynically, it simply means that support will come from one source for a particular project and from another source for a different proposal. A donor or legislator who does not support your proposal may be there the next time you ask. Be certain to behave in a way that allows you to approach that person the next time. Do not assume that people who do not agree with you are badly motivated.

■ *Keep in touch.* Seeking help from community members, legislators, and donors involves building relationships. In any relationship, no one likes to be approached only when they are needed. They like to know what is going on at their institution. Community leaders, donors, and legislators appreciate being involved and consulted with at times when they are not being asked to help directly.

This involvement should be formal as well as informal. At Western State College, we are members of the local "Mayors and Managers," an informal collection of city and county officials who meet regularly to share issues and concerns. We also have a College Advisory Council, composed of key citizens in our area who are kept informed about college programs and problems and who provide advice on those issues. Membership in local chambers of commerce and other groups is also important.

■ *Involve others.* There are certain roles that only the president can perform. Other functions are left to staff members who are delegated those responsibilities. However, there are many others within your college or university who can help. Faculty members, in particular, have invariably played a crucial role with graduates of your institution. Often these individuals were there long before you arrived. At your next alumni function, listen carefully. Your graduates will not only talk about the institution, generally, but about faculty members who shaped their lives and whom they will never forget.

EDUCATION IS DIFFERENT

I began by noting that competition for public and private funds and community support is intense and that unquestioning allegiance to higher education can no longer be assumed. We are inevitably competing for public dollars with public school education, the correctional system, and other public concerns. The share of the budget devoted to public higher education has declined in virtually every state in the nation in the last 20 years. A college education, once rare, has been earned by more than 25 percent of the adult population of our country. Universal access to higher education, the dream of many who preceded us in our work, has nearly been achieved. However, the awe with which a college degree was once regarded, perhaps by our parents, has diminished.

This has caused some to be disheartened. We should not be. The clear evidence is that college and university attendance is valued highly by the American public. Indeed, the greatest concern among the public about higher education is not whether their sons and daughters should attend college, but whether they can afford it. We work in one of the most valued activities in American life. There continues to be much support for our work, both politically and financially. However, we cannot assume that support will be there for every project we think worthy. We must communicate clearly about those important ideas and projects. We must listen to what our critics, most of them friendly, are saying about how we can improve our enterprise.

I have referred to the fact that some presidents, and others in higher education, may find this work slightly distasteful and "political." It is true that we go to our country's capitols for our appropriations, and to donors for private contributions. In that regard, we are like many other causes. However, the tradition we are working to continue when we undertake these activities is unlike any other.

An important part of the tradition of higher education, especially in the United States, is protection from the daily political forces that press upon other organizations. We say that we are different in higher education, and should be treated differently. To demonstrate that, we must act as though we are different. Our relations with the public, community members, alumni, legislators, and governing boards must be impeccable.

It is most important that we behave in ways that are consistent with what we say we believe and that we be timely and accurate in our communications. Because our "product" is ideas, we must be persuasive with the facts. If, in our efforts to promote our institution, we act like just another lobbying group or fund-raising cause, we do great harm to our institutions.

In much of our promotion of higher education, we are harvesting the work of those who preceded us. Donors are more likely to give if they see their college or university going in a good direction, one consistent with its history and tradition. They give because of faculty and staff who worked with them—individuals who, for the most part, made those contributions before we arrived. We must contribute to and perpetuate that legacy.

REFERENCES AND FURTHER READINGS

Cohen, Michael D. and James G. March. *Leadership and Ambiguity.* Berkeley, CA: Carnegie Commission on Higher Education, 1974.

Giamatti, A. Bartlett. "A Free and Ordered Space: The Real World of the University." Gannett Center for Media Studies' 5th Annual Leadership Institute (June, 19, 1989.) New York: Gannett Center for Media Studies, 1989.

Goodall, Leonard E., ed. *When Colleges Lobby States.* Washington, DC: American Association of State Colleges and Universities, 1987.

Immerwahr, John and James Harvey. "What the Public Thinks of Colleges," *Chronicle of Higher Education* (May 12, 1995.)

Murphy, Mary Kay. *The Advancement President and the Academy.* Washington, DC: American Council on Education/ORYX Press, 1997.

Rhodes, Frank H. T. "The Art of the Presidency." Washington, DC: American Council on Education. Spring, 1998.

As we enter the 21st century, the role of institutional leaders in advancement is firmly based in bridge building. They are the shapers and stewards of the university's human and capital resources.

The Role of Academic Leaders in Advancement

Mary Kay Murphy
Vice President for Institutional Advancement
Morris Brown College

African-American writer Ralph Ellison observed that "Education is a matter of building bridges." As we enter the 21st century, the role of institutional leaders in advancement is firmly based in bridge building. They are the shapers and stewards of the university's human and capital resources. The academic deans and department chairs and faculty are the heart of the institution's advocacy program. With presidents, governing board members, and development officers, they form a partnership to advance education. Combining their diverse talents, perspectives, and experiences, they extend their reach to multiple constituencies to advance the mission of the school, college, or university—to build bridges wherever bridges need to be built.

SETTING ACADEMIC PRIORITIES

Deans, department chairs, and faculty operate in a different space and time than do the leaders of institutional advancement. The first bridge that needs to be built is between these two entities of the university—those who teach and those who promote teaching. As the ancient Chinese proverb reminds us, "The journey of a thousand miles

begins with the first step." Advancement professionals take their first and most important step when they work with academic leaders to help set achievable and realistic institutional and academic priorities.

Strategic planning, long the centerpiece of a strong institutional administration, is the cornerstone of focused, systematic, private fund raising. Academic priorities grow out of effective strategic planning. Implicit in the planning process is the continuous review of progress toward the institution's goals, a continuing evaluation and analysis of costs associated with raising money for academic priorities, and timelines related to their achievement.

Setting academic priorities is vital to identifying prospects for support and funding. Without them, donor interests cannot be properly cultivated and donors cannot be appropriately solicited for gifts. At all levels of the institution, donors give in one of two ways, gifts restricted to specific purposes and unrestricted gifts to be used at the discretion of campus leaders. Both types of gifts are important, and both are needed.

Increasingly, donors participate in the planning process. Most often, they participate as trustees of the institution or as alumni leaders on advisory boards in departments, schools, and colleges. They work hand in hand with academic leaders and advancement professionals, building confidence and trust so invaluable to soliciting others' contributions. Donors want to know that their investment will make a difference, not just tomorrow but five or 10 years down the road.

Donors also want to know that the program they are funding has an institutional priority—not just with the faculty member whose work is being funded or with the dean whose facility is being built. They want to know that the project advances the institution's mission and enhances its academic standing among educational peers. How, for example, do the goals of the capital campaign position a school, college, or university to meet institutional objectives? How do the academic priorities relate to positioning the institution to deliver better teaching, research, and public service?

Linking academic priorities to institutional planning results in four primary benefits:

1. It establishes a long-term planning time frame—one that extends out five years or more.
2. It requires that strategic planning be an ongoing, integral activity that engages the whole community, including deans, faculty, department heads, and development officers.
3. It forges ties to external groups that support the college or university. It engages those groups in an ongoing review of priorities and progress toward achieving strategic goals.
4. It enlarges the pool of prospective donors who support the priorities identified in the strategic plan. These include individual, corporate, and foundation donors as well as local, state, and federal government agencies and their respective leaders.

THE ROLES OF TEAM MEMBERS IN ACHIEVING STRATEGIC OBJECTIVES

All members of the institution's strategic planning team participate as the institution moves strategic initiatives from the planning phase to implementation. To begin with, those professionals with communications and marketing expertise must find ways to make a clear and compelling case for institutional needs to both internal and external constituencies. They must help create a climate of support for academic priorities among such diverse constituencies as students, legislators, faculty, and foundation leaders. They must position the institution and its leadership for success.

Complementing their work is the communication from academic leaders themselves—particularly deans, department chairs, and faculty. Apart from their roles in forming program goals and objectives, they often directly communicate with potential donors and supporters, relating in more detail the academic needs that must be met. They can put donors and sponsors directly in touch with students and other beneficiaries of the proposed new initiatives. The dean's role is pivotal. He or she must put a name and a face on the project. The dean must commit time and energy to advocate for it and understand that the project is a long-term commitment—often three to five years or more.

Department chairs and faculty members also have special roles to play, especially when the donors or potential donors are alumni. Their closeness to the curriculum, their knowledge of the students and their fields, their relationships with alumni, their professional reputations, and their visibility with important constituencies make them invaluable to the fund-raising process.

FORGING INTERNAL ALLIANCES

One of the major challenges for academic leaders is to create internal consensus for academic priorities. Each project or program will have its own advocates among deans, department chairs, faculty members, and alumni. But all must come together to determine how those priorities fit into integrated programs. Within the current or emerging goals in the strategic planning process, where do these priorities fit? How do they advance the mission of the college or university? To what program niche or marketing strategy do they relate? How do they mesh with institutional goals in enrollment management, research, continuing education, undergraduate and graduate recruitment, faculty disciplines, academic reputation, student demographics, and trustee and donor support?

Academic leaders, with the president and

> ● ● ●
> **One of the major challenges for academic leaders is to create internal consensus for academic priorities.**

members of his or her cabinet, set academic priorities. Helping to achieve those priorities in concert with academic leaders is the role of advancement leaders. This is especially complicated at large, decentralized institutions where many departments or colleges within the university have their own advancement professionals. Building bridges between internal constituencies is vital. When done well, it is one hallmark of successful institutional advancement programs.

FORGING EXTERNAL ALLIANCES TO ACHIEVE ACADEMIC PRIORITIES

A key step toward reaching academic goals is successful stewardship of current donors to these programs. The best prospects for future gifts are current donors. A vital part of securing additional gifts from current donors is making sure they are informed about the use of their funds and about the success achieved as a result of their investment.

Donors may want to be involved in the work of the academic department or school. Consider inviting them to serve as external advisers either informally or as members of an external advisory board. Increasingly, academic units have come to rely on boards of visitors that meet periodically to review the unit's programs and progress, and to marshal support for that academic unit. Members of such boards often accompany the dean or department chair, and an advancement officer, on calls to prospective donors. They can make persuasive arguments, especially if they themselves are donors to the department and have seen the impact of their gifts at close range. Such boards of visitors have become fertile fields in which to cultivate the next generation of college trustees.

Some prospective donors might prefer to give a lecture to a class in their area of expertise or host a college event at their home or place of business. Whatever the mode of cultivation, the process

helps determine the fit between the individual and the institution—the fit between the institutional opportunity and the interests of the donor.

The process ends where it began, with academic leaders working with advancement professionals to build bridges of support for the institution. The pilings on which those bridges are built include trust, confidence, mutual respect, integrity, and ethics. There is no greater work or any higher calling than building bridges of support for education. It is its own reward.

Alice Duer Miller put it best at a 1939 dinner celebrating the 50th anniversary of Barnard College. "Don't ever dare to take your college (education) as a matter of course," she said, "because, like democracy and freedom, many people you'll never know . . . have broken their hearts to get it for you."

FURTHER READINGS

Bryson, John M. *Strategic Planning for Public and Nonprofit Organizations: A Guide to Strengthening and Sustaining Organizational Achievement.* 2nd ed. San Francisco, CA: Jossey-Bass Publishers, 1995.

Hall, Margarete Rooney. *The Dean's Role in Fund Raising.* Baltimore, MD: Johns Hopkins University Press, 1993.

Hunt, Carle M. et al. *Strategic Planning for Private Higher Education.* Binghamton, NY: Haworth Press, Inc., 1997.

Keller, George. *Academic Strategy.* Baltimore, MD: Johns Hopkins University Press, 1983.

Murphy, Mary Kay. *Building Bridges: Fund Raising for Deans, Faculty, and Development Officers.* Washington, DC: Council for Advancement and Support of Education, 1992.

Murphy, Mary Kay. "Multiply and be Fruitful: Making the Most of Deans and Faculty in Development," CURRENTS 19, no. 8 (September 1993): 49-52.

Nahm, Rick and Robert M. Zemsky. "The Role of Institutional Planning in Fund-Raising," *Trusteeship* 3, no. 3 (May/June 1995): 22-26.

Worth, Michael J, ed. *Educational Fund Raising: Principles and Practice.* Phoenix, AZ: ACE/Oryx Press, 1993.

Being viewed as a leader by the media is much like picking the low-hanging fruit—all we have to do is to stretch out our hands.

Institutional Leaders and the Media Community: Forging a Strong Relationship

Sharon Kha
Associate Vice President for Communications
University of Arizona

You could feel the tension in the large lecture hall. The media covered the talk. The vice president for research, a research biologist himself, was answering questions from a largely hostile crowd about the value of the research that depended on laboratory rats to validate results.

A woman in the audience became increasingly agitated as he described what could be learned from examining brains and livers and kidneys of rats that had received promising new drugs. She clearly believed the vice president was a lost soul and sought to make him aware of his fate if he didn't repent soon.

"What are you going to say when you meet God?" the woman asked in a trembling, angry voice.

The vice president looked thoughtful for a moment. "I hope he's not a rodent," he said.

I felt as though I were watching the long, slow trajectory of a Molotov cocktail being lobbed right into the middle of my precariously balanced public relations plan for the animal research issue. I could see the headlines in the morning paper, the outraged letters to the editor, a chiding editorial about the university's flippant attitude about serious questions.

Animal research had been in the news a lot. Two fires had been set and two labs had been trashed. Twelve hundred rats and mice had been stolen by the Animal Liberation Front. The media had been supportive of the university so far, but the carefully crafted messages could come crashing down.

The next morning I picked up the paper with my eyes averted, trying to see with peripheral vision if there was a bad headline. When I couldn't make out the word "rat" or "God" anywhere, I let my eyes slide across the page. There was an innocuous headline about the lecture on the bottom half of the Metro section. The potentially inflammatory remark was buried. Neither the vice president nor I received so much as a complaint call.

What is it that blows some stories sky high and lets others float to the ground as lightly as a thistle? Dumb luck is one answer; leadership is another.

The vice president in this case was perceived as a leader in the media community. When things were at their worst, and the embers of the arson fires were literally still warm, he talked to people. He was available. He answered questions calmly and fully, and he talked more about the value of the

Institutional
Leaders and
the Media
Community:
Forging a Strong
Relationship

research projects that had been interrupted than about his anger at the arson and vandalism. Nobody was looking for an opportunity to make him look foolish.

The fact is that along with our many other responsibilities at the institutions where we work, there is yet another role for institutional leaders to play: assuming leadership in the media community. It is not enough to represent our institutions or departments well. We must also look for opportunities to lead; we must build up personal and intellectual capital with the community. It isn't only the responsibility of the campus news office. People throughout the institution do and should have relationships with reporters and editors. It is the way to build respect and trust that can sustain the campus during difficult times.

In some senses, the attributes of leadership are visited upon those of us in advancement offices without our asking for them. When reporters have a difficult story with contradictory information, they turn to the university for information that makes their story credible. The media are constantly looking for experts to lend perspective on stories. There is something about the quest for and dissemination of truth that strikes a respectful chord among academics and journalists alike.

Being viewed as a leader by the media is much like picking the low-hanging fruit—all we have to do is to stretch out our hands. Often, however, we keep our hands firmly in our pockets. This is especially true of university administrators who don't have a lot of confidence in the media, or who may not want to appear self-aggrandizing. Those same administrators, however, often get frustrated when their own programs and priorities are not given just due by the local newspaper or TV station.

Therein lies one danger about harvesting the fruits of leadership: if we only reach out because we are greedy for the results, we are likely to glean crab apples.

TAKING THE LEAD WITH MEDIA

So how do institutional leaders, and especially public relations professionals, establish leadership with the media that isn't blatantly self-interested?

■ Help media outlets succeed in reaching their own charitable goals. You see it all the time—the news anchors make an earnest appeal for blankets for the homeless, toys for the children or clothes for a family that is burned out of its home. College campuses are full of idealists—take the lead. Make your office the collection point for blankets or toys; deliver the items to the television or radio station yourself. Make it clear that the people at the university are part of the broader community.

■ Use your own media connections to mentor students and help them find opportunities for internships. It is just a matter of a few years before the junior you introduced to the city desk editor will be covering the university beat and calling you for information. A high school student that I once invited to ride along with me on a television shoot and give me a "three-two-one" countdown became the anchorwoman for the evening news. My investment 10 years ago wasn't much, but the positive feelings that accrued paid me back for years.

■ Weave yourself into the life of the community by joining service clubs, volunteering for community projects such as United Way, and attending fund-raising events that address major issues within your community. Let community leaders, many of whom are connected to the media, know that their priorities matter.

The University of Arizona has a coach that does that. The basketball coach has a spotless image. But one morning, the headlines on the front page announced that he had been caught in wrongdoing. The paper reported that he had paid an outrageous price for basketball uniforms because the company who manufactured the uniforms paid him $10,000 a year to be their consultant.

The story was dead wrong. First of all, the coach had paid about the same as everyone else for uniforms; the reporter had looked at the wrong column of numbers in researching the story. Second, when the company that retained him as a consultant acquired the company that made the basketball uniforms, the coach resigned as a consultant. He was squeaky clean.

It took 4.3 nanoseconds after the story hit

Institutional
Leaders and
the Media
Community:
Forging a Strong
Relationship

until we started hearing that the coach was so steamed he was considering job offers elsewhere. While the news office was scurrying about trying to get a fact sheet together, the university attorney was doing a slow burn himself. The facts of the story were wrong and he knew it.

Without any fanfare, he drove to the newspaper building and asked to speak to the editor. Behind closed doors, the attorney laid out the true story. The next morning, the front page had a story of exactly the same size as the previous day's story. This time, the headline said: "Star Apologizes." The paper laid out the real facts and admitted that it had been very wrong. The apology was deeply satisfying.

Two kinds of leadership were exerted that morning. First, the attorney had an existing relationship with the editor of the paper, even though it wasn't his job to deal with the media. Second, the coach had made himself a citizen of our community by cheerfully doing public service announcements for innumerable local charities, hosting fund-raising dinners, and generally helping the community achieve its own goals. Those who knew the coach because of his participation in the community found it hard to believe that he would have been involved in an underhanded deal and were madder than wet hens when they found out it was all the mistake of an over-eager reporter.

By the morning of the third day, the telephone lines to the newspaper were jammed. Hundreds of people called to cancel subscriptions. Car dealerships canceled huge blocks of advertising. By the end of the year, the three people at the newspaper most involved in the story had found jobs elsewhere.

Why don't we get that kind of response every time the media gets a story wrong? Well, OK, so we aren't all popular basketball coaches. But this coach got an extraordinary response in large part because he was perceived to be a leader outside the basketball arena.

Weaving ourselves into the life of the community is an opportunity that advancement officers cannot afford to ignore. If we want the community to consider us as an essential part of their lives, we must pay attention to the needs of our neighbors.

● ● ●

Let community leaders, many of whom are connected to the media, know that their priorities matter.

Unfortunately, our university presidents, deans, and faculty often live in a global academic community with more intensity than they live in their own neighborhoods. They flash daily e-mails around the globe to colleagues, and attend national and international meetings. But the fact that there is a shortage of food in their local food bank often eludes them. National recognition is gratifying, but it's how the local PTA views us that may make the most difference to the amount of support we get from the people we serve. If the university is going to truly advance, the university community needs to be better neighbors.

Almost every advancement person has the same story to tell. The trustees or the chancellor or the faculty or the deans are unhappy with the quantity and quality of attention the university gets from the media.

"We're the best kept secret in the state," they say. "We've got to get the word out there!" (This is usually accompanied by a broad sweep of the arm.) "Nobody knows about all the positive things that happen in this place."

And so news directors measure column inches, publish information about the latest rankings, and send news clips to administrators. And still the complaints go on. People at cocktail parties rant and rave about the failings of the university.

In fact, goodwill from the community will never be measured in column inches, and the cocktail party stories will continue to gall university leaders regardless of the good press about the latest research awards. What does change attitudes is the institution's willingness to take on a leadership role in the community, even if it isn't in its immediate self interest.

Leadership that translates into support in the media community is low hanging fruit. Reach out. Pluck it. The harvest is sweet and worth your while.

FURTHER READINGS

Carter, Lindy Keane. "Communicating in a Crisis: The Good News is that Candor, Credibility, and Cool Heads Can Keep the Bad News from Getting Worse," CURRENTS 13, no. 10 (November/December 1987): 14-18,20.

CASE. *Classic Currents: Media Relations Practice: Working With Reporters, Broadcast Media, International Public*

Relations. Washington, DC: Council for Advancement and Support of Education, 1998.

Geuder Maridith Walker. "Convincing Your Faculty: Specific Steps to Show the Value of Talking with Reporters," Currents 20, no. 9 (October 1994): 15.

"Just the Facts: Campus PR Pros Must Be Active in Assuring Accurate Reporting," CURRENTS 24, no. 4 (April 1998): 7.

● ● ●

At successful campuses, all administrators take ownership of the goals and needs of the institution—from faculty compensation to student recruitment—and they talk freely and often to each other and to both internal and external constituencies in an effort to solve problems.

Internal Communications: A Two-Way Street

Terry Shepard
Vice President for Public Affairs
Rice University

Debra J. Thomas
Director of Public Relations
Jesse H. Jones Graduate School of Management, Rice University

The public relations unit within institutional advancement usually has the responsibility for the public's awareness of the good (and bad) result of actions by all people, at all levels, all the time. Public relations are neither more nor less than how our publics perceive us. And how our publics perceive us can never be controlled, or even greatly influenced, solely by those who are assigned titles that carry some responsibility for that perception.

A potent technique that makes every administrator a partner in public relations and institutional advancement is simply two-way communications. We need to talk to one another.

THE COMMUNICATIONS FLOW

Past reviews at universities and colleges, large and small, private and public, helped form our perspective for this chapter. However otherwise distinctive each institution is from another, where there is success, it stems from a good flow in communications and a common understanding of institutional priorities. Where there are problems, there is a stark and simple common problem: those on the administrative team aren't talking to each other.

Good presidents take their messages far beyond their cabinet room; effective vice presidents communicate across the campus. At successful campuses, all administrators take ownership of the goals and needs of the institution—from faculty compensation to student recruitment—and they talk freely and often to each other and to both internal and external constituencies in an effort to solve problems.

EXAMPLES TO LIVE BY

To illustrate the power of talking, or not talking to each other, here are several case studies that include solutions:

1. A president criticized a vice president of university relations for letting "her" people print newspaper and magazine articles the president found unsupportive. Her news staff, on the other hand, felt that university leaders were stifling their freedom to "tell it as they saw it." Caught in the middle, the VP realized that her news staff didn't have enough access and information to really understand the university. She began a monthly series of lunches during which the president, provost, deans, and other university leaders talk informally with the news staff about their operations, challenges, and priorities. The mutual education is paying dividends

in ensuring media coverage that satisfies the concerns of all parties.

2. The new public relations director of a small college quickly diagnosed a major problem confronting the school and its public image: lack of good communication and trust among the senior management team. The college was experiencing financial problems and was on accreditation probation. The president wasn't all that committed to the school; the faculty was unhappy; and other administrators complained openly about the president and conditions at the college. Many of the leaders with whom the new staff member talked criticized others on the management team and the college.

The director's assignment: *Mission Impossible*. He was asked to help build enrollment by increasing the visibility and attractiveness of the college. But talking more widely, the director found that the faculty was truly committed to teaching and was very good at it. Students felt the college gave them a second chance to succeed. He created public relations themes around the caring faculty, and around the college as a place where personal attention to the students helps them succeed. The campaign was a success but only after overcoming obstacles that the leaders and faculty created for themselves.

3. Talking to each other results in a mutual understanding of how institutional administrators can help each other. A senior forum on student-to-student sexual assaults, sponsored by the Council for Advancement and Support of Education, brought together deans of student life and public relations professionals. At the end of a useful day, one dean thanked CASE for inviting the deans, saying he'd never realized how much public relations could help—or hurt—an institution because he had always been focused on students. From that time on, the dean and the communications director met regularly to discuss students and student concerns. The dean gave the director many media opportunities by telling her about unusually interesting programs and

students, ideas for magazine articles, and the like. The director was able to address the dean's concerns in recruitment publications, thereby helping to prepare students for college life even before they enrolled. The two offices created a new publication—a parents' newsletter with something of a difference. Rather than rehash news about the university, available in other publications sent to parents, this newsletter addressed the ways parents can make their children's college experience more meaningful, including tough advice about when to leave the kids alone.

4. Talking together also breeds trust. At another CASE senior forum for legal counsel and public relations professionals, many participants were startled to hear one institutional lawyer declare that she would never tell her communications people anything for fear that they would leak it to the media. Whatever the origin of such mistrust, that university is not served well by either its counsel or its public relations people. Lawyers are necessary legal protectors; public relations people are necessary interpreters of the public mood. Getting the two together and creating a mutual bond of trust and respect gives them both a context for decision making and thereby better serves the institution.

COMMUNICATIONS: A TWO-WAY STREET

Talking, of course, includes listening. When people say: "No one tells me anything," they often mean: "No one asks my advice." A public relations officer who feels no one tells her anything may not be asking for the advice she needs. Institutional advancement people need everyone's advice. And all administrators need to keep their communications people in the loop. It is every bit as important that we know the "whys" of a decision as it is to know the "whats." Without that knowledge, the spokesperson does not understand and can say little that will help the institution.

By now, you may be thinking that all this communication sounds wonderful but it is totally unrealistic in the busy world of running our educa-

● ● ●
A potent technique that makes every administrator a partner in public relations and institutional advancement is simply two-way communications. We need to talk to one another.

tional institutions. You would be happy if your deans, public safety officials, and other administrators would simply come to you before talking to reporters. Many communications people try to set themselves up as gatekeepers or filters as the only contact with the news media. A few even succeed. Even if this works with the media, it won't stop people from talking to everyone else. An education reporter once called a public relations person to take him to task for not telling her about the closing of some graduate departments of which he was unaware. The reporter had learned about it from someone at a nearby college!

Acting as a media gatekeeper or filter can never be enough. All administrators need to talk to their communications people and, preferably, be trained by them to talk to the media. Each institutional leader needs to recognize that advancing the whole institution is part of his or her job. What administrators say about their institution to neighbors, professional associates, or mere acquaintances can have far more impact than a front-page story in the local newspaper.

Sure, the professional staff with the training and the skills can guide the way when appropriate, but just as the head, chancellor, or president of the institution is the chief public relations professional, so too is every member of his or her administration involved with advancement. Learn from each other. Be humble and generous, and avoid the hubris of believing any one of us is the expert and the only expert.

FURTHER READINGS

Council for Advancement and Support of Education. *Creating Campus Community: A CASE Issues Paper for Advancement Professionals,* No. 10. Washington, DC: CASE, 1992.

Denbow, Terry. "Breaking Out of the Box: How to Stop Closing Yourself Off from Reality," CURRENTS 17, no. 2 (February 1991): 6-10.

Hale, Don. "High-Tech PR: Five Case Studies in Computerized Communications: A Campuswide Network Helps Carnegie Mellon Shop Around for Better Internal Communications," CURRENTS 19, no. 4 (April 1993): 18-19.

Shoemaker, Donna. "They Pledge Allegiance: PR People and Their Presidents Tell How They Forge a Bond Through Open, Honest Communication," CURRENTS 19, no. 9 (October 1993): 20-23.

Stubbee, Melinda. "The FAQs on Intranets: You've Heard of These Hot New Tools. Now Consider Whether Building One Can Make Internal Communication on Your Campus Easier, Faster, and Cheaper," CURRENTS 23, no. 7 (July/August 1997): 18-20, 22.

*A student's personal story of how the school or college
has treated him or her is worth 100 brochures or news
stories. And an alumna's testimonial to the difference
the school has made to her life and career is worth a
dozen job fairs.*

Students and Alumni: Important Partners in Institutional Leadership

Bruce Darling
Vice President, University and External Relations
University of California

Linda Weimer
Vice President for University Relations
University of Wisconsin System

When we think of institutional leaders, we are tempted to look solely at those in the president's or chancellor's cabinet. But presidents and advancement professionals, perhaps more than others in academia, know that two of the most important partners in institutional leadership are students and alumni.

Students and alumni are considered together in this chapter because they are two sides of the same coin. Increasingly, we have come to realize that student leaders often become alumni leaders. But beyond that, they can serve some of the same roles for the institution. And what is good advice when working with alumni is often good advice when working with students. There is also great benefit in bringing alumni leaders and student leaders together. They can educate each other and reinforce an affection for our institutions in ways that we cannot.

A student's personal story of how the school or college has treated him or her is worth 100 brochures or news stories. And an alumna's testimonial to the difference the school has made in her life and career is worth a dozen job fairs.

In chronicling the many kinds of alumni and student leaders, the men and women who serve on our boards of trustees or regents come immediately to mind. Their leadership is critical. They select the president. They must concur in the appointment of the institution's officers. They approve the budget, tuition and fees, admission standards, building projects, and a myriad of other programs and policies that determine the future direction of the school. In private institutions, and with some exceptions, public institutions as well, they also pick their successors. The influence that they have on the institutions they serve is profound. Alumni are commonly found on an institution's governing board. Students less often serve in that capacity but a growing number of schools have added students to their governing boards.

Advancement professionals know that trustees serve another extremely important function for our institutions—they are the chief volunteers, institutional consciences, fund raisers, donors, mentors, friends, and sometimes, loving critics. They are ambassadors for the institution and most often bring to the table distinguished careers in business, law, medicine, politics, and public service that can contribute to the institution's credibility.

There are other alumni leaders in our institutions as well. The alumni board, the foundation board, and alumni who are engaged in mentoring students and faculty as members of "boards of advisers" in individual departments and schools are a few examples.

This latter group often plays a key role in fund raising, serving with deans, directors, and department chairs to spearhead targeted campaigns and to call on donor prospects. Another role, though less apparent, is also critical. Alumni and student leaders connect the campus to the community.

COMMUNITY CONNECTIONS

One outstanding example of how alumni can strengthen ties to a community is at the University of California, San Diego. An arts committee, composed of community leaders and alumni, decided to help make the university more visible in the arts community. The group organized an annual dinner event that has become an important way to connect student and faculty artists with community arts patrons.

Each year, about 300 people attend a dinner held at the university. Faculty art is displayed in the art gallery and attendees can visit student and faculty studios. After the dinner, there is a student dramatic or musical performance. This has become a "can't miss" event for city arts officials, museum leaders, foundation trustees, and other civic leaders—all thanks to the efforts of the UC San Diego Board of Overseers.

This is just one of hundreds of roles that alumni play in bringing the university and the San Diego community together. Alumni who are civic leaders tap faculty and students to help solve city problems; alumni in business and industry involve faculty and students in their research and development programs; alumni draft faculty and staff to serve on the boards of nonprofit agencies and to help in the community's United Way campaign.

Alumni leaders in the community also involve the university or college when special events take place. When San Diego hosted the Republican National Convention, a member of the foundation board chaired the city's nonpartisan host committee. Another alumni leader designed the convention space and the university hosted nonpartisan events

at its world-renowned aquarium and other facilities. When Los Angeles hosted the summer Olympics, UCLA hosted the tennis competition and provided housing for athletes. Other local universities also provided support. These were win-win situations for the cities and universities alike.

Students, too, play a critical role in community relations. Public service has long been central to a college education. On any given day, students can be found tutoring at local elementary schools; serving as interns at a nearby TV station; working in medical clinics for the indigent; reading to the elderly; and engaged in more structured programs like Americorps or Habitat for Humanity.

ALUMNI AS ADVISERS AND ADVOCATES

Alumni and student leaders also serve as trusted advisers to deans, department chairs, faculty, and other administrators on our campuses. Increasingly, presidents and chancellors are placing alumni leaders—and in some cases, student leaders—on search and screen committees when recruiting for senior positions. While this has long been standard practice in choosing an athletic director, it is now more common in choosing academic and administrative leaders, too.

Alumni who serve on search committees bring important professional experience to the committee and they are good judges of whether the candidates have the management and leadership skills to run a professional school or a research program. At the same time, this engagement provides alumni with a sense of deep and substantive involvement. They have a stake in the success of the chosen candidate, and a sense of commitment to the program that can be rewarding to both the college and the alumni.

When a school or university looks at major issues such as international education or enrollment management, alumni can play an advisory role. When UC San Diego created a new undergraduate college to focus on the making of the modern world, it consulted alumni and professional leaders who enriched the vision for the program and its development.

Schools and colleges also have been turning to alumni in the marketing and public relations

● ● ●

Time spent by administrators or advancement officers meeting regularly with student government leaders to keep them well informed is time well spent.

fields for advice and help. Often, alumni who own advertising, marketing, or survey research firms offer their services *pro bono* to their alma mater. They can help assess public awareness and opinion. They can help craft a plan based on the outcome of that research, and they can play a role in executing that plan to build a climate of support among key constituents.

ALUMNI AND POLITICS

Alumni provide a wealth of advice and influence in the political world. Many alumni serve, or have served, as local, state, and federal leaders or on the staffs of such leaders. It is important to identify and keep in touch with them on a regular basis. Then, when need be, the campus can seek their help when facing political challenges.

More and more, public institutions are creating alumni advocacy networks composed of influential citizens of the state who are willing to speak on behalf of these institutions when legislators determine budget appropriations or voters consider ballot measures.

A recent bond campaign in California illustrates the benefits of such involvement. On November 3, 1998, California voters passed the largest bond measure in the history of the United States. By a vote of 62.5 percent to 37.5 percent, they passed Proposition 1A, which provided $9.2 billion in funding over a four-year period to both K-12 and higher education. The bond measure provided $2.5 billion in funding for capital projects and infrastructure improvements in higher education, of which roughly $840 million funded building projects at the University of California.

Alumni leaders were involved in this project from the start. UC's alumni advocates worked with legislators to ensure that the controversial bond measure secured a place on the ballot. During the intense two-month campaign to inform voters about Prop 1A, alumni and campus leaders as well as members of the UC Board of Regents, were active participants.

Regents and campus foundation trustees attended civic gatherings and media events in support of Prop 1A, sent letters and opinion pieces to their local newspapers, and worked as advocates for Prop 1A's passage. They garnered contributions and endorsements for the Prop 1A campaign from business and civic leaders. The outcome was a successful campaign.

Alumni with political influence can attract distinguished public figures to the campus. A visit from the U.S. President, First Lady, Vice President, or a governor gives students an invaluable opportunity and brings recognition to the school. For example, an alumnus working for Vice President Al Gore persuaded him to hold a town meeting on the UC Berkeley campus early in 1997.

STUDENTS AS ADVISERS AND AMBASSADORS

Student leaders, our institutions' primary customers, are very important sources of advice and influence. Many university leaders have some formal or informal student advisory network. Student body presidents have long been included in commencements, convocations, and other ceremonial functions on campus. They also are likely to offer their views at the dean's conference table.

Alumni organizations have long recognized the benefits of involving students in their programs. In recent years, it has become common to involve students in fund-raising, public relations, and advocacy programs as well. For example, the Council for Advancement and Support of Education (CASE) has a staff member in its Washington, DC headquarters who serves as the leader of the Association of Student Advancement Programs (ASAP), an organization for more than 3,000 institutions of higher education interested in student advancement programs.

ASAP functions primarily as a communication link among student alumni associations, student foundations, and other institutional advancement programs (such as ambassador and spirit groups) throughout North America. It sponsors an annual international convention, produces a membership directory and various handbooks, and publishes the *Advancement Quarterly* newsletter. More information is available at *www.case.org/asap.*

Students are very effective ambassadors and advocates for schools and colleges. As tour guides on campuses, they win over prospective students and their families with personal stories of campus life. They also make effective advocates with opinion leaders.

The University of California makes a point of bringing together legislators and students in informal settings where they can learn from each other. A student's view of the high quality of teaching and mentoring he or she is getting on a big research campus can allay a legislator's mistaken impression that such students are just numbers, not names, to the faculty.

Students also can play a role in more formalized advocacy programs. In the California bond campaign, for example, students conducted voter registration campaigns, handed out leaflets on the measure, and spoke to student and community organizations.

TIPS FOR WORKING WITH ALUMNI AND STUDENT LEADERS

These simple rules of thumb can enrich the institution's relationships with key alumni and students:

- *No Surprises:* Whether it's good news or bad, let alumni and student leaders hear it from you first. You'd rather they hear it from you than from the local TV reporter or newspaper editor. This is easily done, especially with e-mail networks. If you don't trust cyberspace with sensitive news, fax the information around to your key contacts or rely on an old fashioned phone tree.

- *Listen to complaints:* An alumnus or student who has had a bad experience can be a very credible critic and can hurt the university by influencing public opinion. If you get wind of such a situation, address it immediately. You may not be able to reverse the outcome but you can ameliorate it. We have all seen an alumnus who didn't have a perfect experience harbor ill will toward an institution. It is gratifying beyond measure to see that person become involved and gain a new perspective.

- *They know things you don't know:* When you spend most of your waking hours working somewhere, it is tempting to think that you know it far better than any alumnus or student could. Not so. Students, in particular, can educate you in ways that will surprise you. You may

be delighted to learn about a good experience they are having with a particular professor, or you may be horrified to learn how easy it is to buy drugs on the quad. You can use this information to good effect if you keep your ears and mind open. By the same token, alumni who are out in the community and working in professions that bring them into contact with the university can often give you new perspectives on your institution.

- *You know things they don't know:* Alumni, in particular, may have an outdated notion of the campus they once attended. Make sure alumni volunteers are well briefed. At UC Berkeley, a Cal Parent who had been a Cal student some 25 years before lectured the parents of incoming freshmen with misinformation, outmoded observations, and bad advice. It was a lesson learned the hard way. Since then, Cal Parents have been well briefed before doing new student/parent orientations.

Student government leaders also may feel they know the institution better than they actually do and may second guess the reasons behind a policy or funding decision. Time spent by administrators or advancement officers meeting regularly with student government leaders to keep them well informed is time well spent.

In sum, alumni and student leaders always have played—and will continue to play—vital roles in the lives of our educational institutions. They are education's *raison d'être*.

The founders of the University of California weren't thinking of establishing campuses, creating research powerhouses, or employing teachers. They were looking to create leaders for California. They wanted to cultivate an educated citizenry and lay a foundation in mechanical arts, agriculture, literature, humanities, and the arts that would help turn the state, with its raw natural resources and striking beauty, into the economic and cultural engine that it is today. It is only fitting, therefore, that we in university relations should turn to alumni and students as full partners in advancing education in a new century.

FURTHER READINGS:

Jackson, Laura Christion. "On the Road to Alumni: If You Want Involved Graduates Tomorrow, Steer Your Students in the Right Direction Today. This Year-By-Year Road Map Can Help," CURRENTS 20, no. 9 (October 1994): 20-24.

Kobara, John. "Helping Others, Helping Ourselves: Community Service Programs Don't Just Benefit Society. They Bring Alumni Offices Greater Participation and Increased Campus Value," CURRENTS 20, no. 3 (March 1994): 50-51, 53-55.

Koral, Mimi. "Political Performance: If You Want Campus Support From Legislators, Alumni Volunteers are Instrumental to Your Success. Here's How to Fine-Tune Your Advocacy Efforts," CURRENTS 24, no. 1 (January 1998): 46-52.

Lennon, Chuck. "Service With a Smile: Helping Alumni Reach Out and Make a Difference in Their Communities," CURRENTS 17, no. 6 (June 1991): 56.

McDaniel, Sheila A. "Joint Ventures in Volunteering: Community Service Projects Can Bring Current and Former Students Closer to Campus—And Each Other," CURRENTS 20, no. 3 (March 1994): 52.

Scalzo, Teresa. "The Power of Politics: How to Turn Supportive Alumni Into Political Capital for Alma Mater," CURRENTS 18, no. 3 (March 1992): 20-24.

Scalzo, Teresa. "United Efforts: A Look at Five Campus Programs That Bring Students and Alumni Together," CURRENTS 20, no. 9 (October 1994): 34-39.

Educated parents, who are so often eager to give of their time, talent, and resources, can be an enormous asset to an institutional advancement program.

The Role of Parents in Institutional Advancement: An Independent School Perspective

Deirdre A. Ling
Head
Middlesex School

In the early 21st century, parents who have children attending independent schools represent a broad range of ages, interests, and attitudes. From those who began their families shortly after marriage in their early 20s to those who deferred having their first child until their late 30s or early 40s, the parents of today may have come of age in the McCarthy Era or during the final years of the Vietnam War. Shaped by the times in which they grew up, these parents may differ widely in their opinions about child rearing, discipline, religion, and a variety of social issues. It can be a challenge, therefore, for schools to recognize and comprehend the complex set of attitudes that exist among the "baby boomers" who are now the parents of their students. When it comes to the education of their children, however, present-day parents have much in common with one another, and these commonalties are an extremely important part of the relationship between schools and parents.

BOOMER PARENTS

For baby boomer parents, education is entitlement. The generation that came of age in the 1960s, for example, has enjoyed greater access to education than has any other in American history. These parents have high aspirations for their children and many take a keen interest in the schools to which they entrust their sons and daughters. They throw themselves into helping their children with their nightly homework assignments or college admissions essays with the same energy they brought to tackling big picture problems like reinventing government, reengineering corporations, reforming religion, and redefining community. They want only the best for their kids.

While a number of boomer parents were raised on a diet of healthy skepticism about organized religion and institutions like the military, many have come to feel a deep sense of loyalty to the schools and colleges that set them on the path to their success. That sense of indebtedness, in turn, is often extended to the schools that their children choose. Capitalizing on that wellspring of good feeling by providing an outlet for their generosity of spirit and resources can garner great benefits for the institutions that are astute enough to match interests to needs. In short, educated parents, who are so often eager to give of their time, talent, and resources, can be an enormous asset to an institutional advancement program.

The Role of
Parents in
Institutional
Advancement:
An Independent
School
Perspective

WAYS TO INVOLVE PARENTS

From hosting a reception for prospective parents to providing a moving testimonial to the job that an independent school has done in educating their child, parents provide support the school cannot itself provide. Grateful parents bolster and promote a school in myriad ways. Such involvement need not be viewed as a benefit limited only to the years that parents have children enrolled in a particular school. In fact, past parents—and grandparents, too—often continue to support an independent school long after a child has graduated. Schools that wisely maintain the interest of this important constituency through recognition in publications, appointments to advisory committees, and other forms of cultivation will continue to ensure that their institutions remain on the list of philanthropies these individuals support year after year.

At the highest and perhaps most influential institutional level, current and past parents, in reasonable proportion to the school's alumni, can provide a valuable perspective by serving on the board of trustees. Their experiences with the institution as it exists today can leaven the perspective of alumni whose vision may be colored by nostalgia and the passage of time. And their enthusiasm for the school's current activities and achievements can revitalize others whose contact with the school is less immediate. Parent committees and associations are frequently a useful means of identifying parents who would serve a school well at the board level with their leadership experience, imagination, interest, and resources.

At many independent schools, parents committees are an important fund-raising arm of the development office. Soliciting other parents for their annual fund gift to the school is a role many parents are willing to assume and these parents can be highly effective. The power of peer leadership in fund raising among parents should not be underestimated. It is an excellent way to leverage gifts to higher levels. In the final months before graduation, parents of senior students at many independent schools often raise large sums for a special purpose, such as a scholarship or other endowed fund. Their gift serves as a lasting legacy to the school

● ● ●

Loyal alumni are not born but made—all the more reason for school administrators to invite parents to participate in the life of their children's school.

that has nurtured their sons and daughters, preparing them well for the colleges and universities of their choice.

Parents associations—usually separate from fund-raising committees—also can be key organizations. They apprise other parents of activities at the school and invite their participation in academic, athletic, and social events. Through these associations, parents' energy can be tapped to extend the institution's resources dramatically to benefit students and faculty alike.

Parents might host "sports teas" after athletic games or entertain boarding students with unexpected dorm surprises. Parents associations produce informative monthly newsletters and calendars of current events. In short, parents will find numerous, creative ways of contributing to the school that welcomes their meaningful participation.

Parents so encouraged may volunteer to sponsor independent study courses for students interested in a given career, enriching the school's curriculum with classes offering real-world experience with working professionals. Parents who may be uncomfortable making telephone solicitations for the school's annual fund may nonetheless enjoy organizing and taking part in book or bake sales to raise funds for the school library or an academic program. It is incumbent upon the school's administrators to suggest helpful ways that parents can get involved, and to ensure that these activities are clearly aligned with the school's policies and procedures.

WAYS NOT TO INVOLVE PARENTS

Conversely, the head of every independent school has a story about the litigious parent whose child can do no wrong. Disciplining a wayward student whose parent is overly invested in the success of a son or daughter—to the detriment of the school community—can become the bane of a CEO's existence. At the outset of the school-parent relationship, it is critical to outline clearly the expectations between school and parents with regard to rules and standards of behavior. A published handbook in this regard is very helpful and may keep things from going awry in the future.

The Role of
Parents in
Institutional
Advancement:
An Independent
School
Perspective

The head of a parents committee or parents association who attempts to use the position to lobby for a policy change at the school is another example of the misguided kind of involvement that can occur on occasion. It is crucial that there be clarity between the policy-making prerogative of the Board of Trustees and the advisory nature of most parent groups. Reviewing the mission and goals of the parents committee or association with its members at the start of each school year—or whenever there is a change in leadership—is an invaluable exercise for all parties involved.

In a similar vein, every development director knows of a parent donor who wanted to restrict his or her gift in such a way that it failed to match institutional needs, or, even worse, a parent with a political agenda that was at odds with the institution's mission. The endowed chair offered to add a faculty member of a particular ideological bent is an endowed chair that should be graciously but firmly refused lest it set a precedent for future gifts to the school.

SETTING AN EXAMPLE

Despite these occasional pitfalls, the inclusion of parents in the everyday life of their child's school—and, consequently, in the advancement of that institution—is a highly recommended practice that will undoubtedly help all those involved. Parents exert a powerful influence on their chil-dren. Children identify with and imitate their parents. It is difficult if not impossible to involve secondary school students in advancement activities; their first responsibility must be to their academic and extracurricular activities. But parents active in their children's school set an example of involvement that is likely to rub off on their children. Thus, loyal alumni are not born but made—all the more reason for school administrators to invite parents to participate in the life of their children's school.

FURTHER READINGS

Dessoff, Alan L. "Welcome to the Family: Use Parents and Students to Offer Prospects the Straight Story about Life on Your Campus," CURRENTS 20, no. 1 (January 1994): 44-47.

Lindemuth, Tim. "A Relative Success: Casting Parents in Leading Roles Can Bring Box-Office Hits to Your Campus," CURRENTS 17, no. 4 (April 1991): 12-13, 15-17.

McNamee, Thomas A. "Ask and Ye Shall Receive: A Survey Helps Hartwick College Find New Ways to Involve Parents in Everything from Internship Programs to Fund Raising," CURRENTS 11, no. 6 (June 1985): 16-18.

Schaefer, Kristina Gulick. "Keeping It in the Family: When Your Annual Fund Plans Include Parents, Everyone Feels More Involved," CURRENTS 17, no. 4 (April 1991): 18-20, 22.

Weiss, Larry J., ed. *Parents Programs: How to Create Lasting Ties.* Washington, DC: Council for Advancement and Support of Education, 1989.

Index